EASTERN
AFRICA
SERIES

REMAKING
MUTIRIKWI

Eastern Africa Series

Remaking Mutirikwi

Landscape, Water
and Belonging
in Southern Zimbabwe

JOOST FONTEIN

JC JAMES CURREY

James Currey
an imprint of Boydell & Brewer Ltd
PO Box 9, Woodbridge, Suffolk IP12 3DF (GB)

and of
Boydell & Brewer Inc.
668 Mt Hope Avenue, Rochester, NY 14620–2731 (US)
www.boydellandbrewer.com
www.jamescurrey.com

Published in association with The British Institute in Eastern Africa

The publisher has no responsibility for the continued existence or accuracy of URLs for
external or third-party internet websites referred to in this book, and does not guarantee
that any content on such websites is, or will remain, accurate or appropriate.

British Library Cataloguing in Publication Data
is available from the British Library

ISBN 978-1-84701-112-1 (James Currey Cloth)
ISBN 978-1-84701-125-1 (James Currey Africa-only paperback)
ISBN 978-1-84701-211-1 (James Currey Paperback)

Typeset in 10/12pt Cordale
by CPI Typesetting

Dedication

Dedicated to Tashamiswa,
for the joy you bring.

Contents

Illustrations

Maps

Photographs

Acknowledgements

Many people assisted in making this book. The British Academy funded my postdoctoral fellowship during which much of its research was done, and I am also thankful for small grants from the Munro, Tweedy and Hayter funds. More significant has been the friendship, intellectual stimulation and wise counsel of many colleagues in Edinburgh. John Harries, Tom Molony, Dimitri Tsintjiloni, Sara Dorman and Paul Nugent deserve particular mention. My much missed late friend and mentor Charles Jedrej inspired me to do this project, and it is a continuing sadness that he could not witness its completion. Jeanne Cannizzo is another much missed colleague, now enjoying well-deserved retirement. I am also grateful to my PhD students who made me think harder in my own work. Some of them are already building academic careers. In Oxford I benefitted from Terry Ranger's enormous experience and generous engagement, often within hours of unruly drafts appearing in his inbox. His death in January 2015, just before this book went to press, has robbed African Studies of one its greatest and most committed scholars. Colleagues at the *Journal of Southern African Studies* too deserve a mention for their enthusiastic and critical encouragement, particularly Lyn Schumacher, Matthew Engelke, Joss Alexander, JoAnn McGregor and Dick Werbner. In Nairobi, Susan Ongoro produced a wonderful map of Lake Mutirikwi.

In Zimbabwe there are far too many people to name all individually. Gerald Mazarire remains my true 'comrade at arms', and amongst the very best of Zimbabwean scholars. Another promising scholar is Joseph Mujere, whose PhD I was fortunate to supervise, and who now holds the fort at the University of Zimbabwe. The National Archives repository in Harare remains an unrivalled resource, and I am grateful to all its staff who have kept this valuable institution thriving. Around Mutirikwi there are simply too many people to whom I owe gratitude; their names and voices appear throughout this book. I hope I have done justice to their enthusiasm. Particular mention must go to the late Matopos Murinye, to Ambuya VaZarira and Peter Manyuki, all exceptionally articulate, warm and committed people, whose contribution to this research remains unrivalled. I must thank Baba Lisa who accompanied me throughout my fieldwork. As we grappled with Mutirikwi's complex landscapes he became a close friend, and I won't forget all the fun we had.

It is almost twenty years since I first visited Masvingo. Throughout that time I have been repeatedly welcomed by the Rukasha family with whom I have shared many of life's ups and downs, laughter and tears. My debt to them is one not easily settled – I only hope my presence has been tolerable, and sometimes enjoyable. In Harare I shared so many fun moments with Apronia, Shelter, Bernard, Tendai and Baba Enoch, and my old friend Mike. You have all put up with my moodiness too many times, and with good humour. But the two people who have endured the writing of this book more than anyone else are Barbara and our daughter Tashamiswa, to whom I dedicate this book. Thank you both. It wouldn't have happened without you.

Note on Fieldwork, Notes & Sources

The main ethnographic fieldwork and interviews for this book were carried out around Lake Mutirikwi in Masvingo district in southern Zimbabwe in 2005/06, although I also refer to previous visits and periods of fieldwork in 1997, 2000/01 and 2004, and subsequent visits in 2008 and 2011. Archival research was carried out at the National Archives of Zimbabwe (NAZ) in Harare in 2005/06, and in August 2008. I also sometimes refer to notes taken doing previous periods of archival research in 2000/01. All interviews were conducted in either Shona or English, or often a bit of both, and were noted through hand written scribbles at the time, and then fully typed up and recorded in my fieldnotes in English (including particular Shona phrases where appropriate) immediately afterwards – later the same day or early the next day. I also digitally recorded many of these interviews, but these recordings were never transcribed, and only very rarely referred to as I wrote up my fieldnotes, to clarify particular names, Shona phrases used or other details. They remain in my possession, as do thousands of pages of field and archival notes. In what follows, footnote references to people and dates refer to these interviews, which were normally pre-arranged during earlier prior visits. References to 'Fieldnotes' refer to ad hoc and less formal conversations, visits and events that I participated in or witnessed during ethnographic fieldwork. I was also fortunate to be able to spend several days working through files held by Zimbabwe's National Parks and Wildlife Authority at their offices at the Kyle Recreational Park, and I occasionally refer to notes taken from the National Museums and Monuments files at Great Zimbabwe in 2000/01. In addition to field and archival work in Zimbabwe, I also had a very engaging interview with Simon Bright in Bristol, United Kingdom, in 2008.

Baba	father
Baba mukuru	father's elder brother (lit. great father)
Babamunini	father's younger brother (lit. little father)
Badza (pl. *mapadza)*	hoe
Bira (pl. *mabira)*	ancestral ritual, possession ceremony
Bute	snuff
Chimurenga	liberation struggle; first *Chimurenga* comprised the rebellions of 1896; second *Chimurenga* was the liberation struggle of the 1960s and 1970s; third *Chimurenga* is fast-track land reform in the 2000s, also referred to as *hondo yeminda*
Chikaranga	Karanga dialect of Shona, also loosely used to refer to 'culture' or 'tradition' (see *chivanhu*)
Chimwido	female youth who assisted guerrilla fighters during the war
Chisi	ancestral rest day
Chivanhu	(loosely) 'culture', 'tradition' (lit. of people)
Dagga	mud
Dambo	wet lands
Dare	meeting, court, meeting place
Dhumbu	apron or skirt made of animal skin
Dzimba dzeushe	houses of the chieftainship
Dziva	pool
Fast-track	land reform programme that followed and formalised the land occupations begun in 2000
Gadzingo	sacred place, associated with particular clans and 19th-century chieftainship, often related to or same as *mapa*, and where chieftainship is/was conferred upon new chiefs
Gukurahundi	massacres committed between 1983 and 1987 by the North-Korean-trained fifth brigade, and other government forces, in Matabeleland and the Midlands, under the guise of rooting out so-called dissidents, in which an estimated 20,000 people were killed

Hondo yeminda	war of the fields, see also Third *Chimurenga*
Ivhu kuvanhu	soil to the people
Jambanja	chaos, violence, normally associated with land occupations of 2000/01
(Ka)Ngwena	(small) crocodile
Kare	long ago
Kubata maoko	to offer condolences (e.g. at funeral) (lit. to shake hands)
Kuchengeta vhu	to look after the soil
Kugadzikana nyika	to settle the land
Kupira	to appease, or praise (ancestors)
Kusasika	to dry out, preserve through heat, mummify.
Kuuraya	to kill
Madzishe (sing. *ishe*)	chiefs
Madzitateguru (sing. *Tateguru*)	ancestors
Madzimambo	chiefs
Mahakakurimwi	so-called 'traditional' mourning practice after death of chief or senior elder, involving a ban on all agricultural work for a set period of time
Makandiwa (sing. *kandiwa*)	contour ridges
Makuva (sing. *guva*)	graves
Maline	linear settlements constructed in the Native Reserves through centralisation policies of the 1930s–40s (lit. lines)
Manyusa (sing. *nyusa*)	*Mwari* cult messengers
Mapa	sacred places, usually graves, of chiefs and/or clan ancestors
Marambatemwa	sacred grove or forest (lit. refusal to be felled)
Mashanje/Mashuku	fruit of wild loquat tree (*uapaca kirkiana*)
Mashave	'Foreign', 'alien' of 'animal' spirits, often associated with healing, or special talents
Masvikiro (sing. *svikiro*)	spirit mediums
Masvingo	post-independence name of what had been Fort Victoria, Victoria district and Victoria province; means stones, also used to refer to Great Zimbabwe
Matongo (sing. *dongo*)	ruins (of former homestead), birthplace
Mhondoro	clan, 'tribal' or royal ancestors, or lion spirit
Mhosva	crime
Miganhu	boundaries
Minda mirefu	resettlement plots (lit. long fields)
Misha yakavauraya	the (people of the) villages killed him
Mitemo yenyika	rules of the land
Mitoro (sing. *mutoro*)	rituals to request for rain, see also *mukwerere*
Moyo	heart; a totem (i.e. *Moyo Muduma*)

Muchakata	wild cork tree (*parinari curatellifoliai*), a sacred tree – often *bira* and rain-making events are held beneath them. In times of drought people eat its fruit, but normally describe it as foul tasting
Mudzimu (pl. *mi-* or *va-*)	ancestor/ancestral spirit
Mudzimu wemvura	ancestor of water/rain
Mudzviti	raider, usually referring to 19th-century Ndebele and Nguni raiders, also used in Masvingo to refer to Native Commissioner and later District Administrator
Mujiba	male youth who assisted guerrillas during the war
Mukoma	older brother
Mukwasha	son-in-law
Mukwerere	ritual to request for rain, see also *mitoro*
Muneri	missionaries
Munyai	messenger, go between
Murungu	white person
Musha (pl. *mi-*)	home, village
Mushonga	medicine, potion, magic, witchcraft
Musikavanhu	god, creator of people; see also *Mwari* and *Nyadenga*
Mutero weminda	field tax
Mutupo	totem
Muzukuru	grandchild, nephew/niece
Mvura	water
Mwari (*Mwali* in Ndebele)	God, or high god, associated with the Matonjeni, Njelele and other shrines in the Matopos, in southern Matabeleland; see also *Musikavanhu* and Nyadenga
Mweya wetsvina	dirty or evil spirits
N'anga	'traditional' healer, diviner, herbalist
New farmer	resettlement farmer, particularly fast-track resettlement
Ndari	party or event for which millet is brewed for sale, as opposed to a *bira* ceremony when beer is brewed to venerate the ancestors
Ngozi	frightening and dangerous avenging or aggrieved spirit, often of someone murdered and/or not buried properly
Nhare	cave, tunnel, rock shelter
Njuzu	water spirit, or creature, sometimes translated as mermaid, associated with water, especially specific rivers, springs and pools, and with healing; known to abduct people, especially children, who may become powerful healers
Nyadenga	God (lit. 'of the sky'); see also *Mwari* and *Musikavanhu*

Nyembe	title, also used to refer to chief's medal
Nyika	land, territory
Nzara	hunger, drought
Operation *Murambatsvina*	government programme of urban clearances, 2005
Pamberi neZANU PF, Pasi neMDC	slogan 'Forward with ZANU PF, Down with MDC!'
Pungwe	night time political rallies
Rapoko/rukwesa	finger millet
Rukuvhute	umbilical cord
Ruware	bare granite outcrop
Sabhuku	village head (lit. of the book)
Sadunhu	headman
Sadza	staple food, stiff porridge made from maize meal
Sango	bush
Sekuru	grandfather, mothers' brother, also general term of respect for male elders, and sometimes for ancestors
Shato	python
Shoko (or *Tsoko*)	monkey; a totem (i.e. *shoko mbire*, or *shoko mukanya*)
Shumba	lion; a totem (i.e. *Shumba sipambi*)
Tezvara	father-in-law
Thovela	rain god of the Venda people
Ukama	blood or patrilineal kin group
Vana vevhu	children of the soil, used to refer to comrades/ guerrilla fighters during the war
Varidzi venyika	owners of the land
Varimi/varungu vanhasi	farmers/white people of today
Vatengesi	sell outs/traitors
Vatete	paternal aunt
Vatorwa	strangers, incomers, foreigners
Vlei	marshy wetland
Zitete	great aunt
Zunde ramambo	old system of communal fields and harvests controlled by chiefs, to provide food for the elderly, orphans and the infirm; subject to high profile revival in the mid-2000s
Zvitubu (sing. *chitubu*)	springs

Acronyms & Abbreviations

A1 resettlement	Smallholder farms, which could be either small self-contained plots or villagisation schemes where homes, fields and communal grazing areas were divided
A2 resettlement	Larger self-contained farms, designed for medium scale commercial farming.
AIDS	Acquired Immune Deficiency Syndrome
AIPPA	Access to Information and Protection of Privacy Act
ARC	African Reformed Church
ARDA	Agricultural and Rural Development Authority
AREX (formerly Agritex)	Agricultural Extension Service
AZTREC	Association of Zimbabwean Traditional Ecologists
BSACo	British South Africa Company
BSAP	British South Africa Police
CAF	Central African Federation
CAMPFIRE	Communal Areas Management Programme for Indigenous Resources
CEO	Chief Executive Officer
CFU	Commercial Farmer's Union
CIO	Central Intelligence Organisation
CNC	Chief Native Commissioner
COPAC	Constitutional Parliamentary Select Committee
DA	District Administrator
DC	District Commissioner
DDF	District Development Fund
DRC	Dutch Reformed Church
GMB	Grain Marketing Board
GNU	Government of National Unity
GPA	Global Political Agreement
GZ	Great Zimbabwe
GP	Growth Point
IG	Inclusive Government (see GNU)
JOMIC	Joint Monitoring and Implementation Committee
LAA	Land Apportionment Act

LDO	Land Development Officer
MDC	Movement for Democratic Change
MET	Meteorological Service Department
MIA	Ministry of Internal Affairs
MOU	Memorandum of Understanding
MP	Member of Parliament
National Parks	Zimbabwe Parks and Wildlife Management Authority
NAZ	National Archives of Zimbabwe
NC	Native Commissioner
NGO	Non-Government Organisation
NLHA	Native Land Husbandry Act
NMMR	National Museums and Monuments of Rhodesia
NMMZ	National Museums and Monuments of Zimbabwe
ONHRI	Organ on National Healing, Reconciliation and Integration
PA	Provincial Administrator
PC	Provincial Commissioner
PM	Prime Minister
POSA	Public Order and Security Act
RAR	Rhodesian African Rifles
RDC	Rural District Council
SADC	Southern African Development Community
SiN	Superintendent of Natives
TTL	Tribal Trust Lands (Native Reserves until 1965)
UDI	Unilateral Declaration of Independence (1965)
UNWTO	United Nations World Tourism Organisation
VAT	Value Added Tax
VIDCO	Village Development Committee
WADCO	Ward Development Committee
WFP	World Food Programme
WWII	World War II
ZANU PF	Zimbabwe African National Union Patriotic Front
ZANLA	Zimbabwe African National Liberation Army
ZAPU	Zimbabwe African People's Union
ZEC	Zimbabwe Electoral Commission
ZHRC	Zimbabwe Human Rights Commission
ZIPRA	Zimbabwe Peoples Revolutionary Army
ZINWA	Zimbabwe National Water Authority
ZNA	Zimbabwe National Army
ZIRRCON	Zimbabwean Institute of Religious and Ecological Conservation

Chronology

Early 19th century	Duma clans of Murinye, Chikwanda, Shumba, Chibwe and Mugabe arrive and settle in what is now Masvingo district. They are the last in a series of Karanga clans who began arriving in the area in the 18th century.
1890	Cecil Rhodes' pioneer column invades Mashonaland. Fort Victoria town is established. Its location is moved three years later due to water supply problems. Many farms around and under where Lake Mutirikwi now lies were first pegged during the following decade.
1891	Morgenster mission founded.
1893	The Matabele war, and the Victoria agreement.
1895	First native reserves established in Victoria district.
1896/97	First *Chimurenga*. Mediums Ambuya Nehanda and Sekuru Kaguvi executed by Rhodesians for instigating the revolt.
1912	Severe drought coincides with death of Chief Masungunye, most senior of all Duma chiefs and renowned rain maker.
1920s	Investigations begin into the possibility of two large irrigation schemes in Victoria District, at Umshandige (Mushandike) and Popotekwe (Pokoteke). Umshandige dam is built in the late 1930s. Discussions about a Popotekwe dam continue until the project is finally shelved in the late 1950s.
1921	Mudarikwa Murinye born on Oatlands Farm.
1923	Murray MacDougall builds Jatala Weir across the Mutirikwi river in the lowveld.
1924	Native Regulations Act.
1930	Land Apportionment Act (LAA).

1940s	Centralisation of native reserves in Victoria district that was begun in the 1920s accelerates and is completed. Mass evictions in wake of LAA take place. Most people around Mutirikwi in the 2000s remember being evicted from European farms during this decade. After World War II there is large influx of new white settlers into Southern Rhodesia, many ex-serviceman attracted to new settlement schemes.
1941	Native Resources Act.
1944	Murray MacDougall's sugar industry at Triangle is nationalised.
1945	Jarios Haruzvivishe and others removed from Mzero farm to Gwana in the Victoria reserve, under Chief Mugabe.
1947	Chieftainship of Chikwanda abolished. Sir Alexander Gibb commissioned to survey the Save valley for possible irrigation schemes. His report is published in 1948.
1949	Mudarikwa Murinye and others removed from The Retreat farm, in the Boroma area across the Mutirikwi river, into the Mtilikwe Reserve. Exploratory diamond drilling takes place at proposed Kyle dam site, at the same time as at Popotekwe site.
1951	Native Land Husbandry Act (NLHA).
1952	*Report on Large-Scale Irrigation Development in Southern Rhodesia* is published.
1953	Beginning of the Central African Federation (CAF) consisting of Southern Rhodesia (Zimbabwe), Nyasaland (Malawi) and Northern Rhodesia (Zambia).
1954	Triangle Estate sold to syndicate of Natal sugar planters, who commit £300,000 to building a dam across the Mutirikwi river. A year later it is sold to Guy Hulett, who reconfirms the previous agreement to fund the dam, later signing the Kyle Agreement committing the majority of its waters to Triangle's sugar estate.
1957	Hippo Valley Agreement (and Act in 1958) between government and Ray Stockil. Government promises to build Bangala dam after Kyle dam is complete, committing the majority of its waters to Hippo Valley.
1959	Kariba dam is finished. Building of Kyle (Mutirikwi) dam begins. Zano people removed from Chinango and Nyangani areas to be flooded by the dam. Kelvingrove and other farms on northern border of Mtilikwe reserve are purchased for their resettlement.

1960	The Kyle dam is completed in December, and formally opened in early 1961. Stocking of wildlife reserve begins immediately.
1962	Native Land Husbandry Act is repealed, as African nationalism gains ground.
1963	Federation is dissolved.
1964	Kyle Game Reserve opened to the public for the first time. Murray MacDougall dies. Ian Smith becomes prime minister. Michael Mawema is arrested in Fort Victoria in March, followed by Ndabaningi Sithole in June.
1965	Ian Smith makes his Unilateral Declaration of Independence (UDI). This signals the move from nationalist mobilisation to liberation struggle, and the Second *Chimurenga*. The Murray MacDougall Scenic Drive is created around Lake Kyle.
1967	Kyle Game Reserve is reclassified as a national park.
1968	Jairos Haruzvivishe's elder brother, Joseph Chikudo Mugabe becomes Chief Mugabe, and moves to Chikarudzo on Morgenster Mission Farm, when that area was informally returned to and resettled by Mugabe people by the mission.
1972	The liberation struggle and incursions by guerrillas from camps in Zambia, and later Mozambique increase. The war intensifies.
1974	Kyle dam finally spills, 14 years after its completion.
1975	Kyle National Park becomes Kyle Recreational Park. In the mid-1970s the fishing co-operative is established in Zano, on Mutirikwi's eastern shores. Removable radial gates fitted to Kyle dam, raising water level by one meter.
1978	Ndabaningi Sithole announces the Internal Settlement in Fort Victoria.
1979	Ceasefire.
1980	Zimbabwean Independence. Chieftainship of Chikwanda re-instated. Sophia Muchini returns to Great Zimbabwe. A wave of squatting on state lands and farms begins around Lake Mutirikwi.
1981	Abraham and Margaret Roux and Helena van As and her grandson Philip are killed in what became known as the Victoria East farm killings. Sophia Muchini and former guerrilla fighters with her are arrested after a shoot-out at Great Zimbabwe, and she is later found guilty in the high court in Salisbury (Harare).

1987	Last of Mutirikwi's squatters evicted from Mzero farm, which officially becomes a game park, although no animals are ever moved there. Resettlement schemes and small irrigation schemes are established at Boroma, Longdale and elsewhere.
1992	The worst drought in Zimbabwe since independence.
1998	ZINWA (Zimbabwe National Water Authority) Act. Early land occupations in Svosve and elsewhere.
1999	Traditional Leaders Act.
2000	After the constitutional referendum of February, war-veteran-led land invasions begin in Masvingo province, and spread throughout the country. Areas of state land as well as farms all around Lake Mutirikwi are (re)occupied. Later, after the parliamentary elections of June that year, the land invasions are formalised as fast-track land reform.
2002	Chief Mudarikwa Murinye, and his son, Matopos Murinye, return to Boroma. Presidential elections won by Robert Mugabe.
2004	Chief Mudarikwa Murinye dies and is buried, in secret, in the Murinye *mapa* on Boroma. His death is not announced for another three months.
2005	Parliamentary elections are followed by the urban clearances spreading from Harare to Bulawayo and other major towns and cities, known as *Operation Murambatsvina*. Annual 'national *bira*' and *zunde ramambo* projects initiated by government for the first time.
2008	ZANU PF (Zimbabwe African National Union – Patriotic Front) loses the combined parliamentary and presidential elections of March 2008. The announcement of the official results is delayed for several weeks, as a wave of violence and intimidation is unleashed across the country, particularly in ZANU PF's former rural strongholds. MDC leader Morgan Tsvangirai pulls out of the presidential 'run-off' election, and Robert Mugabe is re-elected unopposed. Under enormous regional pressure ZANU PF and the two opposition MDC parties sign a Memorandum of Understanding (MOU) in July, followed by the Global Political Agreement (GPA) in September, paving the way for the formation of a Government of National Unity (GNU) in February 2009. Between September 2008 and January 2009, Zimbabwe is hit by a devastating cholera epidemic.

2009   In February the GNU is formed, with Robert Mugabe as President, and Morgan Tsvangirai as Prime Minister.

2010   Acting Chief Matopos Murinye is replaced by Ephais Munodawafa Murinye, who is made the new substantive Chief Murinye. Matopos dies in early 2011.

2013   ZANU PF wins the combined parliamentary and presidential elections of July.

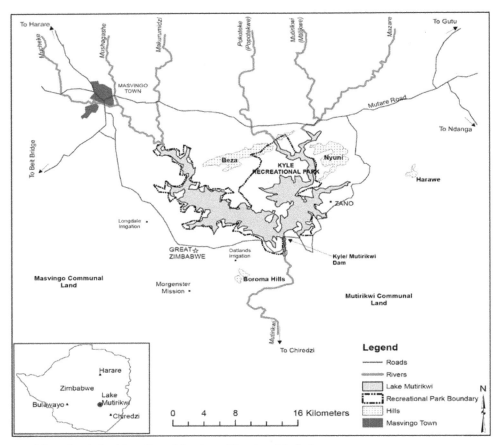

Map 1   Lake Mutirikwi, Masvingo District, Zimbabwe
(Drawing by Susan Ongogo)

Remaking Mutirikwi:
An Introduction

The Mutirikwi river was dammed in the early 1960s to make Zimbabwe's second largest lake. This was a key moment in the 'Europeanisation' of Mutirikwi's landscapes, which had begun with colonial land appropriations in the 1890s. But African landscapes were not obliterated by what became known as the Kyle dam. They remained active and affective. At independence in 1980, local clans re-asserted ancestral land claims in a wave of squatting around Mutirikwi. But they were soon evicted as the new government asserted its control over the remaking of Mutirikwi's landscapes. Amid fast-track land reform in the 2000s, the same people returned again to reclaim and remake Mutirikwi's landscapes. Many returned to the graves and ruins of past lives forged in the very substance of the soil, and even incoming war veterans and land reform's so-called 'new farmers' appealed to local clans' autochthonous knowledge to 'make safe' their own resettlements. This book explores those re-occupations – and the complex contests over land, water, belonging and authority they provoked – both ethnographically and historically. It offers a detailed ethnographic and historical study of land reform in Zimbabwe from the perspective of those involved in land occupations around Lake Mutirikwi, including local clans, chiefs and spirit mediums, as well as government technocrats, war veterans, and new farmers.

Through analytical lenses focused on the political materialities of water and land, it reveals how the ongoing remaking of Mutirikwi's landscapes has always been deeply entangled in changing strategies of colonial and postcolonial statecraft. It highlights how the active traces of different past regimes of rule – Rhodesian and Zimbabwean, developmentalist, traditionalist and everything in between – intertwine in contemporary politics through the active and enduring yet emergent forms and substances of landscape. The 2000s may have heralded a long-delayed 're-Africanisation' of Mutirikwi's landscapes, but just as African presence was never obliterated by the dam, so colonial and white presence too remains active and affective through Rhodesian-era discourses, place-names and the materialities of ruined farms, contour ridging and old irrigation schemes. *Remaking Mutirikwi* therefore focuses on how claims and practices of belonging and autochthony articulate with practices of authority and power in the present, through the enduring yet emergent

1

materialities of water and landscape. Deploying both anthropology and history, it examines how local contests provoked by land occupations around Lake Mutirikwi in the 2000s are animated by the entangled material and imaginative remnants of the past colonial and postcolonial regimes of rule through the form and substance of landscape.

Setting the scene: a visit '*Kubata maoko*'

In September 2005 I began fieldwork in Masvingo district in southern Zimbabwe by visiting acting Chief Matopos Murinye. My purpose was to offer my condolences ('*kubata maoko*', lit. 'to shake hands') for the death of his father, Chief David Mudarikwa Murinye, who had died late the previous year; and to seek assistance for my new research around Lake Mutirikwi. We set off early one Sunday morning from Nemanwa, south of the lake, into the Mutirikwi communal areas where I had interviewed the late Chief Mudarikwa and his *dare* (court) during previous fieldwork in 2001(Fontein 2006a). From Great Zimbabwe the road took us towards the Mutirikwi dam, passing various hotels and chalets, and recently re-occupied areas of the (formally delineated but never actualised) 'game park' buffering the lake's southern shores, and past older resettlements established on former farms around the Boroma hills in the 1980s. After the dam wall, the narrow tar road winds up to the township of Topora. There we left the tar of the Murray MacDougal Drive circling on around the lake – named after the lowveld sugar pioneer who, according to many, first championed the damming of the Mutirikwi – and descended a steep gravel road into the old Mtilikwe reserve. Arriving dusty, rattled and hot, we were told that Matopos, the acting chief, no longer lived there. Both the late Mudarikwa and his son had moved to the Boroma hills in 2002, which we had passed almost an hour before. We would find Matopos down a newly carved track through woodland, marked by an improvised wooden sign indicating the 'Muchakata bus stop'. We were also warned he was very sick, and may not be able to see us.

Turning back up the treacherous hill to Topora, onto the tar and across the dam, we turned off at the new Muchakata bus stop, two miles or so after the Kyle Boat Club – another remnant of the white recreational landscape that Rhodesians forged around the new lake in the 1960s. Here, on the grazing area of a *minda mirefu* (long fields) resettlement established in the 1980s, new fields had been cut, woodland cleared, and pole and *dagga* (mud) homesteads built, marking recent occupations by new settlers; an aesthetic of resettlement very familiar across Zimbabwe in the early 2000s. It was already evident the acting chief (and his late father) were re-occupying state lands, just as the 'game park' further west had been re-occupied by Haruzvivishe people of the Mugabe clan; who also interpreted the fast-track context as an opportunity to return to ancestral lands from where they had been evicted twice before: during the colonial period and again in 1987 after the failure of early post-war efforts to reclaim them.

Entering acting Chief Murinye's pole and *dagga* homestead, I was again told that he was very sick. After explaining that I had worked closely with both his father and the senior Duma *svikiro* (spirit medium) Ambuya VaZarira, we were shown inside a hut, where a radio was noisily reporting a local football match. As my eyes adjusted to the dark, I was shocked by what we saw.

> I scarcely recognised the man, who is fairly young, but now shrunken into skin and bones, with bulging eyes. He took a while to recognise me. I explained that I had come *'kubata maoko'* ... over the death of his father ... I also explained that I was planning to do more research once my papers came out. He said that Duma chiefs had been carrying on with their traditions since the last time I was here. He explained that I would be shown everything that had happened, and even the secret places where the Duma chiefs are buried, but first he would have to talk to Ambuya VaZarira. I explained that I was planning to visit VaZarira soon, and he said ... I should tell her that Chief Murinye is very sick, and that there is a very big *bira* [ancestral ceremony] planned for 24th September, to be held on a small hill in the bush nearby.[1]

Wishing him a swift recovery we left, accompanied by the acting chief's son. He explained that Matopos had become ill suddenly in August, and 'there were days when he wasn't even talking'. Since going to Masvingo provincial hospital, he 'had got a little better'. As we walked we were told that some of the new settlers living around them were 'squatters', but 'we are not squatters' Matopos's son added emphatically. On the Boroma hillside, smoke from a fire was dancing in the hot breeze, caused we were told by those 'people clearing fields from the bush'.[2]

After that first visit it was already clear that Murinye people and their chief too were invoking ancestral claims to belonging and entitlement to legitimise occupations of state land around Mutirikwi. Furthermore the burial of the late Chief Mudarikwa in late 2004 was finely intertwined with their recent resettlement at Boroma. Later I discovered that the hills lie at the centre of a volatile boundary dispute between Chiefs Mugabe and Murinye, and that claims to ancestral authority over land, knowledge of its sacred hills, caves, and springs, and especially graves and burial practices *in* the landscape, are of recurring significance around the lake; even on commercial farms to its north resettled under the fast-track programme. Indeed graves and burials are key to the stories I trace in this book.

But I was also pessimistic that the acting chief would survive long enough to assist me with the enthusiasm he promised. He looked so very close to death. Since my last fieldwork in the area (Fontein 2006a), death had almost become an everyday matter. So many people had died, or were dying. I struggle to remember them all. Fields around rural homesteads had become littered with graves. AIDS was obviously a large determinate of Zimbabwe's enormous mortality rates, among the highest in the world,[3] but equally significant in its decade of misery,

---

[1] Fieldnotes 04/09/05.
[2] Ibid.
[3] In the late 1990s to early 2000s, prevalence was widely estimated at 30 per cent (UNAIDS/UNICEF/WHO 2004). Since then this has reduced significantly, as awareness campaigns (Duffy 2005), and antiretroviral treatment programmes have expanded (www.unaids.org/en/resources/presscentre/featurestories/2013/may/20130514zimbabwe, accessed 16/05/13).

Photo I   Acting Chief Matopos
Murinye, with the plans for
his 'palace'
(Source: author, 2006)

were the exacerbating everyday hardships of hunger, inflation, shortages, poverty, and sometimes violence, through which Zimbabweans
endured the deepening economic, political and social crises of the 2000s.
In 2005 this general zeitgeist of misery was compounded by recurrent
drought and the devastating urban clearances known as Operation Murambatsvina (Fontein 2009a; Potts 2006; Bratton & Masunungure 2006;
Kamete 2006; Vambe 2008) from which Masvingo's rural dwellers were
hardly immune. It was, in many respects, a terrible time and fieldwork in
2005/06 was a difficult endurance, mirroring (albeit minutely) the daily
struggles of people with whom I lived in Masvingo.

After my visit in September 2005 I hardly expected Matopos Murinye
to survive. But remarkably he did. As he grew stronger we often travelled
around Lake Mutirikwi together, to visit Ambuya VaZarira at Mazare, or
the office of the *mudzviti* (District Administrator).[4] He became an important informant for this book. His words and understandings are layered
thickly throughout it. Later Matopos explained his illness in terms of the
struggles that often surround chiefly succession; implying that, as with
his father's accession in the 1950s, he had been victim to witchcraft by
jealous rivals. In so doing he both illustrated the contentious nature of
chiefly succession, and legitimated his claim by linking his recovery to
the historical precedence provided by his father's emergence as chief
after similar misfortunes, a position Mudarikwa subsequently held for
over half a century. Matopos's confidence that he would become the
substantive chief, and that he and other Murinye 'returnees' would

---

[4] Literally this means 'raider', and refers to 19th-century Ndebele and Nguni
raiders. In Masvingo it also often refers to the District Administrator.

continue living on their ancestral lands around Boroma, and avoid a third eviction, was manifest in the enthusiasm with which he often discussed the 'palace' he was building on a small granite knoll not far from his pole and *dagga* homestead.

Almost a year later, in July 2006, on my last day of fieldwork, Matopos Murinye led us – myself, Baba Lisa (my friend and assistant), and Peter Manyuki (VaZarira's son) – as he had promised, to his father's grave, in a cave, in the sacred *mapa* (ancestral grave) on Boroma. It is a place guarded by fierce baboons and strict taboos, where several generations of Murinye chiefs lie buried amidst the traces of even earlier peoples who buried (and maybe dried) their dead there; and where 19th-century people hid from Ndebele raiders. That special visit into the Boroma caves inspired me to interrogate the immanence of the past and the materi-alities of belonging, which have become central themes of this book. It focused my attention upon how the affective presence of old graves and ruins, new burials and homesteads, as well as state-led technocratic land and water interventions, materialise past and present occupations *in*, en-gagements *with*, and regimes of rule *over* landscape. This materialisation animates localist contests over autochthony, sovereignty and belonging even as they are implicated in broader reconfigurations of authority and statecraft provoked by the upheavals of land reform in the 2000s.

LANDSCAPE, MEMORY AND THE IMMANENCE OF THE PAST

The 1990s heralded a move away from conventional (European) under-standings of landscape as 'static repository' for the past sedimented into it, towards an understanding of landscape as part of contested processes of memory work through which the present and the past are constituted (cf. Kuchler 1993, 1999; Morphy 1993, 1995; Hirsch and O'Hanlon 1995; Harrison 2004). More recently, aligning with a broader turn towards questions of materiality and a 'return to things', Domańska (2006:338) and others (Runia 2006; Pinney 2005) have turned further away from the symbolic or metaphorical value of objects, things and landscape in nar-rative, discursive and textual constructions of the past, to focus on the immanence of the past through material presence. This examines how the enduring *thingness* or autonomy of objects, things and landscapes can have metonymic (rather than metaphorical) affects that confront or confirm, afford or enable, demand or contest normative efforts to constitute or stabilise meaning about past and place. This challenges conventional temporalities of causality and effect, and change, conti-nuity and difference. Domańska (2006), in particular, emphasises the tensions between presence and absence emergent in the materiality of things, a vein of thought that has been particularly productive for re-search on the materialities of human remains (Domańska 2005; Fontein 2014; Filippucci et al. 2012; Harries 2010). It is equally productive for understanding how the ambivalent presence/absence of the past in the forms and properties of landscape around Mutirikwi both constitutes and is constituted by the contested politics of land occupations in the present. Therefore, the significance of the sacred Murinye *mapa* on Boroma, and of Mudarikwa's burial there in 2004, for the resurgent territorial politics of neighbouring chiefs, resettlement farmers, and various state authorities are in part constituted by the *longue durée* of past Murinye occupations and burials as manifest by its numerous older graves and ruins. But equally, re-emergent territorial politics, and the different contestations they involve, themselves re-constitute the significance of the *mapa,* and other material ruins of past Murinye occupation in the landscape, and Mudarikwa's burial in it.

Much of this book is about what was happening at Boroma and elsewhere around Mutirikwi during fieldwork in 2005/06, a period bounded by visits to Matopos Murinye for *kubata maoko* and to Mudarikwa's grave almost a year later. More loosely, it is about the cultural politics of land occupations all around Mutirikwi, since the war-veteran-led land invasions and *jambanja* (violence or chaos) of 2000 turned, hesitantly, into government-sponsored, politically animated but technocratically legitimated, fast-track land reform across Zimbabwe. However – and this is a key principle behind this book – although conventional personal, family, societal and broader national histories are often presented as punctuated by a series of moments that herald, provoke or come to represent important periods and processes of social and political change, more often than not such critical events and the changes they articulate, find traction only in the context of enduring continuities of meaning and practice, particularly as they relate to the immanence of the past manifest in the affective materialities of landscape. This is one of the reasons for structuring the book as I have – backwards. Rather than writing the history of Lake Mutirikwi in a linear narrative beginning at a more or less arbitrary point in the past and unfolding into the present – a narrative form which assumes a particular (fairly conventional) kind of temporality – this book begins with five chapters exploring the politics of belonging, entitlement and sovereignty involved in remaking Mutirikwi's landscapes in the 2000s. In part two we turn to consider earlier remakings before, during and after the dam was built, the traces of which continued to animate the events of the 2000s. In writing the book in this way, my emphasis is upon how the politics of the past may be less about competing narratives that seek to instil the legitimacy of rupture and precedence onto the present, than about how the material presence (and absence) of the past makes the politics of the present, and indeed of the future, possible in the first place.

Mirroring the return to things animating recent anthropological debates, in African studies this renewed focus on the enduring significance, indeed co-existence, of the past in the present has come about, in part, as a result of lengthy debates about the so-called 'invention' or 're-imagination' of 'tradition' and particularly 'ethnicity', heralded by Hobsbawm and Ranger's much (and often mis-) cited book (1983). As Nugent (2008) and others (Spear 2003) have discussed, this highly constructivist approach to the past, with its emphasis on colonial rupture, provoked a wealth of debate which has turned, of late, into a remarkable consensus about the need to refocus attention on pre-colonial African histories, and the enduring social, cultural and political continuities through which the ruptures of colonialism and postcolonialism gain traction and make sense (cf. Landau 2010; Gulbrandsen 2012). Not only has this resulted in a promising, renewed emphasis on the importance of pre-colonial African history, and a much less naïve return to oral history first heralded in the 1960s (cf. Mazarire 2010), perhaps most promising are the possibilities offered by a renewed enthusiasm for pre-colonial African archaeologies (cf. Delius & Marks 2012). This book does not draw directly on these new archaeological turns, but it is closely aligned to them exactly because exploring the continuing affectivity and political efficacy of the material presence of different African and European pasts co-existent in close historical and material proximity in the forms and substance of Mutirikwi's always emergent landscapes, involves a profound rethinking of the relationship between not only matter and meaning, but also difference and temporality. This is a project in which the disciplines of archaeology and anthropology have found a new, shared concern (cf. Shankland 2012).

BEYOND THE BIOGRAPHY OF A DAM

This book is therefore not simply a biography of a late colonial dam. Taking its mould from the 'social life' or 'cultural biography' of things (Appadurai 1986; Kopytoff 1986) such an approach could be productive in reflecting the shifting meanings and values associated with the dam and its landscapes, as its social, political and cultural contexts change through time, and with the ebb and flow of people, ideas and political systems. Since Colson's seminal work (1971) on the devastating social consequences of resettlement for Tonga people displaced by Kariba, exploring the after-effects of dam building has almost become a genre of its own. There are now many books about the after-effects and downstream consequences of dams, and such an approach is hardly novel, even if too many emphasise only the often considerable social and environmental damage that dams do, rather than explore their social, cultural and political productivity (Tsikata 2006; Isaacman & Isaacman 2013; Barker & Gildertson 2006; Hoag 2005; McCully 1996; Adams 1995). Hughes's work (2006a, 2006b, 2010) on the political productivity of hydrological engineering, watery shorelines and 'wilderness', for forging 'white African' belonging in Rhodesia and Zimbabwe is a remarkable exception, and I have drawn much inspiration from it here.

McGregor's *Crossing the Zambezi* (2009), although more about a river than a dam, has also been an important influence because of its determination to bring the Zambezi's complex and multiple pasts together into the story of the continuing contestations, claims and appropriations that articulate its ongoing becoming. McGregor presents a complex history animated by struggles for meaning, livelihoods and state-making, wherein the Zambezi appears (amongst other things) as a continuing

source of identity for its long marginalised 'river people', a moral justi-
fication for colonial rule or of late colonial developmentalist pride, and
simultaneously or sequentially, as a conduit and a boundary, a frontier
and an international border, a fishery and wildlife park (2009:1–19). Yet
Crossing the Zambezi is by McGregor's own admission (2009:5–7), more
'a history of claims' than an exploration of the 'complex reciprocity'
(Beinart 2000:287) that marks the 'imbrication of the semiotic and the
material' (Deleuze & Guattari 1987:337; Moore 2005:24), which has animated this Mutirikwi study.

This is an important point so let me explain. McGregor argues she
deliberately 'cast the claim-makers as its primary actors', thereby writing 'against much recent interest in the agency of the non-human world,
which has involved various means of trying to equalise human and non-
human actors and to blur the categorical boundaries that separate them'
(2009:5). Her strategy reflects how, in her view, across the period she
examines, 'the impact of human agency has been disproportionate, and
it is important to understand the ideas that drove those interventions',
particularly because 'non-representational conceptions of power (used
to incorporate non-human actors) can result in de-politicised and ahistorical narratives' (2009:5). I am sympathetic to McGregor's position. If
the turn to materiality is in part a reaction to some of the extremes of
social constructivism, then there may be a danger that we are returning
to a new, ahistorical or rather ahistoriographical form of determinism,
wherein human consciousness and agency no longer really matter. Are
we at risk of returning to a kind of objectivist History, with a capital
H, and ignoring historiography, the history of history? In some ways
these concerns are well founded. Latour has been criticised for being
ahistorical, although I think what is really meant is ahistoriographical,
in the sense that his networks of human and non-human actors not only
appear flattened (Navaro-Yashin 2012:162–5), they also seem not to include much space for human imagination, awareness and contestations
of time and the past. Similarly, Navaro-Yashin (2009) has criticised the
'affective turn' for focusing too much on the affects that objects, things
and landscapes exude, without reference to the complex subjectivities
and historical consciousness necessarily intertwined with such affec-
tivities. I agree with both McGregor and Navaro-Yashin that we must not
lose sight of the contested play of meanings and imaginations of place
and the past, nor of the complex subjectivities, creativity and agency of
people living in or *with* it, if we are to understand the complex politics of
remaking Mutirikwi's landscapes.

But I am still interested in what *stuff* does, allows, enables and constrains. Indeed as Ingold (2012a:3) suggests, there is a need to question
the commonplace 'chasm between perception and imagination'. Therefore in Chapter 7 I consider the materialities of imagination involved in
building the Kyle (Mutirikwi) dam, and the remaking of Fort Victorian
(Masvingo) landscapes that it entailed. If the materiality turn is a timely
response to the excesses of deconstruction and social constructivism,
then swinging to the other side of the pendulum in the excitement of

focusing on what *stuff* does, and so ignore consciousness, meaning and imagination, and by extension politics and historiography, is hardly the solution. So in my quest to understand the political materialities of land and water around, under, before and after Lake Mutirikwi, I stress how stuff and meaning are always intertwined, entangled, and emergent in politically implicated ways. This is what I mean by seeking to explore the 'complex reciprocity' (Beinart 2000:287) marking the imbrication of matter and meaning. In other words, I seek to understand how material-ity matters not just for History with a capital H, but for historiography. The 'social life' or 'cultural biography' of things approach – heralded by Kopytof (1986) and Appadurai (1986) in the 1980s – does not go far enough because it assumes that the meanings, values and political im-plications of a thing, an object or landscape derives from the changing social, political and cultural webs of meaning and action in which it is situated at any moment, or through time, rather than exploring how those meanings and actions find traction in their entanglement with the materialities of milieu.

In this respect Moore's *Suffering for Territory* (2005) has been an es-pecially important influence. Moore articulates how such a perspective led him to utilise the notion of 'assemblage' – derived from Deleuze and Guattari (1987) – as an analytical tool.

> If landscapes are integrally entangled in power relations, then analysts need to take more seriously the environmental and site specific materialities enmeshed in rule, unequal resource distribution, and governmental projects. While eschewing environmental determinism, what conceptual tools enable my analytic of landscape and power? In my vision *assemblages* displace humans as the sovereign makers of history. Humans are not the only entities making mixtures not of their choosing. Kaerezi is alive with nature-culture hybrids: SaGumbo's irrigation channel, his wife's neatly planted rows of maize and beans, and cook-hut fires that burn harvested trees. Assemblages arrange provisionally, giving emergent force to contingent alignments of social relations, material substance, and cultural meaning. And like places, assemblages foreground multiplicities irreducible to a single sense, structure or logic. They span the divide between nature and culture, humans and non-humans, symbol and substance, marking the 'imbrication of the *semiotic* and the *material*'. In such a vision, history and politics are inflected with the *consequential materiality* of milieu, of nonhuman entities and artefacts. (Moore 2005:23–24, original italics)

Whether the notion of assemblages contains sufficient mileage remains debatable. For McGregor, 'theories of assemblages ... seek not to understand the perspective of human actors, but to analyse the con-straining role of provisional and material arrangements of human and non-human things, to provide an interpretation of the power of non-hu-man actors' (2009:6, fn. 8). My reading is slightly different. If for Moore assemblages are 'contingent alignments of social relations, material substance, and cultural meaning', then 'understanding the perspective of human actors' remains central to the equation. Certainly around Mutirikwi the perspective of different human actors has been of central concern and I hope this is apparent throughout this book. But perhaps of greater theoretical significance in Moore's deployment is how the notion of agency is reconfigured, displacing *both* humans and environment as singular, 'sovereign makers of history'. This recalls Ingold's discussion of the 'mutual constitution of persons and environment', and in particular the relationality of 'effectivities and affordances – between the action capabilities of subjects and the possibilities for action offered by objects' (1992:51–52).

Ingold developed his argument for an 'alternative ecological anthropology' in response to debates 'for and against various versions of environmental and cultural determinism' (1992:42). It is also clear he was writing against a postmodernist perspective in which there is no environment, only landscape (Layton & Ucko 1999:3). More recently Ingold has critiqued approaches to materiality by emphasising the properties and flows of materials (2007), as he worked through his 'conception of the human being as a singular nexus of creative growth within a continually unfolding field of relationships', a 'process of growth ... tantamount to a movement along a way of life' (2011:xii). Over more than two decades, Ingold's work has shown remarkable consistency, particularly in its critique of how the notion of agency has often been deployed in anthropological analysis. Importantly, for Ingold the 'cultural construction of the environment is not so much a *prelude* to practical action as an (optional) epilogue' (1992:52).

Yet, like McGregor, it seems to me that there is no need to set aside in this way the heightened awareness of the complex intricacies of the politics of representations that the postmodern turn provoked. If practical action *in* the world by humans is not necessarily determined by detached cultural/social understandings *of* it, that does not mean that culturally/ socially constructed (and contested) meanings are not the cause or subject of intense *political* actions. Indeed to imply a sharp separation between practical and political human engagements with the world seems naïve, in the same way that the distinction between perception and imagination looks increasingly frail. Furthermore, representations, meanings, knowledges, rules and discourses also have 'affordances' or 'use-values' that enable or limit particular types of practical/political action and thought – as much as do material things, landscapes and environments. This was especially clear in 2005/06 on resettled farms north of Lake Mutirikwi, where the ancestral languages and practices of competing autochthonous land claimants and so-called 'traditional' authorities were gaining increasing purchase alongside legacies of suffering, eviction and loss, and appeals to productivity, soil conservation and technocratic land planning, as *jambanja* was giving way to more formalised resettlement.

Furthermore, rain and drought are inherently political, but rain making, dam building, contour ridging and all sorts of other languages and practices of water and land (Fontein 2006b) can also be forms of symbolic capital, in the remaking of authority over land around Mutirikwi. Rain has its affordances in political, social and ecological terms, but so do the practices and languages associated with it. Indeed, we can deepen our understanding of the political imbrications of rain, water and land – and of the technologies, practices, regimes of rule and registers of meaning, associated with them – by exploring the *materiality of signs*. Keane (2003, 2005) and Engelke's (2007) expansion upon Peirce's 'semeiotic' approach (1955) illustrates how the material qualities of some signs in part condition, enable and constrain meanings. This allows us to consider how socialities, historicity, contestation and political efficacy are *in part* determined independently of human agency, even as the materiality of signs can only gain political efficacy in relation to the constant play of contested 'semiotic ideologies'. This approach is deliberately open-ended and ultimately indeterminate. In Chapters 3 and 4 I use it to understand the divergent ways in which water, with all of its material forms and properties (as rivers, dams, irrigation or run-off but especially as rain) can be an *index of power* in the contested play of sovereignty and legitimacy amidst Mutirikwi's changing landscapes. This open-endedness is central to understanding not only how the materialities of land and water are key to both History and historiography, but also how, for example, rain making and dam building are linked in the politics of colonial and postcolonial state-making.

Therefore, in steering a path between environmental determinism and social constructivism, while maintaining a sharp historical focus on the entanglement of power in all human thought and action, recognition of 'the imbrication of the *semiotic* and the *material*' (Moore 2005:24, original emphasis) becomes an essential part of the endeavour. If Ingold reminds us that the material engagements *in* and *with* the world matter, then Moore re-affirms that it is 'history and politics [that] are inflected with the *consequential materiality* of milieu, of nonhuman entities and artefacts' (2005:24, emphasis added). This focus on the political materialities of landscape around Mutirikwi returns attention to the central dynamic that has made landscape, at its best, such a productive analytical concept: its 'useful ambiguity' (Gosden & Head 1994:113). Too often this analytical potential has not been realised, due either to an overly poststructuralist concern with the endless play of meanings – 'like the flickering text of a computer screen' (Daniels & Cosgrove 1988:8) – or because latent cultural or environmental determinisms have made landscapes 'appear pre-determined or even transcendental' (McGregor 2009:8).

DIFFERENCE, TIME AND LANDSCAPE

In 2011 Ranger anticipated that this book's central focus would be 'the Africanisation of a European landscape at Lake Kyle' (2011a:661). In many respects he was right. We can read the appeals to autochthony and ancestral practices, through which land occupations were being substantiated around Mutirikwi in the 2000s, as part of a longer historical process of re-Africanising landscape marked by the heavy imprint of European settlement and colonial rule. A remaking of landscape suffused with the remakings of Rhodesian rule: from the grandiose 'heroic' engineering of the dam wall to the celebrated beauty of Mutirikwi's rocky shoreline, and the wildlife park, fishing and recreational facilities established around it, but also the productive, bureaucratic and technocratic land and water planning imposed differentially in the white farming areas and African reserves of its wider milieu.

Yet for many of its protagonists – particularly those asserting (what I will call) 'genealogical geographies' in the form and substance of the soil (Chapter 5) – this already is, and always was, an African landscape. Traces of colonial remakings are merely brief blips in the far longer continuities they are seeking to restore. Many re-settlers in 2005/06 remembered their eviction from lands they were now resettling – in the 1940s and 1950s, in the delayed wake of the Land Apportionment Act (LAA 1930) but before the dam was built. With the important exception of the Zano people removed from the Chinango and Nyangani areas of the Mtilikwi reserve ahead of the dam's rising waters, it is those critical moments in the wake of the LAA, not the delineation of farms or the making the reserves in the late 1890s and early 1900s, nor the dam's completion in 1961, which mark the rupture of these continuities. This points to the different temporalities at play in the remaking of Mutirikwi's landscapes. My purpose is to explore how these colonial and postcolonial remakings of landscape, and the different temporalities they suggest, are made possible and even conceivable only because of the enduring materialities of landscape and the immanence of the past. If graves, the remains of homesteads, and sometimes much older stone ruins, all mark the *longue durée* of African presence persistent around Mutirikwi despite the imposition of re-imagined Rhodesian landscapes, colonial re-orderings and vast hydrological engineering, then these traces of white remakings too continue to animate and confront recent resettlement. As the active traces of these all different pasts co-exist and endure in close proximity through the shared materialities of landscape, the long history of efforts to inscribe *difference* into the shifting substances, forms and temporalities of space begins to falter.

Contests over land not only take place in the landscape but actively reshape it (Moore 1998). Because the history of state-making in Rhodesia and Zimbabwe has always been about land, 'just as the politics of land was centrally about state-making' (Alexander 2006:10), we can read this history of land and state-making off the very topography of milieu as an ongoing – but ultimately flawed – process of imposing, and re-imposing divergent and contested notions of difference into the very fabric of landscape. This imposition and re-imposition of difference into the substance of space and place, is both enabled and undermined by the materialities of milieu and the immanence of the past therein. Just as Rhodesian remakings of Mutirikwi as a productive and recreational landscape of white belonging could not obliterate the pre-existing African landscapes so re-emergent in the 2000s, neither can the resettlements and re-occupations of the 2000s obliterate the ruins of white settlement in the land (or of older post-war resettlement schemes) but rather builds off them. Just as change and rupture only make sense in the context of enduring continuities then, so does difference inscribed and re-inscribed in the form and substances of landscape only gain traction through shared engagements in the materialities of milieu. As I argue in Chapter 2, an analytic of co-existence and proximity in shared material landscapes does not eschew difference or change in favour of similarity or continuity so much as seek to provide a framework for understanding both at the same time.

A good way to think about this co-existence and proximity of different imaginative and material engagements in shared landscapes, confound-ing the arrow of time, is to consider place-names. To be sure, Rhodesian settlement and remakings of Mutirikwi's landscapes did involve the imposition of different, new visions, imaginations and experiences into colonial delineations of space and milieu. It was a process inflected with white settler needs to inscribe belonging into material landscapes they were re-forging as their own. This remains evident in the 'white' farm names that continued to be used by resettlement planners in the 2000s. Many reveal the origins of the Rhodesian pioneers, settlers, and survey-ors who first pegged them in the 1890s and early 1900s. Yet often they reflect not simply the inscription of new articulations of belonging into existing African landscapes as if they were a blank slate, but rather an entanglement of past memories, new aesthetic experiences and future aspirations. Perhaps the best example is the name 'Kyle' itself, the first, Rhodesian name for the Mutirikwi dam and lake, still widely used today despite renaming in the 1980s to reflect the principle river feeding it. It derives from the name of a farm located exactly where the dam was built, at the convergence of the Mutirikwi and Mushagashe rivers, a small area of land sub-divided from Oatlands farm near Boroma, which later gave its name to the irrigation scheme established there in 1988 (FAO & SAFR 2000). Kyle farm was so named because Mrs Francis – wife of Gordon Francis who bought it from Alfred Gifford in 1926 to use as 'a holding sta-tion for their cattle near Fort Victoria' (Masvingo town) – was reminded by the watery, rocky landscape where these two rivers converged of the Kyle of Lochalsh on Scotland's west coast where she grew up.[5] The name therefore reflects equally the memories and origins of its Rhodesian set-tlers and an aesthetic experience of the materiality of milieu.[6]

Many farm names betray the Scottish or Dutch/Afrikaner origins of the settlers and surveyors who pegged them (for example, Kelvingrove, Desmondale, Bannockburn, Niekerk's Rust, Twee Fontein and so on). Elsewhere farm names reflect poorly translated (or understood), pre-ex-isting African landscapes and territorialities. For example, 'Mzero farm' after the Muzviro river that has long been a territorial divide between the

[5] James Alfred Gifford 04/12/70, Dunollie Farm, Fort Victoria (NAZ Oral/G1 2f3, NAZ). But note that Saunders (1989:53) argues Alfred Gifford named the farm 'Kyle' after 'the Kyle Tea estate in Darjeeling in India where he was born'.
[6] A similar story is told about Glenlivet, on Nyuni mountain on Mutirikwi's eastern shores, later a well-known hotel, named by Mr Gilfillan, a government surveyor, who told Harry Harper that its view was 'a duplicate of the lovely valley of the River Spey, caressing Glenlivet Mountain in my own county of Banffshire, in the highlands of Scotland' (Sayce 1978:112–3).

Mugabe, Nemanwa and Charumbira clans; 'Beza farm' in the Beza hills, where a previous medium for the Duma ancestor Zarira lies buried and which Ambuya VaZarira claims as her own; 'Arawi' and 'Inyoni' reflecting the important hills of Harawe and Nyuni for the Chikwanda clan; and so on. Other farm names reflect early colonial efforts to delineate white farmland and African reserves; such as 'Mlinya farm' on the Mushagashe river, where Alfred Drew, one of Victoria's early Native Commissioners, located the small 'Mlinya [Murinye] reserve', before the reserves were remade again in the early 1900s.

That many less formal place-names in use around Mutirikwi today refer to the Shona nicknames ascribed to prominent white farmers ('Shephards', 'KwaBhani', 'KwaRoy'), only further illustrates the immanence of many pasts in place, and its potential to work against formal orderings of difference imposed into landscape. Similarly, the fact that A.A. Louw, founder of the Dutch Reformed Mission at Morgenster, chose that site because of its close proximity to Great Zimbabwe (as well as for its water supplies) illustrates, like Cecil Rhodes's posthumous appropriation of sacred African graves in the Matopos (Ranger 2012), how pre-colonial African ways of investing meaning in the landscape could animate colonial settlement, as part of European efforts to remake landscape to their economic, political, social and cultural needs. That such incorporation into existent landscapes by white incomers entangled with older forms of territoriality and assimilation around Mutirikwi (Mazarire 2013a), further illustrates the continuities that straddle ruptures of change and difference imposed into space. Likewise the remains of pottery, stone walling, and pre-Duma graves encountered in Murinye's Boroma *mapa* during our visit in July 2006, points not only to the immanence of many pasts in the materialities of place, but also the continuities in meaning, practice and rule that these can engender and make possible.

The immanence of diverse past practices, interventions and occupations in the active political materialities of landscape, is therefore a major theme running through this book. It appears in many forms: from the way the dam's presence continues to animate technocratic demands for soil conservation as well as local appeals for access to fishing and irrigation, and for protection from hippos, to the way that graves and ruins of earlier African occupants afford new autochthonous land claims and make ritual demands upon new farmers and re-settlers. Similarly, in the way that movement through, and recent resettlement of, former African reserves and white commercial farmland was and is shaped by the traces of previous efforts to enable, control or contest white or black movement through the landscape, in the forms of roads, bridges, fences, homesteads and fields. These measures were themselves afforded, in part, by the topographic and material qualities of rivers, hills, caves, rocks and soil, which later became the focus of guerrilla action to subvert imposed landscapes of white Rhodesian control during the liberation war.

Yet the immanence of the past does not only emerge through the active material remains of graves, ruins, dams, roads and fences. The past can animate the present in other ways that also point to the co-existence and proximity of different ways of engaging with it. In Chapter 2 I discuss how the ancestral and autochthonous knowledge of Mutirik-wi's African landscapes, and its sacred places, rituals and taboos, meets the uncanny presence of white ghosts on former Rhodesian farms, to illustrate how the immanence of multiple pasts can confront the ruptures of change and difference across divergent registers of meaning and practice. Encounters with ghosts and spirit possession can be very different kinds of experience, because ghosts are rarely *made* to appear, and when they do they usually point to an uncanny 'power of absence' (Domańska 2006:346), unlike the over-determinations common to spirit possession through which ancestors are made *decidedly* present. Spirit possession in Zimbabwe, particularly by known ancestors, involves learnt, repeated, and socially validated, embodied practices through which mediums are both 'subjected to power and history, but nevertheless manage to constitute [themselves] as subjects in their own right' (Lambek 2002a:25). In mediumship, as opposed to ghosts, the immanence of the past is therefore in part manifest through the generative capacities inherent to habitus: the repeated bodily practices and dispositions through which mediums form mutually constitutive relationships with their spirits (Perman 2011:850) and creatively 'choose to subject themselves' (Lambek 2002a:38) to their will, and to the social, historical, political and moral expectations of those around them, upon whose recognition mediums' authority depends (Fontein 2006a:47–72).

But ancestral spirits can also defy the creative, embodied dispositions and practices of mediums, and the social expectations through which they are authenticated and legitimated. Like ghosts, they can appear unexpectedly in odd places, moments and unexpected contexts, as wind, rain, drought, fire, sickness and misfortune, or through encounters with animals, like *mhondoro* (ancestral) lions, angry baboons, dangerous hippos and crocodiles, or through the merged substances of graves, bodies and soil. There always remains something uncertain, excessive and other to spirit encounters, which confronts not just ethnographers but all participants, including mediums themselves. There is always some doubt about the authenticity, identity or motivation of any spirit, medium, or possession event. Reaching beyond the confines of *mudzimu* ancestral spirits to grasp the entire complexity of the spirit world around Mutirikwi – including (amongst many others)[7] the *njuzu* water spirits/creatures that abduct people into springs, rivers and dams – the shared capacities of ghosts and other kinds of spirit to intrude unexpectedly into the present become much more salient.

Amidst this wider cacophony of spirit encounters, both ghosts and ancestral spirits, like graves and ruins, point to capacity of the past to intrude upon and disrupt the present. Furthermore, uncanny or not, encounters with ghosts, spirit possession or abductions by *njuzu,* carry decidedly moral and political implications that point not only to the

---

[7] Such as *mashave* (healing and/or animal spirits), frightening *ngozi* (avenging) spirits, and *chidhoma* and *chikwambo* (witchcraft familiars).

past, but to the future. Lambek's emphasis on the creative and moral dimensions of memory practices – what he calls 'poesis' and 'phronesis' (2002b) – links the immanence of the past to the politics of contested futures. Like spirit possession, rain making and encounters with *njuzu* or ghosts, all engagements with, or interventions in, landscape face forward or are enacted in anticipation of enduring affects and what is to come, however much they may also respond to or derive from the past, or be enacted within a politics of the present. The immanence of the past emergent in both the materialities of landscape and visceral encounters with spirits further collapses conventional linear temporalities, so that it is the present that appears subdued as the past spills or intrudes into (or out of) anticipated futures (cf. Hodges 2008; Nielsen 2011). As 2005 turned into 2006 this became apparent to me when an unexpected optimism spread across Mutirikwi's resettling landscapes, as first the wild *mashuku* harvest[8] and then the rains finally bore fruit.

OPTIMISM, RAIN AND LAND REFORM

One of the defining features of fieldwork in 2005/06 was an unfolding sense of optimism I encountered as the rainy season finally bore fruit, reversing several years of variable rains and poor harvests. I first came across it visiting Matopos Murinye in September 2005. For a man who had recently lost his father and seemed so close to death himself, his enthusiasm to explain how the 'Duma chiefs had been carrying on with their traditions', and to show me 'the secret places where the Duma chiefs are buried' was startling,[9] especially given the hardships of Zimbabwe's wider economic and political strife. In the following months I became increasingly aware how for many of Masvingo's diverse new land occupiers the fast-track context offered opportunities to realise a multiplicity of long-held aspirations that turned on access to land and fertile soils in different ways (cf. Moyo 2001; Moyo & Yeros 2005). These included, amongst others, the fulfilment of the 'peasant option' (Ranger 1985), the return of ancestral landscapes and traditionalist forms of authority, the completion of Zimbabwe's rural 'revolution' (Sadomba 2011), new entrepreneurial possibilities that the access to fertile lands offered, or any combination of these. This multiplicity of aspirations reflected the diversity of overlapping languages and practices of entitlement, belonging and authority deployed by new farmers, war veterans, and returning autochthons to legitimise their land occupations.

Local and provincial land planners and technocrats at AREX[10] and the

---

[8] Fruit of the *mushuku* (wild loquat) tree, *uapaca kirkiana* (Daneel 1998:306).
[9] Fieldnotes 04/09/05.
[10] Department of Agriculture and Rural Extension. At the time of my research the old AGRITEX had been merged with agricultural research departments to form AREX. This was later reversed. See www.worldwide-extension.org/africa/ zimbabwe, accessed on 21/5/13; also 'Zimbabwe: Agritex Revives Land Use Planning Dept', *The Herald*, 11/08/11.

Department of Lands too revealed genuine enthusiasm for fast-track land reform, despite their exclusion from the initial land invasions, and the severe funding limitations and political interferences they endured. Many understood fast-track as a revitalisation of early post-independence efforts to promote smallholder agriculture (Kinsey 1999). The fact that civil servants were prominent amongst the beneficiaries of land reform in Masvingo (Scoones et al. 2010:53) reiterates, rather than negates, the significance of their optimism. It illustrates how land reform could be understood as a response to a diversity of long-standing aspirations, reflecting a diversity of past engagements in the land and the entanglement of different aspired futures. This sense that the fast-track context enabled a multiplicity of long-standing, delayed, localised aspirations, grievances and demands to be realised is important for understanding the optimism I encountered as 2005 turned into 2006. But it is not enough. All of these elements were already in play before the 2005/06 agricultural season began. So what was it about that year that provoked this diversity of shared optimism? The answer, in short, is that it rained.

In 2005 rural communities in Masvingo were again suffering drought and poor harvests. In part this explains why a six-week ban on agricultural activities, imposed in mourning after Chief Mudarikwa Murinye's death, was so unpopular.[11] More broadly, however, the recurrent droughts of the early 2000s had begun to call into the question the legitimacy of the government's land reform programme. True enough, ZANU PF often, perhaps erroneously (Richardson 2007), cited poor rainfall to explain dramatic declines in agricultural production as Zimbabwe's agricultural sector was so profoundly reconfigured. But the political significance of rain and drought in Zimbabwe is not simply a question of agricultural productivity (cf. Lan 1985; Ranger 2003; Vijfhuizen 1997). Around Mutirikwi the recurrent failure of the rains had provoked difficult questions about the way fast-track was being implemented. Spirit mediums pointed to the failing rains as indicative of their marginalisation from land reform. In January 2001 Ambuya VaZarira told war veterans and new farmers that 'the lack of adequate rain they had experienced that season was because the government was not adequately consulting with the spirit mediums'.[12] When the same war veterans came back later that year to urge VaZarira to return to her ancestor's *mapa* on Beza, because they were having problems there with '*mhondoro* lions' (ancestral lions), she told them she 'was not interested in the fast-track ... I want to go back there with *chivanhu*' (tradition).[13] Such problems with rain and *mhondoro* lions are amongst the reasons why many war veterans, and new farmers around Mutirikwi turned to mediums and autochthonous clans as they sought to 'make safe' their occupation of resettled farms, an effect also reported elsewhere (cf. Chaumba et al. 2003b: 601).

---

[11] 'Zimbabwe: Villagers protest against 6-week ban on fieldwork', *The Herald*, 18/07/05.
[12] Fieldnotes 26–27/01/01.
[13] Ambuya VaZarira, 16/08/01.

The imbrication of rain in the politics of land has a long history, and represents one of the continuities entangled with the materialities of milieu this book examines. In 1912 a severe drought in Masvingo was attributed to 'the recent death of Chief Mazungunye', the most senior Duma chief and a widely renowned rainmaker (Sayce 1978:111). The good rains that followed in 1913, however, did not lead to a renewal of the Mazungunye chieftaincy and its rain-making powers, but became embroiled in tensions between the Duma rain cult at Mandara Hill, and the 'encroachment of the *Mwari* cult from the west' (Sayce 1978:59,111). With the 1896 revolt (Ranger 1967), and the prominent role of the Matopos *Mwari* shrines fresh in their minds, Rhodesian settlers 'evacuated ... to the town ... until things settled down' (Sayce 1978:111), illustrating how even then the politics of rain making was imbricated in colonial politics. The 1912/13 drought and then abundant rains culminated an assemblage of events and 'external pressures' that contributed to the demise of the Mandara cult – and subsequently the whole 'Duma Confederacy' (Mtetwa 1976) – amidst growing incursions by the *Mwari* shrines, Ndebele and Nguni raids, and deepening interference by Rhodesian settlers, the British South Africa Company (BSACo), and Christian evangelists from the end of the 19th century (Sayce 1978:58).

These events illustrate how rain, drought and rain making have long been imbricated in localised contests around Mutirikwi with wider reverberating effects. Reminiscent of 1912/13, in 1992 Zimbabwe's most devastating drought since independence brought renewed tensions between so-called 'African spirituality' and Zionist and Pentecostal churches to the foreground, resulting in the emergence of various traditionalist religious movements, including the Juliana cult (Ranger 2003, 2011b; Mafu 1995; Mawere & Wilson 1995). Juliana's meteoric rise and subsequent demise – because she failed to make it rain – illustrates how the fortunes of those claiming ancestral or divine legitimacy can be intimately linked to the vagaries of weather. The 1992 drought is equally well-remembered for bringing the ancestral legitimacy of the state into question, illustrating how the politics of water is closely related to its material qualities as rain or run-off, in its ability to reverberate across different political and geographical scales. Even President Mugabe himself was forced that year to ask 'the spirit mediums to bring rain', a request many refused 'on the grounds that president should consult with them on all matters, not just ... when there was a crisis (Derman 2003:71).

In 2005/06, recurrent drought followed by successful rains again entangled complex localised disputes with wider political events. Before the rains VaZarira became embroiled in contestations over Chief Chikwanda's legitimacy, in which drought was articulated with his failure to secure food aid as well as frightening encounters with *njuzu* spirits. VaZarira and acting Chief Murinye also spent much effort seeking funds, fuel and transport to enable a high-profile visit to the Matopos to request rain to relieve the parched lands. She sought assistance from the new senator Dzikamai Mavhaire, whose political legitimacy for her clearly depended upon his recognition of her authority as a key Duma medium;[14] illustrating how national politicians are entangled within localist performances of sovereignty and legitimacy, and implying their fortunes too are linked to the vagaries of rain and drought. This was further demonstrated in early 2006 when countrywide 'national *biras*' (instigated by government for the first time in September 2005) were heralded an enormous success because the abundant rains of the 2005/6 season had delivered 'bumper' harvests in many areas.[15] For many around Mutirikwi the ancestral legitimacy of land reform had been restored.[16]

This then accounts, in part, for the optimism around Mutirikwi in 2005/6. For many the successful rains confirmed that fast-track land reform might enable long-delayed, localised aspirations to be realised; a sense that government, party and state mechanisms were now, to some extent, working *for* them, and their aspired futures. But not everyone perceived the successful harvests of 2005/06 as indicative of government and land reform's legitimacy.[17] Nor did the rains necessarily resolve the many localised disputes between, war veterans, new farmers, mediums, chiefs and technocrats that land occupations had provoked. Although traditionalist languages and practices of land and water (Fontein 2006b) like rain making, have had an unusually *longue durée* of significance, there are many registers of meaning and regimes of rule to do with water in play around Mutirikwi. Indeed a theme recurrent throughout this book is how water in its various manifestations (rain, run-off, rivers, pools, dams) and with its various material qualities (as a volume, medium or line; its fluid, pooling, erosive qualities) features in an array of overlapping performances and reconfigurations of power and sovereignty, authority and legitimacy. The politics of rain is one way among many in which water can be an *index of power*; indicative of the contested entanglements of *both* demonstrative, performative and sometimes coercive assertions of sovereignty, autonomy and capacity, *and* productive and pastoral appeals to legitimacy, developmentalism, moral authority and consent. Rain making is a good example because it is

---

[14] As she put it, it is a 'test ... to see if he keeps his promises, because the work that I am doing is for ... the country and since they are the government it is work that they should be doing ... so they should send me a car to take me where I need to go' (Fieldnotes 29/11/05).

[15] *Daily Mirror*, 04/03/06.

[16] 'Newsflash: Divine backing for land reform', *Zimbabwe Independent*, 06/01/06.

[17] Despite widespread rains ('Zimbabwe: bumper harvest prospects still high', *The Herald*, 23/02/06; 'Country receives above normal rainfall', *Daily Mirror*, 17/05/06) harvests were not abundant everywhere and food still needed to be imported. Some argued that poor harvests despite the good rains, were the result of continuing shortages of fertilisers, seed and other inputs ('Zimbabwe crops fail despite good rain', *The Telegraph*, 01/02/06; 'Zimbabwe faces worst harvest on record', *Voice of America*, 31/01/06; '650,000 people need food aid in Masvingo province', *ZimOnline*, 24/07/06, accessed 05/10/14). The government was also accused of inflating figures ('Zimbabwe accused of inflating maize harvest figures', *ZimOnline*, 17/05/06, accessed 05/10/14; 'Zimbabwe Officials admit severe food deficit', *ZimOnline*, 25/08/06, accessed 05/10/14; 'Food Shortages are looming', *IRIN (UN)*, 29/08/06).

both demonstrative of the autonomy and capacity of rainmakers, ancestors and *Mwari*, yet also responsive to peoples' livelihood needs. But dam building, borehole digging, contour ridging (as well as fishing, wildlife conservation and irrigation) can equally incorporate both 'repressive and productive mechanisms of power' (Navaro-Yashin 2002:53).

It is important to emphasise, therefore, that the link between the optimism of 2005/06 and the successful rains was not necessarily dependent upon a commitment to the ancestral ownership of land or divine provision of rain. That was simply one (albeit important) way in which the potentialities offered by rain, fertile soils and land could be articulated, assembled and understood. Rather, rain and promising harvests engendered optimism across divergent registers of meaning and practice because it materialised – made real – the possibility that land reform could be responsive to a whole host of localised aspirations that turned on access to land in diverse ways. It was the rain and abundant harvests that made reachable and tangible the diversity of aspired futures invested into re-occupying land by new farmers, autochthonous land claimants and others, just as the prolonged droughts of previous years had made land reform look tentative, uncertain and doubtful. If resettling the farms involved considerable commitments of time, labour and resources (cf. Scoones et al. 2010: 77– 93), as well as profound social, political and imaginative investments, it was the successful rains which transformed these efforts into the realisable possibility of substantiating new livelihoods, return to ancestral lands, or the completion of an unfinished programme of national liberation, and so on. All of which fed into and out of diverse imaginations for what a good, modern, legitimate postcolonial state should be about. If hope entails 'a vision of a transcendent perfection' that is 'anchored' into the future, and optimism 'results from tangible or assumed success' in the here and now (Deneen 1999:577,581), then the unfolding optimism I encountered around Mutirikwi as the rains at last bore fruit, was really a kind of hope with optimism. If so, then it was the rain which enabled the materialities of the past unfolding in the tangible actualities of the present to spill forward into anticipated and aspired futures, linking optimism to hope and thereby performing a profound temporal trick in which the enduring hardships of the present almost, for a moment, disappeared.

But it did not last. As I discuss in the Epilogue, in the years that followed devastating droughts returned and the hardships endured by Zimbabweans worsened profoundly, amid rocketing inflation, failing infrastructure, and deepening political crisis. The March 2008 elections were followed by a brutal wave of violence across Masvingo and the country (cf. Sachikonye 2011). Just as prevalent was the unremitting hunger. Few harvested more than a tin-full[18] of maize after a prolonged dry spell caused crops to wilt. People resorted to harvesting, and sometimes fighting over, the unpleasant fruit of wild *muchakata* trees[19]

---

[18] A common every-day measurement used for selling grain in local markets, normally a fairly standard re-used cooking-oil or other 'tin' or container, about 25x25 cm square x50 cm high.

[19] The wild cork tree, *Parinari curatellifolia* (Daneel 1998:304)

washing and grinding commercial maize seed (treated with pesticides), or collecting maize spilt from passing trucks, as prices rocketed and shelves remained empty.[20] ZANU PF's suspension of food relief by international NGOs exacerbated the situation and hungry, brutalised rural folk often had nowhere left to turn.[21] As Matopos Murinye explained when I visited him in August 2008:

> After the March elections when it became clear that the opposition had won, the people in government from ZANU PF, they could not accept that. So that was when this recent violence began. People's houses were burnt, they were beaten, and some were even killed. Things were very difficult particularly in places like Bikita and Zaka, which were more affected than we were here. But then there was this memorandum of understanding, and things have become quieter now, but things are still not better. The big problem we have now is *nzara* [hunger]. The harvest was bad this year, and now that the government has suspended the operations of NGOs like CARE, people are very hungry. Everyday I have people coming to me telling me they have nothing to eat. In some places they go for some days without food. There are some people who have resorted to washing *mbeu* [commercial maize seed treated with pesticides] and grinding that to get *sadza* [thick maize-meal porridge] to eat. Things are very very bad.[22]

Later that year, Zimbabwe's miseries were compounded by a cholera outbreak that caused more than 4000 deaths across the country (Mason 2009).

The hope with optimism of 2005/06 proved as ephemeral as the rains that had provoked it. When I next visited in 2011 things had changed again. The Government of National Unity (GNU) formed in 2009 and the desertion of the Zimbabwean dollar arrested crippling inflation and, for a time, political violence. For some, this new economic and political context offered renewed hope and perhaps a little optimism. But by then acting Chief Matopos Murinye's conviction, so apparent in 2005/06, that he could substantiate his position as chief had already been quashed. A fierce succession dispute had arisen and amid much controversy a new chief was installed in 2010, Ephias Munodawafa Murinye, who immediately exacerbated many of the territorial disputes his predecessor had faced. As my visits *kubata maoko* in September 2005 and to Mudarikwa Murinye's grave in July 2006 were among the critical events that had structured my 2005-06 fieldwork, it was with great sadness that I learnt in December 2011 of Matopos Murinye's subsequent death. To compound this, his family were denied permission to bury him in the sacred Murinye *mapa* on Boroma as he had wanted. Having finally succumbed to his sickness of 2005 even his hopes of being buried alongside his father were denied.

There have been many changes around Mutirikwi since 2005/06. Yet in the multiple contests that land occupations provoked, it is the enduring political materialities of landscape, across diverse regimes of meaning, practice and rule, which appear most striking. The remaking of Mutirikwi's landscapes charts many profound re-alignments over the

---

[20] Fieldnotes 22–24/08/08 and 28/11–22/12/11.
[21] 'Zimbabwe: NGO ban starting to bite', *IRIN*, 07/07/08.
[22] Acting Chief Matopos Murinye 22–24/08/08.

last century, before, during and after the dam was built, over the last decade, and even over the period it was written. More often than not, however, they have gained traction in the context of important continuities. Enduring across the perceived ruptures of History, these often derive from the immanence of the past emergent in the materialities of landscape, across the contested play of sovereignty and legitimacy inherent to the politics of water and land.

Land reform in the 2000s not only contributed to the polarisation of Zimbabwe's political sphere, it has also divided commentators and scholars working within and outside the country. In the early 2000s many rushed to condemn the land invasions as the cynical and violent manipulations of an embattled ruling party. Yet if the 'history of claims' and 'the ideas that drove interventions matter' (McGregor 2009:5) in the assemblages of human/non-human actors, material processes, meanings and practices involved in the re-configuration of land, authority and the state, then understanding land occupations around Mutirikwi without recourse to the immanent pasts and imagined futures of people involved in them, or the emergent material contexts within which they gain traction and coherence, is to see only part of the picture. I am confident that there is now a wealth of empirical scholarship emerging on and coming out from Zimbabwe, which is better placed to take up this challenge than the polarised debates on land reform were in much of the 2000s. This book is my modest contribution to that larger project, and that of many protagonists remaking Mutirikwi in the 2000s, whose voices I hope are clear throughout it.

BOOK STRUCTURE

The book is structured into two parts. Part One focuses on the remaking of Mutirikwi's landscapes in the 2000s, and Part Two on older remakings before, during and after the dam was built. Chapter 1 introduces the historical and localised complexity of what in the early 2000s was often over-simplistically characterised as 'Zimbabwe's authoritarian turn'. It considers how members of different clans around Mutirikwi, occupying state land, earlier resettlement schemes or resettled farms, made very specific claims to land which appealed to autochthonous knowledge, and invoked memories of past occupation, eviction and the burial of ancestors in the soil. Such claims were reinforced by the official 'return' of the powers of chiefs over resettlement areas, and sat uneasily next to both the increasing participation of technocratic planners, and the waning authority of war veterans who had spearheaded land occupations in 2000.

Chapter 2 discusses resurgent disputes over autochthony and belonging around Mutirikwi in relation to recent approaches to materiality, which have explored the agency, affordances and affective qualities of things, materials and landscapes. Linking these discussions to anthropology's recent, 'ontological turn', it explores how material forms of different past and present landscape practices reveal and materialise proximities and co-existences even as they are often articulated in political processes of differentiation.

Chapter 3 considers the significance of rain making, *njuzu* water spirits, and national *bira*s, to pursue the notion that water acts as an *index of power*, of the contested play of legitimacy and sovereignty, across many different registers of meaning. This theme is continued in Chapter 4, which discusses disputes over fishing, wildlife and irrigation around the lake to explore how water's many material potentialities gain political purchase across divergent yet co-existent regimes of rule.

Chapter 5 hinges Part One's focus on the political materialities of belonging, sovereignty and legitimacy in the 2000s with Part Two's focus on the contested Rhodesian futures embedded in the materialities of irrigation planning and dam building in the mid-20th century. It explores the contested genealogical geographies deployed by chiefs and clans around Mutirikwi, and what they tell us about history, historiography and changing notions of territoriality. Such genealogical geographies challenge conventional temporalities that assume discrete pre-colonial, colonial and postcolonial periods are properly meaningful, by making the colonial period appear like a brief gap in much longer continuities imbricated in the materialities of landscape.

The chapters in Part Two explore what happened during this gap. Chapter 6 reveals how Rhodesian irrigation planning and dam building was bound up with hotly contested, imagined white futures, at a time of both 'high-modernist' optimism and growing momentum for decolonisation across British colonial Africa. These futures circulated around the possibilities irrigation offered for increased white settlement, agricultural production and industrialisation. The building of the Kyle dam was deeply entangled within the complex tensions that beset the Southern Rhodesian and Federal governments.

Chapter 7 explores how the nexus of imagined futures, engineering and water planning that dam building involved was at once both a highly abstracted and yet a profoundly material affair. It provoked deep tensions between Victoria residents and the sugar planters and industrialists of the lowveld. While the lion's share of Mutirikwi's waters transformed the lowveld's 'wilderness' into one of Rhodesia's industrial heartlands, constituted around sugar production, long-standing demands of Victoria residents for local irrigation remained muted as the lake was remade into a game and recreational park for fishing, boating and other watery activities.

Chapters 8 and 9 consider what happened in the wake of the dam. Although Victoria residents built their 'playground' with great gusto, and the lowveld sugar industries rapidly expanded, African nationalism and war quickly brought danger and insecurity to Mutirikwi's landscapes. As white futures looked more precarious, African futures were increasingly full of promise. For many, cultural nationalism anticipated new futures offering diverse promises of return. With independence these materialised in a wave of restless squatting. This is considered in Chapter 9, written around the story of Sofia Muchini, a Nehanda medium who became deeply embroiled in the murders of white farmers during that un-settled period. By the end of the 1980s many returnees had been evicted again, as older management plans for the Mutirikwi's recreational park were re-asserted. Some promised returns did take hold and the Europe-anisation of Mutirikwi's landscapes was at least partially undone. But many were frustrated. By the century's turn many around Mutirikwi felt independence had not delivered its radical promises. This set the scene for the return of radicalism in the 2000s. As one land claimant put it, explaining his second return to Mzero farm in 2000: 'the government said *ivhu kuvanhu*' (soil to the people) and that is indeed what happened.

This takes the book back to its beginning. It is a story about the re-assertion of African pasts and presence around Mutirikwi, which the dam failed to obliterate. It is also a story of African futures frustrated in the wake of war. Furthermore, it is story in which the commonly perceived ruptures of history – of the dam, war, independence, and of eviction and return – diminish in context of material and imaginative endurances, co-existences and proximities. The optimism and insecuri-ties of the 1970s, and the euphoria and frustrations of the 1980s, tell of the accumulative, open-ended and emergent becoming of landscape, of the enduring political materialities of land and water, of the proximity and co-existence of different regimes of rule, and registers of meaning and practice entangled with it. This is what I reflect upon in the Epilogue, which assesses events around Mutirikwi in more recent years.

PART ONE

Remaking Mutirikwi
in the 2000s

I

New Farmers,
Old Claims[1]

OPTIMISM, ENTHUSIASM AND HARD WORK

Gore rino ndinoda kuzadza GMB nechibage changu!
[This year I want to fill up the Grain Marketing Board with my own maize!]
(New farmer, 19/12/05, Masvingo District)[2]

But in terms of the broader vision, I have to stress that I think this land reform programme is one of the most wonderful programmes for a third world country to embark upon.
JF: So you are actually very optimistic?
Yes I am optimistic. I think it is a great thing for a third world country, it really is.
(Chief Lands Officer, 5/06/06, Masvingo Province)[3]

You asked me ... what were the major changes that I have seen since the 1970s ... and I said that at independence ... there were very dramatic changes ... in agricultural development and extension. But now, having had our conversation ... I think that even the period we are going through now is one of profound ... change. It is a very exciting period, especially in terms of land tenure ... Since the 1980s there were not many changes in land tenure, but then all of a sudden in 2000 there was this revolution, which has thrown up all sorts of new challenges.... And some of us need to have a paradigm shift in the way that we do things.
(Provincial Agricultural Extension Service (AREX) Officer, 28/04/06, Masvingo Province)[4]

One remarkable feature of the comments above is the optimism they convey. This optimism and enthusiasm of many involved in land resettlement around Mutirikwi in 2005/06, was remarkable in the face of not only the huge volume of criticism levied at Zimbabwe's agrarian reform programme, but also the severe economic, social and political problems that nearly all Zimbabweans faced throughout that decade.[5] Accompanying land reform in the 2000s a new brand of 'authoritarian nationalism'

---

[1] An earlier version of this chapter was published in *African Studies Quarterly*, 10/04/09. I am grateful for permission to include a revised version here.

[2] Mafuma Mutsambwa 19/12/05.

[3] Joseph Munyanyi 05/06/06.

[4] Nyasha Pambirei 28/04/06.

[5] For examples of NGO reports critical of 'fast-track' land reform see: UNDP, January 2002, *Zimbabwe land reform and resettlement: assessment and suggested framework for the future*; Human Rights Watch, March 2002, *Zimbabwe: fast-track land reform in Zimbabwe*, 14, 1(A); International Peace Academy, *Democracy and Land Reform in Zimbabwe*, 25/02/02.

(Raftopoulos 2003:217) emerged, involving increasingly 'extreme and violent political intolerance' (Alexander 2003:99) of any perceived opposition to the ruling party, as well as continuing economic decline, very high unemployment and, in 2005, a grossly disproportionate government attack on the informal economy and urban housing. All of this was punctuated by ever more restrictive legislation on citizenship, the media and NGOs, and by a series of controversial and sometimes violent elections (2000, 2002, 2005 and especially 2008).[6] In addition, Zimbabwe was terribly affected by the AIDS catastrophe, with thousands dying every week; a situation exacerbated by failing urban infrastructure, health services and particularly sanitation and water supplies.[7] To compound this, from 2001 to 2005 severe droughts dramatically worsened food shortages, undermining, even among apparent loyalists, enthusiasm for the land reform programme.[8]

In this broader context, one could wonder what the optimism of 2005/06 was all about. The immediate answer relates to drought and hunger, given that the rains that year were in many areas plentiful and

---

[6] The elections of 2008 witnessed Zimbabwe's worst violence since the 1980s (Sachikonye 2011). In August 2008, inflation reached an astonishing 350,000 per cent ('Zimbabwe March inflation surges to 355,000%, Independent says' 16/05/08 *Bloomberg*). On *Murambatsvina* see UN Tibaijuka Report, 18/07/05 *'Report of the Fact-Finding Mission to Zimbabwe to assess the scope and impact of Operation Murambatsvina by the UN Special Envoy'*; also Sokwanele, 18/06/05, *'Operation Murambatsvina': An Overview and Summary*, (www.sokwanele. com, accessed 29/05/13). On legislation, see AIPPA (Access to Information and Protection of Privacy Act, 2002); POSA (Public Order and Security Act, 2002); ZEC ACT (Zimbabwe Electoral Commission Act, 2004); and the NGO Act (Non Governmental Organisations Act) December 2004. See also Amnesty International Report, 10/05/05, *Zimbabwe: Human rights defenders under siege*. In August 2007 the Interception of Communications Act was passed allowing state security to intercept email and telephone communications (*Financial Times*, 'New law allows Mugabe to eavesdrop', 05/08/07).

[7] In 2003 rough estimates suggested between 1,000 and 3,500 people were dying from Aids every week (*Zimbabwe Standard*, 23/03/03, 'Zimbabwe Aids Statistics in Shambles'). Urban sanitation dramatically worsened towards the end of the decade, provoking a recurring outbreaks of typhoid and cholera. In late 2008 a cholera epidemic infected 60,000 and killed over 4,000 ('Global, national efforts must be urgently intensified to control Zimbabwe cholera outbreak', www.who. int/mediacentre/news/releases/2009/cholera_zim_20090130/en/index.html, accessed 29/5/13).

[8] By the elections of March 2008, even ZANU PF's rural support began to dwindle, and several prominent politicians, new farmers and war veterans, including in Masvingo, renounced support for ZANU PF in favour of independent candidates or even Morgan Tsvangirai's MDC. ('Dumiso Dabengwa quits Zanu PF (Mugabe Faction) for Zanu PF (Makoni Faction)?' 01/03/08 (www. zimdaily.com /news/117/ARTICLE/2406/2008-03-01.html, accessed 29/05/13); 'Mbudzi warns CIO against making Makoni target', (www.newzimbabwe. com/ pages/zanupf 14.17700.html, accessed 29/05/13); 'Zvinavashe concedes after recount, takes aim at Mugabe', 24/04/08 (www.newzimbabwe.com/pages/ electoral244.18100.html, accessed 29/05/13); 'General Vitalis Zvinavashe concedes defeat, blames Mugabe', *The Zimbabwean*, 24/04/08.

promising of good harvests.[9] A related point is soil fertility and the productive potential of land on the resettled farms. Mafuma Mutsambwa,
who came from communal areas in Zaka – 'where the soil is now very
poor' – to occupy a farm along Masvingo–Mutare road in February 2000,
exclaimed there would be no need to use fertiliser on his land – 'not for
a hundred years!' – so good was the soil.[10] Rain, soil fertility and good
harvests were hugely important in complex ways, and I return to them
in later chapters. But there was more to it than that. To adequately
understand this optimism requires careful reflection on the overlapping
trajectories of individual and shared memories and aspirations, within
wider, shared and contested, imagined futures. This includes *imaginations of*, or *aspirations for*, what a good, functioning postcolonial state
should be; or in Ferguson's words (1999) the 'expectations of modernity'
that people and states foster. Here is the focus of this chapter: to explore the complex entanglement of different, overlapping, sometimes
contested and often highly localist aspirations for land, with broader
imaginations of postcolonial stateness as manifest through land reform
around Mutirikwi. In particular, how localised ideas and practices of
landscape, livelihoods and the past inevitably entangled with contemporary discourses of, and imagined futures for, the postcolonial state.

Along with the mood of optimism across Masvingo in 2005/06, another
under-reported aspect of Zimbabwe's land reform is the hard physical
work invested in resettlement plots and redistributed farms, which reflected importantly upon the individual commitment of so-called 'new
farmers'. In the early 2000s, and since, the national and international
independent press have tended to focus upon the violence of the initial
'land invasions', the exclusion of farm workers and women (Derman
& Hellum 2007), poor take-up rates, abandoned plots and the un-
derutilisation of resettled land, on the poor farming techniques, limited
agricultural knowledge, inputs and resources available to new farmers,
as well as on cronyism, corrupt land allocation, and multiple farm ownership.[11] The government-owned press sometimes joined these debates
although it tended, not surprisingly, to emphasise success stories. It took
an active part in a lively discourse surrounding resettled farmers, and
began to publish a monthly magazine called the *New Farmer*. Less benign

---

[9] Others researching land reform in Masvingo Province also indicated that some
new farmers produced good crops during 2005/06 (Cousins 2009; Scoones 2008).
This was not the case everywhere. Masvingo's southern districts of Chiredzi,
Chivi and Mwenezi experienced poor harvests and nationally food shortages
continued despite the rains (*Reuters*, 'WFP says 1.4 mln in Zimbabwe will need
food aid', 11/10/06; *Zim Online*, 'Zimbabwe runs out of mealie-meal', 15/08/06,
accessed 05/10/14; *Zim Online* 'Zimbabwe officials admit severe food deficits',
24/08/06, accessed 05/10/14).

[10] Mutsambwa 19/12/05.

[11] Others too have highlighted how, despite enormous international coverage,
'very little attention [was] paid to understanding the complexities of the
programme, especially at point of implementation, specifically at a local level
and on the farms themselves' (Matondi 2012:7–8; see also Scoones 2008; Scoones
et al. 2010).

Photo 2 VaKurasva, war
veteran, Desmondale Farm
(Source: author, 2006)

renderings for resettlement farmers as 'cell phone farmers', or *varimi/
varungu vanhasi* (farmers/white people of today) appeared on the street,
in muffled beer hall conversations and the independent media, pointing
towards the dynamic and contrary conversation taking place about land
reform. It was (and to some extent remains) difficult to enter this discussion without being shunted to one or other end of the polarised debates
about Zimbabwe's multiple 'crises' (Hammar & Raftopoulos 2003:17).
Even scholars found themselves trapped by these emotive 'discursive
divides' (Cliffe et al. 2011:907), as was demonstrated when Mamdani
waded into the discussion in 2008.[12] Similarly critical and sometimes
shrill reactions have been provoked by recent far more thoroughly re-
searched accounts, illustrating how fraught the subject remains, despite
the wealth of empirical research now emerging.[13]

Nevertheless, it is clear that for many new settlers around Mutirikwi
at least, especially poorer A1 (small-scale) resettlement farmers and
their families, the experience of establishing a homestead and fields on
resettled farms, once the *jambanja* of the initial invasions was over, involved huge personal commitments of labour, time and resources. 'When
we first came in here' VaKurasva, a war veteran and 'new farmer' on Desmondale Farm explained, 'there was no AREX and there was no pegging.
There were no agricultural officers at all, we were doing everything our-

[12] See Mamdani (2008) and the many critical responses this provoked (Jacobs &
Mundy 2009).
[13] Cliffe et al. 2011; Moyo 2011; Matondi 2012; Hanlon et al. 2012; Sadomba 2011;
Scoones et al. 2010; Scoones et al. 2011; Dekker & Kinsey 2011; Mutupo 2011;
Zamchiya 2011; Chambati 2011; Marongwe 2011; Mujere 2011; Murisa 2011;
Moyo et al. 2009; Scoones 2008; Mavedzenge et al. 2008.

selves'.[14] Like many others, VaKurasva felled, de-stumped and planted his new fields with *mapadza* (hoes) almost single-handedly. As another war veteran and new farmer described: 'Yes, this involves a lot of effort here on the farms ... it's not easy. You have to sacrifice ... It is not the government who will do the planting and harvesting. It is you yourself who will have to take the risk, and it will show at the end of the harvest if you have managed to do well'.[15] In January 2006, one prominent white commercial farmer in Masvingo – who had had several farms acquired for resettlement since 2000 but at the time remained with one to continue farming – expressed sympathy with the work new farmers faced on their allocated plots. While agreeing with his wife that 'many have no knowledge of farming at all', he acknowledged that others 'are obviously good farmers', adding 'I wouldn't do what they are doing: cutting down bush, ploughing and planting without tractors ... that is quite impressive given that they have no inputs whatsoever ... it is very very hard for them'.[16]

This huge investment of labour and resources suggests people did have confidence in their future on resettled farms, even if many kept a foothold in communal lands or employment in urban areas (cf. Sithole et al. 2003). It also indicates that many did have a serious commitment to their new opportunities, despite commonplace remarks about new farmers' lack of it. Furthermore, these material commitments were often accompanied by imaginative investment in, or creative engagement with broader aspirations for the possibilities of new or re-imagined postcolonial futures. Doubtlessly, some acted simply (and cynically) out of self-interest, looking for land and resources. Yet 'agents are always partly constructed through their acts' and, by 'rendering themselves subject to specific liturgical, political and discursive regimes', people 'simultaneously lay claim to and accept the terms through which their subsequent acts will be judged' (Lambek 2002a: 37–38). The moral investments accompanying the material commitments of new farmers may have amounted, for some, to direct, active and uncritical support for the ruling party, its political aims, practices, ideologies and alliances. Clearly it was not entirely coincidental that the 'land invasions' occurred when and *as* they did, at a moment when ZANU PF faced, for the first time in 20 years, a credible political threat in parliamentary elections (Derman & Hellum 2007: 177; Alexander 2006:186–7). But for others around Mutirikwi, perhaps a majority, this was not necessarily the case. It was far more complex than that. People engaged with a myriad of different discourses and practices, all of which invoked or appealed to different re-membered pasts and imagined futures, and a variety of entangled aspirations of what the postcolonial state could be, even as they were grounded within very localised politics and livelihood strategies. The complex aspirations, motivations and subjectivities of people involved in land occupations mattered and continue to matter intensely. Emergent in both language and practice, they are sites for the possible

---

[14] VaKurasva 17/04/06.
[15] Robby Mtetwa 29/06/06.
[16] Ant and Helen Mitchel 9/01/06.

construction of alternative imaginations of what could be, from those offered by either side of the polarised political debates about Zimbabwe's land reform in the 2000s; between the renewed, but narrowed African nationalism of ZANU PF, and the liberal appeals to civic nationalism, development and human rights of opposition groups.

This chapter describes these aspirations as they appeared in the actions and words of war veterans, new farmers and land occupiers, as well as technocrats and local officials, around Mutirikwi in 2005/06, to investigate how they appealed to and engaged with an entanglement of different ideas of 'stateness' based on divergent remembered pasts and imagined futures. Like Mamdani's (2008) emphasis on the importance of consent as well as coercion in ZANU PF's politics of land, my argument assumes that those 'in power', the 'potentate' (Mbembe 2001), are sometimes forced to engage with and respond to such alternative imaginings and aspirations. This sets the scene for the following chapters, which focus on the materialities of belonging, sovereignty and rule around Mutirikwi in the 2000s.

NEW YET AUTOCHTHONOUS FARMERS

As Nyasha Pambirei, the provincial AREX officer, told me in April 2006, the Mutirikwi area is particularly interesting for exploring the entanglement of different remembered pasts, imagined futures and aspirations for postcolonial stateness in the context of fast-track land reform, because of the variety different landscapes that co-exist around the lake.

> The Mutirikwi habitat is peculiar in the province because there is the water from the dam ... [and] there is quite a variety of different land uses in the area. Of course there are the commercial farms ... which have been affected by the land reform programme, but also there are other commercial activities, the hotels, the fishing industry, tourism, boating and so on. Some of those things, AREX is not involved in at all. But AREX is concerned with the agriculture around the dam and there are both farms and communal areas adjacent to that dam and in its broader catchment area. The farms have been taken up and resettled. Mostly it is model A1 resettlement but also some model A2, and we should not forget that there are still some old commercial farms operating too. There are also some special settlement areas, like the small-scale farms at Sikato, where there are 100 or 150 ARDA [Agricultural and Rural Development Authority] plots. Those ARDA plots are individual plots that pre-date the land reform begun in 2000. So in terms of the land scenario there have been changes, mainly the partitioning of the commercial farms into A1 and A2 models.[17]

Pambirei might also have mentioned several other, earlier post-independence resettlement and irrigation schemes (Longdale and Oatlands, see FAO & SAFR 2000) dating to the 1980s and 1990s, as well as areas which 'reverted' to communal lands, either when the dam was built in the early 1960s to settle people removed to make way for it (around Zano, east of the lake), or after independence (Mzero farm, south of the lake). There is a game reserve to the north occupying several former

[17] Pambirei 28/04/06.

farms, and a recreational park roughly equating with a buffer zone or servitude area surrounding the entire lake. The area also contains Zimbabwe's most important national heritage site, Great Zimbabwe (Fontein 2006a), and several even older rock art sites.

Alongside all these different formal land uses and divisions, Mutirikwi also hosts the hotly contested 'history-scapes' (Fontein 2006a: 19–46) and 'genealogical geographies' (see Chapter 5) of different clans, spirit mediums and chiefs, which refer to very real places on the landscape, including sacred hills, springs, trees, and importantly, *makuva* (graves) and *matongo* (ruined homesteads) of past occupation. These are not just articulated in ongoing disputes over places such as Great Zimbabwe or recently resettled commercial farms, but also areas of state land reserved as the lake's servitude area, its recreational and game parks, and the older post-independence resettlement schemes. In the early 1980s, soon after independence, there was a wave of spontaneous land occupation or 'squatting' in these areas by claimants from competing local clans, in which prominent chiefs and mediums were directly involved. In most cases these people were later evicted when formal resettlement schemes were established, putting many *vatorwa* (strangers) onto the land. Similar to the Dande resettlement schemes of northern Zimbabwe discussed by Spierenburg (2004), this settling of strangers – people from elsewhere in Zimbabwe with no autochthonous claims or specific genealogical geographies to deploy – has long been contentious around Mutirikwi. Amid the farm invasions of 2000, these state lands were re-occupied again, often by the same people who had occupied them in the early 1980s. Many claimed to be returning again to the places their fathers and grandfathers were evicted from by European settlers. In their view, they were again living amongst the *makuva* and *matongo* of their kith and kin. The genealogical geographies deployed to legitimise such re-occupations, questioned and denied the rights of the 'strangers' formally resettled on those schemes. Crucially, they are based on 'knowing' the landscape, its sacred places, graves and ruins, and the taboos that surround them. This particular kind of knowledge, more inherent than learned, is based on kinship and relatedness with the past and landscape, and often involves different performances of the past (Fontein 2006a: 47–72).

All these different, co-existing landscapes around Mutirikwi are, in a sense, the material manifestations of different ways of understanding of time and space. They are the active sedimentations of different teleologies – different understandings of the past, present and future, and the movement or 'progression' between them – into and out of emergent material landscapes. The question is how these different visions and materialities of time intermingled in the fast-track context around Mutirikwi in the 2000s, and what the implications were for Zimbabwean state-making. As Ferguson (1999:24) noted, following Fabian (1983) and Appadurai (1988), 'modern western ways of knowing have mapped out ethnologically "different" places in a spatial array of distinct "topics" and evolutionary "stages" ... as if they represented a sequence of historical epochs or evolutionary stages, laid out in space instead of time'. In this way 'modern', 'western' knowledge understood cultural differences in terms of time, and then laid them out spatially. It is not just anthropology that used this teleological, spatial technique to construct its 'other'. Colonial authorities used similar approaches to divide up land and authority (Mamdani 1996; Worby 1994). In Rhodesia they were manifest, through a series of legislative measures (especially the Land Apportionment Act of 1930 and the Native Land Husbandry Act of 1951), in the sharp division between African 'native reserves' (later 'Tribal Trust Lands' (TTLs), and now 'communal areas') and European farming areas, with the African Purchase Areas (Shutt 1997) forming a kind of middle stage between the two. The teleological nature of these colonial land divisions is apparent in the language often used to describe them. For example, it is only in relation to reified notions of 'traditional' and 'modern' forms of land tenure that the notion of farms 'reverting' to communal land makes any sense.

This racial and teleological division of the land continued after independence, with only cosmetic changes serving as a reminder that something had changed. By the late 1980s early land reform efforts had waned, and the state's focus shifted from redistributing 'commercial' farmland to re-organising 'communal areas', recalling the 'high-modernist' efforts of the 1940s and 50s to 'remake' the reserves (Alexander 2006:44; Spierenburg 2004). As Pambirei noted,[18] renewed focus on agricultural extension in smallholder and communal areas did have early success in terms of increased maize and cotton production (Rukuni & Eicher 1994), although this stalled in the 1990s.[19] Despite this and the fact that by 1999 over 70,000 people had been resettled (far fewer than the promised 162,000), the old dualistic land divisions largely continued up to 2000. Could fast-track land reform therefore be understood as representing, at last, a determined effort to overcome solidified, colonial distinctions between commercial and communal land, between productive and subsistence farming, between so-called 'modern' and 'traditional' forms of land tenure? In June 2006 I discussed this with Joseph Munyanyi, Masvingo Province's Chief Land Officer. In his response he described the differences between A1 and A2 resettlement in fast-track land reform:

> A1 farms are almost like the communal areas, it includes villages that have communal grazing areas, or small plots. In those areas there really is a focus on the equity issue. The aim is to bring people from communal areas, where they live under their chiefs, and to preserve their value system. ... The A1 scheme ... is allocated by the district land committees in which chiefs play an important role. For a long time there was a lot of play with VIDCOs [Village Development Committees] and WADCOs [Ward Development Committees], but those structures they never really took off ... They were meant to flatten out the administration but it was found that the strength of rural people is resident in

---

[18] Pambirei 28/04/06.

[19] With the combined effects of droughts, structural adjustment and economic decline. Some argue that set against the goals of poverty alleviation, welfare and increased agricultural productivity, many early resettlement schemes performed well (Kinsey 1999; Hoogeveen & Kinsey 2001).

the chiefdoms. When people have problems they go and talk to the *sabhuku* [village head] or the chief, they don't go to the VIDCO chairman. The chiefs are linked to the land in the communal areas and people go to them to resolve their disputes. This value system is like a religion or a way of life, the chief as custodian of people's heritage ... So it was realised that those VIDCOs in communal areas were not effective, and in the old resettlements, the resettlement councils and chairmen, and even in the new resettlements, where that role was played by base commanders, all of that is now going to be under the chiefs.

In A2 there is something different going on ... the aim is to distribute land to people who will be able to do commercial farming ... to redistribute that wealth. The white farmers were in a position of being like the custodians of those commercial farms, of that access to wealth ... It is a process of indigenising commercial farming. And it is solely the bureaucracy which administers that. That is the real territory of the Ministry of Lands, which is the acquiring authority. That is not really where chiefs come in. Having said that, however, even here the chiefs have recently been saying they want access to farms for the *zunde ramambo*. So there are discussions going on about providing particular farms for chiefs to use to feed their people under the *zunde ramambo*.[20]

This suggests that something of the old dualistic land divisions was being reproduced in new guises through fast-track land reform. This was reinforced by the fact that all new farmers went through some form of vetting, assessing not only political loyalties, but capacity to farm productively. Particularly for A2 farmers,[21] there was considerable pressure to occupy allocated lands productively, echoing notions of 'beneficial occupation' which long preoccupied Rhodesian authorities.[22] With continuing food and foreign currency shortages, official concern about the productive utilisation of resettled farms was increasingly expressed at highest echelons of government in the mid-2000s. There was a series of high-profile 'land audits' and in November 2006 President Mugabe gave fierce warnings to new farmers on A2 farms, that government retained the right to withdraw their '99 year leases' and remove them from the land, if they were not farming productively.[23] Such statements echoed past and present opponents to land reform who had long argued 'the utmost caution should be exercised in transferring land from commercial

[20] Joseph Manyanyi 05/06/06. *Zunde ramambo* was a pre-colonial institution in which people worked in communal fields to produce food for widows, cripples and orphans. Recently it was formally re-instituted (Kaseke 2006) as part of the functions of chiefs.

[21] The A2 schemes were also often more subject to cronyism and patronage, sometimes pitting technocratic criteria against political expediency so that neat 'planning' distinctions between A1 and A2 farm sizes became blurred and ill-defined (Scoones et al. 2010:25; Marongwe 2011:1069).

[22] With the BSACo's growing concerns about absentee landlords, in the late 1890s white settlers were required to demonstrate 'beneficial occupation' of their farms (e.g. *Rhodesian Herald* 15/09/1897). Requirements of productivity continued to be central to post-WWII settlement schemes for ex-servicemen.

[23] *Financial Gazette*, 15/11/06; 'Yet another land audit' *News24 (SA)*, 04/11/06. All resettled land is owned by the state, which grants 'permits of occupation' to A1 farmers and '99 year leases' to A2 farmers. These were supposed to enable new farmers to take out loans. In June 2004 (*The Herald*, 08/06/04) the now late John Nkomo announced all land was to be nationalised, however this was hastily withdrawn a few days later (*The Herald*, 15/06/04).

farmers to inexperienced operators because of the risks posed to aggregate agricultural output' (Bratton 1994:73), concerns that in the short term proved dramatically correct in hungry post-2000 Zimbabwe.

Munyanyi's suggestion that A2 farming was about 'indigenizing wealth' and 'Africanising' commercial agriculture, and A1 farming about 'preserving that value system' in which chiefs are 'custodians of peoples' heritage', clearly resonated with older, teleological distinctions between white 'commercial' and African 'communal' farming areas. But there was more going on, a hint of which lay in his comment about chiefs demanding farms for their *zunde ramambo*. This became clearer as Munyanyi continued:

> And then the chiefs are saying in relation to those A2 areas, this is our land, so they are involved in that sense ... Because even though the A2 farms are distributed through the provincial level offices, we are also responsive to the district land committees, which have to be consulted in all A2 resettlement. And through those district land committees the chiefs are involved too. So for example in the issue of which white farmers are allowed to stay on their farms, this is often left with the chiefs, who might say this white farmer is ok he should stay, or whatever, because they will have the knowledge and experience of those farmers. So the chiefs do have a role in the distribution of A2 land, but we at the Ministry of Lands carry out the administration. If something does not have the blessing of the chief of that particular area, then we could go straight ahead, but it will cause us other problems in those areas. So as stakeholders the chiefs are consulted.
>
> But there is something going on here in terms of that 'value system'. Along the way there was return to the chiefs by those people who initiated the land reform, who began the land invasions. The fast-track land reform programme was motivated by war vets, they started this, and they put up temporary structures of authority, in terms of base commanders and so on. Fast-track started as *jambanja* [violence or disorder] with the land invasions. I don't want to say it was chaos, but it was *jambanja*, it was carried out with a great deal of speed. And initially those war vets did not consult the chiefs, they ignored them, and set up their own structures. But along the way people went back to that value system, they went back to the chiefs to give them that custodial role.
>
> On the A2 farms, like in A1 and communal areas, people still feel like they need to be under a chief. People still yearn for that value system. You know, Zimbabweans, we have like a dual citizenship. We want to belong to our roots, and we want to be modern people. So on A2 farms, most people really want that traditional function, and no one says no to that. Yes some people are challenging chiefs in those areas. Many are more educated and have more resources, that is part of the criteria of being granted A2 land. Some may be saying 'what can the chiefs tell us?' but still then at the back of their minds, they have that sense of allegiance to the chiefs, to that 'value system'.[24]

This growing influence of or 'going back to' chiefs, as many framed it – in 'commercial' A2 areas as well as the more 'communal' A1 resettlements – suggests something different was going on across Zimbabwe's agrarian landscapes during the 2000s. Certainly informants around Mutirikwi often spoke in such terms, frequently invoking diverse notions of return with distinct temporal implications. The *jambanja* of the land invasions, when war veteran 'base commanders' established their own structures of authority, did later change in response to growing concerns for the 'autochthonous knowledge' of the landscape that people

[24] Manyanyi 05/06/06.

making ancestral claims offered. Sometimes this began straight away. VaKurasva explained how when he first occupied Desmondale farm, he and his comrades relied on particular farm workers 'who have been living here from long ago, like Sekuru Makwinye here', because 'they know all the sacred places not to be disturbed and the rules to be followed. I was walking everywhere during those days with this *sekuru'*. Not only familiar with the land's sacred places and taboos through having long worked it, farmworkers like Makwinye also sometimes claimed direct kinship with the Chikwanda clan and their *svikiro* (medium) VaZarira, who once ruled the landscape surrounding nearby Beza.[25]

Amidst war veterans' growing recognition of such autochthonous knowledge, some new farmers made their own ancestral claims to land they were occupying. Several such 'new but autochthonous' farmers described how when they first accompanied war veterans spearheading the occupations in 2000, they made no mention of their own historical claims, emphasising only their desire for access to fertile land. Only later, when other settlers, war veterans and local government officials began to recognise the significance of so-called 'traditional' knowledge, they announced their own autochthonous claims.

> Varirai M. Chikwanda – we came back here in February 2000, but how it happened that we came back *here*, well, these are things of the soil [implying ancestral intervention]
> Mutsambwa – The war vets came here first, they started the invasions, and then we followed ... first we didn't say we are coming back to our land. We just told the base commander we were coming for our own piece of land. But later, when the farm was pegged, people from the DA's [District Administrator] office were saying we don't want to use the English names, we want real names of this area, and we want someone who comes from here, a son of the land, to tell us. That is when we said we are from Chikwanda, and VaChikwanda here [pointing to his companion] was made a *sadunhu* [headman]. That was 2001. They wanted someone who knew the land, who could appease the ancestors and knows the sacred places.[26]

The significance of autochthonous landscape knowledge was often recognised when its new occupiers faced unexpected difficulties associated with the unhappiness of its ancestral spirits (cf. Chaumba et al. 2003b:601). New farmers sought autochthonous knowledge in order to 'make safe' their occupations (Fontein 2006b:237–43, also 2006c). Solomon Makasva, another 'new yet autochthonous' farmer resettled on land near Beza, where he claimed his grandfather had once been a 'big chief', explained how his name was recognised when he applied for land from the DA; and how he was appointed headman (*sadunhu*) under Chief Chikwanda:

> This is what caused me to come to this place, because they were looking in the books saying this person is a chief, so let him come and stay where his *mapa*

---

[25] VaKurasva 17/04/06. Makwinye claimed to have been born at Harawe and to be a *muzukuru* (maternal grandchild-in-law) of the Chikwanda clan. He moved to Mlinya farm and then Desmondale with his parents who were farmworkers. Long ago, he told me, the land around Desmondale was under Chief Chikwanda and Ambuya VaZarira (Sekuru Makwinye Mavuka 15/11/05).

[26] Varirai Chikwanda and Mafuma Mutsambwa 12/01/06.

Photo 3   VaSolomon Makasva
in his field, with Baba Lisa,
my research assistant
(Source: author, 2006)

[sacred site/ ancestral grave] are. I went to the DA, saying I want a piece of land to farm. He asked me who I was. I told him my name was Solomon Bvungudzire Makasva, and he said yes, you are the man we have been looking for, someone who knows and is from this land. Then I went to a meeting of the Governor and the DA, and he said 'As he goes there, give him the chieftainship'. But the DA said 'No I have already given that land to Chief Chikwanda. And I said 'But Chikwanda is of the same people as I am. So I came here and I brewed beer and Chief Chikwanda gave me the title of Sadunhu Bvungudzire.[27]

In a strange twist, as war veteran base commanders increasingly deferred to such autochthonous knowledge, some 'new yet autochthonous' farmers began to describe them and other new farmers around them as *vatorwa*, in a way reminiscent of the adverse attitudes taken against many beneficiaries of the earlier resettlement schemes around Mutirikwi, by disgruntled people evicted after the squatting of the 1980s. Such denunciations are part of a repertoire of rhetorical and practical means of reinforcing individual assertions of belonging and entitlement, through which highly complex, localised struggles over legitimacy and authority were played out, implicating overlapping tensions and loyalties among competing political factions, different war veteran groups, as well as chiefs, mediums, clans and kin, and different churches (Scoones et al. 2010:71–72). Mutsambwa explained how, as *vatorwa*, some war veterans were relying on Chief Chikwanda's patronage, who in turn relied on them to buttress his waning legitimacy among his own clan, in the face of criticism about his refusal to work with the medium VaZarira.

VaChuma and Ziki [war vets] are not our relations, we do not know them, they are *vatorwa*, so they go to that present chief and he is happy to put strangers

[27] Solomon Makasva, Beza 14/01/06.

here on Chikwanda land as *sabhuku* because he needs their support. The present chief is happy about having these strangers here because they won't oppose him. Right now, the *nyika* [land] of Chikwanda needs a chief who recognises the *svikiro* [medium] Ambuya VaZarira.[28]

Unsurprisingly, while most war veterans described how '*basa reBase Commander rakapera* [the work of base commanders finished]' once the initial land occupations were over, several also stressed their continuing role on the new 'committees of seven' set up on farms to work alongside the village heads and headmen that 'returning' chiefs were tasked to establish in all resettlement areas.[29] Others explained their continuing role as 'soldiers' of the Third *Chimurenga* (liberation struggle) – or as the 'eyes of the government' – would ensure the political gains of the ruling party were not reversed.

> If they put a *sabhuku* here, that person will do the work of *kuchengeta vhu* [looking after the soil]. It will be good if they put a *sabhuku* here of the Chikwanda clan, who knows the land and its sacred places to protect and the trees that should not be cut down. I will be happy because of that issue of *mitemo wenyika* [rules of the land]. The committee of seven will not just disappear because that *sabhuku* has been put here. No! We will do the other things, making sure the rules of the land committees are being followed. I am on the political side; that is what the committee of seven will do. We are like the eyes of the government, looking out for opposition and ensuring the government rules are followed. But if someone does something that is wrong in terms of the traditional rules of the soil, they will have to go to the *sabhuku*, and from the *sabhuku* to the chief.[30]

The DA for Masvingo too was at pains (in part, no doubt, for his own political reasons) to stress that despite the formal return of traditional leaders to resettled farms, war veterans continued to play an important role and their prominent presence on land committees at district and provincial levels certainly substantiated this.[31]

If traditional authorities did not entirely replace war veterans on resettled farms then they also did not merely displaced the system of rural councils, ward and village committees instituted after independence to promote more representative local government. Rather, they nudged in alongside them in complex ways. There was, in the words of Felix Chikovo, Masvingo's PA (Provincial Administrator), a marriage of 'democratic and traditional leaders'.

> It is ministry policy that there should be sound local government. We are under mandate to emplace traditional leaders into the former commercial farming areas. It has been decided that the way to go is to establish the traditional leader who was in place prior to the change in land use [i.e. the colonial appropriation of land for European farms]. Where there is no conflict over different claims and boundaries, we are able to place the leader. Where there are one or two conflicts,

---

[28] Varirai Chikwanda and Mutsambwa 12/01/06.

[29] Obediningo Chuma, war veteran and new farmer, Green Hills farm 12/06/06.

[30] VaKurasva 17/04/06.

[31] James Mazvidza, DA Masvingo 21/03/06. Also Mubvumba 2005. The continuing role of war veterans in Masvingo materialised again in a wave of political violence and farm invasions during the fraught elections of 2008.

we are resolving those disputes, so we can put the proper traditional leader in place.

Those early resettlement schemes were definitely not under chiefs. It was policy that resettlement land was not communal. The new policy is to emplace all resettlements under traditional leaders. That includes both new resettlements and old resettlements. So traditional leaders now act outside of just communal areas. This was the result of two pieces of legislation: the Traditional Leaders Act and Rural District Councils Act. These acts married together the democratic leaders and the traditional leaders. For example, the village head is now also chairman of the village assembly, which is a substructure of the RDC [Rural District Council]. There has been a marrying of traditional leaders and development structures. The village head is the chairman of the VIDCO and the WADCO. The ward assembly is headed by a chief or headman who reports to the RDC. So the new policy has moved what was once the preserve of communal areas only, to all areas.[32]

This illustrates something of the dynamic re-structuring of authority over land taking place during the 2000s. It amplifies why land reform was understood, by some at least, as decisive for overcoming the bifur-cated system of land and authority inherited at independence, even if for others it was about the return of ancestral graves and territories, or the final stage of anti-colonial struggle (or Third *Chimurenga*). It also echoes Manyanyi's suggestion that the return of chiefs, and 'that value system', reflected a widespread desire to both 'belong to our roots and be modern people'. The was further amplified by the increasing involve-ment of different government departments, including National Parks, and the Ministry of Lands, Natural Resources and ZINWA (Zimbabwe National Water Authority) focused on soil and water conservation, and the protection of the lake. Like the emphasis on productive occupation, as well as the return to chiefs and 'autochthons', such environmental imperatives too recalled older landscape interventions harking back to the technocratic impulses of the late 1940s, when Rhodesian officials set about remaking the reserves and modernising African agriculture (Alex-ander 2006:44–62). In the 2000s concerns around Mutirikwi were again focused on the threat that soil erosion and siltation posed to the long-term future of the dam. As Chikovo explained, what 'is urgently required is that the land taken for resettlement does not become quickly eroded, overpopulated, overgrazed or wrongly tilled'. Even 'during the initial land reform stages we had to be careful in case we affected the dam'. 'That is why there is not too much A1 villagisation there, because of soil erosion ... we concentrated on A1 plots where everyone would have their own land, to encourage effective self-management.'[33]

Clearly concerns about 'sound local government', environmental conservation and appropriate forms of land use continued to inform local administrators and officials. At the same time, however, the of-ficial return of traditional leaders to resettled farms caused a seemingly endless series of localised disputes over boundaries, authority and seniority, in which many alternative claims to autochthony, belong-ing and sovereignty, and competing versions of landscape and the past

---

[32] Felix Chikovo, PA Masvingo 23/05/06.
[33] Chikovo 23/05/06

were contested. If land and state-making in Rhodesia/Zimbabwe have always been mutually imbricated (Alexander 2006:10), then it seems clear the many 'minor theatres of power' (Worby 1998:563) emergent in the complex 'new political terrain' (Chaumba et al. 2003b:604) of the 2000s, were minutely involved in an ongoing and highly localised process of re-imagining and remaking the Zimbabwean state. While Chaumba et al. (2003a:543–4) identified a 'reassertion of technocracy' as war veterans employed technical planning to peg fields on occupied farms, the return of chiefs and re-assertion of autochthony I encountered around Mutirikwi indicates a *variety* of old forms and motifs were being re-assembled into something new (Alexander 2006:191). One of this book's larger purposes is to explore how the enduring yet immanent and emergent materialities of many different, past engagements *in* and *with* the land (and crucially water) were imbricated in these reconfigurations of authority over it, through the different languages and practices of belonging, sovereignty and legitimacy at play in the remaking of Mutirikwi's landscapes.

DIVERSE ASPIRATIONS, STATE-MAKING AND LAND REFORM

In *Expectations of Modernity*, Ferguson (1999:14) describes the defeated optimism he encountered in Zambia's Copperbelt in the late 1980s, as the 'myth of modernity' and confidence of a developing Zambia was replaced by a 'cynical scepticism'. For many this was a 'world-shattering life experience' that provoked depressing predictions of 'reversed modernisation', with the future promising not progress but irreversible decline. This was 'modernisation through the looking glass, where modernity is the object of nostalgic reverie, and "backwardness" the anticipated (or dreaded) future' (1999:13). Much literature on Zimbabwe in the early 2000s employed a similarly reversed teleological perspective. Many commentators posited 'Zimbabwe's crisis' as a 'retreat from' or 'end of modernity', deploying metaphors of 'exhaustion' or 'plunging' (cf. Bond & Manyanya 2003; Campbell 2003) to suggest that as the 'developmental' and 'democratising' imperatives of the state were abandoned, and the government became increasingly authoritarian, 'promises of development and modernity' were traded in for a narrow and divisive redistribution of resources.

In contrast Worby (2003) argued that events in the 2000s represented less a 'retreat from modernity' than a redefinition of the nation/state. 'Political modernity' he suggested, has always involved a tension between 'sovereignty' and 'development', and currently the 'see-saw of political modernity has tipped to one side – the side of sovereignty' (2003:68). This echoes Chatterjee's argument that the failure of postcolonial states has not been an 'inability to think out new forms of modern community but in our surrender to the old forms of the modern state' (1993:11; 1996:222). In other words, the developmental imagination of the modern state enacted after independence, which some now suggested was in retreat, was never able to fully deliver on the diverse, often localised, promises of postcolonial stateness. In this respect, ZANU PF's refocusing upon sovereignty and the redistribution of resources – and the emergence of 'patriotic history' (Ranger 2004) as a new streak of its 'whole, coherent and self-perpetuating postcolonial master fiction' (Primorac 2005:2) – were part of a revitalised nationalism that appealed to other, previously excluded aspirations. These included the frustrated promises of return so apparent around Mutirikwi. While Zimbabwe's authoritarian turn excluded many, particularly the urban poor, farm workers, and women, it *did* appeal to such other, localised aspirations thwarted since 1980.[34] In this sense, the redistribution of land, however corrupt, politicised and violent the process may have been, were astute political moves.

It is here that observers who emphasised the ideological continuities of post-2000 land reform with that of the 1980s and 1990s, made an important point (Moyo 2001; Moyo & Yeros 2005; also Marongwe 2003). The desire for land reform in Zimbabwe has, since independence, been a central tenet of many people's livelihood aspirations, and many diverse imaginations of what a good postcolonial and modern state should be about (Moyo 2001, also Alexander 2003:99). The motivations and ma-terialisations of such aspirations were multiple and diverse: from the desire to return to ancestral lands, to the opportunity to take forward the 'peasant option' (Ranger 1985) on fertile A1 plots, or 'a renewed "mer-chant path" of urban professionals, petty bourgeois and bureaucrats' on larger A2 farms; or any combination of these (Marongwe 2003:174; Fon-tein 2006b & 2006d; Moyo & Yeros 2005:195). Some involved profoundly different teleologies – alternative ways of understanding movement through time (and space) towards a goal or destiny – perhaps best exemplified by the way the temporality of ancestral land claims could reduce the colonial past to a brief interlude in much longer continuing relationships between specific kin-based clans, their ancestors and par-ticular territories.[35] In any case, however much it was accompanied by an increasingly authoritarian, violent and exclusive kind of nationalist politics, it was not *only* coercion which enabled land reform to be imple-mented, or allowed ZANU PF to maintain its political hegemony, until March 2008 at least.

The repeated occupations and evictions of state land and resettlement schemes around Mutirikwi since independence indicate the longevity of particular localised aspirations acted out in the fast-track context of the 2000s. Such land aspirations based on memories of eviction and appeals to restitution have long recurred across Zimbabwe (cf. Knight 1999; Marongwe 2003; Moore 2005; Palmer 1990). Citing the 'conspicuous ex-amples' of Tangwena people in Kaerezi, Sekuru Mushore in the Nharira

---

[34] On marginalisation of farm workers, women and others see Rutherford 2001 & 2003; Derman & Hellum 2007. For other histories of thwarted aspirations for land between 1980 and 2000 see Alexander 2006, Moore 2005 and Hughes 2006c.

[35] I must credit this point to a deeply engaging conversation with historians at the University of Zimbabwe in June 2006.

hills, Ndau people in Chiranda forest, and Chief Manhenga's claims over Gumbuli Farm, Marongwe (2003:186) argues that 'one of the underlying causes of land demands and conflicts ... has been the non-recognition by policy makers of such historical claims'. This chimes with Alexander's account of land reform in the 1980s, when the state 'certainly responded to popular demands, but ... allowed little in the way of popular participation ... Only the state was deemed capable of ensuring that redistribution occurred in a rational and productive manner' (2006:111). In this context, the question of whether fast-track did, in contrast to earlier efforts, successfully appeal to such widespread aspirations for land as a kind of restitution, takes on particular urgency. In contrast to Manzungu's claim that 'in Zimbabwe, unlike in South Africa, the concept of land restitution does not apply' (2004a:66), statements by the Council of Chiefs, the inclusion of chiefs on district land committees, and efforts to install chiefs, headmen and village heads on resettled farms; and around Mutirikwi, the importance placed upon autochthonous knowledge of the landscape by war veterans, new farmers and others, suggest that it did.[36]

Similarly, war veterans in Masvingo were clear that in 2000 they had felt strongly enough about the unresolved land issue to act, and that the government then responded. As one described,

> When we were fighting for this country we were fighting for the soil ... in 2000 after the refusal of that constitution [the constitutional referendum of February 2000] ... we sat down as comrades and said no, if we continue like this we will have no land until we die. So then we decided to force the landowners out and to occupy the land. But actually they are not landowners because the land is ours![37]

Dubbing land reform as the 'Third *Chimurenga*' reflected more than war veterans' central role in it, or the 'celebrated lawlessness' of the invasions known as *jambanja*, it was a deliberate effort to appeal to rural nationalist aspirations by emphasising that it was the final stage of an unfinished programme of liberation (Alexander 2006:193; Derman & Hellum 2007:161). For many war veterans, the land occupations that started in Masvingo in February 2000[38] were not a ruling party response to waning political support (cf Manzungu 2004a:54; Alexander 2006:186), but rather provoked by a need to complete a task directed by the ancestors, which many traced to Ambuya Nehanda's legendary last words before she was hanged in 1897 for rebelling against Rhodesian rule. As war veterans told me in 2001:

> You see we have not yet finished the war of taking back the land ... we have not yet finished the mission left by our ancestors. Ambuya Nehanda said 'my bones will rise'. We haven't yet accomplished [what] we, the bones, were tasked to fulfil ... to liberate all the land that we were given by our ancestors. The land of our ancestors must be free ... Unless we fulfil this task ... there is not going to be any peace in this country. We are not going to rest. Even our comrades ... who died besides us when we were fighting the war, they are now the spirits ...

---

[36] *The Herald*, 03/12/00, 06/05/04, 08/05/04; *Zimbabwe Independent*, 14/05/04; *The Masvingo Star*, 23–29/07/04.
[37] Obediningo Chuma 12/06/06.
[38] VaMhike 26/06/01.

driving us forward. So we have got a lot of pressure from behind ... to liberate our country, to go forward for our people. [39]

In this perspective, fast-track land reform was a government response not only to the unresolved aspirations of living war veterans, but also to ancestral demands, and those of dead comrades killed during the war. It illustrates how the fast-track programme could, like the exhumation and reburial of liberation war dead (Fontein 2009b; 2010; 2014), engage with the shared, sometimes convivial, often demanding, war legacies of mediums and war veterans (Fontein 2006c). And it is this conviction of an ongoing legacy of ancestrally guided struggle, which the ruling party invoked through its rhetoric of patriotic history (Ranger 2004).

If the liberation of ancestral lands through fast-track land reform could be seen as a government response to the frustrated aspirations of war veterans and mediums, then a host of other reforms (the 'national *biras*'; the return of chiefs' judicial powers; their new authority over re-settlements, on rural councils and land committees; the *zunde ramambo* project; the amendment of the Witchcraft Suppression Act; and so on)[40] could be similarly understood as responsive to the long-standing aspi-rations of chiefs, headmen and village heads. All these thwarted and frustrated aspirations, and the perceived delays in the state's response to them, suggest that at the centre of the grievances of war veterans, chiefs, mediums and others was a shared sense of exclusion from state-making at local and national levels. By being seen as responsive to such aspirations, the ruling party was, in a sense, re-opening access to state-making processes, revitalising the possibility, at least for some, of making the state work towards their interests. This counters com-monplace suggestions that traditional leaders and war veterans were, in different ways, merely 'co-opted' into the ruling party's authoritarian project. Other scholarship on war veterans also suggests a more complex picture than a framework of co-optation allows, in which the ruling party and veterans have long, 'manipulated and shaped each other as they have pursued their distinct and overlapping agendas' (Kriger 2003:208; also McGregor 2002; Sadomba & Andrew 2006; Sadomba 2011). Simi-larly, the relationships of chiefs and government, whether colonial or postcolonial, have always been much more nuanced than is captured by 'co-optation' (cf. Ranger 1999; Alexander 1995, 2006; Maxwell 1999; Mubvumba 2005; Hadzoi 2003). Government relationships with spirit mediums have long been marked by even greater ambivalence. Some mediums, like VaZarira, complained bitterly of being ignored in the land distribution process. Others (in Masvingo and elsewhere) were deeply involved from early on, though sometimes with very mixed results

[39] VaKanda, VaMadiri and VaMuchina 16/03/01; for a longer extract of this interview, see Fontein 2006c.
[40] *Zimdaily*, 28/09/05, 'Govt Blows Unbudgeted $95 billion On National Biras'; *Newsnet Zimbabwe*, 25/09/05, 'National Biras gather momentum in various parts of the country'. On the amendment of the Witchcraft Suppression Act see *The Herald*, 10/05/06.

(Sadomba 2011:181–5). VaZarira was often consulted by war veterans and new farmers around her home in Mazare. She was also involved in many occupations of state lands by those for whom the rhetoric of *ivhu kuvanhu* (soil to the people) offered renewed opportunity to return to ancestral landscapes. In 2001, for example, she attended *bira* ceremonies hosted by Haruzvivishe elders in the re-occupied 'game park' on former Mzero farm and in 2004 (as we shall see in the next chapter) she directed the burial of Mudarikwa Murinye in the sacred *mapa* on Boroma.

While Chaumba et al. (2003b: 600–1) identified a 'contradiction be-tween a simultaneously reinvigorated and disempowered chieftaincy' in tensions between 'the new political authority of war veterans and the old authority of chiefs and ancestors' in Chiredzi, around Mutirikwi many people did gain a 'sense of empowerment' from the government's programme; including the civil servants, land planners and technocrats noticeable amongst its beneficiaries.[41] Although he sees the 2000 land invasions as part of ZANU PF's 'official campaign strategy', Marongwe agrees 'this does not negate the sense of empowerment that some occu-piers experienced during the process' (2003:165). He also notes that this was later often undermined by the land committees' lack of transpar-ency (2003:187).[42] In 2006 Masvingo's Chief Lands Officer was adamant about people's new confidence to vocalise demands for land:

> People are now bold enough to demand land that they want or claim is theirs, not just on the farms but in the old resettlements and other areas not opened for resettlement. This has resulted from this land reform programme. It's quite impressive really, and means there is a need to involve all stakeholders ... this needs politicians to engage with it seriously. It's a very sensitive thing. You can't just send people off land they have occupied because they are on the grazing area of an old resettlement scheme. I would become a very unpopular Chief Lands Officer! You have to have a sensitive approach, and to be careful, if you upset the wrong people you might find yourself labelled MDC.[43]

The way fast-track offered the realisation of diverse, long-delayed, localised aspirations for land – in *traction* with that year's rains making them *tangible* and *realisable* – accounts for the seemingly out-of-place optimism around Mutirikwi during 2005–6. For those benefitting from it, fast-track land reform represented not a 'retreat' or 'plunge' from moder-nity, but the realisation, however imperfect, of aspirations and imagined futures sidelined since independence. We could frame this, like Worby (2003), in terms of a tension between sovereignty and development, and suggest the 'see-saw' of political modernity has swung to the side of sov-ereignty. Or suggest, like Alexander (2003:114), that the ideology behind the 2000 occupations reflected a re-imagined nationalism 'reconstituted

---

[41] Scoones et al. (2010:53) show that civil servants were significant beneficiaries of land refom (also Zamchiya 2011). The question of 'who got what' is still much debated (Cliffe et al. 2011:924–5).

[42] This was echoed around Mutirikwi (and elsewhere, Sadomba 2011) where reports of villagers being removed from farms in favour of local elites after painstakingly clearing fields and building homes caused great anger (VaKurasva 17/04/06).

[43] Manyanyi 05/06/06.

as authoritarian anti-colonialism, not modernising developmentalism'. But the problem with these positions is that they imply that for new farmers the price of land was 'modernising developmentalism', as if sovereignty could only come at the cost of development. I don't think this characterisation accurately reflects the aspirations of new farmers and other land occupiers around Mutirikwi at all. The new farmers I met resembled Gable's (2006) 'Manjaco village cosmopolitans' much more than 'modernity's malcontents'. For them, unlike the 'broken lives and shattered expectations' of the Zambian Copperbelt (Ferguson 1999:18), the possibility of past promises being fulfilled, of achieving entangled aspirations for land and livelihoods – of 'belonging to our roots' and being 'modern people'– were not so much of the past, but still of the future.

DEVELOPMENTAL ASPIRATIONS AND LIMITATIONS

The diverse, overlapping aspirations of war veterans, new farmers and other land occupiers around Mutirikwi did not exclude the technocratic interventions, bureaucratic order or commercially productive agriculture normally associated with modernising developmentalism. Most new farmers emphasised their need for tractors, irrigation, soil conservation, agricultural extension, credit facilities, schools, clinics and so on. Sometimes new communities organised the building of new schools or clinics by themselves. In lieu of any international assistance for the programme (cf. Hanlon et al. 2012), I was often asked if I could communicate with donors and NGOs about supporting local projects, supplying irrigation, tillage equipment and so on. Similar demands fiercely animated ZANU PF meetings on resettled farms north of Mutirikwi, ahead of the senate elections that year, alongside the continuing insistence of some war veterans and ZANU PF activists that the few remaining white-owned farms in the area at the time still needed resettlement.

I attended one such meeting in November 2005. The same concerns that critics of fast-track often raised were the source of much acrimony among new farmers and war veterans in the area. These included cronyism, new farmers selling their plots, or squatting on others' or unallocated areas, as well as the lack of credit facilities, agricultural inputs, and the need for schools, clinics and other infrastructural development. There was much discussion about a land audit then underway. Stating that they were 'very concerned about soil erosion' and that it was 'important proper land pegging procedures are followed', party officials told people to co-operate with local government officials running the audit, and emphasised that everyone's paper work needed to be in order, to demonstrate they were 'following the rules properly', or they risked losing their allocated lands. Amid fists thrown into the air to chants of '*pamberi neZANU PF*' (forward with ZANU PF), '*pamberi nedevelopment*' (forward with development) '*pasi neMDC*' (down with the MDC), one party offical announced that 'because we are ZANU PF, and not MDC, we have to show everyone that we do things properly'. Another stressed that 'people need to learn how to farm properly and especially about how to use credit, in order to become good commercial farmers'.[44]

Accordingly, many new farmers I spoke to discussed digging their own contour ridges to prevent soil erosion in their new fields; a remarkable thing given the unpopularity of such coercively enforced soil conservation measures during the high-modernist fervour of the 1940s and 50s. This had fed enormous support for African nationalism (Drinkwater 1989), and is well remembered around Mutirikwi today. When I asked about this apparent contradiction, I was often given the same answer: 'the ideas behind contour ridges and soil conservation were good, but the coercive implementation was wrong'. This epitomises how, in some ways, older modernising notions of agricultural productivity, soil conservation and centralised, bureaucratic land planning again persisted through land reform in 2000s, despite (or rather in the wake of) the *jambanja* characterising the initial land invasions. As in the late 1980s, 'technocratic planning has by no means had its day in Zimbabwe' (Drinkwater 1989:287), reiterating the co-existence of multiple spatialities of rule in the 'articulation' and 'entanglement' of grounded livelihood practices, localised aspirations and nationalist legacies of 'promised postcolonial freedom' (Moore 2005:17–25).

Despite the enthusiasm fast-track land reform provoked around Mutirikwi, there was often much disappointment at the inability of local government to provide the developmental assistance new farmers required. These developmental limitations placed extra demands upon the commitment of 'new farmers' to their new opportunities. As one war veteran put it:

> AREX has a big shortage of manpower. In this whole area ... there is only one AREX person, from the Popoteke [river] to Mhunga. That is too big for one person. We are still in need of AREX. They need to have more field officers. What we would like is one officer for each farm. This farm, Green Hills, has 3,100 hectares on which live 389 families. Some families live in the two villages, A & B, the rest on the plots. The Department of Natural Resources have been running courses there at the Farmers Hall, just past Mhunga, but they have not yet really started to enter the farms ... AREX came to peg but only pegged the plots, not the fields. But I don't have to wait for them, I can build a contour ridge. This year, with all that rain, I have seen a place where water is carrying away the soil from the field, so I will have to prepare a contour ridge in that spot. I don't have to wait for AREX, because I can see where the problem is. [45]

These comments echoed those of many others about the 'effort' and 'sacrifice' needed 'to achieve something' on resettled lands.[46] Although confident that fast-track was 'one of the most wonderful programmes for a third world country to embark upon', pointing to the 'huge potential being opened up', and the 'huge amount more land being farmed' because of it, Masvingo's Chief Lands Officer acknowledged that:

[44] ZANU PF meeting at Mazare, Zvishumbe Primary School, with Ambuya VaZarira. Fieldnotes 05/11/05.
[45] Chuma 12/06/06.
[46] Robby Mtetwa, 29/06/06; ZANU PF meeting, Fieldnotes 05/11/05.

Maybe the only problem has been that it is too big. Too much all at once, when all the systems were not yet geared up for it ... It needed all the systems to be in place, so we could have, say, put a farmer into six weeks of training before he was granted his plot or farm, and then for extension officers to have gone with him to the land to provide training on the spot. What we needed was a more holistic approach that included all these parallel support systems. They need a lot of resources. So yes perhaps the programme was just too massive.[47]

If the government's fast-track programme was an astute political move that pandered at last to the popular demands of certain sections of society (even as it excluded many others), then whatever pressures new farmers faced to demonstrate commitment to their new opportunities, the need to provide 'developmental' support too was something officials had to respond to. Hence there was much effort by government in the second half of the 2000s to assist, or be seen to be assisting, new farmers through access to loans, credit, and agricultural support in the form of tillage, seeds, fertiliser and fuel. Before the March 2008 elections, for example, President Mugabe himself handed out tractors, ploughs and other agricultural equipment to new farmers in an effort to appeal to voters.[48] Similarly, announcements in 2006 about plans for a new 100-hectare irrigation scheme drawing water from Lake Mutirikwi for communal farmers in Zano, on its eastern shores, were a belated realisation of much older promises that had accompanied their removal to that area when the dam was built in the late 1950s.[49]

In this context, the 'reassertion of technocracy' (Chaumba et al. 2003a) that followed the *jambanja* of the land invasions was to be expected, because it reflected how the multiple, diverse aspirations to which fast-track appeared responsive, were not necessarily opposed to notions of developmental modernity. Rather those notions too were invoked along-side appeals to anti-colonial restitutive justice, the return of the chiefs and the ancestral ownership of land, in ways that undermined (even as they could also appeal to) assumed polarisations between modernity and tradition or sovereignty and development. For ZANU PF other interests were at stake too such as the need to demonstrate the programme's success, and therefore food security, productivity, allegations of cronyism, and adequate land utilisation all became highly sensitive issues.[50] But this further suggests that despite its anti-colonialist rhetoric, ZANU PF was sensitive to the need to respond to other lingering, developmental aspirations, and the grounded livelihood practices of new farmers on resettled land.

---

[47] Munyanyi 05/06/06.
[48] 'Mugabe dishes out tractors, food, money to buy election votes', 07/03/08, *Afrik*, www.afrik-news.com/article12763.html, accessed 02/02/15.
[49] Chikovo 23/05/06.
[50] This was reflected in, amongst other things, the controversies that surrounded 'land audits'. See 'Mutasa suppresses damning land audit', *The Zimbabwean*, 20/04/08.

FACTIONALISM, PATRONAGE AND CHIEFS

If official responses to such developmental aspirations recalled the Rhodesian high modernism of the 1940s–50s, when native reserves were centralised into *maline* (linear settlements) amid drastic destocking and the coercive construction of many miles of contour ridges, then the accelerated return of the chiefs in the 2000s recalled the turn to 'customary rule' that followed the demise of the Native Land Husbandry Act in the 1960s (Alexander 2006:63; Drinkwater 1989). Both the incorporation of developmental technocracy and the return of the chiefs into the fast-track programme therefore illustrate how past efforts to remake the land and authority over it, continued to reappear in the remaking of Mutirikwi's landscapes in the 2000s. It is important to acknowledge, however, that patronage, violence, elitism and factionalism also marked Zimbabwe's land reform. This too was part of the crucial context that enabled land reform to take place as it did. Equally important to recognise is that many of the divergent aspirations that fed enthusiasm for land reform and the Third *Chimurenga* were not ultimately realised, as impoverished new farmers sometimes returned to more secure land holdings in communal areas, or were victim to a series of evictions and re-occupations as new violent acquisitions later took hold (Moore 2012; Thebe 2012; Marongwe 2011; Zamchiya 2011). Around Mutirikwi and elsewhere this sometimes provoked profound disillusionment as *jambanja* was too often asserted upon *jambanja* (Sadomba 2011:217).

After Zimbabwe's unity government was formed in 2009, the significance of patronage, factionalism, and the 'ZANU PF-isation' and 'informalisation' of state institutions became increasingly apparent. Some argued ZANU PF's rule operated 'increasingly through informal networks rather than institutions qua institutions', blurring 'the distinction between state and nonstate ... coercive and noncoercive institutions, and public and private organisations', amounting to 'a parallel government that effectively sabotages the IG [Inclusive Government]' (Kriger 2012:11–12). Although the significance of such informal networks undoubtedly changed after 2009, many of these elements were already in play in the 2000s (cf. McGregor 2002). Around Mutirikwi the politics of patronage and informal networks were already evident in 2005/06, for example in the distribution of food relief in which some chiefs were heavily embroiled. The politicisation of local state institutions was also evident. But most obvious and enduring was ZANU PF's internal factionalism, long a defining feature of Masvingo politics; particularly between those aligned to the late Eddison Zvobgo and Dzikamai Mavhaire on one hand, and the late vice president Simon Muzenda, the late Stan Mudenge, former governor Josiah Hungwe and Chief Charumbira on the other. This long-running factionalism entangles the politics of chiefs and clans with that of district administrators, councillors and politicians, and found new manifestations in the fast-track context of the 2000s. The pervasiveness of Masvingo's factionalism is notoriously difficult to research empirically, yet is widely evident. For example, councillors, administrators and particular chiefs and clans are often aligned so that chiefly boundary and successions disputes can take on distinct 'factional' dimensions.[51] In wake of the unity government, various high-profile deaths (Muzenda in 2003; Zvobgo in 2004; Mudenge in 2012), and ZANU PF's own succession battles, Masvingo's factional alignments have become much more volatile and changeable.[52] Yet political factionalism, patronage, and informal networks continue to be implicated in the localised politics remaking Mutirikwi's landscapes.

In 2005/06 I glimpsed how this operates during long journeys with Matopos Murinye, as he sought to secure his chieftaincy and its claim to Boroma. Besides everyday administrative tasks, these journeys involved, for example, visiting the DA at his ARDA plot on Sikato farm with the gift of a goat. Another time there were negotiations with Clement Makwarimba, CEO of Masvingo Rural District Council, about council assistance to transport materials for his new 'palace'. Matopos also ensured he attended ZANU PF's 2005 conference in Bulawayo, and sought support across factional divides in his boundary dispute with Chief Mugabe. We also drove VaZarira to visit local businesses, district and provincial officials, the governor and local war veterans, seeking transport for her proposed trip to request rain at Matonjeni. Matopos Murinye was not unusual in making these efforts, all chiefs and headmen are involved in forging, utilising and cementing informal networks. They illustrate how relationships between chiefs and ZANU PF are more complex than the notion of co-optation allows, questioning assumptions that they are inevitably compromised by ZANU PF's politics of patronage, accumulation and violence. Yes, traditional leaders have been courted, as evidenced by their increased salaries, vehicles, electrification and other state benefits. Their powers have increased, and some have been implicated in violence and electioneering.[53] Others have been victim to it. But, analytically, co-optation is not robust enough to capture the complexity of strategies, agendas and conflicting imperatives in which they are situated. Some are closely aligned to particular factions.[54] Others forge relationships with

[51] For example, the DA is of the Charumbira clan, close to Makwarimba (CEO of the RDC), and associated with the Mudenge/Hungwe faction. Trust Mugabe is both a local councillor, a local party chairman, and a former acting chief. The Duma clans are sometimes said to be aligned with Svobgo/Mavhaire, and Charumbira/Nemanwa with Mudenge/Hungwe, although such older alignments have become more complex in recent years.

[52] 'Showdown looms in Masvingo', 10/01/13 *Newsday*.

[53] 'Violent chief fined', 23/03/13, *Newsday*; 'Army, chiefs plan violent election', 07/11/12, *The Zimbabwean*; 'Charumbira threatens chiefs over anti-sanctions petition', 21/03/11, *Newsday*; 'Influential Chief accused of destabilising outreach program', 06/07/10, *SW Radio Africa*; 'Masvingo violence exposed', 13/11/10, *The Zimbabwean*.

[54] Chief Fortune Charumbira (like his late father Zepheniah, a senator in the late 1970s) is a good example, and a key member of one of Masvingo's ZANU PF factions. In the early 2000s, as Deputy Minister of Local Government, he facilitated the appointment of loyalists into key local government positions. Since he was removed from his ministerial position in a move orchestrated, some rumours suggest, by ZANU PF figures in Harare determined to curb his

party protagonists in order to realise the local aspirations to which they too must be responsive. Most are careful to maintain public perceptions about their loyalty to ZANU PF. In late 2005 I was asked to leave a meeting hosted by Chief Mugabe because, to paraphrase his words, 'we are near to the road, and someone passing might think I am MDC if they see a white person at my meeting'.[55] It was partially in jest, but only partially; no one laughed. It reminded me of chiefs' vulnerability. That Chief Mugabe's sudden death in November 2009 was attributed by some to witchcraft illustrates exactly the complex webs of political demands, factional loyalties and local expectations within which chiefs are located.[56]

However much fast-track offered renewed opportunity for a diversity of delayed aspirations and imagined futures, chiefs clearly occupy an unenviable position amongst an array of demands, imperatives and agendas, of which ZANU PF politicking is but one complex dimension. This is not a recent development. When nationalist struggle brought war and danger to Mutirikwi in the 1970s, chiefs were often caught between the contradictory pressures of Rhodesian forces, nationalists and guerrilla fighters. Matopos Murinye often told me the difficulties his father Mudarikwa faced during the war, including attempts on his life and internment. But he survived and successfully negotiated chieftainship in postcolonial Zimbabwe for another twenty years. Matopos was not as successful. That his replacement explained his own 2010 inauguration in terms of Mudarikwa's perceived opposition to ZANU PF during the war indicates the salience and longevity of the politics surrounding chieftaincy. This is perhaps the best illustration of how the past can continue to intrude upon the present and structure the future.

THE POLITICS OF RESEARCHING ZIMBABWEAN LAND REFORM

In 'the ambiguity of state-society relations', the politics of *both* inclusion and exclusion was central to Zimbabwean politics in the 2000s (Dorman 2003:845). However authoritarian and intolerant the state became – culminating in the terrible violence of 2008 – it also at times appealed to a diversity of unresolved, overlapping, and highly localised aspirations. This was reflected in the seemingly out-of-place optimism around Mutirikwi in 2005/06. It substantiates the argument that 'the exercise of government in all modern states entails the articulation of ... pastoral care with ... sovereign power' (Hammar 2003:130–1; Dean 2001:53). Consent as well as coercion was key to the politics of land in the 2000s. In the

---

(contd)   ambitions, as President of the Council of Chiefs, he has driven efforts to re-establish the authority of chiefs.

[55] Ironically some time later, when we met by chance, Chief Mugabe admonished me for not attending a public celebration he had hosted to celebrate his *zunde ramambo*, which I had heard about but decided not to attend without an unambiguous invitation!

[56] His wife told me, '*misha yakavauraya* [the villages killed him]' (Fieldnotes 12/12/11).

highly charged debates about Zimbabwe's multiple crises, this argument is not intended as an apology for ZANU PF's haughty authoritarianism, but rather to recognise that the diverse aspirations, remembered pasts and imagined futures of war veterans, chiefs, new farmers and others resettling farms and occupying state lands around Mutirikwi mattered, not just for academics but for its officials, land planners and politicians.

When I first wrote about the unexpected optimism of 2005/06 in a precursor to this chapter, I had considerable problems getting published. No doubt this reflected my own shortcomings, but it also revealed how the divisive polarities of Zimbabwe's social and political arenas in the 2000s were mirrored in academic spheres. It sometimes seemed like few commentators were willing to consider more nuanced understandings of land reform. Those who did often found themselves shunted to one or other side of Zimbabwe's polarised political divides, derided as apologists for ZANU PF (Moyo 2001; Moyo & Yeros 2005) or for the MDC and the conglomeration of civil society and foreign opinion perceived to lie behind it. The venom provoked by Mamdani's foray into these discussions (cf. Jacobs & Mundy 2009), which has also enveloped more recent studies,[57] is illustrative of how divided academics writing on Zimbabwe could be. I am thankful that a new wealth of scholarship has begun to present a more nuanced picture of both the profound problems and sometimes remarkable outcomes of land reform across highly variable, localised contexts.[58] Although debates remain critical, contentious, and far from consensus, few now doubt that it was irreversible. Many acknowledge that in some places, in some ways, it was surprisingly successful, widening access to fertile land and offering new possibilities for smallholder farming and rural entrepreneurship. Although older acrimonies continue (cf. Phimister 2012), most scholars recognise that whatever ZANU PF's motivations, the war veteran-led land invasions of 2000, and the fast-track programme that followed, only found traction in their engagement with a diversity of long-standing, localised aspirations that turned on remembered pasts and imagined futures in complex ways. This new scholarship is only beginning to make sense of how profoundly Zimbabwe's social, economic and political landscapes have been reshaped. Just as the liberation struggle continues after 34 years to provoke intense debate, the events of the 2000s will be debated for many years to come, as their long-term implications unfold. Much of this book, however, looks in the other direction, at the active materialities of the past immanent in the remaking of Mutirikwi's landscapes in the 2000s.

[57] See the reception that both Scoones et al. (2010), and Hanlon et al. (2012) have received: 'For he's a jolly evil fellow', 11/05/13, available at www.zimvigil. co.uk, accessed 3/6/13; 'Scoones defends controversial findings', *Zimbabwe Independent*, 07/12/12; Dale Doré, 'Myths, Reality and The Inconvenient Truth about Zimbabwe's Land Resettlement Programme', 13/11/12 www.sokwanele. com, accessed 03/06/13.

[58] Matondi 2012; Hanlon et al. 2012; Sadomba 2011; Scoones et al. 2010, 2011; Moyo 2011; Moyo et al. 2009; Dekker & Kinsey 2011; Mutupo 2011; Zamchiya 2011; Chambati 2011; Marongwe 2011; Mujere 2011; Murisa 2011; Mavedzenge et al. 2008.

2

Graves, Ruins and Belonging[1]

This chapter has three purposes. First, I discuss contestations over autochthony and belonging taking place in the context of fast-track land reform around Mutirikwi in the 2000s, in order to contribute to a growing body of work[2] exploring how land reform is part of an ongoing remaking of the (postcolonial) state. Second, I consider this micro-politics of belonging in relation to recent, diverse (but often complementary) approaches to 'materiality', which have sought to decentre the agency of human subjects by exploring the agency, affordances and affective qualities of things, materials and landscapes (Miller 2005; Gell 1998; Latour 1999; Ingold 1992 & 2007; Navaro-Yashin 2009; Stoler 2008; Edensor 2005). Finally, I link these discussions to anthropology's recent, 'ontological turn', which has seen a renewed and 'deepened' concern with 'radical difference' (Henare et al. 2006; Carrithers et al. 2008), to make a case for focusing on discursive, historical and material co-existences and proximities. How do the material forms of different past and present practices in the landscape reveal and materialise proximities and co-existences even as they are often articulated in political processes of differentiation? What is the significance for anthropology of such material and historical proximities and co-existences in shared landscapes? I suggest that, in social and historical contexts where difference is increasingly politicised as the contours of political inclusion and exclusion are dramatically redrawn, such as in post-2000 Zimbabwe, sensitivity to peoples' material engagements with space and substance can offer a way of writing against such politicised differences rather than re-asserting them on ever more abstract philosophical grounds.

---

[1] An earlier version of this chapter was published in *Journal of the Royal Anthropological Institute* 17, 4 (706-27). See Fontein 2011. I am grateful for permission to include a revised version here.

[2] Alexander 2006; Hammar et al. 2003; Chaumba et al. 2003a & 2003b; Matondi 2012; Marongwe 2003; Muzondidya 2007; Mubvumba 2005; Sadomba 2008; Scoones 2008; Scoones et al. 2010; Hanlon et al. 2012; Kriger 2006; McGregor 2002; Cousins 2006; Rutherford 2008; Raftopoulos 2007; Moyo 2001; Moyo & Yeros 2005.

THE BOROMA HILLS

I begin by discussing two apparently unrelated phenomena that have taken place around the Boroma hills, in order to introduce how the remains of different pasts are 'active' in ongoing, entangled discourses and practices of belonging and autochthony. These hills lie to the south of Lake Mutirikwi, on the boundary of what were once the farms of Oatlands, Le Rhone, Clifton and The Retreat, and are now at the centre of localised contests over authority and belonging between the two neighbouring Duma chiefs, Murinye and Mugabe and their clans, and between the inhabitants of several resettlement schemes established soon after independence when these farms became state land. These schemes' grazing areas, as well as swathes of other land bordering the lake, were occupied by so-called 'squatters' during the land invasions of the early 2000s. Although these occupations were not officially part of ZANU PF's so-called Third *Chimurenga*, its broader upheavals and fast-track rhetoric did provide an appropriate political milieu for what some saw as the return of long-claimed ancestral territory. These recent occupations were mirrored all around Mutirikwi, where resettled commercial farms and state lands have been claimed by a variety of chiefs and their clans, many of whom remember being evicted not only after previous waves of squatting soon after independence, but also much earlier during the colonial period. The area surrounding Boroma is notable because it lies on older colonial boundaries between white commercial farms and two former native reserves, and sits on the edge of the middle-veld escarpment, where it leads down to the hot, dry but fertile plains of the lowveld.[3] The area's complex historical geography is reflected in a myriad of debates between government institutions over different land uses around the lake, including national parkland, 'old' and 'new' resettlements, communal areas, and a protective boundary zone to prevent the lake's siltation.[4] Often these struggles reflect and exacerbate tensions between local ZANU PF factions, drawing in complex alliances with war veteran groups, local chiefs, councillors and others.

The two phenomena I begin with are the 2004 burial of Chief Murinye in Boroma, and the ghost of George Sheppard who often appears to guests at the nearby Ancient City hotel, which Sheppard himself built next to Great Zimbabwe in the 1930s. These examples introduce a broader consideration of how the remains of different pasts present in the landscape, as ghosts and ancestors, graves and ruins are active in the varying ways they materialise, constrain, enable and structure dif-

---

[3] For archaeologists this geography explains Great Zimbabwe's location nearby. It also explains, partly, why Le Rhone became a Rhodesian battle camp during the war, and why the dam was built there, at the confluence of the Mushagashe and Mutirikwi rivers, where gravity could feed water to the Chiredzi sugar fields many kilometres downstream.

[4] These have also involved the National Museums and Monuments of Zimbabwe at Great Zimbabwe (Fontein 2006a), and have entangled with government intentions to build a new university in the area (see Fontein 2006b:231,245, Fn. 23).

ferent, entangled discourses and practices of autochthony and belonging in the re-configuration of authority over land and wider remaking of the state provoked by fast-track land reform. This provides the context for a discussion of recent anthropological interest in questions of materiality, ruination and affect, and leads into my larger argument about the need to re-consider the historical, conceptual and material co-existences and proximities that anthropology's long history of allegiance to 'difference' tends to eschew.

THE BURIAL OF CHIEF MURINYE

In late 2004 Chief David Mudarikwa Murinye died. Having been chief for over fifty years, his death and subsequent burial amongst the graves of past Murinye chiefs in the Boroma hills was bound to be a significant event. By all accounts he had led a remarkable life.[5] Born around 1921 on a small hill on Oatlands farm,[6] Mudarikwa spent his childhood living at a granite *ruware* (bare rock outcrop) below Boroma known as Chingomana, on the nearby farm known as The Retreat.[7] In the 1940s Mudarikwa was removed, with many others, from Boroma to the Mtilikwe reserve beyond the Mutirikwi River,[8] at a time when Africans were removed from European farms all over the country, after the infamous Land Apportionment Act (1930).[9]

---

[5] This information came from long conversations with his son Matopos, the acting chief in 2005/06 (see also National Archives of Zimbabwe (NAZ), S2995/8/5, and Mtetwa (1976)).

[6] 'You can still see the tree that marks the spot where the homestead was' (Fieldnotes 22/05/06).

[7] Fieldnotes 13/06/06.

[8] Murinye's family had already been subject to various, less well remembered, movements. The late chief's father, Wurayayi, had lived in the short-lived 'Mlinyis' reserve, drawn up by the Native Commissioner Alfred Drew in 1901, west of where the lake is now. This later became Ivylands and Mlinya farms, and it is likely that was when Wurayayi moved to Boroma, where Mudarikwa was born and grew up (NAZ,Victoria reserves, sketches by A. Drew, 04/03/1901, n3/24/34; Victoria reserves L2/2/117/46; file S2111/42).

[9] Others remembered being moved in the 1950s, and it is likely people were moved at different times, depending on the nature of their tenancy or employment on the farms. It may be that Murinye's eviction from The Retreat coincided with its transfer from 'Shumba' Wallace, Great Zimbabwe's first curator, to Jack Sawyer (Interview with Bhodo Mukuvare 19/11/05a; Interview with Sekuru Chinengo' 26/05/06). Certainly Wallace had been looking to sell The Retreat since 1944, when post-war resettlement schemes for ex-servicemen were already being devised. It was described as a rather 'neglected' farm, overrun with 'native agriculture'; '50% ...comprised of bare granite kopjes' with only 300 acres of arable land, but 'well watered' along 'a long river frontage on the Umtilikwe river'. Morgenster Mission were not keen to entertain the government's proposal to exchange their farm Arawe (where it wanted to resettle ex-servicemen) for Wallace's Retreat, so that sale fell through (Land Inspector Cobham to Under Secretary, Lands, 21/1/44, NAZ S2136/51/1990).

The late chief's uncle, Chief Mabika was buried at Boroma,[10] as was his grandfather Chief Wushe. His father (Chief Wurayayi) was installed there sometime before they were evicted in 1949. When Mudarikwa became chief he suffered a series of witchcraft-induced afflictions, including a snakebite which left him with a lifelong limp. Later the old chief witnessed the building of the dam and lived through the turmoil of the liberation struggle. Shortly after independence he and many of his people (and other squatters) re-occupied Boroma, reclaiming it as their own, before being removed for a second time to make room for the *minda mirefu* (long fields) resettlements of the 1980s. In 2002, at the height of fast-track, he returned to Boroma again, now an old man, to claim his birthplace and ancestral *mapa* (sacred grave/site), where he was finally interred in 2004.

In the context of wider upheavals over land, authority and belonging, Murinye's burial in the landscape was a politically motivated as well as emotionally charged event. As directed by his ancestors, the late chief had before his death indicated the precise spot where he wanted to be buried, in a cave which constitutes a major ancestral *mapa*, near to his own birthplace and childhood, alongside the *makuva* (graves) of his ancestors and the *matongo* (ruined homesteads) of his fathers. With his son, Matopos, the acting chief, embroiled in a continuing boundary dispute with neighbouring Chief Mugabe, amid ongoing tensions between 'returnees' and members of the older resettlements, and with a complicating myriad of state institutions (local government administrators, lands, natural resources, agriculture, water and so on) involved, it is clear this burial was an intensely political act that sought to materialise Murinye's claims to autochthony and belonging, in order to substantiate claims of authority and sovereignty over land in the area. Matopos had moved with his father to Boroma in 2002, and by 2005/06 was building his house on a carefully chosen site below the hills.[11]

But Murinye's burial was not merely an instrumental exercise. It was also the result of the nostalgic longings of an old man, and a response to the ancestrally directed need to live amongst and guard over the *matongo* and *makuva* of ancestral forebears. The controversies that surrounded the burial were more complex than simply the contested claims of rival chiefs over boundaries. Chief Murinye died in December 2004, and was buried the next day in secret with only a handful of elders present. No announcement was made until the public funeral three months later. Later that year, after the harvests, the acting chief imposed a six-week ban on all agricultural work across his chiefdom, a mourning practice known as *mahakurimwi*. This angered many Murinye 'subjects' concerned about their loss of earnings, especially given the difficult macro-economic conditions. The burial organisers, the acting chief and the medium VaZarira, saw these strict conditions as the proper ('traditional') funerary procedures for a Murinye chief, ensuring his transformation into a protective ancestor (Lan

[10] Although just outside the *mapa* itself, because his epilepsy, associated with witchcraft, prohibited burial within the caves (Fieldnotes 22/05/06).
[11] Fieldnotes 22/05/06.

Photo 4 Mudarikwa Murinye's grave in the *mapa* on Boroma, with acting Chief Matopos Murinye in background, and Peter Manyuki and Baba Lisa in foreground
(Source: author, 2006)

1985:31–5). Both described how the late chief was buried in a wet skin of a black bull, seated upright on a throne of stones, overlooking the valley below, walled up in a cave opening that was once the *dare* (meeting place) of the late chief's grandfather Chief Wushe.[12] As VaZarira continued:

> We wrapped him in a cattle skin and no one knew what was taking place, even his wives did not know... That is our rule, because Murinye is the eldest chief around here. After three months, we told the *sabhuku* [village heads] ... that is when the whole land knew the chief is no more ... Chief Charumbira turned up ... he said to me 'Ambuya what you have done is amazing ... what you have done is very original to your ancestors'... That was how we buried your friend, Joe [this author], and even Charumbira was afraid of that.[13]

For VaZarira Chief Charumbira's response was very significant. The Charumbira clan is not only an historical rival to the Duma clans, the current chief is also a major rival for political influence across the district, as powerful head of the Council of Chiefs, and an influential member of ZANU PF. In July 2005 he publicly defended the imposition of *mahakurimwi*, in response to villagers' complaints reported in *The Herald* (18/07/05). Given Charumbira's well-known advocacy for a return of chiefs' powers, it is perhaps not surprising that he defended the actions of a chief who many might position as his historical rival. VaZarira's comment that 'even Charumbira was afraid of that' points to this rivalry, but also to a shared sense of the 'power' that can accumulate from follow-

---

[12] Fieldnotes 29/06/06 & 22/05/06. These descriptions resemble accounts of the Ndebele King, Mzilikazi's burial in the Matopos, 'sitting upright in a stone chair, looking out from the cave in which his body had been embalmed, over a wonderful stretch of country he had conquered' (Sir James McDonald cited in Ranger 2012:4).
[13] Fieldnotes 12/12/05.

ing 'proper traditions' or *chivanhu*. There is a kind of moral conviviality (Fontein 2006c),[14] a shared moral episteme, in which all chiefs, mediums and other so-called 'traditional leaders' are located, despite personal animosities, religious or political differences, and historical contests between clans. A central tenet is recognition that living descendants of dead chiefs have privileged access to particular knowledge about the land, its sacred places, taboos and ritual practices, which ensures adequate rainfall, prosperity, and protection from disease and misfortune. This 'moral conviviality' is one important facet, alongside a diversity of technocratic imperatives, appeals to developmentalism, and differing versions of traditional rule, not to mention the complex political agendas of ZANU PF patrons, feeding into the ongoing re-structuring of authority over land across Zimbabwe's changing rural landscapes. In this context, Mudarikwa's burial in the *mapa* of his ancestors was not only about materialising autochthony for the purposes of claiming land, but also about renegotiating regimes of rule and re-configuring structures of sovereignty over territory and people, a process which gained new salience in the fast-track context (Alexander 2006; Hammar et al. 2003; Chaumba et al. 2003a & 2003b; Marongwe 2003; Muzondidya 2007; Mubvumba 2005; Sadomba 2008). In other words, the politics of Murinye's burial are as implicated in a wider remaking of the state as they are about substantiating Murinye claims in historical contests with neighbouring chiefs.

Villagers' grumblings about the agricultural ban illustrate how Murinye's burial was also implicated in the internal politics of chiefly rule; particularly in the tension between assertions of ancestral authority and the demands of pastoral care. The ancestral dimension of this internal politics was demonstrated at Boroma again later that year, when a series of unexplained fires were interpreted by some as an ancestral response to unruly new settlers breaking taboos by cutting firewood and setting traps in the sacred *mapa*.[15] The concern the new chief and VaZarira showed about these fires highlights both how seriously they take the protection of sacred sites and ancestral taboos, and how their own authority, even among people living in fairly close vicinity, was not necessarily a given, particularly in recent, unplanned (and informally) resettled areas such as around Boroma.

A newspaper report in November 2006 indicated that some in the area were deeply concerned about 'the massive environmental degradation' caused by 'illegal settlers who include war veterans, ordinary villagers and their leader, Chief Murinye', who had 'invaded an area on the banks of the lake reserved for wild animals'.[16] The acting chief agreed

---

[14] See also Mercer & Page 2010 and Mercer, Page & Evans 2008: 3–31, who use a similar notion of 'moral conviviality' but in a very different context.

[15] Fieldnotes 14/12/05. For others these fires were a 'serious *mhosva*' (crime) caused by careless people that might lead to future ancestral problems.

[16] 'Lake Mutirikwi invaded', *Zimbabwe Standard*, 12/11/06. The acting chief carefully differentiated between 'illegal settlers' who settled themselves or were encouraged by rival chiefs, and those accompanying his father and himself in returning to Murinye's ancestral land.

environmental degradation was a concern and that new settlers must respond to technocratic demands, but also deftly argued that such eco-logical concerns further demonstrated why ancestral lands needed to be properly occupied by autochthons who 'know the land' and are best able to protect it. Clearly traditional leaders' authority over land in which they have resettled themselves does not exist in simple opposition to the governmental regimes of formally planned resettlement, but rather intertwines with them in complex ways.

THE GHOST OF GEORGE SHEPPARD

George Sheppard was born to a fishing family in Grimsby, England. He went to South Africa to fight in the Second South African war but arrived too late, so joined Cecil Rhodes's British South Africa Police in 1904. After working in Bulawayo, he moved to Fort Victoria (now Masvingo town) to work in the Victoria Hotel. Later he bought Le Rhone farm, between Great Zimbabwe and the Boroma hills, next to The Retreat where Mudarikwa Murinye grew up. There, in the early 1930s, he built Sheppard's Hotel,[17] on a site still referred to locally (and on maps) as 'Sheppard's plot', where the Ancient City hotel now stands. In 1952 he died from black water fever.[18] From 1953 Le Rhone was run as a cattle ranch by Sheppard's daughter Joan until it was sold in 1968 when, as her son Simon Bright explained, she left the country with her family as 'part of a whole generation of liberal whites ... driven out by Ian Smith'.[19] It is not clear where George Sheppard was buried. Some believe that 'Magi-gan', as he was locally known, was buried near his hotel, or on his farm. His grandson Simon does not know either, but like many locals, he does refer to stories about Sheppard's ghost appearing to guests and haunting managers at his old hotel: 'he's been a spirit around there for a long time ... local people always respond when I say I am the grandson of Magigan ... I have ... poured whiskey onto the ground for his spirit ... but I have never seen his ghost myself'.[20]

Simon himself fondly remembers and has a deep attachment or 'ob-session with ... the landscape of my childhood' around Boroma. Stories about his grandfather's ghost and offerings of whisky substantiate this personal sense of belonging by materialising his family's history in the landscape. In August 2008 Simon reminisced of school holidays on the farm, 'playing with the local African kids', 'chasing baboons', 'collecting *mashanje* fruits', and so on.[21] There are striking resemblances between

---

[17] On a disputed boundary with the Great Zimbabwe estate (Letter from A.M. Williams to Minister of Transport & Commerce, 31/1/34, NAZ S914/12/7).

[18] Bright, 04/08/08.

[19] Colin Bristo bought the ranch and ran it as a wildlife park, until it was abandoned during the war and became a Rhodesian army camp. Later it was a demobilisation camp, and then became a resettlement scheme.

[20] Bright 04/08/08.

[21] Bright 04/08/08.

Simon's memories of the area as the 'landscape of his childhood', and acting Chief Murinye's description of his late father's stories of herding goats as a child and hunting with dogs around Boroma. While these stories sometimes refer to wrath of the white farmer who owned The Retreat, 'Shumba' Wallace (Sheppard's neighbour),[22] indicating the very different childhood experiences of the late Murinye before 1949, as the son of African tenants/workers on a white farm, from those of Simon Bright after 1953, as the child of white farm owners, both accounts do illustrate how attachments to landscape, indeed a sense of belonging, can involve deeply personal and affective memories of past experiences. In both accounts there is also a sense that such memories become particularly acute exactly in historical contexts of migration, dispossession and return.

But there are also obviously different purposes for narrating such stories. Bright was not embroiled in the same array of contests with neighbouring chiefs, land settlers and government structures as the late chief and his son were since their return in 2002. He was not trying to legitimise a claim to land through appeals to autochthony, and nor was he able to narrate a history of violent, state institutionalised, racialised dispossession, even if he did leave Rhodesia to avoid Smith's increasingly right-wing politics. Yet Simon did describe how he returned two years after independence 'keen as mustard' to do something for the new country and particularly for the area around his family's former farm. He joined Agritex (now AREX) and became involved in rural development. In the 1990s he contributed to various projects near Boroma with his childhood friend Thomas Mapanda. For Bright, his own childhood memories and friendships, but equally his family's history in the area bequeathed him with a right of access, a right 'to roam the landscape' involving *not* the 'terrible weight of responsibility that ownership brings' but rather a strong desire to re-establish past relationships with people and the land and to do 'something good'. Most interestingly Simon described what he saw as his inherited right to visit, and responsibility to keep secret, the sacred Boroma caves, which his grandfather had first been shown by a local spirit medium called Ndavanga (his friend Mapanda's father). In his words 'it says something about my grandfather's reputation with the locals that he was shown these sacred caves ... whenever I have been to those caves, I have made offerings to the spirits ... and we have kept that commitment to keeping the caves secret'.

The importance of the sacred Boroma caves for both the late Murinye and his son, and George Sheppard and his grandson is striking, even if they are quite possibly talking about different caves – the late chief's grave lies on the other side of the Boroma hills from those described by

[22] 'One time ... my father was herding goats near those ruins over there. The white farmer used to stand on the stone walls and shout at his workers ... one day ... the white farmer ... fell down and broke his leg! ... everyone was laughing ... but they had to turn their heads to one side so that they would not been seen ... And the white man was cursing ... look you use your witchcraft to make me break my leg ...' (Matopos Murinye 11/06/06).

Bright, and there are many hilltops, caves and rocks in the area. Even more striking are the resemblances in how belonging is understood in terms of kin-based, inherited responsibilities over the land, and the protection of secret knowledge about sacred places and ancestral rituals. But the resemblances do not stop there. Most significantly, in 2001, before leaving Zimbabwe for a second time, Bright (re)buried his parent's remains 'there on The Retreat, at a place with a lovely view overlooking the lake', under a stone bench below a Mukwa tree.[23]

While this quiet reburial materialises Bright's understanding of his parents', and his own, relationship with the land, and so it does resemble Murinye's burial in nearby Boroma, it is not clear what the late chief or his son (or others in the area) made of this. It happened before or just as they were returning to the area. Bright acquired the granite slab for the bench from people on nearby resettlements, and there had been some problems afterwards: 'but the grave was not desecrated or anything like that, as far as I know. I just did it!' Simon joked.[24] Exception could have been taken to this burial in the same way that neighbouring chiefs (particularly Chief Mugabe) took exception to Murinye's subsequent burial in Boroma, but it may also be that there was no objection as long as the correct rituals had taken place to ensure the ancestors were placated. Graves and burials intersect with the politics of recognition (Englund & Nyamnjoh 2004) in very complex ways, drawing in not only the graves of colonial settlers and returning, competing chiefs, but also those of earlier clans displaced or subsumed when the Duma first occupied the area in the 19th century (Mtetwa 1976). Maybe a clue to how the acting chief might have responded lies in his descriptions of Sheppard's ghost at the Ancient City hotel. Long before I met Simon Bright, I had already heard about Sheppard's ghost when Matopos Murinye explained problems he was having in 2006 with the new hotel management, who were refusing access to carry out annual rituals at some Murinye graves located at the same site. As the acting chief explained, these annual rituals are essential to ward off ancestral problems that in the past had manifest as swarms of flies, ticks or troubling snakes:

> [E]ven Mr Sheppard himself has appeared on several occasions ... They find him sitting on the bed holding his ivory walking stick, talking about things that are being done wrong at the place and what the other spirits are saying. The staff would call us and we would come, do these rituals, put snuff down and these problems would go away.[25]

The way that Sheppard's ghostly presence has been incorporated in this 'autochthonous' account of Murinye's ritual responsibilities at the hotel indicates it is quite possible that the burial of Bright's parents'

---

[23] His mother died in the early 1980s, her ashes were scattered in Harare's Warren Park cemetery. After his father died, Simon buried his remains near the lake with soil from that cemetery and some of his mother's belongings (Bright 04/08/08).

[24] Bright 04/08/08.

[25] Fieldnotes 24/04/06.

remains near Boroma will not cause any significant problems. Indeed, perhaps like Sheppard, their presence too will be incorporated into the autochthony of others so that, in a sense, they too can ultimately belong.[26]

What particularly interests me about the demanding presence of Sheppard's ghost alongside Murinye graves at the hotel is how these very different pasts coincide and co-exist in close and active proximity in the same place and time. If, as I argue, the remains and presence of different pasts in the landscape (as ghosts and ancestors, graves and ruins, *makuva* and *matongo*) are active in the varying ways that they materialise, constrain, enable and structure different entangled discourses and practices of autochthony and belonging, then there is, I suggest, a need to explore the historical, conceptual and material proximities of such discourses and practices that derives from the shared nature of material landscapes. The ghost of George Sheppard may be exceptional – there are not very many other white ghosts in the area[27] – but the material remains of white occupation in the landscape are all around, from ruined farmhouses, graves, old irrigation schemes and dilapidated farm tracks, to signs, place-names and boundaries, not to mention the commanding presence of Mutirikwi's dam itself. The contrast drawn here between traces of white colonial occupation and those of Africans once removed and now returning is a deliberately stark and polarised portrayal of a much more complex array of co-existences and proximities always present and active in any landscape. There are a multitude of differences, not reductive to 'race' or 'culture', the proximities and co-existences of which may be of interest around Mutirikwi: between 'autochthons' and 'strangers', competing chiefs and clans, technocrats and traditional elders, local councillors and government bureaucrats, war veterans and spirit mediums, political parties or factions within them, and so on. What I want to explore is how the material forms of all these different past and present practices in the landscape reveal and materialise proximities and co-existences even as they are often articulated in political processes of differentiation. What do all these material traces, this presence of different but shared pasts, do in ongoing struggles of authority, sovereignty, autochthony and belonging around Mutirikwi? What is the significance

[26] Such incorporation of 'strangers', even 'invaders', into existing religious structures has long historical precedence (see Lan 1985; Ranger 1999).

[27] But they do exist. For example the ghost of 'Shumba' Wallace: 'One of the Mutevedzi [Charumbira] people used to work for him. In fact Mutevedzi was his *tezvara* [father-in-law], he was *mukwasha* [son-in-law]. And when he died he left his cars, and some money to his favourite workers ... So that Mutevedzi took that car and property, and Wallace was coming into his dreams telling him what to do with the money, car, etc. But Mutevedzi then decided to go to Gokwe to sell that car. When he was there, Wallace came to him and said "why are you not doing what I told you to do, I gave you all this property...". Then that Mutevedzi died'. I heard another story about a ghost 'near Mavhaire's farm... Apparently there is an old house where a *murungu* [white person] lived called Chikitty [lit. 'small cat'] ... if you go into that old house you will always find the dinner table set, even though the house has been unlived in for many years' (Fieldnotes 28/05/06).

for anthropology of these kinds of material and historical proximities and co-existences in shared landscapes?

LANDSCAPES OF BELONGING

As Geschiere and others (Cohen & Odhiambo 1992; Shipton 2009) have noted, funerals in Africa often 'constitute a high point for the reaffirmation of belonging', even where 'quite different modalities of belonging are at stake' (Geschiere 2005:59). As 'true festivals of belonging', 'the funeral offers an occasion to link "soil" and "body" in all sorts of naturalising ways ... and of course, the climax of a funeral anywhere is when the body of the deceased is committed to the soil' (Geschiere 2009:18,30). Yet despite the prominence given to funerals in this literature, and the well-recognised fact that autochthony implies a claim to a 'special link to the soil' (2009:2), little attention is paid to what we might call materialities of belonging, and of graves in particular, beyond emphasising the immediate significance of how they link autochthony to place (Geschiere and Nyamnjoh 2000). What seems missing is an exploration of the 'consequential materiality' (Moore 2005:24) of interred bodies and burials, beyond merely *locating* belonging in the landscape. Graves and burial sites are not simply passive and inert 'criteria' for assertions of belonging, as 'symbolic focal points of human attachments' (Shipton 2009:20) or 'geographical markers' or 'evidence of ownership' (Evers 2005:223–4). Around Mutirikwi at least, graves and indeed ruins have a more active and affective presence.

The anthropology of landscape provides more analytical tools with which to consider how 'things and places are active agents of identity rather than pale reflections of pre-existing ideas and socio-political relations'; with 'real and ideological effects on persons and social relations, things and places can be regarded as much subjects as objects of identity' (Tilley 2006:17–18). This perspective can be productively merged with Geschiere's emphasis on subjectivity, shared aesthetics, religious symbols and style, and the emotive appeals of autochthony. For Geschiere 'the special and highly variable meaning imputed to the soil ... can offer a vantage point ... for explaining autochthony's varying trajectories' (2009:35). Certainly around Mutirikwi, 'soil' does take on different meanings in different languages of belonging being articulated – from evocative descriptions of war veterans as '*vana vevhu*' (sons of the soil); to spirit mediums' assertions that *ivhu rakatsamwa* (the soil is angry) at the perceived failures of chiefs, new settlers and others *kuchengeta vhu* (to protect the soil); all of which intertwine with land and water planners' concerns about soil erosion and agriculturalists' classifications of good and bad soils. But this focus on meanings imputed to soil falls short of explaining how soil, like 'things and places', can be an 'active agent of identity'. If Geschiere's emphasis on funerals highlights how subjectivity is important for understanding autochthony's emotive appeal then, like Navaro-Yashin (2009) suggests, we need to combine such a focus on 'internal' subjectivities with an understanding of the 'external' affects of objects and landscapes. Murinye's burial was significant both for the political implications of the funeral process itself, and the emotive and kinship-based subjectivities involved, as well as its further material substantiation of the Boroma hills as an active landscape of Murinye belonging. If autochthony is highly mutable yet must involve a claim to the soil, then funerals are important not just as 'festivals of belonging' but in the way they create material landscapes of belonging.

GRAVES AND RUINS, MATERIALITY AND AFFECT

The lack of attention to materialities of landscape in the autochthony and belonging literature is surprising because clearly one important aspect of the politics of burial concerns what the presence of graves may cause, enable or constrain in the future. Across Zimbabwe, and indeed the region, the politics of burial often circulates exactly around what the presence of graves might subsequently lead to – from offending ancestors and causing drought or pestilence, to undermining official histories of past violence, or to substantiating (or not) the efficacy of new kinds of claims to land, resources, and authority (Werbner 1998; Posel & Gupta 2009; James 2009; Fontein 2009b, 2010, 2014; Mujere 2011, 2013). In this context, the graves and commemorative monuments of colonial settlers, such as Bright's parents' grave near Boroma, or the prospective graves of recently evicted white farmers still determined to be buried on their former farms,[28] or the various memorial chapels overlooking the lake,[29] may all entangle with or provoke new, unforeseen, kinds of politics. Similarly the graves of deceased farm workers or other colonial-era African migrants continue to have a latent potential to provoke future controversy.[30] For people removed when the dam was built in 1961, the presence of graves of their kith and kin under the lake's waters, or among the hilltops that poke out as islands from its surface, are intertwined

---

[28] Pat Potgeiter, a former commercial farmer, insisted that he was born and would be buried in a family cemetery on his former farm, Bon Air, next to his uncle who was shot during the war in East Africa (Potgeiter 15/01/06). Similarly, Ray Sparrow told me that although his 1000 hectare farm next to the Kyle Game reserve had been threatened many times 'I really hope we will be able to keep it' because 'one of our sons is buried there on that farm' (Sparrow 15-06/06/06).

[29] There are two such chapels. One was built by Italian prisoners of war in the 1940s, and contains the remains of 71 Italian prisoners who died in captivity (see www.nmmz.co.zw/web2.0/index.php?option=com_content&view=article&id=22&Itemid=29, accessed 5/6/13). The other, near the dam wall, was built by the step grandfather of Mr Errol Edwards, commodore of the Kyle Boat Club, in memory of his daughter (Errol's dad's half-sister) who was killed in a car accident (Fieldnotes 25/05/06).

[30] Such as the Basotho, whose short-lived ownership of Erichstahl farm in the 1930s continues to be marked by graves in what is now a National Park (Mujere 2011, 2012).

with continuing demands for fishing rights, or long promised but not yet delivered irrigation schemes.

Around Mutirikwi such problematic politics of burial long pre-date the 2004 interment of Murinye in Boroma. Burials in resettled areas have often provoked tensions between returning autochthonous clans and incoming *vatorwa*.[31] Such burials can be problematic not just because they may provide future efficacy to competing claims and histories, but due to anticipated problems from offended ancestors or from dangerous *ngozi* spirits demanding to be returned home (Fontein 2010). Burials can create future obligations, as well as rights to the land, through the intermingling materials and substances of kin and soil; as witnessed, for example, by the troubling fires, ghosts and ticks at Murinye graves on Boroma and at the Ancient City hotel. Another example is VaZarira's obligation to return to her spirit's grave on Beza, north of the lake, 'to clean the bones and sweep the *mapa*'.[32] Similarly, many war veterans, technocrats and government administrators have acknowledged that, beyond official demands for agricultural productivity and environmental protection, existing graves and sacred places on resettled farms create particular kinds of obligations for new farmers towards autochthonous chiefs and their ancestral rules and taboos. Even National Parks rangers admitted to sweeping old Basotho graves in the game reserve (Mujere 2012), because they realised 'it is in our interest to do that'.[33] Elsewhere drought, crop failure, misfortune, sickness and even economic crisis have all been understood as the result of ancestral anger at the failures of new farmers, war veterans, government employees, and sometimes chiefs themselves, to respond to the obligations imposed by specific ancestral graves and sacred places in the landscape. This is true at Great Zimbabwe (Fontein 2006a), but also north-east of the lake where Chief Chikwanda's perceived denigration of ancestral rules at Mafuse, a *mapa* where Chikwanda chiefs were once dried and buried, led some to accuse him of failing to look after the soil (*kuchengeta vhu*), undermining his authority within his own clan. Meanwhile his neighbour Chief Makore blamed poor rains and failing harvests on 'those fast-track people' who 'do not know the land', and challenged Chikwanda's attempt to settle nearby Zishumbe hill, claiming it is Makore's sacred *mapa* where their founding ancestor Risipambi lies buried (dried).[34]

---

[31] Settlers on parts of Mzero farm that 'reverted' to communal land after 1980, have often faced opposition from Nemanwa elders for burying relatives of different clan identities at their homesteads. Mai Rukasha explained that she faced particular difficulties when she buried her father near her home in the 1980s, because her father was of a different and 'unknown' totem. Similar problems re-occurred when other relatives, of different clan and totemic identities were buried at the same plot more recently (Fieldnotes 16/04/06).

[32] Fieldnotes 12/12/05.

[33] Warden and rangers, at Kyle Recreational Park, 25/11/05.

[34] Chief Chikwanda and Chief Makore have been involved in a deep boundary dispute provoked, as around Boroma and elsewhere, by land occupations. The late Chief Makore was particularly angry about a local councillor, closely aligned to Chikwanda, who occupied one of Makore's sacred hills (Fieldnotes 26/06/06).

But it is not just graves that act in the landscape. Ruins and other traces of past occupation, of other regimes of rule, too are important features in landscapes of belonging. One reason for linking graves and ruins in this way is ethnographic. In justifying current occupations and claims to land, people referred not only to the *makuva* of their kith and kin, but also to *matongo* – ruined homesteads and birthplaces. Like graves, *matongo* too materialise belonging in the merging substances of bodies and soil through the burial of umbilical cords (*rukuvhute*) of new-borns in homesteads or cattle kraals, so that 'home is where their *rukuvhute* is and ... ideally where they should be buried after death, to complete the cycle of life where it began (Mazarire 2013a:10). Both Murinye's son, recounting his return and burial, and of course Simon Bright, referred to old houses and material features of the landscapes of their childhood, and this is repeated all around Mutirikwi.[35] As with the motif of 'suffering for territory' that Moore identified in Zimbabwe's Eastern Highlands (2005), around Mutirikwi too, legacies of remembered eviction and dispossession have often merged with such claims to ancestral autochthony.

Ruins and traces of past material interventions in the landscape can be articulated with very different kinds of claims to belonging. Hughes (2006a, 2006b, 2010), for example, discusses how, for colonial settlers and 'Euro-Africans' refusing to engage with Africans around them, agricultural improvements and particularly water engineering, became a mechanism for inscribing legitimacy and belonging into the landscape. The construction of Kariba, Lake Mutirikwi and later smaller farm dams really was an 'heroic', 'hydrology of hope', engineering 'nature' to satisfy white settlers' aesthetic needs for watery landscapes, for entertainment, 'wilderness' and most significantly, a claim to the soil (Hughes 2006b). Like graves, these kinds of ruins, traces of past regimes of rule in the substance of landscapes, also continue to be active in the way that they enable, constrain and structure contests of belonging, entitlement and authority. Lake Mutirikwi's commanding presence and concerns about soil erosion and siltation have dictated attitudes amongst government officials about surrounding land use, which land occupiers like Murinye at Boroma have had to engage with in very practical as well as discursive

(contd)   The tensions between these related Duma chiefs have involved local spirit mediums, including Mai Macharaga and VaZarira (Fieldnotes 14/04/06 – see also Scoones et al. 2010: 198). They escalated when the acting chief Makore (son of the senior chief) was assaulted by youths allegedly working for Chikwanda (*The Herald* 09/07/08). In 2010 the elder Makore died and his son was embroiled in new disputes after imposing a two-week agricultural ban ('Zimbabwean villagers forced to donate at chief's funeral' www.radiovop.com, 13/01/10, accessed 05/10/14).

[35] References to *makuva* and *matongo* are repeated among many different people making autochthonous claims to land, including Haruzvivishe people next to Great Zimbabwe, Chikwanda occupiers north and east of the lake, and Charumbira people to the west. Although I have not heard of the burial of umbilical cords by white Zimbabweans, former white farmers too frequently made references to birth places, 'landscapes of their childhood' and family graves on former farms (Sparrow 15–06/06/06; Potgeiter 15/01/06).

ways. Upon returning in 2002 the late Chief Murinye and his son deliberately located their new homes topographically, where any run-off
threatens not the lake but feeds into the Mutirikwi river downstream
of the dam, because, as the DA (District Administrator) put it 'he knows
why he was removed from this side of the hill' in the 1980s.[36]

There is a growing literature on ruins, ruination and affect, and this is
my second reason for linking graves and ruins here. As Stoler puts it, to
explore colonial ruins and ruination is to examine 'the material and social
afterlife of structures, sensibilities and things ... the focus is not on inert
remains but on their vital refiguration' (2008:194). Travelling across
former white farms I became accustomed to encountering material
traces of settler occupation and colonial rule. Old farm tracks, fencing
standards, ruined buildings, and old dips conjure up images of particular
pasts just as readily as caves, sacred springs and ancestral graves can.
Visiting Boroma we drove along an old gravel farm-track, still signposted
'Old Retreat road', which used to be an entry point into the Victoria reserve. Large concrete drains once dug under the road, form treacherously
steep humps that confront cars, drivers and passengers with the area's
colonial pasts but also with postcolonial failures to maintain roads and
infrastructure, feeding localised struggles between chiefs and councillors for authority and developmental legitimacy.[37] Another day I picked
up a rusty bullet as we rested from the sun – sparking my imagination
with a wave of conflicting, emotive images of colonials hunting baboons,
beating workers, evicting locals, and of liberation era 'contacts' with
'guerrillas'.[38] Later that day I listened as similar melancholic imaginings
were evoked in discussions between acting Chief Murinye and VaZarira's son Peter Manyuki as we explored the Boroma caves – of past chiefs
feasting and holding court, or seeking refugee from 19th-century Ndebele raiders – provoked by the affective objects which we encountered,
including pottery shards, grinding stones and walled-up graves.[39]

Similarly, travelling across communal areas, I became increasingly
aware of the magnitude of Alvord's modernisation and centralisation
projects in native reserves during the 1940s. Hundreds of kilometres of
coercively constructed contour ridges are still visible today. They remain
active and affective in the memories of people forced to build them,[40]

---

[36]   This may not be not enough to prevent future eviction given the 'catchment
wide' concerns of water planners (DA, James Mazvidza, 21/03/06).

[37]   Fieldnotes 11/06/06.

[38]   Fieldnotes 29/06/06.

[39]   Another time Manyuki showed me BSACo buttons, tags, bullet casings, and
beads retrieved from VaZarira's *mapa* on Bannockburn farm on Beza (where they
lived in the 1980s), pondering out aloud about what might have happened there
in the past (Fieldnotes, 12/12/05). Similarly if stone ruins visible on the lake's
islands recall the graves of Zano people removed when the dam was built (as well
as much older archaeology) then the 'old Zimbabwe road' and the ruined farm
houses that re-appeared when the lake almost dried up in 1992, were a reminder
that white farms too were flooded by the dam in the early 1960s.

[40] One person remembered a colonial official nicknamed Gabarinocheka (Tin
can that cuts) who 'was mad about contour ridges' ('*vaipengesa makandiwa*')

alongside the drastic destocking that decimated African wealth, and are recalled in legacies of suffering/eviction sometimes deployed in land claims, as well as in the continuing insistence of land technocrats on the prevention of soil erosion through contour ploughing, ridging and pro-hibitions on river-bank cultivation. With the continuing use of colonial place-names (farm names but also nicknames ascribed to settler-farm-ers), these kinds of traces, like Sheppard's ghost, illustrate how just as African presences were not obliterated by colonial land appropriations, so European settler presence continues to be active and affective in com-plex ways today.

Such politically salient melancholia inspired by affective objects and places is not separate from memories, imaginations or discursive constructions of the past; rather they are entangled and mutually con-stitutive. As Navaro-Yashin (2009) argues, one of the weaknesses of the recent affective turn is a deliberate disavowal of the discursive and imaginative dimensions of affect – as if what Edensor calls the 'sensual immanence of the experience of travelling through a ruin' is somehow dependent upon the 'usual uncertainty about what went on within these abandoned buildings' that he experienced exploring industrial ruins in the United Kingdom (2005:15). Around Mutirikwi, as with Cypriot land-scapes, experiencing the affectivity of ruins and material remnants of the past is not dependent upon a lack of historical knowledge or imagination but fundamentally intertwined with them (Navaro-Yashin 2009:14–15).

In recent literature, processes of ruination have also received attention (cf. Stoler 2008). Drawing on Walter Benjamin, the violation of ruina-tion is 'the underlying condition for the production of emergent forms of politics and social life' (Navaro-Yashin 2009:7). Like Northern Cyprus, around Mutirikwi new configurations of localised authority have or are being fashioned 'out of appropriating, using, and exchanging objects cap-tured by violation from other people' (2009:8). A good example is the way former farm houses, buildings and removable property have sometimes provoked nasty disputes on resettled farms. In some areas farmhouses and their contents have been claimed, occupied or taken by local elites; elsewhere buildings have been stripped of reusable materials including window and door frames, roofing, fence posts, wire, and so on.[41] But it is not just 'abject objects' but languages and practices, things, places and

(contd) and used to drive his Land Rover along contour ridges to check their width and construction (Tobias Mandebvu 15/03/06).

[41] Elsewhere farm buildings were turned into temporary schools or clinics, for and by new communities on resettled farms. Such 'ruination' amidst resettlement is not new: at the Boroma irrigation scheme established in the 1980s people still lament the destruction of farm buildings on Le Rhone by the 'squatters' who had preceded them, as indeed did Simon Bright when he 'mourned' the destruction of the farmstead he remembered from his childhood, which he too felt would have been more productively used as a school. Such contests over the use of ruined materials echo larger debates pitting 'anti-colonial restitution' against 'developmental appeals' to 'productive redistribution', highlighting further how the 'thingliness of politics' (Navaro-Yashin 2009:8) is intertwined in the remaking of the state provoked by 'fast-track' land reform in the 2000s.

ideas, that have 'been consumed, and this consumption has been gen-erative of new subjectivities and a new political system' (Navaro-Yashin 2009:6), in a kind of bricolage of old elements reconfigured into something new. Just as colonial-era evictions and land appropriations were not able to fully obliterate pre-colonial African languages and practices of belonging and rule around Mutirikwi, so post- and anti-colonial political movements designed to obliterate colonial pasts inevitably draw in the objects of their ruination. Such theories of ruination provide us with a framework not only for understanding how objects can have affects, but also how such affective objects, places and landscapes are intimately involved in political processes of change. These processes of change necessarily involve continuities deriving in part from material and con-ceptual co-existences and proximities with the very ruins of those past political orders. This is despite the politics of differentiation and exclusion such processes often involve.

Navaro-Yashin eloquently uses this ambivalent notion of ruination to argue that academic (particularly anthropological) knowledge produc-tion has a tendency to catastrophically 'ruin' old 'paradigms', and then set them up in deliberate, exaggerated, antithesis to the new theoretical fad of the moment. In this ruination there is an artificial distancing between theoretical perspectives which ethnography cannot justify; 'beyond paradigmatic shifts and wars, theories of affect and subjectivity, as well as of objects and symbolisation, demand to be merged' (2009:17). Around Mutirikwi the active, affective presence of graves and ruins too crosses over such polarised divides between theories of affect and subjectivity, and object-orientated approaches and social constructivism. In fact I think we could go further. The burgeoning of interest in materiality and affect, means that there is now a wide array of analytical tools for considering how graves and ruins can have an active presence in discourses, practices and contestations of autochthony and belonging. One perspective shared by all these approaches is the problematisation of Cartesian distinctions between subject and object, mind and matter, in exploration of the 'im-brication of the semiotic and the material' (Deleuze & Guattari 1987: 337).

A contrast has often been drawn (e.g. Miller 2005) between Gell's 'theory of abduction' and the 'inferred intentionality' of art (1998) and Latour's notion of objects as non-conscious 'actants' in 'networks of hybrids' (1999).[42] Different as these perspectives might be, in my view they are most usefully seen as complementary rather than mutually exclusive. Just as bones and bodies animate Zimbabwe's 'politics of the dead' in differing ways (Fontein 2009b, 2010), so both are reflected in the way graves and ruins are active around Mutirikwi. Gell's notion finds resonances in the way ancestral graves and sacred *mapa* create social obligations and can cause drought, sickness, misfortune or even political

---

[42] While theories of affect find an antecedent in Williams' 'structures of feeling', Gell finds a precursor in Mauss's *The Gift* (1954) and Latour's approach can be seen 'as a partial throwback to structuralism' because 'what matters may often not be the entities themselves … but rather the network of agents and the relationships between them' (Miller 2005:11).

and economic strife. Here the agency of sacred places derives, ultimately, from the intentionality of the spirits (whether ancestors or troubling, dangerous *ngozi*), and war veterans, new farmers, chiefs, even members of Pentecostal and African Independent Churches[43], as well as government administrators and technocrats, must, in some way respond to that. Other things like hydrological engineering works such as the dam, or contour ridges, can also be indexes (Gell 1998) carrying the distributed agency of their designers. But although the remains of technocratic landscapes can continue to carry some of their intended disciplining affects, this is not all that they do. Often, highly planned landscapes, perhaps particularly (but not necessarily) those in ruin and decay, are active not as 'a congealed residue of performance and agency in object-form ... via which their agency can be communicated' (Gell 1998:68), but rather more like Latour's unintentional 'actants'. For example, when the qualities of soil or the presence of a nearby dam, topography, or indeed the availability of 'abject objects' to be looted, determines, enables or constrains what happens where, how and by whom in the construction of new systems of rule provoked through fast-track land reform.

The way that graves, ruins, soil, contour ridges, and so on, can act both as indexes of distributed human intentionality (Gell), and as non-human actants in complex 'hybrid' networks (Latour), provokes the larger question, beyond the scope of this chapter, of what this suggests about 'agency' itself (Ingold 2007:11). We can explore parallels here with work by phenomenological thinkers. Ingold's discussion (developed from Gibson 1979) of the 'mutual constitution' (1992:40) and 'dialectics of the interface between persons and environment', between the 'affordances' or 'use-values' of objects and the 'effectivities' of subjects (1992:51–52) in some ways recalls Latour's emphasis on networks because of its emphasis on 'agentful' relationships and processes. We can think about how graves, ruins, soil and contour ridges have affordances in political, social and ecological terms, as of course do the practices, languages or 'effectivities' associated with them. More recently, Ingold's critique of materiality in favour of the properties, flows and transformations of materials (2007), further enriches our understanding of how objects/materials do things in Zimbabwe; by highlighting, for example, how the containment, transferences and merging of materials, such as bodily substances into soil, often animates the politics of violence and burial (Fontein 2010, 2014).

For Ingold, materials matter because to talk of the 'materiality of an object' is an abstraction. I am sympathetic. Certainly the significance of *makuva* and *matongo* in contests over belonging around Mutirikwi relates intimately to the merging of substances, of bodies into the soil, and Ingold's perspective can help us understand that what matters is not necessarily pre-constituted, bounded objects like 'the body', 'graves', or indeed the soil, but rather the properties and flows of materials between them. Yet more, I sense, can be achieved by reaching for complementarity

---

[43] As, for example, when Chief Chikwanda was obliged to contribute to ancestral events in 2005, despite his own apostolic faith.

than by staging dramatic antitheses. One result of a determination to focus on materials and substances is that inevitably attention is reverted back to how materials *become* 'objects', physically but also conceptually, historically and politically. We could ask, how was the Mutirikwi dam constructed? What were the material as well as social, historical and political (not to mention conceptual) affordances, effectivities and processes that enabled such an object to become, with its own subsequent (material, social, political and conceptual) consequences? Or how are graves and ruins constituted as, and how do they become, active and affective objects from the merging substances of body, clay and soil? Beyond overcoming conventional Cartesian dualities, Ingold's emphasis on materials, much like Brown's 'Thing theory' (2001), points to the complex, and always incomplete processes of becoming, through which both objects and subjects are constantly being (re-)constituted, transformed and re-assembled; and in turn how things, materials and stuff are always both more and less than the objects and subjects that they constitute – substantive qualities that are in excess of, yet imbricated in their own becomings and unbecomings (Filippucci et al. 2012; Harries & Fontein 2010).

If Ingold's emphasis on materials therefore enriches our repertoire of tools with which to understand how materials/substances do things, then like Navaro-Yashin, I think we need to deploy our scrutinising gaze 'against the grain of "ruination" in being anti-, trans- or multi-paradigmatic' (2009:17) in favour of an emphasis on how the ruins of theoretical ruination are necessarily constitutive of the new. One way of doing this is to explore how theories too often opposed to each other, can be complementary when viewed in close proximity.

ONTOLOGY AND DIFFERENCE

There is another strand of work that makes an important contribution to questions of materiality. This is best represented by the introduction to Henare et al.'s *Thinking Through Things* (2006). Also determined to take 'conventional' dualisms to task, it focuses sharply on a distinction between 'ontology' and 'epistemology', between 'other worlds' and 'other worldviews'. The authors argue for a new ('more ethical') methodology, both radically essentialist and radically constructivist, through which artefacts and things, encountered ethnographically, without *a priori* assumptions distinguishing meanings from things or perceiving from conceiving, may offer the opportunity to create new analytical concepts. Drawing its inspiration from the so-called 'ontological turn' (vanguard by Viveiros de Castro 1998), this approach has provoked considerable debate (Carrithers et al. 2008), enthusiasm, unease and frustration within anthropology. One reason for the frustration maybe the endless circularity of academics accusing each other of reifying 'latent dualisms';[44] another the conceit of claiming to propound a more 'decent',

---

[44] Miller 07/03/07, (see www.materialworldblog.com/2006/12/thinking-through-things, accessed 02/08/13)

'ethical' position (framed as a 'return to (analytical) innocence' or 'radical humility'), advocating a 'science of the ontological self-determination of the world's peoples' (Viveiros de Castro 2003:18), yet one that is radically anti-humanist in its eschewal of empathy with informants, on the basis of not presuming to be able to say anything about them.[45]

While I sympathise with the main tenet proposed – that we can use things/artefacts encountered in fieldwork to challenge our own assumptions at profound levels – I do wonder how 'radically new' this approach really is. I remember my first ethnographic encounter with spirit possession in Zimbabwe. I made a conscious decision not to foreclose the possibility that the medium in front of me was genuinely possessed by an ancestral spirit speaking through his body. This suspension of disbelief was not merely to better understand another *worldview*, but to explore what a world inhabited by protective, dangerous and demanding spirits is actually like. I suspect the ethnographic stances taken by anthropologists have long been indeterminate in similar ways, agnostic rather than atheist if you like. On our visit to Murinye's grave in July 2006 we got lost in tangled thicket, so the acting Chief put down snuff as an ancestral offering to announce our presence and request permission to enter. We quickly found the correct path through the dense undergrowth to the *mapa*. The wonderment I shared with my companions was not because I had achieved some kind of privileged ethnographic access to another worldview, rather precisely because I felt I had entered another world. Later, after exploring the caves, graves, ruins and rocks of the *mapa*, baboons in nearby trees suddenly became extremely aggressive in their barking, informing us we had overstayed our welcome. We promptly left the *mapa*, and found our way out of the dense undergrowth of the hilltop.

The most significant aspect of the 'ontological turn' is the renewed and 'deepened' recognition of the possibility of 'radical difference' or 'alterity', even if this alterity is reified into rarefied philosophical realms, rather than located in the excessive potentiality of material substance, as other theorists of things would probably advocate (Brown 2001; Filippucci et al. 2012; Pinney 2005). This is why the question of ontology's relationship to the (older) culture concept – anthropology's 'traditional' way of dealing with difference – has been subject to such debate (Carrithers et al. 2008). An 'ontological perspective' insists we take seriously the possibility of alterity – of radically different worlds not reducible to different worldviews – and that such profound differences should be used to question our own deepest assumptions. It is, if you like, another fundamental unpeeling of the onion, painful as that may be on the eyes. Fortunately, as Carrithers et al. (2008) and others have stressed, anthropology does not have to become 'ontography', and an interest in ontology can be part of the broader anthropological project, without swamping it.[46]

[45] Holbraad 04/03/07, (see www.materialworldblog.com/2006/12/thinking-through-things, accessed 02/08/13).
[46] Miller, 14/12/06 & 04/03/07; Holbraad 04/03/07 (www.materialworldblog.com/2006/12/thinking-through-things, accessed 02/08/13).

A good example of how an ontological approach can be deployed in anthropology that remains focused on people is Scott's *The Severed Snake*. His model of 'onto-praxis' – 'the organization of praxis as the situational engagement of social actors with ontological categories' (2007:20) – does offer a way of taking ontology seriously without denigrating the social/political lives of our informants themselves. Importantly such onto-praxis may be fundamental to understanding how otherwise 'superficial', 'political phenomena' relate to, derive from and are entangled with 'deep ontological problematics', as Scott does in his analysis of the cosmic tensions of unity and diversity between 'multiple ontologically distinct matrilineages' at play in the politics of chiefs and warriors in pre- and postcolonial Arosi, in the Solomon Islands (2007:21–22).

This approach has the benefit of taking the politics of difference occurring within our ethnographic fields as seriously as the power involved in the relationship between anthropologists and informants – which is what an 'ontological method' as proposed in Henare et al. (2006) risks privileging in its 'decent' refusal of the possibility of saying anything about informants' lives. Of course radical ontological differences do raise important questions of politics and power almost immediately. Maintaining focus on the politics of difference/sameness as appearing in ethnographic settings means that questions of consciousness soon come to the fore. We can easily foresee the rhetorical trick an 'ontologist' might perform here by relegating consciousness to questions of epistemology – of different 'worldviews' rather than 'other worlds' – but in practice it may be very difficult to make such distinctions empirically and ethnographically. As Gluckman might have said, there is a 'structuralist orthodoxy' here that 'leaves the native unconscious' (Werbner 2008:3). It is indeed 'a contradiction to reserve consciousness and reflexiveness for the anthropologist exclusively and yet to call for a level playing field, with equal self-determination for all' (2008:3). Surely the politics of difference crosses such strata in complex ways, and an ethnographic perspective must inform us that deep ontological differences are not separate from 'shallow' epistemological or 'even shallower' social, historical and political ones. Indeed as Povinelli's work (2001) has shown, the politics of commensuration/incommensuration inevitably involve a social, historical and sometimes violent process.

This brings us back to the politics of belonging and exclusion around Mutirikwi – in which landscapes are active/affective in a myriad of ways – and towards the argument I want to finish with for the value of focusing less on 'radical difference' and more on material, historical and conceptual proximities. We can certainly imagine there are radical ontological differences at play in southern Zimbabwe. Upon close inspection we might, for example, discover fundamental ontological differences in the way that places 'do' things – between say chiefs, traditionalists and spirit mediums, and members of African churches, or government technocrats and land planners. We might also identify, like Scott, a kind of 'poly-ontology' of diverse origins, of 'small-scale mono-ontologies' (2007:15) in the contested assertions of autochthony articulated by competing clans. This might also confront a 'racialised' ontology where radical difference is posited between Africans and Europeans, as for example in some extreme manifestations of ZANU PF's political rhetoric. In all these cases it is not clear where ontology gives way to epistemology – all these differences are articulated politically and consciously. Indeed maybe ontologically there are no profound differences here at all. On the other hand, such politicised differences are sometimes used to imply radical ontological difference: as when people say whites are not affected by witchcraft, or do not have ancestors only ghosts; or that these new settlers cannot look after the soil (*kuchengeta vhu*) because they are *vatorwa* (strangers) not *varidzi venyika* (owners of the land); or in the very claim that war veterans are *vana vevhu* (sons of the soil); or in the claim often articulated around Mutirikwi that, 'the problems that exist are because the land is not with whom it belongs'.[47] All these statements are deeply political, but also maybe deeply ontological.

But, having pointed out how the politics of difference entangle across such strata, implying that the epistemological, ontological, social and political are finely intertwined, what is left to explore? Deploying a *Thinking Through Things* methodology to create new analytical concepts may not help us gain a better understanding of the complex politics of belonging and the active/affective role of graves and ruins around Mutirikwi. I suggest that what follows the identification of difference, and indeed of processes of differentiation, should be a consideration of the co-existences and proximities that can cross over and confront distances/differences. As Scott acknowledges, 'ontology-based investigation' necessarily 'confronts the fact that, in any given social context, more than one cosmological system – and therefore more than one deep ontology – may coexist in tension' (2007:35). As both his work on the Solomon Islands and the situation around Mutirikwi demonstrates, this co-existence in close proximity is historical, material and perhaps ultimately conceptual. Importantly, an analytic of proximity does not eschew difference or change in favour of similarity or continuity; rather it seeks to provide a framework for understanding both at the same time.

CO-EXISTENCE AND PROXIMITY

My research has led me to be interested in proximity in three ways. Ethnographically, I am struck by the multiple material, historical and conceptual proximities taking place around Mutirikwi and suspect they are inter-related. I do not think the significance of Murinye's burial in Boroma is only coincidentally related to Bright's burial of his parents' nearby, nor is the presence of Sheppard's ghost at a hotel sited on the graves of Murinye ancestors, whatever different purposes or worldviews they encapsulate or in whatever 'different worlds' they exist. Similarly, I am struck that the Boroma hills are sacred and demand particular rituals and responsibilities for both Bright and the late Mudarikwa and his

[47] Samuel Haruzvivishe 21/07/04.

son Matopos, just as war veterans and new farmers occupying farms too were often drawn into others' autochthonous rituals. Indeed, as many informants suggested, even white settler-farmers sometimes engaged in ritual events on their farms during (and after) the colonial period, by providing beer, grain or meat for rain-making ceremonies, and did so, I suspect, not simply to placate 'their' workers but because they, too, needed rain.[48] Just as President Mugabe famously appealed to mediums to bring rain in 1992, perhaps provincial government funds were once set aside for rain-making visits to the Matopos, as Peter Manyuki claimed.[49] Likewise, accounts of Rhodesian dam builders turning to local chiefs to placate troublesome *njuzu* (water spirits/creatures) during the construction of the Mutirikwi dam, too point to such material, historical, and conceptual proximities.[50]

---

[48] I frequently heard this around Mutirikwi. Simon Charumbira remembered white farmers who assisted with rain making events, or trips to 'ask for rain from *Mabwe*' (*Mwari* shrines in the Matopos). 'We used to have a white man here who knew that is what brings the rain, [and] would give *rukwesa* [finger millet], or even a cow to slaughter' (Fieldnotes 27/05/06). In part, no doubt, such assertions reflect ways of remembering, assessing, and ascribing the moral standing of different white farmers, at the same time as asserting autochthony and sovereignty. VaZarira, for example, claimed that Mr Coventry invited her to live on his farm, Bannockburn, on Beza in the 1980s because of troubles he was having with ancestral lions (*mhondoro*), and because he needed rain (Fieldnotes 17/02/01 & 16/8/01), although his wife suggested Mr Coventry was deeply sceptical of VaZarira's claims, particularly after their relationship soured (Fieldnotes 01/11/05). Such claims point to a profound ontological uncertainty, which also appeared when discussing *n'anga* (traditional healers) and witchcraft with former white farmers. Pat Potgeiter told me how, during the war, he 'had a *n'anga* ... put down *mushonga* [medicine/potion/magic] at my home to protect me', even though 'it isn't strictly speaking allowed by my church'. That 'old *n'anga*', he continued, 'boy, he was something. He was from Egypt, and he was brilliant. I used him to get medicine for my son who had an ear infection ... then he warned me about a snake harming my son. The next day I was with my son in the garage working on the car and he was saying to me "look daddy, look" ... When I eventually looked there was big puff adder at his feet. I told my son not to move and held his arm and sharply pulled him away. Then I shot that snake. That was the snake that *n'anga* had warned me about' (Potgeiter 15/01/06).

[49] Fieldnotes 17/03/06

[50] 'When they built the dam they consulted the elders. When they finished they killed a black bull and gave Chief Murinye the skin and our fathers the head' (Geri Zano, 23/03/06). Others were less generous, and many referred to the accidents builders faced at the dam site (VaChinengo 26/05/06; Chief Mugabe 19/11/05; Sekuru Bhodo Mukuvare 19/11/05). For Matopos Murinye these accidents were due to the Italian contractors sleeping with local women, 'giving them gonorrhoea' and 'not following the rules set by the rituals' his father had performed at the request of the native commissioner (Fieldnotes 13/06/06). Everyone agreed such problems forced officials to ask local elders to appease the ancestors and angered *njuzu*, but given resurgent boundary contests, many disagreed over which chief was responsible for ritually placating the angered *njuzu*, and allowing the dam to be built. Mazarire describes similar events in relation to the much delayed Tokwe-Mukorsi dam project (2008:757–8).

I also suspect the entanglement of different languages and practices of belonging all around Mutirikwi is intimately related to the historical and material co-existences and proximities of shared landscapes. Conceptual proximities can sometimes derive from historical and material co-existences, even if this does not necessarily reduce the profound differences that may exist between, say, technocratic land management and ritual responses to ancestral demands, or between what the ghost of a colonial settler might mean for his European descendent, and what a white ghost signifies in the much more sophisticated spiritual repertoire to which Shona people refer.

Sometimes material proximities are deliberate political moves: such as A.A. Louw's decision to site Morgenster mission near Great Zimbabwe, or Cecil Rhodes's burial at 'World's View' in the Matopos, which sought to supplant Mzilikazi's prominent burial at Entumbane, yet unknowingly took place only yards from a prominent pre-Ndebele shrine called Malinda-Dzimu Matosi-po.[51] But perhaps more often they are unintended but with equally profound results. A good example is Morphy's (1993) discussion of how colonial and indigenous landscapes came to be orientated around the same physical features in the Roper Bar Police Reserve of Australia's Northern territory, which was subject to a land claim in the 1980s by an aborigine group known as the Ngalakan. Here, 'by a great irony of the colonial process Aborigines and Europeans developed their strongest emotional attachments to precisely the same places though the attachments are constructed on a quite different basis' (1993:239). This 'irony' is perhaps the proximity that I am discussing here. The material and historical proximity of different understandings of landscape – of difference of worlds if you like – has real affects, it causes real changes, even as it may also allow, or be enabled by, certain continuing, fundamental differences.

Bernault (2006) illustrates how such proximity can reduce otherwise radical alterity in very profound ways. Concluding her discussion of how both Europeans and Africans 'participated in the re-enchanting of the human body' (2006: 207) in colonial Equatorial Africa, through controversies surrounding the traffic and use of body parts, Bernault argues:

> the formulaic similarity of white and black visions of the body and power suggests that the reconfigurations sparked by the colonial encounter can also be explained by the premise of historical proximity. To suggest that colonizers and Africans shared mutually intelligible ideas and symbolic systems ... pushes intricate issues first uncovered by the premise of difference further ... the latent compatibility between European and African symbolic systems did not stem from mere existence of inert repertoires across the racial divide ... Colonial confrontations encouraged African and Europeans to transform their representations of the corporeal sacred, and to engage in an extensive refetishization of the human body (2006:236).

Such historical proximities can undermine ostensive differences because they involve not co-existences of 'inert repertoires' but active

---

[51] See Ranger 2012:3; also1999. Mission stations in the Matopos too were deliberately sited close to cult shrines (Ranger 1999; Nyathi 2003),

encounters. Just as graves and ruins around Mutirikwi are not inert material expressions of politically deployed languages of belonging and authority, but rather are active and affective in complex ways, so we should envisage historical, material and conceptual proximities as involving active, changing engagements between peoples, things, epistemologies and even ontologies. Such engagements do not 'make colonial differences disappear under the thick veil of resemblance'; they merely locate 'cultural and ideological conflicts on a different plane', amplifying how the politics of difference usually 'crystallized less from existing symbolic or material discrepancies than from conscious or unconscious strategies of organising ... difference' (2006:238).

This is my second reason for being interested in proximities. Zimbabwe's post-2000 politics of land and state-making have manifested around Mutirikwi in a myriad of contested claims to belonging/non-belonging which have often been articulated around politically motivated assertions of difference. These localised (and localist) assertions replicate, however imperfectly, reconfigurations of political inclusion and exclusion at a national level, simultaneously resonating within a 'global conjuncture of belonging' (Li 2000 cited in Geschiere & Jackson 2006:3). In this broader and historical (Mamdani 1996) context, the renewed emphasis on radical difference implied in anthropology's 'ontological turn', needs to be handled very carefully indeed. As Ferguson warned of studies of 'postcolonial mimicry', the 'ontological turn' too risks becoming a means by which 'anthropological otherness is salvaged' (2002:554) and older premises of cultural distance and heterogeneity restored.[52] We may do better not by emphasising radical difference but rather by cultivating an acute sensitivity to the proximities, co-existences and continuities that derive from peoples' shared material and historical engagements, as a way of writing against politicised differences rather than re-asserting them on ever more abstract philosophical grounds.

There are clear and important resonances here with older debates about social field theory, particularly Gluckman's 'The bridge' (1958), even if my concern with active/affective landscapes, and ontology, reflects more recent turns. So the third reason for my interest in proximity relates to anthropological knowledge production. If ruination correctly involves a re-incorporation of old elements in the new, then we should recognise that staging radical antithesis or distance between new and old theoretical fads is unconstructive. In this way, an anthropology of proximity involves not just renewed conceptual reflexivity (or indeed creation) of the ilk ontologists might enthuse about, but also a better historical sensibility. Perhaps anthropology can learn something from the 'tidy consensus' that has emerged in Africanist debates about ethnicity, which in recognising that ethnicities are 'neither rooted in a timeless past nor simple colonial fabrications', has highlighted the need 'to map the *historical* trajectories of contemporary identities' (Nugent 2008: 948). In a similar way anthropology needs to re-consider not only the histori-

---

[52] A similar argument has been debated about the notion of 'indigenous' peoples (Kuper 2003; Barnard 2006).

cal trajectories of its own knowledge production, but also the historical, material and conceptual co-existences and proximities that our discipline's long history of allegiance to difference tends to eschew. Across Zimbabwe's changing landscapes, such an anthropology of proximity might reveal the significant co-existence of far more than just white colonial ghosts and pre-colonial African ancestors.

3

Rain, Power and Sovereignty

CENSORING THE WEATHER FORECAST

In November 2010 a senior government meteorologist revealed that for much of the previous decade Zimbabwe's weather forecast had been censored on a daily basis by the President's Office. The admission came in response to journalists' questions about 'why the meteorological service department (MET) had over the years denied possible droughts' that were later experienced despite predictions that 'the country was expecting above average rainfall every year'. Also blaming 'obsolete weather equipment' and the loss of experienced personnel for the 'inaccurate weather forecasting', Washington Zhakata 'admitted that there is heavy political interference and censorship of the weather forecasts in Zimbabwe before it is issued out to the public'. 'This information', he said, 'was seen as sensitive'.[1]

What this sensitivity amounts to is the subject of this chapter. A clue can be found in a much earlier news item in the international press, which had reported (amid official denials) that 'the president's office took control of the forecasting service' in 2003 'after learning that the drought-affected country is facing two more years of low rainfall'. Then a series of droughts had coincided with the first three years of fast-track land reform, deepening economic and political crises, and widening discontent about food shortages.

> 'The government does not want any information on the weather to be leaked' an official from the Meteorological Office said. 'All our forecasts are to be sent to the president's office, and only then can they be released' ... Informed sources said Mr Mugabe feared that the revelation that no early end to the drought was in sight would heighten discontent at a time when nearly half the country's 13 million people are going hungry. Food riots have already erupted in the capital, Harare, and the south-western city of Bulawayo this month. The development came as the World Food Programme said the harvest of the staple maize would be poor for the next two years ... The impact of the regional drought has been compounded by Mr Mugabe's crude land redistribution program, which has crippled the country's agricultural sector and left swathes of fertile land unplanted.[2]

[1] 'Political interference in Zim weather forecast' www.radiovop.com, 17/11/10, accessed 05/10/14.

[2] 'Mugabe seizes weather service', *Sunday Telegraph*, 27/01/03.

Although the political consequences of food shortages and rising prices are undoubtedly of great significance in Zimbabwe's recent history, they do not alone adequately explain this long-term commitment to daily interference in the weather forecast.[3] It is hard to make sense of ZANU PF's impulse to censor the weather forecast in the 2000s without reference to the localised reconfigurations of authority over land and the remaking of the state provoked by the fast-track programme. If for many, fast-track offered the realisation of long delayed, localised aspirations and imagined futures that turned on access to land and fertile soils in divergent ways, the recurrent droughts of the early 2000s were politically significant because they called into question the legitimacy of land reform, and the Third *Chimurenga* (liberation struggle) constituted around it.

It is true that government often, perhaps erroneously (Richardson 2007), blamed recurring drought for the dramatic fall in agricultural production during this period when its commercial farming sector was so profoundly reconfigured.[4] But the political significance of rain and drought in Zimbabwe is not simply a question of agricultural productivity (cf. Lan 1985; Ranger 2003; Vijfhuizen 1997; Mafu 1995; Mawere & Wilson 1995; Garbett 1977). Across the region, rainfall and drought have long been measures of contested political legitimacy in far more complex ways (Sanders 2008; Jedrej 1992; James 1972; Southall 1953; Packard 1981; Akong'a 1987; Krige & Krige 1943). From the politics of floods and elections in Mozambique (Bertelsen 2004), to the collaborations of rainmakers and guerrillas in the Dande in the 1970s (Lan 1985), or the drought-invoking cosmic 'unordering' and pollution of the land caused by violence in Matabeleland (Werbner 1995:201; 1991:188; 1998:98),[5] rain and drought are political in ways that intertwine with, but are not limited to the politics of food, famine and agricultural production. Around Mutirikwi, this is true not just for mediums, chiefs and other traditionalist authorities for whom rain-making practices are well established means of demonstrating autochthony, sovereignty and legitimacy, but also for war veterans, new farmers, government technocrats and others involved in land reform in the 2000s.

This is what I examine here. Whilst I focus particularly on the significance of rain making, encounters with *njuzu* water spirits/creatures, and national *biras* (ancestral possession ceremonies) in 2005/06, the larger point being pursued is that water often acts as an *index of power* – of the entangled, contested play of legitimacy and sovereignty – across

---

[3] Protests about food shortages and rising prices had been a feature of Zimbabwe's political landscape since 1997 ('Zimbabwe police fight food price protesters', *Reuters*, 17/10/00; 'Zimbabwe food riots spread' *BBC News*, 06/01/03). The situation dramatically worsened in the 2000s, but it also created new spheres for ZANU PF patronage, particularly through the politicisation of food distribution (Human Rights Watch 2003).

[4] 'Don't blame it on the weather: CFU', *Zimbabwean*, 01/08/12.

[5] Also 'No rain in Zimbabwe's Matabeleland south', *Radio Netherlands Worldwide*, 27/06/11.

many different registers of meaning and regimes of rule in which it is saturated. Towards the end of the chapter I turn to Keane (2003; 2005) and Engelke's (2007) elaboration of Peirce's theory of signs (1955), and build upon others (James 1972; Jedrej 1992) who have long argued that rain-making 'traditions' across eastern, central and southern Africa are less a form of applied meteorology and more an idiom of politics and power, in order to argue that they are necessarily *both* at the same time. After all, the unfolding (if short-lived) optimism I encountered around Mutirikwi in 2005/06 was directly related to the successful rains of that season, because they *made real* the possibility that a diversity of long-delayed, aspired futures might now be substantiated, just as the recurring droughts of previous years had begun to make land reform look tentative, uncertain and doubtful.

RAIN MAKING IN ZIMBABWE

In Zimbabwe the ancestral or divine provision (or denial) of rain, and rituals associated with it, have long been fundamental to so-called traditionalist forms of authority over people and land. This derives from the sovereignty of ancestral owners of the land from whom they descend or by whom they are possessed, and in turn from the high divinity *Mwari* (or *Mwali*, 'God'), widely accredited as the ultimate provider of rain. There are marked regional and historical differences in the relative role of different ancestral and divine cults in the provision of the rain, and these relate both to long and complex pre-colonial and colonial histories, and their contemporary invocation and re-imagination in ongoing contestations of belonging and rule.

For example, Lan (1985:72–117) explored the historical relationships between autochthonous Tavara and Tande clans and invading but now ruling Korekore lineages in northern Zimbabwe, where the *mhondoro* (royal ancestors/lion spirits) of the former retained a special place in the hierarchical sequence of offerings by which requests for rain are passed up to the distant divinity *Mwari* (cf. Garbett 1992). These ancestral relations were mirrored and contested in the unfurling relations between clans, mediums, chiefs and guerrilla fighters during the liberation struggle. Working in the same area over a decade later, Spierenburg (2004) explored similar dynamics in relation to later incoming peoples or *vatorwa* (strangers) resettled by the postcolonial government in the 1980s. In Masvingo, the role of *Mwari* in the provision of rain has historically been much more immediate, and there are no *mhondoro* cults of the ilk apparent in northern Zimbabwe. Instead a system of *manyusa* and *munyai* (shrine messengers) once travelled annually between the *mukwerere* or *mitoro* (rain-making) rituals held in individual chiefdoms, and the *Mwari* shrines at Matonjeni, Dula, Zhame and Njelele in the Matopos, southern Matabeleland, where the voice of *Musikavanhu* (creator of people) made the divine a much less distant entity. Although few *manyusa* still make these journeys, their past significance and the continuing importance of the *Mwari* shrines is evident in the ongoing efforts of some mediums and chiefs, as well as war veterans,[6] to visit the Matopos.

It is important to avoid any assumption that pre-colonial rain making was any less contested than the politics of rain and drought are today. The Matopos shrines themselves have long been embroiled in complex localised contests between competing clans, shrines and shrine keepers (Ranger 1999; Werbner 1989; Nyathi 2003). Furthermore, their crucial position at the pinnacle of regional rain offerings was not always consistent across Masvingo. Mazarire (2010) discusses the historical tensions between the various groups (Hera, Venda, VaRemba and Duma) who jostled for political and religious authority over land and water resources after the demise of the Rozvi Nechishanga polity in the 18th century. Similarly, the 19th Duma confederacy (Mtetwa 1976) was much more oriented eastward, towards the Pfupajena cult at Mandara hill, than the westward focus towards the Matopos many remember today. The influence of the *Mwari* cult among Masvingo's Duma clans was only firmly cemented in the early 20th century after the death of Chief Mazungunye, a renowned rainmaker, had coincided with a severe drought in 1912. The 1912 drought and abundant rains that followed culminated in an assemblage of meteorological and political events contributing to the Mandara cult's demise, amidst the growing incursions of the *Mwari* emissaries, Ndebele and Nguni raids, and the deepening interference of Rhodesian settlers, the BSACo and Christian missionaries from the end of the 19th century (Sayce 1978:58).

Around Mutirikwi in the mid-2000s, such entangled political, religious and ecological histories lay in the background of many resurgent disputes over territory, autochthony and authority among mediums, chiefs and clans. Just as the 'flood' of *Mwari* cult emissaries into Masvingo in the early 20th century (Sayce 1978:58) had alarmed Rhodesian settlers, and therefore fed into colonial state-making – alert as they were to the role of mediums and the *Mwari* cult in the 1896 rebellions (Ranger 1967)[7]

---

[6] There has been a proliferation of controversial war veteran visits to Matopos in recent years, especially Njelele ('War vets Njelele trip slammed', *Newsday*, 29/04/11; 'Blood soaked war Vets' Njelele sacrilege', *Newsday*, 02/05/11; 'War veterans fight over Njelele shrine', *Standard*, 20/05/12).

[7] Officials were highly sensitive to the threat posed by mediums and *Mwari* cult messengers after the 1896 rebellions. In October 1899 the Chief Native Commissioner (CNC) told the Native Commissioner (NC) for Gutu, that 'your chiefs should be warned against listening to any foolish advice or prophecies by their witchdoctors or "mswikiros"' (Circular, CNC to NC Gutu, 02/10/1899, NAZ NVG 1/2/1). A year later, the assistant NC Gutu was requested to investigate reports 'quietly and without alarming the Natives' suspicions', that 'M'wri of Matabeleland has instructed Gutu's people not to sow any Rapoko [finger millet] this year, but only to sow Munga or Nyauti [sorghum], and has told them something is going to happen'. In 1904 the NC Charter district requested that the NC Gutu 'collect evidence ... to support a charge of endeavoring to incite natives to rebellion', against Manyanga, a 'Mlimo [or *mwari*] messenger' spreading a 'Mlimo message' amongst the chiefs of Gutu and Chilimanzi 'to the effect that that the whites would be driven out of the country by a gale' (NC Charter to NC Gutu, 07/03/1904, NAZ NVG1/2/1). As late as March 1936 a messenger called

– so drought and the politics of rain making continued to be woven into postcolonial state-making. The terrible 1992 drought, in particular, brought the question of the ancestral legitimacy of the state into sharp relief, so that even President Mugabe was forced to ask 'the spirit mediums to bring rain'; a request that many refused (Derman 2003:71). The 1992 drought equally brought tensions between 'African spirituality' and Zionist and Pentecostal churches to the foreground (Ranger 2011b), resulting in the (re-)emergence of various traditionalist movements, particularly the short-lived but high-impact Juliana cult (Mawere and Wilson 1995; Mafu 1995; Ranger 2003). Indeed both Juliana's dramatic rise and her equally rapid demise – after she failed to make it rain (Ranger 2011b:6) – illustrate how political, religious and meteorological fortunes are often intertwined.

If the fortunes of those who claim to bring or 'hold up' the rain are intimately connected with the vagaries of weather, there can clearly be much wider reverberations. Through the *longue durée* of the highly contingent and localised politics of rain making, we can begin to make sense of ZANU PF's concern to censor the weather forecast throughout the 2000s. The recurrent droughts of the early 2000s not only undermined agricultural productivity already destabilised by land reform, but raised questions about its ancestral or divine legitimacy. Mediums often suggested the failing rains were indicative of the ancestors' marginalisation from the fast-track programme. In January 2001 Ambuya VaZarira told war veterans and new farmers that 'the lack of adequate rain they had been receiving was because the government was not adequately consulting with spirit mediums'.[8] Failing rains and poor harvests were amongst the reasons why many around Mutirikwi turned to mediums and autochthonous chiefs, as they sought to 'make safe' their own resettlements. Similarly, countrywide national *bira* ceremonies initiated by government for the first time in 2005, but organised locally by individual chiefs, point exactly to the entanglement of local and national regimes of rule within localised performances of sovereignty and legitimacy linked to rain making. Later the good rains of 2005/06 were often attributed accordingly. Yet if these government-sponsored events illustrate how the entangled sovereignty and legitimacy of chiefs and government could be mutually beneficial, they also rode roughshod over complex local histories of struggles between clans, chiefs, mediums and different rain making cults. It is no surprise that some around Mutirikwi met the na-

(contd)   Koko, possessed by the rain making spirit Mbedeze, from Matonjeni, was stopped in the Mtilikwe reserve and taken to police at Fort Victoria, where he signed a statement explaining he was collecting 'contributions from all chiefs, headmen and kraal heads ... so that rain sent by the Spirit would fall'. He would take them to Matonjeni and then return with 'a certain kind of seed grain' for contributors to mix with their own seed to 'strengthen their crops so they could resist drought'. By then official anxieties had eased, and the NC was more concerned about 'fraud' than rebellion, adding that Koko 'appears to be a victim of Machokoto' the 'principle offender' (Statement by Koko, 12/03/36, NC to BSAP, Victoria, 12/03/36, 'NC Victoria: correspondence, 1935–36 NAZ S1043).
[8] Fieldnotes 26–27/01/01.

tional *biras* of 2005 with suspicion, particularly those mediums who felt marginalised by the government's ever-closer association with chiefs.

If the 'reach of the postcolonial state' is 'conditioned' by 'locally proved realities of alliances within, between and beyond communities at the periphery' (Werbner 1999:70), then the control of water, I argue, invokes the very ambiguity of power – both as assertions of sovereignty, and in governmental dimensions of legitimacy and rule. This political tension is inherent to the material, cultural and ecological qualities and flows of water intertwining the local and national, crossing over different repertoires and techniques of water management (from rain making to dams, irrigation and contour ridging). The saturation of water across diverse regimes of rule and registers of meaning emphasises the specifically hydrological dimensions of the 'consequential materiality of milieu' (Moore 2005:24). If the politics of water has long been as central to Zimbabwean state-making as that of land (Alexander 2006), then my primary purpose here is to examine how water featured in localised struggles over sovereignty and legitimacy around Mutirikwi in 2005/06 in ways that replicated and were finely intertwined with water's centrality to Zimbabwean statecraft.

THE POLITICAL PROPERTIES OF WATER

As Wittfogel (1957) demonstrated, the control of water – whether for irrigation, sanitation or safe drinking water, or in managing run-off, erosion and siltation – is often central to the spatialities of power involved in statecraft (cf. Mosse 2003; Fontein 2008). The politics of water are rarely entirely separate from those of land. Water and land may be different kinds of resources, their different qualities shaping different kinds of politics, yet their histories and history-making are inevitably intertwined (Mosse 2008:939). My purpose is to focus attention upon how water in its various manifestations (rain, run off, rivers, pools, dams), and with its diverse material qualities (as a volume or a line, its fluidity, pooling, erosiveness, cruciality for life), features in complex reconfigurations of power around Mutirikwi. I build on the basic premise that any regime of rule – whether of 'the state' at large, local officials or the localised authority of chiefs, mediums, and war veterans – 'persists through both repressive and productive mechanisms of power' (Navaro-Yashin 2002:154), involving 'the articulation ... of pastoral care with sovereign power' (Hammar 2003:130–1). Across diverse 'regimes of rule' and 'registers of meaning', water is often central to both demonstrative, performative and sometimes coercive assertions of sovereignty, autonomy and capacity on the one hand, and to those productive, disciplining, governmental dimensions of power that circulate around appeals to legitimacy, moral authority and consent on the other hand.[9]

[9] In other words, the politics of water embodies both Gramscian notions of hegemony, at the intersection of coercion and consent, and Foucauldian notions of discipline, techniques of the self and governmentality (cf. Moore 2005:9).

These forms of power exist in tension, are unstable and often mutually productive. They are not exclusive to each other, nor historically sequential as Foucault himself implied (Navaro-Yashin 2002:154). It is important to avoid privileging particular 'texts, taxonomies, and forms of knowledge produced by the state', or identifying *singular* rationalities of power, at the expense of the multiple co-existing, contingent assemblages of 'situated practices', discourses, and materialities of rule (Moore 2005:7). Hence 'sovereign', 'productive' and 'responsive' forms of power materialise through different processes and technologies of ecological and hydrological control co-existent in close proximity around Mutirikwi. These include the rain-making rituals, ancestral ceremonies, and the ritual protection of sacred groves, pools and springs, which are the main focus of this chapter. They equally include both colonial and postcolonial developmental, technocratic rationalisations of space and water, such as contour ridging, dam building and irrigation, and the regulation of fishing, wildlife, and recreational landscapes that reappear in later chapters.

An important example is the continuing official insistence that land surrounding the lake must be properly protected to prevent soil erosion and siltation. This involves performances of sovereignty (such as the coercive construction of contour ridges in the 1940–50s) alongside more productive mechanisms of power forging particular political subjectivities and regimented, disciplining landscapes, amid appeals to conservation, developmentalism and governmental legitimacy. Such regimes of rule are not separate from the historically contingent, contested structures animating the politics of rain and the ritual protection of sacred places, but rather intertwine with them. After all chiefs, headmen and village heads have long been charged with ensuring compliancy with soil protection strategies, even as they must lead the government-sponsored national *biras* introduced in 2005. Regimes of rule entangle across levels, and chiefs can be simultaneously involved in rain making and technocratic soil conservation with no apparent contradiction.

But beyond simply examining how the control/provision of water is imbricated in emergent struggles for legitimacy, sovereignty and rule around Mutirikwi, my larger purpose is to explore the 'complex reciprocity' (Beinart 2000:287) of water's diverse material qualities and the different meanings and politics to which these give shape. Exploring the political salience of water's diverse materialities offers an opportunity to consider the relationship between a 'semiotics of water' and the political materiality of signs. If water/rain partly determines what kinds of politics gain traction around Mutirikwi – just as graves and ruins are active and affective in complex ways in the politics of autochthony and belonging – then what things, places and substances like water and rain, graves and ruins *do*, relates intimately to what/how they *mean* in any context. This involves examining how meaning and matter are not distinct but mutually implicated. As an *index of power*, what water signifies in any context depends in part upon its form and material qualities, as well as the unstable registers of meaning (or 'semiotic ideologies',

Keane 2003) that are at play. After all, it is good rains, at the right time, in sufficient quantities, and not destructive of crops or houses, that can signify the legitimacy of chiefs, clans, mediums, and the moral wellbeing of community, government, or even the state at large. Bad rains, or no rain at all, question such claims to legitimacy, even as they demonstrate perhaps most forcefully the ultimate sovereignty of the ancestors and of *Mwari,* as owners of the land and the provider of rain respectively. In this regard, the localised, topographical nature of rainfall in Zimbabwe is very significant. Good rains can fall in one area whilst nearby crops wilt under a heavy sun. At the same time, however, the effects of drought, rainfall and run-off flow beyond localities, encompassing larger catchment areas, geographical zones and political terrains. The same is true of technological provisions of water, from irrigation to urban water supplies. So droughts at Lake Mutirikwi have profound effects downstream, particularly for the enormous Chiredzi sugar estates that financed the dam in the late 1950s.

The diverse regimes of rule and registers of meaning to do with water therefore relate directly to its multiple, changing and fluid material properties and forms, reflecting an uncertainty which easily defies singular rationalities of meaning and rule. The focus of this chapter is necessarily narrowed, for sake of clarity, to the contested languages and practices of water – involving *njuzu* water spirits/creatures, national *biras* and rain making – invoked around Mutirikwi in the re-emergent traditionalist politics of the 2000s. But water's ability to cross, defy or even collapse different registers of meaning is important, because this fluidity of matter and meaning is what makes it difficult to grasp conceptually but also politically. If water is to be understood as *an index of power* – of the contested interplay of legitimacy and sovereignty – across the different regimes of rule it saturates, then often it is not clear whose, or what kind of, legitimacy and/or sovereignty it actually indexes. It is this, I suggest, which animates the profound ambivalence towards it witnessed by ZANU PF's apparent determination to censure the weather forecast through the 2000s. The same ambivalence animates the way mediums and rain makers have long been treated, even as chiefs and headmen have been drawn ever closer into government structures.

MVURA YAKATSAMWA, IVHU RAKATSAMWA NOKUTI MADZISHE HAASI KUWIRIRANA
(The water is angry, the soil is angry because the chiefs are quarrelling)[10]

In October 2005 I visited Ambuya VaZarira. Arriving at her Mazare homestead, north of the lake, I found *seven days* millet beer[11] had been

---

[10] Peter Manyuki, Fieldnotes 29/10/05.

[11] An opaque local beer, made from fermented finger millet, and used for 'traditional' ancestral rituals and *bira* ceremonies. The process of making it is said to take seven days (although that is not always exactly true) hence it is often referred to as 'seven days'.

brewed for a *bira* event. Shoes at the door and animated voices suggested a small but vocal group of people had gathered for the event. Peter Manyuki, VaZarira's son, stood up to greet me, and urged me to sit next to Ambuya, as I was handed a plate of *sadza* (maize-meal porridge) and goat meat. I looked around the dark room at familiar and unknown faces, listening to the intense discussions going on.

Most people present lived locally, on farming plots at Mazare resettlement scheme or on recently resettled farms nearby. Many were members of the Chikwanda clan, and there were war veterans and local ZANU PF committee members present. The severe drought and failed harvest of the previous season (2004/05) meant the discussions revolved around, among other things, the (non-)functioning of the local party welfare committee, promised but undelivered food aid, the ineptitude of a local councillor, and the imposition of a new field tax (*mutero weminda*). Many referred to Masvingo's infamous factionalism, in which competing local chiefs and clans are involved in opaque ways. Although multifaceted, the heated discussions culminated in a consensus that all these grievances originated in the failures of the incumbent Chief Chikwanda (who was not present), whose authority and legitimacy was directly challenged.

> One person says 'the Charumbira people are getting food whilst we are starving here'... 'No matter how much money we get together we can't see even a single truck of food here because we are not recognised, unless there is a chief to stand up for us' [...]
> People suggest the chief is just a political appointment because he is close to the party. Some accuse him of taking food meant for old people, orphans and the handicapped ... and selling it on to make money.
> Everyone seems to agree that they want to choose their own chief from the proper house now in line for the chieftainship. ... There is a great deal of animated discussion about this. One person suggests that when the Chikwanda people choose their chief they should choose someone because he is Chikwanda and not because he is an important figure in the party ... 'A chief chosen because he is prominent in the party may use that position against us. We need a chief who will put Chikwanda people first'.[12]

For some, Chief Chikwanda's illegitimacy was based on his ineffectual or corrupt leadership, and his inability to ensure food assistance during a debilitating drought. Others challenged his legitimacy according to widely muted, but always contestable, forms of collateral succession, arguing that other houses – suggesting particular people present – were now in line for the position. Therefore the dispute, while circulating around broader grievances, pitted the agendas of particular claimants against Chief Chikwanda. VaZarira's own agenda was scarcely veiled, her complaint focusing on the incumbent's membership of an apostolic church that frowns upon ancestor veneration, for her an affront to her spirits and her authority as the senior Duma medium. As discussions heated up, Peter Manyuki announced there was another issue to be considered.

---

[12] Fieldnotes 29/10/05.

> Peter says that the people gathered should be discussing the issue of people and cows drowning in pools of water nearby. He mentions the case of a young boy, in grade two at school, who disappeared last week and was not found for three days. He was eventually found by Ambuya [VaZarira] in a pool in the partly dried up riverbed of the Mutirikwi river near Mazare township. Police and others had been looking in the pool but could not find him. Ambuya went there, put down *bute* [snuff] and then the boy was found seated under water, dead. More recently two cows went missing and were found under water in the same pool ... For two cases like that to happen at the same pool at the same time is very unusual and must mean that there is something going on. Peter mentions another case of a person rescued from a nearby dam. Peter mentions *njuzu* in the water, and explains that the water and the soil are angry: *mvura yakatsamwa, ivhu rakatsamwa nokuti madzishe haasi kuwirirana* [the water is angry, the soil is angry because the chiefs are quarrelling].
>
> These things are happening because the current chief is not the proper chief at all. He is a member of an apostolic church and does not follow the rules of the soil, nor does he listen to what the spirit mediums say. For VaZarira to go and tell him what she has been told by the ancestors, whose land this is, is impossible because he won't listen to her and does not respect her.[13]

This, Peter told those gathered, is what they should be discussing. VaZarira then prompted a huge response by suggesting they choose another person for the Chikwanda chieftainship, and bring him to her. 'If you come with someone today' she said 'I will take him to the DA tomorrow!' This provoked a huge cheer, and some individuals stood up to perform impromptu dance moves in celebration. Soon drums were being beaten and everyone began to dance. The discussions were over for that day.

This was my first introduction to an ongoing dispute within the Chikwanda clan about the legitimacy of the current chief. It is but the latest in the clan's particularly turbulent history, dating back to the ra- cialised dispossession of their land in the early 20th century, their forced dispersal and the removal of the chieftainship in the 1947, followed by the reinstatement of the chieftainship after independence and later, much more gradually, some of its territory. Many farms resettled under fast-track north of Mutirikwi have 'reverted' to Chief Chikwanda, who has appointed *sabhuku* (village heads) and *sadunhu* (headmen) across the area. In the context of government policy to (re)install traditional leaders on all resettled land (Mubvumba 2005), the re-establishment of Chikwanda's place in a local order of chiefs, clans and territory was as- sured even as it provoked a new intensity of disputes within the clan and with neighbouring chiefs.

But what struck me most was how this very specific dispute over a chief's legitimacy was inexorably linked to broader political, social and, importantly, ecological events. Severe drought, the non-arrival of promised food aid, and the drowning of a boy by *njuzu* in an almost dried up riverbed, were linked and understood as the material manifesta- tions of Chief Chikwanda's illegitimacy. The politics of food distribution apparent here are important, linking drought to questions of political legitimacy and illustrating how the contested authority of chiefs is nec-

[13] Ibid.

Photo 5   Chief Chikwanda
(Source: author, 2006)

essarily intertwined with regional and national politics.[14] But what I wish to focus on particularly is how all these different dimensions of Chief Chikwanda's alleged illegitimacy were linked to the troubling presence of *njuzu*, and how this indicated the anger of the water and the soil. Manyuki and VaZarira's invocation of a connection between *njuzu*, drought and Chief Chikwanda's illegitimacy is consistent with the broader literature on religion, ecology, rain making and politics across southern and eastern Africa. *Njuzu* feature prominently, alongside sacred pools (*dziva*) and snakes – particularly the python (*shato*) – across Zimbabwe's wide diversity of ecological, rain making, fertility and healing cults (cf. Reynolds 1996:158–60; Gelfand 1959; Shoko 2007; Aschwanden 1989; Schoffeleers 1979; Rennie 1979; Bourdillon 1987; Mawere & Wilson 1995; Ranger 2003; Daneel 1998). Their continuing social and political significance is amply evidenced by the frequency with which *njuzu* are blamed for (amongst other things) the abduction of children, interfering with dams and boreholes, and for denying rain. This proliferation of *njuzu* across Zimbabwe's rivers, pools and dams, and across its divergent often highly localised cults, makes them rather hard to interpret. Establishing exactly how *njuzu* feature in this complex cultural nexus – as powerful water creatures, perhaps half human/half animal or perhaps spirits, associated with healing and water, believed to live below ground and jealously guard specific pools, rivers and springs in the landscape – and what their link is to the ancestors who own the land

[14] If ZANU PF has often been implicated in politicising food distribution, frequently it is chiefs who have been directly accused of restricting aid to party supporters only. ('Cases of politicised food aid growing, says MDC', 17/01/03, *Daily News*; 'Villagers walk out on Chief Charumbira', *Daily News*, 04/06/13).

and *Mwari* who provides the rain, is not straight forward. Many around Mutirikwi were unable to articulate a clear account of the cosmological order of spirits, ancestors and the divinity *Mwari*, and their different, inter-related relationships to land and water, sacred places and rain. This reflects both complex histories of migration, shifting authority, and the waxing/waning influence of divergent ancestral/divine cults across southern Zimbabwe, and the uncertain political properties of water I have been describing.

AMBIVALENT *NJUZU*

Often (perhaps erroneously) translated as 'mermaids', descriptions of *njuzu* I encountered were decidedly varied, divergent and uncertain, even as most agreed that they constitute (or once constituted) a power-ful presence in the landscape. Some suggested that while the ancestors are associated with the land that they own through the soil, caves and mountains in which they are buried, it is through the water of the sacred pools, rivers and springs which they inhabit and guard that *njuzu* are associated with *Mwari* who provides the rain, and with the *manyusa* messengers who once linked specific ancestral territories to the Matopos shrines. So, in June 2006, VaZarira explained: 'We need to have a *bira* for those *njuzu* because they have made sure that there were plenty of rains this year. We need to thank them, because there is no hunger this year ... Yes *muzukuru* [grandchild – referring to the author] *njuzu* bring the rain. They go straight to *Mwari, Musikavanhu, Nyadenga* to ask for rain. That is why we need to cook a very big *bira* for them'.[15]

Aschwanden too suggests that many Karanga-speaking[16] people consider *njuzu* to be 'messengers from the Matopos' (1989:188), even if others deny this connection. *Njuzu* 'announce an imminent rainfall' and 'if, in the hot season, one hears distant thunder without seeing lighten-ing, this is *njuzu*'s voice'. Similarly 'if a whirlwind sweeps the country and one hears the noises of *njuzu* in the pool at the same time, the old Karanga say: "Mwari [God] has passed by"'(Aschwanden 1989:189). Yet most people I spoke to stated clearly that it was for the ancestors that beer should be 'cooked' to request rain.[17] Older people remembered *man-yusa* who used to travel to the Matopos carrying *rapoko* (finger millet) and other rain offerings, but very few suggested *bira* events should held for *njuzu* specifically.[18] Even VaZarira's close associate, acting

---

[15] VaZarira 10/06/06.
[16] Karanga is dialect of Shona, spoken across Masvingo province.
[17] Aschwanden also noted that requests for rain were rarely made directly to *njuzu*, although 'in reply ... one occasionally hears a noise coming from the caves, which is made by the *njuzu*' (1989:189). Only 'during persistent aridity' did people in the past 'make a "human sacrifice" to the *njuzu*' – by leaving a child by a pool to become an *njuzu*– 'to ask the ancestors and god for the life-saving rain' (1989:189–90).
[18] Simon Charumbira 27/05/06; Bhodo Mukuvare 19/11/05a.

Chief Murinye felt that: 'people go to the *mudzimu wemvura* [ancestor of water] to ask for rain, not the *njuzu* ... people have their *mutoro* [rain-making event] and they ask their *mudzimu* to ask for rain from *Mwari* and then they go to Matonjeni to ask for rain. People don't go to *njuzu* to ask for rain. The *njuzu* is for those places where water comes from, that is where the *njuzu* lives, in wells, springs and rivers'.[19] Yet Murinye agreed that '*njuzu* and *mudzimu* do work like a hand in a glove: the *njuzu* looking after springs and rivers and *mudzimu* after the land and the rain'.[20] This was echoed by others, including VaMakasva, who cited an old proverb '*mudzimu wakupa chironda wati nunzi dzinodya*' (lit. 'an ancestor gives you a wound so that the flies can eat') to illustrate the co-operation of *mudzimu* and *njuzu*.

The association of potentially dangerous *njuzu* (and their taboos) with particular sacred water sources links them to the ancestors through the autochthonous knowledge of the landscape held and enforced by local chiefs, mediums and clans, which incoming war veterans and new farmers sought to 'make safe' their farm occupations. The dangers of watery places associated with *njuzu* faced on the farms were frequently discussed around Mutirikwi. Like the crocodiles encountered by Kariba's fishermen etching out increasingly precarious livelihoods after 2000, for Masvingo's new farmers, and its fishermen,[21] *njuzu* could appear part of a 'diverse assemblage of human and non-human adversaries' to be dealt with (McGregor 2008:868). I was often told that the use of soap and ash, and the washing of dirty pots or linen is prohibited at pools, springs and rivers associated with *njuzu*, and the defilement of such places can have grave consequences. In such accounts, *njuzu* appear ambivalently both as indices of ancestral and chiefly authority over the land (through the landscape knowledge claimed by autochthonous clans), and yet through their association with water and rain they also index the ulti-mate sovereignty of *Mwari*, the bringer of rain. This ambiguity of what authority or sovereignty *njuzu* index (cf. Aschwanden 1989:186–200; Bourdillon 1987; Lan 1985; Mukamuri 1995) reflects the fluidity of water, and its changing material forms and qualities across divergent registers of meaning and regimes of rule. Indeed, in a sense, *njuzu* manifest the link between the 'territorial' authority of ancestors and the ultimate 'rain-providing' sovereignty of *Mwari,* just as 'their' watery places mate-rially link the rain to the land.

In his symbolic analysis of Karanga mythology, Aschwanden (1989: 186–200) too faced the ambivalence I encountered trying to locate the cosmological ties linking *njuzu* to ancestors, and the *Mwari* cult. He focused attention on their 'doubtful descent' and their hybrid nature; half human, half creature, or 'human animals' (1989:197). For him 'the question of *njuzu* descent has never been answered absolutely satisfac-torily or without contradiction' exactly because 'the undefined nature of a phenomena is its essential characteristic' (1989:189). This uncertainty

---

[19] Acting Chief Murinye 13/06/06.
[20] Ibid.
[21] VaChigohwe 10/05/06.

surrounding *njuzu* reflected 'the exchange between man and nature', which is 'made real by letting something in the pool descend from man, and something in man from the pool and its creatures' (1989:197). For Aschwanden the 'symbolically and mythologically related relationship between nature and man' can only be understood through the existence of hybrid *njuzu* in the 'Karanga weitbild's' 'pool complex'. In his analysis, the pool and its creatures are symbolically linked to woman, witchcraft and the 'marriage-and-incest problem' (1989:197) because 'the idea of the stranger is also immanent in the pool', and 'as the woman who bears children, or becomes a witch, is always a stranger, so all the spirits from the pool ... are always genuine alien spirits [*mashave*]'. 'The "pool" from which a man obtains his children [ie woman]' is therefore 'always alien to him because the child is in the uterus surrounded by alien blood, in the same way as non-consanguine ancestral spirits rule the "pool"' (1989:198).

In this structuralist understanding, ancestors who own the land and are of the soil, are linked reciprocally to *njuzu*, who are of the water, pools and rivers. *Njuzu* are connected to ancestors in the same way that incoming wives and affines are linked to their autochthonous husbands – they are the strangers who enable life to be renewed.[22] So for Aschwanden, 'the woman who creates life, or destroys it by refusing her role, is the pool through which nature lives or dies', just as '*njuzu* lives in these waters in order to safeguard the life and prosperity of nature and the rivers'. 'But if *njuzu* is too much interfered with, it disappears and leaves drought, death and destruction' (1989:198–9). This offers a powerful explanation for Manyuki's linking of the 'anger of the soil' and that 'of the water', as expressed by the drowning of the young boy by *njuzu* in the Mutirikwi river. It is also a powerful analysis of the ontological significance of the ambivalence of *njuzu*, finding important echoes in the autochthonous claims of some clans that their ancestors 'germinated' from the land, or were married to, abducted by, or descended from *njuzu* who emerged from sacred springs.[23]

But if Aschwanden's symbolic analysis of the Karanga pool complex offers a sophisticated account of *njuzu*'s powerful but ambivalent presence in mythology and landscape around Mutirikwi, his is also a decidedly synchronic and ahistorical approach. The uncertainty that circulates around the respective roles of ancestors, chiefs, *njuzu*, *manyusa* and *Mwari* shrines in the provision of rain, the protection of sacred water sources, and the conferment of ancestral and divine legitimacy, equally reflects the multi-layered history of alternative regimes of rule and

---

[22] As Lyn Schumacher pointed out (personal communication December 2012), 'in northern Zambia it is just the opposite – the men are the incomer 'strangers' who must marry into the matrilineage of the 'owners of the land', eventually becoming owners themselves when subsequently buried in the land'.

[23] For example at Great Zimbabwe (Fontein 2006a: 19–41), where the little girl *Chisikana*, who was taken by *njuzu* and emerged from a sacred spring, is claimed as a founding ancestor or as an affine, by both the Nemanwa and the Mugabe clans, in their continuing disputes over the custodianship of the site.

contested spheres of political/religious influence that waxed and waned during the area's complex pre-colonial pasts. Such pasts are materialised through the affective presence of graves, ruins, rivers and sacred places, which are to varying degrees available for imaginative re-deployment in the present. Just as there was an ebb and flow to the reach of the Matopos shrines and other rain cults as different dynasties moved, set-tled and ruled across pre-colonial southern Zimbabwe, so it is unlikely that *njuzu*'s salience has remained constant. In other words, as well as complex ontological and structural continuities, there are also important histories and historiographies at play in the ambivalent significance of *njuzu* around Mutirikwi. This reminds us that so-called 'traditionalist' regimes of rule are as contested, multiple and overlapping as 'modern', technocratic governmental structures of rule can be – and always have been.

Whatever these structural and historical complexities, however, it is clear that drownings attributed to *njuzu* are often taken as a sign that the rules of the soil have not been respected, that the ancestral owners of the land and/or *Mwari* the provider of rain are displeased. Many around Mutirikwi remember drownings and accidents attributed to disturbed *njuzu* when the dam was being built in 1959–61; and how future accidents were prevented by rituals held by local chiefs as the 'autochthonous' guardians of the land being inundated.[24] Similarly, *njuzu* drownings in the Mutirikwi river in late 2005 revealed that 'something has gone wrong'. As VaZarira exclaimed: 'these days *njuzu* are being seen everywhere, and even [I] am now afraid to go out. There must be a reason for this, somewhere something has gone wrong and steps will have to be taken to correct that'.[25] Clearly, the appearance of *njuzu* – like the falling of good, fertile rains, or bad, destructive rains, or even the lack of rain altogether – are indicative of the moral wellbeing of people, land and the state, and therefore can be seen, like rain and drought, as *indexes of power*; even if it is not always clear whose or what form of legitimacy and sovereignty (or lack of it) is being indexed. In 2005, the drowning of the young boy in the Mutirikwi river was for many an index of Chief Chikwanda's illegitimacy. But it also allowed VaZarira to demonstrate (by finding the dead boy in the pool) her capacity as a powerful Duma medium, a position that for some empowered her to be an arbitrator for the troubled chieftainship.[26] In turn the drowning of the boy by the *njuzu* could be equally demonstrative of the sovereignty of ancestors as owners of the land and of *Mwari* as the provider of rain. After all, Chief Chikwanda's apostolic faith, his failure to follow the rules of the soil and to respect VaZarira, was also an affront to them.

[24] VaChikami (water bailiff) 06/11/05; VaChinengo 26/05/06; Geri Zano 23/03/06; Chief Mugabe 19/11/05; Bhodo Mukuvare 19/11/05; Matopos Murinye 13/06/06. See chapter 2 fn 50.
[25] Fieldnotes 02/11/05.
[26] Fieldnotes 24/11/05.

NATIONAL *BIRAS*

If drought provoked difficult questions about Chief Chikwanda's legitimacy, then in late 2005 fears grew amongst disgruntled clan members that his alleged failure to conduct a proper *bira* at their sacred *mapa*, Mafuse, on Mt Harawe, when government was sponsoring national *bira*s throughout the country, threatened further crop failure.[27] Manyuki told me Chief Chikwanda refused to allow a *bira* at Mafuse, because his religious beliefs denigrated ancestral events.[28] Later, after the first rains had fallen in the district but not in Chikwanda's area, these fears were heightened as good rains were promising elsewhere. VaMutsambwa complained that Chief Chikwanda's refusal to involve VaZarira in his national *bira* meant that 'in late November/December everywhere else was getting rain, but we weren't here because *denga nemidzimu vakatsamwa* [the sky and ancestors are angry]'.[29] Chief Chikwanda told me that despite his apostolic faith, he *had* organised (though not attended) a *bira* at Mafuse, indicating how the government's commitment to a resurgent traditionalism could compel even chiefs of different religious persuasion to take part. Later, when it became clear good rains were widespread, some did recognise Chikwanda's event as successful, even if VaZarira attributed the good rains to *Mwari* and even *njuzu*. According to Furere Mashuro, a *sabhuku* in Zano, east of the lake, 'this year our chief did a good job. He told everyone to prepare their beer ... so ... the rains were good, everyone will harvest and there won't be hunger'.[30]

In fact the government's new national *bira*s of September 2005 proved hugely significant as the rainy season bore fruit.[31] For many across Masvingo, they signalled government was at last listening to chiefs and mediums, and recognising that their legitimacy sprung from the ancestors and *Mwari*. Indeed for some the good rains demonstrated how, as 'intermediaries between human beings and the Creator' the authority of ancestors and mediums 'supersedes that of *madzimambo* [chiefs]'.[32] As Trust Mugabe, councillor for Ward 13, explained:

[27] Ibid.

[28] 'People were preparing to have their *bira* there at ... Mafuse, but the chief ... sent them away... These *bira*s should be done at the sacred places not in someone's house. The problem is that he is a Zion and that is why he doesn't want anything to do with *chikaranga* [loosely: 'tradition'] and *bira*s. Even though he wears the *nyembe* [title] of the chief, which comes from the elders [ancestors], he refuses to respect them, and even calls them *mweya wetsvina* [dirty/evil spirits]' (Manyuki 29/11/05).

[29] VaMutsambwa 19/12/05.

[30] Sabhuku Furere Mashuro/Gundura 12/04/06.

[31] The *bira*s were celebrated on television, and in the government press ('Message from Manhize: Dzimbahwe speaks with Muhera wekwaPfumojena' *Daily Mirror on Saturday*, 04/03/06), although some reports chided that they could not 'ask for crucial inputs [i.e. seed and fertiliser] from the other world', which still 'had to be met by the responsible ministry' ('No more rhetoric: heads should roll' *Sunday Mirror*, 26/02/06).

[32] 'Dzimbahwe speaks' *Daily Mirror on Saturday*, 04/03/06.

We had many years of drought and the *masvikiro* [mediums] were saying we need *biras*, for the chiefs to respect their *vadzimu* [ancestors]. That's when we saw the government was serious about *masvikiro* after many years of poor rains. That is why this year the rains have fallen well. It was only this year that the *masvikiro* were given attention, and the rains were good, just as the *masvikiro* said they would be. [But] even in some places there is still not enough rain ... because they are not respecting the *masvikiro* all the time. In south Matabeleland there is still not enough rain ... and in other parts of the country too ... there is still *nzara* [hunger]. All this is caused by the government not respecting the *masvikiro*.[33]

In April 2006 I waited patiently for a chance to speak to Chief Fortune Charumbira – President of the Council of Chiefs,[34] highly influential in Masvingo and closely tied into ZANU PF politics – at his well-attended weekly *dare* (meeting/court). I was fascinated to overhear his telephone interview with a journalist from the state-owned newspaper *The Herald*, discussing the successful rains of 2005/06 and the national *biras* of the previous September.

In the waiting room ... we hear everything going on. The chief is hearing cases, and his loud voice booms out from next door. He often gets phone calls, and always takes them, dealing with all sorts of business at the same time. He gets a call from a journalist ... They are discussing the chief's regalia and in particular the pith helmet and red cloak which are part of a chief's official outfit.
Chief Fortune explains: This regalia ... was given to the chiefs during the colonial government ... so now that we have independence we want to change it. So we are looking into preparing a new outfit, which will restore the dignity, yes dignity, and we can say identity. You see this is about building our own identity as black Zimbabweans, our dignity and our identity through restoring our Zimbabwean traditions. This is part of our wider efforts to restore our own identity, which was ignored, sidelined or destroyed by the colonial government. ... This goes along with our efforts to restore our traditions, like here ... we had the return of the Zimbabwe Bird, and also we have our identity as Zimbabwean warriors. We are warriors, Zimbabweans are warriors. We have fought the First *Chimurenga* and the Second and now the Third *Chimurenga*, so we want restore our identity. So that is the first thing, the chiefs' regalia.
Second, we have Statutory instrument 17 of 2006, and ... the main thing is the restoration of the full powers of chiefs. This statutory instrument 17 is about the power of enforcement. The chiefs will have the power to enforce their findings from their courts. Previously ... the chief needed to go to the magistrate, and the messenger of court would have the power to enforce the judgement of the chiefs, now that power to enforce is going back to the chiefs, so that they enforce their own judgements. Whether that means the payment of a cow or a goat or money, the chiefs will be able to send their own messenger to collect those goats or whatever ... Yes ... they deal with civil cases not criminal cases, which will remain with the police and the courts. The chiefs have the power to fine up to a maximum of 100 million dollars, and this is why we are having workshops with the chiefs to teach them about their restored roles and what they should now be doing.
This ... is but one part of ongoing efforts to restore the traditional role of chiefs. Last year, yes, we had those *mabira* [national *biras*], that was very important. And you see this year the rain fell very well and we are hearing ... that ... in most of the country there are bumper harvests because the rains fell after those *mabira*. And the *zunde ramambo* ... every chief should have a *zunde ramambo*. Those stray cattle collected and sold by the police, that money should also go

---

[33] Trust Mugabe 16/03/06.
[34] He was elected president of the council of chiefs, replacing Jonathan Mangwende, in April 2005 ('Zimbabwe: Charumbira Elected Chiefs' Council President' *Herald*, 07/04/05).

into the *zunde ramambo*. No, the *zunde ramambo* is not for the chiefs' own fields … it's for feeding the orphans. There are many orphans out there.[35]

Charumbira's comments illustrate brilliantly how the national *biras* fitted his traditionalist agenda, and how that located chiefs within ZANU PF's broader strategy of remaking the state through its rhetoric of patriotic history (Ranger 2004). They also illustrate how Charumbira's particular agenda (wherein chiefs rather than mediums were especially trumpeted) envisaged a regime of rule in which a complexity of productive, coercive, governmental and hegemonic mechanisms of power are intertwined, entangling a plethora of sources/forms of sovereignty and legitimacy. While the question of the chiefs' regalia points to the symbolic and demonstrative stylistics of chiefly rule, the discussion of Zimbabweans' 'warrior identity' directly complemented ZANU PF's hegemonic patriotic history and Third *Chimurenga* project. The reference to Statutory Instrument 17 located this traditionalist agenda within wider legislative changes (cf. Mubvumba 2005), pegging the 'return' of chiefs' authority within a legal structure that points to the ultimate sovereignty of law and the state. At the same time, the *zunde ramambo* project points to the pastoral dimensions of chiefly rule and the imperative to be responsive to peoples' needs. The references to national *biras* and 'bumper harvests' too fulfils such responsive requirements, but importantly do so in a way that implicates not the sovereignty of the state or law, but rather the legitimacy deriving from the sovereignty of the ancestral owners of the land, from whom chiefs descend. For Charumbira the national *biras'* success, as manifest in that year's good rains, was a personal triumph as well as an indication of the potency of government's renewed commitment to re-imagined traditionalist rule in which chiefs had a central role. I was even more fascinated to read the resulting news report the following day.[36] It faithfully reproduced the discussions I had overheard with the startling exception of the chief's emphasis on the national *biras*. This was subtly transformed into a triumphalist announcement about 'bumper harvests', with little mention of the national *biras* that for many around Mutirikwi were responsible for the fertile rains. Perhaps not everyone in Harare felt that trumpeting the successful rains as an indication of the potency of traditionalist regimes of rule – thereby pointing to the legitimacy chiefs receive from ancestral and divine sovereignty – necessarily served ZANU PF's wider political purposes.

Nevertheless, if many chiefs around Masvingo felt vindicated by the apparent success of the national *biras*, for war veterans and new farmers the good rains served to re-legitimise faltering land reform and no doubt contributed to the optimism of that year. Several acknowledged not enough attention had been paid to mediums and ancestors during the early *jambanja* stages of land reform in 2000–02. As the war veteran Va-Chuma, explained 'we knew we were doing something good [by taking the land] but saw that some things were not going very well, like those

---

[35] Fieldnotes 23/04/06.
[36] 'Zimbabwe produces better harvests: Chiefs', *Herald*, 24/04/06.

droughts ... things were not yet settled'. 'Later,' he continued, 'we knew that people should follow the rules of the land ... to respect the land. We decided to ask VaZarira ... what we should do. And the chiefs ... decided they should brew beer to give thanks for getting the land back for their *sekurus* [lit. grandfathers, meaning ancestors here]'. 'So every chief in the whole country brewed beer last year and that is why the rains were good and there is enough to eat this year'.[37] Another war veteran, VaKurasva, on Desmondale farm, agreed.[38] VaMakasva, living below Beza, felt that war veterans 'should have worked with the *masvikiro*' when they first re-occupied the farms; 'that is why the rains refused ... these last few years'. He agreed the good rains resulted from the national *biras*, but warned that although 'things are a bit more stable' they were 'not yet properly sorted out'. 'There is need to prepare more *biras* and call all the *masvikiro* to do our things properly', he told me.[39]

Not everyone was unanimous about the success of the *biras*, particularly during the anxious months of October and November 2005, when early signs provoked much concern that the rains would again fail. VaZarira and her supporters were often extremely sceptical. Complaints were diverse, reflecting widespread confusion about the national *biras*' purpose; whether to request for rain, assistance with land reform, or to announce the success of the *hondo yeminda* (war of the fields) or, as some claimed,[40] to do with the unresolved legacies of liberation war dead in mass graves in Mozambique and Zambia (Fontein 2009b, 2010), or all of these together. According to Manyuki each of these issues needed to be dealt with individually. He felt this lack of clarity, their televised nature, and the sight of chiefs wearing shoes and performing for the cameras, all reflected the inauthentic nature of the government-instigated *biras*. His views were shared by others. The problem, he said, 'is that they are working with these very young chiefs who do not know the traditions properly, instead of working with the old people and the *masvikiro*'.[41] This sentiment was shared by Bhodo Mukuvare who attended Murinye's *bira* but lamented:

> *Vakapira mudzimu wekare* [they appeased the ancestor from long ago], there was dancing and beer and food. I want the things from long ago. This life of today I don't like it. There was no *vadzimu* [ancestors] who came out [possessed mediums] because there were only youngsters there, no one knows. Me, I am not

[37] VaChuma 12/06/06.
[38] 'Why there was no rain last year? There were some problems with leadership and the *masvikiro* and ancestors who felt they were being ignored. So then they had those *mabira*. It was an issue to do with *chivanhu chedu* [our culture]. So government told us to brew beer to appease the ancestors, because they were being disturbed ... they held those *biras* and that is why this year it rained a lot, which showed us that some of those problems have now been sorted out' (VaKurasva 17/04/06).
[39] VaMakasva 14/01/06.
[40] Robbie Mtetwa 29/06/06.
[41] Manyuki 05/11/05.

seeing it. Even the *manyusa* are no longer. The *vadzimu* are there, they are not happy. It is quite a big problem. Can you see the rain is not coming?[42]

Such complaints echoed concerns that the national *biras* celebrated chiefs and war veterans but excluded mediums. Mai Makasva, a *sabhuku* under Chief Mugabe, attended both an earlier *bira* organised by VaZarira, and later, Chief Mugabe's own national *bira*. Worrying about the late rains in November 2005, she acknowledged that the national *biras* had been unusual because they were organised by chiefs and war veterans in the absence of *masvikiro*:

> We do not know why the rain is refusing to rain ... we cooked beer and held *biras*. We had a *bira* recently. It was big. Everyone was there, the *masvikiro*, even from Mashava, Matopos, even Harare. But even then the rains have not come. We did it in July, VaZarira cooked the beer there at that mountain Chasosa. [And] the national *biras* were done well. We had ours at Chikarudzo. It is true they were different. That one, *doro harina kupirwa nemasvikiro* but *nemadzishe* ['that beer was not appeased by the spirit mediums but the chiefs'] and the comrades, but the first *bira* we had in July was done by the *masvikiro*.[43]

For VaZarira, such concerns not only reflected her ongoing dispute with Chief Chikwanda, but longer-standing grievances about the marginalisation of *masvikiro*.[44] For her mediums' exclusion from the national *biras* was merely the latest in a long series of exclusions, even as chiefs were increasingly courted by ZANU PF. Such complaints illustrate how contested traditionalist regimes of rule are, and reflect ZANU PF's uneasy relationship with mediums, particularly in comparison to the relatively pliant regime of chiefs, headman and village heads.[45] Unlike chiefs, whose authority and legitimacy is more dependent upon political allegiances and state structures, mediums depend on the efficacy of their performances and their ability to demonstratively submit their subjectivity to the agency and sovereignty of the spirits possessing them, even as they too must be responsive to their various local audiences (Fontein 2006a:47–70). This has a longer history than ZANU PF's re-found traditionalism over the last decade, dating back to the 'ultra-traditionalism'

[42] Mukuvare 19/11/05.

[43] Mai Makasva 26/11/05.

[44] As she put it: 'When the Second *Chimurenga* first started a few freedom fighters came into the country to fight and they were all killed. That was when they realised that they needed the support of the *masvikiro* and we helped them. That is why we got independence. But since independence they have forgotten about us and the important work we do. That is why there are now problems of fuel, money and rain. Then they started to say we need to take back our land, and of course the land has to be returned but they have done it in the wrong way. They have forgotten about the *masvikiro*. They have chased away the whites from the land not thinking that the country needs money, and the land needs to be returned properly, with the *masvikiro*. That is why there is no fuel, no food or money and no rain' (Fieldnotes 03/11/05).

[45] A similar argument could be made for Zimbabwe's diverse array of churches. Since 2008 there is growing evidence of a concerted campaign by ZANU PF to court churches of all varieties, including Zimbabwe's many Pentecostal churches. This was not particularly prevalent around Mutirikwi in the mid-2000s.

of the 1960s, after the demise of the Native Land Husbandry Act, when chiefs 'stood at the centre of the Rhodesian's state's struggle to remake its authority over land and people' (Alexander 2006:83), and mediums became increasingly (but not unfalteringly) influential for Zimbabwean nationalism.

These inherent tensions between chiefs and *masvikiro*, and the localised nature of the *biras*, also meant that criticisms reflected and sometimes exacerbated long-standing tensions within and between different clans. The contested nature of Chief Chikwanda's *bira* at Mafuse is a case in point, but disgruntlement also circulated around a national *bira* allegedly held at Great Zimbabwe by Chief Charumbira, which fed into the enduring tensions surrounding that site (Fontein 2006a). As delayed rains in some areas in late 2005 raised fears of another drought, VaZarira, Chief Mugabe and others vocalised concerns about Charumbira's rumoured involvement at Great Zimbabwe.[46] Both felt a single national *bira* with all the mediums and chiefs should have been held at the site to signify both its national importance and, of course, its proper custodianship by those with valid autochthonous claims to it. As Chief Mugabe explained:

> The government organised those *biras*, each chief at their home, with only his own people. That is not the *bira* of all the *masvikiro* at GZ [Great Zimbabwe] that is needed to make the rains fall ... The keys of the rain are there at GZ. It was clever of them to organise the *biras* at chiefs' homesteads instead of GZ, they didn't want it to work properly. GZ is now very dirty, it needs to be cleaned with the rains. The foundation of GZ is Duma. Charumbira is not happy about that ... At GZ the person who has to *kupira* the ancestors would have to be me, and not him, even as head of the chiefs. I heard a rumour that in secret, late at night, Charumbira did go in there. That is why the rain is not falling. We don't know what *mushonga* [medicine/witchcraft] he went into GZ with, but the rain is not falling.'

> As we leave the building, Chief Mugabe points to the sky. 'Look, the clouds were being built by the heat but now the wind is breaking them down. The rain has already passed by. It will not rain today'.[47]

[46] VaZarira told me: 'there has still been no rain. It is a big, big problem. There is definitely something that has been done wrong ... In the old days in November if the rain had come, it had come, but this wind is taking the rain away. The reason the rain is not falling is because of those national *biras* in September. They should have been held with all the chiefs at Great Zimbabwe [GZ], instead of just Charumbira by himself. It is not his place, none of his forefathers are buried there. Beer should have been cooked in the *sango* [bush] outside of GZ. Then those elders who have graves in GZ, should have gone in with their beer, *bute* [snuff] and black cloths to pray to their ancestors there. It is only Mugabe and Nemanwa, and maybe Murinye, but not Charumbira. There are Haruzvivishe graves there, right on top of that mountain. I would like to see Charumbira showing us his ancestors' graves there.' Peter Manyuki chimed in saying '*kwakapinda politics ipapo* [there were politics involved there] ... that is why Charumbira alone went in there, because he is the chairman of the chiefs' (Fieldnotes 29/11/05). Haruzvivishe made similar complaints against Charumbira, saying the lack of a proper *bira* at Great Zimbabwe and the failure to consult the *masvikiro*, meant that 'if you see that the rain does not fall this year, it is because of that'. But he also did not attend Chief Mugabe's *bira* because he continued to dispute his claim to the chieftaincy (Fieldnotes 06/10/05).

[47] Fieldnotes 19/11/05.

A VISIT TO MATONJENI?

However parochial these tensions around Great Zimbabwe often appear, for Chief Mugabe, VaZarira and others they clearly have far wider significance. VaZarira has long been involved in efforts to reclaim and re-sanctify it as a key sacred site of national significance. In 2005 she did participate in acting Chief Murinye's national *bira* at Boroma, but over the following months her attention focused on organising a visit to Matonjeni in the Matopos.[48]

> The conversation turns to her efforts to arrange the trip to Matonjeni to ask for rain. That is why she is trying to meet the chiefs. She stresses that when she is working to ask for rain it is 'for the whole country', but 'the government refuses to help us. Seven years I worked with the comrades during the war but now they have forgotten us. During the [national] *bira*s some people were saying they were to appease the spirits of the dead comrades, others that it was to ask for rain, but no it was to welcome the new country, to thank the ancestors for independence'. She mentions another *bira* which she organised a long time ago when she wrote angrily to the president himself, and was eventually helped with bags of maize, *rapoko* [finger millet] and two beasts, which 'the president said was for Ambuya to use as she knows how'. 'But at this recent *bira* they were making the war vets and chiefs important but not the *masvikiro*. Now I have to go Matonjeni to ask for rain, but they are not helping me. It is as if they don't understand. I need to go to Matonjeni where a voice speaks out of the rock'.[49]

As 2005 turned into 2006 VaZarira and acting Chief Murinye made great efforts to secure financial support from local ZANU PF politicians, businessmen and government administrators for transport and fuel to make this visit.[50] She saw her approach to the recently elected Senator Mavhaire, in particular, as a test of his recognition of where sovereignty over land and rain ultimately lay. As she put it 'I want to ... see if he keeps his promises, because the work that I am doing is for ... the country and since they are the government it is work that they should be doing ... so they should send me a car to take me where I need to go'.[51] For VaZarira, Mavhaire's legitimacy (as with Chief Chikwanda) clearly depended upon his recognition of her authority as the medium of an ancestral owner of the land, and in turn of *Mwari*'s ultimate sovereignty as the provider of rain. Her comments reveal a commitment to a traditionalist regime of rule in which mediums, ancestors and the Matopos shrines, rather than chiefs, are key to the provision of rain. The significance of failing or successful rains was therefore ultimately less as index of the legitimacy (or illegitimacy) of chiefs, than of the sovereignty of the ancestors, their *masvikiro*, and most of all *Mwari*. In other words, hers was an attempt to secure a place for *masvikiro* and the Matopos shrines in the re-configuration of authority over land and people ongoing since independence, but

[48] As indeed she had successfully done when I was researching Great Zimbabwe five years earlier.
[49] Fieldnotes 02/11/05.
[50] In these efforts the district and provincial administrators, the now-former provincial Governor Chiwewe, the now-late, retired General Zvinavashe as well as the then-new senator Mavhaire were all approached, without success.
[51] Fieldnotes 29/11/05.

drastically revived since 2000. This encompasses a moral vision of the future that gains traction ecologically and materially through rain and water, but builds on particular readings of past regimes of ecological and political control.

VaZarira and Murinye's unsuccessful efforts throughout 2005/06 to visit Matonjeni – first to ask for rain and then, after the rains had come, to offer thanks – do reflect older histories linking Masvingo to the Matopos. Their determination acknowledged even as it reconstructed a past when *manyusa* linked individual chiefdoms to the *Mwari* shrines, and were responsible for requesting rain, while mediums and chiefs focused on problems to do with the land. As acting Chief Murinye explained:

> Rain is the job of the *manyusa*. They come from each chiefdom, where they collect money and gifts to help them on their way to Matonjeni to ask for good rains. They can even go by themselves if they are not sent by the chief, and usually they would travel on foot. The chiefs and *masvikiro* should also go Matonjeni to thank for good rains or even to ask for rain, because there have not been *manyusa* in this area for a long time. But traditionally it is the role of *manyusa* to ask for rain. The chiefs and *masvikiro* go there to speak to the Voice of the rock ... to deal with the problems of the *nyika* [land, territory]. *Manyusa* go there for *mvura* [water]. Chiefs and *masvikiro* might go there to address problems of army worms or locusts, or disease affecting people, or lightening strikes killing people and burning houses. Or if a chief is having problems with people not ... following the traditional rules. Maybe people are not burying children in the wet soils by rivers as they should, but rather in the hard soils. Or cutting sacred trees or not following other rules ... to protect the country. There are so many rules. Chiefs and *masvikiro* go there *kugadzikana nyika* [to settle the land].[52]

This offers a different traditionalist vision to ZANU PF's growing embracement of chiefs and headmen since the late 1990s, as most actively advocated by actors like Chief Charumbira. Perhaps ZANU PF's heavily politicised rhetoric is unable to deal with the localised, historical complexities of contested territorial and rain-making cults. Yet VaZarira and Murinye's determination to visit Matonjeni also re-forged a past in which the 19th-century influence of the Pfupajena and Musikavanhu cults, for example, and of the rain-making practices of pre-Duma Karanga clans, are also conveniently set aside.[53]

Murinye and VaZarira's efforts also reflect their individual histories and aspirations. For Murinye, a visit to the Matopos shrines offered opportunity to replicate his late father's visits, from which he had acquired his own name, Matopos.[54] His father, Mudarikwa, had last visited Matonjeni around 2003 with a delegation led by VaZarira, and his son's desired visit in 2005/06 was in part intended to solidify his authority as

[52] Fieldnotes 17/03/06.
[53] VaChinengo 26/05/06.
[54] Matopos Murinye explained: 'One time my father went to the Matonjeni with a delegation. At that time he had not had any sons yet and he said this to the voice at Matonjeni and the voice said that when he returned he would find that one of his wives who was pregnant had had a son. He was told to name his son Matopos, and much later on I myself had to go to the Matopos to thank the voice that speaks from the rock there' (Fieldnotes 17/03/06).

chief within his own clan, from whom he collected funds for the trip. For her part, VaZarira had utilised NGO funding to make several high-profile visits to the Matopos during the 1990s (see Daneel 1998), where she was received with great honour by the *Voice* at Dzilo shrine. No doubt her authority within the Duma clans was invigorated by these visits (Fontein 2006a:64). Sharp reductions in NGO funding in the 2000s, amid deepening political crisis and government suspicion, are part of the back-drop to VaZarira's search for funds among Masvingo's political leaders in 2005/06. Fuel shortages meant transport was a particular problem and VaZarira even approached a local transport company, Mhunga buses, seeking help with transport, diesel or food.[55] Later Murinye acquired diesel from relatives in Mozambique.[56] Despite promises made during the senate elections of November 2005, Masvingo's politicians did not ultimately facilitate VaZarira's intended visit to Matonjeni in 2005/06, confirming what her son Manyuki already suspected, that: 'politicians often make promises they don't keep, especially at election time'.[57] Clearly, a rain-requesting visit to Matonjeni did not have the same signif-icance for local ZANU PF politicians, as it did for VaZarira and Matopos Murinye. Perhaps once the rains had come, they no longer saw the need. Or it reflected the continued unease with which state, government and party structures have long dealt with mediums, rainmakers and the Matopos shrines.

MEDIUMS AND THE STATE

Manyuki claimed a former Masvingo provincial administrator (PA) once told him that in the past 'there used to be [local government] budget allocation for visits to Matonjeni'. Furthermore, 'during the time of Smith and Rhodesia there was always money for that and people used to go very frequently with help ... from the PA'.[58] This echoes accounts of white settler-farmers sponsoring rain-making ceremonies on their farms in the past, reflecting historical co-existence and proximity with existing African communities in material landscapes around Mutirikwi, and their shared need for rain. Whether provincial funds were ever set aside to fund trips to Matonjeni, or not, it is clear that relations between mediums and different arms of government has, since independence, been characterised by a profound ambivalence, unlike the increasing re-incorporation of chiefs and headmen into local state structures. The ambivalence sometimes shown by nationalist political elite to mediums during the liberation struggle (cf. Chung 1995:146) has largely continued since independence. At times, such as during the 1992 drought (Mawere & Wilson 1995), mediums have been embraced at the very highest

---

[55] Fieldnotes 24/04/06, also 17/03/06.
[56] Acting Chief Murinye 22/5/06.
[57] Fieldnotes 24/11/05.
[58] Fieldnotes 17/03/06.

levels, but this has never amounted to sustained incorporation into local government structures in the way chiefs have been.

The alternating celebration followed by frequent denigration of mediums of Zimbabwe's highest profile ancestors (Nehanda, Chaminuka, and most recently Changamire Dombo) at the hands of ZANU PF, point precisely to this ambivalence. Numerous examples attest to this. Nehanda was celebrated during the liberation struggle due to her role during the First *Chimurenga* of 1896–97 (Ranger 1967; Lan 1985). Guerrillas famously carried Nehanda's elderly medium over the border to Mozambique (and back again after she died).[59] But, as I discuss in greater detail in Chapter 9, at Great Zimbabwe shortly after independence, another Nehanda medium called Sophia Muchini was initially courted by senior politicians but then implicated in attacks on white farmers east of Mutirikwi, and convicted of murder. At her trial 'she declared that ... the claimed independence was a mockery ... [and] Mugabe was a puppet of the whites', to which ZANU PF spokesmen retorted 'that the party had made Nehanda rather than Nehanda the party and that it was treason to dispute Mugabe's right to determine peace' (Ranger 2010a:10). In the early 1990s in northern Zimbabwe some mediums (including another Nehanda medium) did receive substantial rewards for their work during the struggle, although many interpreted them as officials' attempt to get mediums' approval for unpopular, 'rationalising' land reforms then being implemented (Spierenburg 2004). More recently, reports emerged that police destroyed the home of a new farmer in Chinhoyi, on the orders of Lina Govera, another Nehanda medium in northern Zimbabwe.[60] Conversely Sadomba (2011) discusses the mixed fortunes of another four competing Nehanda mediums involved in fast-track in Masowe and subsequently evicted from resettled lands in favour of more senior political clients. This was despite announcements by ZANU PF's most strident recent ideologue, Tafataona Mahoso, that Nehanda herself was inspiring war veterans in the Third *Chimurenga* (Ranger 2010a:10); a sentiment I often encountered amongst war veterans around Mutirikwi.

Part of the problem often cited by authorities is establishing the authenticity of mediums. In March 2005 then-president of the Council of Chiefs, Jonathan Mangwende, told *The Herald* that 'that the whole country is filled with people claiming to be possessed by Ambuya Nehanda or Sekuru Kaguvi. There are now lots of bogus and greedy spirit mediums'.[61] Urging 'all people who claim to be possessed ... to first approach traditional leaders in their areas because tradition just like anything else has its own rules, procedures and processes', he revealed mediums' need to maintain local support bases, but also implied a vision of traditional rule in which chiefs preside over mediums' authenticity/

---

[59] Mhanda (2011) describes how, during the war, guerrilla fighters had returned the remains of Nehanda, who died 'in exile' in Mozambique, to Zimbabwe for burial before the struggle could be continued.

[60] 'Police destroy home on orders from Spirit Medium', *Zimbabwe Independent*, 05/03/10.

[61] 'Bogus national spirit mediums hammered', *Herald*, 08/03/05.

legitimacy, and not vice-versa, as VaZarira and others would advocate. Questions of authenticity and local legitimacy were also a feature of the death of Muchetera, a famous Chaminuka medium killed in 1977 by guerrillas concerned about his Rhodesian sympathies (Ranger 1982b). More recently, descendants of the original Chaminuka medium, Pasipamire, famously killed in 1883 by Lobengula, collected his remains from Matabeleland and re-interred them in a new shrine in Seke communal lands near Harare, to await the 'resurrection of the legendary medium', which will result 'in all the problems facing the country disappearing'. NMMZ became involved 'at the shrine ... to preserve it as a cultural heritage', thereby setting 'the stage for a tough battle between the National Monuments and Museums and the family'.[62]

Another case worth citing is that of the 'diesel *n'anga*' Rotina Mavhunga, self-proclaimed medium of the Rozvi ancestor Changamire Dombo, who was courted by ZANU PF ministers, as well as local chiefs, after claiming she discovered diesel flowing from rocks near Chinoyi in northern Zimbabwe in 2007. She received '$5 billion [Zimbabwean dollars], a farm and other services' before her fraud was discovered; lifting 'the lid on how deep belief in superstition and sorcery among the country's political leaders runs', as one newspaper chided.[63] But if the diesel *n'anga* case revealed the credulity of some within ZANU PF, becoming the source of great ridicule,[64] it also illustrated how mediums can be victim to the machinations of politicians who court them (Fontein 2012). A similar argument applies for Sophia Muchini, whose involvement in farm murders around Mutirikwi after independence insinuated political manipulation by the then Minister of Health, Ushewokunze (Clark 1985:133). The medium Tenzi Nehoreka is another recent example, whose noisy visits to Great Zimbabwe, Njelele and other shrines, with large war veteran entourages, have provoked deep consternation among shrine keepers, local officials and ZANU PF; particularly after he 'allegedly stripped Chief Tandi ... of his chieftainship badge', leading to a court trial and, significantly, subsequent acquittal.[65] The sinister 'carrot and stick' role played by the CIO (Zimbabwe's feared intelligence organisation) in the guarding, surveillance and rewarding of mediums further reveals how ZANU PF and security branches of the state, do not take the influence mediums wield lightly. Spierenburg recalls encountering CIO agents guarding a Nehanda medium behind barbed wire at a house in Hurungwe, and argues the government's reaction to resistance by *mhondoro* mediums to land re-structuring in the 1990s, was characteristically

[62] 'Chaminuka: the resurrection?' *Herald*, 14/12/09, cited in Ranger 2010:14.
[63] 'Saga could land Mudede in court' *Financial Gazette*, 02/11/07. The same report implicated the Registrar-General Tobaiwa Mudede for obstructing justice by harbouring Rotina Mavhunga after the fraud was discovered.
[64] For example 'Zimbabwe's person of the year' 18/01/08; 'Changamire Dombo on trial' 09/04/08; blog: 'The world according to Gappah', available at http://petinagappah.blogspot.co.uk, accessed 18/06/13.
[65] 'War vet Tenzi Nehoreka acquitted' *Nehandaradio*, 20/04/14; 'War veterans vow to defy Zanu PF', *Standard*, 24/06/12.

ambivalent: 'On the one hand ... mediums' arguments were not taken seriously at all ... DDF and Agritex continued attempts to implement the land reforms ... On the other hand, government did try to bribe the mediums of Chidyamauyu and Nehanda, and kept the latter under close surveillance, indicating that it did not consider the Mhondoro mediums' challenges harmless at all' (2004:222).

There is evidence of similar CIO activity in Masvingo more recently. In early 2006 nine Chiweshe mediums turned up at Headman Nemanwa's household with the intention of holding a *bira* for rain at Great Zimbabwe. They were under the obvious surveillance and custody of CIO minders who delivered them and periodically returned during their extended, if unwelcome, stay.[66] Ahead of elections in July 2013, several different groups of mediums from all over Zimbabwe slaughtered cows and made offerings 'for peace' at Great Zimbabwe, chaperoned separately by unrelated CIO agents.[67] These included another significant but controversial medium around Mutirikwi, Mai Macharaga, a war veteran closely involved in directing land occupations in Masvingo in the early 2000s, and a former associate of VaZarira, who claimed in 2006 that she received substantial CIO support.

> In terms of '*matraditional*' things are better now ... and *bira*s asking for rain are being organised. I have been organising a big *bira* at Great Zimbabwe soon with members of the CIO and the President's Office in Masvingo. Because of the droughts of recent years I had been telling the authorities that it was important that *bira*s be arranged at Great Zimbabwe, as well as trips to Matonjeni to ask for rain. At first they ignored us, but later people from the President's office came to organise *bira*s because the rains were not falling. Before the national *mabira* of last September there was a *bira* organised in Muchakata where VaZarira and Murinye, Mugabe, Chikwanda and other Duma chiefs were invited. But I did not go because I was still unhappy about having been sidelined ... Later they came back and I did attend a following event held in Great Zimbabwe. It was there that the authorities were told that those national *bira*s had to be held across the country ... But things are not always easy. Even last year when I prophesised that there would be very good rains ... they did not believe me at first, but later they saw that it happened.[68]

This account, and other conversations with Macharaga in 2006, revealed that her relationship with VaZarira had become strained since previous research in 2000/01 when they had been forged in a closer alliance. This is not surprising given Macharaga's claims to be organising a *bira* at Great Zimbabwe, affronting VaZarira's own claims to the site. This is important because it says something about the different ways in which mediums establish their legitimacy, and illustrates how tensions between chiefs and mediums can be replicated between different mediums. A comparison between Macharaga and VaZarira is illustrative. As medium for not only the ancestor Zarira but Murinye himself, the most senior Duma ancestor in the district, VaZarira's popular support is based largely upon on her clan loyalties, her alliances with Duma chiefs, and

---

[66] Fieldnotes 07/03/06, 16/03/06, 19/03/06, 28/03/06, 20/04/06.
[67] Fieldnotes 09–15/12/13.
[68] Mai Macharaga 25/03/06.

upon the effectiveness of her performances as a medium. Conversely, without such clan loyalties to draw upon, Macharaga's legitimacy is based to a much greater extent on her war veteran past. In this respect it is no surprise that of all Masvingo's mediums, she was most closely involved in land occupations around Mutirikwi, and for a time, an influential member of the district land committee. This does not mean she is more politically malleable than VaZarira, or feels less marginalised from state processes than other mediums.[69] Yet it does suggest that she may have more to gain from close association with agents of the President's office.

But the consequences of this kind of official attention can be very severe. In 2002 a 70-year-old medium called Takatukwa Mamhova Mupawaenda was killed for 'mobilising chiefs, headmen and other traditional leaders against President Mugabe in the presidential poll', prompting condemnation from other mediums who pointed out that in the 1897 Kaguvi and Nehanda had been killed by Rhodesians 'for standing up to the same brutal policies now being perpetrated by Zanu PF'.[70] Active, articulate mediums like VaZarira and Macharaga clearly have to tread carefully. In 2006 I sensed growing unease from VaZarira, and those around her, as she became increasingly aware of being under CIO surveillance. Yet ultimately such attention by the feared security arms of central government is also a strong indication that the potential political efficacy of mediums' claims about the sovereignty of the ancestors as the owners of the land, and of *Mwari* as the provider of rain, however contested, has been recognised far beyond the remaking of Mutirikwi's landscapes by war veterans, new farmers, chiefs and mediums in the 2000s.

WATER AND THE MATERIALITY OF SIGNS

The multi-layered political imbrication of rain and water around Mutirikwi I have been describing is not unique to Zimbabwe. It re-occurs in different forms throughout the region. Reviewing rain-making practices across eastern and central Africa,[71] Jedrej pointed to the 'highly ambivalent power' of people credited with controlling the rain, noting how the extent to which 'weather is experienced as benign or malignant' is often 'indicative of the general state of the community' and 'its moral well being' (1992:292). Furthermore, 'those enjoying sovereign powers … not expressed as a rain making cult', he argued, 'appreciate the threat

[69] Her confrontation with the provincial governor Josiah Hungwe in 2001 is a good illustration of both her own disaffection, and how she too, like VaZarira, is imbricated in the nitty-gritty of ZANU PF's complex factionalism (*Masvingo Star*, 02–08 & 09–15/03/01, also Fontein 2006c:183–4).

[70] 'Spirit mediums condemn Terror', *Daily News*, 07/03/02.

[71] From Sudan and Ethiopia to the Eastern Congo and down to Zimbabwe (Southall 1953; James 1972; Packard 1981; Akong'a 1987; Krige & Krige 1943; Lan 1985).

Photo 6   Mai Macharaga
(Source: author, 2006)

Photo 7   Ambuya VaZarira
(Source: author, 2001)

posed by the appearance within their domains of such techniques and their practitioners' (1992:292). Although his example is articulated spatially, across the 'definite boundary to the spread of rain making techniques [that] can be detected along the Nile-Zaire watershed', this sense of threat posed to 'non-rain-making' sovereignties is clearly applicable to the ambivalence with which party and state officials have long engaged mediums in Zimbabwe.

Jedrej also made the important point that 'there is no useful correlation between rainfall distribution and the distribution of rain making institutions', nor is the 'unreliability of rainfall' a 'sufficient condition' for explaining the 'emergence and persistence of rain making institutions' (1992:290–1). Rather, citing Packard's study of the Bashu of Eastern Congo (1981), Jedrej pointed to the 'ambivalent attributes of rain', including its variability and unpredictable quantity, quality and periodicity, which can cause crops to wilt and harvests to fail, regardless of high annual rainfall figures. These qualitative properties of rain, and particularly of the timings of different types of rainfall in relation to crop growth cycles and decisions about when to plant, are hugely significant for farmers in Zimbabwe.[72] It means that farmers in communal areas, and on resettled farms without irrigation, do 'live in a world in which plenty and famine can and do follow one another unpredictably' (Jedrej 1992:291). Similarly, the localised and topographical nature of precipitation is equally significant in the hilly, middle-veld escarpment area around Mutirikwi.

These 'ambivalent attributes of rain' are linked in Jedrej's argument to the ambivalent power of rainmakers, but ultimately he concluded that it is the 'political quality of indigenous meteorological institutions which accounts for their distribution and persistence rather than the physical properties of the climatic environment with which people have to contend' (1992:292). 'Rain magic' is therefore more 'an idiom' or 'language' of political power than 'applied meteorology' (1992:290 & 293), and it is the embedded-ness of rain-making institutions in political and social hierarchies that accounts for their continuing salience. It is on this point that I find myself in disagreement with my late friend and mentor. Jedrej's essay contributed to a volume (Fradenburg 1992) exploring the role of women and gender in structures of dominance and resistance (Jedrej 1992:298), an admirable framework for a discussion of African environmental religions elaborated in further detail by others, notably Ranger (2003) and Sanders (2008). My purpose here has been somewhat different. I have sought to explore the political efficacy of rain (and water more generally) as imbricated in contested traditionalist regimes of rule and registers of meaning in southern Zimbabwe, without succumbing to a naïve environmental determinism or a simplistic functionalism, rightly warned against by Jedrej. My framework derives from recent debates about materiality and, in particular, questioning commonplace

---

[72] In the past, rain offerings across Zimbabwe were closely aligned with the agricultural season to ensure the right kind of rain fell at the right moment in the annual cycle (Lan 1985; Bourdillon 1987; Garbett 1977, 1992).

distinctions between matter and meaning, semiotics and materiality, focusing attention on the materiality of signs (cf. Keane 2003; 2005). This leads me to question whether a valid distinction can in fact be made between rain making as an *idiom* or language of power, and as applied meteorology. I would argue that for many people around Mutirikwi, it is necessarily both these things.

Although recent debates about materiality are often presented as something critical and new, they have many precursors.[73] A precursor of sorts for my argument can be found in James's 1972 essay 'The politics of rain control among the Uduk'. Her discussion has strong echoes with Jedrej's paper (which drew on it) and the situation I describe in Masvingo. For example, how 'control over the rain is one of the main idioms through which power relations are worked out in Uduk society'; the salience of rain's variable, localised and topographical qualities, forms and periodicity; and the 'double-edged power to bless or curse' that 'he who controls the rain' possesses (1972:34, 35, 37). While Jedrej (1992) and Ranger (2003) might point out that this 'he' is often a 'she', I draw attention to an interesting analogy Wendy James made between rain making and currency. In her words:

> To perform a rain ritual is not simply to carry out a naïve 'symbolic' act ... supposed to have instrumental efficacy; it is to make a calculated move in a very real game of social and political manoeuvre. That moves in the local power game are often of a 'symbolic' character should require no special explanation, as symbolic action is bound up with politics everywhere. Politics is played not only with such obvious symbols as flags, banquets and cricket matches, *which may be opposed in the mind to the reality they symbolize; but also with symbols which are themselves a reality*, a means of social articulation and political control. Currency is such a symbol, the circulation of money and financial policy being in them selves the stuff of politics. (James 1972:33, emphasis added)

Later, in her conclusion, James returns to her analogy with currency:

> The symbols of rain-control are in a broadly similar way a system of giving shape and substance to social and political credit. One could not compare a rain stone with a piece of money, true; but one could suggest a parallel between rights over rain stones and, say, shares in an insurance company. To ask: 'why do you believe in rain stones' is in some ways parallel to asking 'why do you believe in the Sudanese pound?' – *and not at all parallel to the question 'why do you believe in the radio-forecast'.* Belief in rain stones, as in currency, is rooted in local political structures of confidence and credit between people. (James 1972:57, emphasis added)

As with Jedrej's comment about rain making not being applied meteorology, I am also inclined to disagree with James's suggestion that belief in rain making is not parallel to a belief in the radio forecast. In part, I think we should, as Henare et al. (2006) imply, take our informants more literally. But James's comment about symbols not 'opposed in the mind to the reality they symbolize but also ... themselves a reality' does offer an opportunity to consider *both* how 'belief in rain stones ... is rooted in

[73] Similarly, Mauss's *The Gift* (1954) anticipated Gell's *Art and Agency* (1998), and Williams' (1977) notion of 'structures of feeling' anticipated recent interest in notions of affect.

local political structures of confidence and credit' and for understanding how the contingent forms and moments through which such beliefs gain traction socially and politically are in part dependent upon meteorological materialities.

This is where Keane (2003; 2005) and Engelke's (2007) elaboration upon Peirce's theory of signs (1955) is significant. For Pierce, 'words are not all that signify' and 'in his work there were three aspects of signs, each of which has a different kind of material relation to the world' (Engelke 2007:31). These are iconic, indexical and symbolic. If the meanings of symbols are based on convention, and therefore arbitrary, then the meanings of icons and indexes are based on a material relationship between these signs and what they represent; they 'are defined, at least in part, by the qualities of their materiality' (Engelke 2007:32). Icons are 'likenesses ... of the objects they represent', so pictures and maps resemble what they represent. But an index 'points to something', and this 'pointing-to can also involve (or imply) causality' (Engelke 2007:32); the object being represented in some way causes the index. Engelke provides the usefully meteorological example of a weather vane – 'so if the wind is blowing east, the weather vane points east; that is, the index (the weather vain pointing east) is caused by the object (the easterly wind)' (2007:32) – but we could equally consider an appropriately hydrological example, such as rain or flow gauges or even pre-paid water meters (cf. von Schnitzler 2008). This is the basis of my argument about water, particularly rain, being an *index of power*: successful or failing rains can index the legitimacy of chiefs, mediums and even government, and in turn the sovereignty of ancestors as owners of the land, and ultimately, of *Mwari* as the provider of rain.

The significance of this take on the 'materiality of signs' is that it allows analysis which does not reduce everything to the endless conceptual play of discourse and meanings, separate to the material world. Rather than the significance of the material world amounting simply to the way it reflects the politicised play of language, symbol, culture, memory and even ontology, Peirce's approach incorporates how the material qualities of signs in part condition, enable and constrain meanings. In this way it does have 'a much easier time incorporating the stuff of ethnography' (Engelke 2007:32). Sociality, historicity, contestation and political efficacy are *in part* determined independently of human agency, because matter and meaning are fundamentally intertwined. So rainfall really can, in part, determine political fortune.

Importantly, this argument is not to denigrate James and Jedrej's reflections on how rain making is rooted in the play of symbols embedded in political structures, because the materiality of signs gains political efficacy in relation to the constant play of contested 'semiotic ideologies' (Keane 2003:419), shared 'basic assumptions about what signs are and how they function in the world'. This approach is therefore deliberately open-ended and ultimately indeterminate; the efficacy of particular semiotic ideologies is contingent and gains traction in relation to the material world, even as the material world or features of it achieve their contingent significance in relation to particular semiotic ideologies. So around Mutirikwi not only the legitimacy of particular chiefs, mediums or senators is at stake when the rains are promising or fail, or when children are abducted by *njuzu*, but also the different, contested traditionalist regimes of rule put forward in the localised processes of remaking authority over land. In a context were droughts are recurrent and unpredictable, yet to be expected, water is of course always politically salient, but how this salience is realised is dependent both upon its unstable material qualities (and in relation to other material substances and forms – landscape, soil, climate and so on), and the unstable registers of meanings and regimes of rule with which these are intertwined.

In Engelke's work (2007) on the *Masowe weChishanu* Church (Friday Masowe Church) in Harare, who are unusual because of their deliberate rejection of the Bible, he argues that for them water is so common it is therefore mundane. Unlike other substances like pebbles and honey, and especially the anxiety provoking, unstable materiality of the Bible, water's ubiquity of religious and political significance, from healing to rain making, and across many different religious contexts, is so widespread that Apostolics can make no special claim to it. Water's meaningfulness is so imbued, so intrinsic, it causes no particular anxiety because it is 'a lost cause' (2005:133–4). Unlike Engelke's Apostolics, I am less convinced about the innocuousness of water's ubiquity. Around Mutirikwi, water's ability to cross, defy or even collapse the different registers of meaning and regimes of rule in which it is imbricated – its fluidity of matter and meaning – can be the cause of much anxiety and contestation. How to make sense of all the different meanings and political significances of water's many different forms/qualities, from rain to runoff, boundary rivers and conduits, from healing substance to irrigation, from cholera to drowning, and *njuzu* spirits to soil erosion? Water is significant in so many different registers of meaning and political salience. Even within the broadly shared recognition around Mutirikwi that rain is ultimately provided by *Mwari*, through the intervention of ancestors, *njuzu*, mediums and chiefs, there are a range of contested semiotic ideologies and regimes of rule at play. What water means in any moment is dependent upon its many different forms and qualities: as rain that falls after the sun's heat has built towering clouds, as *njuzu* drowning children, as destructive rain ruining crops and collapsing houses, or drought signifying poorly performed *mukwerere* ceremonies; the list seems endless. What then about irrigation, water supplies and boreholes? Or soil erosion, contour ridging and dam building? What does water index in all of these differing registers and in all of its variable qualities and forms?

The answer I have been working towards is that water is an *index of power*. But not power simply as something someone has to wield over someone else, nor omnipresent productive power as reified by Foucault. But power as contingently all of these: in tension, unstable, contested and mutually productive. Water can index productive, pastoral, governmental forms of power circulating around appeals to legitimacy, developmentalism, moral authority and consent, as well as performative and sometimes coercive assertions of capacity, autonomy and sovereignty. Around Mutirikwi water as rain, and as dangerous *njuzu*, indexes the authority and (il)legitimacy of chiefs and mediums, but also the (il)legitimacy of government and state. Indeed the very ambivalence with which ZANU PF have treated mediums since independence is, in this respect, indicative of its own uncertainty about water. Unlike Engelke's *weChishanu* apostolics then, the ubiquity of water's salience – its excessive, imbued meaningfulness and unstable materialities – does not make it innocuous, but rather provokes deep anxiety not only for new farmers, chiefs and mediums waiting for rain, but also for state officials and politicians. It is this uncertainty about the ambivalent ubiquity of water that, I suggest, can help us understand ZANU PF's impulse to moderate the weather forecast throughout the 2000s.

4

Hippos, Fishing and Irrigation

If the politics of rain discussed in the previous chapter illustrate how water can index the contested play of sovereignty and legitimacy in ongoing reconfigurations of traditionalist rule, then a similar argument can be made for other, more technocratic regimes related to water around Mutirikwi. Continuing official insistence upon the prevention of soil erosion and dam siltation is an example I have already discussed, which too involves performances of sovereignty alongside more productive mechanisms of power shaping political subjectivities and regimented landscapes amid appeals to developmentalism and governmental legitimacy. Such technocratic regimes exist in close proximity to and intertwine with the politics of rain and the ritual protection of sacred places through chiefs long charged with ensuring adherence to soil conservation strategies[1] even as they lead government-sponsored national *biras* (ancestral possession ceremonies). So-called traditionalist and technocratic regimes of rule entangle across various levels, and chiefs, mediums, war veterans, new farmers and others can be simultaneously involved in rain making and technocratic soil conservation without contradiction, because all gain traction through the material potentialities of water and land.

The significance of soil conservation strategies for my larger arguments about the political materialities of land and water in Zimbabwean state-making, and the entanglement of multiple regimes of rule and registers of meaning through the active remnants of past landscape interventions, are hard to exaggerate. It reappears repeatedly in the literature (Drinkwater 1989; Scoones and Cousins 1991; Scoones 1997; Beinart 2000; Moore 2005; Alexander 2006; McGregor 1995b), and throughout this book. This chapter, however, focuses on two other concerns to do with water that were salient around Mutirikwi in 2005/06: local demands for access to fishing and for irrigation from the lake's waters. Like rain making and national *biras*, both gained particular renewed efficacy in the context of recurring drought and economic crisis, even as they recalled

---

[1] In November 2005 Chief Mugabe discussed soil erosion at a public meeting, warning people against riverbank gardening, and announcing 'a sabhuku has been appointed to ... impose fines on those who persist' (Fieldnotes 02/11/05; 19/11/05). Also 'Enact laws to protect environment, chiefs told', *Herald*, 06/04/12.

the contested aspirations and imagined futures entangled with Rhodesia irrigation planning and the remaking of Mutirikwi's landscapes in the 1950s and 1960s, which are discussed in later chapters.

Irrigation, soil erosion and even fishing point, like rain, to water's productive and excessive/destructive material potentialities. Like rain making, regimes of rule to do with irrigation, soil erosion and fishing are charged with optimising and minimising water's productive and excessive potentialities respectively. Soil conservation is the flipside to irrigation because whilst both engage with water's fluid qualities, one does so in relation to its excess, the other its scarcity. As with rain making, both gain salience exactly because of the uncertainties of me-teorology and rain. Yet the commanding presence of the Mutirikwi dam itself also affords particular efficacy to water's productive and excessive potentialities. The dam sharpens the need for soil conservation around it even as it animates local demands for irrigation and fishing, so apparent in 2005/06. Neither could have the same political purchase without the dam. Even as the very possibility of, and imperative for, the dam was afforded *in part* by the vagaries of climate and topography, the dam itself affords water's productive and excessive potentialities to gain particular purchase in watery regimes reconfigured around it. The politics of fishing, irrigation and soil erosion around Mutirikwi are, therefore, in part, a continuing after-effect of the dam's construction during the Rho-desian period. But however much they made it possible, desirable and necessary, the dam has not elided the political affordances of climate, topography and the excessive materialities of water so much as com-plicated them. Rainfall, dam and topography are caught up in complex assemblages in which water's potentialities gain particular political pur-chase across divergent, co-existent regimes of rule/registers of meaning. It is water's material potentialities that entangle so-called traditionalist and technocratic regimes around Mutirikwi despite normative and rhe-torical efforts to differentiate them. If soil conservation, rain making and the protection of sacred places entangle most visibly through the figure of the chief, then in governmental regimes over fishing and irrigation, it is the recurring dangers of *njuzu* (water spirits), hippos and sometimes crocodiles which, I argue here, point most clearly to the entangled co-existence and proximity of multiple, contested regimes of sovereignty and legitimacy over Mutirikwi's waters.

Control over fishing and irrigation around Mutirikwi are administered through two parastatal bodies that exercise rule with very different styles. Zimbabwe's Parks and Wildlife Management Authority (here-after National Parks) is a long-established paramilitary organisation whose rule over wildlife around Mutirikwi manifests a tension between the demands of tourism, scientific research, and the imperatives of enforcement.[2] Established much more recently, after water reforms in

---

[2] The Kyle Game Reserve was envisaged before the dam was built. Wildlife was introduced and it opened to the public in 1964. In 1967 it was reclassified as a National Park, and in 1975 became the 'Kyle Recreational Park'. It was extended with additional neighbouring lands several times.

the late 1990s, Zimbabwe National Water Authority (ZINWA) struggled over the 2000s to establish its more regulatory authority over Mutirikwi's waters.[3] Despite ZANU PF interference,[4] both have attempted (in differing ways) to be responsive to the demands of local legitimacy. In 2005/06 these manifest particularly through appeals for local access to fishing and irrigation. As with land occupations, such demands typically invoked a diverse plethora of assertions of belonging and entitlement around the lake. Because fishing and irrigation draw people into the governmental regimes managing them, examining such demands offers opportunity to consider how, as an *index of power*, water involves not only the interplay of different kinds of sovereignty and legitimacy, but also the production of complex moral/political subjectivities (cf. von Schnitzler 2008), as people inevitably straddle conventional distinctions between different regimes of rule/registers of meaning.

Fishermen, poachers, National Parks rangers, new farmers, war veterans, chiefs, mediums and others are all differentially situated between diverse, co-existent regimes over water in play around Mutirikwi. Water and its related resources have different political efficacies in varying contexts, not just because of changing material properties, but because of the fraught, mutually constitutive nature of subjects and objects, substance and society, matter and meaning (cf. Miller 2005; Moore 2005:4). If the possibility for alterity/difference, for different regimes of meaning and rule – and therefore also their contestation – exists less in rarefied cultural, epistemological or ontological realms and more in the excessive potentiality of stuff to be (re)constituted in different ways (Filippucci et al. 2012; Pinney 2005), then this potentiality is not enlivened or realised in and of itself so much as in relation to particular historically, politically and socially inflected contexts and subjectivities. In this chapter I suggest it is dangerous encounters with *njuzu*, hippos and crocodiles, threatening fishermen and farmers that best illustrate the complexity of sovereignties, legitimacies and subjectivities involved in water's role as an index of power across co-existent, entangled regimes of rule and meaning. The ambivalent significance of hippos in particular – as

---

[3] Like land, Zimbabwe's water reforms have been the subject of much literature (Ferguson & Derman 1999; Derman & Ferguson 2003; Manzungu & Kujinga 2002; Manzungu 2003, 2004b; Derman & Manzungu 2012; Latham 2002; Musemwa 2008).

[4] ZINWA was established in the late 1990s, replacing Rhodesian-era water courts. Although reforms were built around the 'user pays' principle, they also instituted stakeholder participation through catchment councils. Land reform meant many ZINWA reforms were not adequately implemented. In the mid-2000s, for political reasons, urban water was placed under ZINWA (Musemwa 2008, 2006; Mapira 2011). National Parks too suffered ZANU PF interference, from the redistribution of high-value hunting licenses and game conservancies to rumoured involvement in poaching syndicates ('Conservancy slams "criminal" handover of hunting permits to ZPF' *SW Radio* 13/08/12; 'Zanu PF linked to Zim poaching syndicate' *SW Radio*, 04/05/11; 'Wildlife land reform enacted' *Zimbabwean*, 11/03/11; 'ZANU minister clash over Save' *Zimbabwean*, 17/10/12; 'Save invasions threaten US$30m safari business' *Standard*, 02/09/12.

materialisations of *njuzu* for some, as totemic taboos for others, or as protected but hugely destructive wildlife – points to the indeterminacies of meaning and rule in complex, emergent assemblages of people, spirits, animals, things, water and landscape. As dangerous protected wildlife, hippos manifest the primacy of National Parks rule around the lake, yet as manifestations of *njuzu* they exist at the very margins of its registers of meaning, demonstrating the limits of its rule. Similarly, the presence of *njuzu* in dams and irrigation schemes illustrates how 'water in its multiple African forms, practices and meanings not only pre-exists but co-exists with "high-modernist" schemes' (Ranger cited in Fontein 2008:740; Bender 2008).

NATIONAL PARKS, POACHING AND THE KYLE GAME RESERVE

Around the same time as the boy drowned in the Mutirikwi River at Mazare, (discussed in the previous chapter) – linking anxieties about *njuzu*, drought and displeased ancestors with questions about Chief Chikwanda's legitimacy – south of the lake another drowning had taken place. On 28 October 2005, a local newspaper reported that a man suspected of illegal fishing had drowned in the lake after being chased by National Parks rangers.[5] Many were deeply angered by this drowning, and suspected it had been deliberate. My friend and field assistant, Ernest Nzou told me that the man had been floating on an inner tube trying to get away, when rangers shot the tyre and he drowned. Ernest thought it was not an accident as reported, but a deliberate action by the National Parks guards in response to the recent death of another guard by a poacher.[6] Some weeks later Vincent Matende, a relative of the drowned man and resident of Oatlands irrigation scheme at Boroma, complained bitterly about National Parks who, in his view, had killed his *muzukuru* (father's sister's son). 'They fire live rounds at us with their guns. They even killed someone recently, at the Matende household of my *baba mukuru* (father's elder brother) in Chikwanda at Zano. He was my *muzukuru*, the son ... of my *vatete* (paternal aunt)', he explained.[7]

The killing of poachers in the name of wildlife conservation is not rare in southern and eastern Africa (cf. Duffy 2010, 2000; Brockington 2002). Despite the introduction of both private conservancies (Wolmer 2007) and community-led wildlife resource management,[8] since 'the 1980s, conservation practice has been progressively militarized' across the region (Duffy 2010:78). Although poaching is frequently said to have peaked in Zimbabwe in the 1980s, the land occupations, drought and political, economic and social turmoil of the 2000s resulted in, or coin-

[5] 'Poacher drowns in Dam', *Masvingo Mirror*, 28/10/05–03/11/05
[6] Fieldnotes 28/10/05 & 29/10/05.
[7] Vincent Matende 18/12/05.
[8] Such as the Communal Areas Management Programme for Indigenous Resources (CAMPFIRE), (Alexander & McGregor 2000; Hughes 2006c; Duffy 2000; Dzingirai 2003).

cided with, a dramatic increase in illegal hunting.[9] Zimbabwe's lowveld, especially around Chiredzi, the Save conservancy, the Great Limpopo Transfrontier Park (Spierenburg 2011; Wolmer 2003), were particularly badly affected.[10] Many private conservancies established in the 1990s (Wolmer 2007) have been occupied, resettled and subjected to deeply contested processes of 'indigenisation',[11] at the same time witnessing a resurgence in high-value wildlife poaching, shootings and increasing numbers of poachers killed by police and rangers.[12] Sometimes poachers have included members of the Zimbabwean army, and rumours frequently circulate about politically connected, international poaching syndicates trading wildlife products like ivory and rhino horn.[13]

The Kyle Game Reserve has long been targeted for high-value poaching because of the rhino kept there.[14] This was demonstrated again in

[9] 'Zimbabwe: nation warned over Rhino poaching', *SW Radio*, 04/01/13; 'Wildlife worth millions killed', *Zimbabwean*, 06/06/12; 'Poachers devise new tricks to evade detection', *Standard*, 28/08/11; 'Zimbabwe arrests 10 for Rhino, elephant poaching', *Mail & Guardian*, 22/07/11; 'Farmers encroach on wildlife', *Timeslive*, 31/07/11; 'Hunting of black Rhinos on farms on the increase', *Zimbabwean*, 04/07/11; 'Transfrontier conservancy hit by rampant poaching', *SW Radio*, 11/07/11; 'Chinese poison elephants', *Newsday*, 15/07/11; 'Former CAMPFIRE director blames rampant poaching on land reform', *Standard*, 01/05/11; 'Upsurge in Rhino poaching in Zimbabwe', *Science Daily*, 07/01/08; '241 poachers arrested countrywide in March', *Herald*, 10/04/06; 'We can't put a policeman behind every animal', *Financial Times Weekend Supplement*, 02–03/08/03; 'Daring poachers wreak havoc', *Herald*, 20/07/12.

[10] 'Zimbabwe is dropped from game park plan', *Telegraph*, 11/12/02.

[11] 'Mudenge fingered in conservancy destruction', *New Zimbabwe*, 04/04/12; 'ZANU ministers clash over SAVE', *Zimbabwean*, 17/10/12; 'Chiefs want conservancy seizure reversed', *New Zimbabwe*, 03/09/12; 'Save invasions threaten US$30 million safari business', *Standard*, 02/09/12; 'ZANU PF factions take Save conservancy dispute to courts', *VOA Zimbabwe*, 31/08/12; 'Endangered wildlife under threat as hunting is 'indigenised', *SW Radio*, 10/08/12; 'Indigenisation of conservancies starts', *Herald*, 10/08/12.

[12] 'Two armed poachers killed in Mkanga safari area', 26/02/12 www.zimparks.org/index.php?option=com_content&view=article&id=139&Itemid=29, accessed 24/06/13; 'Cop shot in encounter with suspected poachers', *Daily News*, 14/05/10; 'Four poachers die in shootout', *Herald*, 10/06/09; 'Poacher shot dead in Binga Blitz', *New Zimbabwe*, 28/05/12; 'Chinoyi teenager jailed for killing poacher', *Daily Mirror*, 02/03/06.

[13] 'ZANU PF linked to Zim poaching syndicate', *SW Radio*, 04/05/11; 'CIO chief among ZANU PF officials linked to illegal hunting in Zim', *SW Radio*, 17/10/12; 'Four poachers die in shootout', *Herald*, 10/06/09; 'Soldiers involved in poaching', *Zimbabwean*, 29/09/07; 'Poaching blamed on Zim soldiers', *News24*, 11/02/10; 'Zimbabwe arrests 10 for rhino, elephant poaching', *Mail & Guardian*, 22/07/11.

[14] White rhino were first moved there in 1962 from Natal. By 1966 they numbered 30. Many other species (zebra, giraffe, ostriche, kudu, eland, buffalo and wildebeest, and twenty breeds of fish) were introduced in the 1960s and 70s. Poaching began almost immediately. In 1964, 'a large number of snares ... capable of killing rhino' were discovered. 'Frequent patrols were carried out on horseback, by boat, by land rover and on foot'. By 1996 these measures had reduced poaching 'although the reserve remained vulnerable to poachers' with 'access from the lake' (Annual reports, Kyle Game Park Files).

2009 by the fatal shooting of an ex-army officer found dehorning a dead rhino in the park.[15] A year later two more rhino were killed, and a gang of eight poachers later arrested.[16] Yet this kind of high-value poaching is comparatively rare. Subsistence poaching, illegal grazing, grass collection and fence cutting are far more common everyday concerns. In 2005, Mr Nyathi, senior warden at Kyle, admitted that amidst the numerous problems fast-track around Mutirikwi had caused for National Parks – new farmers encroaching on the game reserve to the north, and land occupiers building homesteads, cutting fields and stealing fences on its southern shores – illegal subsistence fishing/poaching was one of their biggest concerns.[17] What the killing of Vincent Matende's *muzukuru* in 2005 demonstrated was that little difference is necessarily made between local subsistence fishing, and the high-value poaching for the international market. In either case, National Parks claim absolute authority and sovereignty over wildlife resources in/around Mutirikwi, and have the capacity to demonstrate this through the use of extreme, even lethal, violence. As Matopos Murinye exclaimed: 'if we go fishing we risk being beaten by National Parks for poaching'.[18] Similarly, VaMakasva explained, 'if you want to live with the National Parks people, then don't hunt. Its like my dogs, they always stay here to guard my house ... and at my field to guard them at night when wild pigs come ... If National Parks see dogs in the bush, they will shoot them ... if I need to go to the bush then I don't go with dogs'.[19]

The extent to which National Parks can exercise their authority over wildlife far more severely and absolutely than other local and para-statal arms of government around Mutirikwi, was further revealed by Makasva's lament that they could not hunt the wild buck which emerged as they cooked beer for his *bira* near Mt Beza that year; a sign that for him indicated ancestral approval for his preparations. 'If there wasn't a game reserve over there, we would have killed that animal, but we didn't because they would arrest us' he explained.[20] Unlike war veterans, new farmers, National Museums and Monuments of Zimbabwe (NMMZ), the council, Agricultural Extension Service (AREX), and even sometimes local administrators, National Parks rarely has to yield to ancestral regimes of rule over landscape. When I asked Mr Nyathi about the relationship between the 'traditional conservation' of sacred places, and National Parks, he explained that 'there is a big difference': 'For a tree to be sacred, certain individuals have to declare that it is sacred, but at Na-

---

[15] 'Six Soldiers Shot Dead in Zimbabwe', *RadioVOP*, 08/06/09, accessed 05/10/14. 'Poacher killed in Masvingo', *GreatZimbabweNews*, 26/04/09.

[16] '8 suspected poachers in court', *Herald*, 13/10/10.

[17] Mr Nyathi 25/11/05. 'Lake Mutirikwi invaded', *Standard*, 16/11/06. Problems with subsistence fishing began soon after the lake was established. In 1967 'illegal fishing' was 'rife' and during the year 'nine Africans were arrested for fishing offences and ... sentenced ... to a fine of 5s each', but this did 'nothing to deter Africans from illegal fishing' (Annual reports, Kyle Game Park files).

[18] Matopos Murinye/Acting Chief Murinye 13/06/06.

[19] VaMakasva 14/01/06.

[20] Ibid.

tional Parks we don't have to be told by anyone ... to protect animals and other natural resources. It's the law, we have an act of parliament. Museums, who have ... the task of protecting sacred places ... cannot preserve a hill or a tree or other sacred place unless people who know its history are pushing for it. They need a community to say that is our sacred rock, tree or whatever. We do not need that. We know what we have to do. We do not preserve sacred places'.[21]

In many respects, for National Parks locals are 'cast as abusers of fish and ecology', revealing a long legacy of preference for wildlife over people that derives from older, white Rhodesian efforts to 'escape African people' and 'belong ecologically in Africa' (Hughes 2010: 6, 51–2). Rangers and wardens described the problems they faced from local communities, not only poaching and illegal fishing, or stealing wire, but also contraventions like collecting firewood, grass for thatching, or poles for building, or grazing cattle. One revealed what National Parks control over land defined as game reserve usually amounted to: 'If we see people in the park we arrest them and charge them with illegally entering a game park. If we suspect them of hunting we charge them with illegal hunting, or hunting without a licence, or fishing without a license; even a person who is ... just walking in the park without a valid reason.'[22] National Parks' capacity to demonstrate its authority and sovereignty over wildlife is echoed across the region, where increasing recognition that community resource management is much harder to achieve than its rhetoric implies, has meant that the kind of 'fortress conservation' marking wildlife management in the 1980s has often been revived (Duffy 2000, 2008, 2010; Brockington 2002). For the most part, African wildlife conservation remains outside of or exceptional to normal processes of law and bureaucratic regimes. In Zimbabwe, National Parks' paramilitary role has been strengthened in recent years despite the profound upheavals to structures of authority over other natural resources, such as land.

Mbembe (2003) has argued that killing is the ultimate performance of sovereignty, reversing – as Bernault (2010:372) notes – Foucault's principle of bio-power as that to 'make live and let die'. 'The ultimate expression of sovereignty resides, to a large degree, in the power and the capacity to dictate who may live and who must die' (Mbembe 2003:11). He builds on Agamben's notions (1998) of '*Homo Sacer*' and 'the state of exception' (2005), which highlights those spaces or moments outside of the normal functioning of the law and governmentalism, where people are reduced to 'bare life' and subjected to extra-judicial coercion and violence. Resonating with Turner (1969) and van Gennep's (1960) identification of liminal 'anti-structure' and 'communitas' in ritual as vital moments for the re-affirmation of symbolic order and structures of society, these spaces/moments of 'exception' are conceptualised as the essential 'outside', re-affirming normal mechanisms of judicial and governmental rule. In other words, legitimate, productive mechanisms

[21] Fieldnotes 25/11/05.
[22] Naphtal Ndube 25/11/05.

of power and normative regimes of rule necessarily rely on those exceptional moments/spaces where questions of judicial legitimacy are put aside in favour of coercive and repressive power; where rule is reduced to performances of sovereign power and subjects to 'bare life'.

We can see how this logic might be applied to the killing of wildlife poachers. Other examples from Zimbabwe include the election violence of 2008 (Sachikonye 2011), the extra-judicial killings of Chiadzwa's informal diamond miners, *Operation Murambatsvina* in 2005 (Potts 2006; Vambe 2008), or police refusal to investigate 'political crimes' during the *jambanja* of 2000/01.[23] But such spaces/moments of exception are usually not indefinite, and rarely exist entirely outside of more productive, bureaucratic, governmental regimes of rule. Violent assertions of sovereignty are never entirely uncontested, and rarely simply demonstrations of might and capacity. Just as a 'reassertion of technocracy' followed the *jambanja* of the land invasions (Chaumba et al. 2003a), and *Operation Murambatsvina's* 'tsunami' did not entirely ignore older aspirations to urban order (Fontein 2009a), so National Parks' sovereignty over wildlife, game reserves and Mutirikwi's waters is not entirely unfettered. Sometimes game wardens are held accountable for the killing of poachers.[24] Those I spoke to emphasised they *arrest* suspected poachers, even if patrols are routinely armed. Similarly, police investigations following the drowning in October 2005 indicate that, whatever their outcome, even National Parks must respond to someone.[25] Aside from rumours of political interference, corruption and of game commandeered to feed ZANU PF conferences,[26] around Mutirikwi the acknowledgement by rangers that they must allow VaZarira and others to sweep Basotho graves in the game reserve (Mujere 2012), or do the sweeping themselves,[27] similarly suggests they are conscious of the limits of their rule, that there are dimensions to the management of land defined as game reserve which are beyond their capacity.

---

[23] See Human Rights Watch reports (all accessed 25/06/13): 2003 'Under a Shadow: Civil and Political Rights in Zimbabwe', www.hrw.org/legacy/ backgrounder/africa/ zimbabwe060603.htm; 2005 '"Clear the Filth" Mass Evictions and Demolitions in Zimbabwe', www.hrw.org/sites/default/files/ reports/zimbabwe0905.pdf; 2008 '"Bullets for Each of You" State-Sponsored Violence since Zimbabwe's March 29 Elections', www.hrw.org/sites/ default/ files/reports/zimbabwe0608.pdf; 2009 'Diamonds in the Rough: Human Rights Abuses in the Marange Diamond Fields of Zimbabwe', www.hrw.org/sites/ default/files/reports /zimbabwe0609web.pdf; 2011 'Perpetual Fear: Impunity and Cycles of Violence in Zimbabwe', www.hrw.org/sites/default/files/reports/ zimbabwe0311NoPage8Full.pdf.

[24] 'Chinoyi teenager jailed for killing poacher', *Daily Mirror*, 02/03/06.

[25] 'Poacher drowns in Dam', *Masvingo Mirror*, 28/10/05–03/11/05. It is not clear what the outcome of these investigations was.

[26] Fieldnotes 09/01/05; 'Zanu PF linked to Zim poaching syndicate', *SW Radio*, 04/05/11; 'CIO chief among ZANU PF officials linked to illegal hunting in Zim', *SW Radio*, 17/10/12.

[27] Fieldnotes 25/11/05.

FISHING MUTIRIKWI

Although National Parks does use its paramilitary capacity to demonstrate sovereignty over wildlife resources in and around Mutirikwi, they also do so in ways more responsive to popular demands, and more governmental in style. Fishing on Mutirikwi began almost as soon as the dam was built. Outside of subsistence fishing – normally defined as 'poaching' and therefore subject to heavy-handed control – recreational and commercial fishing has long been regulated through two separate regimes.[28] These define how, when, where and by whom fish can be legitimately caught, mapping (albeit imperfectly) onto two distinct user groups: African small-scale, commercial fishermen based at the co-operative at Zano, east of the lake; and recreational fishermen who are mainly (but not exclusively) white,[29] and include both local residents and returning tourists from South Africa and beyond.

As a place of recreation, and for generating tourist income, the opportunities of fishing, boating and sailing on the lake obviously added value to the game reserve alongside it. It also coalesced with 'Euro-Africans' aesthetic need for wilderness, shorelines and watery landscapes (Hughes 2010; Wolmer 2007), buttressing the 'beautiful'[30] dam's significance for white Rhodesian assertions of belonging. When the dam was completed Rhodesians, and Victoria residents in particular, embraced fishing on the lake, and for many it remains 'the greatest bass challenge in the country'.[31] But if recreational fishing with rod and line was encouraged as part of the dam's second *raison d'etre*, then local commercial fishing using nets, by African co-operatives and small businesses in communal areas east of the lake too has long been permitted, albeit

---

[28] Both began a few years after the dam. After it was declared a national park in 1967, 'commercial fishing by Africans under permit' was allowed and by 1971 'fishing in waters off the Mtilikwe Tribal Trust Lands' remained 'under close supervision', amid continuing problems with poaching. 'Local [white] public who [had] enjoyed free boating and fishing' too now required permits and fishing licences, and registered boats had reached 200. The following year a ferry service began, and competitors from Malawi and South Africa took part in an international bass tournament (Annual reports, Kyle Game Park files).

[29] I asked Errol and Daryl Edwards about Kyle Boat Club membership, and whether it was 'mainly a white Rhodesian thing': 'In the past, yes, but, membership has been open to all since before independence. The water bailiff and the head of National Parks are both honorary members ... and we want the club to be representative', but 'still today there are very few black Zimbabwean members ... there are more black Zimbabweans owning boats to go fishing. Much less for sailing and water ski-ing' (25/05/06).

[30] As Errol Edwards put it: 'Kyle has an amazing beauty, [which] means that even if we go out and catch no fish, that's no problem because there is a peace there. It has a tranquillity, we can enjoy the nature side of it ... Going onto the lake is therapeutic ... Many of our members do not own boats. They just come to sit at the boat club ... for solitude, peace and quiet' (Edwards 25/05/06).

[31] Edwards 25/05/06.

closely regulated.[32] For National Parks, allowing locals access to fishing, particularly those at Zano displaced by the dam, was a way of ensuring local legitimacy, but they may also have other motives. Zano's fishing co-op was established in the mid-1970s by its vice-chairman VaChigohwe. As he explained:

> In 1965 I started working with National Parks and worked with them for ten years, there at Chinango, at the Kyle Game Park. Mr Norris, a white man and the ecologist there, sent me to start this co-operative because he wanted to find out more about how the fish moved … So they [used to] put rings on bass fish there at Mushagashe [river] and this side, where the Mutirikwi [river] flows into the lake. The co-op started because Mr Norris wanted to know how the fished moved in the water, and the idea of having a fishing co-operative was [to offer] some benefit for local communities.[33]

This illustrates how National Parks regulation of fishing attempts to fulfil pastoral and responsive dimensions of rule even as it draws subjects into disciplining, governmental systems producing and monitoring knowledge about natural resources under its control. VaChigohwe explained how they still record catches and complete monthly returns, contributing to the volumes of wildlife and fishery surveys archived at National Parks offices, dating back to the 1960s. Aside from these knowledge-producing practices, how the co-op does its fishing is also determined by National Parks rules: fishing at night 'because they want to know how the fish move', and measures to preserve fish stocks, such as prescribed net sizes and prohibitions on fishing in breeding areas. In some ways the co-op is much more closely regulated than recreational fishing. It is therefore not surprising that members complained bitterly about local 'poachers' purchasing recreational fishing permits and then using nets (or spear guns), thereby catching far larger hauls and avoiding not only the co-op's licence payments, but also its financial commitments (maintaining boats, and so on) and the 10 per cent levy and VAT charged on sales.[34]

In 2006 VaChigohwe worried, like Kariba's commercial fishermen,[35] that the rising costs of licences and taxes, and competition from illegal fishing, might force the co-operative's closure. Another commercial fishing outfit that once operated from the Mutirikwi lakeside lodges had closed due to similar concerns.[36] For VaChigohwe the difficulties of the mid-2000s were a far cry from 1975, when 'there was no VAT, no levy and the taxes were much less; in those days we could live off fishing alone'.[37] This echoed Errol Edwards, commodore of the Kyle Boat Club

---

[32] Matopos Murinye ran his father's fishing business in the 1960s and 1970s until it collapsed because his father 'spent all the money acquiring new wives' (Acting Chief Murinye 24/04/06).

[33] VaChigohwe 10/05/06.

[34] Ibid.

[35] 'Fishing tariffs go up by 2000%', Daily Mirror, 22/02/06; 'New $750 kapenta fishing permit fee too high', *Sunday Mail*, 30/40/06–06/05/06.

[36] Edwards 25/05/06; also Masunga et al. (2004).

[37] VaChigohwe 10/5/06.

(from where much recreational fishing takes place), who lamented the collapse of Mutirikwi's once vibrant tourism due to Zimbabwe's economic and political crises, stressing that 'the whole community needs tourists to come back' to its 'magnificent facilities'.[38] In this context, neither recreational anglers nor co-operative members were particularly critical of each other. Both saved their grievances for poachers who refused to play by the rules, threatening the lake with over-fishing, using spear guns or nets without licences, and fishing in prohibited areas.[39] In 2005/06 both seemed equally frustrated by the effects of wider economic and political problems; not just increases in illegal fishing, but also declining fish stocks, the spreading water hyacinth weed, and pollution.[40] This complimented deepening disaffection with huge increases in fishing permits, launching and license fees, which affected both commercial and recreational fishing,[41] and was exacerbated by a sense that National Parks was no longer successful managing or restocking the lake's fisheries.[42]

Despite their very different orientations towards (and methods of) fishing – particularly the livelihood imperatives of Zano's co-operative compared to the less urgent needs of recreational anglers[43] – both described fishing on the lake in remarkably similar terms. For both, finding fish involved detailed knowledge of the lake's waters, its bays, shorelines and inlets, its seasonal changes, and especially the nature of the land and soils under its surface. Many talked about rotting trees under the water (predominantly soft wood, unlike at Kariba)[44] as a valuable food source for fish, determining at different times of year and according to water

---

[38] Edwards 25/05/06. See 'A poignant reminder of President Mugabe's warped economic policies in Masvingo', *Standard*, 20/08/02; 'CIO invade holiday resorts', Standard, 26/09/04; 'Masvingo fails to fully exploit vast tourism potential', *Herald*, 14/07/06.

[39] Edwards 25/05/06.

[40] 'PA not being honest on Lake Mutirikwi disaster', *Standard*, 07/01/07; 'Raw sewage poses pollution threat to Lake Mutirikwi', *Standard*, 20/03/11; 'Water authority sues Masvingo council', *Daily News*, 02/05/03; 'Masvingo faces heavy pollution fine', *Standard*, 18/01/03; 'Severe pollution threatens Zimbabwe's largest reservoir', *Standard*, 05/01/03; 'Water hyacinth problem creating controversy in Zimbabwean lakes; weevils, toxic chemicals or inaction?' *Daily News*, 12/09/02.

[41] 'Fishing tariffs go up by 2000%', *Daily Mirror*, 22/2/06; 'New $750 kapenta fishing permit fee too high', *Sunday Mail*, 30/04/06–06/05/06.

[42] 'A poignant reminder of President Mugabe's warped economic policies in Masvingo', *Standard*, 20/08/02. As Daryl Edwards put it: 'Yes they [National Parks] are heavy handed, we do have some problems with them. Like we have to pay a launching fee, but where we launch from is our land, so why should we pay? ... And the fees have risen so much ... what do National Parks do with all that money? There is no restocking' (25/05/06).

[43] In 2005/06 this difference was eroded by the difficult economic context. Daryl Edwards explained that 'fishing now costs about 1 million [Zimbabwe dollars] a day! It means you throw less back ... you are going take whatever you can get.' (25/05/06).

[44] Ibid; also 'Boat trip with Brandon Edwards', Fieldnotes 22/06/06.

levels, where fish might be caught.[45] It was also agreed that some sewage pollution from Masvingo town, although exacerbating water hyacinth problems, could benefit fish stocks in what Edwards described as 'quite a sterile lake' with 'not too many nutrients' due to its 'catchment over sand veld'.[46] Zano's co-op secretary agreed 'sewage might even increase the fish in the lake'.[47] Shared experiences on the lake do, to some extent, produce shared knowledge.

But there are also important differences. Recreational fishermen often have better equipment, such as powerboats and depth finders, while co-operative fishermen rely upon rowing boats and nets, requiring far more labour. Different technologies mean different practices, knowledge and experiences, despite shared understandings of the lake's geography and where best to find fish. Similarly, although everyone on the lake faces its peculiar hazards – encounters with crocodiles and hippos, and the sudden winds creating swells over a metre high[48] – these threaten co-op rowing boats much more than recreational powerboats; not to mention local poachers who sometimes wade up to their necks to catch fish. I often heard stories of dangerous encounters between (legal and illegal) fishermen, hippos and crocodiles.[49] VaChigohwe told me how a co-operative fisherman, VaJeriman, was attacked by a hippo in the late 1970s: 'The boat capsized and he fell in and drowned. Someone else with him managed to get back to the boat, but Jeriman died. They finally got the body back after four days. He is buried just over there.'[50] So, even as fishing is of far more livelihood significance for them, co-operative fishermen (and poachers) also appear much more vulnerable to Mutirikwi's dangers. Importantly, these include not only its hippos and crocodiles, but also *njuzu*. As VaChigohwe explained:

---

[45] At Kariba too 'anglers valued the submerged remains of huts and granaries' which 'provided ideal habitat for certain sport fish' (Hughes 2010:53).

[46] Edwards 25/05/06.

[47] Fieldnotes 10/05/06.

[48] Fieldnotes 22/06/06. From the early 1960s National Parks ran a 'rescue service' and in 1967 'staff rescued seven people from boats which had got into difficulties' (Annual reports, Kyle Game Park files). In the mid-1970s, the ferry sank during a sudden storm (Edwards 25/05/06). In December 2000 seven South Africans 'went missing for two days ... while cruising on Lake Mutirikwi' (*Daily News*, 28/12/00), after refilling their boat with contaminated black market fuel. During two days adrift they endured a heavy storm, a fire, and were eventually stranded on an island until rescued by National Parks.

[49] Matopos Murinye recalled being attacked by a hippo when he ran his father's fishing business (24/04/06). In Nemanwa, a well-known story recounts how a local ZANU PF chairman was bitten by a 'small' crocodile [*kangwena*], when he waded into the lake to fish. More recently a suspected poacher was killed by a hippo in Triangle ('Masvingo man killed in Hippo attack', *NewsdzeZimbabwe*, 27/02/13). Such dangers recur at Zimbabwe's other lakes (cf. McGregor 2009:6). After Leonard Tichareva survived a crocodile attack at Lake Chivero, National Parks confirmed that eight other fishermen had been eaten by crocodiles 'in recent weeks' ('Lucky to be alive', *Newsday*, 03/02/10).

[50] VaChigohwe 10/05/06.

> *Njuzu* trouble some people. It's like some people have something in their bodies, which acts like a magnet for *njuzu* ... So let's say somebody comes to work in the co-op. When we go out fishing, some go one way and others fish somewhere else. When we have finished we come back and tell the others what has happened. If someone has had problems with hippos or crocodiles, that is when we learn that that person maybe has that something which attracts *njuzu*, that they have that magnet ... If a person has that happen to them, and they think it's because of an *njuzu*, they can decide to stop. Some won't even go into a boat at all![51]

Crocodiles and hippos 'biting chunks out of boats' are a hazard also faced by recreational anglers (and National Parks staff),[52] but such encounters were rarely, if ever, associated with *njuzu*, despite Brandon Edwards' comment that he must 'have a thing with crocodiles' because he frequently came across them.[53] Nor were such encounters often put down to witchcraft, as with Kariba's Tonga fishermen (McGregor 2008:871). This indicates the different 'semiotic ideologies' (Keane 2003:419) at play. Although not unheard of, co-op fishermen and local subsistence poachers rarely linked crocodile and hippo encounters to witchcraft.[54] Much more prevalent were references to *njuzu*. This reflects the continuing efficacy of autochthonous landscape knowledge, but also relates to specific totemic taboos shared by the Duma clans around Mutirikwi.[55] When I expressed curiosity about eating hippo meat, Matopos Murinye's disgust was visceral. He explained why: 'because of my totem I am not allowed to eat hippo or crocodile':

> There is an old mad man in Murinye, of the *Moyo muDuma* totem. One day he came across a shot hippo and took some of the meat home. His wife told him he shouldn't be eating that but he said it doesn't matter and began to cook the meat. While cooking, he lifted the pot's lid and the smell of the meat went into his nostrils, and he became very sick. He was sick for a long time, maybe six months. No one knew why because the man had become mad and wasn't able to explain, until they went to a *n'anga* [traditional healer] who explained what happened. He eventually got better but is still not entirely right in his mind. There was another case of young boy who came across a shot hippo and cut some meat and took it home. Before eating it he became very sick with a swollen head. They rushed him to hospital and he later died. Yes, we have to take our *mutupo* [totem] very seriously; otherwise there might be serious consequences.[56]

Entangled with such divergent semiotic ideologies are diverse historical relationships with landscape, reflecting different pasts and different persisting regimes of rule. Co-op fishermen, poachers from communal areas and resettled farms, and recreational anglers from across Zimba-

[51] Ibid.
[52] In December 1971 there was an accident between a hippo and a car on Mtilikwi bridge. Later 'an attempt to move a hippo herd from Bompst bay using thunder flashes was successful, but they returned the next day' (24/12/71). Scouts also faced ostrich attacks (July 1968) and in 1973 'rhino number 19 took to chasing scouts on patrols' (Aug 1973, Annual reports Kyle Game Park Files).
[53] Fieldnotes 22/06/06.
[54] Aschwanden argues crocodiles are 'the animal of the witch', 'symbolising evil', in Karanga mythology (1989:190–1).
[55] 'We don't eat hippo because of our *mutupo*' (E. Mandebvu 15/03/06).
[56] Fieldnotes 24/04/06.

bwe and beyond, have different geographical, historical, cultural and social orientations and reference points in, on and around the lake. This is most obviously reflected in how past land divisions are manifest in the launching sites used by different fishermen. During the 1960s and 1970s, African fishing was restricted to areas adjacent to the Mtilikwe Tribal Trust Lands (TTLs), and Zano's co-operative continues to launch their boats from that area. The Kyle Boat Club, on the other hand, owns its launch site south of the lake. With the exception of its eastern shores, when the national park was declared in 1967 most of Mutirikwi remained 'in the category of European land'.[57] These different, co-existent, over-lapping historical landscapes are materialised in the ruins of inundated structures visible around the lake's shorelines, or on hilltops jutting as islands from its surface. During our boat trip Brandon Edwards pointed out where relatives and people he knew lived around the lake, and other spots with particular significance for him. He showed us the remains of chalets at Sikato bay flooded in the 1970s when the dam's waters rose higher than expected, and much older African stone ruins visible on the lake's rocky islands.[58] But he made no reference to the graves of people removed from Chinango and Nyangani when the dam was built, which remain under Mutirikwi's waters or on its hilltop islands, and are still a pre-occupation for many at Zano. Neither did he mention the hills and islands that some say contain a *nhare* (cave) used as a guerrilla base during the war,[59] or the flooded sacred sites where VaChigohwe claimed those '*njuzu* are now found'.[60] So, although Mutirikwi's co-operative and recreational fishermen faced similar 'assemblages of human and non-hu-man adversaries' (McGregor 2008:868) in 2005/06 – the macro-economic crises, National Parks' increasing regulatory demands, and the lake's physical and wildlife hazards – the efficacy and particularity of these di-verse assemblages is also partly determined by differing historical, social and political relations with each other, the landscape and the different regimes over it. Subsistence poachers too are uniquely situated within such assemblages and for them National Parks appear like particularly coercive and hostile adversaries.

Yet in 2005/06 by far the greatest number of people fishing on the lake probably did so without permits – outside of National Parks rule. I often saw them on my drives around the lake, running to hide at the sound of passing vehicles. Macro political and economic strife, and dramatic shortages in cash and fuel, meant few South African tourists were coming to fish Mutirikwi's waters. Massive price hikes in licence fees, and the prohibitive cost of transport and taxes made co-operative fishing ventures much less viable. Indeed the Zano co-op was very small, and the only one in operation around the lake. At the same time, drought,

[57] Annual report 1967, Kyle Game Park files.
[58] These were regularly reported by National Parks. For example, in January 1974 an 'ancient settlement was found' on 'Vutami East Kopjie' adjacent to the TTL (Kyle Game Park files).
[59] Fieldnotes 23/03/06.
[60] Fieldnotes 10/05/06.

unemployment and shortages of meat and relish made illegal fishing an attractive source of subsistence for local communities. Given the threatening presence of highly organised, armed poaching syndicates, it is not surprising that National Parks are heavy handed with poachers. It is equally unsurprising that many locals were deeply disturbed that subsistence fishing provoked similarly robust and sometimes violent responses. In the fast-track context, complaints against National Parks were often expressed through assertions of entitlement, particularly by those claiming ancestral ties to land around, or inundated by the lake. As Jairos Haruzvivishe, a *sabhuku* under Chief Mugabe occupying state land on Mutirikwi's southern shores, put it: 'on this issue of poaching, the people here ... the dam is in their area but they cannot get anything from it. Can we really be in need of fish, when there is a dam just there?' 'At Zano, people ... fish without paying,' he continued, 'it would be better if people could fish for free here too'.[61] Such sentiments were shared widely. Vincent Matende (whose *muzukuru* drowned in October 2005) complained 'we are not benefiting anything from this dam. If we go fishing we get chased away. We benefit nothing from a dam built over our ancestors' graves. At that time they just told us to leave ... It would have been better if there had been laws ... so that our children and our children's children would have something.'[62]

Such claims are different to contests over Chishanga's rivers (Mazarire 2008), because it is not the ownership of the lake's waters that is at stake, rather that ancestral ownership of land under and around it should allow access to its watery wildlife resources. Such claims, like illegal fishing and wildlife poaching, are a challenge to National Parks' sovereignty over the lake and its wildlife. Perhaps this further explains their sometimes heavy-handed response to illegal local fishing. Certainly National Parks are aware of how such ancestral assertions feed into local subsistence poaching. As the senior warden Mr Nyathi explained:

> Yes we have problems with local communities. There is a conflict of interest. They want to harvest fish in the lake. They say 'who was here first, the dam or ourselves?' They tell us 'you only say these fish are yours but you cannot prove it!' Most of these problems are from Chikwanda country in Zano, where the communal lands are ... not everywhere around the lake. On the northern side there are new A2 settlers, and we have other problems there. On the south side, Chief Mugabe is troublesome because he is claiming GZ [Great Zimbabwe] as his, putting his people on the lakeshore because he wants to surround GZ ... to control the area. So the fishing problems are more to the south and over at Zano.[63]

Mr Nyathi is a former policeman from Matabeleland and this is important for what it says about National Parks. 'My role is to educate and provide a background of law enforcement. National Parks is a paramilitary organisation and a police background is one of the entry systems.' 'The other', he continued, 'is the natural resource management route,

---

[61] Sabhuku Manunure 27/11/05.
[62] Matende 18/12/05.
[63] VaNyathi 25/11/05.

through [the] Natural Resource Management College ... in Masvingo'.[64] If these two 'entry systems', and staff divisions between 'scientific' and 'operations' wardens,[65] say something about internal tensions between the demands of research and of enforcement, they also indicate how juxtaposed these entangled regimes can *appear* against local clans' ancestral claims and the autochthonous landscape knowledge they assert.

But most people are located differently *between* such diverse regimes of rule and registers of meaning. VaChigohwe, the co-op's vice-chairman, is a good example not just as a former National Parks employee, or someone closely involved in fishing and monitoring Mutirikwi's fish stocks, but in other ways too. Born in Mushawasha, his father was a member of the Charumbira clan who married a woman from Murinye. This means he can make no autochthonous claims around Zano, where he first arrived in 1975 when the co-op began, even if his maternal links did facilitate this move, particularly because at that time the area was under Chief Murinye.[66] His lack of paternal, ancestral links to lands and graves around Zano means he cannot organise rituals to appease *njuzu* associated with sacred places inundated by the lake. He explained: 'I am not from here, but people who are, have the things they do, things of *chivanhu* [culture/tradition], but not us, we don't do those things'.[67] Yet, granted land to farm in Zano in 1980, when the area returned to Chikwanda, he and other co-op members are still, like new farmers and war veterans on resettled farms, subject to the chief, his *sabhuku*, and their autochthonous landscape knowledge; even if, as Mr Nyathi acknowledged, 'the whole community' often seemed 'against that co-operative'.[68] While other fishermen, including some subsistence poachers, do claim autochthonous links to the land, and have recourse to ancestral rituals, VaChigohwe's distance from them is further amplified by his allegiance to the Member in Christ Church. 'We don't believe in *chivanhu*, we believe in Jesus Christ', he told me. 'Those things, even of *njuzu*, are things people long ago believed in, these days there is nothing like that.'[69] This contradicted his earlier comments about encounters between fishermen, hippos and *njuzu*, and contrasted with others' views – including ZINWA's water bailiff (stationed at the dam) and officials in the DA's office, among many others[70] – who often warned of the lake's *njuzu*. In a sense, VaChigohwe's ambivalence about *njuzu* captures perfectly his unique location between different regimes of rule and meaning,

---

[64] Ibid.

[65] Naphtal Ndube, National Parks, 25/11/05.

[66] When Zano was settled by people removed from the dam, it came under Chief Murinye. After independence, Zano and nearby resettlement areas were 'returned' to Chikwanda. Many people however continue to identify with Murinye.

[67] Fieldnotes 10/05/06.

[68] VaNyathi 25/11/05.

[69] Fieldnotes 10/05/06.

[70] VaChikami, Water Bailiff 06/11/05. See '"Mermaid" sightings in Zimbabwe spark debate over traditional beliefs', *VOA News*, 03/02/12.

overlapping, entangling and competing for space around Mutirikwi, even as his later dismissal of *njuzu* echoed one warden's view that 'that happened long ago, now life has changed'.[71]

SOVEREIGN HIPPOS

If such references to *njuzu* reveal how, despite National Parks' powerful grip on the lake, other registers of meaning, regimes of rule, and other pasts do co-exist unevenly with it, then encounters with hippos more readily materialise the play of both sovereignty and legitimacy *within* National Parks' rule over Mutirikwi's wildlife. In the sense that both *njuzu* and hippos really can kill, both reveal (as with the killing of poachers) how water, in its widest sense, can index the coercive and sovereign dimensions of power. But hippos register across different regimes of rule in ways that *njuzu* do not. If hippos are a serious hazard for fishermen, they are also a serious problem for people farming the lake's eastern shores, and on resettled farms to the north.[72] People removed from Nyangani to Zano when the dam was built often lament they have never been able to use their allocated fields, because hippos destroy their crops and attack people, as indeed happened in March 2006.[73] That same month *The Herald* reported 'rampaging hippopotamuses ... destroyed crops belonging to resettled and communal farmers near Mutirikwi' who 'accused the Parks and Wildlife Management Authority of not doing enough'.[74] This was the most consistent complaint of people in Zano, who did not refer to *njuzu* when discussing hippo problems in their fields, instead blaming National Parks for failing to build fences,[75] and 'demanding compensation for our destroyed crops'.[76] As Furerere Mashuro put it: 'The rains are good this year, everyone will harvest and there won't be hunger. But hippos are a problem. We have told National Parks about this and they promised that every time a hippo comes out of the water, they would kill it. This month they have already killed three'.[77]

[71] Naphtal Ndube 25/11/05.
[72] VaKurasva 17/04/06; L. Mandebvu 19/04/06; E. Mandebvu 15/03/06; Mai Coventry 01/11/05.
[73] 'Last week a son of Shindi was trampled by a hippo. He was hurt on his arms and legs. He saw hippos trying to get into the fields. He tried to chase them away but he didn't see a hippo with its baby behind him' (E. Mandebvu 15/03/06).
[74] 'Hippos destroy crops in Masvingo', *Herald*, 30/03/06. These problems echo those faced with elephants elsewhere ('Chief appeals to Parks to contain stray elephants', *Herald*, 10/04/12; 'Stray jumbos cause havoc in Kariba', *Daily Mirror*, 03/06/06; 'Elephants destroy fields in Mat North', *Daily Mirror*, 06/04/06).
[75] 'We keep asking them to put a fence to stop hippos coming into our fields ... Why do they let them come in here like cattle? National Parks should keep the animals way from us.' (E. Mandebvu 15/03/06).
[76] 'Hippos destroy crops in Masvingo', *Herald*, 30/03/06.
[77] Furere Mashuro 12/04/06.

Not only are hippos extremely dangerous they are also protected by National Parks' legislation. Hippos affect farmers along the Mutirikwi river, up and downstream of the dam, and there is a seasonality to such encounters which reflects fluctuating water levels. It is widely agreed that hippo numbers entering fields and destroying crops have increased greatly since the 1960s because of the lake and its game reserve.[78] Acknowledging 'hippos have a tendency to move upstream during [the] rains ... near areas where people live', Retired Major Mbewe of National Parks insisted that 'hippos are our national heritage like other wild animals and there is nothing which ties us to compensate crops ... destroyed by these animals'.[79] Despite such comments, however, dangerous hippo encounters do enable something of the more responsive dimensions of National Parks' rule to be revealed. This is most clearly demonstrated by the routine shooting of problem hippos. If killing is indeed the ultimate demonstration of sovereignty, then both the threats that hippos pose – regularly killing people – and the fact that only National Parks are permitted to kill them (and maybe only they are capable of doing this), is of huge significance. Yet the killing of problem hippos, and the local sale of their meat, is also a 'CAMPFIRE'-esque effort to promote local support for National Parks activities. In this respect, however, the totemic taboos against hippo (and crocodile) meat shared by the Duma clans dominating Mutirikwi's immediate milieu mean they cannot benefit from culled hippos, thereby further reinforcing how hippos index National Parks rule. In the past, Bhodo Mukuvare lamented it was spirit mediums who chased away problem hippos, 'not these youngsters of today'. When 'hippos used to come out and eat our crops ... the old Zarira ... would come ... the *mudzimu* [ancestral spirit] would come out [ie possess the medium] and start shouting and screaming and then we would know that ... the hippos would no longer eat our crops'.[80]

In a sense, therefore, hippos do materialise the primacy of National Parks' rule over the lake, manifesting both demonstrative acts of sovereignty and sometimes more responsive dimensions of its rule. However, that at the same time hippos are for some people sometimes indicative of dangerous *njuzu*, or protected by totemic taboo, illustrates the continuing efficacy of other, older regimes of rule, beyond the limits of National Parks' capacity and on the margins of its registers of meaning. The continuing presence of *njuzu* in the lake, and in the many smaller dams, rivers and streams feeding it, does a similar thing for other watery regimes of rule around it, particularly those to do with irrigation. These are the domain of a host of other institutions much more amenable to the myriad local concerns and registers in play around Mutirikwi, than the para-militarism of National Parks.

[78] Many locals were clear that the hippo problems they face are a result of the dam (L. Mandebvu, 19/04/06; E. Mandebvu 15/03/06).
[79] 'Hippos destroy crops in Masvingo', *Herald*, 30/03/06
[80] Bhodo Mukuvare 19/11/05.

IRRIGATION

In Zano, concerns about hippos were matched by disappointment about unfulfilled promises that people's removal to the area in the late 1950s would be eased by a local irrigation scheme. This resonated historically with the role promised irrigation played in the imagined futures of white residents of Victoria in the decades before the Mutirikwi dam was built, discussed later in this book. At an *ndari*[81] drinking party in Zano in May 2006, there was optimism about recently announced plans to develop a 'Zano irrigation scheme', particularly because it renewed hope that fencing would be provided to keep out hippos.[82] Later in 2006, Chief Chikwanda 'appealed to government to speedily set up irrigation infrastructure ... for villagers to benefit from Lake Mutirikwi', as it was 'painful that the sprawling Chikwanda communal lands has perennially been stalked by drought despite abundant water' in the lake.[83] Acting Chief Murinye too expressed desire for irrigation, stressing his area's proximity to the dam, both around Boroma and further downstream around Topora, adding that 'although we are very near to that dam, we actually benefit very little from it'.[84]

If such appeals for local irrigation were based not only on physical proximity to the dam but also on past, unfulfilled promises, then they also gained traction (as with fishing) in terms of ancestral land claims around the lake. Jairos Haruzvivishe explained he had 'not yet used any ZINWA water' on state lands he was occupying south of the lake, but 'we do have an issue because the dam was built in our area [yet] people are suffering from drought here. It would be better if ZINWA built us some tanks so we can have water and irrigation. Then we could do something about the hunger in this land'.[85] New and 'returning' farmers on former farms north of the lake also expressed desire for irrigation from the lake and the rivers flowing into it. Such desire for irrigation intertwined with hopes for improved livelihood opportunities empowered by land resettlement. VaMakasva, occupying land below Beza, on the Popoteke river, told me that:

> Irrigation is the type of farming I have been thinking about. That is why I was asking if you can find a donor who can give me an engine so I can pump water to irrigate my fields from the Popoteke river ... If I take water from there I will have to pay ZINWA, which is fine because I can pay for the water, but money for an engine [or pump] I don't have. If I do irrigation then I want to build a tank so I can pump water up there, then around the house. For this field I can use ground irrigation, but I will need to pump it to the big field over there.[86]

[81] These are events where millet beer is brewed and sold to raise cash, rather than in honour of the ancestors.
[82] Fieldnotes 24/05/06; also Provincial Administrator (PA) Felix Chikovo 24/05/06; District engineer Darlington Chenjerai 23/06/06. Also 'Politicians dupe gullible villagers', *Financial Gazette*, 16–22/03/06; 'RBZ avails $150million for irrigation scheme', *Herald*, 10/01/07.
[83] 'Chief appeals for irrigation development', *Herald*, 13/10/06.
[84] Matopos Murinye 13/06/06.
[85] Jairos Haruzvivishe 27/11/05.
[86] VaMakasva 14/01/06.

Mai Macharaga also planned to irrigate her fields on Eland's Kopje farm next to the Mutirikwi river, and her biggest impediment too was equipment.[87] Similarly for Mai Coventry, left farming just a small plot on Desmondale farm, the lack of a working pump limited her intentions to irrigate from the Makurumidzi river feeding into the northeast of the lake.[88]

This need for equipment and infrastructure illustrates the logistical and developmental limitations of the fast-track programme, as Masvingo's Chief Lands Officer acknowledged.[89] Resettled farmers' enthusiasm for irrigation also meant that proximity to water sources featured in the complex politics of land allocation and the 'looting' of 'abject' material this often involved.[90] Scoones et al. (2010:193–4) describe what happened at the 'Sanangwe A1 site', north of the lake, where 'invaders pegged plots on richer soils along the banks of the Mutirikwi river ... positioning their fields along the river ... [to] ... allow them to irrigate the land and get water for their homes'. Despite taking measures 'to avoid erosion, including bush fencing along the riverbank' and identifying watering spots for cattle, 'the settlers were soon shifted ... when re-pegging occurred, and the land-use planning criteria in use since the 1930s were invoked, moving the settlement and fields to the crest of the hill and leaving the low lying areas for grazing'. As a result 'the rich alluvial soils are under-used and they must farm on the dry and sandy top lands', which not only 'negatively affected the success of their resettlement', but also meant travelling 'a long distance back to the river to fetch water' whenever their single, unreliable borehole malfunctioned. To make matters worse, the 'richer riverine soils' from where they were removed were later re-allocated to others from elsewhere, who therefore harvested 'higher yields' than the first occupiers, 'generating much resentment' (2010:193–4). Such events illustrate how water, soil quality and the possibilities of irrigation, as well as older technocratic imperatives, informed where and how new farmers settled (and resettled) on occupied farms. This echoed historically with the way problems of water supply had animated the making and remaking of the reserves in the early 20th century

---

[87] Fieldnotes 25/03/06.

[88] Mai Coventry is the daughter of farm workers from Chinyango, where the lake is now, who worked on Bannockburn and Desmondale farms where she was born. In the 1980s she married the white farmer Vernon Coventry who died in 2003. After fast-track she kept a 50 hectare plot on Desmondale farm. With an old water right, in 2005/06 she intended to irrigate from the river until her diesel pump was stolen. She told me that in recent years they had experienced more problems with hippo, crocodiles and *njuzu* in the river (Mai Coventry 01/11/05).

[89] Joseph Munyani 05/06/06.

[90] See 'Police, war vets surrender loot' *Standard* 05/03/06. There was a high premium on a1 and a2 resettlement plots with access to water and more so for those with irrigation infrastructure. The prominent presence of civil servants and politicians on Sikato Farm's irrigated plots, a government project resettled in the late 1990s – is illustrative, mirroring the allocation of Rippling Waters estate, along Masvingo–Mutare road, to influential war veterans shortly before the same people organised land invasions across the district (Robby Mtetwa 29/06/06).

(Cleaver 1995). It also resonated powerfully with recurring disputes at earlier, post-independence irrigation schemes around Mutirikwi, such as Longdale and Oatlands, and elsewhere such as Mushandike, indicating how access to irrigated resettlement has long been contested in the district.[91]

Before the successful rains of 2005/6, demands for irrigation around Mutirikwi once again became acute after yet another drought. A year later there were signs such demands had been noticed within local, parastatal and central government structures. As with censorship of the weather forecast, official announcements about expanding irrigation indicate how such local demands could intersect with wider concerns about political legitimacy, especially in the context of recurring food shortages. Shortly after ascending to the vice-presidency, Joyce Mujuru embarked upon 'a programme of visiting rural areas to ... see how the government can ... improve their standard of living'. 'My priority' she claimed, 'is to make sure there is enough food for families in the countryside and that each and every one of our nationals live in peace. We want people to understand what the government is doing to better their lives'.[92] Water and irrigation featured prominently in publicity surrounding Mujuru's tour, and in her statements about government plans to assist agriculture, bolster land reform and restore food security. This resonated historically with Rhodesian enthusiasm after the Second World War for large-scale irrigation planning, which too had turned on issues of food security. In May, *The Herald* reported that 'to ensure food security at household level, government was ... developing and resuscitating irrigations schemes ... to exploit ... abundant water resources in dams dotted around the country'.[93] Visiting Siya Dam in Zaka, where 'government would set up an irrigation scheme ... [for] Nhema communal lands', Mujuru told *The Herald* that 'if we were using all our water resources fully' there would be enough food every year, allowing 'the government to repay ... loans instead of buying food'. Echoing demands for irrigation around Mutirikwi, Mujuru added that 'it was disheartening that water from Siya Dam was being used to irrigate sugarcane fields in the lowveld – about 150 kilometres away – yet villagers next to the dam were perennially plagued by food shortages owing to drought'.[94]

The proposed scheme at Siya (and another at Matezva dam) was part of a new provincial 'irrigation master plan' being discussed at the time. According to Felix Chikovo, the PA, irrigation had been prioritised in Masvingo's five year development strategy. Although the lowveld was 'a priority because it has certain advantages' – its fertile soils and the vast sugar industry already established there – Felix stressed that a new irrigation scheme at Zano was being planned. 'On the advice of His Excellency', he explained, a provincial irrigation committee had been tasked

[91] Matende 18/12/05; also 'Charumbira ordered headman's kidnap', *Financial Gazette*, 07/06/07;

[92] 'Mujuru assures nation of peace, enough food', *Herald*, 21/04/06.

[93] 'Utilise land to end unemployment', *Herald*, 18/05/06.

[94] Ibid.

to expand existing irrigation, rehabilitate 'defective schemes' and to address 'under-utilised water in all dams in the province', as well as to plan future irrigation from the incomplete Tokwe Mukorsi dam. In particular 'an accelerated irrigation development plan for the first block of 100 hectares' at Zano had been prioritised after 'His Excellency directed that water from the Mutirikwi dam be utilised immediately for the people'. This was already costed and only awaited the 'release of resources'.[95]

Given the dire economic situation and government's long failure to deliver its promises on dams and irrigation in the province these new plans met much scepticism.[96] A month after the *ndari* in Zano, Mukani Muzarira was much less convinced by the government's promise: 'of course they are talking about irrigation again, but we don't know if it will materialise'.[97] Nevertheless, renewed official calls for the productive use of Mutirikwi's water for local irrigation was part of wider efforts at the time to re-assert the government and ZANU PF's developmentalist credentials, in the context of deepening concerns about food insecurity. In this sense it was a parallel strategy to the promotion of national *biras*. Both concerned the legitimacy of government's land and agricultural policies, both circulated around water as an index of that legitimacy, and both gained traction around Mutirikwi because of rain's unpredictability.

But if meteorological uncertainty was the context in which both irrigation and national *biras* gained political traction, topography also informed the new irrigation plans, and the scepticism they provoked. Jonathan Maphenduka complained in the *Financial Gazette* that politicians had 'duped' villagers in 'Murinye's mountainous domain east of Mutirikwi Dam' by urging the utilisation of 'available water resources' without pausing to consider 'how irrigation could be developed in that rugged terrain'. 'Even with all the good will and engineering know-how in the world ... irrigation is not possible. This is why Mutirikwi was built for the lowveld'.[98] In fact, whatever politicians' motivations, for water planners the affordances of topography and soil were of key consideration, as they had been during the heyday of dam planning in the 1950s. The political imperatives of providing local irrigation whilst maintaining water supplies for the lowveld, had to be carefully calculated in relation to the availability of suitably large, flat areas of appropriate soil for cost-effective irrigated agriculture. As Darlington Chenjerai, the district engineer explained:

> There is potential for further growth in irrigation development around Lake Mutirikwi, which is what government is now pushing, so we can economically empower ourselves through farming ... The construction of the lake was for irrigation in the lowveld. The government took a 10 per cent stake for other activities in the local area of the dam. Now the government's thrust for irrigation development in the immediate area of the dam [means] there is need for a greater stake in water for local communities, so they too can benefit. There

[95] Felix Chikovo, PA 24/05/06.

[96] See 'Unfinished projects rile Masvingo' *The Standard,* 23/04/06; 'Politicians dupe gullible villagers' *Financial Gazette,* 16–22/03/06.

[97] Mukani Muzarira & Last Matsuro 23/06/06.

[98] 'Politicians dupe gullible villagers' *Financial Gazette,* 16–22/03/06.

needs to be a compromise with the water [for] the lowveld. This is particularly the case in the area along Mashate–Chenowe road, towards Nyajena from Murinye's area. It is relatively flat, unlike the hilly areas immediately around the dam. That gives good potential for irrigation development … There was a plan to put irrigation there … but now it looks likely [there will be] an irrigation scheme in the Zano area. It's a new plan. We had targeted Rukovo for irrigation. But … it was felt a larger area of land had to be developed. At Zano the irrigated area is much larger, so there will be more benefits. Given that irrigation development is very costly it was decided it is better value for money irrigating at Zano first.[99]

The importance of topography for irrigation was not lost on local communities demanding water from the lake. Although he complained of benefitting 'very little' from the lake, Matopos Murinye acknowledged that 'in this area we are not able to divert rivers for irrigation … not like in Nyanga where people divert mountain streams for irrigation'. 'That is why for us' he continued, 'rain is so important, and … why the role of *mudzimu* is bigger than *njuzu*, because we need the rain for our crops to have enough food to eat. So we go to the *mudzimu* for rain. For water in our fields we rely on rain; that is why rain making is such an important part of our culture here.'[100]

By linking the need for irrigation, rainfall's unpredictability and the limitations of topography with the relevant saliency of *mudzimu* and *njuzu*, acting Chief Murinye's comment mirrors my suggestion that government's renewed irrigation enthusiasm and the national *biras* were driven by similar factors. They also illustrate how ostensibly different regimes of rule/registers of meaning over water and landscape co-exist and intertwine. Again *njuzu* have an important, if ambiguous, part to play. Not everyone differentiated *njuzu* from rain making in the way Matopos Murinye did. The diversity of ways in which relationships between *njuzu*, ancestors, *Mwari* (high god) and rain can be articulated reflects complex, contested histories between mediums, ancestral cults, and *Mwari* shrines. Despite his comments about the saliency of 'rain making' over irrigation, and the relative importance of ancestors over *njuzu*, Matopos Murinye insisted *njuzu* presence in rivers and springs must be protected by chiefs whose ancestors are buried in the land. He identified springs on Boroma where 'mysterious things happen' and 'strange sounds' of 'heavy rain', or 'raging torrents', or 'of cattle bellowing' and other animals', which 'show us there is an *njuzu*, that this place is sacred, and needs to be protected'. 'No one is allowed to wash their clothes or bring dirty black pots to wash at those spots. If they do the *njuzu* will be angry, leave and the water will dry up', he explained.[101]

Importantly, *njuzu* are not just found in springs and rivers but also in the dams that supply irrigation schemes. This includes not just Lake Mutirikwi itself – which I was often told is home to many *njuzu* – but also much smaller farm dams, such as that supplying water for Oatlands scheme near Boroma. Murinye explained how 'the water that fills that dam comes from a stream and spring further up the mountain … at that

[99] Darlington Chenjerai, District engineer 23/06/06.
[100] Matopos Murinye 13/06/06.
[101] Ibid.

spring there are those strange noises which show that there is an *njuzu*, and that the place needs to be protected to make the water stay there'.[102] Vincent Mutende agreed there is an *njuzu* at Oatland's dam, citing 'an incident maybe 3 or 4 years ago when someone died there, who was taken by an *njuzu*'.[103] Just as ancestors and the provision of rain require regular rituals, so *njuzu* demand particular prohibitions to protect water sources and prevent drownings. Enforced by chiefs, mediums and autochthonous clans, they point to the other sovereignties, subjectivities and regimes of rule at play in the otherwise much more technocratic regulatory systems typically governing irrigation schemes (cf. Bender 2008).

Of course *njuzu* do not always easily co-exist with dams and irrigation schemes. Many people remembered problems caused by *njuzu* disturbed by the construction of the Mutirikwi dam. According to Chief Mugabe 'many white people died ... [or] disappeared in those tunnels ... caused by the *njuzu* fighting back'. Only after 'elders came and appeased the ancestors so the *njuzu* would stop' could they build the dam.[104] Several people, including VaChikami the water bailiff, suggested *njuzu* were causing similar problems at the Tokwe Mukorsi dam site, explaining long delays there.[105] Such complaints illustrate how so-called technocratic and traditionalist regimes over water do not necessarily intertwine, they can also confront. This echoes Ambuya Julianna in the early 1990s blaming 'drought on government development plans ... and on dynamiting for dams'. 'A holy silence needs to be restored', reported Ranger, so '*njuzu* can again operate' (2003:86). Acting Chief Nemanwa also described the troubles he encountered in 1992, when unprecedented water shortages meant Nemanwa's sacred spring came under increasing pressure from people desperate for water.

> There is a big, very sacred spring near the Matambo bus stop, soon after Chirichoga school. My great grandfather died near that spot and that is exactly where my mother gave birth to me. I was born where my grandfather died. We don't know where he was buried because the whites took him away, but his spirit now possesses me. NMMZ used to ask me what they could do with that spring and I said no, that spring is very sacred. I was trying to protect it. There were problems in 1992 when there was very severe drought. There was no water in Nemanwa or Morgenster. People from the GP [Growth Point] were coming to the spring to wash. The whole place stank of soap and that destroyed the water there. *Njuzu* do not like soap. The water dried up and people were very worried. They came to me because they knew the spirit on me has something to do with that spring. I said no, there should be no soap here. I asked people to pick up all the rubbish around there. Then I said lets cover up that spring with branches. We did that and the same day, before sunset, water started running again. Then council people thought they could just dig a borehole nearby to extract that water. But when they were drilling, their big machine just fell over. People could have died. The same night a very big snake came to where those workers were staying and chased them away. They never came back to dig a borehole there again. They wanted to use that water to supply the GP and Morgenster hospital but I said no. So that place is really very sacred.[106]

[102] Ibid.
[103] Vincent Matende 18/12/05.
[104] Chief Mugabe 19/11/05.
[105] VaChikami 06/11/05.
[106] Chief Nemanwa & VaChirengarenga 25/04/06.

In the 2000s similar confrontations affected ZINWA's attempts to institutionalise itself as the new parastatal managing river catchments and water delivery, particularly among war veterans and new farmers spearheading land reform. There is no space here to do justice to the complexities of ZINWA's efforts to establish its rule over water since the late 1990s. However, one of the (many) issues facing ZINWA in Masvingo in 2005/06 was the collection of fees, both from errant councils, and from new farmers on resettled farms.[107] Indeed as government drove to assist new farmers to better utilise water resources, new farmers often questioned why they should pay for water used in irrigation. In April 2006 *The Herald* (25/04/06) reported that 'ZINWA has received a lot of criticism ... about why farmers need to pay for the water they use. Most farmers argue water is god given and ZINWA has no right to demand payment from water users'. The problem was so widespread that ZINWA's exhibition at Zimbabwe's 2006 International Trade Fair (entitled 'Water, Water for Agriculture: Spearheading Economic Revival') focused on educating new farmers on 'the social and economic aspects of water'. 'The social part is the right of every Zimbabwean to have access to water,' it stated, but 'the provision of that water comes at a cost, which is the economic part'.[108]

Besides reflecting how a tension between water as 'human right' and as 'commodity' frequently animates debates about water governance (Hellum & Derman 2004; Fontein 2008:742), this also exemplified how, despite ZANU PF's urban water politics, ZINWA adopted a much less privatisation-orientated approach than its South African equivalents (cf. Von Schnitzler 2008). Indeed, ZINWA's insistence that water per se is not for sale but rather its provision and the infrastructure supporting it,[109] is not so far away from the assertion common around Mutirikwi that water comes ultimately from *Mwari*, the provider of rain, through the mediation of mediums, ancestors, *njuzu*, *manyusa* (cult messengers) or the Matopos shrines. Through this lens what is at stake is, exactly as ZINWA officials would have it, the *provision* of water; or, in my terms, the regime of rule that enables it, whether chiefs and mediums organising *bira* ceremonies, *manyusa* visiting the Matopos shrines, the ritual protection of sacred springs, or new farmers subjecting themselves to ZINWA regulations on irrigation schemes. Despite confrontations between *njuzu* and dam builders, or new farmers and ZINWA officials, the existence of *njuzu* in dams and the continuing efficacy of rain making for people on irrigation schemes suggest that more often than not, different co-existent regimes of rule over water do intertwine. Many making ancestral claims around Mutirikwi – like VaMakasva on the Popoteke river below Beza – did apply to ZINWA to use water for irrigation, and signalled they were willing to pay for it. Even Jairos Haruzvivishe, re-occupying ancestral lands near Great Zimbabwe, had 'made an ap-

---

[107] VaMare, Runde Catchment manager 11/04/06; VaChikami 06/11/05.
[108] 'ZINWA to showcase info on water management', *The Herald*, 25/04/06.
[109] As VaMare, ZINWA's Runde catchment manager, put it: 'we are not selling water, what we charge for is the infrastructure providing it' (11/04/06).

plication to ZINWA', and was only awaiting 'a meter so they can record the water I use' before deciding whether to use it 'for both domestic and irrigation purposes [depending] on how much it will cost'.[110]

As with pre-paid water meters in Johannesburg (Von Schnitzler 2008), and like National Parks' requirement that Zano's fishing co-op record its catches – the metering of water usage is not simply about ensuring correct allocations or cost recovery. It is also about forging particular political subjectivities. Even Mujuru's announcements about utilising land 'to end unemployment', and 'resuscitating irrigation' to ensure food security, was qualified by her demand for 'Zimbabweans to pay taxes' as 'the only way government could get the funds to build key infrastructure'.[111] Rain making, *bira* ceremonies, the ritual protection of *njuzu* springs and sacred *mapa* too all forge complex political subjectivities. Most people are situated in differing, unique and complex ways between such entangled political regimes, practices and technologies: whether chiefs enforcing soil conservation and leading national *biras*; co-operative fishermen monitoring fish stocks, wary yet ambivalent about dangerous hippos and *njuzu*; game wardens asserting militarised authority over wildlife yet sweeping Basotho graves; AREX officials, war veterans and new farmers enforcing technocracy, or *jambanja*, yet deferring to the autochthony of chiefs, mediums and local clans.

ENTANGLED MULTIPLICITIES

Given the proximity and co-existence of different registers of meaning and rule around Mutirikwi, it is not surprising some 'new but autochthonous' farmers and land occupiers were willing to pay ZINWA's water levies, even if not everyone appreciated the catchment and water-table orientated concerns of water managers.[112] The same can be said for the role some chiefs have played in developing irrigation in their areas. Matopos Murinye was clear that a chief's functions include promoting development as well as protecting sacred sites, ancestral taboos and so on.[113] If in 2005/06 the government used both national *biras* and the promise of irrigation to bolster land reform's faltering legitimacy, a similar argument could be made for chiefs. Their legitimacy too, in part, depends upon developmental credibility. Besides recurring drought and the drowning of the boy by an *njuzu*, Chief Chikwanda's legitimacy was undermined, in part, by the failure to secure food aid. Both he and acting Chief Murinye appealed for irrigation from Lake Mutirikwi to improve local livelihoods. Chief Mugabe went one step further, not only establishing the most successful *Zunde ramambo* in the district in 2006,[114] but also

---

[110] Jairos Haruzvivishe 27/11/05.

[111] *Herald*, 18/05/06.

[112] VaMare 11/04/06.

[113] Matopos Murinye 13/06/06.

[114] In early 2006, Chief Mugabe hosted a large party to celebrate the acclaimed success of his *zunde ramambo*, a scheme rolled out by government the year before.

claiming responsibility for a successful irrigation project at Chikarudzo, which too is inhabited by *njuzu*.[115]

While everyone occupies unique positions between contingent regimes of meaning and rule around Mutirikwi, and the material potentialities of water imbricated with them, in many respects chiefs best embody the nexus where multiple registers and regimes to do with water (rain, run-off, soil erosion, fishing and irrigation) intersect. The play of legitimacy and sovereignty chiefs are involved in cross and collapse normative distinctions between technocratic and traditional structures and performances of authority and rule. Yet perhaps the presence of *njuzu*, hippos and crocodiles better materialises the complexity of water's role as an index of power in entangled regimes around Mutirikwi, because it points to the indeterminacies of materiality, meaning and rule in emergent assemblages of people, spirits, wildlife, ruins, water, landscape, climate and topography. If the violence, destruction and danger of protected hippos point to the primacy of National Parks authority over Mutirikwi's fishing and wildlife, then the fact that hippo encounters can be interpreted as manifestations of *njuzu*, not to mention the totemic taboos associated with them, illustrates how even its militarised rule cannot entirely eclipse other registers of water and land around the lake. The association of hippos with *njuzu* also links the regulation of fishing/wildlife to the politics of rain making and irrigation. The dangers of *njuzu* in dams, as well as springs and rivers, materialises the complexity of different past and continuing assemblages of rule over water sources in the land. The historical ambiguities surrounding *njuzu*, as dangerous but also healing spirits or creatures, their relationship to watery places but also to rain, linked to *mudzimu* and mediums as well as *manyusa* and the Matopos shrines, point in turn to older, contested historiographies of meaning, materiality and rule enduring in close proximity with modern hydrological politics, planning and regulation.

To some extent all of this revolves around the provision of livelihoods, of making life possible (bio-power), but also the determination of death (necro-politics) and therefore sovereignty. In all regimes of rule over water, sovereignties and legitimacies are intertwined. So dam building and rain making are both 'heroic' demonstrations of capacity, and interventions responsive to demands, needs and aspirations. In the way that all regimes of sovereignty and legitimacy are politically productive, such entangled multiplicities forge complex subjectivities that defy normative distinctions between different forms and structures of meaning and authority. So water indexes the complex play of sovereignties, legitimacies and subjectivities around Mutirikwi in which everyone is implicated.

---

[115] Chief Mugabe 19/11/05.

5

Genealogical Geographies

After 2000, land occupations around Mutirikwi meant disputes be-tween rival chiefs and clans over boundaries, people and 'ancestral territories' re-emerged with new immediacy. These related directly to re-imagined and re-membered pre-colonial landscapes, involving contested 'history-scapes' (Fontein 2006a:19) and what I shall call 'genealogical geographies'. In 2005/06 such disputes were particularly prominent on occupied state lands bordering the lake's southern shores, which had been subject to squatting, and in some places formal resettlement, in the 1980s. But they also took place on farms to the north being resettled for the first time, as well as to the east around Zano, which had 'reverted' to native reserve in the late 1950s to settle people removed for the dam.

At Boroma, the grazing areas of *minda mirefu* (long fields) resettle-ments and an irrigation scheme from the 1980s were re-occupied in 2002 by the late Chief Mudarikwa Murinye and his people, provoking new boundary disputes with Chief Mugabe. As territorial markers rivers fea-tured prominently (especially the inundated Mutirikwi river), as did the graves and ruins of past occupations and new burials, such as Mudarik-wa's own burial in 2004. With prevailing droughts these disputes also reverberated through the distribution of food aid, as chiefly territories were conflated with new ward boundaries, and hungry people crossed disputed boundaries to seek assistance from whoever was able to source it. Not far from Boroma, Chief Mugabe placed settlers on state lands between the lakeshore and parts of former Mzero and Le Rhone farms, a section of the lake's protective boundary zone later earmarked for the Great Zimbabwe University. Besides his own clan these settlers included *vatorwa* incomers, some of whom became *sabhuku* (village heads) as the chief tried to increase these under his jurisdiction to bolster his status among local rivals.[1] In a contiguous stretch of land between the lake and Great Zimbabwe, long-standing tensions between Mugabe, Nemanwa and Charumbira, as well as *within* the Mugabe clan, re-emerged as various Haruzvivishe 'houses' (particular branches or families within the clan) re-occupied lands they had been removed from twice before: by Morgenster mission in the 1940s and 1950s, and by the independ-ent government after earlier re-occupations in the 1980s. Further west,

---

[1] Mai Makasva 26/11/05.

around the Longdale irrigation scheme below Ruvuri mountain, boundary tensions re-emerged between Nemanwa and Charumbira, until the former's new headman was granted land to live on by Chief Charumbira in late 2005.[2]

Similar disputes emerged on resettled farms north of the lake. This area had been dominated by farms for a much longer period; from the early 20th century (after the Chikwanda people were dispersed and their reserve split, shrunk and moved repeatedly) right up to the land invasions of 2000. By 1913 the Native Commissioner (NC) for Gutu had already acknowledged the Chikwanda reserve no longer bore any relation to its name (Mtetwa 1976:313) and by 1947 the entire chieftaincy was abolished.[3] The chieftaincy was 'resuscitated' in early 1980s, but little land returned. In the 2000s Chief Chikwanda's claims to an enormous stretch of territory – from Ndanga district to Nyuni and Harawe mountains, up into Gutu district and along the Beza range towards Masvingo town – were challenged by other chiefs and clans, including Charumbira, Murinye, and most of all, Makore.[4] Across this former commercial farmland, such disputes were complicated by the presence of war veterans, ZANU PF 'big men' on A2 (commercial) farms, and local land officials, as well as by Ambuya VaZarira's powerful claims over Beza. Challenges also came from former farm workers claiming both their own autochthonous ties to the landscape, and to the Chikwanda clan. But most of all, Chief Chikwanda's aspirations were overwhelmed by the internal clan disputes he faced, to do with his perceived failure to secure food aid, or carry out effective rain-making events at Mafuse. Disgruntled Chikwanda people also complained bitterly about his appointment of incoming new farmers and war veterans as *sabhuku* on resettled farms.

All these disputes around Mutirikwi turned, in part, on the deployment of contested history-scapes, invoking particular, pre-colonial and

[2] Chief Charumbira has also been implicated in violent struggles with the Bere clan over irrigated resettlements at Mushandike. In 2007, he was involved in the assault of a headman who he accused of 'denying 13 villagers' access to water ('Charumbira order's headman's kidnap', 07/06/07, *Financial Gazette*). Also 'Senator orders release of suspects from police cells', 28/02/08, *Wezhira Community Radio*; 'ZANU PF sticks to threats', 06/07/10, *Zimbabwe Telegraph*).

[3] Chikwanda people were terribly affected by the remaking of the reserves in the early 20th century (NAZ L2/2/117/46), because their 'reserve' (allocated in the late 1890s) lay on fertile lands much desired by white settlers, who put immense pressure on officials. A schismatic group of 'Dutch farmers' around Fort Victoria led by Mr Richards made a great deal of noise, and several, such as Mr Vermaak and the Rademeyer brothers, defied instructions to leave land they had pegged in the Chikwanda reserve, staying put until the reserve boundaries were, in effect, split, shifted and reduced around them. Chikwanda people were left with no reserve of their own, living on un-alienated state lands, or as tenants or workers on settler farms, or moved to reserves in neighbouring districts, culminating in the abolition of the chieftaincy in 1947.

[4] The dispute between Chikwanda and Makore was particularly nasty, dragging in VaZarira and Mai Macharaga, and resulting in Chief Makore being severely beaten in 2006 (Fieldnotes 14/04/06, 26/06/06; *The Herald*, 09/07/08; also Scoones et al. 2010: 198).

colonial pasts of arrival, settlement and eviction. These linked competing autochthonies and clan genealogies to the landscape through graves,
ruins (*makuva, matongo*) and other sacred places. Although provoked
by the government's stated intention to 'return' chiefs and headmen to
all resettled lands (Mubvumba 2005), these revitalised disputes did not
simply revolve around competing claims to land per se. Nor did they
simply involve competing versions of the past. Rather they turned on
'the mountains, ancestral graves and sacred forests that [had] qualified
Karanga political geography for most of the 19th century' (Mazarire
2013a:14). In other words, alongside different versions of history and
territory, these disputes invoked different historiographies and territorialities long co-existent and active in close proximity around Mutirikwi.

The importance of mountains, graves and ruins in the 2000s points to
how the 'principles of territoriality' (Mazarire 2013a:4) that had defined
19th-century Karanga politics have become intertwined with the more
cadastral kinds of territoriality that dominated Rhodesian land politics,
technocracy and state-making through most of the 20th century. Amidst
Masvingo's granite kopjes, and the fertile wetlands peppered between
them (Scoones 1997:618–9), 19th-century Karanga territoriality had
turned symbolically, materially and politically on the *gadzingo* (sacred
place) complex of sacred mountains, rivers, ancestral graves, refuge
caves (*nhare*), forests (*marambotemwa*), and abandoned homesteads
(*matongo*) (Mazarire 2013a). The material remnants of these pre-colonial
Karanga regimes of rule had renewed efficacy in the 2000s, even as new
farmers, war veterans and other land occupiers were simultaneously
utilising Rhodesian-era maps, technocratically pegging plots, fields and
homesteads, and sometimes digging contour ridges.

In the resurgent disputes of chiefs and clans in the 2000s, therefore,
both old and new graves, and ruined and new homesteads have been
hugely significant, just as different forms of genealogical and cadastral
territoriality have become increasingly entangled. They reflect important mechanisms through which conflicts over territory are imbricated
into land: deriving from, taking place through and giving shape to the
material forms and substances of landscape itself (cf. Moore 1998). The
notion of contested history-scapes reflects how such disputes can turn
on different, overlapping versions of the past and place, located within
a shared discursive as well as physical landscape (Fontein 2006a:19).
This is useful for understanding how the politics of the past inflect
complex historiographies closely linked to shared physical landscapes.
But it is not adequate for exploring the materialities of belonging and
territoriality in which kinship and relatedness with the substance of soil
and landscape become salient, entangled with the 'cadastral politics'
(Hughes 2006c:11) of maps and boundaries that characterised Rhodesian
rule. Nor does it illuminate how the affective, metonymic qualities of
different pasts (and futures) – of different regimes of rule – present in the
properties of landscape around Mutirikwi, are imbricated in the emergent
politics of the present. For this I use 'genealogical geographies'.

This chapter examines contested genealogical geographies around

Mutirikwi for what they tell about history, historiography and changing notions of territoriality. One central feature is the incongruence between a tendency to point to the evictions of the 1940s and 50s as the moment ancestral landscapes were lost, and the archival records that indicate European farms and native reserves were demarcated much earlier, in the 1890s. This illustrates how material legacies of occupation and eviction (as well as of colonial planning) are central to the politics of belonging and entitlement today, and shows how genealogical geographies challenge conventional temporalities which assume discrete pre-colonial, colonial and postcolonial periods are properly meaningful. According to Mutirikwi's genealogical geographies, the colonial period often appears like a brief gap in much longer continuities of belonging imbricated in the materialities of landscape. This sets the scene for Part Two of the book, which examines the profound remaking of Mutirikwi's landscapes that took place during this gap – between the evictions of the 1940s and 50s, and the first returns of the 1980s.

GUVA RAGUNDIRO AND DUMA GENEALOGICAL GEOGRAPHIES

During our frequent journeys to visit his *zitete* (great aunt), the Duma medium VaZarira, at Mazare north of the lake, acting Chief Matopos Murinye and I often discussed the history of 19th-century Duma settlement in Masvingo district. The account he gave was a story of hills and graves in the landscape. In common with others, he described a great, anti-clockwise, circular movement, almost as if the lake had always existed.

> Acting Chief Matopos Murinye tells us how when his father was nearing his death he began to tell all the stories he knew about the land and its past, [and] about Murinye coming from Bikita, along the direction of what is now Mutare road. 'In those days Murinye would not stay in one place for a long time, but would arrive somewhere and leave his son in charge while he moved on. So this area here is now under Chikwanda because Chikwanda was the first son of Murinye. His place is centred on Harawe. Further on, he arrived at Great Zimbabwe and there he stayed for only a short time ... He moved on and came to where Morgenster is now. There he left his son Mugabe, and that is how Mugabe got his chieftainship. He did the same with Shumba further along from there. Later Murinye came to Chinango, and he gave Beza to his *svikiro* [medium] Zarira. Then Murinye went to live at Boroma where my father was born and lived until he was chased away by whites who took the area for their farms. At Beza is where the first Zarira was buried, the second was buried at Boroma, and the third is Ambuya who is still alive.'[5]

This account of Duma arrival and settlement is typical of the genealogical geographies in play around Mutirikwi. Yet VaZarira herself offered a slightly different version. According to her, 'the real, old Zarira never saw any white people. She used to rule in that area of Beza, long ago before the whites came'. 'She used to have her own *dare* [court], sitting like a man wearing a *dhumbu* [animal skin apron],' and 'she divided

[5] Fieldnotes 17/03/06.

the land into the Duma chieftainships here, because they were the children of her brother'. 'No chief can put a hand on Beza and say it is theirs,' she stressed, 'that is a lie. Zarira divided the land among the children of her brother, Pfupajena'.[6]

The differences between these accounts reflect the tensions that can exist between chiefs and mediums, even two so closely aligned. It illustrates how genealogical geographies can be highly mutable and contested even between close allies. Given the long rapport between the current VaZarira and the late Mudarikwa Murinye, continued by his son Matopos in 2005/06, the question of who between Murinye and Zarira divided the Duma lands, and how Beza became Zarira's place, was not of particular consequence at that time. VaZarira and acting Chief Murinye were pre-occupied with other shared concerns: raising funds for the visit to the Matopos shrines, VaZarira's return to Beza, the problems surrounding Chief Chikwanda, and Murinye's various boundary disputes with Mugabe, Chikwanda and others. Despite her assertion that it was Zarira who divided the Duma lands, she agreed with Murinye that 'Mugabe has no ancestor at Boroma', and that 'there is no *nyembe* [title] which came to those [Duma] chiefs, which does not come from Murinye'. Murinye, she stressed, is the 'father of them all'. [7]

Not surprisingly Chikwanda people often narrated Duma arrival in Masvingo differently, even those seeking VaZarira's support in their challenges to the incumbent chief. For example, Varirai Mhinda Chikwanda traced the history of Duma settlement back to a person called Sanguwi.[8] In his story a man called Gundiro, son of Pfuwayi, was a founding Chikwanda ancestor.

> The first Duma to come here was Sanguwi, son of Muchangavanhu WaMabika. When Sanguwi died, his relatives in Bikita realised that the land here was empty. They decided to give the land to the younger brother of Mabika, who was [also] Sanguwi's father. They were looking for someone who had many sons who could take over the chieftainship. So the chieftainship was given to Gundiro, son of Pfuwayi. Pfuwayi was the *mukoma* [older brother] of Murinye, Shumba, Mugabe and Chibwe. Therefore Chikwanda was the son of Pfuwayi, and Murinye is our *babamunini* [younger paternal uncle]. We just say *Baba*. Gundiro Mutonhodza was the first Chikwanda chief.[9]

Although their accounts differ, in both cases Murinye's status as father of Chikwanda is based on the original Murinye being the brother of Chikwanda's father. In Shona, paternal uncles are known as father or '*baba*', and differentiated according to age, so a key issue here is whether Murinye was Chikwanda's *baba mukuru* or *babamunini* (senior or junior paternal uncle). VaZarira agreed the Chikwanda clan are the 'children of Pfuwayi', and related this genealogy directly to the *mapa* (sacred place) at Mafuse. 'Pfuwayi' she explained 'was given land there at Mafuse, so that hill Mafuse is where the children of Pfuwayi, the sons of Chikwanda,

---

[6] VaZarira 12/12/05.
[7] Ibid.
[8] Who Mtetwa identified as 'Munguwi', the son of Mabika (1976:50, 68).
[9] VaChikwanda 12/01/06

should be buried, with their wives, wearing bands of beads around their foreheads, and bangles'.[10] However, according to Varirai Chikwanda, the original Zarira lived at Beza *under* Gundiro, the first Chikwanda, and not under Murinye, nor under her own authority, as sister to Pfupajena (the most senior Duma ancestor), and the person who divided the Duma lands, as VaZarira claimed. Yet Varirai did acknowledge VaZarira's central role as a Chikwanda medium, just as Murinye and Mugabe recognise her importance for them. Zarira's different genealogical positions in these varying accounts reflects and reiterates the tricky position VaZarira often finds herself in between the sometimes conflicting demands of Masvingo's different Duma clans.

Varirai's account demonstrated the extent of the territory being reclaimed by Chikwanda people in the 2000s, and is useful for illustrating how genealogical geographies are imbricated with the material textures of graves and hills around Mutirikwi. In his words:

> Chikwanda's territory was very big! Where Ndanga hospital is now, at Kusala, was the boundary in that direction, from there up to Jichidza. This side the land went right up to the Makurumidzi river [near Desmondale farm]. On the other side, was the *nyika* [territory/land/country] of Zarira at Beza, after the Mahurumidze river. Zarira was the *svikiro* and had her own territory under Gundiro, where she stayed with her people, because a *svikiro* cannot stay alone. But the land where she lived was under Chikwanda. Chinango is the name of a small hill now under the dam. That place belongs to Chikwanda. All of the area of the Kyle [Mutirikwi] dam belongs to Chikwanda. A small section on the other side was Murinye's or Mugabe's, but most of it was Chikwanda.
> There are many sacred mountains here. There is Beza, Nyuni, Mafuse and Chipangamano. Beza is where Zarira stayed. Nyuni is where Chief Chikwanda lived, the one called Mashura. There is a spring there where water always runs. That spring supplies Glenlivet hotel. Mafuse is where all our ancestors are buried. That is where they used to be dried – *kusasika* – before they were buried. All those ancestors who were dried long ago are there. Even now, that is where our chief is supposed to be buried. At Chipangamano there is a *nhare* [cave/ tunnel] where my own ancestors are buried, where we used to keep our granaries, and other important things, and where we used to hide from *madzviti* [Ndebele raiders]. My own ancestor, Mutamba YaShata, fought with the *madzviti*. He is buried at Chipangamano.
> There is another hill of bare granite, where Gundiro was buried, but it is now under water. When Gundiro died, lightning struck that rock and it split, and that is how he was buried. That story is very important for us now. Chikwanda's ruling chief must always stay near that place and go there. Although some of the hill is under water, where the grave is, on the other side, is not. We must do a *bira* to appease our ancestor there. Last year we wanted to do that. We told our *svikiro* Zarira and she agreed a *bira* should be done, but we failed to organise it. The problem we have is this present chief who has our *ushe* [chieftaincy]. He doesn't want to work with our *svikiro*. But we must go to that place to do our *bira*, and to Beza and to Mafuse, all these places. There are even some sacred places that we do not know, but our elders, our ancestors, they can tell us.[11]

I was also told about Gundiro's grave by acting Chief Murinye, but for him Gundiro occupied a very different place in Duma genealogies. Gundiro was, he told me, 'one of Murinye's sons', the youngest son, 'who got the smaller *nyembe* of headman rather than a full chieftaincy' and whose descendants 'are now the Chibwe people' with their own head-

[10] Fieldnotes 12/12/05.
[11] VaChikwanda 12/01/06.

man under Murinye. Gundiro 'came to live somewhere near Beza' until 'one day there was a lightning strike against a big rock', causing it 'to split into two pieces'. 'Gundiro went into the split, the rock closed up over him, and he died and was buried there'. That place 'is still known as *Guva raGundiro* [Gundiro's grave]'. 'Even my father wanted to do a *bira* there, but he was not able to do it before he died'. 'You see' he continued, 'these things are important *kugadzikana nyika* [to settle the land] and I too will need to do a *bira* there at *Guva raGundiro* sometime.[12]

Gundiro is clearly important in the genealogical geographies of 19th-century Duma settlement in Masvingo, even if his genealogical location remains unclear and contested. Aquina's research in Victoria District in the 1960s too identified Gundiro as a senior Duma ancestor, however in her version he was the son of Masungunye, who fathered Chikwanda, Mugabe, Zarira and Murinye (Aquina 1965:10). This challenges the common view that Murinye is the most senior, or father, of Masvingo's Duma clans. Yet it is remarkably close to the current Chief Chikwanda's account of Gundiro's role in Chikwanda genealogies.[13] As he explained:

> Gundiro had four children who were Chikwanda, Murinye, Mugabe and Chibwe. As Chibwe was the youngest brother, the others said you should have the smaller title and he became a headman, under Murinye. Chibwe's area is called Shongani, but now there is a school there called Zivazanu. All the others were chiefs. Shumba was the son of Murinye. Gundiro also had a last child, a girl called Zariro [he emphasises the 'o']. Zariro was the last born of Gundiro, that is why she is the *svikiro* of Chikwanda ... [and has] that name Zariro because there were no more children after her. Most people don't know the real story, they just call her Zarira.
> JF – so do you work with the *svikiro*?
> Chief Chikwanda – Chiefs don't work with the *svikiro*. Rather the *svikiro* works with the chief, because the chieftainship was there before the *svikiro* was.[14]

This illustrates something of the problems between VaZarira and Chief Chikwanda. It also exemplifies how mediums like VaZarira are not just arbitrators in complex clan disputes, they are themselves finely implicated in the contested genealogical geographies through which such disputes take/make place. In this respect it is important to note that for Murinye, VaZarira's significance depends upon her mediumship of the spirit Murinye, 'the fighter, the lion of the forest',[15] but for other Duma chiefs it turns on her mediumship of another spirit – Zarira – from whom she gets her name.

Acting Chief Murinye's claim that Gundiro was a son of Murinye, from whom the Chibwe people descend, is unusual. It probably reflects his attempt to challenge Chikwanda efforts to reclaim huge territories north

---

[12] Fieldnotes 17/03/06.

[13] Chief Chikwanda's account is based, in part, on his reading of Aquina's research. He was deeply instrumental, with his late brother (the previous chief), in lobbying for the resuscitation of the chieftaincy after independence, and it is clear he used official, Native Affairs department documents to do so, some of which he showed me during my visit to his homestead (Fieldnotes 22/12/05).

[14] Chief Chikwanda 22/12/05.

[15] Fieldnotes 26–27/01/01.

and east of the lake, particularly around Zarira's *mapa* on Beza, but also in the Mutirikwi communal lands between Topora and Zano. He likened these to his disputes with Chief Mugabe around Boroma. In both cases he disputed their genealogical geographies, but also their conflation of recent ward boundaries with 19th-century chiefly territories.[16] Yet the fact that both he and Varirai Chikwanda agreed a *bira* ceremony was needed at Gundiro's grave, despite differing accounts of Gundiro's genealogical significance, illustrates how genealogical disputes are inherently geographical and emergent, both taking place in and remaking shared landscapes, just as struggles over ancestral territories and seniority are inherently genealogical.

KARANGA EXPANSION AND DUMA SETTLEMENT IN MASVINGO IN THE 19TH CENTURY

Clan genealogies invoked in contemporary territorial disputes may appear sedimented into place, but they are not static. Their very contestation, now and in the past, points to the ongoing becoming of both landscape and the past. Furthermore, such genealogical geographies often tell histories of mobility, conflict and movement. With the exception of Nemanwa, who claim to have 'germinated' at Great Zimbabwe (Fontein 2006a: 43), all of Mutiriwki's clans acknowledge their ancestors came from elsewhere and conquered, displaced, incorporated, or married peoples already living where they settled. These pasts point to the complex history of Karanga and Duma settlement in Masvingo during the 18th and early 19th centuries, as the 'Rozvi confederacy' was disintegrating 'under pressure from invading Nguni groups from south of the Limpopo ... ejected by the *mfecane* wars' (Mazarire 2008:759). Across Masvingo a whole host of earlier groups were subsumed, displaced and conquered by these Karanga expansions, of which the Duma arrivals in the early 19th century were the last.[17]

Many of the other Karanga groups, who arrived with or before the Duma, were later recognised and granted their own reserves by Native Commissioners in the 1890s, and some are still prominent in the area. But the earlier pre-Karanga groups are much harder to recover. Most were incorporated into the clans and polities that overran them. There

---

[16] Matopos Murinye 13/06/06.

[17] For example, when Shumba Chekai arrived in Mshawasha he 'over ran the Nhire from Vuzeze' who had themselves displaced earlier Vashawasha people of the *shoko-watinaye* totem (Mazarire 2010:66, 60). When Murinye settled at Boroma it was occupied by 'Chasura's *shiri*' and '*shoko-vudzijena* groups were scattered on nearby hills'. 'The extreme southern part of the Mtilikwe-Chivaka confluence ... was already inhabited by the Tembo people under Jiri at Nyaringwe hill' when Chibwe settled there (Mtetwa 1976:68). Likewise, north of Mutirikwi, 'Shoko and Shiri groups ... were conquered by the Gurajena Dziva from ... Chipinga ...who occupied firstly Beza hill near the present Kyle Dam, and later moved to Mazambara hill between the Popoteke and Mushagashe rivers in the early nineteenth century' (Mtetwa 1976: 44–45).

is 'untapped' oral history in totemic lineages and praise poetry that can be effectively utilised, as both Mtetwa (1976) and especially Mazarire (2010) demonstrate. Yet the geographical genealogies of clans reclaiming/re-occupying land around Mutirikwi since 2000 only rarely mention the groups that pre-dated their 19th-century arrival.[18] Members of the Charumbira and Nemanwa clans very rarely, if ever, speak of the Rombo and Gwadzi who pre-dated their arrival (Mtetwa 1976:185; Mazarire 2010:68), although references to the *shoko mbire* people in rain-making ceremonies do point to the enduring significance of older pre-colonial pasts. Sometimes I heard references to other *shoko* lineages, such as when VaChinengo discussed in hushed tones the *shoko mukanya* lineage his father belonged to, who pre-existed Murinye settlement around Boroma.[19] Varirai Chikwanda mentioned the NeChiHarawe people, also of the *shoko mbire* totem, who lived at Harawe 'when we first came here, and ... was killed by our forefathers and we took the land. That is why this land is of Chikwanda'.[20]

NeChiHarawe may have been killed by Chikwanda, but often the Duma arrivals created marriage alliances with pre-existing groups, as illustrated by both VaChinengo and Bhodo Mukuvare's contemporary status as senior *muzukuru* to Murinye, and by the well-known marriage of Pabva, Murinye's first son, to one of Nemanwa's daughters (Mtetwa 1976:68). Similarly Varirai Chikwanda referred to the *shumba* people who mined and smithed iron from Nyuni during the 19th century and married a Chikwanda daughter.[21] But such references to pre-Karanga and pre-Duma groups around Mutirikwi are comparatively rare. More often than not, for chiefs and clans re-occupying land around Mutirikwi in the 2000s, the important and relevant history begins when their groups settled the area in the late 18th and early 19th centuries, when their kith and kin were first buried into the landscape and their genealogical geographies first materialised into place.

There is an important question here concerning the graves, ruins and sacred places of these pre-Karanga groups around Mutirikwi. Is it likely that just as new farmers, war veterans and others resettling farms in the fast-track context, have had to respond to the demanding presence of the graves, ruins, pools and *njuzu* (water spirits) that make up existing sacred landscapes, similar demands were put upon the Karanga and Duma arrivals of the 18th and 19th century?[22] One would have thought

---

[18] Traces of earlier groups are sometimes found 'safely captured in their historic names before the coming of the immigrant Karanga groups such as the Shava-vaHera, some Shumba groups and the Moyo-vaDuma' (Mazarire 2010:61). Mazarire reconstructs this complex pre-Karanga past for the southern parts of Masvingo district, showing how the names Chishanga and Mushawasha, once tributary polities of the 'Rozvi confederacy' (2010:1), continued in 'imagined geographies' of groups that followed them.

[19] VaChinengo 26/05/06.

[20] VaChikwanda 12/01/06.

[21] Ibid.

[22] I am grateful to Terence Ranger who raised this question in conversation in 2009, although the answer is very much my own.

so, even if the nature, form and purpose of the responses must have been shaped by the specific social, political and cultural contexts of those moments. Certainly Mazarire's account of 19th-century Karanga 'principles of territoriality' suggests so (2013a:4). Mutirikwi's landscapes are littered with ruins and graves amidst its granite hills, caves and rivers. Many, or at least some (but probably not all), became the sacred graves, *mapa*, springs and pools of the incoming Karanga and Duma clans, just as the Matopos shrines pre-existed and then co-existed with the Ndebele state after Mzilikazi's arrival in the early 19th century, because its autochthonous, moral and political potency was recognised (Ranger 1999; Nyathi 2003). The hill at Great Zimbabwe, long sacred for Nemanwa, became Mugabe's *mapa* where their key ancestor Chipfunhu (amongst others) lies buried. The Chisikana spring there remains sacred for both clans, and the source of ongoing dispute. Similarly at Boroma, acting Chief Murinye acknowledged that hilltops and rock shelters around Murinye's *mapa* contain many, much older graves, including the dried remains of pre-Duma chiefs.[23] It is also likely that Harawe and Nyuni mountains around which Chikwanda's pre-colonial territory was centred, too had great significance for the earlier peoples supplanted by the Duma clans' arrival.

In a similar vein, Mazarire describes how, as Mapanzure's Hera consolidated their rule over Chishanga further south, they established a new ancestral burial ground or *gadzingo*, and a sacred forest (*marambotemwa*) on and around Zhou mountain (2008:765). As a newcomer, Mapanzure had to 'find a means of legitimising his "sacred chieftaincy"'. They did so by appealing to 'the autochthonous Mhizha'; a Venda group welcomed into the previous NeChishanga polity, who had established themselves as a powerful rain-making cult by transforming the landscape 'into a sacred zone with water secrets known only to them, associated with ... *njuzu* and rain-making powers drawn from the Venda rain god *Thovela*' (Mazarire 2008:761,765). Mapanzure married a Mhizha woman and their son Mazorodze was 'in turn, able to consolidate all the earlier efforts to combine the secular and religious powers of the land' (2008:765).

It is likely therefore that although pre-Karanga and pre-Duma groups are often scarcely acknowledged by those reclaiming land around Mutirikwi now, their (muted) presence endures not only through totemic lineages and praise poetry, but also through the very graves, ruins and rivers so central to the genealogical geographies and materialities of autochthony and belonging at play in the context of recent land reform. Furthermore, the kind of spiritual supplanting that missionaries, settlers and colonialists later sought to achieve by deliberately siting missions and graves in close proximity to existing African sacred places, probably already had a great deal of pre-colonial precedence. Rhodes's grave in the Matopos may have been unknowingly sited only hundreds of yards from royal pre-Ndebele Banyubi graves, but it was certainly designed 'to replace Mzi-

---

[23] In 2011 many such graves were disturbed when Chinese contractors for a mobile phone company drove a road through the Boroma hillside, causing an uproar with NMMZ and local communities.

likazi' – buried at Entumbane in the eastern Matopos – 'as spiritual owner of the land' (Ranger 2012:8). Similarly, Rhodes's efforts to 'ideologically expropriate Great Zimbabwe' through the burial of the ill-fated Allan Wilson patrol there (before they were re-interned alongside him at 'World's View' – Ranger 2012:3)[24], not only mirrored the careful placement of missions amongst the Matopos shrines (Ranger 1999; Nyathi 2003), it too fitted existing pre-colonial, African ways of appropriating already sacred landscapes. Likewise Rev. A.A. Louw's fascination with founding a mission 'for the proclamation of the Gospel' at Morgenster, 'near the famous Zimbabwe ruins which in all probability ... had been the centre of pagan worship',[25] may have intended a kind of 'spiritual replacement', yet it inadvertently continued practices already long established in the area; a point doubtlessly recognised by Africans at the time.

This dynamic partly explains the continuing secrecy that often surrounds clan *mapa,* springs and sacred forests. But if early colonial interventions did engage, however unwittingly, with existent principles of 19th-century Karanga territoriality, the land politics that became central to Rhodesian state-making (cf. Alexander 2006) in the 20th century also introduced new repertoires of claiming, taking measure of, and refashioning landscape, which nestled uneasily alongside, intertwining with and changing, but not entirely transforming, what was already there.

CADASTRAL POLITICS AND THE (RE)MAKING OF THE RESERVES

It has frequently been argued that pre-colonial politics across sub-Saharan Africa turned more on a politics of people, than of land or territory. The relative scarcity of human resources and abundance of land meant patriarchal authority was vested in a 'wealth in people' (Guyer 1993, 1995), while land, as Berry suggests for pre-colonial Ghana, was 'valued primarily as a means to attract followers, rather than as an asset in its own right' (2001:9). Such arguments imply that in southern Africa's colonial settler states a new 'cadastral politics' emerged through processes of territorialisation accompanying colonial land grabbing, so that 'land displace[d] people as the locus of political culture' and 'discourses of enslavement g[a]ve way to ... enclosure, boundaries and maps' (Hughes 2006c:11). Comparing colonial land and labour policies across the Zimbabwe-Mozambique border, Hughes argues that land appropriations and the fixing of boundaries involved in Rhodesian settler rule led to a territorialisation of chieftaincy, so that a pre-colonial politics of people was replaced by a colonial politics of land and territory. Chiefs,

---

[24] Allan Wilson was an officer in the Victoria Volunteer forces who fought in the First Matabele War in the early 1890s. In 1893 he and the 33-man patrol he led were searching for King Lobengula north of the Shangani river when they were attacked and killed by Ndebele fighters. Their deaths and 'last stand' became the stuff of Rhodesian legend, and after initially being buried at Great Zimbabwe, they were later removed and buried near Cecil Rhodes's grave in the Matopos.
[25] van der Merwe 1953:184, cited in Aquina 1965:11.

and native departments may have 'defended' (and in part 'invented')
'customary land tenure' in African reserves, but they also *'appropriated
the cadastral mentality'* (emphasis original) to keep Europeans and 'land
merchants' out of their 'coveted' reserves (2006c:10). Such analyses
imply that boundaries asserted by chiefs reclaiming ancestral territories
around Mutirikwi in the 2000s, are less a reflection of pre-colonial pasts
(as they claim) and more an effect of colonial processes of land alienation, delineation and 'ethnic mapping' (cf. Worby 1994; Moore 2005).

But I am not sure I agree. I suspect a dialectical relationship has always
existed between the control of people and land, just as politics always
turns, to some degree, on tensions between sovereignty and legitimacy.[26]
Both Maxwell (1999) and Mazarire (2010; 2013) offer a different, more
persuasive, picture of the 'territorial basis' or 'principles of territoriality'
of pre-colonial chieftaincy in Zimbabwe. Not only does Maxwell's description (1999:12) of the pre-colonial 'Katerere polity' in eastern Zimbabwe as 'a history of its hills' better reflect, like Mazarire's 'Karanga in
granite hypothesis' (2013a), the genealogical geographies in play around
Mutirikwi, but both approaches also question whether a valid distinction
can be maintained between a pre-colonial politics of 'power over people'
versus a colonial/postcolonial politics of 'power over land'. My emphasis
on exploring the co-existence and proximity of different regimes of rule/
registers of meaning through the shared materialities of landscape under-
mines the validity of positing such historical ruptures without reference
to the continuities that make them meaningful in the first place.

Yet current territorial disputes around Mutirikwi do *in part* reflect
colonial cadastral politics, as well as enduring principles of 19th-century
Karanga territoriality. This has to do with Rhodesian obsessions with
mapping and surveying, which became crucial to the delineation of European farms, the making and remaking of the reserves, and the 'ethnic
spatial fix' involved (Moore 2005:153–83), as well as the large-scale irrigation planning of the 1950s and 60s discussed in Part Two of this book.
When Victoria's native reserves were first delineated by Alfred Drew in
the late 1890s/early 1900s, they were numbered and assigned, for the
most part, to individual chiefs/clans. In 1895 the Assistant Native Commissioner (NC) warned against 'amalgamating them', and if they were to
'all be in the same reserve there would have to be a boundary marked out
for each of them', or there would be 'continual and incessant trouble'.[27]
Drew included sketches and descriptions of each reserve's boundaries,
topography, populations and their (often tenuous) relationship to each
chief's *nyika* prior to 1890.[28] The short-lived (misnamed) 'Mlinyis' or
'Mlinya' [Murinye] reserve, for example, was located between 'Ruvuli
[Ruvuri] mountain', along the boundaries of Longdale, Sikato and
Bompst farms, and stretched across the Mushagashe river. It was

---

[26] Hughes warns against overstating the distinction between 'power over people'
and 'land' arguing they are 'forms of political culture' reflecting 'ideal types' that
help 'to clarify a social reality that is still more complex' (2006c:11).
[27] NC Victoria annual report 1895 (NAZ N1/1/1–12).
[28] NAZ N3/24/34.

(under-)estimated to hold 3000 people, with 'not more than 7000 acres of land fit for cultivating', and placed 'partly in Mlinyis' country and partly in Charambila's country ... [as] the other part of Mlinyis' country is quite taken up by farms'.[29]

In the early 20th century, as land pressure from white settlers increased, surveying and mapping improved, and the segregation of 'Native' and 'European' lands solidified, Victoria's reserves were 're-adjusted' several times, and more land 'opened' for European farms, particularly around where the lake now lies.[30] Smaller reserves, with better land, or located close to Victoria, such as the Mlinya and Bere reserves, were 'thrown open for farming'.[31] This was when Mudarikwa Murinye's father Wurayayi moved to Boroma, after Mlinya reserve became Iyylands and Mlinya farms, still visible today. It was during this period that, under pressure from aggressive Afrikaner settler-farmers like Rademeyer and Vermaak,[32] the Chikwanda reserve was first enlarged and transferred to Gutu, then split, moved and shrunk several times, until it no longer resembled Chikwanda's claimed territories nor contained many of its people (Mtetwa 1976:295–350). During this extended process deeply unpopular efforts were made to consolidate Africans into fewer larger reserves, such as the Victoria and Mtilikwe reserves south of Mutirikwi, more or less where the Mutirikwi and Masvingo 'communal areas' still are today.[33]

Native Affairs officials were acutely aware the formation of Victoria's reserves would cause 'great dissatisfaction amongst the Natives', because, as Drew noted in 1898, 'nothing hurts the Natives more than being taken away from their lands'.[34] As the increasingly crowded reserves were repeatedly adjusted, moved, abolished or amalgamated in the early 20th century, Africans remained deeply reluctant to move into them, especially where 'the graves of their ancestors are on the reverted land'.[35] Many 'chose to remain on their ancestral lands', casting doubt on the official policy of inducing 'gradual "voluntary" movement' (Palmer

[29] NC Victoria to Chief Native Commissioner (CNC), 04/03/1901 (NAZ N3/24/34).

[30] Administrative boundaries were also tweaked, and some reserves and chiefs (like Makore, the remnants of the initial Chikwanda reserve, and Gurajena and Nyajena) crossed to the neighbouring districts of Gutu, Chilimanzi and Ndanga, after various commissions (NAZ A3/3/20/5; Mtetwa 1976:336; Palmer 1977:104–94,267–8).

[31] For example, Superintendant of Natives (hereafter SiN), Victoria, to CNC 17/03/1909 (NAZ L2/2/117:46–48); also Palmer 1977:268).

[32] NAZ L2/2/117/46.

[33] NAZ L2/2/117 46–8; NAZ N3/24/34 1898–1913; NAZ A3/3/20/5; Mtetwa 1976:295–350; Palmer 1977:80–194,267–8.

[34] NC Victoria, March 1898, NAZ N9/1/4.

[35] NC Ndanga to SiN Victoria, 06/10/18, (NAZ A3/18/39/23). In 1909 Gutu's NC acknowledged the difficulties Chief Chiwara faced being moved to Ndanga district: 'it is very hard on him to leave a country which for centuries past his ancestors have occupied. A well known custom of the tribe is to bury the chief on a certain hill named "Binga"; all the graves of past chiefs are to be seen here, not less than six Chiwaras' (NC Gutu to SiN Victoria, 15/02/09 NAZ L2/2/117/47).

1977:150). In 1924 the 'refusal of Chief Charumbila [Charumbira] and some 4000 of his people to vacate the surrendered Mlinya reserve … for which there were many European applicants' (Palmer 1977:150) so incensed C.L. Carbutt, Victoria's Superintendent of Natives (SiN), that he requested authorisation to use force, commenting 'it will probably be necessary to turn the people out of their huts … and then burn the huts, before they move'.[36] NCs' powers to move Africans into the reserves were later strengthened with the 1924 Native Regulations Act (Palmer 1977:150). A year later the Morris Carter Land Commission was appointed, eventually leading to the infamous Land Apportionment Act (LAA) of 1930. The segregation it heralded would spell 'separateness but not equality' (Palmer 1977:187), and led eventually to alienation of most of the land that Lake Kyle/Mutirikwi later flooded.

If these early Rhodesian efforts to delineate African reserves and European farms first introduced 'cadastral' forms of territoriality around Mutirikwi, in the delayed wake of the LAA this was enormously augmented by increasingly draconian interventions into African agriculture; particularly the 'soil conservation' planning that accompanied the 'development of the reserves' and E.D. Alvord's 'Gospel of the Plough' (Moore 2005:80–83).[37] As it was realised that 'the Native reserves of the Colony are inadequate for the accommodation of the indigenous Native population',[38] 'a great deal of effort' was 'devoted … to increase their carrying capacity' (Palmer 1977:197), although this was complicated both by settler concerns about competition from 'native' agriculture, and their need for African labour. Determined to solidify the segregation of European and African lands and yet ensure a supply of African labour for white farms, the LAA 'envisaged that all rent-paying agreements on European farms should cease by 1937' (Palmer 1977:205), to be replaced by labour agreements. The impossible time-scale meant that in 1936 the LAA was amended and the deadline extended to 1941. Despite 'progress' in Victoria, further delays followed, causing Victoria's NC to worry that the 'regrettable' postponements 'led to considerable confusion in the Native mind'.[39]

---

[36] SiN Victoria to CNC 29/05/24, NAZ S1561/33.

[37] Alvord was an American agriculturalist and missionary, who combined religious zeal with 'developmentalist' impulse, and led deepening interventions into 'Native Agriculture' from the mid-1920s, aiming 'to curtail "shifting cultivation" and what he saw as the poor [African] farming techniques that caused environmental degradation' (Moore 2005:80). Concerned more with agricultural improvement than with 'conservation *per se*' (McGregor 1995b:261), his 'civilizing' mission of 'demonstration' and 'conversion' became much more coercive with the centralisation of the reserves, contour ridging, destocking in the 1930s and 1940s, and the 'rapidly expanding technical corps' of the Native Affairs department (Alexander 2006:24–25), culminating in the ultimately doomed Native Land Husbandry Act (NLHA) of 1951. He was Director Native Agriculture from 1944–55, and memorialised in the 'Alvord Provincial Training Institute' established in north Victoria district in 1942.

[38] CNC to Secretary of PM 21/08/33, (NAZ S1542/I1).

[39] NC Victoria, Annual Report 1940 (NAZ S1050).

The 'centralisation' of the reserves begun in the late 1920s – moving African farmers off slopes and into demarcated, linear villages (*maline*) with separate arable and grazing lands – was now moving quickly, at least in Victoria. In 1939 the NC reported that 'the centralisation of the Victoria reserve … was completed this year', and despite initial 'opposition from a small but noisy section', most 'inhabitants … have now realised that the scheme imposes no hardships'.[40] But the NC's optimistic tone hid the resentment and resistance these measures often (but not always – McGregor 1995b) provoked. The 'centralisation' efforts of land development officers (LDO) required continuous attention. In late 1945, LDO Miller (much remembered around Mutirikwi today) sought authorisation from the Chief Native Commissioner (CNC) to remove 12 'kraals' under Chief Mugabe, from designated 'grazing areas' on slopes 'north west of Gwana school' in the Victoria reserve.[41] These people had lived on Morgenster farm, but after leaving it, or being sent off, 'took up their abode in the hills nearby'. For two years after 'centralisation they were warned to leave the places in the hills which are in the grazing area and move to the flat country below' but repeatedly ignored the Provincial NC's warnings. 'The Natives do not want to go and will not move unless they are constrained to do so' reported the exasperated PNC, so 'the removal of these people by order of the Governor is sought. They have had more than ample warning' and 'continued cultivation of the land …will re-act to the detriment of soil and pasture'.[42] Authorisation was granted in December 1945, but in February 1946 the LDO reported that these 'kraal heads with their people' continued to resist removal.[43]

However fraught it frequently was, centralisation affected 'lineage-based practices of land distribution and access' in the reserves in often contradictory ways (Moore 2005:83; Ranger 1985:72–75). Sometimes it provoked challenges to the chiefs' and headmen's authority, particularly where it interfered with 'privileged access to land spirits' (McGregor 1995a:272). Other times it could 'grant new authority to village heads in the allocation of fields', as the demarcation of *maline* was 'incorporated into shifting ideas about custom', despite Alvord's fervent disdain for 'African superstition' and 'custom' (Alexander 2006:24–25). Apart from productivity and soil conservation, centralisation was also clearly about 'discipline'; making African rural lives and lands 'legible' and 'visible' (Moore 2005:82–83; Alexander 2006:24).[44] Little wonder it often inspired

---

[40] NC Victoria, Annual Report 1939 (NAZ S1050).

[41] CNC to PNC 07/12/45; LDO to PNC 25/01/46; LDO to PNC 12/10/45; PNC to CNC 27/10/45 (NAZ S1048 Victoria PNC, General correspondence 1945–50).

[42] PNC to CNC, 27/10/45 (NAZ S1048 Victoria SiN, General correspondence 1945–50).

[43] LDO to PNC 25/01/46 and scribbled note, dated 06/02/46, on Memo from CNC to PNC, 07/12/45, (NAZ S1048 Victoria SiN, 1945–50).

[44] In Shurugwi 'centralisation' was 'justified in different ways to different audiences and changed over time' (McGregor 1995b:263). Its 'conservation value' was often only stressed afterwards to placate settler concerns about competition from African farmers. In the reserves 'local leaders had their own reasons for adopting centralisation' and sometimes *sabhuku*, headmen and chiefs benefitted

resentment. Despite unpopularity, increasingly coercive soil conservation interventions and destocking regulations were accelerated with the
1941 Natural Resources Act, and particularly the 1951 Native Land Husbandry Act (NLHA) of 1951 (Alexander 2006:44–59; Moore 2005:83–87;
Duggan 1980). This would feed African nationalist support in the late
1950s, and provoke 'the greatest crisis of authority the settler state had
faced since its foundation' (Alexander 2006:44).

As Africans all over Victoria were gradually moved from farms into
the reserves in the LAA's slow wake, the appropriation of Mutirikwi's
landscapes for European farms was consolidated. By the early 1940s
'approximately three-quarters of the district was European land' and an
'estimated 50,000 Africans had been moved into the reserves' across the
country (Palmer 1977:268,222). Yet around Mutirikwi many Africans
still remained on European lands, as rent-paying tenants, under 'labour
agreements', or as 'squatters' on unalienated crown lands, dating from
when the farms had initially been surveyed, pegged and delineated
around them, sometimes decades before.[45] Unlike elsewhere, farmworkers around Mutirikwi would remain predominantly drawn from local
clans.[46] Only with the influx of new settlers after the Second World
War, were the mass evictions of the LAA were finally realised; between
1945 and 1955 'at least 100,000 people were moved, often forcibly, into
the reserves' (Palmer 1977:243). This is the period when most people
re-occupying lands around Mutirikwi in the 2000s recalled being evicted
from their ancestral lands.

Planning, both *for* and *against* water (boreholes, earth dams, mechanical soil conservation works, the movement of fields to watersheds,
the fencing of 'headwaters' and regulations against cultivating slopes
and wetlands), was central to the 'development' and remaking of the
reserves after 1930.[47] The surveying, mapping and pegging such (often
coercive) 'technocratic' interventions demanded reinforced cadastral

(contd)   by gaining authority over new evictees coming into the reserves, or over
errant dependents, or allocated themselves much larger holdings, and so on.
Other chiefs in Shurugwi, however, resisted fiercely.

[45] In 1939, Victoria's NC recorded 32632 'natives' living in the reserves, 2649 on
Native Purchase Areas (NPA), 5316 on alienated land (European farms) and 327
in mines and towns. The next year it was 36704 in reserves, 2319 on alienated
lands (Labour agreements & Private locations), 2654 in NPAs, and 1371 in towns
and mines (NAZ S1050, NC annual reports 1933–40). By 1945 there were 34346
people reported living in the reserves, 3220 in the NPAs, 2568 on alienated
European lands and only 250 permanent residents in town (at Mashaba mines)
(NAZ s1051,1945).

[46] Ray Sparrow, 15/6/06.

[47] 'Water Preservation, Native Reserves, 1923–33' NAZ CNC S138/7; a'Water
Development Reserves, 1933–9' NAZ S1542:w5 vol.1–3. Providing water was
particularly important in the dryer reserves of Matabeleland and Midlands, such
as Gwanda, Gwai, Mphoeng, Semokwe, Shangani, Gwelo, Insizva as 'it was soon
realized that many of the areas ... were incapable of occupation unless adequate
water supplies were provided' (Irrigation & Agriculture engineer to Director
Agriculture, 5/11/23, NAZ CNC S138/7). See Palmer 1977: 151, 201–5, 209,
218–222, 257–8; Cleaver 1995; McGregor 1995a & 1995b; Wilson 1995.

forms of engaging with landscape. While priorities moved from securing land and labour for European farming, to 'modernising' African agriculture and tenure (with the NLHA), and then later 'back' to 'tribal custom' and 'community development' (after the NLHA's demise), whatever the official framework of the moment all these massive interventions were at least partly driven by the need to ensure the viability of the African reserves upon which Rhodesia's deeply racialised land divisions depended (Alexander 2006:3–4). African agriculture changed profoundly, from the cultivation of fertile, wetland *dambos* characterising pre-colonial farming (Scoones 1997:618–9), to the dryland farming on poor soils in overpopulated reserves that characterised much African farming during the Rhodesian period.

The territoriality inherent to rural politics in Zimbabwe inevitably changed through the complex interplay of all these colonial interventions. Surveys, maps and fixed boundaries do now carry considerable weight as techniques, artefacts and idioms of claiming authority over land and people. In 2000, and again in 2005, Radison Haruzvivishe showed me a map from the 1960s he had retrieved from the National Archives – reflecting Chief Mugabe's enlarged territory as once delineated by Native Affairs – in order to legitimate Mugabe occupations of state lands on former Mzero farm.[48] District and provincial land committees were also using such maps, and the District Administrator has an enormous map covering the entire district, pinned to a wall overlooking his office. Just as war veterans and new farmers were busy pegging their own plots on occupied farms throughout the province (Chaumba et al. 2003a), so chiefs all around Mutirikwi (but especially Chikwanda)[49] were using Rhodesian-era planning maps alongside genealogies constructed by Native Affairs delineation reports to reclaim ancestral 'territories'.[50] All these efforts reflect how the territoriality of chiefly politics is now minutely intertwined with past and continuing state-led surveying, technocratic interventions and ethnic mapping.

In 2005/06 this 'cadastral politics' took a new turn as some chiefs conflated ward boundaries with clan territories, and even ancestral *nyika*, exemplifying how bureaucratic/technocratic ways of making landscape legible and governable are part of the repertoire of chiefs/clans reclaiming territory, as different regimes of rule increasingly overlapped. Matopos Murinye felt both Chief Mugabe and Chikwanda were 'taking advantage of the issue of ward boundaries to claim the whole ward to be under their chiefdomship'. 'Long ago' he insisted 'the boundaries of chiefs were not the same as those wards today'.[51] For his part, Chief Mugabe encapsulated perfectly how recent ward divisions, rivers as territorial markers, and the provision of food aid, as well as the burial of dead chiefs, all entangle in disputes between chiefs over people and territory:

[48] Fieldnotes 26/11/05 (and Fontein 2006a: 51).
[49] Fieldnotes 22/12/05
[50] Delineation reports, NAZ 2929/8/5.
[51] Act. Chief Murinye 17/03/06.

Boroma is under Mugabe because it is in ward 13, which runs from Chikarudzo to Mutirikwi [river]. That area is under Mugabe, but now there are Murinye people living there and it is causing problems, as they say they are under Murinye. They have even buried their dead chief there at Boroma, saying it is theirs. But it is not under Murinye. Their area is ward 15, on the other side of the dam and the Mutirikwi river. Boroma is clearly in ward 13 and the chief responsible there is Mugabe, that is me. Because he can't supply them with food, only I can do that. You see this pile of papers here? That is all the names of people who have asked to get food, that is my work and I am doing that for my area. From Mutirikwi to Musuka that is Mugabe.[52]

Bhodo Mukuvare agreed with Matopos Murinye that the conflation of ward and chiefly territories was very recent, and did not reflect older territorial boundaries. Speaking on his old resettlement plot at Boroma, he explained that when he 'was given this plot by the government, we lived under the council', but 'it changed with this struggle of the chiefs recently':

Right now Chief Mugabe is saying this area is his because it is ward 13, but we know this land is of Murinye, from long ago. Ahhh! We used to live very well here long ago, but not these days. Now it is all trouble and poverty. This started last year with the issue of wards, it is very bad ... now even our wives are going to Mugabe to get what they want like food and other things, because of these wards.[53]

Bhodo Mukuvare recalled living as a child with his parents under Chief Murinye 'at a small hill called Chiramba Mumvuri' on an area of Mzero farm adjacent to Great Zimbabwe.

We had our *musha* [home/village] there and lived there a long time, maybe twenty or thirty years. We lived there under Chief Murinye. Chiramba Mumvuri is on the other side of the road from Sheppards ... near Muza [one of the Haruzvivishe houses of the Mugabe clan re-occupying the area]. We lived near the son of Muza Elikias who was a teacher in the school there, *kare*, long ago. But we lived under Murinye. Long ago the boundary between Mugabe and Murinye was the Chisikana river [from the spring at Great Zimbabwe]. Where we were, was under Murinye, but where Elikias lived was under Mugabe. That area became the farm of the *muneri* [missionaries]. The *muneri* took the land and we had to leave. That was when we came back to Boroma.[54]

Taken together, these accounts illustrate how different notions of land – as chiefly/clan territories marked by hills, caves and bounded by rivers, as delineated farms alienated by Rhodesian surveyors, farmers and missions, as post-independence resettlement schemes governed by rural councils, and more recent conflations of clan territories and council wards – overlap and intertwine in contested ways with the politics of people's loyalties. These become particularly acute in periods of drought and hunger, as Chief Mugabe's distribution of food aid among Murinye re-settlers around Boroma indicates.

But none of this excludes older forms of territoriality co-existent with colonial/postcolonial bureaucratic processes and technocratic mapping

---

[52] Chief Mugabe 19/11/05(b).
[53] Bhodo Mukuvare 19/11/05(a).
[54] Ibid.

and, more recently, the politics of food distribution. Just as scholars in the 1990s began to recognise how forms of 'indigenous' mapping (Bender 1999; Harley 1992b; Kuchler 1993) variably pre-existed, resisted and co-existed with colonial mapping across a wide variety of contexts, so the territoriality of chiefs/clans around Mutirikwi is not restricted to the two dimensional, visually-orientated, mapping/surveying that made the land and its peoples legible for Rhodesians. Rather, the territoriality of chiefs/clans continues to manifest forms of relatedness materialised through genealogical geographies, enduring and intertwining with colonial forms of mapping. Rhodesian cadastral politics did not obliterate pre-existing African landscapes, but layered unevenly over them. Indeed pre-colonial place-names for mountains and rivers can sometimes be read in colonial maps, pre-dating post-independence efforts to rename prominent towns, hills and dams.[55] Early Rhodesian maps of 'Victoria' district refer to 'Zalila' (i.e. Zarira) on Mt Beza, Mzero farm from the Muzviro river running through it, 'Mlinya' farm where the reserve once lay, Arawe farm, where Chikwanda's sacred hill Harawe is located, and the 'Mtilikwe' reserve, from the Mutirikwi river, to mention only some.

As with the deliberate siting of missions and Rhodesian monuments near African sites like Great Zimbabwe or in the Matopos, such examples illustrate how aspects of '19th-century Karanga territoriality' became materialised through the very techniques by which cadastral politics took hold. Just as the Ngalakan of Australia's northern territory used European settler maps to reclaim sacred lands in the 1990s, exactly because they reflected the historical co-existence and proximity of colonial and indigenous landscapes (Morphy 1993), chiefs/clans around Mutirikwi can use the techniques, artefacts and idioms of Rhodesian mapping to reclaim the graves, ruins, caves, mountains and rivers through which pre-colonial 'principles of territoriality' operated. This is exactly what many were doing in the 2000s.

A HISTORY OF GRAVES, RUINS, HILLS AND RIVERS

It is through graves, ruins, mountains and rivers that ancestral genealogies are turned into the substance and form of landscape. That is also how they point to the dialectical relationship between 'control over people' and 'over land', defying ruptures others identify. Graves and ruins are active and affective in contemporary politics of belonging through their materialisation of different forms of social relatedness, kinship and clientship – central to a politics of people – into genealogical geographies and forms of territoriality more amenable to cadastral techniques.

Maxwell (1999) offers an important caveat to how genealogical geographies naturalise fixed associations between chiefs, patrilineal clans and territories. Critiquing assumptions about the domination of 'clans'

[55] Such as, for a short while 'Nyanda', and then 'Masvingo' for Fort Victoria, and Mutirikwi, for the 'Kyle' dam/lake.

and 'segmentary lineages', in pre-colonial African politics, he argues that 19th-century Hwesa politics was *'territorially ... rather than descent based'* (emphasis original), and 'kinship was complicated by numerous other social ties', including 'clientship and personal loyalties' (1999:11– 12). This kind of territoriality captures how pre-colonial politics was both about 'power over people' and 'power over land', resonating with Mazarire's account of Chishanga (2010) as well as the genealogical ge- ographies I encountered around Mutirikwi. Descent was an ideology of authority that equally revolved around controlling 'others', especially affines and *vatorwa* (strangers), in ways that echo the complex politics of sovereignty and belonging between war vets, 'new farmers', state officials, chiefs and mediums thrown up by land reform in the 2000s. The kind of pre-colonial territoriality Maxwell describes was not of the bounded, cadastral and ethnic form Rhodesian officials assumed, but 'an extension from hills at the centre, with only vague borders' (1999:26). The history of the 'Katerere polity' was 'a history of its hills', and 'through their association with past leaders, as places of their settle- ment, burial, and dwelling for their spirits, ... mountains were sources of political legitimacy' (1999:26).

This description closely matches the 'territoriality' of 19th-century Karanga/Duma politics (Mazarire 2010; 2013a; Mtetwa 1976), enduring through genealogical geographies in the 2000s. Mutirikwi's 19th-century political history too is a 'history of its hills'. Karanga and Duma groups, and those before them, occupied defensive granite hilltops against rivals and Ndebele/Nguni raids, but also as sacred centres of political author- ity, *gadzingo* or *mapa*, associated with rain making and the instalment and burial of chiefs. Through these hills – like Boroma (Murinye), Beza (Zarira), Mafuse (Chikwanda/Makore), Harawe (Chikwanda), and Great Zimbabwe (Nemanwa/Mugabe), to name only the most prominent – past forms of territoriality, relatedness, kinship and clientism continue to be made present, even as new burials and occupations remake these pasts and places into emergent futures.

Rivers, springs and fertile, wetland *dambo*s too were important for pre-colonial politics, animating territorial contests (Mazarire 2013a:8) that continued to resonate in the genealogical geographies of the 2000s. This evidenced by the recurring (if uncertain) significance of *njuzu* across different regimes of meaning and rule around Mutirikwi. As pres- sure on land fuelled exaggerated (Scoones 1997) concerns about soil erosion in the early 20th century, bans were imposed upon the *dambo* and river-bank cultivation that had been central to pre-colonial agricul- ture (Scoones and Cousins 1991; Scoones 1997; Mabedza and Mawere 2012; Mazarire 2013a), and centralisation shifted African agriculture to dryland watersheds (McGregor 1995b:259, 273). But *dambo* and river- bank cultivation would recur sporadically, despite or as a response to deeply resented colonial regulations. It again intensified in the context of drought, hunger and land reform in the 2000s (Mabedza and Mawere 2012; Scoones et al 2010:193–4). Although chiefs and headmen around Mutirikwi sometimes tolerate the cultivation of wetlands and river banks, often provoking intense local rivalries, they are still expected to enforce colonial-era conservation regulations.

Rivers and wetlands were important for pre-colonial territoriality in other ways too, beyond agriculture and *njuzu* encounters. In Chishanga, the control of headwaters was highly significant to the establishment of Mapanzure's *gadzingo* on Zhou mountain (Mazarire 2010; 2008). This was repeated elsewhere and continued in various guises throughout the 20th century.[56] Rivers featured in the struggles of rival Duma and Karanga clans, and even those swallowed by the lake continue as contested markers of the ancestral *nyika* chiefs seek to restore. In 2005/06 Chiefs Murinye and Mugabe cited different rivers, of vastly different scale – the Mutirikwi river and the Chiskana stream respectively – as their shared boundary, and the Muzviro continues as an important boundary between Mugabe, Nemanwa and Charumbira, just as it did in the remaking of Victoria's southern reserves in the early 20th century. Elsewhere the Mucheke, Mushagashe, Makurumidzi, Popoteke and Mutirikwi rivers have all been cited in resurgent clan disputes since 2000.

Like graves and ruins, rivers are not simply markers of pre-existent territories and belonging. They are part of ongoing processes through which territoriality and belonging are materialised, contested, made real. One way this works is through the constraints that rivers make on mobility. Before or beyond the reach of tarred roads and bridges, rivers limit movement, depending on the rise and fall of waters, both seasonally, and rapidly after heavy rain. This animated pre-colonial politics (and Ndebele/Nguni raiding) around Mutirikwi (cf. Mtetwa 1976), as much as it hindered 19th-century explorers, pioneers and settlers (Sayce 1978:97), and later NCs patrolling the reserves in the 1930s. As useful lines on maps (cf. Hughes 2001) rivers were key to the delineation of farms, reserves, and whole administrative districts (like Victoria – Sayce 1978:58). But their potential to limit movement equally animated their significance for Rhodesia's fledging administration.

In the early 20th century, Victoria's 'popular Koetslich brothers' ran an impromptu ferry service 'on the Mshagashe river in the wet season' using 'a boat rigged to a winch', so that 'people and goods were carried safely across the river', until they were charged with 'operating a ferry without a licence' (Sayce 1978:97). In the 1920s and 1930s, noisy settler farmer associations put considerable pressure on Rhodesian officials to build bridges across the Sabi, Mutirikwi, Munyapi Ndarama, and Popotekwe rivers, amongst others. The 'loss and inconvenience caused by the Popotekwe in flood' was 'particularly serious', as 'one of the swiftest and most treacherous rivers in the country' that could come 'down very suddenly, cutting off farmers from ... Chatsworth for days at a time'.[57] The administrative need for bridges across unpredictable rivers was often acute. In 1936 Victoria's NC urged it was 'most essential for administrative purposes' that the 'Mtilikwe river dividing the Victoria and Mtilikwe

---

[56] Hughes considers the role of rivers in chiefly disputes, and 'the cadastral ambiguities that inevitably arose at their head waters' (2006:7).

[57] Minute to Secretary, Mines & Works, 27/06/30 (NAZ S12:6:426,992).

Photo 8   Footbridge over Mtilikwe (Mutirikwi) river, 1926
(Source: National Archives of Zimbabwe; NAZ 624.5[756.36])

reserves' be bridged, because 'during the rainy season the natives …
cannot cross the Mtilikwe river'.[58] In January 1938, while returning
'from a patrol in the Victoria reserve' the acting assistant NC's car was
suddenly 'submerged in a flooded river' causing the loss of twenty-one
'native dog badges'.[59] Later, during the liberation war, bridges were
targeted by guerrillas exactly to hinder Rhodesian movement across
farms and reserves, even as they too used rivers to divide operational
zones.[60] In the mid-2000s, bridges destroyed by floods following Cyclone
Eline hampered movement across communal areas. In January 2008, ten
people from 'Murinye's communal area' were 'marooned' for five days,
'on an island along the Mutirikwi river … when water levels suddenly
rose and trapped them while they were crossing the river'.[61]

Beyond limiting movement, rivers could also enable it, and often lay

[58] Annual report NC Victoria, 1936 (NAZ S1050, 1933–40).
[59] Act. Ass. NC to Controller, Stores and transport, Salisbury, 12/01/38 (NAZ
S1043).
[60] In 2005/06 Headman Nemanwa's wife explained how she and others had
helped guerrillas blow up a bridge near Chikarudzo, on Morgenster farm
(Fieldnotes, 23/11/05). On the use of rivers by rival guerrilla groups to demarcate
operational areas see for example 'Terr Faction fights in Maranda area', *Fort
Victoria Advertiser*, 09/09/77.
[61] 'Zimbabwe: 10 marooned in river for five days', *Herald*, 14/01/08.

at the very centre of social and political life, as McGregor (2009, 2011) and McKittrick (2008) show for the Zambezi and Kavanga rivers respectively, and Mazarire (2010, 2008) for Chishanga's contested waters. Today's focus on rivers as boundary markers may in part reflect the mapping schemes of colonial surveyors, but it also resonates with pre- and early colonial histories of movement and river sociality, illustrating further how a politics of people entangles with that of territory. Rivers, pools, springs – like rain making and dam building – also link a politics of people to that of land through water's productive, life-bearing qualities, as reflected in their continuing sacred character, and the proliferation of *njuzu*. Just as land occupations around Mutirikwi in 2000s became animated by potentialities for irrigation, so the availability of water, boreholes and earth damming had been central to Rhodesian settlement and land appropriations in the early 20th century (cf. Cleaver 1995). As I discuss in Part Two, as Rhodesian planning *for* water increased phenomenally in scale with the massive dam schemes of the 1950s and 1960s, it became central to the imagination of new Rhodesian futures.

LANDSCAPE, MEMORY AND GENEALOGICAL GEOGRAPHIES

My approach refuses any simple teleological argument positing an historical transition from a politics of people to one of land. Territoriality became more cadastral through the colonial period, just as pre-colonial politics was more complex than competition between descent groups. But older forms of territoriality, kinship, and relatedness to the land continued matter. The pre-colonial *nyika* of Duma and Karanga chiefs 'changed from time to time' (Mtetwa 1976:8); people and their loyalties were mobile and changeable. The 19th century was a period of great turmoil, witnessing the rise and demise of the Duma confederacy, Nguni incursions and Ndebele raids, and eventually Rhodesian occupation. Boundaries were not as fixed or static as colonial mapping, settler pegging and fences tried to make them – or as disputing chiefs/clans might now suggest. Territorial rule was an 'extension from hills at the centre' (Maxwell 1999:26), materialising genealogical geographies through which older territorialities continued to operate, however entangled with cadastral politics they became. 'Duma were and are still a minority ruling over a large non-Duma majority' (Mtetwa 1976:8), and territorial politics was about controlling outsiders: pre-existing groups, later arrivals, affines and captives, and others of all sorts. Chiefs consolidated or lost power by retaining, gaining, or losing subjects, just as their authority on the resettled lands in the 2000s turned, in part, on the ability to gain, retain or lose the fragile loyalties of non-autochthonous *vatorwa* – war veterans, new farmers, landless people, affines and so on – as exemplified by contested appointments of village heads and food-aid distribution, as well as rain making and burials.

Given these historical and political entanglements of landscape, people and territoriality around Mutirikwi, establishing clear genealogies for chiefs/clans can be difficult. Yet genealogies are often delivered through lengthy recitals of hills associated with particular ancestors and houses within clans. Being able to make such recitals commands respect.[62] In anthropology's increasingly sophisticated understanding of the relationship between memory and landscape – landscape *as* rather than *of* memory (Kuchler 1993) – a recurring theme has been how time and the past can be fixed or collapsed into place and space, so that journeys through landscape take on profound (sometimes carefully directed) temporal dimensions (cf. Morphy 1995). Such processes often involve mechanisms that mask their own historicity, producing static, ahistorical landscapes *of* memory (cf. McGregor 2005). In this way landscapes appear both integral to memory work, but are also politically embedded, historical processes. This fixing of the past into place, and time into space, is part of the constant, emergent, open-ended becoming of landscapes, pasts and futures. This is exactly what genealogical geographies around Mutirikwi do and are: historically and politically situated processes whereby particular pasts and emergent futures find presence and are contingently fixed through the materialities of landscape, obscuring their own historicity. How this works is well illustrated by the genealogical geographies that animated the occupations of state lands south of the lake by Haruzvivishe people in the 2000s.

THE BOOKS OF THE *MASABHUKU* WERE ALWAYS THERE

When the so-called 'game park' on former Mzero farm was re-occupied in 2000, it was divided into different *sabhuku*, referring at once to particular hills and graves, and to particular Haruzvivishe houses of the Mugabe clan. Although not instigated by Chief Mugabe, he supported the occupations. 'To begin with they just went in and chose locations for their houses and fields', he explained, 'but then we got involved ... to look after the trees and soil ... so I appointed *sabhuku* for the area'.

> I gave books to four or five people there ... several belong to houses of the chieftainship [*dzimba dzeushe*]. There is Haruzvivishe, the most senior of them all. Then there is Muza, Manunure and Gwauya. These are all different houses of the chieftainship. Another *sabhuku* is Makasva who is not a house of the chieftainship but is Duma and someone who we respect. Finally there is Sithole, my *mukwasha* [son-in-law]. He lives near the tar [road]. I thought I should give something for my daughter and *mukwasha* so he is also a *sabhuku*.[63]

Apart from Sithole and Makasva, each of these houses derive from different sons of the last Mugabe custodian of Great Zimbabwe, Rufu Haruzvivishe, who lived there into the early 20th century (Fontein 2006a:30). This genealogical geography is therefore fairly recent, established over only two or three generations, across the transition from

---

[62] In November 2005, Bhodo Mukuvare recited the name of every one of the 25 or so hills, rocky outcrops and peaks spread in panorama before us, explaining the stories behind each as he did so (Fieldnotes 19/11/05a).
[63] Chief Mugabe 19/11/05b.

pre- to early colonial periods. It is not fictitious,[64] yet it is selective in the pasts it compresses into space. It ignores competing historical claims by rival clans (Nemanwa, Charumbira and Murinye), minimalizing pre-colonial movements and conflicts in the area, but also the histories of those (such as Bhodo Mukuvare) who lived there after they became settler farms. Many locals became tenants (and later workers) as farms were pegged around them in the 1890s and early 1900s, even though absentee landlords and derelict farms were a growing problem for officials.[65] As Chief Mugabe acknowledged, 'when white settlers came they overpowered the people living there ... [who] either moved away or became farm workers ... People became very mixed up. Nemanwa, Charumbira and Mugabe [people] all lived and worked on those farms'.[66] Yet the arrival of Rhodesian settlers, the surveying of farms, the 'mixing up' it provoked, and even the vagaries of lives lived as tenants or labourers, was of scarce relevance for those reclaiming ancestral lands in the 2000s. It is the loss of ancestral landscapes after the delayed evictions of the LAA that is prioritised. Like Mudarikwa Murinye's removal from Boroma in 1949, the loss of Chikwanda's chieftaincy in 1947, and similar histories of removal all around Mutirikwi, most Haruzvivishe people on Mzero farm remembered being removed in the 1940s and 1950s.

Describing how he came to re-occupy the land where his *baba mukuru* (senior paternal uncle) once lived, which he had returned to once before, Jairos Haruzvivishe (Sabhuku Manunure) illustrated how histories of movement, eviction, and resettlement transform into fixed genealogical geographies, linking living kin to ancestral fore-bearers through the active materialities of graves and ruins. His account illustrates the multiple movements between European and mission farms, and nearby reserves that people undertook, after losing their lands in the middle of the 20th century, and the repeated efforts some made to return since independence in 1980, often less than 40 years after their initial evictions.

> My *sekuru* [grandfather] lived there in *Masvingo* [Great Zimbabwe] until he died. His name was Haruzvivishe. My father had his *musha* [village] where the GP [Nemanwa Growth Point] is now [then also Mzero farm, owned by Morgenster Mission]. His name was Jonas Mutero Mugabe. I lived there, but from 1945, after the Land Apportionment Act, we were moved and placed in Gwana [in the Victoria reserve]. We lived under Chief Mugabe. My father's *mukoma* [elder brother] was then chief. His name was Muza. We lived there until 1968, when my *mukoma* became chief. His name was Joseph Chikudo Mugabe. We went to Chikarudzo. That place was under the missionaries at Morgenester, but at that time it was released to Chief Mugabe to live, and that is why we went there. We lived in Chikarudzo until the ceasefire.
> In 1979 we came back right *here*, where we are now, because this was the place of our ancestors, where they lived. My father's *mukoma* lived here, he was called Manunure, and another older *mukoma* of my father, who was called Gutuza. He lived over there where the NMMZ [National Museums and Monuments of

[64] It is supported by other evidence. In the national archives there are references to Manunure living on Sikato farm (next to Mzero) in 1911, in correspondence about a veld fire 'caused by Manunure's child' (Halliday to NC Victoria, 02/09/11, 29/08/11, 24/08/11, NAZ s665).

[65] Victoria Farms, NAZ DV3/9/1; also Sayce 1978:62.

[66] Chief Mugabe 19/11/05b.

Zimbabwe] buildings are now. There was even a school over there called after my forefather, Manunure. It was on that *ruware* [granite outcrop] called Chasosa hill. In 1987 the government thought to put a game park here, so we were told to go back where we came from. Some just left but I stayed for another year, me, Amon Matumbwa and Richard Muza, the *mukoma* of Radison [now Sabhuku Muza]. After one year we were given a letter from the police commissioner saying 'if you refuse to go we will burn your houses'. So I went to Barahanga, on the other side of Chikarudzo.

There are many graves here. We came back when the government said *ivhu kuvanhu* [soil to the people]. That was 2000. Since we didn't have enough land to farm, that made it necessary for us to come back here and plough. But we told our chief and he agreed, very much so. The people who had lived here before were the first to come again in 2000. They went where they had lived before. Later others followed, and entered new places that weren't already occupied.

The books of the *masabhuku* were always there. Some new people, we gave them places to live. Others entered by themselves. But they cannot cause problems here because this area was already under Manunure. We told everyone who came here that Manunure stretches from this point to that point, so they understood that. There were no problems. The area of Manunure is between Makasva, and then up to Muza, on the other side of that hill. Long ago, Manunure was the elder brother and he was given his place here and Muza was given his place on the other side there. These areas of land were given by Sekuru Haruzvivishe to his sons, Manunure, Muza, Gutuza or Nyanyiwa, and Gwauya, and Jonas, Mukono. Sekuru had many children and I cannot remember the others.[67]

This rendition of the past and place, this fixing of Haruzvivishe genealogies into landscape, is a very specific way of doing history. Exemplifying how land occupations took their lead from personal kinship histories linked to place and soil, it shows how the fixing of genealogies into geography continued across the ruptures of colonial rule, and the cadastral politics this introduced. It continued long after the formal alienation of European farms around Mutirikwi, illustrating the long co-existence of different territorialities. Although Jairos insisted 'the books of ... were always there', they probably date to the early colonial period. After all, his grandfather Rufu Haruzvivishe became chief upon the death of Chipfunhu in 1894 (Fontein 2006a:30). Sikato, Mzero and neighbouring farms (Longdale, Bompst, Le Rhone, Morgenster) were already pegged and surveyed (if not actually occupied) by the early 1900s.[68]

More than continuing *despite* the many disruptions of Rhodesian rule, the fixing of such genealogical geographies was in many ways deeply entangled with them, notwithstanding many omissions in accounts like the above. Jairos Haruzvivishe's description of the succession of chiefs is corroborated by Aquina's account of how 'Haruzvivishe was succeeded by his son Muza, and he by his brother Gwauya, who died in 1957' (Aquina 1965:11). But he did not mention that Chikudo's succession was imposed by the NC (Aquina 1965:11), or that shortly afterwards Mugabe's chieftaincy was temporarily demoted to a headmanship under neighbouring Shumba Chekai.[69] Similarly the 19th-century Mugabe-Nemanwa wars (Fontein 2006a:20–22), and Rhodesian and Morgenster

---

[67] Jairos Haruzvivishe 27/11/05.
[68] Victoria farms 1892–98, NAZ L7/11/8; NAZ DV 10/3/1–3; NAZ DV3/9/1.
[69] Delineation reports, Victoria District, 1965, NAZ 2929/8/5:66.

Photo 9   Jairos Haruzvivishe
(Sabhuku Manunure), with
his family on Mzero farm
(Source: author, 2006)

Photo 10   Chief Mugabe,
with Baba Lisa
(Source: author, 2006)

mission's support for Mugabe during them, is brushed over.[70] Nor did he mention that when he lived 'where the GP is now' it had long been occupied by Nemanwa people who were removed to Nemasuva in the Victoria reserve (under Chief Charumbira) around the same time as he went to Gwana, when the LAA was finally being implemented in the 1940s. Moreover, he barely acknowledged that it was Morgenster's long relationship with the Mugabe clan (dating back to the 1890s) that enabled his *mukoma,* as Chief Mugabe, to live at Chikarudzo in the late 1960s.

Many, if not most, of the graves and ruins cited by Haruzvivishe people to legitimise their re-occupation of Mzero farm in 2000, were of their grandfathers' and fathers' generations, who they remember being buried or even themselves buried, before their evictions in the 1940s. But the graves and ruined homesteads of their earlier re-occupations immediately after the war too animated how they re-occupied the game park/Mzero farm in the 2000s. People returned to the places where they had returned to before. The material remnants of the seven years they re-occupied Mzero (up until 1987 when it officially became a 'game park') further imbricated their relatedness to the substance of the land, re-forging active landscapes of belonging. Like the dangerous landscapes of resettled farms that war veterans and new farmers sought to make safe in the 2000s, this had tangible effects. During an early visit in the late 1990s – only a decade after the Haruzvivishe squatters had been removed – I walked through the game park looking for firewood with people from Nemanwa. When we encountered the scattered bricks, rusty pots and other remnants of a ruined homestead from the 1980s, I was told firmly to leave it all well alone. It belonged to someone and was dangerous. Although short-lived, the re-occupations of the 1980s re-invigorated the genealogical geographies of Haruzvivishe people, and through the *makuva* [graves] and *matongo* [ruins] left behind, reconstituted active landscapes of belonging, defying their second eviction and the imposition of a game park to which 'no animals ever came'.[71]

Mai Makasva's return to Mzero as *sabhuku* in the 2000s is a final story worth citing here, because it reveals how genealogical geographies can incorporate outsiders and non-kin into active landscapes of autochthonous belonging, further illustrating how the politics of people and territory entangle. Her husband and father-in-law only came onto the land she now occupies in 1959, after they were evicted from ancestral

---

[70] See Mtetwa 1976:192–8; Sayce 1978:37; Fontein 2006a:20–22). Nemanwa lost all its territory when the missionaries 'recognised Mugabe as the local chief, and … expelled Nemanwa's people from their property' (Aquina 1965:9). Nemanwa became a headman under Charumbira in the Victoria reserve. In the late 1970s parts of Mzero farm were returned for Nemanwa settlement, where the Growth Point was later built. In the early 1980s, when the rest of Mzero farm was returned to settle Nemanwa people displaced by the Growth Point, tensions with Mugabe resurfaced, especially when Haruzvivishe people re-occupied areas of Mzero farm not earmarked not for resettlement.

[71] Fred Mahuto Haruzvivishe 12/09/04.

lands on Beza.[72] This was after most Haruzvivishe people had already been evicted. Three years later they were removed again:

> I first came here in 1980. We were looking for new fields to farm. But this area is of the Makasva people. My husband and his father came here in 1959, but then went to live in Chikarudzo in 1962, because this land was taken by Morgenster mission, who wanted it to graze their cattle. Before 1959 they lived at Beza, but many farms were put at Beza, and they were removed and came here. That was a long time ago. My husband was born at Beza in the 1920s or 1930s. At that time Beza was under Bvungudzire. Bvungudzire and Mugabe are of the same *ukama* [blood or patrilineal kin group]. Bvungidzire is our *madzitateguru* [ancestor]. The graves of Bvungudzire and the oldest Makasva are here, that is the father of the father of my husband, very nearby. The father of my husband died in 1980 just after we came to live here. He was buried there, where his father was also buried, they are buried together.[73]

Given that her father-in-law and husband only occupied the area for three years before 1962, Mai Makasva's claim that 'this area is of the Makasva people' seems largely based on the presence of their graves. Yet she also linked these to much older ancestral genealogies (i.e. Bvungudzire) through which she asserted relatedness to both the soil and the Mugabe clan. Chief Mugabe's acknowledgement that Makasva is 'not of the chieftainship but is Duma and someone who we respect' justified her appointment as a *sabhuku*, alongside his *mukwasha* Sithole, and both are part of an ongoing politics of people which might yet become fixed into genealogical geographies and re-forged landscapes of belonging, so that they too can claim that 'their books were always there'.

All these graves and ruins of past occupation – pre-dating the evictions of the 1940s evictions and those from the returns of the 1980s – drew people back in the 2000s. The new re-occupations further fixed genealogical geographies into the fabric of landscape, as people cut new fields, built new homesteads and dug new graves. When VaZarira attended a *bira* hosted by Samuel Haruzvivishe in 2000, to celebrate their re-occupation of ancestral lands on Mzero, it was these graves – as well as much older graves in nearby Great Zimbabwe – that were the focus of attention (Fontein 2006a:58–62, 2006b:229). Four years later VaZarira led Mudarikwa Murinye's secret burial on Boroma, reinvigorating active landscapes of Murinye belonging, and reigniting territorial disputes with Chief Mugabe.

The re-occupations of Mzero farm illustrate the historical, political and material processes through which genealogical geographies animated land re-occupations around Mutirikwi in the 2000s. They show how colonial delineations of farms and reserves, the recursive movements that successive colonial policies provoked, and previous attempts to return to lost lands following independence, are all part of longer historical processes and older territorialities through which active landscapes of belonging are constituted. This reveals the continuing *historicity* of genealogical geographies, despite their tendency to project fixed, static

---

[72] Where other members of the Makasva family have resettled, such as VaMakasva (14/01/06).
[73] Mai Makasva 26/11/05.

continuities with re-imagined pre-colonial territories through specific ancestral relationships entangled in the substance and form of landscape. By emphasising the historical and geographical continuities linking kin, clans, and houses to specific hills, graves and ruins, the upheavals of the early colonial period are minimalized and the impact of Rhodesian rule compressed into a period marked by removal from ancestral landscapes. Such genealogical geographies therefore turn on a distinct temporality in which the Rhodesian period and all its disruptions are reduced to a gap or brief interlude in longer continuities stretching forward into new aspired futures; a gap defined by the evictions of the mid-20th century and recurring efforts to return after 1979. It is therefore a good story with which to finish Part One of this book, taking us to the middle of the 20th century and the chapters in Part Two, which consider what happened during this gap, when large-scale irrigation planning and dam building deeply accelerated Rhodesian efforts to remake Mutirikwi's landscapes.

PART TWO

**Damming Mutirikwi
1940s–1990s**

6

New White Futures, New Rhodesian Settlers and Large-scale Irrigation, 1940s–1950s

The building of the Mutirikwi or Kyle dam was completed in December 1960. It was formally opened in early 1961, culminating a period of increasingly ambitious irrigation and water planning across Southern Rhodesia. This chapter examines how dam building and irrigation planning, at Mutirikwi and elsewhere, between the late 1940s and 1960s – around the decade of the Central African Federation (1953–63) – was closely bound up with new contested, imagined futures for Southern Rhodesia, the Federation, and more generally European presence and belonging in the region, at a time of both 'high-modernist' optimism and growing momentum for decolonisation across the continent. These futures circulated around the potential that irrigation offered for increased agricultural production, for self-sufficiency in food, and for the industrialisation and European settlement of Southern Rhodesia's lowveld. They were also entangled with the complex and ultimately unresolved politics of how responsibility for European and Native irrigation planning, agriculture, natural resources and immigration, were to be divided up between the Southern Rhodesian and Federal governments. Apart from the politics of the Federation and its Territories (Southern Rhodesia, Northern Rhodesia and Nyasaland), the building of the Kyle dam was also bound up with older tensions between divergent localised futures and aspirations, particularly between Victoria residents and lowveld planters and industrialists.

In Rhodesia's early days water was key to securing white settlement, the appropriation of land for farms, and for the viability of native reserves.[1] Between the late 1940s and the 1960s, however, water planning,

[1] There is no space here to discuss the diverse ways that water was crucial to establishing settler rule in Rhodesia. When the 'fort' at Victoria was moved in 1893, it was because 'what little water there was in the Old Township bore a striking resemblance to pea soup' (Sayce 1978:70,29). Later Wallace at Great Zimbabwe pleaded with the Public Works department to improve water supplies, complaining that between August and November 'I have to carry by hand all my water from the Temple a mile away' (Wallace to Director, Public Works, 13/09/26, NAZ S533/T312/79). Seven years later concerns about Great Zimbabwe's water reached the Prime Minister, when the poor 'sanitary arrangements' at Mundell's hotel increasingly worried officials ('Zimbabwe Ruins Hotel, 1933–9' NAZ S917/a312/800). NCs at distant stations too often

especially dams for irrigation, achieved a new scale of significance. This was the period of intense modernisation across British colonial Africa that some have called the 'second colonial occupation' (Low and Lonsdale 1976:12–16). In Southern Rhodesia, it was marked by the optimism of the tobacco boom and growing industrialisation. It was also a time of labour shortages and shortfalls in food production. Both needed to be imported. These years witnessed renewed efforts to attract European settlers into the country – particularly soldiers demobilised after the Second World War but also sugar planters from South Africa, Holland and Mauritius – even as this provoked a new politics of protectionism, particularly between the Federal and Southern Rhodesian governments. Limited capital resources and the 'Federal government's policy', as one cabinet minister later recalled, 'to encourage more development in Northern Rhodesia and Nyasaland to balance it all up', meant new forms of 'contractor finance' were devised to fund Southern Rhodesia's industrial development, including the Kyle dam.[2] This was also when the large-scale evictions of the Land Apportionment Act (LAA) took place and when most people around Mutirikwi remember losing their ancestral lands. The Kyle dam's completion in December 1960, and the removal of people from Chinango and Nyangani on the Mtilikwe reserve's northern edges before they were flooded, marked the culmination of white land appropriations in the area, even if most of what was inundated had been European farms for many decades. With the expansion of wildlife and recreational facilities over the following decades, the dam and its ancillary developments signalled the most decisive and apparently final Europeanisation of Mutirikwi's landscapes, both in its immediate environs and on the vast sugar estates of Triangle and Hippo Valley in the Chiredzi lowveld.

The proliferation of state policies, expanded bureaucracies and technocratic interventions into land and water planning continued in both European and African areas during this period of high modernism. The scale, impact and longevity of conservation interventions, centralisation

(contd)   struggled securing water, as in Chibi where 'the very serious situation' in 1928 meant 'it may be necessary ... to withdraw officials' (CNC to Secretary of Premier, 24/11/28, NAZ CNC S138/7). Water problems turned not only on supplies for settlements, towns, or the reserves where the need for water (NAZ CNC S138/7; NAZ S1542:w5 vol.1–3) coagulated with deepening obsessions about soil conservation (Cleaver 1995; McGregor 1995a & 1995b; Wilson 1995). It also related to transport and communication (NAZ S1050; NAZ S1043; NAZ S12:6: 426 & 992). Victoria residents complained constantly about the poor road to Great Zimbabwe (NAZM3/10/312). Water-associated diseases like rinderpest (for cattle), typhoid, malaria and blackwater fever were also deeply significant for pioneer, prospector and transporter towns like Victoria (Sayce 1978:10,81,88,99). Settlers quickly learnt to avoid wetland vleis, and settle 'on higher ground where water would have to be carried'. Some, like Fort Victoria's Johann Herbst ignored the advice. After he succumbed to fever, 'old Mr. A.S Gifford', 'buried him and found his children roaming around the veld almost berserk' (NAZ Oral/G1 2f3; Sayce 1978:75). At the DRC's Pamusha mission 'fever had led to the death or departure of fifteen missionaries in 1903 alone' (Sayce 1978:100).

[2]   Geoffrey Ellman-Brown, NAZ Oral/235, p. 18 & 27.

Photo 11   Kyle (Mutirikwi) Dam (Source: author, 2006)

Photo 12   Opening of the Kyle Dam, 1961
(Source: National Archives of Zimbabwe; NAZ 627.8[756.30])

and hydrological landscaping in the reserves easily matched the grandiose pomposity of the large dam schemes that followed. Yet dam building and irrigation planning came to be about much more than agricultural productivity, or the viability of racialised land divisions, despite the paternalistic terms of 'partnership' and 'development' heralded by the Native Land Husbandry Act (NLHA) of 1951 and the relatively liberal policies of the Federation. The heroic dam building of the 1950s and 1960s – the Kyle dam, its larger sibling Kariba and many others – was about the imagination of ambitious, optimistic new European futures in southern Africa, in an era when decolonisation was gaining rapid momentum elsewhere. Throughout this period, the importance of dam and irrigation schemes for European-dominated industry, agriculture and settlement, and equally for recreation and white aesthetic sensibilities for pristine wilderness, wildlife and watery shorelines was recognised by both Federal and Territorial governments, feeding into and out of long-standing 'Euro-African' attempts to construct belonging and a claim to the land (cf. Hughes 2010; 2006a; 2006b; Wolmer 2007). The imagined futures so deeply coupled with dam building and irrigation planning during this period were not uniform, homogenous or uncontested. Nor were they as easy to implement as their purveyors often suggested. Yet as tensions flared up between Federal and Southern Rhodesian officials, and the many other interests involved, the influence of hydrologists and engineers at the irrigation department headed by C.L. Robertson, P.H. Haviland, and R.H. Roberts grew to match that already enjoyed by Native Affairs technocrats.

What these divergent futures involved at Kyle and elsewhere, and how they were imagined, planned, and sometimes materialised – the political materialities of their becoming – and what new pasts these imagined futures would inspire, is the subject of this chapter and the next. Some futures were obsolete almost as soon as the Kyle dam was built. Others survived changing circumstances, were remade and thrived, particularly the Triangle and Hippo Valley sugar estates which continue to benefit most from Mutirikwi's waters. Many tensions heralded by the Kyle dam continued to fester, particularly about differential water allocations for township supplies, local irrigation, and the huge conglomerate irrigators of the lowveld who largely funded it. Calls for local irrigation around Mutirikwi in the 2000s recalled plans first muted in the 1930s for a dam at Popotekwe gorge that were ultimately thwarted by changing measurements of hydrology, soil and topography in the productivity and profitability calculations of water planners in the 1950s.

These kinds of calculations offer insight into how the nexus of imagined futures and water planning is at once a highly abstracted and profoundly material affair. Building the Kyle dam and its many sibling schemes involved huge imaginative efforts and a jostle of aspired futures. But these imaginative processes were firmly rooted in increasingly microscopic and mathematical engagements with the materiality of climate, topography and milieu. Yet even as it became more sophisticated, dam building and irrigation planning remained imperfect and in many respects an exercise in guesswork. In the middle of the Kyle dam's construction in 1959, its height was increased after new hydrological information became available.[3] Apart from changing hydrological calculations, dams remained subject to the vagaries of weather, catchment and climate. Recurring drought meant Kyle took much longer to fill than expected. When it finally spilled in 1974, amid much celebration, the reach of its waters confounded hydrological and topographical expectations, flooding newly built lakeside lodges on its southern shores.

If water planning and its imagined futures were inevitably subject to climate, soil and topography, then the new pasts afforded and required by the dam too engaged with the materialities of place. The name 'Kyle', contested at the time and changed to Mutirikwi since independence, derived from the small 'Kyle farm' where it was built. It reflected the farm-owner's origins and her aesthetic experiences of its milieu, reminding her of the Kyle of Lochalsh in the Scottish highlands.[4] Similarly, when another Scot, the lowveld pioneer Murray MacDougall, built his last house on a spot overlooking Kyle where he 'had sat thirty years previously and dreamt of a great dam to irrigate the lowveld' (Saunders 1989:28), he called it Dunollie after his 'ancestral home' in Argyle. But these new pasts would not always fair better than the imagined futures that irrigation planning inspired, despite a new spurt of Rhodesian self-memorialisation in the 1970s. Mutirikwi's African pasts were not so easily engineered away. Within a decade or so of the dam's construction, the African pasts this Europeanised landscape tried to banish, began to re-emerge amidst new African futures forged as the struggle for majority rule took hold.

Rhodesian dam building in the middle of the 20th century was therefore about imagining, planning and making new futures and new pasts through re-engineering the fabric of topography. These imagined futures and their pasts were contested, emergent, and unstable. This chapter focuses on the imagined futures imbricated with irrigation planning around Victoria (Masvingo) and the lowveld. We will return to the question of new pasts in the next chapter. If water can be an index of power – of the contested entanglement of sovereignty and legitimacy – then dam building might indeed be like rain making, involving both a massive demonstration of sovereignty and a powerful appeal to legitimacy. Yet as with rain making, national *biras* (ancestral rituals) and *njuzu* (water spirit) encounters in the 2000s, it was not always clear what or whose sovereignty and legitimacy was at stake, and what or whose future was being devised. Which, whose and what kind of futures would the colossal damming of Southern Rhodesia's rivers and the irrigation of the lowveld enable? Southern Rhodesia? The Central African Federation? Fort Victoria (Masvingo) town and its white ranchers? The Chiredzi lowveld? South-African-based and other international sugar companies? The Native Affairs department? Rhodesian settler associations? Many

---

[3] *Kyle Dam Operation and Maintenance Manual* Ministry of Energy, Water Resources and Development, February 1989:17.
[4] James Alfred Gifford (NAZ oral/G1 2f3).

interests and long-held aspirations coagulated in the planning and building of the Kyle dam and its sibling schemes, and these tensions often long pre-dated the particular projects in which they became manifest.

THE UMSHANDIGE AND POPOTEKWE SCHEMES OF THE 1930S

Dam building and irrigation planning in Southern Rhodesia did not begin in the 1940s. In 1923 Murray MacDougall famously built his Jatala Weir across the Mutirikwi river on his lowveld estate at Triangle, selecting a different site to that surveyed by the Irrigation department, much to their displeasure. The feeling was mutual and he often referred to them as the 'irritation department' (Saunders 1989:16). For the next seven years his Shangaan and Shona workers carved a canal through two 450 meter granite tunnels and onto his fields eight miles away.[5] In 1931 the first waters for his scheme flowed, by which time sceptics at the Irrigation department had been replaced by C.L. Robertson and his team of engineers, who rapidly began to explore the possibilities that irrigation afforded for agriculture across the country. During the 1930s Native Affairs also built earth dams in the reserves, but this was about making the reserves viable, rather than improving livelihoods.[6] In November 1935 Alvord, the most avid and evangelical agricultural moderniser in the Native Affairs department, wrote himself that the policy was not 'to finance irrigation schemes for use in irrigation of winter crops, but for the production of ordinary summer food crops for Natives in areas where rainfall cannot be relied upon'.[7] Throughout the 1930s, 1940s and later, irrigation planning for European farming continued to be administered separately, received much more government attention, and was often tied to securing productive land to attract new settlers.

As early as the late 1920s and early 1930s, investigations for two possible schemes in Victoria district were under way: a 'western' irrigation scheme at 'Umshandige' (Mushandike) gorge west of Fort Victoria, and an 'eastern' scheme at the Popotekwe gorge.[8] In the late 1920s Robertson (then Chief Irrigation Engineer) inspected the Umshandige site with Mr Haviland (Irrigation Engineer for Matabeleland), followed by officials from the Lands department, the Minister for Agriculture, and even the Prime Minister. For much of 1930–31, a team of surveyors camped at the two sites, investigating 'the possibilities of storing water for irrigation'.[9]

---

[5] While Rhodesians celebrated MacDougall's 'herculean task, undertaken against all odds and contrary to professional opinion' (Saunders 1989:15), his Shangaan and Shona workers have remained 'nameless and faceless' (Wolmer 2007:94; Mlambo & Pangeti 1996). These early irrigation works were later declared a national monument.

[6] 'Water Preservation, Native Reserves, 1923–33' (NAZ CNC S138/7); 'Water Development Reserves, 1933–9' (NAZ S1542:w5 vol.1–3).

[7] Alvord to CNC, 19/11/35. (NAZ CNC S1542/w5 vol. 1).

[8] 'Letter to Editor, Ernest G. Birch', *Bulawayo Chronicle*, 20/06/31.

[9] Haviland to Birch, 06/09/29 (NAZ S2975/-4).

The investigations ranged from determining water flows, topography and soil in the proposed irrigable areas, to examining 'rock formation in the vicinity of and at the gorge itself'.[10] Not only were these schemes targeted to benefit European agriculture, the practical science that planning demanded was also deeply racialised. E.G. Birch, on whose Maybrook farm the Umshandige investigations took place, wrote to the *Bulawayo Chronicle* with not a little glee, that when the chemist 'took samples of earth for analysis at the Government laboratories [he] did not let the "munt" [sl. 'African'] take his samples', rather 'he stuck his own head and shoulders downstairs and took samples carefully from the different sections exposed'.[11] Unsurprisingly, in other correspondence to Haviland, he expressed 'regret' about the 'difficulty obtaining boys for your job here', adding there was 'some superstition locally ... for the gorge, ... that it was used as a spot for execution in the early years, or perhaps the local boys have omitted to put stones in the pile'.[12]

If dam and irrigation planning during the 1930s was primarily focused on improving European agriculture, it also caused many parochial contests between settlers around Victoria. Birch's letter to the *Bulawayo Chronicle* (20/06/31) was a response to lobbying by two different settler associations: the Eastern Fort Victoria Farmers Association's resolution to 'urge the government to abandon the two big irrigation schemes ... [and] concentrate on assisting the owners of small irrigation schemes', and the Fort Victoria Publicity Association's strong support of the Popotekwe scheme as the only one 'deserving of attention'. Both groups, Birch suggested, were biased by the location of their farms, and several had their own smaller schemes whose viability the proposed dams threatened. Birch was 'interested in the western scheme' because of his farm's location. But, he added, 'I sincerely hope ... both schemes will ultimately materialize' because they would be 'the backbone' for Victoria's growing export beef industry, and 'there are ... hundreds of other advantages as well – wheat, barley, onions and potatoes are being imported in huge quantities today'.[13]

Only the Umshandige dam was built in the late 1930s. It created an irrigation scheme both for existing farmers, and to attract new settlers 'of the right type' under 'Agreement to purchase' leases.[14] 'This type of settlement' Robertson explained, 'would be suitable for the growing of lucerne or other fodder crops and the growing of wheat'.[15] Later emphasis would shift to overcoming Southern Rhodesia's food shortages. Before the dam was completed, its canal was extended across 'Victoria–Beitbridge road' for watering cattle in the northwest of the Victoria reserve, where 'the water question ... has always been very acute'. It offered

[10] Birch, *Bulawayo Chronicle,* 20/06/31.
[11] Ibid.
[12] Birch to Haviland, 27/03/30. (NAZ S2975/2).
[13] Birch 20/06/31 *Bulawayo Chronicle.*
[14] Robertson to Secretary, Agriculture and Lands 16/02/37 (NAZ S2975/3).
[15] Ibid.

Africans the 'tail waters' of a scheme built primarily for white settlers.[16] As one of Rhodesia's earliest large dams, data on its flow, seepage and evaporation rates often appeared in the calculations of hydrologists and engineers working on later schemes. It later became clear Umshandige's planners had been over-optimistic. In 1950 'poor runoff ... from the last four years ... confirmed ... that demands being made on the dam are beyond its capacity'. The number of settlers were reduced and existing sub-divisions reviewed according to new soil surveys, 'in order to make the fullest use of water available'.[17] With Umshandige, dam building had moved on from the 1920s when it depended on the resolve of strong-willed settlers and the toils of their African labourers, but large-scale irrigation planning was still in its infancy.

The Popotekwe dam was not built but neither was it shelved, at least not yet. As discussed in the next chapter, throughout the 1940s and well into the 1950s, the possibility of a Popotekwe dam was held open. In 1949 exploratory diamond drilling took place at the proposed dam site around the same time as at Kyle. By then Popotekwe's competition was less for another local irrigation project in Victoria, then for its place in a much grander scheme supplying Mutirikwi's waters to the lowveld. Popotekwe survived the transition from the localised schemes of the 1930s, to the enormous hydrological planning of the 1940s–60s, and the inflated imagined futures these encompassed. But it was never built. As soil surveying, hydrology and engineering improved, and the projected demand for water from the lowveld's sugar industries became increasingly dominant, Popotekwe was finally declared obsolete before it was even built; it was permanently shelved in the late 1950s, only a year or two before Kyle's construction began, to the disappointment of its long-term supporters around Fort Victoria.

FOOD SHORTAGES, INDUSTRIAL DEVELOPMENT AND LARGE-SCALE IRRIGATION PLANNING IN THE 1940S AND 1950S

In the 1940s attention turned to much larger schemes. In particular, the possibilities offered by irrigating the rich alluvial but dry soils of the lowveld increasingly preoccupied government planners. By the late 1930s MacDougall had demonstrated sugar could be grown in the lowveld, but

---

[16] NC to Irrigation Engineer, Bulawayo, 09/08/38 (NAZ S2975/4); Water Bailiff to Director, Irrigation, 4/9/39 (NAZ S2976:4). Also correspondence between Robertson, NC Victoria and CNC (NAZ S1542/w5 Vol.2 1936–7). Only after independence were irrigated resettlement schemes established for Africans below Mushandike. Since 2000 these have been 're-occupied' and Chief Charumbira and his clan have been active in making ancestral claims to the area (Chief Charumbira and his *dare* 24/05/06; Simon Charumbira & Adamson Zvitambo 27/05/06), provoking similar kinds of disputes as around Mutirikwi ('Charumbira order's headman's kidnap', *Financial Gazette*, 07/06/07; Senator orders release of suspects from police cells', *Wezhira Community Radio*, 28/2/08; 'ZANU PF sticks to threats', *Zimbabwe Telegraph*, 06/07/10).

[17] Haviland to Minister, Agriculture and Lands, 12/05/50 (NAZ 1194/1512/7).

his ventures were plagued by financial insecurity and debt. In 1944 the government finally agreed to nationalise his Triangle sugar company, forming the Sugar Industry Board to take it (and its debts) over. The era of large-scale irrigation planning in Southern Rhodesia had begun.

The possibilities of water engineering in south-eastern Zimbabwe fired many imaginations during this period. Sharpened by concerns about growing food shortages in the immediate post-war context, government increasingly focused on the 'irrigable potential of the Save basin' (Wolmer 2007:95). In 1947 Sir Alexander Gibb was appointed to survey 'the irrigable potential of the Save valley ... for the production of wheat, sugar, vegetables and fruit, and dairy produce'. He concluded that 'at least 100,000 hectares of the lowveld could be properly utilized, and recommended the building of dams ... an agricultural research station and a 10,000 hectares pilot scheme' (Wolmer 2007:95; for full report see Gibb & Partners 1948). He also recommended that sugar at Triangle 'should be going forward ... preceding full development of the lower valley'. 'It is most fortunate that the government already has this estate ... and can consequently extend the crop to the economic limit of the present factory [the mill MacDougall constructed in the 1939], so soon as sufficient water is available'.[18]

In the decade after purchasing Triangle, the Sugar Industry Board expanded sugar production, lengthened canals, and built further weirs and storage dams. Although still beset by financial difficulties and problems with smut infestation, frost and drought, in 1954 Triangle was sold to a syndicate of Natal sugar planters. Three years later it was sold to Guy Hulett, who 'initiated a period of major infrastructural development in the lowveld, as South African capital and technology was brought to bear in transforming the landscape' (Wolmer 2007:95; Saunders 1989:48–62; Eastwood 1996). Under Hulett successful negotiations took place with the Irrigation department enabling the Kyle dam, already under consideration for a decade, to be financed and built in 1959–61, with huge preferential water allocations for Triangle.[19] Massive expansions followed in the 1960s, with rival estates emerging at Hippo Valley and later Mkwasine, new dams built at Bangala, Manjirenji and elsewhere, as well as a new sugar mill at Triangle, a tarred road, an airport at Buffalo range, the whole town of Chiredzi, and even a railway to Mozambique.

The broader context for Gibb's 1948 report was the 'lack of co-ordination between industry and primary production', meaning that 'in few ... civilized countries has ... food production kept pace with industrial development'. The 'expansion of the war industries ... high wages attracting workers from the land ... higher nutritional standards and ...

---

[18] Para. 55, *Interim report*, Sir William Gavin, 'Agricultural aspects of the Sabi-Lundi development project' 17/05/48 (NAZ S1194/1512).

[19] Hulett's own fortunes did not survive very long. In 1962 his corporation was taken over by a new consortium of Natal sugar companies, and later it and Hippo Valley became subsidiaries of Anglo-American, although rivalries between the two estates, a marked feature of Hulett's period, continued for a long time (Saunders 1989:48–77).

increasing populations, has so accelerated this maladjustment that the world faces the most serious food crisis in history', he told Southern Rhodesia's prime minister. His plan was 'formidable' but 'its preparation indicates that the Government … are aware of the seriousness of the problem'. The 'Sabi valley project cannot … be regarded as a local or an eastern province one. It is of national, even international importance' he insisted, involving 'nearly a quarter of the colony and … some of its most fertile soils'.[20] Lowveld irrigation planning was being tied to larger and grander ambitions. Eventually Gibb's recommendations 'came to fruition with the establishment of the Sabi-Limpopo Authority' in the 1960s, 'the largest and most ambitious project ever conceived in Southern Rhodesia' and modelled 'on the Tennesse Valley authority … with wide powers over nearly a sixth of Zimbabwe' (Wolmer 2007:96). By 1963 'Rhodesia was exporting sugar, thousands of workers had been brought in from Nyasaland (Malawi) and parts of the lowveld landscape had been unrecognizably transformed'. For white Rhodesians 'the lowveld had become symbolic of growth, development, unlimited future potential and a badge of national pride' (2007:96–97).

The optimism invested in heroic water engineering during this period did not only focus on the lowveld, important as that became. It reached across Zimbabwe. Its extent was perhaps best captured by a 1948 article in *The Liberal*, by Arthur Thornton, advocating a 3,000 square mile lake in the south-east of Rhodesia in order 'to humidify our prevailing wind'.[21] Such a colossal dam on the lower Sabi (Save) or Lundi (Rundi) rivers, he argued, would increase rainfall across Southern Rhodesia. 'Man can conquer his environment' he insisted, and 'Southern Rhodesia can be made a well-watered country with a greater average rainfall … twice, if not more, as great as before'.[22] Criticising the allocations of the water courts and urban municipalities, Thornton also called for better, coordinated water planning at a national level between the demands of towns and farmers, arguing that 'no imagination seems to have existed and each for himself has apparently been the slogan'. 'I firmly believe', he concluded, 'that Southern Rhodesia could be made an agricultural and industrial paradise' if there was 'proper long term planning, particularly with regard to that most vital and indispensable commodity, WATER' (original emphasis).[23]

Thornton's piece raised eyebrows in various ministries, particularly because he was 'preaching his dam gospel' in Bulawayo.[24] The Director of Irrigation suggested 'a campaign is being conducted against the natural resources board, the water court and this department' and recommended 'some reply in public would be advisable'.[25] He calculated that evapora-

[20] Gibb & Partners to PM Southern Rhodesia, 18/06/48 (NAZ S1194/1512).
[21] A.Thornton, 'Wet and dry belts in Africa, 3000-sq. mile Rhodesian Lake advocated', *The Liberal*, 09/01/48, (NAZ file S1194/1512/1–5).
[22] Ibid.
[23] Ibid.
[24] Director, Irrigation to Secretary, Agriculture & Lands, 240/2/48 (NAZ S1194/1512/1–5).
[25] Ibid.

tion from a 3,000 square mile lake would be about '14000 cusecs', and that such a dam would require '70,000 sq. miles of catchment' covering 'practically half the colony'. The dam itself would have to be many miles long. The Director of Meteorological services was consulted, and rejected the idea that a large dam could affect the weather much, noting that most of the air passing over Rhodesia had usually already passed over many thousands of square miles of ocean. The 'lack of rain is due rather to anti-cyclonic subsidence and resulting dryness of the upper layers, than to humidity conditions at the surface' he explained.[26] 'The most that could be expected' the meteorologist continued, 'would be night showers over the lake itself and a small increase of convective showers within ten to fifteen miles of the leeward shore of the lake'. Furthermore, Thornton's argument was 'putting the cart before the horse' because 'the rainfall in the southern part of Rhodesia would ... be inadequate to maintain a lake of such size in a high evaporation area'.[27] Dam building was not rain making after all.

However far-fetched the idea that an enormous dam could bring rain, Thornton's article reflected both the period's optimism for large dams, and recurrent tensions between Rhodesian settlers and the amalgam of different government departments responsible for agriculture, irrigation and natural resources. Yet the sentiment 'that Southern Rhodesia could be made an agricultural and industrial paradise' through proper water planning was one that civil servants and ministers shared with settlers, farmers and entrepreneurs. It was an axiom for the age. In 1952 R.H. Roberts, then Director of Irrigation, illustrated this perfectly:

> Water will without doubt prove to be one of the major limiting powers in the economic development of Southern Rhodesia, and the importance of planning for the best possible utilisation ... cannot therefore be overstated. It affects practically every major development, whether it be growth of towns, the generation of electricity, the development of railways and other communications, the essential supply of water to major industries and mines, or ... the attainment of a reasonable self-sufficiency in ... food ... The colony's water potential ... is definitely limited. How limited has not yet been sufficiently appreciated. Certain rivers, or portions of rivers are already fully allocated, and others are rapidly approaching that point ... The orderly development of water resources will directly affect the expenditure of many millions of pounds, and will indirectly affect vastly larger sums of money. Failure to plan in good time will result in chaos, and in waste of money on expedients and hasty makeshifts and ill-considered schemes.[28]

That same year the 'Report on Large-Scale Irrigation Development in Southern Rhodesia' was published.[29] From now on water planning was of highest priority. Before it was even published, a 'standing committee

[26] Director, Meteorological services, to Director, Irrigation, 19/02/48, (NAZ S1194/1512/1–5).

[27] Ibid. and Director, Irrigation to Secretary Agriculture & Lands, 24/02/48 (NAZ S1194/1512/1–5).

[28] Memo, Roberts, 15/09/52 (NAZ S1194/1512/1/11).

[29] In 1950 a 'Departmental Working Party', 'with Dr. S. Makings, Chief Agricultural Economist, as chairman' was set up to 'Report on large-scale irrigation development in Southern Rhodesia', 1952:1. (NAZ F149/con/120).

of senior departmental officials to advise ... on matters relating to irrigation development' was established.[30] Its chairman reported that without
'major changes in food production ... shortfalls in basic foodstuffs, which
present a major embarrassment ... today, are likely to [become] a
crippling handicap *within the next decade*'.[31] The 1952 report focused
particularly on the economic possibilities of irrigated agriculture, but too
gave 'due weight to our lack of self-sufficiency in basic foodstuffs ... at a
time when external supplies are precarious'.[32] It covered a huge range of
low and high veld, intensive and extensive irrigation schemes, varying
greatly in scale, purpose and location.[33] It 'purposely' did not consider the
Zambezi schemes, because while 'the possibility for irrigation from this
large permanent river' were 'at least as great as that from the combined
schemes of the rest of the colony', the 'problems involved are so vast and
of such importance' that this required its own investigation of the same
ilk as Gibb's Save Valley report.[34] It did consider the 'Popotekwe and
Triangle Estate Scheme', envisaging 'the storage of water at one or more
of three possible dam sites on the Mtilikwe river system' (Popotekwe,
Kyle and Bangala), and included plans for irrigation immediately below
Popotekwe (much of which was later flooded by Kyle), and for '15,800
acres of sugar-cane ... at Triangle'. With detailed calculations of the cost
of water delivered per acre-foot (c. 1,233 cubic metres), and of annual
net profits per unit of 100 acres, the 1952 report recommended that the
lowveld be prioritised for intensive irrigation development,[35] and that
'the necessary preliminary work', in particular 'large-scale air mapping,
detailed soil surveys and the collection of hydrographic data' be started
immediately.[36] Furthermore government 'must accept the principle of
subsidizing such development ... either temporally or permanently', with
land 'given out on leasehold tenure to approved settlers' until a settler
proved 'to be an efficient irrigation farmer', when the option of purchasing the freehold would become available.[37]

---

[30] Ibid.

[31] Undated memo, R.R. Staples, Chairman, Standing Committee on large-scale
irrigation (NAZ F1/4/R/10/01).

[32] 'Report on Large-Scale Irrigation' 1952:2. (NAZ F149/con/120).

[33] E.g. Umfuli scheme for industrial, domestic and agricultural purposes in
Hartley and Gatooma (Kadoma); the 'Ngesi dam', with lined canals on the
Sebakwe river for irrigation, and the Umniati power station and other industrial
purposes in Que Que; and others at 'Poorti' in Shamva, 'Concession' and
'Bindura', 'Hunyani', 'Maquadsi' and Essexvale; to name only some (ibid).

[34] Ibid.

[35] Extensive 'high veld irrigation schemes should not be developed until ... also
required to provide water for other purposes', with the exception of the Hunyani,
Ngesi and Umfuli schemes (ibid.:37,38).

[36] Ibid.:39.

[37] Ibid.:37–39.

NEW SETTLERS: HOLLANDERS, NATAL SUGAR PLANTERS, ITALIANS, MAURITIANS AND FORMER SERVICEMEN

Apart from agricultural production and food security, the development of large irrigation schemes was also about attracting new, preferably skilled, and definitely white, settler-farmers to the colony. Indeed the growing settler population made the food situation much more urgent. Both Gibb and the 1952 report discussed irrigation development for Europeans and Africans separately, laying their emphasis on the former. Both also emphasised the importance of ensuring 'beneficial', 'productive' use of irrigated lands by Rhodesian settler-farmers, which could not be assumed. As Gibb warned:

> We are inclined to blame the Native for working his land merely to get sufficient food for himself and his family without regard to the country's need for increased production. Is the European entirely free from the same charge if we substitute ... the word 'money' for 'food'? I think not and ... there seems room for wider knowledge of modern methods of dealing with light tropical soils, cultivations, humus conservation, fertilisers ... the more readily land is available, the more difficult it is to get it well farmed.[38]

As Rhodesia's urban white population was growing, efforts to attract new farmers expanded, while the British government sought land in its colonies for servicemen demobilised from the Second World War. Geoffrey Ellman-Brown, a member of Godfrey Huggin's post-war government (and later Garfield Todd's during the Federation), explained how the 'tremendous influx of immigrants' after the war meant they were 'desperately short of houses'.[39] In eastern Victoria new settler schemes for ex-servicemen were being devised,[40] something not forgotten by

---

[38] *Interim report*, Sir William Gavin, (NAZ S1194/1512):7, para 27.

[39] Ellman-Brown, NAZ Oral/235:18,27.

[40] The 'Chaka' irrigated resettlement was being devised in 1943–45, even before the Second World War was finished, on a line of existing farms – including Cheveden, Arawe (then owned by Morgenster), Histonhurst, Thankerton, Campsie Glen and Niekerk's Rust – along the Bevumi river, purchased by government, resurveyed and sub-divided, for 'post-war settlement of ex-servicemen' (NAZ S2136/51/199; S2111:41). There were many neglected farms at the time, where 'little farming beyond cattle raising was done in recent years' and 'Native squatters' appeared to have 'had a free hand' (Land Inspector, 19/01/44, S2136/51/199). The impending LAA placed a burden on such farm-owners, and government's farm purchases for post-war settlement schemes offered some a way out. The land inspector was confident 'the recovery of land from this type of Native farming ... should not be a protracted business' and indeed these schemes contributed to the large-scale evictions of Africans during this period.

war veterans occupying farms in the early 2000s.[41] In the lowveld plans were afoot to bring 'Hollanders' into the Sabi scheme, once irrigation facilities were established. In May 1950 the secretaries of Agriculture and of Internal Affairs corresponded about the 'organised immigration of Netherlanders' for '100 acre irrigated farms in the Sabi valley around a central butter and canning factory'. The Agriculture secretary strongly supported the 'scheme to introduce Hollanders to produce food' and felt 'everything possible should be done to encourage' it.[42]

As settler immigration continued, irrigation planning was also envisaged as key to the de-centralisation of growing white populations in Salisbury and Bulawayo. Roberts reported in 1956 that the 'decentralization of population must depend to a very large extent on the development of water resources to supply it'. Water development would 'enable the domestic and industrial requirements of the population at the smaller centres to be expanded' and was 'required for irrigation to provide food for these smaller areas'. 'The proposed Kyle dam' he argued, was a good 'example of how de-centralisation can be encouraged by the development of available water resources', involving 'the development of large-scale irrigation in the district' and 'through the attraction of tourists to the beautiful lake that will be created, both of which can be expected to promote the rapid growth of Fort Victoria'. In addition 'the town will also be able to draw its future water supplies from the Kyle dam'.[43]

The desire to attract white settlers to new irrigation schemes was also closely tied to plans for sugar estates in the lowveld. The Natal syndicate took over Triangle in 1954, after overcoming a rival bid from 'a group of Hollanders with interests in the East Indies'. 'One factor influencing

---

[41] One war veteran explained 'our target was European farms issued as pensions for fighting in the Second World War, because they did not buy the soil ... They were not fighting here, they were fighting somewhere in Malaysia, but they were given our land as pension. So we took those farms. (VaChuma 12/06/06).

[42] Acting Secretary, Internal affairs 16/05/50; Secretary Agriculture 22/05/50, (NAZ S1194/1512/1/7).

[43] 'Decentralization thorough water development' Roberts, 05/10/56 (NAZ F149/con/220).

Photo 13   Aerial view of lands north of where Lake Mutirikwi later flooded, showing Mt Beza to the left, and Fort Victoria's war-time internment camp for Italians in the foreground, 1944. Italians interred there during WWII built the small 'Italian Chapel' which later became part of the 'heritage' trial that Victorians constructed around the new lake in late 1960s and 1970s. (Source: National Archives of Zimbabwe; NAZ 71/72[756.4]75).

government to sell to the syndicate was the intention ... enthusiastically supported by the government, that a major settlement
scheme involving immigration of young farmers from Natal, should
be responsible for the production of the bulk of the cane to be milled
at Triangle when adequate water ... became available' (Saunders
1989:45). It is not clear if Natal farmers were preferred over 'Hollanders' for other reasons, but concerns about the 'type' of white
settler, and particularly preference for Rhodesians did emerge. The
Natal Syndicate placed three '"guinea-pig" or experimental settlers
on the land' to investigate 'the economic requirements of such a
scheme' (Saunders 1989:45–46). The three chosen reflected perfectly
government concerns about the type of new farmer they hoped to
attract. M.N. Starling came from 'a well known Natal family' and
had 'considerable knowledge of and experience in the growing of
sugar'; W.H. Hingeston, was a former airman from South Africa
who had flown in the middle east in the Second World War; and
the third was a Rhodesian, J.H.R. Eastwood (Saunders 1989:46–47).

When Hulett took over Triangle, no more settler/planter farms were
allocated and the existing three were only very reluctantly held on.
Hulett 'could not abide the thought that anybody else had a stake in
his empire' and 'refused to take over Triangle under the previous concept of a large scale resettlement scheme' (Saunders 1989:54). 'We ...
were very keen to have settlers there' Ellman-Brown later explained,
but 'he refused point blank' saying 'they were more of a nuisance than
an asset'.[44] This reflects different visions of the relationship between
private funding, individual enterprise and government in irrigation
planning at the time. Later, however, as water infrastructure was expanded and its availability increased, even Triangle became involved
in outgrower schemes, particularly at the Mkwasine venture shared
with Hippo Valley. After 2000, these outgrower sugar farms became
the focus of elite farm redistributions to army officers, politicians and
civil servants.[45]

Hulett's attitude contrasted strongly with his rival at Hippo Valley,
Ray Stockil, then MP and Leader of the Opposition, who originally
focused on citrus fruit but soon followed Triangle into sugar. Stockil's
scheme attracted the Southern Rhodesian government's attention in the
mid-1950s, and was quickly envisaged as a settlement project for settler-

---

[44] Ellman-Brown, (NAZ Oral/235:18–27).
[45] 'Triangle Visit', Fieldnotes 15–16/6/06. 'Government in bid to harmonise
relations at Mkwasine estates', *Herald*, 22/03/06; 'A2 farmers call for government
intervention over sugarcane dispute', *Herald*, 18/05/06; 'New farm takeovers
threaten sugarcane production', *Herald*, 07/06/06; 'Top army officials and war
vets jostle for farms', *RadioVOP*, 05/06/09; 'War vets, ZANU-PF lock horns over
farmer', *Zimbabwe Times*, 02/06/09; 'Officials of Zimbabwe's ZANU-PF Party eye
Sugar Plantations for takeover', *voanews.com*, 19/01/11; 'Chiefs grab sugarcane
farms', *Zimbabwean*, 07/11/12.

planters contracted to provide sugar to Hippo Valley.[46] In the 1957 Hippo Valley Agreement (and Act 1958) government promised to build the Bangala dam to massively augment the very limited water allocations Hippo Valley would receive from Kyle. The government promised to 'assist ... and facilitate the immigration of settlers', demanding involvement 'with the selection of suitable settlers, all of whom shall be of European origin, PROVIDED ALWAYS that not less than one half of the settlers shall be drawn from ... the British Commonwealth of Nations'.[47]

Stockil's scheme, and the immigration of new European settlers involved, sent ripples of worry through the Southern Rhodesian Government and particularly at Federal levels. Although the desire to increase white settlement in the colony continued unabated, concerns focused on the kinds of immigrants arriving. In July 1958 the prospect of a large 'intake' of Italians particularly concerned Eddie G.G. Marsh in the Federal Ministry for Home Affairs, who urged the Federal Prime Minister (PM) to advise the Southern Rhodesian government to 'reduce the intake of alien immigrants' and 'keep their proportion within the 10/12 per cent of total intake ... accepted in the past'.[48] He was especially worried about 'the high ratio of Italians', noting that 'during the past 3 years 2,236 Italians have entered the Federation, easily the largest nationality group'. Blaming both 'the Intergovernmental Committee for European Migration' and 'the considerable interest in the Federation being shown by the Italian Government and ... financial and trading concerns', he argued against 'any arrangement ... committing us to accepting further Italian immigrants in appreciable numbers' but would 'naturally be prepared to consider any specific project such as the Kyle dam scheme on its merits'.[49] Although the settlement scheme was still at least two or three years off (awaiting water from Kyle), in September 1958 Federal officials were pleased to learn 'the company has now dropped the idea of ... a mass invasion of Italians'.[50]

The threat of a 'mass invasion of Italians' at Hippo Valley was soon replaced by requests for entry permits for more Italians from C. Kirkpatrick, director of Sir Alfred McAlpine and Son (Rhodesia), contracted to build the Kyle dam. These were 'very highly experienced technical personnel' brought in 'for particular jobs and purposes', to remain 'until such a time as their services are no longer necessary.' Kirkpatrick emphasised they were 'vitally necessary for the construction work', adding that 'the total number of Europeans ... employed ... is between 90–100, all of whom, with the exception of 9 or 10 of the specialists ... have been recruited locally'.[51] Colonel Laird from Southern Rhodesia's Home Affairs

---

[46] Ellman-Brown (NAZ Oral/235:18 –27).

[47] Hippo Valley Act (NAZ F119/imm9/6):13, para 30A.

[48] Secretary, Home Affairs, EGG Marsh, to PM and Cabinet Office (Fed.gov.) 09/07/58 ('Kyle dam project 1958–63', NAZ F119/imm9/6).

[49] Ibid.

[50] Memo to Marsh 01/09/58 (NAZ F119/imm9/6).

[51] Letter (25/09/58) from C. Kirk Patrick, Sir Alfred McAlpine and son (Rhodesia) Ltd to Colonel Laird, Secretary, Home affairs (SR gov) (NAZ F119/imm9/6).

supported Kirkpatrick's request and assumed the Federal government would 'not oppose the entry of ten alien specialists'. He reassured them the specialists would 'be admitted on aliens temporary residence permits valid for one year' and 'subject to cancellation should a holder prove to be an undesirable resident'.[52] Such worries about 'undesirable residents' echoed older concerns about 'poor types' of farmer. When an immigration liaison officer visited Triangle and Hippo Valley later that year, he warned it was 'quite obvious that any new settlers … to the Kyle dam area will have to live "on the smell of an oil rag" for the first few years and unless due care is exercised in the selection of settlers and … the amount of assistance given … the settlement area could well become a breeding ground for the "poor" type of farmer'.[53]

Soon concerns about invasions of Italians and poor types of farmer were dwarfed by worries about settlers from Mauritius. This was provoked by Stockil's widely reported[54] negotiations with Mauritian sugar companies. The *Evening Standard* (23/01/59) fretted that the shift from citrus to sugar would mean an 'influx of Mauritian settlers', after Stockil announced that 'Mauritian sugar interests have bought a substantial number of shares' and 'the general manager of the new sugar estates will be a Mauritian'. Noting that the Hippo Valley Act required '50% of the settlers … be drawn from commonwealth nations', and that 'Mauritius, though French speaking, is a British possession and its people are British subjects', it concluded that 'legally … there would appear to be no objection to white Mauritians as settlers on the scheme'. A cutting of the article was pinned to the government file with a note that Stockil had been written to by both the Federal and Southern Rhodesian governments.[55] Later that month, W.S. Harris (Home Affairs) spelled out the Federal government's acutely racialised concerns:

> The act refers to the selection of suitable settlers … of European origin, but if the recent press reports are to be believed … certain Mauritians have been appointed as directors and it is … proposed that others be appointed in a managerial capacity but that no land settlement by Mauritians is envisaged. It is understood that the majority of the inhabitants of Mauritius are of mixed race, mainly of Asian origin and if the company proposes to import either as employees or as settlers Mauritians who are non-Europeans it would be a matter of concern, in view of the longstanding policy in regard to Asiatic and coloured immigration and also of the present employment prospects for Europeans, coloured and African residents of the Federation … The increased production of sugar in the Federation is a matter of considerable importance and this ministry would wish to give the company every assistance possible, within immigration policy, but you will readily appreciate that with the example of Natal before us, great care must be exercised in relation to the entry of persons of Asiatic descent or of mixed race.[56]

[52] Laird, 26/09/58 (NAZ F119/imm9/6).
[53] 'Extract from Immigration Liaison officer's report on Fort Victoria, visited 03–04/11/58 (NAZ F119/imm9/6).
[54] See for example 'Multi-million sugar plan for SR', *Sunday Mail*, 14/09/58.
[55] *Evening Standard,* 23/01/59, (NAZ F119/imm9/6).
[56] Harris to PM & External Affairs, 31/01/59, (NAZ F119/imm9/6).

At the same time, the possibilities of a large irrigated settlement scheme at Hippo Valley generated excitement in London. In February W.H. Hammond, high commissioner for Rhodesia and Nyasaland, wrote to the Federal Ministry of Home Affairs enquiring about settling former servicemen on the scheme.

> In the Rhodesian Herald of the 4th Feb. was a news item concerning the resignation of Ray Stockil as leader of the Opposition. This particular piece of information did not set me alight with pleasure, but what followed ... did give me cause to think. The statement detailed ... the future prospects of the Hippo Valley sugar scheme and I gathered that Stockil ... expected to have some 10,000 acres of sugar land under irrigation with water from the Kyle dam by about 1961. Further, and this is where my interest really perked up, the 10,000 acres was to be sub-divided into small holdings of about 150 acres each. Now reckoning 60 tons of sugar cane per acre, 100 acres on a smallholding would produce 6,000 tons. I am not sure how much this is worth, but I imagine ... quite a substantial sum, sufficient ... to provide a farmer with a good living. That being so, it seems to me that Stockil's 10,000 acres could support ...100 settlers. What about making the settlers 'axed' servicemen? They could do their training during the next two years and ... take up their small-holdings just as soon as the water from the Kyle dam began to flow. At this distance and without any background information I may be talking through my hat. On the other hand there may be a possibility that Stockil's 10,000 acres is but a portion of the land available, in which case, with a little anticipation we might be able to place several hundred 'axed' servicemen.[57]

In response Marsh explained that as 'the bulk of the capital for sugar growing and processing is being put up by Mauritians, people from that country will have the first claim'. Furthermore, it was likely that 'the company will say that they wish to introduce settlers with experience in sugar growing'. Not for ex-servicemen then. But having 'feared that the tie-up with Mauritian interests would mean an attempt to introduce a good deal of non-European labour from that island' Marsh did reassure Hammond that 'we have now had assurance ... that ... the technicians ... will all be British subjects of European descent'.[58]

Extended negotiations took place between Stockil's Mauritius Development Company of Rhodesia, and the Federal and Territorial governments about the settlement of British Mauritian subjects at Hippo Valley. One of the company's directors, Mr Dacombe, reassured the Federal government 'that it is this company's policy to introduce as many Europeans as possible into the lowveld, and ... few, if any, people of mixed origin will be employed by the company'.[59] When Dacombe met Marsh the following month, he explained that 'the company planned to import most of its own staff from Mauritius, since Mauritians had invested capital and had the "know-how"', but 'these would be British subjects, of European descent, on the managerial and technical staff, all earning over £1,500 p.a.'. This suited Marsh because 'there appeared to be no immigration difficulties for such British, European technicians'. However, Dacomb also explained their 'wish to introduce 1 or 2 persons

[57] Hammond, to Marsh, 18/02/59 (NAZ F119/imm9/6).
[58] Marsh to Hammond, 25/02/59 (NAZ F119/imm9/6).
[59] Mr Dacombe, to Secretary, Home Affairs, 19/02/59, (NAZ F119/imm9/6).

of mixed descent ... for such operations as pan-boiling and sugar purifying'. Marsh insisted upon 'consultation before the company recruited such staff' because they 'were generally not accepted for permanent residence', only 'for a limited period ... if the ministry were satisfied that no suitable local labour was available', and on the condition that 'the importations would train local persons'.[60]

In the first instance only three or so 'experimental farms' were to be established, and 'of the three, one would probably be Rhodesian, one Mauritian, of European descent and a British subject' – echoing the experimental farmers settled on nearby Triangle. A further 50–80 farms would eventually become available with water from the Bangala dam, and Marsh insisted the company 'should be aware of Immigration policy, so that its selections could be made in accordance with that policy, to avoid embarrassment'. A year later four experimental farms had been allocated, to 'two Rhodesians and one sugar grower each from Natal and Mauritius'.[61] When fifty further farms became available, Stockil estimated 'the proportion of Rhodesians among settlers will exceed that percentage' reserved in the Hippo Valley Act for settlers from commonwealth countries.[62]

Over the following years Dacombe's reassurances that only one or two 'coloured' Mauritians would be 'imported' to work on the sugar pans proved wrong. Permission was repeatedly sought to 'import' various Mauritian 'coloured', 'mixed race' and 'creole' technicians. In 1962 alone permission was sought for an extra '25 creoles'.[63] Mrs Johnson, sent by Home Affairs to visit Hippo Valley in June 1962, reported that:

> The duty of the creoles is to supervise and instruct Africans and they will gradually be returned to Mauritius as their trainees become capable of taking over. When the company first found that insufficient creoles had been imported it was hoped that sufficient Africans would be trained in time to supplement them and enable two shifts to be worked, but after a month it became clear that this would not be possible. Permission is now being sought, therefore, to import more creoles and it is planned to lay them off gradually, except for the sugar pan boilers, over a period of 2 or 3 years. Mr Stockil emphasized that no Africans would be laid off ... in fact he would probably have to take on a few more. He went on to point out that as a result of his factory's slow start and a slight hitch at Triangle, Rhodesian refineries had had to import another 2000 tons of unrefined sugar. I was shown over the mill and saw Africans working under the supervision of creoles, except at the sugar pan boilers. The whole process depends on each stage working smoothly and without hitch. Care has to be taken that the right amount of material is fed forward at each stage. I could well see the need for reliable men to supervise the operators and it would appear that it will take rather longer than was thought to train Africans for this work.[64]

[60] Note of a meeting between Marsh and Dacombe 23/03/59 (NAZ F119/imm9/6).

[61] 'Two Rhodesians and growers from Natal and Mauritius to start at Hippo valley', *Rhodesian Herald*, 24/02/60.

[62] Ibid.

[63] Dacomb, Hippo Valley Estates, to Federal Chief Immigration Officer, 26/06/62 (NAZ F119/imm9/6).

[64] Mrs Johnson to Minister, Home Affairs, 30/06/62 (NAZ F119/imm9/6)

Federal immigration officials took their duties rather seriously. In 1959 a permanent residence application for a Mauritian employee of Hippo Valley, Maurice France Jacques Desvaux de Marigny, was only granted after the immigration board was 'furnished' with 'a Police Certificate confirming his European Descent'.[65] They were not pleased with the additional, unanticipated immigration requests for 'coloured' technicians, particularly because past experience with temporary 'imports' of Mauritian labour and expertise for other sugar estates at Chirundu had proved, after ten years, anything but short term.[66] Similarly, far more than ten Italian specialists were employed at the Kyle dam site. Of the 230 Europeans employed there more than 50 per cent were Italians.[67]

The 1962 requests from Hippo Valley were therefore reluctantly approved 'on the strict understanding that every effort will be made to train local workers to replace them'. The Mauritians were 'admitted on temporary permit for a period of 12 months'.[68] In the years that followed increased efforts were made to oblige Hippo Valley to hasten the training of African technicians and return 'imported creoles' back to Mauritius, efforts they seemed increasingly amenable to. Apart from the cost of flying workers to and from Mauritius, Hippo Valley's directors had other reasons for resolving the issue: growing unrest among African labourers. In August 1962 an immigration officer based at Gwelo (Gweru) reported that 'there is no likelihood of Hippo Valley requesting any further intake of Mauritians' after 'African personnel complained against wages paid to Mauritian employees, compared with their own, taking into account that the majority of Mauritians are more African than European'. A strike had been 'averted by the presence of the police' and 'no further trouble' was expected, but 'miscegenation is bound to occur' although there had been 'no reported cases' yet.[69]

The Federal government's heavy-handed control and deeply racialised perspective on the kind of settlers desirable at schemes like Hippo Valley is startling, not only because of its reputation for *relatively* liberal native policies (in comparison to Southern Rhodesia), but also because of its desire (shared with Southern Rhodesia) to increase European settlers in the colony. No doubt Federal policies were enacted, in part, under the guise of protecting employment for Africans, and preventing the kind of labour dispute Gwelo's immigration officer reported in 1962. Two years later Stockil suggested the developing lowveld sugar industries were 'a solution to African unemployment' and 'unrest'.[70] Indeed during that period thousands of workers were brought in from Nyasaland to work as cane cutters and labourers (Wolmer 2007:96). But the sugar industry's

[65] Secretary BISB to Secretary, Home affairs, 05/06/59 (NAZ F119/imm9/6).
[66] Secretary PM & External affairs to Secretary, PM SR, 30/06/62 (NAZ F119/imm9/6).
[67] Kyle dam, Visited Wednesday, 23/09/59 (NAZ F119/imm9/6).
[68] Memo 02/07/62, 'Introduction of Mauritian Labour for the Hippo Valley Sugar Estates Ltd.' (NAZ F119/imm9/6).
[69] Extract from report 02/08/62 Immigration officer Gwelo (NAZ F119/imm9/6).
[70] *Sunday Mail,* 12/01/64.

successes, as with large-scale irrigation development elsewhere during this period, were still mainly reserved for European and particularly Rhodesian settlers. Other non-white, 'aliens' would only benefit as temporary technicians. Africans, local and alien, remained, for the most part, the unskilled labour upon which the industry relied, as they had been for MacDougall's much vaunted Jatala weir and canal nearly forty years before.[71]

NATIVE IRRIGATION AND GROWING TENSIONS BETWEEN SOUTHERN RHODESIA AND THE FEDERATION

Food security, settler population growth, and economic development were clearly not the only issues occupying irrigation planners and civil servants during this period. It is less clear how much the Southern Rhodesian government shared Federal concerns about the importation of different types of white aliens. Both desired irrigated settlement schemes to increase the European settler population. But Southern Rhodesian officials sometimes grew impatient with the Federal government's protection of employment opportunities for local Africans, and its tight immigration controls over types of European settlement.[72] Such tensions no doubt related, in part, to what Ellman-Brown recalled as the Federal government's 'very sticky' reluctance to allocate 'capital funds to Rhodesia, as distinct from Northern Rhodesia and Malawi'.[73] Beyond

---

[71] Despite UDI, war and independence (Saunders 1989:69–87), these labour divisions did not to change much. In the second edition (1989) of his MacDougall 'hagiography', Saunders justified the continued use of mass unskilled African labour at Triangle for the employment it offered (1989:85,89), romanticising it as an 'impressive sight to see a trained Triangle cane cutter, muscles rippling, singing away as he swings his sharp instrument with powerful and accurate strokes and harvests the crop from the lowveld's green gold' (Saunders 1989:93). He also changed the first edition's (1977) references to MacDougall's 'piccanines' to 'hardworking Shangaans'. He scarcely mentioned that cheap labour probably made full mechanisation a less profitable alternative. Triangle did alter its brand after independence, and developed progressive welfare, housing, health, and education programmes (Saunders 1989:116–8). More inclusive outgrower schemes were introduced in the late 1980s and 1990s (Shumba et al. 2011). Yet the sugar industry continued to be dominated by international capital (Mlambo and Pangeti 1996). Only with the land reform in the 2000s, and ZANU PF's populist indigenisation policies, was this challenged. Anglo-American gave up shares in Tongaat Hulett in August 2009 ('Anglo American to sell Tongaat Hulett stake', *Mining Weekly*, 12/08/09), but pressure continued for it 'to focus on milling only' ('Redistribute sugarcane plantations', *Sunday Mail*, 15/07/12; 'Zim: Minister loses patience with "defiant" Tongaat Hulett', *Mail & Guardian*, 20/04/13).

[72] A scribbled note on the *Evening Standard* cutting (23/01/59), gives an indication: 'Stockil should see his Minister (Stumbles) and our own Minister [i.e. Federal Government]. Mr Stumbles is understood to have remarked that the immigration side must be left to the Federal Government. I am not quite sure what he meant as he obviously has no option' (NAZ F119/imm9/6).

[73] Geoffrey Ellman-Brown, NAZ Oral/235:18–27.

funds and immigration policies, the question of responsibility for large-scale dam and irrigation schemes too became a source of increasing tensions during this period, replicating highly localised concerns about the amalgam of different authorities involved with water planning generally. These tensions became increasingly intertwined with changing perspectives on the division of Federal and Territorial responsibilities over European and native land and agriculture, and particularly about the future of irrigation planning for Africans.

In September 1952, Roberts had acknowledged uncertainty about how responsibility for water planning would be organised with the forthcoming Central African Federation's establishment, although for him this did not detract from the urgency to set up a statutory body for water development in Southern Rhodesia.[74] A Ministry of Water Development did later replace the Irrigation Department, but did little to ease concerns about the complexity of different authorities in charge of water planning. A decade later, for example, the *Fort Victoria Advertiser* reported local demands for a single 'Kyle local authority' to promote 'leisure and recreational development' around their new dam, and cut through 'the miles of red tape' between the area's 'many masters', which frequently animated discussions between the town's mayor, council and various associations.[75] The creation of Southern Rhodesia's Ministry of Water Development also did little to ease tensions with the Federal government about the division of responsibilities for water planning, agriculture and irrigation development.

In July 1958 the Federal Government received a request from the Northern Rhodesian government in Lusaka, about whether a proposed irrigation scheme there would under Territorial or Federal authority. C.A. Murray (Federal Director of Conservation and Extension) explained that 'although the question of responsibility for "major" and not "major" irrigation schemes seems rather unsatisfactory, it has sorted itself out quite well in Southern Rhodesia and there is no reason why the same should not happen in Northern Rhodesia'. 'Federal government' has accepted responsibility for only Kariba, Kafue, Shire and Sabi valley schemes', he explained, 'not even Kyle dam ... which is to cost approximately £3,000,000, has been accepted as a Federal Government responsibility. This scheme is being financed by the Southern Rhodesian government.'[76] It seems extraordinary that the Kyle project, which created Zimbabwe's second largest lake (after Kariba), was considered a small-scale scheme. Yet Southern Rhodesia's responsibility for financing it might explain their reticence about succeeding immigration control over its

[74] Memorandum Roberts, 15/09/52, (NAZ S1194/1512/1/11).
[75] 'Mayor again hits out at Kyle red tape', *Fort Victoria Advertiser*, 10/04/64. Also 'Move towards Kyle local authority', 20/3/64; 'Municipal Move to Acquire Land at Kyle' 15/12/64; 'Council pressing again for co-ordinated Kyle development', 17/09/65; 'Publicity still fighting for overall Kyle plan', 29/10/65; 'Austin hits out at Kyle appointments', 20/10/67; all *Fort Victoria Advertiser*.
[76] Murray to C.K.Thompson, Ass. Director Conservation and Extension (NRGov. Lusaka) 08/07/58 (NAZ F149/con/120).

new settlers to the Federal government. When a constitutional review re-examined the Federation's division of responsibilities two years later, Murray no longer felt the 'rather unsatisfactory' arrangement had 'sorted itself out quite well'. The existing situation, he explained, meant the Federal government was directly in charge of all European agriculture in both Southern and Northern Rhodesia, but only *indirectly* in charge of African agriculture in all three countries.[77] Large-scale irrigation was a Federal concern, but small-scale schemes remained with the territorial governments. 'It is generally accepted that while SOIL is a nation's greatest asset WATER is its greatest need' he wrote, and 'there are obvious advantages in having control over this vital resource at central or Federal level'. 'In view of the inseparable link between water, agriculture and sound land use at farm, regional, Territorial and Federal levels' he continued, 'it is ... essential that "water development and irrigation" ... should come under Federal control'.[78]

Murray's concerns extended to the control of natural resources more broadly, which he felt should all come under Federal control. 'The future and prosperity of the Federation' he argued 'is largely dependent on the intelligent use of its natural resources', especially 'its soil and water for the production of food for man and for beast'.[79] Furthermore, the division 'between European and Native agriculture is undesirable' as 'there is no difference in the basic principles of land use as the physical controls set by Nature applies to all land irrespective of whether it is used by Europeans or Africans'.[80] 'In planning and implementing soil and water conservation works it is essential to work on a catchment or watershed basis', he continued.

> Operations in any particular part of a watershed must effect ... any lower portion of the area and artificial boundaries are irrelevant. It is quite obvious that where European and Native areas are situated within the same catchment, the work must be on a co-ordinated basis under the same direction ... At present we have the anomalous position in that while the Natural Resource Boards in Southern Rhodesia and Northern Rhodesia are territorial bodies they devote 90% of their time and effort to European agriculture (which is a Federal responsibility) whereas 90% of the destruction is taking place in African areas. ... The entire problem is a very difficult one but one cannot get away from the principle that the Federal government, which is responsible for broad agricultural and national development policy, should also be responsible for conservation, i.e. the wise use of its natural resources on which all future development must depend.[81]

Murray therefore synthesised a catchment-wide, hydrological view of the importance of soil and water conservation and irrigation planning, with a strongly Federalist perspective. In the process he questioned one of the central tenets of Rhodesian land planning. The novelty wasn't so much that it was now suddenly acknowledged that African farmers

---

[77] Also only indirectly in charge for European agriculture in Nyasaland.
[78] 'Constitutional review: Irrigation and water conservation', c.1960 Murray (NAZ F149/con/120).
[79] Ibid.
[80] Ibid.
[81] Ibid.

too would benefit from dams and irrigation. Native Affairs technocrats had been building earth dams and water conservation works for as long as they had been centralising, destocking, and contour ridging in the reserves. The NLHA's (1951) modernist optimism emphasised the need to improve African agriculture, and top priority had been assigned to developing African irrigation schemes. Irrigation planners all over Southern Rhodesia had been brought into the fold.[82] What *was* novel and far-sighted about Murray's report was its emphasis on the undesirability of 'irrelevant', 'artificial boundaries' separating African and European land and water planning, and its emphasis on the hydrological need for coordinated catchment-wide planning. This is something water planners in Zimbabwe and across the region continued to grapple with in the 1990s and 2000s, albeit now with terms like 'integrated water resource management' (Fontein 2008:741–2). In the late 1950s and early 1960s, despite the NLHA's modernist enthusiasms, irrigation planning was still bifurcated in the way land and agriculture was, and Murray was critical of the way this was unevenly replicated in the divisions of responsibility over water, land and natural resources at Territorial and Federal levels.

In Southern Rhodesia, in particular, water planning for European and African areas was kept determinedly separate throughout the 1950's enthusiasm for large-scale irrigation. The 1948 Gibb report discussed irrigation for both African and European agriculture, but insisted on keeping them separate. Similarly the 1952 report acknowledged large-scale irrigation could serve European and native areas, adding that 'in general the products on which schemes may be successfully based will be common to both'. But it insisted there would be 'marked differences in tenure, layout and size of units' and it was 'convenient' for European and native schemes to be considered separately.[83] Native Affairs' enthusiasm for water development in the reserves was not always replicated by water planners. In 1955, the Water Resources Committee (of the Natural Resources Board) raised concerns that clauses in the LAA intended to protect African rights in the reserves, were holding back water development. In particular, section 15, limiting European occupation in the reserves to such purposes deemed to be 'for the benefit of the Natives residing there', had 'the effect of prohibiting the construction of water storage works' unless directly benefiting 'Natives in the ... area concerned'. This affected 'roughly half of the potential dam sites' and 'could seriously hamper water development ... of benefit to the whole country'. Noting that the 'restriction did not apply in reverse' and 'dams

---

[82] In November 1957, for example, the Midlands Water Development Committee noted 'the importance of intensive settlement on African irrigation schemes'. Min. 6th meeting, Midlands Water Dev. Committee, 22/11/57 (NAZ F149/con/220).

[83] 'The estimated acreage of irrigated land which can be handled by a Native family is 8 acres' the report suggested, much smaller than was envisaged for European settlers. Furthermore, for African irrigated agriculture 'capital would have to be found by the State', 'tenure would be conditional on good farming practice' and 'supervision and control' would need to be 'adequate' ('Report on Large-Scale Irrigation' 1952:12, 19. NAZ F149/con/120).

could be constructed in a European area for the benefit of Natives in an adjoining Native area ... [without] ... direct benefit for the Europeans', the Committee recommended to 'take this matter up with the government' because it 'would restrict the functions of Natural Resources Board'. [84] It is not clear what came of this, but evidently the challenges that the catchment-wide perspective of hydrologists could bring to the bifurcation of Rhodesian land and water planning was not always understood in terms beneficial for African agriculture.

In the end Murray's argument for the Federalisation of natural resource management, agricultural and irrigation planning came to nothing. Like the NLHA's modernising optimism and the relatively liberal Federal context, the catchment-wide concerns of hydrologists and water planners could have offered opportunity to question the stark separation of African and European land planning. But this was only whispered towards the very end of the Federal period. For the most part the Federation maintained 'racial segregation under the slogan of partnership' (Ranger 2013:10). Within a few years the Central African Federation had collapsed. Southern Rhodesian politics took a profound swing to the right with the election of Ian Smith's Rhodesian Front, and the NLHA was rapidly abandoned in the face of growing African nationalist militancy. The more liberal, modernising futures entangled with large-scale dam building and irrigation planning quickly demised, as a new traditionalism came to dominate native policy (Alexander 2006:63–79). After UDI (Unilateral Declaration of Independence) many of Rhodesia's more progressive white population emigrated, increasingly as the liberation war intensified in the late 1960s and 1970s. But the industrial landscapes of the sugar-growing lowveld *were* created, thrived and became of huge symbolic and aspirational significance for how Rhodesia imagined itself, even if they too struggled under the vagaries of UDI politics.[85]

When the Kyle dam was finished in late 1960 not all the futures entangled with it survived its completion. Long-held demands for local irrigation in east Victoria were not fulfilled by the damming of the Mutirikwi river. But Kyle did dramatically alter the landscape under and around it. In so doing it fulfilled less the image of heroic engineers and hydrologists as 'pioneers ...pulling together to carve a new productive landscape from the wastelands', as Wolmer describes the lowveld (2007:99), but rather combined older European sensibilities for watery shorelines, wildlife and nature, with more future-orientated concerns with tourism, recreation, and water sports. The lowveld industrialised on a massive scale – transforming the 'chaos' of 'this drab and dusty'

---

[84] Min. 12 of meeting Water Resources Committee of Natural Resources Board, 22/03/55, Water resources Committee correspondence, 1954–58, (NAZ F149/con/220).

[85] With growing international isolation, embargoes, and the changing 'internal' situation of the late 1960s and 1970s, the sugar industries struggled and were forced to diversify, and 'rescue packages' were 'offered to the settler planters to keep them in business' (Wolmer 2007:98; Mlambo & Pangeti 1996; Saunders 1989:69–86).

wilderness into the 'ordered', 'lush, green "cane culture"' of 'the straight edged, grid-like symmetry' of canals and sugar plantations (Wolmer 2007:100). But Victoria got a beautiful lake, a well-stocked game reserve, and the 'best bass fishery' in the country. The next chapter examines how the debates of the 1950s about which dams to build on the Mutirikwi system – and for what or whose benefit – were only partly determined by the ambitious futures that large-scale irrigation offered, or the capital invested by lowveld industrialists. They were equally determined by increasingly detailed engagements with the materialities of climate, hydrology and topography. The remaking of Mutirikwi's landscapes heralded by the Kyle dam was a profoundly material and imaginative process, and one which called for new pasts as well as new futures to be inscribed in the materiality of milieu.

7

Remaking Fort Victoria's Landscapes, 1950s–1960s

This chapter begins by focusing on the debates of the 1950s about which dams (Popotekwe, Kyle or Bangala) to build on the Mutirikwi river system. Engaging with Ingold's efforts to close the gap between imagining and perceiving landscape – what I term the materialities of imagination – it explores how minute material engagements with the affordances of soil, topography and hydrology were caught up in the divergent demands of Victoria residents and the lowveld sugar industries. Although the grandiose imagined futures of irrigation planning were important for what happened – that the long-muted Popotekwe dam was never built and Mutirikwi's waters were primarily harnessed for industrialising the lowveld – this was never a foregone conclusion. It depended on the changeable catchment, water flow, topography, soil type, productivity and profitability surveys and calculations of water planners in the 1950s. The implications of these calculations – of the political materialities of their imagination and becoming – were quite significant. Extended discussions about augmenting Fort Victoria's unreliable water supplies from the lake matched the disappointed expectations of neighbouring farmers that they too might benefit from its waters. Farmers who lost land to the lake did receive compensation and some drew from its waters, but not very many. Those that did could grow wheat and maize commercially. But the remaking of Fort Victoria's landscapes heralded by Kyle would not fulfil the wilderness-taming aspirations and ordering aesthetics of huge irrigated landscapes, as in the lowveld (cf. Wolmer 2007:99–100). Rather, it manifested something closer to another strand of white settler belonging that revolved around European sensibilities for watery shorelines, wilderness, wildlife and nature (cf. Hughes 2010).

It is remarkable how often Lake Mutirikwi is described in terms of its beauty and aesthetic appeal, even more so that this was already imagined long before the dam was built.[1] But this appeal to wilderness was not inevitably linked to notions of pristine 'old Africa'. It was much more future and development orientated than that. It related to long-standing demands for improved infrastructure to make Fort Victoria a 'holiday playground' to 'seriously challenge any comparison by any inland tourist

[1] Errol and Daryl Edwards 25/05/06; Roberts 'Decentralisation' 05/10/56 (NAZ F149/con/220).

areas'.[2] Such demands recalled the 1900s, when the railway's anticipated arrival (Sayce 1978:117) promised increased visitors to the town.[3] With the dam's completion, local newspapers and noisy associations pressed for development with renewed vigour. While National Parks stocked the new lake and game reserve with wildlife and fish, Victoria residents turned to game ranching, tourism and even the film industry. By the 1970s, Rhodesia had created its own, second playground, matching in facilities and beauty the enormity of Kariba, a landscape for game viewing, fishing, and boating.

This did not mean the past no longer mattered, far from it in fact. The game reserve, fisheries, boat clubs, chalets and camping sites did not easily fit the 'old Africa' trope salient elsewhere (cf. Ranger 1999), but the remaking of Mutirikwi's landscapes heralded by the dam definitely involved complex acts of historiography. More than that, it demanded it. With the exception of much older rock art in the area, and of course Great Zimbabwe, local African pasts were (almost) obliterated, as people were relocated from Chinango and Nyangani leaving behind sacred sites and ancestral graves under the lake's rising waters, or on hilltops that became islands. Some traces of African presence survived as names for the new lake's bays, such as 'Basotho Bay' (above the former Basotho-owned Erichsthal farm – Mujere 2012), matching how farm names sometimes reflected older Karanga landscapes (Arawe/Hararwe, Mzero/Muzviro, Beza). Obscure Rhodesian farm(er) names were also traced onto the lake (Bompst bay, Gifford bay), alongside even blander wildlife references (Rhino bay, Hippo creek). The imagined futures and re-forged landscapes of the lowveld also fed into Mutirikwi's new historiography, as the names MacDougall, Robertson and other irrigation schemers became central to renewed Rhodesian self-memorialisation.[4]

But it didn't all last for long, and the promises of dams do not always deliver. The dam retains its formidable presence and the ruins of white occupation and rule around it continued to have unexpected efficacy into the 2000s. But older African pasts and presence in this re-forged landscape of white pleasure were soon re-asserted as the inevitability of war and majority rule became apparent in the 1970s. As discussed in the next chapter, landscapes of white recreation became filled with danger, as cattle rustling and poaching increased, guerrillas blew up bridges, burnt hotels and ambushed farmers, and local farms became Rhodesian bases. This would resonate with the insecurities of the 2000s, which again kept visitors away, and with the experiences of Zano's fishermen and poachers facing *njuzu* (water spirits), hippos, wardens and crocodiles. Much of what was forged with the building of Kyle could be unmade, even as much would endure. Much of what had pre-existed the dam quickly re-emerged as different pasts and futures came to co-exist in close and active proximity through the materialities of its landscapes.

[2] 'Press statement 314/60', 28/7/60, Federal Information Department (NAZ S3269/35/19).

[3] Mundell 24/09/13 (NAZ L2/1/171).

[4] 'MacDougall's name honoured again', *Fort Victoria Advertiser*, 17/09/65.

IMAGINING, PERCEIVING, (RE)MAKING LANDSCAPE AND THE POLITICAL MATERIALITIES OF BECOMING

When the study of landscape spread beyond geography into archaeology, anthropology, history and literary studies in the 1980s and 1990s, debates turned on what remains the concept's greatest analytical strength: its 'useful ambiguity' (Gosden & Head 1994:113). Landscapes encompass 'both the conceptual and the physical' (1994:113) as 'particular ways of expressing conceptions of the world' and 'a means of referring to physical entities' (Layton & Ucko 1999:1). This distinction mapped onto increasingly problematised Cartesian dichotomies of mind and body, nature and culture, or in Weber's terms, *'explanation* and *understanding'* (Ucko & Layton 1999:3). Studies divided into so-called postmodernist, and phenomenological or 'dwelling' approaches. Both attempted to overcome Cartesian distinctions – a surprisingly tenacious problem – but took to the task in diametrically opposed ways.

Daniels and Cosgrove's *The Iconography of Landscape* (1988) perhaps best represented the former. Reducing landscape to 'a cultural image, a pictorial way of representing, structuring or symbolising surroundings', they understood 'written and verbal representations' of landscape not as 'illustrations ... standing outside it, but as constituent images of its ... meanings' (1988:1). Aligned with social constructivism and its critical reassessment of knowledge production, their emphasis on the endless play of representations was useful for understanding the contested nature of landscape. In a 'thoroughgoing postmodernist perspective', Ucko and Layton observed (1999:3), 'there is no environment only landscape'. The other side of the debate, however, argued that this approach was too static, ignoring process and experience. Ingold (1992, 1993), in particular, engaged with Gibson's 'ecological approach to perception' (1979) to focus on landscape as 'taskscape', of living *in* and *with* the world. A 'dwelling perspective' sought to move beyond 'the sterile opposition between the naturalistic view of the landscape as neutral, external backdrop to human activities, and the culturalistic view that every landscape is a particular cognitive or symbolic ordering of space' (Ingold 1993:152). Landscape, he insisted, is neither built nor unbuilt, but 'perpetually under construction', always a 'work in progress' (1993:162). This meant that 'dwelling in the world, we do not act *upon* it, or do things *to* it; rather we move along *with* it. Our actions do not transform the world, they are part and parcel of the world's transforming of itself. And that is just another way of saying that they belong to time' (Ingold 1993:164).

While some critiqued Ingold for neglecting politics, consciousness, imagination and representation (cf. Bender 1998:37), others attempted to reconcile the two polarised positions. Hirsch and O'Hanlon (1995) described landscape as a 'cultural process' between 'place' and 'space'; between the 'foreground actuality' of 'an ordinary, workaday life' and the 'background potentiality' of 'an ideal, imagined existence'. This avoided the static, representational predominance of *The Iconicity of Landscape* but allowed more space for politics, power, historicity and the play of meanings than Ingold's 'dwelling' perspective. For her part, Bender merged the phenomenological emphasis upon seamless, grounded, local-ised movements and experiences, with the representational aspects of imagined landscapes 'within enlarged worlds', arguing the relationship between the two is suffused with politics and power, and landscapes are therefore 'always in movement, and always becoming' (2001:4).

In the 2000s, such notions of becoming, flow, mutual constitution and emergence, gained wider analytical purchase. Recognising how their polarisations sometimes replicated the very dualisms the debates sought to eclipse, the materiality turn refocused attention upon related distinctions between objects and subjects, humans and animals, and particularly matter and meaning. Often inspired by Deleuzian thought, there has been a collective attempt to move beyond the limits of social constructivism, and in this sense Ingold's contributions have cast the longer shadow. Recently he has turned attention to what his earlier work seemed hardly to abide: the imagination.[5] Seeking to collapse the distinc-tion between imagination and perception, he again builds upon Gibson's refusal to separate the 'perceived' from the 'real' world, but also moves beyond it exactly because Gibson leaves 'no place for the imagination' (2012a:3). For Ingold 'the real world and the perceived world do not lie on opposite sides of an impermeable division between "outside" and "inside"'. Rather we must 'reconsider the significance of imagination: to think of it not just as a capacity to construct images, or as the power of mental representation, but ... as a way of living creatively in a world that is itself crescent, always in formation'. 'To imagine' Ingold insists, 'is not so much to conjure up images of reality "out there", whether virtual or actual, true or false, as to participate from within, through perception and action, in the very becoming of things' (Ingold 2012a:3).

This is the approach I draw upon to explore how the damming of the Mutirikwi was both an imaginative and a material affair; a remaking of landscape at once abstracted yet a profoundly material 'participation from within ... in the very becoming of things'. The Kyle dam and its related schemes might have been designed, financed and built by Rhode-sian planners, Italian technicians and African labourers, and inspired by a host of shared and contested aspirations, in processes that remade the landscape, the past and the future. But this was less the imposition of an imagined, and highly imaginative, engineering order onto inert substrate and topography, than an imaginative/material becoming in which the imaginative, perceptive, and creative dimensions of human involvement were *more or less* seamlessly imbricated with the material properties of land, soil, water and climate; 'a never-ending, contrapuntal interweav-ing of material flows and sensory awareness' (Ingold 2012a:16). The

---

[5] Here Ingold comes close to the ontological project (cf. Holbraad 2006) by challenging 'any division we might attempt to force between the reality of the world and its representation' (2012a:15), rather 'perception that is at once material and imaginative, at once close up, and distant' through which 'the landscape ... imagines and re-imagines itself through the awareness of its perceivers' (2012a:14).

more or less is important. It points to the unstable relationship between the changing imaginative/perceptive capacities and capabilities for action of planners, surveyors and engineers, and the excessive poten- tialities (Pinney 2005:270) of material substances and flows that afford irrigation, dam building, and so on, even as they also exceed it. This changeable space of instability, this *more or less*, or *slippage*, is where historicity and politics emerge, and where big engineering projects may fail to deliver promises or exceed them. This is the open-ended space of guesswork and contestation.

MAPPING MUTIRIKWI

Consider the two images, Maps 2 and 2a below. Map 2 is a photograph of a map from the National Archives in Zimbabwe (originally in colour) show- ing the projected reach of waters of the proposed Kyle Dam (hand drawn in blue pencil on the original). I am very grateful to the National Archives of Zimbabwe for their permission to print this image here.[6] Note the dif- ference in the level of detail for European farming areas compared to the African reserves. The centre of the image shows the estimated extent of Lake Kyle's reach, drawn onto the original colour map in blue pencil by hand, a materialisation of an imaginative projection into the future. There is a hand-drawn line (in red on the original) around the projected lake, in- dicating the area – beyond where the Kyle Dam's waters were expected to reach – that it was estimated would need to be protected from soil erosion to prevent the lake's siltation. Some of this area was later reserved for the lake's proposed game park, illustrating graphically how a dam appropri- ates a far larger reach of land than it floods, just as its waters derive from a larger catchment than its surface area.

Map 2a is a reconstruction of Map 2, indicating the blue shaded area and the red line that were hand drawn on the original map. It also shows, above the projected lake, the faint rubbed-out traces (in blue on the origi- nal) where the map was also, for a time, marked with the projected reach of the Popotekwe dam's waters further north: a dam never built and an imagined future that never became. The list scribbled in the margin above (Map 2) indicates the farms that would have been inundated had the Popotekwe dam been built.

In a 'landscape as image' perspective this map is a landscape; a repre- sentation full of efficacious historical, cultural, and political signs, mean- ings and symbolisms to be read off, interpreted and contested, an image of a 'real' environment, or one that might one day exist. On the other hand, we might say this map certainly exists as a thing in the world, but only as a map, artefact or image functioning as a tool or extension of the imagination, *not* a perceived landscape but an imagined one. In what I pursue here this map is *both*; an imaginative/perceptive engagement *with* the material world that participates in and is part of its endless becoming. As an artefact or tool it might become, as things often do, an

---

[6] Kyle Dam, Popotekwe maps (NAZ S3599/435).

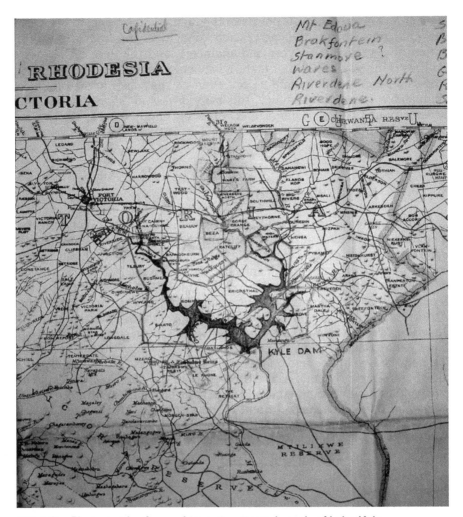

Map 2   Photograph of map showing projected reach of Lake Kyle
(Source: National Archives of Zimbabwe; NAZ S3599/435)

extension of humans *in* or *with* the world, but definitely not *onto* or *out of it*. The map has a material relationship to the world it represents. This may be iconic or indexical (Keane 2005; Engelke 2007) but it is not arbitrary, regardless of how symbolic it may become or how many symbols it contains. However mediated by changing technologies, the map is a 'view from nowhere', yet one materially forged from many *real* locations and *real* actions *in* the world, from the walked measurements and samples of surveyors, lines drawn by cartographers, and the flow projections of hydrologists, to the contours identified by topographers and aerial photographers moving through landscape or flying over it. It is less a representation of abstracted space than the result of numerous material experiences, movements and actions within it. The map was certainly (partly) constitutive of that landscape's becoming, but the landscape is

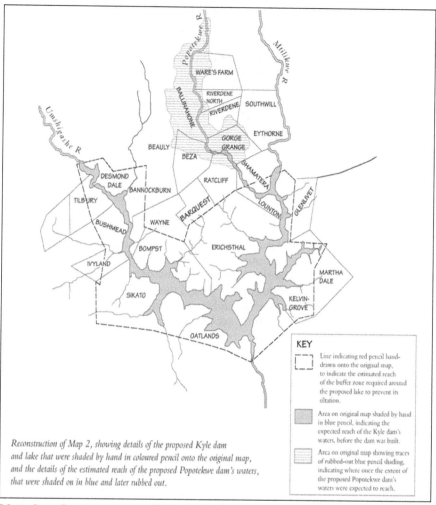

Reconstruction of Map 2, showing details of the proposed Kyle dam and lake that were shaded by hand in coloured pencil onto the original map, and the details of the estimated reach of the proposed Popotekwe dam's waters, that were shaded on in blue and later rubbed out.

KEY

Line indicating red pencil hand-drawn onto the original map, to indicate the estimated reach of the buffer zone required around the proposed lake to prevent its siltation.

Area on original map shaded by hand in blue pencil, indicating the expected reach of the Kyle dam's waters, before the dam was built.

Area on original map showing traces of rubbed-out blue pencil shading, indicating where once the extent of the proposed Popotekwe dam's waters were expected to reach.

Map 2a   Reconstruction of Map 2 showing projected reach of Lake Kyle

equally constitutive of the map's becoming. Like all maps and landscapes, it contains enduring traces of past, incomplete becomings, like ruins and graves or the faded traces of a dam and lake that were never built.

In the 1980s and 1990s scholars of mapping (Harley 1988, 1992a, 1992b; Huggan 1991; Bender 1999) realised just how constructed, symbolic and laden with technologies of power/resistance maps are, and implicated in imperial projects everywhere. The materiality turn demands we recognise maps as both material and abstracted, imaginative and perceptive, projections of the future and reflections of the past, and of past futures and future pasts. The Kyle/Popotekwe map is both product and producer; active and inert; artefact, image and process; metaphor and metonym. It is work in progress, an ongoing assemblage of hands, lines, ideas, desires, soil, water, movement, and substances; part of the very Mutirikwi landscapes its records and remakes. It is decidedly not an arbitrary collection of signs like 'a flickering text ... on the ... screen whose meaning can be created, extended, altered, elaborated and finally obliterated by the nearest touch of a button' (Cosgrove and Daniels 1988:8), but it is fluid, emergent, and politically consequential.

This map (and many others like it) was part of an array of imaginative/perceptive techniques for measuring, surveying, determining and projecting soil, hydrology, topography and climate, which were deployed to investigate irrigation possibilities all around Southern Rhodesia. After surveying the Mutirikwi River in 1951, H.L. Weels (Chief Reconnaissance Engineer) reported that the 'necessity for accurate large scale mapping ... cannot be too strongly emphasized'. 'The economic development of the colony depends ... on such mapping', and 'it must go ahead with accelerated progress'.[7] Ever more detailed surveys of soil, hydrology and topography were central to irrigation planning in this period. This fed a growing demand for surveyors and engineers, and by the late 1950s concerns were raised about a 'worldwide shortage' of 'engineers for development of water resources'.[8] The increasingly sophisticated engagements of colonial scientists, engineers and planners with the stuff of land, water, climate and topography would partly determine which dams would be built, how Mutirikwi's landscapes would be remade, and what imagined futures would become part of the fabric of its history.

POPOTEKWE, KYLE OR BANGALA?

Given MacDougall's extensive memorialisation as *the* pioneer of lowveld irrigation, one could be forgiven for assuming he was responsible for proposing to dam the Mutirikwi on the middle-veld escarpment, below its confluence with the Mushagashe river.[9] This is not true. MacDougall denied he discovered the site, claiming he was shown it by Alfred Gifford in the 1930s, and that two local fishermen called Nolan and Reedman first found it (Saunders 1989:51). It was not even the first proposed dam site considered by government planners in the area. Engineers only investigated it as late as 1948/49, when exploratory diamond drilling at the long-muted Popotekwe also took place.

Serious consideration for a dam at Kyle for lowveld irrigation only began after MacDougall demonstrated sugar cane could be profitably grown. The idea bloomed after the Sugar Board took over Triangle in the 1940s. Well into the 1950s, the Popotekwe dam remained a serious contender, and negotiations continued over the purchase of lands to be inundated by it, or reserved for its irrigation scheme. The proposed road to Mutare was even re-routed, despite government interest beginning to shift towards irrigating the lowveld. By 1952, a very large scheme for both Fort Victorian and lowveld irrigation was being considered,

[7] Weels, 19/12/51 (NAZ S1194/1512/1/9-10).
[8] Roberts, 29/01/57 (NAZ F149/con/220).
[9] MacDougall lives on in folkore. I heard unlikely accounts of him walking the length of the Mutirikwi to identify the dam site (Fieldnotes 06/11/05).

involving dams at any or all of three sites in the Mutirikwi catchment – Popotekwe, Kyle and Bangala:

> *The Popotekwe and Triangle Estate scheme* – This scheme ... envisages the storage of water at one or more of three possible dam sites on the Mtilikwi River system. In magnitude the scheme ranks next to the Sabi. The upper Dam site is on the Popotekwe tributary on Grange Gorge Farm, about 0–12 miles east of Fort Victoria. The Second dam site is on the Mtilikwi river on Kyle farm, just downstream of the Umshagashi confluence, and the third possible site ... still to be investigated in detail, is on the Mtilikwi river some distance upstream of the Bangala falls. It is estimated that normal river flow, supplemented by water from storage at these three sites, would provide a net annual supply of 108,270 acre-feet of water for irrigation development. Of this quantity some 4200 acre-feet would be required for the annual irrigation of 2100 acres of crops under system No. 2 in an area immediately below the Popotekwe Dam. The balance of water would be available for the irrigation of 15,800 acres of sugar cane or such other crops as may be decided upon, at Triangle Estate. With sugar cane the output of raw sugar would be about 40,000 tons per annum.[10]

The extended negotiations of the 1940s and 1950s over what dams and ancillary development to construct, and for what purpose, offer insight into how the political materialities of imagination, perception and becoming involved in large-scale hydrological planning, were intertwined with tensions between the divergent aspirations and demands of Victoria residents and the lowveld interests that financed the dam and, in the end, benefitted most from it. These negotiations were at once minutely concerned with the changing surveys, measurements and properties of soil, topography, climate, water flow, and the fluctuating economics of anticipated costs, productivity and profitability.

In April 1949 Haviland (Director, Irrigation) wrote to the ministry of agriculture and lands (01/04/49) to discuss the relative merits of the three proposals then on the table: a dam at Popotekwe storing 135,000 acre-feet of water for local irrigation, with a second dam at Kyle storing 261,000 acre-feet for the lowveld; or a dam at Popotekwe storing 135,000 acre-feet and a dam at Kyle for 316,000 acre-feet; or thirdly, just a single dam at Kyle to store 412,000 acre-feet, supplying water solely for Triangle.[11] The cheapest in terms of capital expenditure was the third, but as Haviland's project engineer noted, 'from a purely commercial point of view, [all] the projects are unsound'. Haviland advised 'the matter be very carefully investigated ... to ascertain whether the additional expenditure involved in constructing two dams could be justified by returns afforded from irrigation in the close vicinity of Fort Victoria'. This would 'necessitate consideration being given to ... increased output of dairy products ... produced directly at Fort Victoria or elsewhere', and 'in each case comparison made to ascertain the value to the colony between production at Fort Victoria and the production of sugar in the lowveld'.[12]

Later that year new surveys indicated that a proposed 'left bank canal' from the Popotekwe dam would prove 'very long and costly', as 'it would

[10] 'Report on Large-Scale Irrigation', 1952:25 (NAZ F149/con/120)
[11] Haviland Director, Irrigation 01/04/49 (NAZ S1194/1512/4).
[12] Ibid.

be absolutely necessary to have a lined channel'. It could therefore 'never be profitable'. The slope of irrigable land from the 'left bank canal' was also 'far from ideal' and much 'terracing would be required, if water were not to be wasted'. In addition, of the 1,354 acres available, 256 would 'be submerged under the Kyle dam basin'. The engineer recommended abandoning 'this part of the project, if the water can be put to better use elsewhere, for example Triangle', further noting that 'the area on the right bank canal' was also 'not ideal for irrigation and terracing will be necessary'.[13] Topography, hydrology and projected costs were already working against Popotekwe. Later, more detailed engineering and soil surveys would cast even more doubt upon it. Haviland urged his minister that 'before the economies of the scheme can be finally considered, it is necessary to know how much good quality land can be commanded'. 'Pits are being dug and samples will be analysed' but the chief chemist's 'preliminary inspection' was 'most encouraging and there are good hopes that he will find excellent soil for irrigation ... over a large area commanded by the RB [right bank] canal'.[14] With the left bank canal already likely to be abandoned, the right bank canal remained a possibility, keeping Popotekwe in the running.

By September 1949, three possible alternative schemes had become six: the first and second involved the Popotekwe dam alone with either just the left bank canal, or with the right bank canal as well, mainly supplying water for local use and a little to Triangle; the third was just the Kyle dam with all its water for the lowveld; the fourth included Popotekwe and Kyle for both local and lowveld irrigation; and the fifth and sixth were two variations involving only Kyle, with a pumping scheme for irrigation below Popotekwe. For each of the six alternatives, the amount of water available, irrigating different acreages of land at Popotekwe and Triangle, at different times of year, and at different costs per unit of water, was carefully calculated.[15] The introduction of a possible pumping scheme from a single dam at Kyle – meaning Popotekwe was not needed – illustrates the continuing concern for local irrigation, despite deepening questions about viability. Haviland was very aware of the effect on Victoria if the Popotekwe dam was not built. Building Kyle without a pumping arrangement would 'sterilize any further development of water supplies ... above the dam site' and 'irrigation in the vicinity of Victoria will be impossible and any urban or industrial expansion in Fort Victoria ... nullified except at prohibitive cost in providing urban water supplies'.[16]

Victorian futures were clearly of concern for irrigation planners, despite the enormous promise of lowveld sugar. But if a pumping scheme

---

[13] Project engineer, 13/07/49 (NAZ S1194/1512/4).
[14] Haviland, 26/07/49 (NAZ S1194/1512/4).
[15] Haviland 17/09/49; Project engineer 30/09/49 (NAZ S1194/1512/4). The extent of irrigable lands envisaged by the different alternatives in the Popotekwe area ranged between 3000 and 5000 acres, and in Triangle, between 540 and 9,300 acres.
[16] Ibid.

could ensure that Mutirikwi's waters might still offer agricultural or industrial benefit for Victoria residents, even without Popotekwe, then it too had its own costs. The pumping scheme would waste water and reduce Triangle's irrigated acreage, because Kyle's waters would be released throughout the wet season (when not needed at Triangle) to generate electricity to pump water to the Popotekwe lands. One solution was a further storage dam downstream of Kyle, but this introduced substantial new costs, negating any saving made by not building Popotekwe.[17] As dam planning on the Mutirikwi advanced, it escalated sharply in size, ambition and complexity. By 1952 the possibility of a third dam at Bangala had emerged, competing or complementing Kyle and Popotekwe; alternative proposals now juggled variations upon *three* possible dam sites. Damming the Mutirikwi had become very complex.

The 1949 report, detailing six alternatives, was closely and quickly considered by the Department of Irrigation. In October, Roberts (then Assistant Director) recommended 'both the Popotekwe and the Kyle dams should be built'. This would involve 'somewhat higher initial cost than the Kyle dam plus pumping, but very little, if any, more than the Kyle pumping scheme plus additional storage'. 'Annual costs would be lower' and 'control ... greatly simplified as water for the Popotekwe area could be controlled independently of the supply for Triangle'. In addition 'a valuable tourist attraction would be created ... east of Fort Victoria' and the 'future urban needs of Fort Victoria ... provided for, as a supply could be obtained reasonably from the Popotekwe dam, and much less economically from Kyle dam'.[18] This looked like a win-win situation. Trading higher initial costs for lower running costs, Victoria residents would get their irrigation, as well as a tourist attraction and urban water at reasonable rates. Triangle would get its water as it needed. Productive agricultural and recreational landscapes could be forged in Victoria, *alongside* the industrialisation of the lowveld.

It did not last. The following month the viability of the different alternatives changed again, when the Assistant Chief Chemist B.S. Ellis delivered the results of his soil reconnaissance at Popotekwe. Although 'the flooding back of several subsidiary streams and *vleis* by the Kyle dam will not lessen the irrigable area as much as was feared' he reported, 'in the northern part ... quite a stretch of good land will be flooded'. Furthermore 'the Kyle dam will almost certainly raise the soil water table in a considerable area', presenting 'another problem' because 'if the water table is brought to within 10–15 feet of the surface ... irrigation would be dangerous'. 'It is not known for certain ... to what extent the water table will be affected in heavy soil of this type' he added, 'but the danger is to be noted.[19] However, the real crunch came with his new soil analysis. 'Ignoring any such questions and treating the soils on their merits' he stated 'I can only see about 1500 [acres] of good irrigable soil'. Unsurveyed areas in the south may yet have been suitable, increasing

[17] Ibid.
[18] R.H. Roberts, Ass. Director, Irrigation, 07/10/49 (NAZ S1194/1512/4).
[19] Ellis, 22/11/49 (NAZ S1194/1512/4).

'irrigable lands by about 500 acres' but 'it would be safer to consider all the irrigable soils as totalling not more than 1,500 acres'.[20]

The imagination/perception of the soils and irrigable landscapes of the Popotekwe scheme had changed again, so the debate about which dam to build swung in a new direction. This 'puts a somewhat different complexion on the relative merits of the various possible schemes' Roberts explained. Less water would now be required at Popotekwe, and more available for Triangle, but with expected losses in transit 'likely to be relatively heavy' the total acreage of irrigated lands would be 'less than before'. The unit costs of water were also now 'altered slightly in such a way as to be adverse to the building of the Popotekwe dam and more favourable to ... the higher Kyle dam'. 'The balance has been slightly tipped in favour of the Kyle pumping scheme' Roberts concluded.[21] But he was still attached to Popotekwe and urged that other factors deserved attention. Apart from anticipated problems with the pumping scheme, the 'future urban water supply of Fort Victoria would be more economically obtained from the Popotekwe' and it 'would be a valuable tourist attraction'. But he acknowledged that Kyle, 'being only some 5 miles from [Great] Zimbabwe, might also be an attraction to tourist traffic'.[22] Despite Robert's enthusiasm, Popotekwe's fate was now already more or less sealed. By the end of 1949 its viability had diminished not only because its irrigable soils were far fewer than previously thought, but also because Triangle was 'not prepared at this stage to enter into a long-term contract for ... water from the Popotekwe dam'. On the basis of their own 'cost per acre/foot of water' calculations, the Sugar Board preferred increasing storage by heightening the existing Esquelingwe weir, and later another dam near Bangala falls.[23]

Informed by hydrologists, irrigation engineers and soil chemists, fortune had abandoned Popotekwe. But Roberts' enthusiasm for it was shared by politicians, and likely influenced by Victoria's noisy settlers. In November 1949, Haviland, responding to questions by the Ministerial Economic Co-ordination Committee, denied that the option of just building the Popotekwe dam for local irrigation alone had already been determined as uneconomic, and that Kyle dam would flood the Popotekwe dam site. But he also rejected that Victoria residents had 'been promised the Popotekwe dam', claiming his department had 'no knowledge of any such promise'.[24] Haviland also explained why current figures for irrigable lands at Triangle were different from Gibb's more optimistic figures the year before. The problem was 'there are no long term flow observations of the Mtilikwi and its tributaries'. Gibb's estimations were based on mean annual rainfall 'which is insufficient ... to base a reasonable estimate of run-off ... under southern African conditions'.[25] Gibb

[20] Ibid.
[21] Roberts, 25/11/49 (NAZ S1194/1512/4).
[22] Ibid.
[23] Robertson, Chairman, Sugar Board 19/01, 02/49 (NAZ S1194/1512/4).
[24] Haviland, 19/11/49 (NAZ S1194/1512/4).
[25] Haviland, 14/11/49 (NAZ S1194/1512/4).

had also suggested a 150-foot dam at Kyle would hold 310,000 acre-feet of water. New estimates suggested a smaller 145-foot dam would hold 421,000 acre-feet. Furthermore, such a dam would 'overflow only once in 7 years' and was therefore 'of optimum size for the total catchment'.[26] Clearly, alongside shifting understandings of topography and soil, information on rain, run-off and flow in Mutirikwi's catchment too remained tentative, as the perception/imagination of the landscape's properties continued to fluctuate.

The pressure exerted by Victoria residents did not diminish. 'Mindful of ... official assurances that ... under no circumstances would this scheme be dropped', the Victoria Regional Development and Publicity Association was 'somewhat perturbed at certain evidence ... indicat[ing] that the Popotekwe dam scheme is to be shelved indefinitely'. 'In view of ... the vital importance of the Popotekwe scheme to the entire Victoria district', the association's secretary wrote to the Minister of Agriculture asking: 'would you be good enough to indicate at your earliest convenience what is the government's policy in regard to Popotekwe?'[27] The 'Popotekwe Gorge dam is still under active consideration' the minister's private secretary replied, reassuring them that 'no final decisions had yet been made', although soil surveys had 'not come up to original expectation' and rumours 'may have originated from this fact'.[28] The Popotekwe dam was not finally shelved until 1956. Between 1952 and 1956 discussions continued as enthusiasm waxed and waned. Negotiations for land acquisitions continued, although these were affected by more detailed surveying.[29] As projected flood levels fluctuated estimates of the land required changed too, much to the chagrin of local farmers. Given these uncertainties, officials advised against disposing anything already acquired, as 'surplus land held by the government will be of not inconsiderable value for National Park, Hotel, Sports Club, residential and other like purposes'.[30]

Money too remained a problem. In April 1951, Haviland had reported that 'it was agreed some months ago ... that Popotekwe should be proceeded with if funds were available', but now 'there is no money available'. He still included 'the start of the Popotekwe dam in 1952/3' in his 4 year plan.[31] But by 1953 the debates changed again. In April, Haviland preferred a larger dam downstream 'to make more water available for Triangle and to save losses in transit'.[32] As Popotekwe's irrigation potential dwindled with new soil surveys, and the Sugar Board increasingly

[26] Ibid.

[27] Secretary, Victoria Regional Development and Publicity Association, 30/12/49. (NAZ S1194/1512/4).

[28] Reply to Victoria Regional Development and Publicity Association, 09/01/50. (NAZ S1194/1512/4).

[29] R.D. Spitteler, Under Secretary, Lands, 10/05/51 (NAZ S1194/1512/4); Under Secretary Lands, 07/02/52 (NAZ1194/1512/1/9-10).

[30] Under Secretary Lands, 07/02/52 (NAZ1194/1512/1/9-10).

[31] Haviland, 04/04/51 (NAZ S1194/1512/4).

[32] Haviland 11/04/53 (NAZ S1194/1512/1/10).

sought to 'denationalise' Triangle, priorities for damming Mutirikwi shifted more decisively to the lowveld. Concern with avoiding water loss in transit to the lowveld was heightened. Debates refocused on whether to dam at Kyle *or* further downstream at Bangala. Although 'the Kyle site is ... one of the best in the colony ... it is situated some 60 miles above Bangala Falls' meaning 'heavy water transmission losses in the river', or 'a very expensive canal' and losing the 'yield of the considerable catchment between Kyle and Triangle'.[33]

As with soil, topography and hydrology, little reliable data on river transmission losses was available. Furthermore, until the early 1950s, the Mutirikwi river below Kyle had not been properly surveyed for potential dam sites nearer Triangle. Ground and air reconnaissance was carried out in early 1950, but it wasn't until full aerial surveys became available in late 1951 that the Bangala site was identified.[34] With Popotekwe unlikely, serious consideration was now given to a larger Bangala dam *instead* of Kyle, with a 'considerable saving in water, as transmission losses in a 15 mile stretch of river' would be much less than over the 75 miles from Kyle. This would avoid the cost of a lined canal from Kyle.[35] New ground and soil surveys were needed, and new calculations of seepage and evaporation rates. But the idea did not bear fruit. An enlarged Bangala dam, 'to control the whole of the catchment' and 'provide for years of abnormal conditions', would require a dam wall '198 feet' high. It is doubtful the proposed site could accommodate that.[36] Continued pressure from Victoria residents for a local dam may also have contributed, particularly as Popotekwe looked increasingly unlikely.

In 1956 government abandoned Popotekwe and decided to build the Kyle Dam with a concrete-lined canal to Triangle. When the Natal syndicate bought Triangle in 1954, they had committed £300,000 to dam the Mutirikwi.[37] By July 1956 it was 'felt better to raise the [Kyle] dam wall to maximum possible height' and 'obviate any necessity for the Popotekwe dam'.[38] Some long-held land reservations were cancelled, but much of the land acquired for it 'would now be inundated in the Kyle basin'.[39] Plans were briefly entertained for power generation at Kyle, but like the pumping scheme this would restrict the water available for Triangle. With power anticipated from Kariba soon, this was quickly shelved.[40] Within two years, the Kyle Agreement was signed and then-owner Guy

[33] Weels, 19/12/51 (NAZ S1194/1512/1/9-10).

[34] Ibid.

[35] T.W. Easton, Project engineer, 02/01/52 (NAZ S1194/1512/1/9-10).

[36] Ibid.

[37] Roberts, 'The Kyle Project' undated (NAZ F119/imm9/6).

[38] Minutes,16th meeting, Water resources Committee, Natural Resources Board, 23/07/56 (NAZ F149/con/220).

[39] Minutes, 16th meeting, Manicaland regional development committee, 09/08/56; Minutes, 17th meeting, Water Resources committee, Natural Resources Board, 04/09/56 (NAZ F149/con/220).

[40] Ibid. The idea of generating power from Kyle resurfaced several times since its completion, and was briefly again discussed in 2005/06 (VaChikami, Water Bailiff, 06/11/05).

Hulett reconfirmed Triangle's undertaking to contribute £300,000, for which it received four-fifths of Kyle's waters. The subsequent Hippo Valley agreement committed government to building the Bangala dam after Kyle, from which Hippo Valley would receive the largest water allocations.[41] Construction at Bangala began immediately after Kyle was completed in late 1960, and was finished in 1963, by which time its original purpose (tied to the short-lived proposal for a Popotekwe pumping scheme) was long forgotten, eclipsed by the overwhelming imperative to store water for the lowveld.

In sum, it was not simply the financial influence of lowveld sugar interests, nor the promise of food security and export revenue, nor the demands of a growing European settler population that determined which dams were built on the Mutirikwi, and for what purpose. Nor was this determined entirely by the changing calculations, measurements and surveying of an army of soil scientists, hydrologists and engineers. Neither the ambitious, imagined futures of heroic large-scale damming, nor the changeable, increasingly minute, perceptions of the stuff of landscape, water and topography were singularly responsible. Rather it was a finely intertwined combination of both, because in the end the two were inseparable. The result would have important implications for the remaking of Mutirikwi's landscapes, for settlers and Africans alike.

CONTESTING KYLE'S WATER

Detailed preparations for the dam, the canal, the basin and wider catchment began immediately. Clearing the basin of trees was discussed but not carried out because of the high costs incurred at Kariba[42] Fishermen later celebrated this believing submerged trees increase nutrient levels in what is 'quite a sterile lake'.[43] Soil conservation and the protection of the catchment began immediately. In November 1956 Gordon Deedes (Chairman, Natural Resources Board) reported that 'a team of additional conservation and extension officers was being recruited for European areas', and the 'Native Department has already appointed a team of three land development officers'. Efforts concentrated on 'fencing and [the] protection of river banks'.[44] Kyle was already remaking the landscape under and around it, as the machinery of technocratic conservation was brought to bear protecting a dam not yet built. Concerns about siltation would continue into the 2000s, particularly in the wake of fast-track

[41] Hippo Valley Agreement Act, 1958, (NAZ F119/imm9/6); Roberts, 'The Kyle Project' undated (NAZ F119/imm9/6).
[42] 'Kariba Project: Clearing of storage Basin', J. Savory, 14/04/55 (NAZ F149/con/120).
[43] Errol and Daryl Edwards 25/05/06; Ant and Helen Mitchel 09/01/06.
[44] Minutes, 18th meeting Water Resources Board, 09/11/56 (NAZ F149/con/220).

land reform.[45] Other concerns that continued to reverberate after the dam's construction too were anticipated before it was built, such as the invasive water hyacinth weed, pollution and bilharzia.[46] The latter was understood as a particularly 'native problem', requiring 'native housing, washing facilities [and] water supplies', and 'cattle and stock water' to be 'sited away from farrows and dams'.[47]

On the 27 June 1957 the Minister of Irrigation was granted the right to 'impound two hundred and sixty thousand million gallons of public water from the ... Umtilikwe and Umshagashe rivers' by Fort Victoria's Water Court.[48] The acquisition of farmland to be inundated by Kyle's waters, compensation for farm owners, and the removal of 'recoverable materials' began straight away, including fencing standards, wire and poles.[49] Uncertainties persisted, however, about the extent of the lake's reach. When the dam finally spilt in 1974, estimates were proved dramatically wrong when new lakeside lodgings, a restaurant and swimming pool built by the Bristows for a tourist resort at Sikato bay, were flooded.[50] Several local farmers raised formal objections and claims for compensation at the Water Court in June 1957.[51] They were compensated for lost lands, but they were not always satisfied, particularly when the lake's reach extended beyond predictions, and because proximity to the lake did not mean preferential access to water rights for irrigation.[52]

The Water Court asserted that all existing water rights from storage dams and rivers feeding the new dam would be protected. Despite some water allocations for local use, particularly the municipality, it was clear future water applications upstream and around the dam would be affected by the lowveld's huge allocations.[53] This was a point of considerable contention among local farmers, particularly as Popotekwe dam had

[45] In 2006 VaMare, Zinwa's Runde catchment manager, explained that 'the issue of siltation is not yet serious, but it is coming ... like a time bomb waiting to go off. New farmers need to be taught to use contour ridges and stop drains, but we are only just starting with that. There are still lands being allocated. The land is still being opened up. But it is better to do those things now, than wait until the problems really start. Maybe it's because we have had poor rains in recent years, several consecutive droughts, and erosion has not yet become too serious. When the rains really start again then there will more erosion' (VaMare 11/04/06).

[46] Minutes, 11th meeting, Natural Resources Board, 25/01/55; Minutes, 12th meeting Water Resources Committee, Natural Resources Board, 22/03/55; D.Aylen, 03/01/55 (NAZ F149/con/220).

[47] 'Bilharzia and Irrigation' Dr Blair, Director, Preventative Services, 10/12/54 (NAZ F149/con/220).

[48] 'Water Right 4680', Water Court, Fort Victoria, 27/09/57 (NAZ F119/imm/9/6).

[49] Circular Memo, H.N.Booth, 18/07/59 (NAZ S3269/35/19).

[50] Errol and Daryl Edwards 25/05/06.

[51] 'Water Right 4680', 27/09/57 (NAZ F119/imm/9/6).

[52] Mai Coventry 01/11/05.

[53] 'A reservation of the catchment area of the "Kyle" dam in respect of water for the storage of one thousand five hundred million (1,500,000,000) gallons' was made 'in respect of future applications for such storage.' Water Right 4680, 27/09/57 (NAZ F119/imm/9/6).

been abandoned. The dam's water allocations were discussed with farmers across the catchment before the government's application appeared before the Water Court.[54] In the following years the issue continued to trouble Victoria's farmers. Eventually the Water Court relented, albeit in a small way. In 1965, the *Fort Victoria Advertiser* (30/07/65) announced a 'considerable increase of agricultural output in the Victoria Central area may be expected with the approval now given by the Water Court, for two riparian owners on Lake Kyle to extract water ... for irrigation'. Mr J.V. Whithead and Mr W.H. Hewlett were both granted right to 'extract one cusec of water', and 'a further 41/2 cusecs shall be made available between other possible applicants'. In comparison to Triangle's huge allocations, these were very small amounts indeed. Although this enabled some farmers to grow irrigated crops on a commercial scale, many others gave up cropping altogether to focus on raising cattle, or game ranching.[55] With recurrent droughts and the changing of agricultural priorities after UDI (November 1965), Mutirikwi's water allocations continued to provoke debate over the following decade. As Mike Lotter later explained to Fort Victoria's Rotary club, when the dam was built most local farmers concentrated on tobacco and cattle, which needed no irrigation. But 'since the UDI ... farmers are wanting to plant irrigable crops and are applying for water allocations ...[but]... all of the water in the Kyle catchment is allocated to the dam'. This was not unique to Mutirikwi, the same problem was 'apparent in the Hunyani catchment'.[56] In March 1972, a commission of inquiry re-examined Mutirikwi's 'water allocation priorities', but it was clear the lowveld's allocations were secure.[57]

By March 1975, concerns about the over-commitment of Kyle's waters reached new heights. Stakeholders across the catchment – including farmers from Mutirikwi's headwaters in Gutu, lowveld planters, and representatives of the Mayor and Municipality – met the Minister for Water Development, Mr Partridge, at a meeting chaired by Fort Victoria's Member of Parliament (MP), Gordon Olds. Of particular concern was that Victoria farmers with temporary 'riparian rights' to draw from the lake were using 'Municipal water allocations as yet not fully taken up by the town'. Within the next decade the expanding town was likely to require all of its allocations. The minister was adamant 'he had no intention of giving water to the highveld at the expense of the lowveld', and the 'present water allocation to the lowveld was secure'. 'When the dam was built a certain percentage of the water had been allocated to agriculture and to the municipality' he explained, any further allocations would be 'on a first come, first served basis'. Little of the lake's water remained uncommitted. 'Once this was used up no more water would be available'

---

[54] In September 1956, Deedes met with 'landowners in the Gutu-Chatsworth area', in the Mutirikwi's headwaters, to discuss water allocations. Minutes, 17th meeting, Water Resources Committee, 04/09/56 (NAZ F149/con/220).
[55] Pat Potgeiter 15/01/06.
[56] 'Problems of fair water distribution', *Fort Victoria Advertiser*, 21/02/75.
[57] 'Lowveld water supply inquiry', *Rhodesian Herald*, 11/03/72.

and 'farmers would have to weather lack of water during bad drought years'.[58]

The sugar industry's huge water allocations did not change in the following decades, even if a few small irrigation schemes were established around Mutirikwi during the 1980s land resettlements. At particular crisis moments, such as the 1992 drought, urban supplies became so threatened that no more water could be released downstream, but generally the lowveld's allocations were carefully maintained.[59] The ZINWA Act (1998) addressed some of the inequities and inflexibilities of the water court system, emphasising an integrated catchment approach to water management,[60] but did little to change the lowveld's hold over Mutirikwi's waters. Only in the mid-2000s, amidst recurring drought and deepening economic crisis, did the possibility of local irrigation around Mutirikwi receive renewed official attention, as older demands were rehearsed in new forms, albeit with little noticeable effect.

If Victoria's farmers did not benefit much irrigation from Kyle, at least municipal allocations were protected, even if bringing water to town proved difficult and costly, as Roberts, Haviland and others had predicted.[61] The 1957 allocations had anticipated urban growth, but Fort Victoria's long-standing water woes were not solved by the dam. Over the following two decades the issue was as contested and recurrent as disputes over local irrigation. As late as 1958, the municipality entertained the possibility of 'applying for the Popotekwe site' for future urban supplies instead of Kyle, and the minister reluctantly agreed 'as a safe guard' that although 'Popotekwe would not be built in the foreseeable future', the 'new Fort Victoria Birchenough Bridge road would not be run [through] the basin area'.[62] But Popotekwe was never built and Fort Victoria was left devising costly schemes to pipe water from Kyle's western shores. Over the next two decades (and well into the 2000s) water for Fort Victoria/Masvingo town remained a constant source of problems, with town dwellers enduring repeated restrictions while the council re-devised and repeatedly 'augmented' its aptly-named 'Kyle Water augmentation scheme', to increase supplies from the lake.[63]

---

[58] 'Kyle Water almost fully Committed', *Fort Victoria Advertiser*, 28/03/75.

[59] VaChikami, Water Bailiff, 06/11/05.

[60] For more on Zimbabwe's water reform, see Ferguson & Derman 1999; Latham 2002; Manzungu 2003, 2004b; Manzungu & Kujinga 2002.

[61] Roberts, 07/10/49 (NAZ S1194/1512/4).

[62] Minutes of 25th meeting of Water Resources Committee of Natural Resources Board, 17/04/58; and Minutes of 6th meeting of Midlands, regional water development committee, 22/11/57 (NAZ F149/con/220).

[63] 'Council acts to avert grave water shortage', 13/03/64; 'Kyle contract goes to Gwelo firm', 12/06/64; 'Another warning on water' 10/07/64; 'Water crisis may end soon', 02/10/64; 'Water restrictions may end this week', 16/10/64; 'Rapid growth of town enforces increased water storage', 05/11/65; 'Continued dry spell may bring water restrictions', 24/12/65; 'Water crisis', 07/01/66; 'Quick action saved water crisis', 13/03/70; 'Water may have to be restricted', 16/10/70; 'Mayor's appeal to water users', 16/10/70; 'Water consumption reaches new peak', 01/01/71; 'Town keeps ahead of water needs', 14/06/72; 'New water

Occasionally government did try to solve the town's water problems. In 1975 a 'relatively cheap scheme to raise the water level in Lake Kyle by a metre' through fitting 'removable radial gates' increased the town's water supply, even if most of the additional water was again earmarked for the lowveld industries, who paid for it.[64] At other times, such as 1992, the sugar industry had to accept losses because the most basic water supplies had to be maintained for urban needs when the lake dried up completely.[65] But on the whole, Fort Victoria was left to deal with its own water problems. Recurring drought, technical difficulty and the cost of supplying the town from the lake, has meant the water problems 19th-century residents of Fort Victoria first faced were never adequately resolved. Water supplies for the town, and for nearby rural centres like Nemanwa Growth Point are still a recurring problem. Masvingo again faced 'critical water shortages' in July 2012 after poor rains meant the lake fell to just 29 per cent capacity.[66] By October 2012 it was below 15 per cent capacity, prompting Walter Mzembi (Minister for Tourism and Masvingo South MP) to warn of 'an ecological disaster ... unless urgent measures were taken to arrest uncontrolled drawing of water ... to irrigate sugarcane plantations in the lowveld'. Calling for an 'inter-ministerial committee to tackle the issue' – not least because 'the drying up of the dam' would 'impinge on tourism in a big way in Masvingo province' – Mzembi emphasised the need for 'an empowerment model on Lake Mutirikwi to benefit local communities'. This encapsulated per-fectly the local disputes the dam has been embroiled in since before its conception.[67]

BUILDING RHODESIA'S PLAYGROUND

The remaking of Victoria's landscapes heralded by the Kyle dam was not only animated by local disappointments over lost lands, poor compen-sation, miniscule water allocations, and the demise of the Popotekwe scheme. Many Victoria residents, transferred the aspirations of the long-anticipated Popotekwe to their new dam, especially for what it

(contd)   works only a start', 30/06/72; 'Council cautions over water plea', 15/09/72; 'Municipality of Fort Victoria notice: water restrictions', 19/01/73; 'Close watch kept on water position', 19/01/73; 'Water crisis', 02/02/73; 'Water position "frightening" olds tells House', 29/06/73; 'Water restrictions almost inevitable', 17/08/73; 'A short new ban – then water at lib', 07/09/73; 'Restrictions on water lifted', 02/11/72; 'Hesitation on new water scheme', 31/01/75; 'Million dollar water scheme over 4 years', 13/05/77; all in *Fort Victoria Advertiser*.
[64] 'Kyle storage to be boosted', *Fort Victoria Advertiser*, 07/11/75.
[65] Undated notes, Mike Lotter, provided by Errol Edwards 25/05/06; Angus Middleton, 15–16/06/06.
[66] 'Historic Masvingo City faces water shortages', *VOA News*, 09/07/12.
[67] 'Lake Mutirikwi below 15% capacity' *The Herald*, 11/10/12; 'Biggest inland dam in dire straits' *Southern Times*, 13/02/12; 'Deal to ease Masvingo water woes' *Daily News*, 02/09/12; 'Residents in Masvingo go for three days without water' *swradioafrica.com*, 28/06/12.

Photo 14   Mutirikwi Dam, almost completely dry, during drought of 1992
(Source: Jeffrey Davies, 1992)

offered in terms of transforming Victoria into Rhodesia's playground.[68]
Fort Victoria began life in the 1890s as a remote, ramshackle township
of hard-drinking prospectors, independent-minded transport riders, and
belligerent settler-farmers (cf. Sayce 1978). From the early 20th century,
active and noisy local associations had been pushing for improved transport links, accommodation and recreational facilities to promote the
town as a visitor centre. These efforts were built, rather thinly, upon its
pioneer past as the colony's first town, and on the legacies of the Allan
Wilson patrol, the Victoria Agreement, and the 'Victoria volunteers' of
the 1893 Matabele War.[69] They also built upon Fort Victoria's proximity to Great Zimbabwe, fervently re-imagined against all plausibility as
evidence of 'ancient', white, 'non-African' imperial presence in the area
(Kuklick 1992; Fontein 2006a:3–17). None of these, however, had ever
sustained enough visitors or the kind of development to which they
aspired. So the dam, its game reserve and the possibilities of fishing,
boating and other recreation offered renewed hope of prosperity for this
fairly insignificant parochial town, particularly given the picturesque

---

[68] Errol and Daryl Edwards 25/05/06.
[69] On the Victoria Agreement, see NAZ A2 /9/1; NAZ A3/15/24; NAZ L2/2/185.
Also Sayce 1978:46.

aesthetics of the lake's rocky shorelines. Many jumped at the opportunities the dam's 'beautiful' presence offered.

This local enthusiasm began even before the dam was completed. In 1959 Mr Geldenhuys wrote to the government applying for commercial boating rights on the lake. The request was 'one of a large number received ... for varying rights such as trading, fishing, pleasure boating, ferry services, motels etc.'. It was forwarded to the Prime Minister and Cabinet, who reassured him that 'the whole matter of utilization of the surface and surrounding ground of the Kyle lake is being gone into' and his and other applications would be considered 'when this question has been settled'.[70] Victoria residents' enthusiasm was shared by Federal and Southern Rhodesian officials. The following year a Federal press statement announced that 'the new lake will give the Fort Victoria-Zimbabwe area a holiday playground which will seriously challenge any comparison by any inland tourist areas'. The lake 'will contain three islands and will be almost bisected by a long narrow peninsula on which it is planned to create a game reserve'.[71] Announcing the dam's completion later that year, the *Rhodesian Herald* too expected the dam would become 'one of the most outstanding tourist attractions of the Federation' noting that fisheries, a game reserve, gardens and camping sites were already being planned. The 'enthusiasm and optimism' of 'this bold and imaginative project' were 'well founded', it concluded.[72]

With Great Zimbabwe nearby, Kyle was widely promoted for Rhodesia's 'home tourist industry', and Victoria residents took to it with gusto.[73] Numerous articles in the *Fort Victoria Advertiser* over the following two decades show how fierce lobbying for development and road improvements continued, as they established hotels, curio shops, restaurants, a boat club, and tea rooms all around the lake.[74] At Bushmead, stands for new homes overlooking the lake were put up for sale, and a ferry used to take visitors and their cars from chalets south of the lake to the game reserve peninsula, until it later sank.[75] With the game reserve on its northern shores, 'guest farms' and 'game ranches' were established elsewhere, including Vivian Bristow's Le Rhone farm, near Boroma, where Simon Bright had grown up.[76] In 1974 Bristow's tourist resort at Sikato bay flooded when the lake rose above hydrologists' predictions. Le Rhone and the lake were later used to film *Slavers*, starring Trevor Howard, Britt Ekland and Ron Eley. Bristow 'expressed great satisfac-

[70] H.W.H. Wallies to Mr P.A. Geldenhuys, 16/07/59 (NAZ S3269/35/19).

[71] 'Press statement 314/60', 28/07/60, Federal Information Department, NAZ S3269/35/19.

[72] 'Kyle heralds new era', *Rhodesian Herald*, 03/12/60.

[73] 'Kyle part of "home products" campaign', *Fort Victoria Advertiser*, 13/04/64;

[74] E.g. 'Pressure renewed for Kyle-Glenlivet link', *Fort Victoria Advertiser*, 29/01/65; 'Tourism Board backs Kyle road improvement', *Fort Victoria Advertiser*, 10/03/67.

[75] Apparently it sank carrying filming equipment for the *Slavers*. Divers later refloated it, and it was sent to Kariba to become a kapenta (sardine) rig. Errol and Daryl Edwards 25/05/06.

[76] 'Guest farm planned at Kyle', *Fort Victoria Advertiser*, 20/05/66.

tion' that the filmmakers had 'come to Kyle, where the ... natural scenery lends itself well to providing different settings and where it is possible to achieve the illusion of "darkest Africa" ... without the intrusion of noise, people and anachronistic contrivances'.[77]

MacDougall's old home Dunollie became *Norma Jean's*, a popular local eatery.[78] Not far away, the Kyle Boat Club became one of the lake's most enduring entertainment spots, hosting anglers drawn to Kyle's bass fisheries, sailing regattas and power boat races, as well as *braais* and evening dances.[79] In 1975, Rhodesia's president, Clifford Dupont, a keen angler, became the Boat Club's president, and full membership meant a waiting list for new members.[80] Caravan and motorcycle clubs from South Africa held rallies around the lake.[81] 'It used to be incredible, during the 1970s', Errol Edwards (the Boat Club's commodore) told me; 'the place would be very busy with tourists ... South Africans used to pour across the border to come here. All of those resorts were busy'.[82] Sailing events, boat racing, water skiing and fishing competitions became common fare as long-promised Victorian aspirations began to bear fruit. Amid this optimism, even Fort Victoria was given a facelift. Plans were developed for a botanical garden, and remarkably, given the town's continuing water problems, 'the Garden Club and all keen gardeners in Fort Victoria' successfully lobbied council to reduce domestic water charges, arguing it 'would contribute to the beautification of the town'.[83]

Amid this enthusiasm, Victoria residents continued to lobby government for a single authority to control development around the lake.[84] Huge efforts were spent to promote Victoria, as well as the lowveld's successes.[85] When the dam finally spilled in 1974, there were celebrations all round.[86] 'In recognition of Lake Kyle's Scottish connections' one newspaper reported, 'a Highlander piped the arrival of Fort Victorians

[77] 'Slavers Invade Lake Kyle', *Fort Victoria Advertiser*, 08/10/77.

[78] Later becoming Inn on Great Zimbabwe, but then reverting to 'Norma Jeane's Lakeview Resort', www.normajeanslakeview.com, accessed 06/08/13; also Fieldnotes 06/11/05.

[79] 'Boat Club Open day', *Fort Victoria Advertiser*, 10/07/70; 'First sponsored sail on Kyle', *Fort Victoria advertiser*, 13/12/74.

[80] 'Dupont new Boat Club President', *Fort Victoria Advertiser*, 07/11/75.

[81] Tourism Board backs Kyle road improvement', *Fort Victoria Advertiser*, 10/03/67;

[82] Errol and Daryl Edwards 25/05/06.

[83] 'Public catching onto to mini lake idea' *Fort Victoria Advertiser*, 28/03/69.

[84] 'Move towards Kyle local authority', *Fort Victoria Advertiser*, 20/03/64; 'Municipal move to acquire land at Kyle', *Fort Victoria Advertiser*, 15/12/64; 'Mayor again hits out at Kyle red tape', *Fort Victoria Advertiser*, 10/04/64; 'Council pressing again for co-ordinated Kyle development', *Fort Victoria Advertiser*, 17/09/65; 'Publicity still fight for overall Kyle plan', *Fort Victoria Advertiser*, 29/10/65; 'Austin hits out at Kyle appointments', *Fort Victoria Advertiser*, 20/10/67.

[85] See 'Water for prosperity', *Fort Victoria Advertiser*, 03/07/64.

[86] Kyle was not the only dam to take much longer to spill than expected. Umshandige took 13 years. 'Lucky 13 for dams', *Fort Victoria Advertiser*, 13/12/74.

and guests ... from all over Rhodesia, to a party given at the dam to celebrate its spilling', while police mounted 'special patrols', 'in anticipation of streams of sightseers converging on the dam'.[87] Reports circulated that President Dupont and five cabinet members chartered an airplane to see the sight. It was 'a momentous event not only for Fort Victoria but for Rhodesia in view of previous pessimism as to whether the lake would ever fill'.[88]

As Rhodesians took to their new playground with delight, land inspectors raised concerns about the 'unwitting damage being done at Kyle' by 'picnickers and anglers making roads and tracks to the shore'.[89] Ever boisterous, Victoria residents kept a critical eye on changing policies (particularly access charges) at attractions around the lake, including the game reserve and Great Zimbabwe. The fencing of the ruins and later the closure of the golf course, provoked much local disconcertion. So did National Park's closure of the 'Popotekwe arm', to 'provide sanctuary for all aquatic and semi-aquatic animals, reptiles and birds' from noisy boats, yachts and water skiing elsewhere on the lake.[90] When responsibility for Great Zimbabwe later moved to National Monuments, as heritage management became professionalised, this too provoked local anxieties about visitor numbers.[91]

THE AESTHETIC CONSCIENCE OF THE NATION

The dam's recreational potential had long been recognised by planners, even when Popotekwe remained a possibility. Beyond the activities the lake offered, this turned on sentimentalist aesthetic visions of watery shorelines, which Hughes (2010) suggests is a recurring theme in 'Euro-African' hydrological planning. In 1956 Roberts had suggested that 'the attraction of tourists to the beautiful lake' would 'promote the rapid growth of Fort Victoria'.[92] The following twenty years confirmed Robert's prediction, and it is hard to divorce the aesthetic dimensions of watery shorelines from the developmental and recreational opportunities the dam afforded in the remaking of Mutirikwi's landscapes. The two were intertwined from the very beginning, even if they sometimes

---

[87] 'Kyle Spills!', *Fort Victoria Advertiser*, 06/12/74; 'Skirl of pipes and water', *Fort Victoria Advertiser*, 13/12/64.

[88] 'Kyle Spills!', *Fort Victoria Advertiser*, 06/12/74.

[89] 'Unwitting damage being done at Kyle', *Fort Victoria Advertiser*, 19/03/65.

[90] 'Will fence ruin the ruins?' *Fort Victoria Advertiser*, 11/09/70; 'Fencing will run the ruins',*Fort Victoria Advertiser*,08/09/72; 'Improvements at Zimbabwe', *Fort Victoria Advertiser*, 07/09/73; 'Reasons for closing Popotekwe arm', *Fort Victoria Advertiser*, 30/01/76; 'Zimbabwe and Kyle plans under fire', *Fort Victoria Advertiser*, 30/09/76.

[91] 'New plans for Zimbabwe', *Fort Victoria Advertiser*, 12/03/76; 'Zimbabwe and Kyle plans under fire', *Fort Victoria Advertiser*, 30/09/76; 'Stout defence of policy at Zimbabwe', *Fort Victoria Advertiser*, 16/09/77.

[92] 'Decentralisation through water development', Roberts, 05/10/56 (NAZ F149/con/220).

produced conflicting pressures. This contrasts with the damming of the Zambezi in 1958, where the terrible destruction wrought by Kariba took time to be 'redeemed' (Hughes 2010:29–50). At Kyle the anticipated beauty of the lake was always part of the plan, and for many came to carry what Saunders later called 'the aesthetic conscience of the nation'.[93] If for the lowveld damming the Mutirikwi was about harnessing the 'chaos' of 'wilderness' for the production of ordered, irrigated, industrial landscapes (Wolmer 2007:99–100), in Victoria it manifested a different landscape aesthetic, appealing in part to the recurrent longings of the 'children of the glaciers' (Hughes 2010:13–18) for watery shorelines, yet simultaneously forward-looking and development orientated. Victorian enthusiasm for Kyle certainly focused upon the beauty of its rocky shorelines, but also envisaged productive, modern, recreational landscapes. The remaking of Mutirikwi's landscapes afforded by Kyle for Victoria residents was never meant to evoke the 'pristine wilderness' of 'old Africa', even if it could be made to do so for the production of a film.

The game reserve on the lake's northern peninsulas came to occupy a special place in Mutirikwi's remade landscapes. It too was envisaged long before the dam was complete. By 1965, various wildlife (including white rhino) had been brought there, visitor facilities were being constructed, and stocking the lake with bass had begun.[94] National Parks' annual reports give a detailed view of the difficulties involved in 'creating nature', fisheries and a game reserve on what had long been European farms. Fish and animals were brought in, sometimes repeatedly,[95] roads and facilities were created, staffed and maintained, and problems with poaching began almost immediately. The tensions apparent within National Parks in the 2000s, between scientific research, wildlife policing, and the provision of visitor facilities, quickly arose due to the relatively small size of the park and the variety of leisure pursuits established around it. This was not a national park in the 'normal' southern African sense, and parks authorities had to deal with a plethora of different interests and government agencies with diverse responsibilities in the area.

Victoria residents maintained pressure on the need for a single Kyle authority.[96] The 1975 Parks and Wildlife Act created the 'Kyle Recrea-

[93] 'Kyle Recreational Park: a point of view', Confidential Report, Colin Saunders, National Parks Board of Trustees, 02/03/76, Kyle Game Park Files.

[94] In July 1965, £20,000 became available to construct additional chalet accommodation and tearoom facilities for visitors, and to 'provide an all-weather road to the rest camp'. 'These improvements will be a tremendous step forward towards the full exploitation of the tourist potential of Kyle Game Park, with its ever increasing variety of animals, and ... of great significance to the general development of Fort Victoria' ('£20,000 Development for Kyle Game Park', *Fort Victoria Advertiser*, 09/07/65).'Stocking Kyle with Bass has become major operation', *Fort Victoria Advertiser*, 17/12/65.

[95] 'Kyle Bass Stocks to be increased', *Fort Victoria Advertiser*, 26/10/73.

[96] 'Move towards Kyle local authority', *Fort Victoria Advertiser*, 20/03/64; 'Municipal move to acquire land at Kyle', *Fort Victoria Advertiser*, 15/12/64;

tional Park', formally acknowledging that National Parks' role stretched beyond research, conservation, and the provision of game viewing to include the management of recreational facilities all around the lake. This hardly satisfied Victoria's vociferous associations: for some the formation of the 'Recreational Park' was not sufficient, and they continued clamouring for a centralised 'Lake Kyle Planning and Development Authority' to overcome 'the conflict of objectives induced by overlapping and interlocking responsibilities and jurisdictions of a large number of local and national government departments'.[97] However it was significant in the ongoing remaking of Mutirikwi's landscapes. By the mid-1970s, National Parks had lost control of Great Zimbabwe, which had passed to National Museums and Monuments, but were administering expanded Recreational Park boundaries right around the lake.[98] This re-designation appropriated a much larger swath of land than the game reserve itself, just as hydrologists' catchment-wide concerns meant that Kyle laid claims to the water and soil over a much larger area than its surface. National Parks was now charged with 'the long term protection of the environs of Lake Kyle in as natural and aesthetically attractive a state as possible, commensurate with the park's reasonable use as an area where present and future generations of mankind may enjoy and benefit from the pleasures and stimulation of a range of outdoor recreational pursuits'.[99] This echoed Saunders's sentiment that National Parks should acknowledge the 'vitally important principle of acting as the aesthetic conscience of the nation'.[100] 'Lake Kyle lies in a hilly area of superb natural beauty and it is doubtful that there is any similar area of greater beauty in Rhodesia' he stated. While 'the natural features of the lake and the park lend themselves to a wide variety of outdoor pursuits ... it is of the utmost importance that development ... for these tourists ... be done in harmony with the superb natural environment and ... subject to stringent aesthetic requirements'.[101] These aesthetic imperatives stretched into 'the area of state land of rather haphazard boundary surrounding the "outer" shoreline of the lake', where the National Parks should retain a 'right of veto' in 'respect of the usage and development'.[102]

(contd) 'Mayor again hits out at Kyle red tape', *Fort Victoria Advertiser*, 10/04/64; 'Council pressing again for co-ordinated Kyle development', *Fort Victoria Advertiser*, 17/09/65; 'Publicity still fight for overall Kyle plan', *Fort Victoria Advertiser*, 29/10/65; 'Austin hits out at Kyle appointments', *Fort Victoria Advertiser*, 20/10/67.

[97] J. Reardon, Fort Victoria/Zimbabwe Publicity Bureau,09/03/76, Kyle Game Park files.

[98] 'New plans for Zimbabwe', *Fort Victoria Advertiser*, 12/03/76; 'Zimbabwe and Kyle plans under fire', *Fort Victoria Advertiser*, 30/09/76; 'Stout defence of Policy at Zimbabwe', *Fort Victoria Advertiser*, 16/09/77.

[99] 'Policy Document; Kyle Recreational Park, National Parks and Wildlife, Rhodesia, No date. Kyle Game Park Files.

[100] Saunders 'Kyle Recreational Park: a point of view', 02/03/76.

[101] Ibid.

[102] Ibid.

This concern with governing the aesthetic dimensions of Mutirikwi's remade landscapes reveals a tension, common to conservation elsewhere, between 'protecting' wildlife and 'nature' and ensuring developmental potential is realised. But it also illustrates Hughes' (2006a; 2010) view of dam building, and the construction/protection of nature and wilderness often coupled with it, as intimately bound to a politics of white belonging which turns, to a large degree, upon the exclusion of Africans. In the mid- to late 1970s, the two issues were hardly separate at all. It is likely Saunders' aesthetic concerns reflected wider anxieties about the already changing nature of Rhodesia's racialised land divisions, and the encroachment (or return) of Africans – not just poachers, cattle rustlers and freedom fighters but also squatters and land claimants – from nearby Tribal Trust Lands (TTLs). As discussed in the next chapter, the liberation war was coming closer, and security on farms around the lake was becoming problematic.[103] Many would be abandoned by the end of the war, including Bristow's game ranch on Le Rhone, where *Slavers* had been filmed, which became a Rhodesian army camp. Discussions about a new African 'Growth Point' were also under way, envisaged as a way of limiting the movement of 'detribalised Africans' into Fort Victoria.[104] Morgenster Mission had begun negotiations with district authorities about returning sections of Mzero and Morgenster Farms to Nemanwa and Mugabe people crowded in the neighbouring Victoria Tribal Trust Land (TTL).

Haruzvivishe people remember agitating to re-occupy Mzero farm in the late 1970s, and only waited because guerrilla fighters asked them to. During the 'wave of squatting' around Mutirikwi after the war, Mzero was re-occupied by Haruzvivishe people and Mudarikwa Murinye returned to Boroma. But official aesthetic concerns about Mutirikwi's beautiful landscapes also carried into the post-war period. They easily intertwined with technocratic concerns about soil erosion and siltation as both turned on (deeply racialised) assumptions opposing the conservation of nature, soil and wildlife to human and particularly African habitation.[105] In the 1980s such aesthetic and hydrological concerns would drive the eviction of squatters all around the lake, as the Recreational Park's delayed management plan was activated. Mudarikwa Murinye, VaChinengo and others were evicted (for the second time) from Boroma to make room for formal resettlements. Opposite Great Zimbabwe, Haruzvivishe occupiers were driven out of Mzero because 'they told us they wanted to put animals here ... but we did not see any animals

---

[103] Pat Potgeiter recalled that 'right at the beginning of the hostilities, there was big problem with rustling ... hundreds of my cattle were stolen' (Pat Potgeiter 15/01/06). Also 'Rustler killed', *Fort Victoria Advertiser*, 07/09/77.

[104] This too was discussed at the meeting between Minister Partridge and Kyle's various stakeholders in 1975 ('Kyle Water almost fully committed', *Fort Victoria Advertiser*, 28/03/75).

[105] Common comparisons between Mutirikwi's 'beauty' and the 'barren landscapes' around Bangala Dam (which is entirely surrounded by 'communal lands') illustrate how such assumptions continue (VaChikami 06/11/05).

being put here'.[106] When they returned in the 2000s, they provoked responses that again echoed the aesthetic concerns of National Parks' Trustees in the 1970s.[107]

AFRICAN REMOVALS AND NEW RHODESIAN PASTS

The remaking of Mutirikwi's landscapes heralded by Kyle was, therefore, in many ways, a profoundly white project. Its waters irrigated a white sugar industry on the lowveld, supporting the white Rhodesian economy and a growing settler population. For Victoria, it provided some irrigation and urban water, but mainly a landscape of white leisure, recreation, and beauty. African presence was not part of these Europeanised landscapes, except as labour for the vast sugar plantations, or in a kind of celebrated absence as rock art sites and Great Zimbabwe became part of tourist trails around the lake. In the late 1950s, this Europeanisation was not difficult to achieve, given that most of the area had long been European land, and the evictions of the 1940s and 1950s had more or less made this real. But it was not absolute. In the 2000s many remembered problems caused by angered *njuzu*.[108] African graves, ruins and sacred sites under and around Mutirikwi also continued to have an active and affective presence. Mutirikwi's older African landscapes were not so easily Europeanised. Furthermore, although Kyle's waters mostly flooded settler farms, African workers sometimes needed to be relocated.[109] A small northern section of the Mtilikwe reserve was also swallowed by the lake. Some African communities *were* removed to make the dam and its Europeanised landscapes possible.

The 1957 Water Court reported that 'a portion of the Umtilikwe Reserve will be inundated' and 'negotiations are proceeding to make available additional land contiguous to the reserve in exchange'. This 'exchange' meant 'Native interests will not be adversely affected'. Furthermore, water passed from the dam would serve 'the primary requirements of Natives' in downstream reserves.[110] Kelvingrove and Marthadale farms were purchased to resettle people from the flooded lands in an area between the new lake and the Mtilikwe reserve, later

---

[106] Fred Haruzvivishe 12/09/04.

[107] 'Lake Mutirikwi invaded', *Zimbabwe Standard*, 16/11/06: 'They took advantage of the land invasions to settle in a wildlife area, disturbing ... wild animals before they started tilling the banks of the lake ... green vegetation that used to be a marvel to the eyes of tourists who visit Mutirikwi is now history.'

[108] VaChinengo used to prepare food for the labourers at the dam site (26/05/06). Like others he spoke of problems with *njuzu* at the site. Even ZINWA's water bailiff insisted the builders must have involved Murinye elders to appease *njuzu*, otherwise 'they would never had been able to build the dam', and would have faced the 'same problems' as at Tokwe-Mukosi' (VaChikami 06/11/05). Also: Geri Zano 23/03/06; Chief Mugabe 19/11/05; Bhodo Mukuvare, 19/11/05; Matopos Murinye 13/06/06).

[109] Sekuru Makwenye Mavuka 15b/11/05.

[110] Water Court Fort Victoria, 27/09/57 (NAZ F119/imm/9/6).

known as Zano (after one of the families relocated there). Farm work-ers who also lost homes on flooded farms were not compensated,[111] and Kyle never provided much more water for downstream reserves then available before. The people removed to make way for the dam never benefited much from its waters. In 2005/06 many remembered their re-moval from lands at Chinango and Nyangani in 1959. As Headman Louis Mandebvu explained: 'We were told there was a plan to build the Kyle dam, and it was going take a big area including our fields and the graves of our people. People of three *sabhuku* (village heads) – Zano, Muzariri and Mubembe – were moved when the dam was built. Nyangani was right there near the dam site'.[112]

Many remembered the abrupt manner of their removal but also their relief, even enthusiasm, when they saw the rich potential of the soils on their newly allocated lands. 'Before we left that place' Mandebvu ex-plained, 'they held a big meeting and the elders were taken to see where we were being moved to. When they saw the land here, and that it was good for farming, the people were happy'.[113] Others recall receiving mon-etary compensation. 'Everything was done properly', Furere Mashuro insisted.

> When the white people put their water there, the government said we are taking you to a place not far away. Everyone was given money for their things: houses, fields, even trees. The government even prepared our fields for us with those caterpillars [bulldozers]. Our houses were paid for, and we were provided with lorries to come here with our things. There was not a single person who carried their own goods here.[114]

But people also had fond memories of their previous lives and lands, even if for some their new lands had more agricultural potential. As Louis Mandebvu recalled 'Nyangani was a good place, it was our place, but I also remember there were many mountains. Our elders were always telling us it was a good place. Here we have much more land for plough-ing and grazing our cattle, the only problem is that we can no longer plough some of our fields because the hippos destroy our crops.[115] Others fondly recalled the rich alluvial soils and availability of water around Nyangani, and were unhappy to leave them behind. Sometimes enthu-siasm was sparked by the ordered, centralisation of their new lands, and the carefully demarcated fields, pastures and homesteads, indicating that Native Affairs' agriculturalists and planners had already been hard at work. Several people already knew the lands they were removed to,

---

[111] Sekuru Mavuka, was brought up on Mlinya farm, until his family and the other workers were removed when the Lake Mutrikwi's waters rose. They never received compensation, although the white farmer, Mr Coventry, obviously did (Sekuru Makwenye Mavuka 15b/11/05).

[112] Louis Mandebvu 19/04/06.

[113] Ibid.

[114] Furere Mashuro 12/04/06.

[115] Louis Mandebvu 19/04/06.

having worked as labourers on Kelvingrove under its white owner, Mr Page, or 'Burusa'.[116]

Whatever their ambivalence about being moved, many people *were* deeply unhappy about leaving family and ancestral graves behind, an issue that continues to concern them. As Geri Zano, a spirit medium, explained: 'we lived very well at Nyangani. That is where our *sekuru* [grandfathers, or ancestors] are buried. Nyangani is a hill. There is cave in the middle where the *makuva* [graves] are. I am not sure exactly whether it is now underwater or not, but some of those *makuva* were on the side of the hill. Our *sekuru*s were buried there'.[117] For others this proved, with time, to be less of a problem as their new lands were within sight of their previous homes, and because the most important *makuva* are located among the granite hilltops that became the lake's islands and peninsulas, both close by and accessible, yet appropriately secluded. It is likely Zano elders would have made efforts to ensure ancestors were consulted and placated about their move. As Mai Esrian Mandebvu described:

> The people were not very happy about being moved. They were concerned about being far away from the graves of their ancestors. When they realised that we were being put here, not far from the dam they were happier as it was close by. Especially that day we were moved, people did not know where we were being taken. When we arrived here and saw it was not far away, we were not troubled much.
>
> JF – Were ceremonies held to inform the ancestors what was happening?
>
> Mandebvu – There is no way that our elders would not have done that. They told the ancestors: we are now living nearby and asked them to look after us, so we could stay well in our new place. They would have done that because that is what elders have to do, especially in those days. Our ancestors never got angry because they could see that we were given land here to live and farm. But if we had been chased away from here too, then they would have been angry.[118]

There is some indication that when they were settled at Zano, people encountered trouble from Hararwe people of the Chikwanda clan, removed from the area long before but maintaining strong desire to return to their ancestral areas. In the wave of squatting after the war, Chikwanda people did return, provoking new problems with the *vatorwa* (incomers) from Nyangani living at Zano, but many were subsequently removed again when squatters were evicted all around the lake in the 1980s.[119]

Once the game reserve and fisheries were established, some Zano people benefitted from the fishing co-operative established by National Parks, as well as opportunities for (and consequences of) illegal fishing and poaching. In the long run, however, they scarcely benefitted from the dam. Promised irrigation schemes many remembered never arrived. Their move to what had been Chikwanda territory also generated tensions because of their own historical ties to Murinye. Most significantly, their large new arable fields soon became hard to cultivate because of hippo from the

---

[116] Furere Mashuro 12/04/06.
[117] Geri Zano 23/03/06.
[118] Tobias Mandebvu & Mai Esrian Mandebvu 15/03/06.
[119] Geri Zano 23/03/06.

lake. These problems arose shortly after their removal from Nyangani, and were recognised to result from the dam.[120] Both hippo problems and promises of local irrigation remained unresolved in the 2000s.[121]

Except for this short stretch on its eastern shorelines the lake's surroundings were thoroughly Europeanised once the dam was completed. Harnessed for a diversity of white futures, they also became subject to new Rhodesian pasts, as white commemoration became more pronounced once the dam building optimism of the 1950s and 1960s turned fraught with the approaching war. Although Kyle dam got its name from the small farm where it was built, named after Kyle of Lochalsh in Scotland, Victoria's noisy associations clamoured to have its lake named MacDougall. Another influential lobby group demanded it be named after the former director of irrigation, C.L. Robertson (Saunders 1989:28). Government refused all requests and stuck with Kyle. In the following years MacDougall (and to a lesser extent Robertson[122]) became the subject of numerous other commemorations. At Triangle he himself opened the MacDougall School in 1961, and in 1963 his former home there became a museum. MacDougall lived his last days above Kyle, in Dunollie house, named after his clan home in Argyle, Scotland. It later became *Norma Jean's*. According to his 'hagiographer', MacDougall and his wife Marjorie enjoyed Kyle's recreational and aesthetic landscapes, spending 'many happy days and nights on their houseboat "The Gannet"' (Saunders 1989:28). In 2005 elderly locals remembered MacDougall's twilight years there.[123]

Despite government's reticence to rename the lake, efforts to commemorate MacDougall hardly diminished. In Victoria, Tony Carver 'collected funds and bull-dozed both officialdom and granite to create the scenic Murray MacDougall Drive', circling the lake (Saunders 1989:29).[124] In 1962 MacDougall was honoured with an OBE (Order of the British Empire) and was taken for a flight over Triangle's sugar plantations when, according to his ever-reverent biographer, 'there were tears in the old man's eyes as he watched the chained bundles of cane being unloaded at the Triangle Mill' (Saunders 1989:30). In 1964 he was to have been guest of honour at the opening of a new mill by the Rhodesian Front PM, Ian Smith, but died before he could attend. They left a seat empty in his honour and later his ashes were buried under a rock in front of his former Triangle house, already a museum. MacDougall continued to be heralded as *the* lowveld sugar pioneer. His name was used for a museum, school, scenic drive, Triangle's first locomotive, and later its first super-

---

[120] L. Mandebvu 19/04/06.

[121] Tobias Mandebvu & Mai Esrian Mandebvu 15/03/06; Geri Zano 23/03/06; Louis Mandebvu 19/04/06; Furere Mashuro 12/04/06.

[122] In 1977 the lake formed by Darwendale dam near Harare was named Lake C.L. Robertson (Saunders 1989:42).

[123] Fieldnotes 06/11/05. VaChinengo told me he sometimes cooked for him (26/05/06), and Simon Bright remembered visiting MacDougall at his home as a child (04/08/08).

[124] Also 'Pressure renewed for Kyle-Glenlivet link', *Fort Victoria Advertiser*, 29/01/65.

market (Saunders 1989:133–42). Even government later relented: after Manjerenje dam was built they named its waters Lake MacDougall.

All these commemorative efforts began as soon as the dam was completed, illustrating how dramatic change can demand anchoring in re-imagined pasts. They fitted a diversity of long-standing, and sometimes deeply improbable (cf. Kuklick 1991; Fontein 2006a:3–17) attempts to insert white pasts into landscape all around Rhodesia.[125] Such commemoration escalated in the 1970s exactly as Rhodesian futures were rapidly diminishing. With the war being lost and majority rule ever more likely, an era of white colonial nostalgia emerged exactly as the imagined futures intertwined with dam building became more uncertain. As white futures became doubtful, they demanded much more conspicuously materialised pasts. In the 1970s the MacDougall museum was reconstructed and became a national monument alongside Jatala Weir.[126] E.E. Burke of the National Archives was involved, after publishing the first translation of Carl Mauch's journals in 1969, the 19th-century German explorer who 'discovered' Great Zimbabwe in 1872. Another key mover was Saunders, at the same time urging National Parks to take on the 'aesthetic conscience of the nation' around Mutirikwi. Saunders's 'hagiography' of MacDougall was published in 1977, complete with references to the trusty or 'hapless' 'piccanins' of MacDougall's day, and the 'terrorist forces of an alien philosophy' threatening Triangle, which his sanitised second edition (1989) later left out. At the same time National Archives were documenting the oral histories of Rhodesian pioneers, whilst even earlier explorers were receiving new archaeological attention, such as Hodges' excavation of Adam Render's 19th-century homestead on Chigaramboni hill (Hodges 1975). Amidst rising African nationalism, Rhodesian MPs debated censorship of Great Zimbabwe's obvious African origins, prompting archaeologists like Peter Garlake to leave the country in protest (Fontein 2006a:121–3).

In Fort Victoria, the *Advertiser* published extracts from Sayce's research into its pioneer history, urging townsfolk to assist her efforts.[127] In early 1975 the Victoria Museum Society requested former government buildings on, significantly, 'Allan Wilson Street', be converted to a museum.[128] A small chapel dedicated to Saint Andrew built just above the dam by the water bailiff, Mr van Graan, became a memorial before it was even completed after his daughter died in a car crash.[129] Alongside

---

[125] Including the Allan Wilson Patrol first buried at Great Zimbabwe, later moved to Rhodes's grave in the Matopos; farms named after Rhodesian pioneers; the naming of different enclosures at Great Zimbabwe after white explorers; and the statues, monuments and war memorials littering Salisbury, Bulawayo and other smaller towns (Kriger 1995; Fontein 2006a:134–6).

[126] A project shared between the National Archives and National Museums reconstructed the museum's displays (Saunders 1989:133–4).

[127] 'History of Fort Victoria Planned', *Fort Victoria Advertiser*, 13/12/74; 'The first days of Fort Victoria', *Fort Victoria Advertiser*, 31/10/75.

[128] 'Staking a claim', *Fort Victoria Advertiser*, 31/01/75.

[129] 'Unique chapel at Kyle dedicated', *Fort Victoria Advertiser*, 19/02/71; Errol & Daryl Edwards 25/05/06.

Photo 15   A view of the 'beautiful' lake, from Murray MacDougall drive, east of the dam, towards Zano. (Source: author, 2006)

Photo 16   Chapel dedicated to St Andrew, above dam wall, built by Water Bailiff Mr Van Graan, which became a memorial to his daughter who died in car crash as it was still being built. (Source: author 2006)

another chapel built by Italian prisoners of war north of the lake, it joined the Murray MacDougall drive, Great Zimbabwe, and the game reserve's Reolf Attwell Interpretive centre,[130] to offer a Rhodesian 'heritage trail' complementing the hotels, boat clubs, chalets and game viewing already filling visitor itineraries in Mutirikwi's remade landscapes. As white futures became precarious, the historical dimensions of Mutirikwi's beautified, recreational landscapes became part of increasingly shrill efforts to imbricate white Rhodesian pasts into the fabric of topography. African presence around Mutirikwi was tolerated in only very limited ways. Great Zimbabwe's Karanga village was constructed at this time, offering tourists static glimpses into heavily proscribed, apolitical, and decidedly 'over and done with' forms of African tradition, the only sanitised kind of African presence tolerated in Rhodesia's new playground (Fontein 2006a:203–7; Ucko 1994:276). When wardens found graves and ruins on Mutirikwi's kopje islands, they became 'museum specimens' and potential visitor sites, not the active and affective graves and ruins of people removed only a few years before.[131]

But African pasts were not really obliterated in the remaking of Mutirikwi's landscapes heralded by the dam. Local clans remembered the active and affective graves and ruins of their ancestors, the *mapa* (sacred places) of their chiefs, and the *matongo* (ruins) and *makuva* of their families and their youth, around/under the lake, and on its islands. Just as they remembered *njuzu* troubling the dam builders, and the evictions of the 1940s and 1950s, Chinango and Nyangani continued to resonate long after they disappeared under Mutirikwi's waters. By the mid-1970s, with Rhodesia's futures looking frail, the increasingly demanding presence of African pasts and new futures began to be noticed. In Easter 1975 three South African tourists were killed on Beitbridge road, and as the war came closer 'the consequences ... and ... recent collapse of tourism ... in Fort Victoria were obvious to everyone'.[132] Later the Karanga village and hotels at Great Zimbabwe were burnt, farms were attacked, and boat rallies warned to stay away from the lake's eastern shores. In the TTLs guerrillas destroyed bridges and disrupted communications. Staff at Great Zimbabwe were evacuated and visitor numbers dropped sharply. Rhodesia's playground became a place of danger and uncertainty, as demanding African pasts and futures re-asserted their presence in landscapes that only a decade or two before seemed entirely subjugated to the contested futures of the Southern Rhodesian and Federal governments, and the hydrologists, irrigation planners, engineers, lowveld industrialists and noisy Victoria residents who invested so much energy into it. In the political materialities of Mutirikwi's ongoing becoming, much could be unmade as well as remade as confident irrigated white futures became fragile, and older enduring and re-asserted African pasts were re-forged into new African futures.

---

[130] 'Vivid visual display of Lake life', *Fort Victoria Advertiser*, 07/09/77.
[131] E.g. 'Vutami East Kopje', 21/01/74, Kyle Game Park files.
[132] See 'Stout defence of Policy at Zimbabwe', *Fort Victoria Advertiser*, 16/09/77.

8

War & Danger
in the Wake of the Dam,
1970s

AFTER THE DAM

This chapter and the next are about what happened after the dam and after the war that followed, taking us back to the remaking of Mutirikwi's landscapes in the 2000s with which the book began. It is a story about the re-assertion of African pasts and presence that the dam and everything that came with it failed to obliterate. It is also about African futures frustrated in the wake of war, in which the perceived ruptures of history – the dam, war, independence, eviction and return – diminish in context of material and imaginative endurances, co-existences and proximities. Both the optimism and insecurities of the 1970s, and the euphoria and frustrations of the 1980s, tell of the accumulative, open-ended becoming of landscape, of the enduring political materialities of land and water, and the proximity and co-existence of different regimes of rule, meaning and practice entangled with it.

In some respects Kyle dam was obsolete almost as soon as it was built. It did provide water for the expanding lowveld industries, Masvingo town, and the various recreational developments around it. Some of its imagined futures did endure, and its consequential presence in Mutirikwi's landscapes continued to affect land occupations in the 2000s. Yet the optimistic 'axiom of the age', in which heroic dam building promised industrial expansion, food security and new white settler futures, did not fare so well. Traces of this ethic still resound, particularly in the lowveld. In 2006 Ray Sparrow told me, as we watched hippos in a dam below his Chiredzi home, that 'by far the best thing I ever did was bring water to lowveld'.[1] Yet such nostalgic reminiscences reflect, like late Rhodesia's burst of self-commemoration, how the inflated, imagined European futures animating water planning between the 1940s and 60s, proved much more fragile than the dams themselves did.

Shortly after Kyle was completed the Federation dissolved. It had been the nexus of many of these water-inflected European futures (cf. Tischler 2013). With this demise its limited liberalising influences waned. White Rhodesia swung to the parochial right with Garfield Todd's removal by his own cabinet, the Rhodesian Front's election and the

[1] Ray Sparrow 15–16/06/06.

Unilateral Declaration of Independence (UDI) in 1965. Accompanying this changing political mood, the Native Land Husbandry Act (NLHA)'s unpopular, modernising impulses were inverted little more than a decade after being introduced. Africans would again be ruled at arm's length, through chiefs and a restored 'customary rule' in the renamed Tribal Trust Lands (TTLs). African nationalism too changed during this period, 'away from Christian elites and towards locally grounded cultural nationalism' (Alexander 2006:55). In Matabeleland the *Mwari* cult witnessed revival (Ranger & Ncube 1996:38–39); elsewhere spirit mediumship re-emerged as churches were burnt and mediums crossed borders to join refugees and fighters in Mozambique and Zambia (Fry 1976; Lan 1985). Cultural nationalism affected *how* the war was fought across Zimbabwe, as guerrillas in the Dande and elsewhere worked with mediums, autochthonous clans and ancestors to become 'sons of the soil'; even as coercion and generational, class and gendered struggles too contributed to peasant mobilisation (Kriger 1992; Maxwell 1999:119–47; O'Gorman 2011). During the war many of Mutirikwi's mediums first became established, including VaZarira and Macharaga as well as Sophia Muchini (who became notorious immediately after the war). Shared war legacies continue to shape relations between mediums and war veterans (Fontein 2006c).

But people around Mutirikwi also remember the vagaries of life caught between Rhodesian troops and nationalist fighters. The war's arrival certainly turned Rhodesia's playground into a landscape of danger for Victoria residents, but in different ways also for Africans on farms and TTLs around it. Chiefs were often deeply compromised between the administrative demands of the new Ministry of Internal Affairs (MIA), rural expectations and guerrilla demands. The NLHA's demise and the 'return' to customary rule coalesced with rising cultural nationalism in contested ways, so that divergent registers of meaning and rule, index- ing different kinds of sovereignty and legitimacy, were in play. For some, cultural nationalism inspired a 'return' to mediums and rainmakers, displacing unpopular technocrats and administrators, but for others an official 'return of the chiefs' was closely aligned to modernising Christi- anity and developmentalism, which also fed new African futures. Chiefs were often in an impossible position between the new traditionalism of the state, continuing technocratic demands, cultural nationalists and contested localised rural interests.

While white futures invested in the dam and its recreational land- scapes looked more precarious, African futures were full of potential, anticipating diverse promises of return. Like the imaginative/perceptual processes that had imbricated Rhodesian futures with the materialities of water planning and dam building, these 'returning' African futures too entangled local aspirations with material landscapes. Indeed around Mutirikwi demands for land *redistribution* and *restitution* have often been conflated. The war engaged with African pasts not obliterated by the dam through the materialities of landscape, as sacred mountains and caves became guerrilla bases, and local clans agitated to return to lands, graves and ruins from which they were evicted sometimes only two decades before. In the mid-1970s Morgenster mission began negotiating the return of land for Nemanwa and Mugabe resettlement, engaging with genealogical geographies traced in the official Delineation Reports,[2] and other newly collected oral histories (Mtetwa 1976; Aquina 1965), and Chikwanda people too began agitating for the return of their chieftainship.

As discussed in the next chapter, with independence, many impatient aspirations of return materialised in a wave of squatting around Mutirikwi. But these African futures too wavered. Amid violence spilling across the rupture of independence, white farmers were attacked and some killed. Eventually the 'squatting problem' receded amidst robust police responses, ministerial interventions, and numerous prosecutions. By the late 1980s, Haruzvivishe, Murinye, and Chikwanda people around Mutirikwi's southern, eastern and western shores were removed for the second time, in favour of its recreational park and formal resettlements at Boroma, Le Rhone and elsewhere. As government mobilised around development, Sikato became an agricultural research station and Oatlands and Longdale small irrigation schemes. By the end of the 1980s vacant/abandoned land had dried up, and land reform transformed into the *reorganisation* of communal areas, reminiscent of the centralisations of the 1940s (cf. Spierenburg 2004; Drinkwater 1989). The return of autochthonous authority over ancestral landscapes that some desired, was marginalised by local ZANU PF committees and the introduction of Village Development Committees (VIDCOs), Ward Development Committees (WADCOs) (Ncube 2011:90) and Rural District Councils.

But some aspirations *were* realised and some promised returns did take hold. Fairly quickly the Europeanisation of Mutirikwi's landscapes was partially undone. Abandoned farms around its shores *were* quickly resettled, once squatters had been removed. Some of Morgenster's farmland did 'revert' for Mugabe and Nemanwa resettlement, and importantly, the chieftaincy of Chikwanda was quickly re-instated, albeit with little territory. The lake was no longer the white, Rhodesian playground that had been enthusiastically imagined, but it still became a landscape of heritage, tourism and recreation in which (some) African pasts could be celebrated. The 1980s saw renewed efforts to build a landscape of entertainment around Mutirikwi. While the lowveld industries rebranded in alignment with Zimbabwe's independence (without changing very much), the National Museums and Monuments of Zimbabwe (NMMZ)'s uncertainties at Great Zimbabwe (Fontein 2006a: 167–83) reflected wavering all around Mutirikwi about what kinds of African return would be welcomed, tolerated or denied. NMMZ's choice to professionalise is hard to isolate from the wider decision to re-activate 1970s management plans for tourism and protection of the 'beautiful' lake's watery aesthetics, which demanded squatters be removed. Many efforts to reassert Mutirikwi's contested African pasts, ascendant with the imagined futures of the 1970s, would be frustrated and disappointed. This had

[2] Delineation reports (NAZ 2929/8/5).

long consequences. As Samuel Haruzvivishe put it in 2004: 'The problems that exist are because the land is not with whom it belongs'.[3] It is therefore hardly surprising that 1992's terrible drought, and those of the early 2000s, became, for many around Mutirikwi, indexical of the postcolonial government's failure to recognise the sovereignty of ancestors and *Mwari*. With the return of technocratic developmentalism, and land hunger and congestion hardly relieved, many felt by the end of the 1990s that independence had not delivered its radical promises.

THE NATIVE LAND HUSBANDRY ACT'S DEMISE AND THE GROWTH OF NATIONALISM

Three years after the dam was completed, and only months after the Federation was dismantled, two prominent African nationalists were arrested in Fort Victoria. In March 1964, Michael Mawema – a former Morgenster student from Gutu and once president of the NDP (National Democratic Party) – was convicted in Victoria's magistrate's court of 'making subversive statements ... likely to incite disaffection against the government'.[4] He was detained. It was not the first time he or others had been arrested and detained (cf. Ranger 2013a).

In June 1964 Rev. Ndabaningi Sithole, leader of the new Zimbabwe African National Union (ZANU), was arrested in Fort Victoria on a charge of 'distributing subversive leaflets'.[5] He spent the following ten years in detention. In August ZANU was banned, and over the following months and years many other nationalists too were arrested and detained, sometimes multiple times. Fourteen years later in 1978, four years after his release from detention, Sithole was again in Fort Victoria, this time to announce that the 'war is nearly finished'. With the 'internal settlement' (between himself, Bishop Muzorewa's United African National Council and Smith's Rhodesian Front) 'these fellows in the bush' wanted to know 'when the interim government would be set up so that they could lay down their arms', because 'now that ... majority rule had been achieved there was no further point in fighting'.[6] Not only was he wrong, Sithole claimed influence among guerrillas that he did not have (Ngara 1978:348). With the internal settlement's failure, the war intensified for another two years.

Sithole's two contradictory Fort Victoria appearances bracket an important period when Rhodesian self-confidence, as powerfully manifest in its heroic dam building, became increasingly unstuck, and when Mutirikwi's beautiful, recreational landscapes rapidly filled with fear and danger. Mawema and Sithole's 1964 arrests reflect the remarkable rise of African nationalism between the 1950s and 1960s. Although 'mass nationalism had to contend with a range of competing and overlapping political and

---

[3] Samuel Haruzvivishe 21/07/04.
[4] *Fort Victoria Advertiser*, 27/03/64.
[5] 'ZANU leader in Custody', *Fort Victoria Advertiser*, 26/06/64.
[6] '"War is nearly finished" says Sithole', *Fort Victoria Advertiser*, 24/03/78.

identity claims' (Raftopoulos and Mlambo 2009:xx), and a diversity of grievances and aspirations across urban and rural areas, its rise was nevertheless in a large part due to the NLHA's huge unpopularity. 'Undermining the fragile relationships NCs [Native Commissioners] had built with local leaders', 'provoking widespread resistance', and creating 'disaffection and insecurity even where it was not in the end implemented', by the time of its suspension in 1961 the NLHA had created 'the greatest crisis of authority the settler state had faced' (Alexander 2006:44). Nationalists recognised it as their 'best recruiter' (Phimister 1993:228).

Although Mutirikwi's landscapes had been long dominated by European farmland, and the dam was only completed in 1961, the NLHA did have a large impact in its environs. Official concerns about soil erosion and siltation meant efforts to protect its catchment were enforced long before the dam was built. In the Victoria and Mtilikwe reserves, and around Zano, centralisation, contour ridging and destocking continued throughout the NLHA period, and reverberated long after its formal suspension. Around Mutirikwi there are strong memories of the Land Development Officers (LDOs) who enforced centralisation, contour ridging, and particularly destocking. Furere Mashuro described the anger destocking caused, sometimes much stronger than what the coercive construction of *makandiwa* (contour ridges) provoked 'because we saw that they were looking after the soil'. 'Do you think it's good to be told to sell your cattle when you yourself haven't decided to do that?' he asked rhetorically. 'Even I went to Muchakata[7] to sell my goats. I just left them there for nothing. I was told to sell my goats because they were too many!'[8]

Louis Mandebvu also recalled being forced to dig *makandiwa* and to sell cattle at Mashenjere in Murinye's area. One white LDO nicknamed 'Mutupo' (totem), in charge of pegging homesteads and fields at Zano, is particularly well remembered around Mutirikwi. He 'was writing everything that made us sell our cattle', Simon Charumbira explained. Simon himself was forced to sell nine cattle and decided to eat the last one.[9] In Nemanwa an LDO named 'Nhimura' (destocking) is also well remembered for pegging the contour ridges people were forced to dig after their removal from Mzero farm to live in *maline* (linear settlements) at Nemasuva in the Victoria reserve in 1946.[10] 'Gabarinocheka' (tin can that

---

[7] In the Victoria reserve, under Chief Shumba, where a livestock market was established.

[8] Furere Mashuro 12/04/06.

[9] Simon Charumbira 27/05/06. Simon recalled a man nicknamed *Maraire*, 'who began that work of making contour ridges'. Other Charumbira elders recalled *Nhimura*, a white man called *Chimbwa* and an African 'building those contour ridges' known as *Misiki*. They also remembered being forced to live in *maline*, and being prevented from ploughing on slopes (Chief Charumbira and elders 24/05/06).

[10] Chief Nemanwa & VaChirengarenga 25/04/06. Some remembered *Mutupo* and *Nhimura* as two nicknames for the same person, but others remembered them as two different people. *Nhimura* or *Nemura* was identified by VaChinengo as LDO Miller (VaChinengo 26/5/06; see NAZ S1048 Victoria PNC, General correspondence 1945–50).

Photo 17 Contour ridges in the Mutiriwki communal areas, dating from the mid-20th century (Source: author 2006)

cuts) was another LDO who 'was mad about contour ridges!' (*Vaipengesa makandiwa!*). 'If they were not wide enough then you would have to start again … wide enough so that he could drive his car along them', Tobias Mandebvu explained.[11]

In 1951 the NLHA's modernising rhetoric may have signalled a policy change away from squeezing evermore Africans into the reserves, yet technocratic anxieties about over-stocking (Alexander 2006:46) and soil erosion remained ultimately concerned with the viability of the reserves. In an era of large dams these concerns were extenuated by worries about siltation. By the time Kyle was completed, as Rhodesia moved to the right with the Federation's demise, such coercive intrusions into people's lives had stoked deepening unrest.

FROM 'POLITICAL UNREST' TO 'TERRORIST WAR'

The 1960s certainly witnessed growing 'political unrest' in Fort Victoria. In March 1964 (the same day as Mawema's conviction) Paul Hewlett, 'a young Victorian farmer', was fined for 'rowdyism' after throwing 'a log of wood through the window of African quarters at the Victoria Sports club'. 'In times of political unrest such conduct could have far reaching effects' the magistrate warned, as he imposed 'a penalty which would deter others from committing similar actions'.[12] It is not clear if this curbed white rowdyism, but African protests, defiance and sometimes

---

[11] Tobias Mandebvu 15/03/06.
[12] 'Young Farmer fined £20 for Rowdyism', *Fort Victoria Advertiser*, 27/03/64.

violence[13] were certainly beginning to shake white confidence. As 'political unrest' became 'terrorist war' (in settler parlance) over the following decade, Rhodesia's playground became much more dangerous.

Given the anger destocking had provoked, it is unsurprising that cattle rustling became a predominant way in which political unrest materialised around Mutirikwi. It continued with the advent of war, as guerrilla incursions increased dramatically. Pat Potgeiter recalled that 'right at the beginning of the hostilities ... there was a big problem with cattle rustling ... hundreds of my cattle were stolen'.[14] Specialist 'anti-rustling units' were established. In September 1977 a rustler was killed, three others injured and forty cattle recovered, 'in a clash with police anti-rustling units in the Devuli Ranch area'.[15] Despite confidence these new units 'were beginning to achieve good results' the problem did not go away. The following year, 'harassed' by 'continual stock thefts', Victoria East Farmers 'initiated a programme of self-help under the auspices of police reserve'.[16] But only a few months later, Trevor McCusker 'was ambushed and wounded by terrorists on his farm Springfield' while 'on his way to join the anti-stock theft unit operated by Victoria East Farmers'.[17] By this late stage, more than cattle were in danger – the anti-rustlers themselves were in trouble.

Stock theft was not the only form political unrest took in the 1960s, before the onset of guerrilla war. This period witnessed a more general wave of theft, increasing violence, and growing problems with poachers in the game reserve.[18] Newspapers often emphasised the criminal rather than political nature of thefts and attacks. Sometimes perpetrators' nationalist 'pretentions' were mocked. In June 1973, for example, the *Advertiser* reported that 'Pseudo Terrorist' Isaac Zivanayi was 'fined £40 (or 40 days in jail) for threatening a Super Bus Services driver ... in Murinye T.T.L' that 'he would be killed if he took his bus over the Kyle Dam road the following day'.[19] Whether political motivations were involved in this particular case or not – the accused admitted robbery – stock theft and violent robbery around Victoria during this period were often framed in criminal rather than political terms. This may have been a mechanism for containing rising political tensions and fears, or of fortifying Rhodesian grip on an increasingly dubious political/moral high ground. Electioneering in 1974, Mr R. Cowper, Minister for Transport and Power, updated a Rhodesian Front meeting in Fort Victoria on the current 'security situation'. He rejected the 'contention that ... terrorist

---

[13] For example the protests that followed the arrest of NDP leaders, and Bulawayo's Zhii riots (Ranger 2013a:60–87, 2010c:217–43).

[14] Fieldnotes 15/01/06.

[15] 'Rustler Killed' *Fort Victoria Advertiser*, 07/09/77.

[16] 'Move against Stocktheft', *Fort Victoria Advertiser*, 24/03/78.

[17] 'Farmer wounded in Terr attack', *Fort Victoria Advertiser*, 11/08/78.

[18] 'Gunman foiled by storekeeper', *Fort Victoria Advertiser*, 26/02/65; 'Court hears story of Zaka killing', *Fort Victoria Advertiser*, 19/04/68. On poaching, see 'Excerpts from annual reports, Kyle', Kyle Game Park Files.

[19] 'Pseudo Terrorist in Store hold-up', *Fort Victoria Advertiser*, 01/06/73.

infiltration had anything to do with either national or internal policies', stressing that 'the scourge was related only to Communist ideologies'. 'The terrorist pattern had changed in recent months' he explained, and 'attacks on European farmers had largely ceased, changing to attacks of a vicious type on the local African population'. Although 'Rhodesians had been "novices in the game" ' he continued, asserting a confidence that betrayed its absence, 'the tide had turned very much against the infiltrators'. Cowper was 'certain that they would be eradicated in the months ahead'.[20] He was as wrong as Sithole would be four years later.

By the end of September 1975, any pretence that cattle rustling, theft and violence reflected anything other than the deepening struggle for majority rule disappeared with the killings of three South African visitors on Beitbridge road.[21] As efforts to rekindle the war from Mozambique and Zambia took effect (cf. Mhanda 2011), guerrilla incursions into Mutirikwi's landscapes became a pervasive part of life. The security situation rapidly deteriorated and reports of 'Terrorist Attacks', 'Terrs killed', and 'Lucky Escapes' filled the local newspaper.[22] Farmers, farm tracks and farmsteads across Mutirikwi's European areas were targeted, and attacks took place on Dornfontein, Mkwari, Tokwe Grange, Nebraska ranch, Springfield, and Cheveden estates, amongst many others. To shore up confidence, the *Advertiser* reported the 'war efforts' of women's groups 'packing hampers' for 'security forces', and repeatedly alluded to the stoicism of farmers under attack. For example, after Tokwe Grange farm was attacked by guerrillas with machine guns on Christmas eve, the third time in less than a year, the owner's wife, Mrs Ron Vincent said '"Its just one of those things" but added that they were getting rather tired of it'. 'After cleaning up' the paper reported sanguinely, they 'still had an enjoyable Christmas day'.[23] Highlighting the 'terrors' inflicted in the TTLs, the local paper also ran articles about 'the desperate plight of many Rhodesian African children left destitute ... by the terrorist war'[24] and published patronising, heroic biographies of black Rhodesian soldiers stationed (and sometimes killed) in the district.[25] Later it celebrated

[20] 'Cowper predicts early end of terrorism', *Fort Victoria Advertiser*, 19/07/74.

[21] 'Stout defence of Policy at Zimbabwe', *Fort Victoria Advertiser*, 16/09/77.

[22] For example: 'Presence of mind by Terr Victim', 04/02/77; 'Determined to join Terrs', 25/02/77; 'Sundown Terr attack on Kyle Farm', 03/06/77; '16 Terrs killed in 12 days', 01/07/77; 'Quick thinking constable escaped Terrs', 28/10/77; 'Christmas eve Terr attack repelled', 06/01/78; 'Lucky escape from Ambush', 24/02/78; 'Farmer wounded in Terr attack', 11/80/78; 'Farmer missed death by inches in blast', 01/09/78; all from *Fort Victoria Advertiser*.

[23] 'Christmas eve Terr attack repelled', *Fort Victoria Advertiser*, 06/01/78.

[24] For example, 'Victoria "Troopies" branch needed', 25/03/77; 'W.I. makes major war effort', 20/05/77; 'Women in war effort', 10/06/77; 'Women's Institute are going "Great Guns"', 19/08/77; 'War Orphans are in need of care', 27/01/78; all from *Fort Victoria Advertiser*.

[25] For example: 'R.S.M. A terror to the terrorists', 10/02/76; 'Keeping the troops on the move', 23/04/76; 'A fine soldier laid to rest', 22/04/77; 'Quick thinking constable Escaped Terrs', 28/10/77: all from *Fort Victoria Advertiser*.

when the Red Cross determined it would 'not recognize terrorists as prisoners of war'.[26]

Efforts to build Rhodesia's playground continued through this period, but tourism was affected by the deteriorating security situation. Mike Lotter, an engineer who supervised work on the 56 km (35 mile) canal to Triangle, and a keen member of the Boat club, remembered how a 'national sailing regatta at Kyle' in 1975 was guarded by 'two volunteer sticks of police reservists', and 'sailors were warned not to go near the TTL shore beyond the dam wall!'[27] In 1976, National Museums (NMMR) reported a marked decline in visitors at Great Zimbabwe due the security situation, coupled with 'fuel shortages' and the 'indefinite call-up period for Rhodesians'. They had just taken over from National Parks, and a 'certain amount of discipline had to be injected into the African staff'. Poaching and 'snaring has been rife', so a 'BSAP [British South Africa Police] reserve patrol base' was established for 'the Zimbabwe area'. The growing baboon and monkey population also needed reducing, but 'with the security situation it is not possible to discharge firearms'.[28] The following year security continued 'to deteriorate in the district ... staff houses have been fenced and alarms fitted', 'firearms have been received' and 'agri-alert will be fitted ... when available'.[29] Although 'three companies of troops' were now stationed 'at Le Rhone battle camp', there was a 'tremendous drop in tourism in this part of Rhodesia'.

Problems with NMMR's African staff continued. The regional director, P.J. Wright, whinged that he 'personally would not give credit to any of them, they have carried out the work they are paid for and no more'.[30] The following year tourist numbers dwindled further, but 'good relations' were 'maintained with both the army and the police'.[31] In 1978/09 'the security situation dramatically deteriorated', until 'the Officer commanding 4 Brigade ... advised me to caution all visitors against visiting the ruins'. Tourist numbers were 'the lowest ever recorded'. The deepening security concerns caused 'all but two Europeans and six African staff members to desert, resulting eventually in the closure of the monument to the public on 30th June 1979'.[32] Wright's 'labour force had deserted due to intimidation' after the 'Park's office' was burnt down, and the 'museum, tea room and lodges had been vandalised'. 'Two storerooms had also been burgled' and a 'major terrorist attack occurred on the hotel'

---

[26] 'The Red Cross position on terrorists', *Fort Victoria Advertiser*, 20/05/77; 'New Geneva Convention Clarified', *Fort Victoria Advertiser*, 24/6/77.

[27] Notes by Mike Lotter, undated, provided by Errol Edwards 25/05/06.

[28] Annual Report 1975-6, Zimbabwe National Monument, National Museums and Monuments of Rhodesia (NMMZ files), O/3 Annual reports.

[29] Annual Report 1976-7, Zimbabwe National Monument, National Museums and Monuments of Rhodesia (NMMZ files), O/3 Annual reports.

[30] Ibid.

[31] Annual Report 1977–8, Zimbabwe National Monument, National Museums and Monuments of Rhodesia (NMMZ files), O/3 Annual reports.

[32] Annual Report 1978–9, Zimbabwe National Monument, National Museums and Monuments of Rhodesia (NMMZ files), O/3 Annual reports.

and its 'staff house complex'.[33] Later, after fire destroyed lodges and the 'Karanga village', Wright and his wife too 'tendered their resignations'.[34] When National Museums eventually returned after the ceasefire the following year, there was much clearing up to do, and they were immediately immersed in new security concerns caused by Sophia Muchini and her entourage of demobilised guerrillas, as squatting rippled across Mutirikwi's landscapes.

LANDSCAPES OF WAR AND DANGER

In 2001 Comrade Nylon, a guerrilla leader who operated around Mutirikwi during the war, acknowledged that he and others attacked the Great Zimbabwe hotel and 'Machonya', the army camp on Le Rhone (Fontein 2006a). His and others' accounts illustrate how the war took place *within* Mutirikwi's active African landscapes, even as it often seemed targeted *against* excessive Rhodesian attempts to Europeanise them. Such accounts also indicate how landscapes of fear heralded by the onset of guerrilla war not only affected white Victorians but also Africans on farms, in the TTLs, or working for local governmental institutions.

Guerrilla action around Mutirikwi, as elsewhere (Daneel 1998:27–63, 1995; Lan 1985; Ranger 2013b), took place *within* its active landscapes of sacred mountains, rivers and caves. Stories about ancestral guidance, warnings of pending attacks, the healing of wounded comrades by mediums and diviners, and the interpretation of ancestral signs, point to how guerrilla war was fought in engagement with the autochthonous knowledge of mediums, clans and chiefs (cf. Lan 1985; Daneel 1995, 1998; Fontein 2006a). Indeed a key dimension of such collaboration was the access it gave to hills, caves and sacred places. Guerrillas established bases on sacred mountains exactly because it was difficult for others to go there. This resonated with pre-colonial Karanga territorialities, and 19th-century use of caves and mountains as ancestral *mapa*, *gadzingo* (sacred places), or for refuge from Ndebele raiders (Mazarire 2013a; Ranger 2013b), as well as, much later, with war veteran and new farmer efforts to 'make safe' land occupations in the 2000s. 'There are quite a lot of places, especially mountains' Nylon explained, 'there is one ... just before Ngundu, on Beitbridge road, which could burn sometimes, and you could see as far as Nyajena'. 'I and the other comrades could go into those mountains, and put our bases up there' he continued, but 'it was difficult for anyone else to do so ... they would just get lost ... even the enemy, if they tried to come, they would fall off, which just shows the connection between us and the ancestors'.[35] This account was mirrored by VaKurasva, base commander on Desmondale farm. After training in

---

[33] Minutes, 7th meeting, NMMR local Board of Trustees, 09/08/79, NMMZ files, C1a: Trustee correspondence.
[34] Minutes, 8th meeting, NMMR local Board of Trustees, 07/11/79, NMMZ files, C1a: Trustee correspondence.
[35] Comrade Nylon 08/08/01.

Mozambique and Tanzania, VaKurasva returned to Zimbabwe in 1977 through Chimanimani, operating in the Buhera/Birchenough area until the end of the war. He explained how 'when we first entered an area we would ... go to those elders, whether a chief, or a *svikiro* [spirit medium] or a headman. We would explain that we are your children, we have come here to fight this war ... the war of our ancestors, to take back the land. Those elders would tell us the rules of the land, how we should move through it safely and we would be shown the sacred places ... where we could hide'.[36]

But not only did guerrilla war gain traction through enduring African landscapes of sacred caves and hills, it was also fought against white presence in them. Besides obvious military and economic targets, the war engaged with highly symbolic aspects of Mutirikwi's re-forged European-ised landscapes, although not the dam itself. Tourists and hotels were attacked as well as the army base on Le Rhone. Farmsteads were frequently attacked because land grievances were central to rural support for the struggle, but also because of the mistreatment of farmworkers (cf. Da-neel 1995). Perhaps, like cattle rustling, attacks on farmers, tourists and hotels were to be expected. Similarly roads and bridges between farms and in the reserves were targeted with mines and ambushes. Movement through the landscape became almost as restricted for white Rhodesians as it was for Africans. Curfews were established and drivers advised against driving at night. In 1977/8 convoy systems were implemented on main roads north and south of Fort Victoria.[37] Rhodesian farmers armed themselves, fortified homesteads and created 'agri-alert' systems. Across Zimbabwe's TTLs, Internal Affairs created new 'concentration-camp' landscapes of 'keeps' and 'protected villages' to disrupt networks of food and information between rural populations and guerrillas. Life in these camps was difficult, especially for women (O'Gorman 2011:7). Twenty-two were established in Victoria Province alone, although none imme-diately around Mutirikwi. There were many more in other provinces and these, alongside army bases and police camps, left their own imprint upon the war's material and imaginative landscapes.[38]

In diverse ways then, the war took place *in, with* and *against* the active and affective manifestations of past and enduring African and European remakings of Mutirikwi's landscapes. The war was not just motivated by diverse grievances about land, it took place *within* existing landscapes and effectively reshaped them (cf. Moore 2005). Like graves and ruins, material traces of this reshaping continued to be affective into the 2000s. They are still encountered in, for example, rusty security fences clinging to old farmsteads, the fortified homes of older chiefs; ruined

---

[36] VaKurasva 17/04/06.

[37] 'Extended Convoys', *Fort Victoria Advertiser*, 06/01/78.

[38] Manicaland, Mashonaland Central and East provinces had far more – 41, 101 and 57 respectively – and Matabeleland South much fewer (7), reflecting the different war trajectories in these parts of the country. See www. rhodesianforces.org/Intafprotectedvillageprogramme.htm, accessed 18/03/13; and www.freewebs.com/dudleywall/keepsandpvs.htm, accessed 18/03/13.

farm buildings on resettlement schemes, bullet casings encountered on former farms, and patched up bridges in the former TTLs. After severe drought lowered Lake Mutirikwi's waters in 1987, 'grenades and other explosive devices' were exposed on mud flats near the Kyle Boat Club.[39] In December that year dead freedom fighters were reburied in Bikita, as heroes acres were established across the country.[40] Much later, the liberation landscapes of former guerrilla and refugee camps, mass graves and human remains across the country, and in Mozambique and Zambia, would receive renewed attention through NMMZ's liberation heritage project (Fontein 2009b; 2010; 2014).

In the 2000s many around Mutirikwi remembered fighters by their guerrilla names, recalling how their bases and incursions reshaped landscapes, investing them with new significance. VaChinengo remembered comrades (Tendai, Charles, Norn Chiedza, and Dinda Mateinda) coming at night 'to tell us to come to their base camp ... there at Makava'.[41] Charumbira people told me about a base camp at Reshuro mountain, from where comrades Nylon, Chadiwa Chapera, Maplan, Tsuro, Made Nyika and 22Maguerrilla operated.[42] Headman Nemanwa's wife recalled helping guerrillas blow up a bridge between Morgenster and Chikarudzo, pointing out the patch of concrete where it had been repaired.[43] People in Zano remembered guerrilla bases in hills bordering farms and TTLs, and land mine attacks on trucks carrying soldiers.[44] VaChigohwe, of the fishing co-op, recollected helping comrades 'by giving them *sadza* [maize-meal porridge], meat, even clothes and blankets', and of course fish. He explained how guerrillas from Zaka, in the east, established basecamps on hills called Chinyathi, Murangadzi and Chiramba Makozhvo.[45] A young man at Zano told us a story about comrades hiding out in a large hidden *nhare* (cave) on an island on the lake called Rubatagore.[46]

Several people recollected helping comrades as *mujiba* or *chimwido*, boys and girls who would source food, run errands and gather intelligence for guerrillas.[47] Others recalled looking for ways to escape to Mozambique to join the struggle.[48] Many were very young, and this was risky and required endurance. In February 1977 Fort Victoria's magistrate sentenced three young people to five and ten years in prison with hard labour for 'trying to leave Rhodesia to go for terrorist training'. One was only 15 years old. 'The offence' the magistrate said, 'was a serious one as there appeared to have been little or no compulsion on the part of

[39] 'Explosive exposed as lake drops', *Masvingo Advertiser*, 17/07/87.
[40] 'Posthumous honour is a fitting tribute to fallen heroes', *Masvingo Provincial Star*, 04/12/87.
[41] VaChinengo 26/05/06.
[42] Chief Charumbira and elders of his *dare* 24/05/06.
[43] Fieldnotes 13b/05/06.
[44] Geri Zano 23/03/06.
[45] VaChigohwe 10/05/06.
[46] Fieldnotes 23/03/06.
[47] VaMadungwe 12/03/06.
[48] Acting Chief Matopos Murinye 24/04/06.

terrorists to force the accused to go for training' and 'the three had made a determined effort to become terrorists, as they had covered a vast distance ... to reach the Mozambique border'.[49]

But many remembered equally the intimidation and coercion also associated with guerrilla warfare. Furere Mashuro recalled: 'yes the comrades were here, *vaifamba* [they used to walk/travel]' through the 'Harawe lands' at Zano. 'They used to kill' he explained, and 'do what ever they wanted ... They used to stay in this kraal ... leave their guns in the field and come here to eat oranges. Some would take chickens. There was nothing we could do about that'.[50] Similarly, VaChinengo recalled that 'we did not have sides, we were in the middle'. 'When soldiers came we would agree with whatever they told us, and then we would be beaten and they would pass'. Then 'when the comrades came, we would agree with whatever they told us, we would be beaten, and then they too would pass'.[51] Former farm workers too recalled dangerous encounters with both guerrillas and Rhodesian soldiers on roads connecting farms and TTLs east of the lake. Indeed many described being trapped between the demands and violence of both sides, fitting the nuanced picture scholars now have of rural lives during the struggle (cf. O'Gorman 2011; Kriger 1992). As Esrina Mandebvu described:

> During the war we were living with fear, running away from both the soldiers and the comrades, into the mountains because around here it was very dangerous with a tarred road and dam nearby. The soldiers used to beat us a lot. Nowadays I don't have glass in my windows because once when the soldiers ... were beating the people here, they destroyed my windowpanes. This son here [referring to Tobais Mandebvu] was very badly beaten along with his brother. They were arrested and taken to Machonya, a camp for the soldiers there at Shepherds. They were kept there for a month.[52]

The landscapes of fear heralded by war around Mutirikwi affected Africans as much as Europeans. Guerrillas arriving from Mozambique too faced dangers moving around the TTLs and attacking European farms. This involved not only the threat of being 'sold out',[53] poisoned (Mhanda 2011:67), or ambushed by Rhodesian forces, but also because they came as *vatorwa* (strangers) into active autochthonous landscapes. Guerrillas relied on food, clothes and other logistics from 'the masses', but they also needed chiefs and *masvikiro* (spirit mediums) to tell them 'the particular rules of an area' to 'know how to move through it safely'.[54] This is why becoming *vana vevhu*, (sons of the soil) was so important (cf. Lan 1985). This was echoed in the 2000s, as land invasions turned into fast-track land reform, and war veterans and new farmers deferred to the autochthonous knowledge of chiefs, mediums and clans, to 'make safe' their occupations.

[49] 'Determined Effort to Join Terrs', *Fort Victoria Advertiser*, 25/02/77.
[50] Furere Mashuro 12/04/06.
[51] VaChinengo 26/05/06.
[52] Tobias Mandebvu and Esrian Mandebvu 15/03/06.
[53] Tobias Mandebvu with Geri Zano 23/03/06.
[54] VaKurasva 17/04/06.

But of course during the war such dangers usually paled in comparison to the more immediate threats guerrillas brought for Africans living and working in their operational zones. While African staff deserted Great Zimbabwe due to intimidation, the agricultural department in Victoria too experienced pressing staff shortages, especially with Europeans being called up for military service. The NLHA may have been suspended, but pressure for soil conservation and agricultural extension continued. Despite being 'in the midst of war' the 'demand for training increases both from the tribesmen and officially to meet the security situation', Victoria's provincial agricultural officer reported in July 1975.[55] Although 'quite incapable of taking over the management of District staff', and even 'a security risk in such a role', the 'senior African Agricultural officers will, in a holding situation, be used as a district senior agricultural officer' but 'this is likely to be beyond their capabilities' and a 'general break down in development momentum is expected'.[56] The MIA's African agriculturalists too were subject to intimidation, threats and violence in the TTLs, where the legacies of coercive contour ridging, destocking and centralisation meant increasing hostility, further exacerbating staffing problems. A report two years earlier outlined the pressures African staff and 'tribal leaders' were already experiencing in some regions:

> The subjugation of certain tribesmen by terrorist pressures in ... border areas ... has occurred as a result of vicious intimidatory practices against unsophisticated African, numbers of whom have been murdered and tortured ... with extreme brutality. Tribal leaders ... have been subjected to pressures which few Europeans can begin to understand and, as in the case of the late Headman Kandeya, loyalty to Government has even resulted in death at the hands of terrorists. Details concerning the abduction of hundreds of school children from St Alberts by terrorists are well known and ... it speaks well for the officers of this ministry that ... administrative functions of the Ministry have continued ... under extremely difficult circumstances ... District Assistants and African Clerical Assistants and members of the African staff of this ministry have been abducted by terrorists. I cannot speak too highly of the loyalty and devotion to duty shown by those concerned.[57]

African soldiers and police too often encountered trouble when visiting relatives in the TTLs. In October 1977 the *Advertiser* discussed how 'policemen visiting homes in Tribal Trust Lands' were 'coming under increasing pressure from terrorists and terrorist supporters'.[58] It covered the trial of Chitsime and Tinarwo who informed 'terrorists' of Constable Marashe's presence when he visited his father-in-law's (Chitsime's) house to collect his wife. Derided as a 'sell out' Marashe was stripped and beaten 'after terrorists had told [the people] they could do what they liked with him'. He escaped after over-powering a guard and 'pretending

[55] Provincial Agricultural Officer to Internal Affairs, 16/7/75 (NAZ S3780/110/24/1).
[56] Provincial Agricultural officer to Internal affairs, 24/12/74 (NAZ S3780/110/24/1).
[57] 'Notes for Annual Report, Secretary, Internal Affairs, 1973' (NAZ S3708/1).
[58] 'Quick thinking constable escaped Terrs', *Fort Victoria Advertiser*, 28/10/77.

to lob a grenade as a ruse'. Although tainted with a typical celebratory tone, this account of Marashe being informed upon to guerrillas by his father-in-law captures something of the struggles African communities faced in the TTLs.

STRUGGLES WITHIN THE STRUGGLE

Apart from bracketing the period when African nationalism turned into war, Ndabaningi Sithole's two appearances in Fort Victoria also illustrate the internal fractures that became characteristic of Zimbabwe's struggle. Described by Ndabaningi's younger brother, Masipula Sithole (1979) as the 'struggles within the struggle', these turned on divergent aspirations, personalities and ambitions as much as differences of class, ideology and ethnicity (cf. Mhanda 2011; Tekere 2007; Chung 2006). They played out not only in the Zambian and Mozambican guerrilla camps, or the detention camps holding nationalist leaders, but also across rural and urban areas within Zimbabwe, including around Masvingo. In September 1977 'factional' fighting between ZIPRA (Zimbabwe People's Revolutionary Army) and ZANLA (Zimbabwe African National Liberation Army) forces in the Maranda TTLs, killed between five and ten guerrillas. One officer told the *Advertiser* that 'it was inevitable that tribalism would enter the terrorist war and that faction fighting would occur'. These ZANLA/ ZIPRA 'shoot outs' focused on competing 'territorial rights'. Echoing how rivers have long been central to contested territorialities around Masvingo, one 'elderly African man' told the *Advertiser* that 'ZAPU [Zimbabwe African People's Union] say ZANU [Zimbabwe African National Union] must stay east of the Nuanetsi River' and 'ZANU say ZAPU must not cross the Mlelezi River'.[59]

Wartime loyalties and fractures would be long remembered after independence, sometimes replaying in new struggles. Mutirikwi became a ZANU/ZANLA stronghold during the war, so supporters of other nationalist parties remained on the back foot. In the early 1980s, amid widespread concern about squatting, banditry, army desertions and dissidents, ZAPU supporters were particularly victimised (cf. Clark 1985:23, 35, 152–3). Vincent Matende's home in Murinye was looted and burnt by ZANU youth when his father stood as PF ZAPU candidate against ZANU PF's Eddison Zvobgo in the 1985 elections.[60] Similarly, in Nemanwa, former Muzorewa supporters are still remembered. Wartime allegiances, and loyalties have long after-effects. Many would be replayed again in the relationships of mediums and war veterans (Fontein 2006c) during the 1990s and 2000s (cf. Kriger 2003), when ZANU PF's 'patriotic history' (Ranger 2004) and its 'politics of the dead' (Fontein 2009b, 2010) often turned on competing legacies of suffering. But the struggles within the struggle around Mutirikwi, and elsewhere (Kriger 1992; O'Gorman 2011), also turned on much more localised tensions. People used guerrillas to

[59] 'Terr faction fights in Maranda area', *Fort Victoria Advertiser*, 09/09/77.
[60] Vincent Matende 18/12/05.

get even with neighbours and rivals.[61] VaMakasva explained his experiences when he was employed by Rhodesia's electricity authority: 'I worked hard during the war' using 'my own money to go to Mozambique' where comrades would 'give me letters and whatever else ... to [take] to their destinations'. But in 1979 'I had to stop working, without pension' because someone told the comrades 'he is the one who is repairing the electricity that we are trying to destroy'. He was captured at night and 'forced to walk from Chiredzi to Great Zimbabwe'. The comrades then 'agreed to let me go ... but I was to report back after two days'. However, the following day 'the ceasefire had been announced ... so I didn't go back'. 'That was my lucky day', he said, 'a lot of people died during that war', 'once someone had sold you out ... they would kill you'.[62]

If government employees provoked suspicion, African business owners and shopkeepers too suffered deep mistrust, and frequently faced heavy guerrilla demands for supplies, money and food. Vincent Matende's father suffered both. Forced 'to resign from his job as a prison guard' after 'relatives ... were victimised by the comrades', he was expected as a 'businessman' to 'work for the war instead' supplying 'fat cakes, jeans and other things'.[63] Local jealousies meant businessmen and shopkeepers were unusually vulnerable to accusations of witchcraft and/or selling out: the two were often conflated. The persecution of alleged *vatengesi* (sell outs) and witches by guerrillas is a well-known aspect of how local rivalries played out during the struggle (cf. Lan 1985:167–70).[64] VaZarira told me her spirit VaMurinye rescued three people in Zaka before they were killed by guerrillas, after they had been falsely accused of witchcraft.[65]

RHODESIAN TRADITIONALISM, CULTURAL NATIONALISM AND THE RETURN OF THE CHIEFS

If cultural nationalism and war had lasting legacies, then the NLHA and the return to customary rule and state-enforced traditionalism that followed its demise too had continuing after-effects. Both introduced powerful repertoires for asserting belonging, authority and a claim to the land, which continued to reverberate powerfully in the 2000s. There is

---

[61] In Nemanwa, 'Sekuru Sam', visiting from Bulawayo, told me how his brother was killed and his mother shot in the face during the war, when they were living in Zimuto, after 'people in the village told comrades that his brother', who used labour on neighbour farms, 'was working as a soldier for the Rhodesians'. 'Later the whole family who sold out his brother, were found by soldiers protecting the farm where they were working, and they were all killed for sending the comrades to Ambuya's home! It often happened during that war that people sold out their neighbours to the comrades as either sell-outs or as witches, just to settle their own disputes' (Fieldnotes 08/01/06).
[62] VaMakasva 14/01/06.
[63] Vincent Matende 18/12/05.
[64] Tobias Mandebvu 23/03/06.
[65] Ambuya VaZarira 10/11/00.

no space here to do justice to the complexities of how Rhodesian policies changed after 1961, in the troubled wake of the NLHA. Others (notably Alexander 2006) have already done so much more effectively. What is clear is that facing deepening political crisis a host of new repressive legislation was passed, nationalist parties were banned, and the NLHA's high modernist goals were radically altered 'in favour of settling the maximum number of Africans in the reserves under the "customary" authority of chiefs and headmen'. [66] This 'intended to distance the state from its coercive role and to legitimise authority over people and land in customary guise' (Alexander 2006:63). It put chiefs and headmen into increasingly difficult positions.

If the NLHA had sought to repudiate customary and communal land rights in the reserves, it had also turned chiefs and headmen into state functionaries 'with much reduced authority' and 'little ideological purchase', but 'greatly expanded enforcement duties' (Alexander 2006:47). Following its demise, chiefs' powers to adjudicate customary rights in the renamed 'Tribal Trust Lands' were 'returned' and hugely strengthened. Furthermore, to counter African nationalism, 'the government set about recruiting chiefs in national politics' (Alexander 2006:67). A council of chiefs was established, salaries raised and responsibilities over land allocations, judicial matters and soil conservation expanded. Constitutional changes in 1969 brought chiefs into the house and senate. In Victoria, Zepheniah Charumbira, who acquired his chieftaincy after protracted disputes in the early 1970s, became a senator and later president of the Chief's Council (as did his son Fortune in the 2000s).

This new Rhodesian traditionalism coincided uneasily with the rise of cultural nationalism. As the MIA replaced the old Native Affairs Department, notions of community development supplanted the language of technical development, and 'the human sciences displaced those of economics and agriculture' (Alexander 2006:65, 78). The 1960s and 1970s witnessed a huge expansion in official efforts to document 'African custom' and 'tribal structures', in 'an elaborate attempt to find the customary key to African authority on which the state might be built' (Alexander 2006:78–79). This produced the massive delineation exercise of 1965, when the genealogies of chiefs and clans across the country were carefully documented. [67] Research by oral historians like Abraham (1966) and Gelfand (1959) coincided with this new official concern for African history and culture. These works simultaneously fed into cultural nationalism, despite the conservative sympathies of their authors. Indeed the rising importance of ancestors like Chaminuka, Nehanda and

---

[66] This 'overhaul' of 'native policy' (Alexander 2006:65,77) took place through legislative and constitutional reforms from the early to late 1960s. In the process Native Affairs was replaced by Internal Affairs, and Native Commissioners became District and Provincial Commissioners. Officials increasingly condemned the failure of the NLHA due to its inability to accommodate the 'human factor' (2006:65). Under the Rhodesian Front this was turned into a kind of 'ultra-traditionalism', coinciding uneasily with the rise of cultural nationalism during the same period.

[67] Delineation reports (NAZ 2929/8/5).

others, was directly related to these new oral histories (Ranger 1982b). Ranger's own much more radical work (1967) on the 1896 rebellions (the First *Chimurenga*) undoubtedly also fed into cultural nationalism, during what rapidly became known as the Second *Chimurenga*. It is unlikely the re-forged traditionalism of Rhodesian officials, these new oral histories, and the rise of cultural nationalism was entirely coincidental.

As the war heated up, Internal Affairs became increasingly aware of collaborations between mediums and guerrillas in the Dande and else- where. Cognisant of the role played by mediums, rain makers and *Mwari* shrines in the First *Chimurenga*, C.J.K. Latham compiled the 'Spirit Index' for Internal Affairs.[68] He later collated its 'fragmented picture of African religion' into the 'Shamanism Book' which 'gave detailed historical and anthropological accounts of the five major rain-shrine systems in Zimbabwe' (Ranger 2003:73 fn. 4). These complemented and built upon the 1965 Delineation reports and other Internal Affairs files on chiefs and headmen.[69] The Index exhaustively listed mediums, rainmakers, diviners as well as prophets and independent church leaders across the country, noting individual histories, religious affiliations and political sympathies. It also listed all the mountains, ruins, forests, caves and other 'cult places' associated with them, and the ancestral graves of particular chieftainships. There were 847 entries for Victoria province alone. Amongst many others, these included the Boroma hills, listed number 118 as the 'burial place of various Murinye chiefs'; Mandara hill in Bikita, listed number 99 and 'sacred to Duma people'; Maswitsi hill in the Chikwanda TTL, number 519, 'where mummies of the Makore Chiefs are kept'; and Zhou mountain in Victoria TTL, number 442, where Chief Mapanzure, himself a medium, led beer ceremonies and slaughtered black oxen.

The Index offers astonishing insight into the extent and diversity of mediums, *Mwari* messengers, diviners, and Christian leaders active at the time, and their relationships to chiefs, headmen and rural communi- ties. It also provides a wonderful picture of the geographical spread and continuing salience of sacred mountains, caves and forests across the province. Its complex picture defies attempts to link particular practices or movements to particular political sympathies, and any categorisa- tion through the crude filters of 'tradition' or 'modernity'. While Chief Mapanzure led ceremonies on Zhou mountain and sent rain emissaries to the Matopos, in Bikita Chief Mazungunye was 'a Zionist [who] frowns upon traditional religious rituals', even as the continuing importance of Mazungunye's sacred hills (Runyanye, Siya and Mandare) and its me- diums (Pfupajena and Chabata) was also recorded. Still in Bikita, Chief Mabika was 'a bishop of the Zion Apostolic church' but was installed by the medium Zengeya, and appointed 'emissaries to be sent to Musika- vanhu for rain'. The Index includes Zionist prophets as well mediums from Charumbira urging 'people to go and deal with their dead fathers

---

[68] 'Notes on Spirit mediums, healers, church leaders and cult places in Victoria Province, 1974 (NAZ S3276/4).
[69] 'Chiefs & headmen' (NAZ S3277/1&2).

(*midzimu*)', even though Chief Charumbira was a well-known Seventh day Adventist. Meanwhile Zionists under Chief Shumba were 'beating drums on sacred hills in annual ceremonies'. Possessed healers and mediums speaking Shona were listed, but also those speaking Ndebele, Ndau, Basotho, Venda, and even 'Kitchen Kaffir'. Many were consulted by Europeans, and sometimes possessed by them. It also traced the movements of mediums, healers and prophets across TTLs, African purchase areas, European farms, and townships in Victoria, Bulawayo and Salisbury. Ntopa Zingoni from Chibi, for example, had offices in Bulawayo and Salisbury, lived in Mufakose (it listed precise address details) and claimed 'the PM is aware of him and that he has helped police in investigations through his spirits'.[70]

The Index and Shamanism Book reveal the extent of Rhodesian efforts to penetrate, understand and *fix* African customs into landscape across the country. Official determination to clarify 'the spiritual hierarchy within the district' – a demand reiterated to all Victoria's District Commissioners in May 1973[71] – betrayed the static and ahistorical notion of culture upon which Rhodesian traditionalism rested. Yet in some ways this reflected (and reinforced) the genealogical geographies through which contested African pasts had long been sedimented into place around Mutirikwi, which would resurface again in the 2000s. In December 2005 Chief Chikwanda showed me Rhodesian maps, delineation reports and genealogies used for the reinstatement of the chieftainship in the 1980s, which he was then using to assert Chikwanda claims over resettled lands north and east of the lake.[72] Similarly in 2000, Radson Haruzvivishe showed me a map from the 1960s, to demonstrate why the land on former Mzero farm belonged to the Mugabe clan (Fontein 2006a:51).

In some respects, then, in the 1960s and 1970s cultural nationalists, historians, Rhodesian officials, guerrillas, mediums and chiefs around Mutirikwi and elsewhere engaged in diverse discourses and practices of African traditionalism that co-existed in close and uneasy proximity. For Rhodesian officials, as for guerrillas, mediums and chiefs, this turned on the need for rural legitimacy, and each in their own way invoked notions of cultural, racial and perhaps ontological difference.[73] Just as Rhodesian politics had moved away from the more liberal, Federal period, so African nationalism became much more radical. For guerrillas reconstituted as *vana vevhu* (children of the soil) – or Nehanda's arisen bones [74] – close

---

[70] 'Notes on Spirit mediums, 1974' (NAZ S3276/4).
[71] 'Security Information and Psychological warfare' Memo PC, Sumner to DCs Bikita, Chibi, Chiredzi, Gutu, Ndanga, Nuanetsi and Victoria, 11/05/73 (NAZ S3276/4).
[72] Chief Chikwanda 22/12/05.
[73] In 'the heyday of Rhodesian Front racism', Africans 'were reified as essentially different from Europeans, notably in their relationship to land' (Alexander 2006:79 & 63).
[74] VaKanda, VaMadiri and VaMuchina, Fieldnotes 16/03/01; for a longer extract of this interview, see Fontein 2006c.

engagements with the ancestors, mediums and chiefs of autochthonous clans offered unique access to ancestral protection[75] and to sacred land-scapes, unavailable to Rhodesian forces, white or black. These languages and practices engaged with the enduring presence of African pasts through the materialities of landscape, and with mediums' claims about the sovereignty of ancestors and *Mwari,* and clearly appealed to the local aspirations to return to lost lands.

On the other hand, the kind of difference embedded in MIA's ahis-torical traditionalism was racialised and paternalistic, emphasising 'the racial difficulties arising out of differences in "Psyche" between races'.[76] This stressed the need to maintain racial segregation, 'separate develop-ment', and govern Africans through 'long range effort … divesting central government of its involvement in the day to day life of its people'.[77] Of-ficials urged 'careful support for and gentle nurture of chieftainship and the whole tribal system' because 'more local problems … solved by local people' meant 'not only better solutions but often lets government off the hot seat'.[78]

Although aware of the salience of mediums, healers and 'cult places', Internal Affairs could not appeal to the authority of mediums, or the active traces of past African presence as guerrillas did. They did try to limit or manipulate the influence of mediums (cf. Mhanda 2011:112–14,123–4). Latham 'was "in sort of a personal race" with guerrillas "to identify [mediums] of importance"' (Ranger 2003:73 fn. 4). The fate of Pasipamere, a Chaminuka medium killed in the late 1970s, was sealed when guerrillas determined he had been working with Rhodesians (Ranger 1982b). Similarly Nylon was aware of Sophia Muchini's pres-ence around Great Zimbabwe during the war, but was suspicious of her motives, ultimately deciding she was an 'imposter' who 'worked with us as much as she worked with them' (Fontein 2006a:159).

Mediumship clearly was a 'precarious occupation' during the war, as it had long been and would remain (Fontein 2012). Nationalists and guerrillas had divergent opinions about the importance of mediums and ancestors vis-à-vis education and churches, for example, or Marx-ist ideology (Chung 1995:146; Mhanda 2011:123–4), or even what kind of spirits mattered.[79] ZANU PF has continued to treat mediums with ambivalence exactly because they are difficult to control. For similar reasons, in the 1970s MIA focused most attention on supporting 'the tribal structure' of chiefs and headmen. In March 1972 chiefs attending

---

[75] There are many accounts of ancestors intervening to protect guerrillas, in operational zones and in camps in Zambia and Mozambique (cf. Lan 1985; Daneel 1995, 1998). Mhanda (2011:67) describes a mass poisoning at Mboroma camp in Zambia in 1975, when a possessed medium called Chiyamauyu saved many lives.

[76] W.H.H. Nicolle 17/02/64; 27.6.6f/100843 (cited from Alexander 2006:80).

[77] Annual Report, Minister of Internal Affairs, 1973 (NAZ S3708/1).

[78] Annual Report, Internal Affairs, 1973 (NAZ S3708/1).

[79] Nylon stated, for example, that 'we worked with our own personal ancestral spirits' (Fontein 2006a:147) rather than the large ancestors like Nehanda and Chaminuka.

a 'conservation course' in Fort Victoria, were 'told to get tough' with 'intruders threatening their territories' by the Minister of Internal Affairs, Lance Smith. Concerned about a 'serious breakdown in discipline in the country' Smith complained that some chiefs 'had capitulated to a mob of youths' and to intimidation by 'a relatively few people acting under instruction of people alien to the tribe'. Chiefs were told 'to put your house into order' and 'regain ... the confidence of your people ... when these intruders threaten your territory'. 'They are the weevils in your grain' he continued, 'the ticks in your cattle ... the bugs in your beds that will not let you rest. Search them out and deal with them. The law stands behind you to help'.[80]

Chiefs and headmen found themselves caught between the traditionalist impulses of the state, and the demands of cultural nationalism, guerrillas and people in the TTLs. We must avoid positing mediums and guerrillas in simple opposition to discredited chiefs and headmen 'co-opted' into state structures. Across Zimbabwe and the changing trajectories of the struggle, the roles, strategies and motivations of chiefs were more complex and diverse than that. The same applies for churches. Missionary as well as African independent churches[81] were involved in divergent ways in the war (cf. Maxwell 1999; McLaughlin 1995). Morgenster mission, or people working there, did assist guerrilla fighters,[82] although the killing of Father George, a Roman Catholic priest in Mushawasha, indicates that church people faced the same dangers as everyone else.[83] The 'fragmentary' picture presented by the Spirit Index reflects these complexities, even if Rhodesian officials were minded to use it (and the Shamanism Book and Delineation Reports) to fix clan genealogies and tribal structures into time and place.

Older technocratic impulses had not disappeared either.[84] After Internal Affairs took over African agriculture in the 1969, older conservationist concerns merged with the expansion of chiefs' authority. The post of 'chief's pegger' was created to delineate contour ridges and avoid the 'antagonism, threats and intimidation' agricultural officials were receiving. In effect, chiefs were 'to play the same policing roles they had under the NLHA, but now in the name of custom not science' (Alexander 2006:77). Indeed, Lance Smith urged chiefs to punish people caught using erosive 'sleighs', and to give 'leadership' to 'the fickleness of people'

---

[80] 'African Chiefs told to get tough', *Rhodesian Herald*, 28/03/72.

[81] NC reports going back to 1936 report the activities of 'Zionists and Apostles' in Victoria's reserves. Initially provoking 'unanimous protest' by 'native boards' and NCs (e.g. Annual Report, NC Victoria, 1936, NAZs1050), by the 1960s African Independent Churches were well established across Victoria.

[82] Louis Mandebvu's father was teacher at Morgenster, who 'used to help them [comrades] quite a lot', until he was arrested by soldiers and taken to Mutimurefu prison, where he stayed until after the ceasefire (Louis Mandebvu 19/04/06).

[83] VaChinengo 26/05/06.

[84] As 'intense ideological debates' played out within state bureaucracies 'contradictory policies co-existed uncomfortably, highlighting divisions within the state and the tenuousness of its knowledge of – and authority over – its charges and the land' (Alexander 2006:63).

when 'agitators appeared calling for the abandonment of conservation farming'.[85] Chiefs' punitive functions were still enforced from the centre, with warnings, fines and prosecutions for 'below standard' conservation works regularly issued by land inspectors across the province. In April 1975 work in Victoria was 'confined to the Mtilikwe TTL, where the effects of continuing pressure [on] Chief Murinye are apparent'.[86] The following year a report on 'Waterways throughout Tribal Areas' noted problems were 'invariably caused by ... the use of those waterways as roads, and ... the lack of authority by the local Tribal Land Authorities'.[87]

All of this meant that chiefs were in a difficult position, charged with allocating land in increasingly crowded TTLs, without the possibility of land redistribution let alone restitution.[88] Alexander cites Chief Shumba's angry warning, as 'the openly nationalist president of the National Chief's Council', during consultations in Victoria in 1962: 'I have told my people we are going to hear the results of our meeting with the Prime Minister. We are anxious to hear that more land is being given to us ... People will kill us if we don't tell them anything on our return' (Alexander 2006:85). Shumba listed the 'farms from which his people had been evicted' and demanded the 'restoration of his "tribal land"'. He was later removed from the Chiefs Council (Weinrich 1971:21). Yet despite increasing Rhodesian attempts to co-opt them into state structures after the early 1960s, chiefs were not inevitably 'discredited' (Ranger 1982a), or invariably 'lost claim to represent peasants' (Bratton 1978:50). Nor were they necessarily caught between 'the demands of ... the traditional and the modern' or 'rendered irrelevant' by the transfer of their ancestral legitimacy to guerrillas (Alexander 2006:83; Weinrich 1971; Lan 1985; Ranger 1982a, 1985). Whatever the loyalties of individual chiefs, the story of chieftainship during the war was more complex than that.

As Alexander (2006:84) has shown for Chimanimani and Insiva, chieftainship in Masvingo did not simply lose rural legitimacy, however much chiefs were caught between state pressures and fervent nationalist mobilisation. Nylon described how 'the chiefs would guide us to the *masvikiro*' who 'would tell us exactly what they wanted in their places/ areas/land'.[89] Likewise VaKurasva 'would go to those elders, whether a chief, or a *svikiro* or a headman ... so that we would know how to move through it safely'.[90] As in the 2000s, genealogical ties to the substance of the soil and autochthonous knowledge of landscape meant chieftainship 'remained important to the expression of rural demands and obstructions

---

[85] 'African Chiefs told to get tough' *Rhodesian Herald*, 28/03/72.
[86] Monthly report, Victoria District, April 1975, B.Cotton to Chief Inspector Lands, Internal Affairs (NAZ S3708/4).
[87] P.A. Davies, Agricultural Deputy Director to Internal Affairs Natural Resources Board, NAZ S3708/4.
[88] 'The offer of land allocating authority in the absence of land redistribution gave chiefs neither credibility as "Tribal Land Authorities" nor an opportunity to bolster their positions through patronage' (Alexander 2006:85).
[89] Comrade Nylon 08/08/01.
[90] VaKurasva 17/04/06.

of state intervention' (Alexander 2006:84). Yet all these pressures did make chiefs unusually vulnerable, and attacks against them increased.[91] Armed guards and reinforced security fences were placed around chiefs' homesteads, as can still be seen at the late Senator Zepheniah's home, where Fortune Charumbira holds his weekly *dare* (court). Charumbira elders acknowledged that the protection provided for chiefs 'was a problem', but 'it was never serious' and the comrades could still 'work with the chiefs'.[92] When attacks on chiefs increased, however, they were evacuated under armed guard to the chief's hall in Mucheke, Fort Victoria.

In April 2006 acting Chief Matopos Murinye described the troubles his family and particularly his father Mudarikwa suffered during the war. I quote him at length because he offers a wonderful portrait of the different pressures chiefs, their families, youth and rural communities were under during the struggle.

> I lived at home, and the war was hotting up. Some people who were trying to kill my father, mistook my brother for him and he was killed by a hand grenade ... he was blown into pieces. We don't know who it was or why that happened. That was when the District Commissioner [DC] sent armed guards to our house to protect us. He sent guards to protect all the chiefs including Charumbira, because they didn't want them to have contact with the comrades. The DC was called Hansen, he worked quite a long time with my father. While those guards were at home, the comrades attacked. The attack must have lasted about twenty or thirty minutes. After that Hansen, who got on quite well with my father, said: You should come to live in the Chief's Hall in Mucheke for your own protection. So my father went there. He wanted me to come with him but I said: No, I will stay behind to look after the cattle. My mother stayed looking after the fields and the house. Other chiefs living at the Chief's hall then included Chivi, Charumbira, Mapanzure and Zimuto, although Zimuto was only there for a short time.
> At home, my mother negotiated with the comrades to allow my father to come back without being attacked again. My mother was very good at receiving people and making them feel welcome. During that time I was working for *Baba* [father]. He had bought a car, a Peugeot 404. He sold eight cows to buy that car. I was driving that – without a licence then – buying mangoes in the reserves and selling them in Mashava at Kings mine. Later, after the mango season, I was doing the same with fish. My mother was trying to negotiate with the comrades to let my father come home. She invited them to the house and gave them a goat which they slaughtered and ate, and some chickens. At first they did not know if they could trust her, but later they saw that she was ok. My father wanted me to stay at the Chief's hall and my mother wanted me to buys things for the comrades. She asked what they needed, and sent me to buy shoes. I bought four pairs of farmer's shoes for them. It was difficult because I didn't want to deceive my father because he trusted me with his car. But I did do those errands for the comrades. One time I bought loads of cigarettes for them. My mother was still trying to persuade them to let my father come back. Eventually the comrades said: We can let your husband come back but we want to take your son to become one of us.
> My mother didn't want me to go. But she realised there was nothing she could do. I said I could go but I needed to talk to my father. My mother told the comrades that I could go with them but they needed to let my father come back. The comrades agreed *Baba* could come back but without his guards, otherwise

[91] But this 'is evidence less of a rejection of chieftaincy than a repudiation of association with the state: even where individual chiefs were killed, powerful groups within rural society retained an interest in the institution itself' (Alexander 2006:84).

[92] Chief Charumbira and elders 24/05/06.

they would attack again. I went to tell *Baba* that he should come home. The night I drove *Baba* back, he told the guards guarding him that he needed to go to do some rituals or *chivanhu* [approx. tradition/culture] at his home, and asked that they let him go without them. He suggested that they go to the bar while he went to do his *chivanhu*. They went to the bar and I drove my father home. But we had left the spare tyre in town, and when we got near to our home we had a flat tyre. So we walked home. My mother saw this was her chance. That same night she went to the comrades' base. It was quite a long way. She told the comrades that *Baba* was at home without guards. They said that he should come to see them. So she went home and told *Baba*. He didn't trust these comrades at first and said: No they should come and see me here. But eventually he saw there was nothing he could do, so he went there and explained that he had to go back to Mucheke first. The comrades said: Ok, but we are going to Mozambique to get more ammunition. When we come back we want to see you living at home without any guards. So *Baba* went back to the Chiefs hall to see DC Hansen. He told him he was sick and needed to go home to be healed with *chivanhu*. The DC said: I have tried to protect you and the other chiefs from attack, are you sure that you want to go back? *Baba* insisted and we went home. There we stayed. Soon the comrades were coming very often and getting on well with my father. They were looking after him and he was providing them with the things that they needed, food and so on. Baba would put down snuff for them and do the necessary *chivanhu, vachipira vadzimu* [appeasing the ancestors] with the *masvikiro*, for the comrades. The comrades got on well with him, they respected him as chief. They did not force him to come to all those all-night *pungwe* [political rallies] and such things.

After some time, the comrades came to say that they wanted to take me with them. At first my father refused but he realised that if he refused he might lose his son's respect, and he said ok. So I went with the comrades. We went far away in that direction, got a lift in the car of a businessman some of the way, and we got to where we were to spend the night. There were many people there who had been taken to go with the comrades, maybe 150 or 200. Each was assigned to his or her commander, and given the things that they would need to carry. I was told I would be carrying medicines and grenades. They said they would give me a gun later on. The plan was for each commander and their people to go to Mozambique in a different direction, and eventually they would all meet up at the same place at the border. I was supposed to go with them, but that night my mother had followed me, and she pleaded with the comrades, saying she had asthma and was unable to look after herself, that I looked after her and did all the heavy work at home. The comrades said ok, and I stayed behind when the others went on. The comrades said that they would collect me another time because for now I would be looking after my mother.

That night the convoy of people walking to Mozambique was attacked by soldiers and helicopters. Some of those *mujibas* carrying things were captured by the soldiers and taken by helicopter to the Ancient City [Sheppards, next to Great Zimbabwe] where there was a soldiers' camp. Those people were severely beaten and told the soldiers that I too was involved in this. I also heard that comrades were looking for me, to take me as they had said they would do. Now I was in trouble, and didn't know where to go. Going home meant coming past Shepherds where the army camp was. They always had roadblocks here. So I went to Mashava to the Gaths Mine where my brother was living. I became a machine operator, and worked there for a week, but then came back to Masvingo to see a friend of my fathers, a white man called David Avimore. He used to run the ferry that crossed the lake to the game park. I stayed with him, hiding from both the soldiers and the comrades.[93]

The difficult position chiefs often found themselves in during the 1970s, between the demands of Rhodesian officials and guerrillas in the TTLs, resound with the troubles and opportunities many faced in the 2000s, when political loyalties would be tested again. As with mediums and war veterans, the contested war legacies of chiefs can have a long reach. Mudarikwa

[93] Matopos Murinye 24/04/06.

Murinye's wartime loyalties were questioned again during the succession disputes his son faced and lost before his own death in 2011. When I interviewed the controversial new chief, Ephias Munodawafa Murinye, in December 2011, he told me his predecessor Mudarikwa had been 'an uneducated chief', 'tricked by the whites', who 'took him to go and live in Masvingo town there', and 'that is why some people came to see him as traitor'.[94] Matopos Murinye's account presents a more complex portrait, which better reflects the hardships, vulnerabilities and dangers, but also opportunities that war brought Mutirikwi's rural communities.

CHIEFS AND MEDIUMS AFTER THE WAR

In the early 1980s, many commentators predicted the decline of chiefs and headmen, because of their perceived complicity with the Rhodesian state (Lan 1985:149; Bratton 1978:50). In practice, they maintained influence over land in communal areas, 'clandestinely allocating land on the basis of customary, territorial and other claims, despite legislative efforts that formally left them 'with little more than a spiritual function' (Ncube 2011:90). The establishment of rural district councils, VIDCOs and WADCOs in the early 1980s, formally 'divested chiefs of the land allocation powers' granted 'by the Rhodesian front regime of the 1960s', and the Chiefs and Headmen Act (1988) further 'excluded traditional leaders in land administration' (Ncube 2011:90) by not even recognising the system of *sabhuku* (village heads). Yet chiefs remained part of local government structures, however 'divested' of land and judicial powers they were. Three prominent chiefs (Chingombe, Mazungunye and Charumbira) were appointed to Masvingo's new provincial authority in 1981 and Eddison Zvobgo (as Minister of Local Government) warned against 'seeking the removal of a particular chief or chiefs', emphasising that government would not 'permit elements of political parties to remove chiefs from office, or to interfere in national selection procedures, for purely political reasons'.[95]

In the 1990s, after a commission of inquiry found 'widespread resistance to VIDCO/WADCO structures as credible authorities over land', government began to re-empower chiefs and headman (Ncube 2011:90–93), offering concessions, higher salaries and increased authority. The Traditional Leaders Act (1999) has been interpreted as part of ZANU PF's continuing efforts to use chiefs to 'extend its hegemony deeper into rural areas at a time of political discontent' (Chaumba et al. 2003b:599; also Mubvumba 2005). These efforts accelerated during the 2000s, when the authority of chiefs over resettlement areas and on District Land Committees was formalised, their judicial powers and salaries increased several times, they received access to rural electrification schemes, subsidised vehicles and tractors, and became central to the distribution of food aid,

---

[94] Ephias Munodawafa Murinye 19/12/11.
[95] 'Three chiefs elected to Provincial Authority', *Fort Victoria Advertiser*, 30/01/81; '"Hands off chiefs" says Zvobgo', *Fort Victoria Advertiser*, 16/01/81.

seed and fertiliser. The revival of the *zunde ramambo* concept (communal fields and harvests providing food for the needy), national *biras* (ancestral rituals) and new costumes that Fortune Charumbira was involved in 2005/06 as leader of the Chief's Council, were part of this project. As ZANU PF increasingly courted chiefs, Zvobgo's 1981 warnings were long forgotten and closer scrutiny was maintained over the appointment of chiefs, headmen and even *sabhuku*. Throughout the 2000s chiefs and headmen were often reported to be involved in ZANU PF politicking and sometimes violence, while those publicly opposed to the party found themselves deeply compromised. Chiefs, headmen and *sabhuku* around Mutirikwi were certainly very careful to avoid being associated in any way with the MDC opposition. As ZANU PF seemed ever more determined to draw chiefs closer into its ranks, the independent press, Human Rights observers and sometimes academics seemed equally determined to discredit them *en masse* as political stalwarts, just as some had done in the early 1980s. I have tried to show that chieftainship around Mutirikwi in the 2000s, and especially in the fast-track context, was no less complex than in the 1960s and 70s, defying the simplistic political polarisations into which it has often been shunted.

In contrast to ZANU PF's sustained overtures towards chiefs, mediums have rarely received similar concessions, despite their wartime endeavours, their obvious symbolic significance, and shared war legacies with war veterans, not to mention close relationships to particular chieftaincies. The situation is almost exactly the opposite of what many predicted after the war. Now chiefs and headmen receive salaries, hold courts, allocate land in communal and resettlement areas, and have access to government benefits, while mediums receive little formal recognition. Mediums around Mutirikwi often stress how surprised they were to find themselves so marginalised after independence.[96] This was expressed as the anger of the ancestors and of *Mwari*, the owners of the soil and the provider of rain, revealed most forcefully through drought. In 1982 and 1983 Masvingo suffered severe droughts, and again in 1987. But the drought of the early 1990s was the worst, so that even President Mugabe had to ask mediums to make it rain. For mediums who worked hard during the war, this marginalisation came as a profound disappointment. But around Mutirikwi theirs were not the only imagined futures and promised returns frustrated in the wake of war. Even more problematic was the promise of return to ancestral lands. Contrary to expectations of a 'radical redistribution of land and decentralization of power', Zimbabwe's negotiated independence 'ensured the survival of powerful centralized state' and, for the most part, maintained existing land divisions (Alexander 1995:175). This is exactly what the Nehanda medium at Great Zimbabwe, Sophia Muchini, warned about in the early 1980s. It is to her story we now turn.

[96] 'We were expecting a black government would appreciate our work ... [but] today we are being labelled *mweya wetsvina* [dirty/bad spirits]. During the Smith regime we were never labelled that, even though we were not paid, we were not labelled *mweya wetsina*' (VaZarira 27/12/00).

9

Promising Returns
and Frustrated Futures
in the Wake of War,
1980s–1990s

Although the residents of Victoria set about building their 'playground' with great gusto after the dam's completion, and the lowveld sugar industries expanded rapidly once water became available, African nationalism and war had brought danger and insecurity to Mutirikwi. White futures looked more precarious as African futures were increasingly full of promise. While the dangers accompanying war threatened everyone in different ways, for many cultural nationalism anticipated new African futures offering diverse promises of 'return'. African pasts had not been obliterated by the dam and its remaking of Mutirikwi's landscapes. This chapter focuses on what happened around Mutirikwi after the war; a story told, in part, through the troubling biography of the Nehanda medium, Sophia Muchini. With independence in 1980, impatient aspirations of return to ancestral landscapes materialised in a wave of restless 'squatting' around Mutirikwi. But by the end of that decade many returnees had been evicted again, as older management plans for the Mutirikwi's recreational park were re-asserted. Some promised returns did take hold. Chikwanda's chieftaincy was restored; abandoned farms 'reverted' to communal land, or were resettled under smallholder schemes, as the Europeanisation of Mutirikwi's landscapes was partially undone. But many of the imagined African futures ascendant in the 1970s were disappointed. By the turn of the millennium for many independence had not delivered its promises. This set the scene for the return of radicalism and new land occupations in the 2000s, when, as Jairos Haruzvivishe put it, 'the government said *"ivhu kuvanhu"*[soil to the people]'.[1]

SOPHIA MUCHINI AND THE VICTORIA EAST FARM KILLINGS[2]

Sophia Muchini, a self-proclaimed Nehanda medium, first arrived around Mutirikwi in 1974. Comrade Nylon and his men were suspicious of her loyalties, but there is evidence other comrades held her 'in high regard during

[1] Jairos Haruzvishe 27/11/05.
[2] There is now a large body of primary material (including NMMZ files, reports in *Bulawayo Chronicle* and *Fort Victoria Advertiser*, and a detailed account of the police investigation, in Clark 1985), and secondary literature (Garlake 1983; Ucko

the war years'.[3] Garlake noted she recruited people for guerrilla training, and was even 'asked to become a guerrilla leader' (1983:16).[4] Rhodesian forces harassed her, her son was shot dead and she was imprisoned for six weeks in 1978 and again in 1979. After the war she re-established herself at Great Zimbabwe, where she was visited by ex-fighters from across the district and beyond, seeking 'cleansing' after the violence of war.[5] She became involved in plans being discussed by some in the new ZANU PF government, notably Dr Ushewokunze, for a ceremony at Great Zimbabwe, when remains of war dead from Mozambique would be reburied. Later she told Salisbury's high court that 'she had heard a message from God' telling 'her to organize a ceremony to bring an end to "the great chaos all over the country"'.[6] But after the murders of Abraham and Margaret Roux, Helena Van As and her grandson Philip in March 1981, her kraal at Great Zimbabwe was raided by police. She was arrested after a shoot-out in which several former guerrillas around her were wounded or killed.

In the high court later that year some of these ex-fighters admitted the murders, claiming they 'had done so on the orders of a woman who said she was Mbuya Nehanda'.[7] 'The killing of Mr and Mrs Roux was part of a larger plan envisaged by "Mbuya Nehanda" to "destroy" all the white farmers' in Victoria East, after which she would 'give the land to the tribe whose ancestral home it was'.[8] At her own trial – in the Chief's Hall in Mucheke[9] – 'the judge refused ... to allow Miss Muchini to wear traditional medium's attire and to sit on the floor of the dock' as 'this would allow her to retain her "mystique" and ... intimidate witnesses'.[10] One of the former fighters, Tenford Mapfema, refused to testify against her and the trial was postponed. When it re-opened in December in Salisbury, her own children gave evidence against her. A 17-year-old girl told the court she had heard Sophia tell former combatants 'we will kill the Europeans because the *mudzimu* spirit has said that the Europeans must get out because we have taken the country'.[11] In court it became clear Ushewokunze had visited Sophia several times, organised former guerrillas to guard her, and had known about the killings. She was found guilty and sentenced to death by Mr Justice Pitman, who described Ushewok-

(contd)   1994; Ranger 2010a, 2010b; Fontein 2006a: 156–62; Sadomba 2011:77–78; Daneel 1995) about the remarkable events surrounding Sophia Muchini in 1980–81. I am grateful to Terence Ranger for sharing his notes from the *Bulawayo Chronicle* concerning these events.

[3] 'Nehanda told us to kill farmer court told', *Bulawayo Chronicle*, 18/06/81.
[4] Fieldnotes 13/07/01.
[5] 'Nehanda told us to kill farmer court told', *Bulawayo Chronicle* 18/06/81.
[6] 'Medium had message from God', *Bulawayo Chronicle*, 16/12/81. Ushewokunze told the court that 'in a trance' she had said 'a libation ceremony should be staged to stave off impending unrest ... and to restore peace between the races and tribal groups' ('Ushewokunze denies murder plot', *Bulawayo Chronicle*, 18/12/81).
[7] 'Nehanda told us to kill farmer court told', *Bulawayo Chronicle*, 18/06/81.
[8] *Bulawayo Chronicle*, 19/06/81.
[9] 'Police News', *Fort Victoria* Advertiser, 16/10/81.
[10] *Bulawayo Chronicle*, 14/10/81.
[11] *Bulawayo Chronicle*, 12/12/81.

unze's denial of any involvement as 'bald and unconvincing'.[12] Three ex-guerrillas were also given death sentences and two received 20 years in prison. One was acquitted but then rearrested on another attempted murder charge. In a later trial five other ex-fighters arrested during the Great Zimbabwe raid were imprisoned for other attacks and for possessing unlicensed arms. Sophia's death sentence was later reprieved, and she was eventually released in 1986.

Elsewhere I have discussed the problems that Sophia's 'bloody sacrifices'[13] at Great Zimbabwe provoked for the bewildered Regional Director, Cran Cooke, and returning National Museums and Monuments of Zimbabwe (NMMZ) officials after the war (Fontein 2006a: 156–62). Increasing alarm that her activities threatened the fabric of the ruins, tourism, and the security situation meant efforts to remove her became increasingly heavy handed. That account explored how for many mediums and war veterans Great Zimbabwe had become a sacred site where 'national ceremonies' needed to be held to thank the ancestors for independence and to settle the spirits of the war dead – demands frustrated by NMMZ's increasingly professionalised approach to heritage. For Sophia, Great Zimbabwe is a sacred place of considerable importance; she described it as 'God's place'.[14] Her calls for national cleansing ceremonies, the return of Great Zimbabwe's 'sacred treasures', and of war dead from Mozambique, continue to have enormous salience (Matenga 1998:57–60; Fontein 2006a: 220–23, 2009b, 2010, 2012; Ranger 2004). Here I focus less on her Great Zimbabwe activities, than her involvement in attacks on white farmers in East Victoria. These events, like the 2007 diesel *n'anga* saga (see chapter 3), bear marks of significant, but opaque, behind-the-scenes machinations by Ushewokunze and others. Yet Sophia's involvement in those killings also reflected wider aspirations, hugely salient at the time and since, to do with the return of ancestral lands. Like her Great Zimbabwe demands, these too continued to be significant long after her conviction, imprisonment and release, reflecting frustrated futures in the wake of war as, for many around Mutirikwi, the post-independence government failed to deliver long-anticipated promises of return.

'CHIMUKA IS DEAD'

The killings of Abraham and Margaret Roux at Mkwari Ranch on 11 March 1981, and of Helena van As and her grandson on Mudspruit five days later, are well remembered around Mutirikwi. People at Zano remember hearing that their white neighbour, 'Chimuka is dead'. Abraham Roux got this name 'Chimuka' [wake up] because 'he would change his ideas every time he woke up'.[15] Some in Zano remember good relations

---

[12] *Bulawayo Chronicle*, 19/12/81. Pitman also presided over Edgar Tekere's trial (Tekere 2007:128).
[13] C. Cooke to D. Jackson, 28/08/80 (NMMZ file C5).
[14] Fieldnotes 13/07/01; also Clark 1985:127.
[15] Tobias Mandebvu and Esrina Mandebvu 15/03/06.

with their white farmer neighbours before 1980: 'Chimuka' on Mkwari ranch, and 'Stan' on Cheveden. Others remember Abraham Roux differently. As Chief Chikwanda explained: 'Chimuka was very difficult ... there was a group of comrades who had not gone to the assembly points, or who had come back from the assembly points ... they killed Chimuka because he was such a difficult man'.[16] According to Louis Mandebvu, 'at Chimuka's farm there used to be a camp for the soldiers' where 'people ... stopped by the soldiers used to be taken to ... be beaten and punished'. When the war was finished 'those comrades thought to go there to avenge the things that had happened there'.[17]

Masvingo's white farming community remember the Rouxs differently. For them the killings were particularly disturbing,[18] as Pat Potgeiter explained:

> It was after peace had been declared. The people who killed them went to Abe Roux's farm, Mkwari. His wife was outside feeding the lambs and he was in the workshop. They had a shop there and these two guys approached wanting to buy something. He asked them to wait outside saying he would open the shop when he was finished with what he was doing. They went outside, but five minutes later came back in with AKs and killed him. Then they went to his wife and just gunned her down where she was ... Those killings were bad, especially as it was in peacetime, the war was over. They were excellent farmers Abe Roux and his wife.[19]

This matches the account of the white policeman leading the investigation, Henry Clark, who had worked with special branch during the war (1985).[20] What made these killings so shocking was that they came when 'for months Victoria ... had been under ... transformation from war to peaceful co-existence' (Clark 1985:2). Clark reports there was 'a strange peace ... throughout the country during most of 1980' (1985:31), probably related to the relief many Rhodesians felt after Robert Mugabe's reconciliatory Independence Day speech (Fisher 2010:27–54). 'News of the murders' came 'as a great blow' to East Victoria's white community 'lulled by a year of almost total peace' (Clark 1985:25), who quickly gathered at the Farmer's Hall 20 km (12 miles) east of town. This was amplified because despite many serious attacks and woundings, no East Victoria farmers had been killed in during the war, even though it was 'an area where ... terrorists had been particularly dominant ... right until ... the cessation of hostilities' (Clark 1985:10). Mkwari 'bordered tribal

---

[16] Chief Chikwanda 23/06/06.
[17] Louis Mandebvu 19/04/06.
[18] Also 'Police news' column, *Fort Victoria Advertiser*, 20/03/81, 27/03/81, 03/04/81.
[19] Pat Potgeiter 15/01/06.
[20] Although informative, Clark's account is typical of much 'Rhodesiana' in its celebratory, nostalgic and masculinist perspective on the war, its tribalist understandings of ZIPRA/ZANLA tensions, and descriptions of Rhodesians as 'the best bush fighters in the world' (1985:121). It also carries a sense of impending doom, perhaps indicative of much white feeling at the time. After the trials he left the police and the country to go to South Africa ('Police news', *Fort Victoria Advertiser*, 31/07/81).

trust land' and 'had survived four farm attacks' during the war. 'Abe' or 'Chimuka' was himself responsible for killing or wounding several guerrillas on these occasions (1985:19–20). Some worried the killings were motivated by revenge.[21] Victoria's farmers quickly returned to a 'war footing', shouldering wartime rifles, resurrecting community patrols, radio alert systems, and re-instituting techniques and architecture of security around their homesteads,[22] as many would do again during the land invasions of the 2000s.

But these 'bizarre' (Clark 1985) murders did not really come out of the blue and if there was a period of unexpected calm around Mutirikwi immediately after the war, this had dissipated by early 1981. Sophia Muchini was already causing disconcertion at Great Zimbabwe. Farmers around the district faced problems with squatters, poachers and illegal grazing.[23] Armed robbery, housebreaking, stock theft and fence cutting too were continuing concerns.[24] In January two constables were convicted for theft and shoplifting, and a stolen car was found 'being stripped of parts to sell' near the Kyle dam.[25] That same month, Victoria residents received threatening 'anonymous phone calls, mainly by Africans to Europeans'.[26] Later the *Advertiser* worried about increasing cases of witchcraft.[27] There were also problems with banditry, 'dissidents' and desertions from the newly formed Zimbabwe National Army, and from ex-guerrillas refusing to enter assembly points across the country.[28] Much of the infrastructure of Rhodesian security forces was still in place and there were large amounts of unregistered firearms, ammunition and explosives across the district. Amid deepening political concerns about 'arms caches', police organised amnesties to collect (or re-register) such

---

[21] Particularly because two days before the killings Roux 'had mentioned...that the guerrilla he ... wounded during one of the war-time attacks ... was known to have returned to the area' (Clark 1985:27).

[22] The police also drew on Rhodesian security resources, receiving 'a great deal of assistance from 2 R.A.R. and ... helicopters from the airforce' ('Police news', *Fort Victoria Advertiser*, 27/03/81). Horse patrols were also re-established around Kyle and in Victoria East 'just like the old days' ('Police News', *Fort Victoria Advertiser*, 31/07/81, 14/08/81).

[23] 'Police news', Fort Victoria Advertiser, 06/02/81, 27/02/81, 27/03/81, 31/07/81, 14/08/81, 28/08/81, 04/09/81, 11/09/81,18/09/81,16/10/81, 27/11/81, 11/12/81, 29/12/81. Also 'Landless must register with councils', *Fort Victoria Advertiser*, 07/08/81; '12 squatters get maximum sentence', *Fort Victoria Advertiser*, 11/12/81; 'Squatters destroying the country', *Fort Victoria Advertiser*, 30/07/82; 'Police news', *Fort Victoria Advertiser*, 29/01/82.

[24] 'Police news' *Fort Victoria Advertiser*, 27/02/81, 14/08/81, 15/01/82, 29/01/82.

[25] 'Police news' *Fort Victoria Advertiser*, 16/01/81.

[26] 'Police news' *Fort Victoria Advertiser*, 05/03/81.

[27] 'Police news' *Fort Victoria Advertiser*, 18/03/82.

[28] These concerns later coalesced with anxieties about South African infiltrators ('Help beat bandits says governor', *Masvingo Advertiser*, 05/10/84; 'Governor urges self-improvement on Police', *Masvingo Advertiser*, 27/04/84).

weapons.[29] But they also continued to run regular shoots at the 'Combat Pistol' and 'Police Reserve Rifle' clubs.[30]

Simon Bright visited his family's former farm Le Rhone around this time, then still an army camp, and described the tensions between ex-Rhodesian soldiers and ex-guerrillas retraining for the national army.[31] This period also witnessed deepening tensions between former ZIPRA and ZANLA forces, sometimes resulting in open violence, as at Entumbane in Bulawayo. In 2006 a war veteran occupying Green Hills farm along Mutare road, recalled being moved from Foxtrot assembly point in Buhere (where many of Sophia's ex-guerrillas came from) to Entumbane, 'because … there was like a civil war between ZIPRA and ZANLA'.[32] Although Clark reported no ZIPRA/ZANLA violence in Victoria, he did describe increasing desertions by ex-ZIPRA soldiers at the 4th Brigade camp outside Fort Victoria, then commanded by Perence Shiri who was later deeply implicated in the *Gukurahundi* massacres in Matabeleland and the Midlands (1985:23, 35, 152–3). Elsewhere Edgar Tekere faced trial for shooting dead a white farmer near Harare (Tekere 2007: 126–30; Clark 1985:24).

Clark's account implies Ushewokunze, Shiri and others were behind the East Victoria murders, hidden by the 'smokescreen of witchcraft' (1985:153). Before Ushewokunze's visit on 21 February 1981, Sophia 'had confined her activities to cleansing and healing rituals'. Only 'after the minister's visit' had 'she ordered ex-guerrilla callers to arm themselves and to desert the national army'. Previously 'Mbuya Nehanda had never spoken of people in the new government as … "enemies of the people" … "bought by western money"' (1985:133). As with the diesel *n'anga*, it is hard to untangle who manipulated who. The same is true of the ex-fighters who committed the attacks. It is likely some were genuinely motivated 'in this last hour of retribution' by 'the voice of Nehanda' ordering 'the Great Zimbabwe area be cleared of foreign intruders' (Daneel 1995:12–13).[33] Daneel's account (1995) of Weeds Chakarakata's involvement suggests revenge too could have motivated the attacks, as many suspected.[34] Ushewokunze's involvement came to

[29] 'Police news', *Fort Victoria Advertiser*, 05/03/81, 31/07/81. By 04/09/81 'very little' had been handed in and 'there must be a mass of stuff still lying around or possibly at the bottom of Lake Kyle'. On 12/03/82 it warned about the illegal possession of weapons and ammunition 'collected during the "hostilities"', reminding readers that 'after all the scares we have had over arms caches, there are lots of eyes looking out for arms and ammunition'.

[30] 'Police news', *Fort Victoria Advertiser*, 27/02/81.

[31] Simon Bright 04/08/08.

[32] VaChuma 12/06/06.

[33] In Clark's account, one of the former guerrillas, Stephen Pfumo or Tenford Mafema, describes how they genuinely believed 'no harm could come to them' up until one of them was shot during the Great Zimbabwe raid when 'the realization began to dawn on him [Pfumo] that she did not, in fact, possess the great powers she claimed' (1985:118).

[34] Weeds is Cosmas Gonese, later an influential Masvingo war veteran, and Vice President of the National Liberation War Veterans Association. Daneel (1995) suggests he was involved in the Sophia Muchini affair, and imprisoned after

light during Sophia's trial, when witnesses reported his various visits to Sophia.[35] Her daughter told the court she overheard Ushewokunze saying 'he would arrange the killing of white farmers'.[36] Less clear is what his motivations were. Clark speculates he was attempting to challenge Prime Minister Mugabe's authority by undermining government policies of army integration and reconciliation. Before the trial was over he was sacked from his ministerial position, in part due to the publicity it caused. But Clark also points to duplicity in Mugabe's rhetoric of reconciliation, sensed by Victoria's white community at the time. Of particular significance was Mugabe's English/Shona speech in Kariba in February 1981, where the Shona version contradicted the reconciliatory tones of the English version. Both black detectives on Clark's team and Shona-speaking white farmers brought it to his attention, because 'the clear implication' was that 'the average African' would see it 'as a signal for the harassment of ... Europeans ... to make room for Blacks on the land' (1985:61, 137).

Mugabe's apparently contradictory speech reflected the political ambiguities of reconciliation in the wake of a war fought, in the aspirations of many, upon the promised return of land. Later Sophia put ZANU PF into another 'paradoxical position', when she 'declared ... independence was a mockery and ... Mugabe was a puppet of the whites' (Ranger 2010a:10). ZANU PF retorted 'that the party had made Nehanda rather than Nehanda the party and ... it was treason to dispute Mugabe's right to determine peace'. 'They thus found themselves in the paradoxical position of proclaiming that the First *Chimurenga* of 1896 had been led by a Nehanda medium who had heroically refused to surrender while at the same time denying that a living Nehanda could have any power over war and peace' (Ranger 2010a:10). The 'same paradox' re-appeared in the 2000s, when ZANU PF ideologues trumpeted Nehanda's legendary antics during the First and Second *Chimurenga* – and Masvingo war veterans told me Nehanda was inspiring them to 'liberate all the land ... given by our ancestors'[37] – while four different Nehanda mediums leading farm occupations in Mazoe were driven off their land, so it could be 'allocated to ZANU PF clients' (Ranger 2010a:10; Sadomba 2008, 2011).

(contd)   attempting to kill a Gutu farmer who had 'disfigured' his father. He was involved in Daneel's AZTREC (Association of Zimbabwean Traditional Ecologists) until he set up the splinter AZTREC Trust (Daneel 1998). He died in March 2011, and was buried in Masvingo's provincial heroes acre, upsetting war veterans who felt he should have been awarded national hero status ('Cde Cosmas Gonese dies', *ZBC News*, 24/03/11; 'Sibanda attacks politburo over Gonese', 13/04/11).

[35] Which are also apparent from NMMZ files (Fontein 2006a:157–60).

[36] *Bulawayo Chronicle*, 12/12/81.

[37] VaKanda, VaMuchina, MaDiri 16/03/01.

LAND THIRST AND SQUATTING IN THE EARLY 1980s

There was certainly 'land thirst' (Clark 1985:83) in Masvingo in 1980/81. Waves of squatting, illegal grazing, and fence cutting took place on white-owned and abandoned farms all around Mutirikwi, particularly Victoria East.[38] Expectations were high 'that tribespeople would be given white-owned farms if they supported the struggle for "liberation"'. 'This message was beamed constantly to the "masses" ... from Radio Maputo' (Clark 1985:83). But, after independence, government 'made it policy to state that land grazing and squatting by tribespeople was illegal' (Clark 1985:83). Shortly after the farm killings, Minister Hove went into the Mtilikwe and Chikwanda TTLs to dissuade people from squatting, grazing and cutting fences on neighbouring farms. Sometimes 'local people heard him sullenly' but other times 'the minister was shouted down' as 'tribesmen spoke out strongly against present government land policy' (Clark 1985:84). Sydney Sekeramayi, (Minister of Lands, Resettlement and Rural Development), Simon Muzenda (Deputy prime minister) and Eddison Zvobgo (Minister of Local Government and Housing), and numerous government technocrats, also tried to curb the 'squatter problem'.[39] Clearly, contradictions between reconciliation and nationalist promises of land were deeply implicated in Sophia Muchini's activities and the Victoria East killings. Whatever different motives were involved, desire for the return of land around Mutirikwi was the critical to these events. Shortly after the killings, 'tribesmen' were 'overheard praising a former ZANLA combatant ... for having killed white farmers in some other part of Zimbabwe, stating that this was the only way in which their own land objectives were likely to be achieved' (Clark 1985:84). East Victoria's farmers were aware of such sentiments, recognising that the 'friendly mood of co-existence' immediately after independence had 'soured' with the 'realisation that the White-owned farms promised to them ... during the "bush war" were not in fact forthcoming' (Clark 1985:27).

Squatting around Mutirikwi involved both 'land thirsty' people from crowded TTLs and farms elsewhere, and members of local clans making specific ancestral claims to soil, graves and ruins on the landscape. Demands for land redistribution and restitution became deeply entangled, as a complex local politics of belonging and exclusion played out, as would happen again in the 2000s. Clark discusses the 'purchase of a White-owned farm by a prominent Black businessman who ... re-erected broken-down fences at considerable cost' only to find them 'ripped down overnight by people from the adjoining Chikwanda tribal trust land' claiming 'the land belonged to the tribe and no one else, irrespective of who the intending

---

[38] 'Police news', *Fort Victoria Advertiser*, 06/02/81, 27/02/81, 27/03/81, 31/07/81, 14/08/81, 28/08/81, 04/09/81, 11/09/81, 18/09/81, 16/10/81, 27/11/81, 11/12/81, 29/12/81.
[39] 'Landless must register with councils', *Fort Victoria Advertiser*, 07/08/81; '12 squatters get maximum sentence', *Fort Victoria Advertiser*, 11/12/81; 'Squatters destroying the country', *Fort Victoria Advertiser*, 30/07/82.

purchaser might be Black or White'. 'The Chikwanda people named the Black businessman ... an "enemy of the people" and ... the purchase was never concluded'. In fact, Chikwanda people 'were laying claim to all commercial farmland east and north east of Lake Kyle' (Clark 1985:84). The local press covered the squatter problem in great detail. In September 1981, the *Advertiser* reported the continuing 'saga of the Victoria East farmers' as 'squatters' returned 'to the farms with their friends and relatives, disregarding our warnings, those of Government ministers, ZANU (PF) and the land owners themselves', arguing it was 'their ancestral land' and they had 'a right to settle there', even as 'over 100 tribesmen from Ndanga are going to court for their unlawful actions'.[40]

Although in some renderings Sophia Muchini's activities appear broadly motivated – calling for national cleansing ceremonies, the return of sacred objects and for 'the Great Zimbabwe area [to] be cleared of foreign intruders' (Daneel 1995:12–13) – closer examination indicates she engaged with very particular landscape claims. This is true both at Great Zimbabwe where she was linked to Mugabe efforts to reclaim custodianship of the site where their ancestors are buried,[41] and in relation to Chikwanda efforts to return to lands around Harawe east of Mutirikwi. Yet even in relation to these specific local demands, Sophia's interventions were controversial. When VaMakasva re-occupied Mzero shortly after the war, he was shot in the face by 'those people staying with that woman' because 'this Nehanda said I was living across the route of an *njuzu* ... that is why they beat me and everyone else living there. The same day that I was shot, they killed those white people'.[42] Clark recounts what Pfumo, one of the ex-combatants later convicted, told him about the specific instructions they received from Sophia Muchini. It presents a wonderful picture of how mediums could strengthen the resolve of freedom fighters. It also shows Sophia appealing to broad cultural nationalist concerns and engaging with very specific, sacred landscapes around Mutirikwi where squatting was taking place.

> Next day Pfumo and his comrades were again summoned to the medium's presence, and she led them to a stream nearby ... Each was given a leaf to eat, the medium informing them: 'This is the leaf of life'. Then she sipped water from the stream and placing her mouth over that of each comrade in turn she spat water into his mouth, saying: 'Be strong for Zimbabwe, son of the soil' ... She turned to each man ... asking: 'Will you be strong for Zimbabwe?' ... As each comrade ... declared himself strong ... the entire group felt an enormous surge of energy, so that they ran about in the bush and leapt on the rocks ... When they had all settled down ... the medium blessed each comrade's weapons and they were led away ... to an area of high ground. Here the medium pointed to the north-east and told them that was the direction of the mountains known ... as Nyoni. White people lived in that area now, she said, but the land belonged to the 'masses' and to their forefathers; all this land must be returned to the 'people' and ... the Whites ... living there had to be killed. 'Kill, kill! Kill them all, sons of Zimbabwe!' the medium intoned. 'No harm will come to you. Nothing will hurt you. Your fathers will protect you. Kill all!' Now the medium turned to the south-west, pointed at a large mountain ... and said: 'At this mountain, Nyanda, are more

[40] 'Police news', *Fort Victoria Advertiser*, 01/09/81.
[41] Cran Cooke 16/03/81 (NMMZ file C5, cited in Fontein 2006a:159).
[42] VaMakasva 14/01/06.

farms of the White people. All these people must die! ... Sleep one night in the mountain, and then you will know which farm to attack first' (Clark 1985:117).

The court heard a similar account of Sophia blessing the ex-guerrillas and their weapons, telling them 'to kill the whites in the vicinity of Nyoni and Nyanda ... to make the land available for the people of the Zana [Zano] area'.[43] One of the ex-guerrillas on trial, John Ruwizi (or Joseph Rwizi) told the court that if they 'had not transgressed taboos spelt out to them by Muchine [*sic*] ... "we would still be on the rampage, killing, killing, killing"'.[44]

The speed with which squatting took hold around Mutirikwi after the 1979 ceasefire, reflects not only people's intense desire to return to lost landscapes, but also their anticipation that a local politics of belonging and exclusion would soon be provoked. There was much expectation that nationalist promises would provoke intense competition over land once the war was over, both between disputing 'returnees', and with 'land thirsty' 'incoming' *vatorwa* from elsewhere. Furere Mashuro explained that even before the war was over squatting had begun in Victoria East, especially on abandoned farms.[45] South of the lake competition between Nemanwa and Mugabe people heated up in the early 1970s, as Morgenster Mission began negotiating to return land on Mzero and Morgenester farms to Victoria TTL. This anticipation of future land struggles was even encouraged by some white farmers and missionaries, who sensed which way the wind was blowing. As VaChirengarenga (of the Nemanwa clan) explained:

> We didn't like living there at Nemasuwa under Charumbira. We wanted to come back to our own land. During the war comrades were telling us that they had come to fight the war to take back the land. The *VaMuneri* [missionaries] were telling the people who had been moved from their land that they should go back to their original places, before that land got taken away after the war. After the war that is what we did. We came back here. Even those who had been moved to Chikarudzo were told the same thing, to go back before others came to take that land after the war.[46]

Haruzvivishe people (of the Mugabe clan) too wanted to return to Mzero, arguing it had been formally returned to them by the mission in 1969. But the comrades told them to wait as it lay within their field of operations and they feared people might get hurt.[47] A similar story recurs around Boroma, on The Retreat where Mudarikwa Murinye had grown up, once owned by 'Shumba' Wallace and then Mr Sawyer, under whom many Murinye people were evicted. After the war Mudarikwa and other Murinye people immediately returned, provoking contests with Mugabe land occupiers nearby, as well as with landless squatters from elsewhere,

[43] *Bulawayo Chronicle*, 13/10/81.
[44] *Bulawayo Chronicle*, 11/12/81.
[45] Furere Mashuro 12/04/06.
[46] 'Headman Nemanwa and VaChirengerenga 25/04/06.
[47] Jarios Haruzvivishe 27/12/05; also Fred Haruzvivishe 12/09/04; Samuel Haruzvivishe 21/07/04.

not to mention officials worried about soil erosion, siltation and Mutirik-wi's 'beautiful' landscapes. Before the end of the 1980s Mudarikwa and other Murinye returnees were evicted again and replaced with formal resettlement schemes. As VaChinengo explained:

> After the war we went back there. We went back to Sawyers farm [The Retreat] to cut our fields and build our houses. We used to go at night to plough our fields and build our homes and grow our crops. The next day, they would wake up to find the fields ploughed and houses built. We stayed there for almost three or four years until we were again chased away. Then they put all those other people there, and us the people who were born there were not given anything![48]

Nemanwa and Mugabe people returning to Mzero too became embroiled in struggles, not just with each other but with incoming *vatorwa* from elsewhere, as well as government officials from various departments. Charumbira people became involved in similar disputes on Longdale farm, once owned by 'Bani' Richards, where an irrigated resettlement scheme was later established. Similarly, in Victoria East squatting provoked tensions not only between white farmers and competing Makore and Chikwanda people from the TTLs to the north and east, but incoming *vatorwa* land seekers from elsewhere. Around Harawe and Zano tensions emerged between returning Chikwanda 'autochthons' and the people moved there when the dam was built, who had long been affiliated to Murinye. Indeed people at Zano were the only ones around Mutirikwi not to have squatted or reclaimed ancestral land immediately after the war. The dam and its waters meant that they could not go back.

Whatever similarities there were in the politics of autochthony, belonging and exclusion provoked by squatting around Mutirikwi after the war, and whatever resonances there would be with the localised politics thrown up by fast-track resettlement in the 2000s, the histories, aspirations and trajectories of land occupations in the early 1980s were not all the same. They derived from different historical grievances and met with different degrees of success. North and east of the lake, Chikwanda demands to return to ancestral lands around Harawe, Nyuni and elsewhere, were animated by grievances to do with the dispersion of Chikwanda people and the removal of their chieftaincy in 1947. After the war their chieftaincy was returned, but it took much longer for Chikwanda authority over ancestral territories to return. South of the lake, occupations around Mzero, Boroma and elsewhere turned more on inter- and intra-clan rivalries, boundary disputes, and tensions with land officials implementing technical resettlements and irrigation schemes. Here the aesthetics of Mutirikwi's 'beautiful landscapes' were important. Again many people lost out, particularly after evictions from Mzero and Boroma, but some later got access to *minda mirefu* (long fields) resettlements and irrigation schemes established at Oatlands, Longdale, Le Rhone and The Retreat. Yet wherever squatters were replaced by formal resettlements, those who remembered being evicted

---

[48] VaChinengo 26/05/06.

from those lands, those whose relatives and ancestors were buried in it, were often left most aggrieved. It was these claims that re-emerged again after 2000.

THE RETURN OF CHIEF CHIKWANDA

Of all of Mutirikwi's clans, Chikwanda had lost most during settler rule. They lost all of their lands and territory, their sacred *mapa* at Mafuse in Harawe, and in 1947 the chieftaincy was abolished. 'Chikwanda's lands were good and the whites wanted it, so they took it and the chief-domship was ended', Chief Kandiwa Chikwanda explained in 2005.[49] His account closely matches Mtetwa's detailed discussion of how 'the Chikwanda chiefdom ceased to exist as a result of European alienation of land' (1976:314). Most of this was already done by 1914, due to relentless pegging by European settlers across Eastern Victoria and up into Gutu district, during the Jameson period (1890–96) and after the original Chik-wanda reserve was marked out by Native Commissioners (NCs). Like all the Duma reserves it was 'inadequate for agricultural development' – too small and very poor quality. But it had also been marked out across existing 'unsurveyed farms' briefly occupied 'a good many years ear-lier' (Mtetwa 1976:296,299). 'Land in Chikwanda country' was in great demand from cantankerous white settlers like the Rademeyer brothers and Vermaak, who pegged without authority wherever they chose. The Chikwanda reserve was split, moved and shrunk repeatedly until in 1913 Gutu's NC acknowledged it was 'a misnomer since the people of Chief Chikwanda were outside the reserve' (Mtetwa 1976:313).

After eviction from European farms in 1936, Chief Mutubuki Chikwanda lived under Murinye around Chiredza hill, but that only accommodated a few of his people. When his brother Mapaika became chief in 1946 he returned from Ndanga to Harawe hill, already long a European farm, but 'was ordered to leave immediately'. Chief Ndanga would not accommodate him, so 'government took the chief's medal from him' saying it 'would be returned when he had found a suitable area in a reserve to live with his people' (Mtetwa 1976:314). With all their land gone 'Chikwanda people scattered in many places; some went to Zaka, some Bikita, others to live under Chief Shumba, or in Zimuto. Some went as far as Gokwe and Chiredzi'.[50]

The current chief, Kandiwa, was born in 1932 near Harawe, on a farm then known as Arawe, owned by Morgenster. It later became Mkwari ranch where 'Chimuka' Roux and his wife were killed in 1981. That is also where Chikwanda's *mapa*, Mafuse, is located, 'where all the chiefs are buried'. His parents were workers 'for a white man who owned a farm here, known as Madomare. His real name was S.P. Burger. He came here after the war in 1920 or 1930'. During that time 'some Chikwanda people stayed here to work', Kandiwa explained, 'but many others were

[49] Chief Chikwanda 22/12/05.
[50] Ibid.

moved away'; first 'when the farm was taken around the 1920s' when 'only workers remained', then 'again in the late 1940s'. 1953 was 'when the last of the Chikwanda people were removed from here'.[51] Some Chikwanda people moved to reserves in the north under Chief Gutu, 'with the *sadunhu* [headmen] of Chikwanda who remained … Mawere, Rupiri, Mutema, Kufonya, Hunduza and Gurujena'. Others lived under Makore who, long ago, had himself been one of Chikwanda's headmen. Kandiwa Chikwanda explained: 'In 1953, when Elizabeth became Queen, Makore was installed as a chief because the Gumbo people felt that they could not stand for the Chikwanda or Duma people who were there. That is why chief Makore was installed in Gutu, and he still attends the Gutu district offices.[52] Kandiwa himself went to live at Muchakata under Shumba in 1953. Later, when government bought Marthadale and Kelvingrove farms to resettle people moved from the dam, 'some Chikwanda families moved onto that land where they lived under Murinye … 13 *sabhuku* [village heads] of Chikwanda were living there'.[53]

In 1980, as Chikwanda people returned to 'squat' all over Victoria East, their chieftaincy was restored to the current chief's older brother Madzitire. From documents and maps Kandiwa showed me, it is clear Madzitire and his younger brother had been lobbying for the return of the chieftaincy for almost thirty years. Mtetwa described 'a group of Chikwanda descendents seeking the resuscitation of the Chikwanda chieftaincy' in the 1970s (Mtetwa 1976:314). Madzitire died in 1999, and Kandiwa took over as acting chief until formally installed in 2005, much to the chagrin of rival claimants, as well as VaZarira and Chief Makore, with whom he had deep disputes in 2005/06.

Many of the Chikwanda squatters of the 1980s were evicted, some were prosecuted, and many returned several times. Some later received land on resettlements south of the lake, causing problems with Charumbira land claimants there.[54] Some of the very persistent eventually stayed on abandoned farms around Harawe, despite repeat evictions and prosecutions.[55] Given the huge land pressures, local government and party officials were sometimes more restrained about evictions and prosecutions than official policies and rhetoric suggested. Some white farmers also made concessions.[56] Chief Chikwanda explained how the white farmer on Cheveden farm 'divided his land and let us live on one

---

[51] Ibid.

[52] Ibid. This reflects Chikwanda's ongoing struggles with Makore in the 2000s (see Mtetwa 1976:295–350).

[53] Chief Chikwanda 22/12/05.

[54] Simon Charumbira and Adamson Zvitambo 27/05/06.

[55] 'Police News', *Fort Victoria Advertiser*, 11/09/81, 18/09/81, 27/11/81, 11/12/81, '12 Squatters get Maximum sentence', *Fort Victoria Advertiser*, 11/12/81.

[56] Some white farmers tried to accommodate 'land hungry' farmers in TTLs, to counter recurring problems with poaching, fence cutting and illegal grazing. In June 1982, commercial farmers in Central Victoria were offering 'free grazing' for nearby communal farmers suffering shortages due to drought ('Commercial/ communal farmers find common ground' *Fort Victoria Advertiser*, 04/06/82).

side of the farm while he continued to live on the other side'. 'As time went on he left the farm completely and people settled everywhere'.[57] The government also quickly implemented resettlements in the area, acquiring Twee Fontein, Kopje Fontein, Sundown extension, Inyoni and Mudspruit, and 'on all of these farms they put *minda mirefu*'.[58] Officially it became known as the Kyle East Resettlement. Apart from being insufficient to accommodate the numbers of people seeking land, the problem was 'the *minda mirefu* were given to anyone looking for lands', echoing complaints south of the lake. 'Although these people were on Chikwanda land, for a long time they did not know that; they thought they were living on government property'.[59] Resettlement schemes in the 1980s were not administered under chiefs, but fell under the new system of VIDCOs, WADCOs, Rural District Councils, and District Administrators. District Council Conservation Committees were responsible for ensuring adherence to soil conservation measures. This was considered particularly urgent given that across the country 'mechanical conservation measures were abandoned during the war and ... soil conservation ... left unchecked'. With '1000 squatters' on farms intended 'for resettling only 118 people', much of 'the land bordering Kyle is now extremely vulnerable to soil erosion', the Regional Land Inspector reported.[60]

So although their chieftaincy was re-instated, and some did return to Harawe and Zano, many other Chikwanda people were left landless while people from elsewhere were formally resettled on Chikwanda lands. Chief Chikwanda still had little territory and few people to administer, even around Zano. Eventually Chief Murinye returned Zano to Chief Chikwanda. 'Those people who had remained there lived under Murinye' Kandiwa explained, 'but Murinye knew that land belonged to Chikwanda. He said we should take our land back. We had a meeting and decided on the boundaries'.[61] Through the 1990s, as chiefs' powers were revived, their influence in local government and over resettlement areas did increase. So when *vatorwa* on *minda mirefu* were 'told that they were living under Chikwanda ... they understood that'.[62] But there were still many landless Chikwanda aspiring to return to ancestral lands they had lost under settler rule. Much of Chikwanda's claimed territory north of Mutirikwi, from Harawe to Beza, remained commercial farms.

That was until the *jambanja* of the early 2000s, when nearly all those farms were occupied by war veterans, new and 'new but autochthonous' farmers, and sometimes farm workers claiming Chikwanda descent.[63]

---

[57] Chief Chikwanda 22/12/05.

[58] Ibid.

[59] Ibid.

[60] 'Squatters destroying the country', *Fort Victoria Advertiser*, 30/07/82.

[61] 'Before ... that whole area was under Murinye, but then the wards were sorted out in 1982–3, and now it is under Chikwanda' (Chief Chikwanda 22/12/05; also Chief Murinye 13/06/06).

[62] Chief Chikwanda 22/12/05.

[63] VaKurasva explained (16/04/06) that when they occupied Desmondale farm, they offered land to farm workers but not many stayed, with the exception of some claiming Chikwanda descent.

As around Boroma, the grazing areas of *minda mirefu* east of Mutirikwi too saw new squatting by returning Chikwanda people. As ancestral territories were re-asserted across resettled farms everywhere in the 2000s, Chief Chikwanda claimed the largest area of all Mutirikwi's chiefs, just as the Chikwanda clan had lost most during settler rule. This provoked the many overlapping boundary disputes he became involved in, particularly with Makore to the north, but also Charumbira, Murinye and others further west, as well as deep internal rivalries and problems with VaZarira. Complications also arose on Mkwari, where Kandiwa Chikwanda had been born, where the Mafuse *mapa* is located, and where 'Chimuka' and his wife were killed in 1981. Masvingo's former Governor, Willard Chiwewe, grabbed it for himself in 2005, following the death of its black owner Mr Ganyani, a well-known local bus opera- tor. Chief Chikwanda explained how after Chimuka was killed in 1981, the farm went 'to the government' and became 'Mkwari estates'. 'That was when Joshua Nkomo gave it to Ganyani, one of his close advisors'. 'After Ganyani died the farm went to the Governor' he continued, 'but before he died he gave 400 hectares for Chikwanda people to settle, in 2002 or so. Recently when the farm was taken I explained to the district land committee that that land had been given for Chikwanda people, so they were allowed to stay. And the Governor [Chiwewe] is on the remaining areas.'[64]

Later reports suggest that problems between Chiwewe, the Ganyani family and Titus Maluleke, Masvingo's next governor, over Mkwari continued well into 2012.[65] It was finally settled by President Mugabe, who 'ordered Chiwewe out of the farm arguing it was against govern- ment policy to take over a black-owned farm'.[66] It seems likely these events were entangled with Masvingo's complex factionalism.[67] In this context Chief Chikwanda's hope in late 2005, to build a house on Mkwari below the Mafuse *mapa* seems optimistic. He did not mention it again when I visited him in June 2006, when he was still looking for a location to build a new home and establish his own *zunde ramambo*. It remains to be seen if Chikwanda's ongoing disputes with Makore and others have been resolved; and if Chikwanda 'land thirst' and aspira- tions to return to ancestral lands have been adequately quenched by fast-track land reform.

---

[64] Chief Chikwanda 23/06/06.
[65] 'Former Governor evicted from seized farm', *Zimbabwe Times*, 03/08/09; 'Court orders former governor to co-exist with Ganyani family', *Newsday*, 21/07/10; 'Police thump war veterans in Masvingo', *Radio VOP*, 13/02/12.
[66] 'Former Masvingo Governor booted out of farm', *Newsday*, 04/06/12.
[67] 'Minister, war vets' fight for farm', *Zimbabwean*, 23/01/13; 'Police thump war veterans in Masvingo', *Radio VOP*, 13/02/12.

OCCUPATION, DESTRUCTION AND EVICTION SOUTH OF LAKE MUTIRIKWI

Although driven by similar combinations of general 'land thirst' and particular aspirations to return to ancestral lands, events on Mutirikwi's southern shores in the early 1980s took a different trajectory to Victoria East. This was partly due to its different pre-colonial and colonial pasts, but also because the legacies of the dam were different. Here the aesthetic concerns about the destruction of Mutirikwi's 'beautiful landscapes' played a bigger role in official responses to squatters. In September 1981, the police 'were very very concerned ... at the squatting and destruction of vegetation ... south of Lake Kyle'.[68] In December they worried they would be blamed for the 'dreadful destruction of once beautiful land', describing the 'Lake Kyle debacle' as a 'hot potato being dealt with at the very top by the various ministries concerned'.[69] Such aesthetic unease was closely intertwined with technocratic concerns about soil erosion. The 'problem' was not solved quickly. In July the following year the local paper reported that 'squatters have ... been left undisciplined to destroy forest areas and this has not only brought the threat of soil erosion to their affected areas but also affected the natural beauty of one of Zimbabwe's tourist attractions – Lake Kyle'. Mr Matthews, the Land Inspector, claimed that 'although the Kyle Dam will not silt easily, part of the natural scenery around the dam is already dead' and would become 'a scarecrow to tourists visiting the area'.[70]

It wasn't until the second half of the 1980s that squatters on Mutirikwi's southern shores were evicted, as plans from the 1970s, for the recreational park, and to protect 'the aesthetic conscience of the nation', were re-activated.[71] As in preceding decades, the local paper celebrated the re-development of tourism and recreational facilities.[72] It also carried numerous articles expounding the importance of technocratic land planning and soil conservation, particularly for development and resettlements.[73] At Boroma, Mudarikwa, VaChinengo and other

---

[68] 'Police news', *Fort Victoria Advertiser*, 18/09/81.

[69] 'Police news', *Fort Victoria Advertiser*, 11/12/81.

[70] 'Squatters destroying the country', *Fort Victoria Advertiser*, 30/07/82.

[71] 'Kyle Recreational Park: a point of view', Saunders 02/03/76 (Kyle Recreational Park, file three).

[72] 'Ruins had 40,000 visitors', 16/01/81; 'Victoria Hotels slammed at Salisbury Tourist Indaba', 20/02/81; 'Re-planning of site museum at Zimbabwe', 13/03/81; 'President opens new museum', 04/09/81; 'New-look site museum at Zimbabwe', 25/09/81; 'Ray of hope for new road to Zimbabwe', 15/01/82; 'Tourism launches for Kyle', 19/02/82; 'Tourism goes waterborne at Kyle', 24/09/82; 'Mrs Chitepo optimistic on tourist potential', 05/02/82; 'All you need to know about Kyle fishing', date unclear; all from *Fort Victoria Advertiser*. From 1983 it became the *Masvingo Advertiser*: 'Kyle gets lions share of boat racing', 23/09/83; 'Governor speaks on World Tourism day', 05/10/84; 'Tour operators concentrate on Runs/Kyle area', 24/6/83.

[73] 'Mugabe's idea bear fruit', *Fort Victoria Advertiser*, 01/05/81; 'Chilimanzi farmers told old methods must go', *Fort Victoria Advertiser*, 14/08/81; 'Agritex

Murinye occupiers reclaiming landscapes of their birth, and the *mapa* of their ancestors, were evicted for a second time, mainly due to concerns about soil erosion and the protection of the dam. Sandwiched between Great Zimbabwe and the lakeshore, parts of Mzero farm north of the road to Masvingo town occupied by Haruzvivishe people also became subject to such technocratic concerns. In this particular area, however, the revived aesthetic imperatives of the Recreational Park and the Van Reit plan (Fontein 2006a:168–9) were particularly significant. Events on Mzero were further complicated by Morgenster's older efforts to return mission lands during the 1970s, which re-ignited long standing disputes between Nemanwa and Mugabe.

MZERO FARM

Morgenster mission had long been embroiled in the disputes between Nemanwa and Mugabe over Great Zimbabwe and land around it (cf. Fontein 2006a). Between the 1940s and early 1960s the mission was involved in unpopular evictions from its Mzero and Morgenster farms.[74] Both Nemanwa and Mugabe people remember it well.[75] They were told the mission needed the land for grazing.[76] It is likely technocratic concerns about soil erosion adjacent to the new dam were also a factor. For those remaining on Mzero and Morgenster farms, usually under labour contracts (or 'as slaves' as some remember it), the mission imposed difficult, deeply resented rules.[77] As VaChirengarenga and Headman Nemanwa recalled:

> VaChirengarenga – When we went into *maline* at Nemasuwa [in Victoria TTL, under Charumbira] the *vamuneri*, [missionaries] said to us they did not want anyone living in their area who drank beer or had more than one wife. And as it

(contd)   Provincial reorganization', *Fort Victoria Advertiser*, 16/04/82; '"Act now on erosion" councils told', *Masvingo Advertiser*, 25/02/83; 'Resettlement areas must conserve', *Masvingo Advertiser*, 21/10/83; 'Mass conservation campaign led up to tree planting', *Masvingo Advertiser*, `09/12/83; 'Conservation awareness at Nyahombe', *Masvingo Advertiser*, 16/12/83; 'Land use enhanced by availability of irrigation'', *Masvingo Advertiser*, 30/01/87.

[74] The delineation reports described how 'pressure on the land' was a particular concern for Mugabe people in 1965, caused by 'Morgenster Mission enforcing eviction of persons resident on the farm'. At the time Mugabe people were also deeply concerned that their chieftaincy be restored, as they had been temporarily reduced to a Headmanship under Chief Shumba. This was restored soon afterwards. The 'great need' of 'detribalised' Nemanwa was to acquire territory of their own, rather than continue occupying 'Chief Charumbira's country'. Many also lived 'outside tribal trust land'; some on Morgenster farm. The delineating officer felt 'the tribe must inevitably sink more and more into insignificance' (Delineation reports, Victoria, 1965:66,102, NAZ 2929/8/5).

[75] Jarios Haruzvivishe 27/22/05; Radison Haruzvivishe Mugabe 26/11/05; Mai Makasva 26/11/05; Sabhuku Chikutuva 28/11/05; 'Headman Nemanwa & VaChirengarenga 25/04/06.

[76] 'Mai Makasva 26/11/05.

[77] Sabhuku Chikutuva 28/11/05.

was their farm, there was nothing that we could do about it. The only people who could stay were those prepared to stop doing their *chikaranga* ['traditional' practices/'culture'] and those who didn't have more than one wife. Many us said no we don't want to throw away our *chikaranga,* and we can't just divorce our wives, so we moved to Nemasuwa.

Headman Nemanwa – What the *vamuneri* did was not good, it was by force. They forced us to move because they wanted grazing for their cattle. But for those of us who were tough enough to stick to the rules of the mission they stayed but the mission knew that many people would leave and that would give them more land for grazing their cattle, which was what they wanted.[78]

By the late 1960s and early 1970s priorities had changed, as the Dutch Reformed Church (DRC) prepared to hand over its missions to the African Reformed Church of Rhodesia (ARC). Morgenster began negotiations for returning parts of both farms to the neighbouring Victoria TTL. It was anxious that Mugabe and Nemanwa people be given preferential access to land. Chief Mugabe and some of his people were invited to live at Chikarudzo on Morgenster farm, adjacent to his area in the Victoria TTLs, in the late 1960s.[79] This was partly because when the mission's founder A.A. Louw first arrived in the area in 1890, it was Mugabe who granted lands for the mission to occupy. Yet in recognition that this relationship with Mugabe had led to Nemanwa's marginalisation, the mission also granted land for Nemanwa people below Bingura hill on Mzero farm.[80]

As the ARC negotiations proceeded in the mid-1970s, Morgenster became increasingly concerned to ensure their Mugabe tenants at Chikarudzo would be secure. Discussions began with Rhodesian officials to turn over the southern eastern section of Morgenster farm to 'Mugabe's section of Victoria Tribal Trust Land', even though 'the mission have virtually handed this ... over already, bar the legal formalities'.[81] Although keen to secure Mugabe's tenure, Rev. Murray was equally 'anxious that some provision ... be made whereby only those persons living on this land would be allowed to live there in the future'. He did 'not wish Chief Mugabe to flood the area with his friends from elsewhere'. This echoed Internal Affairs' concerns about 'over-stocking' and 'over-cultivation'.[82] Topographical maps were carefully prepared. Concerns about soil suitability and water availability meant officials wanted the mission to make more land available than had been offered, to ensure it was suitable for TTL farming. The mission was reticent because this risked 'a considerable reduction of the beef production on the farm'.[83]

Before the issue was resolved they were compounded by Chief Charumbira's request for land on Mzero farm to be transferred to his area of Victoria TTL, for occupation by Headman Nemanwa and his people. This had arisen because a Growth Point was to be built exactly where

[78] Headman Nemanwa & VaChirengarenga 25/04/06.

[79] Jairos Haruzvivishe 27/11/05.

[80] Rev. G.M. Murray to DC Victoria, 25/05/76 (NAZ S3700/106/6/2).

[81] DC W.E.J. Henson to Secretary, Internal Affairs, 30/06/77 (NAZ S3700/106/6/2).

[82] DC W.E.J. Henson to PC Victoria, 30/05/73 (NAZ S3700/106/6/2).

[83] M.M. Pratt, Internal Affairs, to Secretary, Lands and Natural resources, 07/05/75 (NAZ S3700/106/6/2).

the mission had given Nemanwa land to occupy below Bingura. At 'approximately 500 acres' this would 'deprive ... the present residents of their stands and fields'.[84] By now the ARC negotiations had raised other problems for Internal Affairs, worried about an African church owning, but not legally able to occupy, mission farms in European areas.[85] Furthermore, they had received 'extremely adverse reactions from farmers' on Longdale and Sikato (neighbouring Mzero), who had 'heard rumours of the impending change'. The acting DC sympathised with 'these farmers, knowing how difficult it is to face the fencing, grazing and wood cutting problems caused by a T.T.L. boundary'.[86] He denied the 'extra land will solve T.T.L. problems', warning that 'continued nibbling at the edges is a grave danger to our future economy as a country'. The PC agreed, particularly 'in view of its proximity to [Great] Zimbabwe', and recommended limiting the Growth Point's development instead.[87] DC Henson had a different view and with Rev. Murray 'being pestered by Chief Charumbira and his headman Nemanwa for this land', recommended that Mzero farm north of the road [to Great Zimbabwe] be reserved for 'the re-location of the Zimbabwe Ruins tourist amenities', and 'the portion lying to the south west ... be added to Chief Charumbira's area'.[88] As arguments within Internal Affairs continued, some suggested mission ownership of Mzero be continued and Nemanwa given permits to live there, and others emphasised the need for a 'buffer zone' of state land around Zimbabwe and along the main road, as the Van Reit plan and National Parks had recommended. Everyone was very conscious that pressure from 'local tribesmen' would not be easily resolved.[89]

Eventually they agreed 'the south eastern part of Morgenster farm' would go to 'the Mugabe people ... already residing on the farm' and 'the western area of Mzero farm' to 'Nemanwa people ... due to lose land by the establishment of Nemanwa township'.[90] But the war heated up and nothing was done. After the war events took a different turn, as 'tribesmen became impatient' and squatting rippled across the district.[91] Chief Mugabe and 'his followers' moved onto land all over Morgenster farm, and although 'premature ... nobody objected strongly' the DC reported. Much more problematic were Haruzvivishe occupations of eastern Mzero, bordering the lake and Great Zimbabwe, which had never been earmarked for resettlement. The old disputes and rivalries between Mugabe and Nemanwa resurfaced with renewed fury.

[84] Rev. G.M. Murray to DC Victoria, 25/05/76 (NAZ S3700/106/6/2).
[85] This also involved Zimuto (Copate) farm, north of Fort Victoria, which too had squatters, and was proposed to 'revert' to TTLs (Acting DC J.M. Baker to PC Victoria, 08/06/76, NAZ S3700/106/6/2).
[86] Ibid.
[87] PC R.L. Westcott to Secretary, Internal Affairs, 23/06/76 (NAZ S3700/106/6/2).
[88] DC W.E. Henson to PC Victoria, 29/07/76 (NAZ S3700/106/6/2).
[89] C.J. Herd, Internal Affairs, to Morgenster Mission, 17/08/75 (NAZ S3700/106/6/2).
[90] DC M.M.F. Fox to PC Victoria, 06/04/81 (NAZ 968:91).
[91] Ibid.

Amid adverse publicity about destruction caused by squatting around Mutirikwi, the PC asked the new DC, M.M.F. Fox, to compile a full report on the history of the dispute.[92] Fox drew on the Delineation Reports (1965), scholars like Aquina (1965), Mtetwa (1976) and Garlake (1973), as well as early explorers like Mauch (Burke 1969), Bent (1893) and Hall (1905). He also held meetings with both parties, who appealed to the same, contested genealogical geographies long animating Nemanwa/Mugabe disputes over Great Zimbabwe (Fontein 2006a:19–45). Chief Charumbira was present at the DC's meeting with Nemanwa on 12 January 1981, and submitted his own written statement in support. Nemanwa people had not yet occupied their allotted areas on Mzero, and contested Haruzvivishe occupations of what was 'traditionally and historically a Nemanwa area'. Deeply concerned that 'Chief Mugabe is trying to take over their area', they 'wanted the old boundaries restored to them as they were in 1890'. Furthermore, they had been 'restrained' and 'not illegally settled on this farm', so 'why should they lose out by having been law abiding', while 'Mugabe's people ... illegally settled part of Mzero and ... so far got away with it'.[93]

Chief Mugabe brought a delegation of twenty-one people to his meeting with the DC two days later, including Chief Masungunye from Bikita (the most senior Duma chief) and Chief Mudarikwa Murinye, himself 'squatting' on The Retreat near Boroma. They contested Nemanwa's version and deployed their own genealogical geographies to assert Mugabe's pre-1890 boundaries. Chief Mugabe told the DC 'that old men among [his] followers were born on Mzero farm', as indeed many of the Haruzvivishe people re-occupying the same land again in the 2000s told me. For them 'the books of the *sabhuku* were always there' and the area was full of the graves of their relatives and ancestors.[94] When the DC asked 'why Mugabe's people had settled on land which the Mission had not wanted to part with', he was told 'this land was originally theirs before the missionaries came and [in 1978] the mission agreed to give Mugabe the grazing on Mzero farm'. Later 'the mission removed the wire fences so naturally "our people moved in"'.[95]

Fox concluded 'both sides are trying to justify their claim to Mzero farm by reference to traditional ownership', and that 'in a nutshell ... Nemanwa's people were in the area long before Mugabe's people' but 'during the last century Mugabe's people have become more dominant and asserted themselves whereas Nemanwa's people have declined in influence'.[96] But as formal land resettlement schemes got under way in the 1980s, claims to traditional ownership did not hold much sway

[92] Ibid.
[93] Ibid.
[94] Jairos Haruzvivishe 27/22/05; Radison Haruzvivishe 26/11/05; Mai Makasva 26/11/05; Sabhuku Chikutuva 28/11/05.
[95] DC M.M.F. Fox, to PC Victoria, 06/04/81 (NAZ 968:91). I heard similar accounts from Haruzvivishe 'returnees' re-occupying Mzero farm in 2005/06 (Jairos Haruzvivishe 27/22/05).
[96] DC M.M.F. Fox to PC Victoria, 06/04/81 (NAZ 968:91).

anywhere, least of all in areas as sensitive as Mutirikwi's 'beautiful landscapes'. All Haruzvivishe and Mugabe squatters were removed from the eastern stretches of Mzero in 1987, but the land did not return to Nemanwa, or to Morgenster. Neither did it 'revert' to communal land, nor become a formal resettlement scheme. Rather, aesthetic concerns about Mutirikwi's 'beautiful landscapes' fed into official plans for the Recreational Park, and it became state land, a buffer zone for the lake and officially a game park, although no wildlife was ever put there. The game park, as it became locally known, continued to be used for grazing and firewood by people in communal lands now just across the road, with the tacit approval of council officials. No one was allowed to settle there; only NMMZ's new conservation centre, a new primary school, National Park's tourist lodges and a water pumping station were established there in the following years.

The Growth Point was built and named Nemanwa. A new secondary school was named Chirichoga, after Nemanwa's most senior ancestor, and 'Nemanwa Primary School' replaced 'Manunure school' (named after a Mugabe ancestor). Nemanwa people removed from the Growth Point occupied the western areas of Mzero farm allocated in the late 1970s, which 'reverted' to communal area under Headman Nemanwa. They got back their sacred spring and the remains of a *murambatemwa* (sacred forest).[97] In line with technocratic re-assertions everywhere, land planners pegged contour ridges and boreholes were sunk.[98] Some Nemanwa people also later found land on the irrigation scheme developed at Longdale, much to chagrin of rival Charumbira claimants.

Some of Nemanwa's 'ancestral territory' was therefore returned and their historic presence in the landscape around Great Zimbabwe, however small geographically, was restored. They continued to resist attempts by Haruzvivishe people to resettle in the area, some of whom were later granted plots next the new growth point in an attempt to appease their demands.[99] Nemanwa also struggled fiercely against other *vatorwa* incomers looking for land in the area,[100] and their disputes with the Mugabe over Great Zimbabwe have continued. They also continued to reclaim a chieftainship of their own, rather than remain as Headman under Charumbira, a particularly sore point for them (Fontein 2006a:26). In contrast Chief Mugabe, and particularly the Haruzvivishe family, did not achieve the returns they aspired to. Mugabe's territory on the former Morgenster farm around Chikarudzo and Barahanga did increase

[97] Headman Nemanwa & VaChirengarenga 25/04/06.

[98] Mai Rukwasha, whose family have hosted me since the mid-1990s, came to Nemanwa with her husband from Gutu after the war, managing, against the odds, to acquire land on the section of Mzero that returned to Nemanwa. She explained how she had been required to dig a contour ridge across her field in the 1980s. It has long since been ploughed over numerous times.

[99] Radison Haruzvivishe 26/11/05.

[100] Mai Rukasha described the problems they had as *vatorwa* when they first settled on Mzero farm under Nemanwa. These circulated around the burial of their dead, and continued on occasion into the 2000s, when so many of their extended family died.

when this land also 'reverted' to communal land. But even here Mugabe 'squatters' were removed, particularly from the slopes of Mount Mugabe (where the mission is located) and on Chivange, Muromo Wehoto and other smaller hills adjoining Great Zimbabwe's southern boundaries.[101] In all these areas, concerns about soil erosion intertwined with aesthetic concerns about protecting beautiful landscapes.

After 2000 all these areas were re-occupied again, often by the same people evicted from them in the 1980s. Given how concerns about the destruction caused by squatters had animated events in the 1980s, it is not surprising that when they returned to Mzero, many placed their homesteads topographically, to avoid the criticisms of officials worried about siltation; as indeed Matopos Murinye did at Boroma. In 2000 Radison Haruzvivishe told me the 'land is coming back to Mugabe, but not as communal land, rather as plots, to prevent soil erosion and the siltation of the lake'.[102] Many of these returnees deployed languages and techniques of land planning and soil conservation to legitimise their re-occupations, just as war veterans on resettled farms were pegging plots, fields and digging contour ridges, as planning replaced *jambanja* (Chaumba et al. 2003a) in the transition from land invasions to fast-track land reform after 2000. Yet throughout the 2000s, Haruzvivishe occupations on Mzero hardly looked more secure than in the 1980s, particularly after the area was earmarked for the new Great Zimbabwe University. In September 2001 the PA stressed that this was state land, a designated 'game reserve' and 'because national concerns must always override the claims of individual clans' it was 'inevitable' the 'illegal' settlers would be evicted.[103] Twelve years later, however, they were still there, and the Great Zimbabwe University was not yet built.

'PEOPLE WHO DON'T KNOW THE LAND CAN'T LOOK AFTER IT'

Unlike Mzero, other farms south of the lake did become formal resettlement schemes once squatters had been evicted. Around Boroma, The Retreat, Clifton and Le Rhone became *minda mirefu* in the 1980s and early 1990s. Nestled between them, Oatlands became an irrigation scheme. Further west another irrigation scheme was established on Longdale farm, and later irrigated plots were sold on the ARDA farm at Sikato too (FAO 2000). All these resettlements were formally part of the 'Mushandike resettlement area'. As happened on *minda mirefu* around Harawe, land on these resettlements was predominantly given to landless people on the land register, rather than members of local clans claiming it as their own. Formal technocratic imperatives outweighed so-called traditional claims, and resettlement schemes did not 'return' to chiefs in the way communal lands did. They were firmly under Rural District Council authority to whom they paid rent, with their own resettlement officers

---

[101] VaMadungwe 12/03/06; Fieldnotes 18/12/05.
[102] Fieldnotes 29/10/00.
[103] Alphonse Chikurira PA 10/09/01.

and committee structures. Oatland's chairman, VaMadungwe, stated: 'It was properly done, not like the *jambanja* of recently, this farm was bought by government, and they put a proper resettlement scheme here for landless people to be given land'. Echoing how notions of 'beneficial occupation' animated land allocations throughout the 20th century, 'people were chosen on their experience of farming and their ability to farm'. While it was 'the chiefs who nominated people', they were ... 'mainly young people who were going to actually farm the land, not old people just wanting a place to live, who might sleep on the land, or make a grave yard'.[104] Chiefs had some influence in choosing who was selected for resettlement, but only later was their role in local government strengthened, and only in the 2000s were resettlement areas formally returned to chiefs. By then the grazing areas of many 'old resettlements' were 'invaded' by squatters who again included both *vatorwa* from elsewhere and those returning (for a second time) to reclaim ancestral graves and the landscapes of their childhood, like Mudarikwa and Matopos Murinye at Boroma. This time they had the existing occupiers of the old resettlements as well as government technocrats, bureaucrats and rival chiefs to contend with.

Yet concessions were sometimes made to local demands, and some claiming autochthony or appealing to legacies of colonial-era eviction, did acquire land in the 1980s resettlements. At Longdale, Charumbira as well as Nemanwa people got some land. At Boroma, VaBhodo acquired *minda mirefu* on The Retreat, as did Simon Bright's childhood friend Thomas Mapanda.[105] Vincent Matende's family received an irrigated plot at Oatlands. VaBhodo and Matende are both affinal relations of Murinye. The chairman at Oatlands, VaMadungwe, is a member of the Haruzvivishe family who squatted on Chivange hill (where his parents once lived, just above Nemanwa Growth Point) soon after the war. He is a local ZANU PF political commissar and prominent wartime *mujiba* (male youth who assisted guerrillas), illustrating how political allegiances and war legacies were already carried sway in the early 1980s. Official attempts were made at both Oatlands and Longdale to draw people from nearby communal areas, as well as landless from elsewhere. Yet both schemes endured problems of project ownership and security of tenure,[106] and both were subjected to repeated claims by local clans. VaMadungwe described how Oatlands' twelve irrigated plots were allocated to people 'from the surrounding chiefs: Charumbira, Mugabe, Mapanzure, Murinye and Chikwanda', indicating why these schemes became so entangled in boundary disputes after 2000. 'Each chief was given a number of people' to be 'settled on the scheme'. But 'the number for each chief differed and some chiefs were given less people to resettle ... that is why Charumbira had only one person settled here, but of the

---

[104] VaMadungwe 12/03/06.
[105] Simon Bright 04/08/08.
[106] See FAO (2000) for a close analysis and comparison of these and other smallholder irrigation schemes.

twelve, four are of Mugabe.'[107] In the 2000s Mugabe/Murinye disputes over Boroma would become deeply entangled with the distribution of food aid and re-structuring of ward boundaries,[108] as well as the distribution of irrigated plots at nearby Oatlands.

Given the extent of squatting in the early 1980s, the enormity of 'land thirst' and congestion in communal areas, and the very small numbers accommodated by resettlement schemes, inevitably many seeking to return to lost lands were deeply aggrieved when landless 'strangers' (*vatorwa*) acquired resettlement plots before them. Given the salience of autochthonous landscape knowledge in recurring struggles for belonging and entitlement around Mutirikwi, for many the resettlement of *vatorwa* caused the destruction of the land. This perspective inverts, even as it appeals to, the recurring notion that squatters threatened Mutirikwi's 'beautiful landscapes'. VaChinengo lamented that 'all the "new" people were put on *minda mirefu* at Boroma whilst we the owners were never given a place to stay there'. Furthermore:

> These people who come from nowhere are not able to look after the sacred places because they do not know them. That is why you find them cutting trees and digging where they are not supposed to. How many of them know that the old Murinye chiefs were buried in those caves there? ... They took people not from that area and they put them in that place. Those who used to live in shacks. Not people like us whom came from that area. I was born there. How can it be good? These people cut [around] the *zvitubu* [springs] and through the *marambatema* [sacred woodlands], because they don't know about these sacred places. They cut because they don't know anything ... People who don't know the land can't look after it.
> [The younger man present says] But if you were given land at the *minda mirefu* you would have to pay rent for those fields.
> Ahh [responds VaChinengo] do you think I would pay rent for land on which I was born? No we wouldn't pay. [109]

VaChinengo's reference to 'those people who come from nowhere', who 'live in shacks', shows how people reclaiming ancestral and personal ties to the land do not consider themselves 'squatters'. In this view, it is the people granted land on resettlement schemes who are the squatters. It is a powerful assertion of difference, appealing to active and affective landscapes of ancestral belonging around Mutiriwki, which echoes how 'new yet autochthonous' farmers north of the lake described war veterans and new farmers around them as *vatorwa*. VaChinengo's assertion that he would not 'pay rent for land on which [he] was born' indicates his position between the different registers of ownership, belonging and entitlement in play around Mutirikwi. Yet he was also proud of his old 'master farmer' certificate, emphasising that 'you cannot become a master farmer without knowing how to build *makandiwa* [contour ridges]'. Likewise, he was adamant that acting Chief Murinye's

---

[107] VaMadungwe 12/03/06
[108] Matende explained: 'First this area was under ward 15, under Murinye, but now has changed to ward 13, under Mugabe', 18/12/05.
[109] VaChinengo 26/05/06.

Photo 18   VaChinengo, Mutirikwi communal areas (Source: author, 2006)

Photo 19   VaMadungwe, Oatlands irrigation scheme, Boroma, with Baba Lisa (Source: author, 2006)

successful *mukwerere* [rain-making] ceremony had ensured 'the rains fell well last year', despite his own fervent Seventh day Adventism.[110]

People on the resettlement schemes, particularly those asserting their own autochthonous claims, like VaBhodo on The Retreat, and VaMatende and VaMadungwe at Oatlands, could also find themselves in an uneasy position between different registers of meaning and regimes of rule co-existing in close and active proximity around Mutirikwi. Despite being 'under the council', they respected the ancestral *chisi* rest day, worried about *njuzu* in their dams, and contributed to rain-making events. VaMadungwe agreed 'the rules chiefs tell us to follow, our traditional way of living, respecting the *chisi* [ancestral rest day], not living in certain places and so on ... are very important'. 'Government' he explained, 'is looking into those things now because we had problems with recent dry spells, and in some places with ... *mhondoro* [ancestral lions] killing cattle'.[111] Yet as tensions between Mugabe and Murinye escalated in the 2000s, different resettled families at Oatlands aligned with different chiefs. At the same time they all asserted they were there under the authority of the rural district council to whom they pay rent and tax, even as they often appealed to the autochthonous knowledge of ancestral landscapes and the role of chiefs in the proper allocation of land. VaMadungwe, for whom Oatlands and Boroma clearly fell under Mugabe, put it as follows:

> Yes we have village committees here, those are the structures of the local government, but there are also chiefs involved, as well as resettlement officers. It is the job of resettlement officers to visit the farms along with AREX to see what development is being done and to make sure the land is being farmed properly. The chiefs were involved but then the government tightened the string on chiefs giving out land, because some were giving out land to people who pay money ... So the government said no chief can have the power to give out land. Rather chiefs co-ordinate the allocation of land with the councils; the powers are shared with the chiefs, councils and local government. Even now, on all resettlement areas chiefs have no power to give land, but they are part and parcel of the resettlement committees. There are some issues where the role of the chiefs is very important: without these chiefs people might be settled in places that are important for our cultural heritage. That's why traditional leaders are being invited. All the chiefs around Zimbabwe were removed from their areas by white settlers, so they really know the land, the sacred places, and the *matongo* [ruins] of their forefathers, where people lived *kare* [long ago], where their ancestors used to have their homes.[112]

Given the problems they faced in the 2000s with new settlers/land occupiers on their grazing areas, people on resettlement schemes also often decried the destruction caused by 'squatters', regardless of who they were, where they came from or what their claims where. This included both those who occupied their grazing areas after 2000, who 'came here with the *hondo yeminda*' [war of the fields], and those who had preceded the resettlement schemes of the 1980s. Vincent Matende described the

---

[110] VaChinengo 26/05/06. He was referring to Murniye's 'national *bira*' below Boroma in September 2005.
[111] VaMadungwe 12/03/06.
[112] Ibid.

'damage and vandalism' caused by those who 'settled here illegally' before the Oatlands scheme was established. 'There was a farmhouse just over there, those people destroyed everything. There used to be electricity here, farming equipment, water pipes but everything was destroyed. If it wasn't for those people, this place would have had good development here now' he complained. Now, he added, 'there is a problem with the new settlers that came here recently. They are ploughing near to the dams'.[113]

Both Matende and VaChinengo's laments about the destruction caused by 'squatters' (however defined) recalled, albeit imperfectly, the concerns of government officials, police, local newspapers and Fort Victorians in the early 1980s about the 'dreadful destruction of once beautiful land' around Mutirikwi.[114] They also echoed older Alvordian anxieties about soil erosion, and hydrologists' concerns about protecting river catchments. Furthermore, they reverberated strongly with widespread critiques of fast-track land reform, albeit in different ways: Matende in more developmentalist terms, VaChinengo appealing to autochthonous knowledge of the landscape. They illustrate how concerns about the destruction of landscape caused by the 'wrong kind of' occupation have long resonated across different regimes of rule and meaning around Mutirikwi.

The 'reformed missiologist' Daneel, who grew up at Morgenster, expressed similar sentiments about destruction caused by squatters and 'poorly controlled resettlement' around Mutirikwi in his book *African Earthkeepers* (1998). It comes in a section entitled 'the wounded earth' (1998:11–21), describing his motivation for establishing the 'eco-religious' conservation movements ZIRRCON and AZTREC in the mid-1980s, in which many mediums, chiefs and war veterans, as well as African Independent Churches took part (1998:86).

> Soon after *Chimurenga* a large number of squatters were allowed to settle in the catchment area of Lake Kyle … In no time large sections of the *msasa* and *mutondo* forests were gone, and the sandy soil lay bare in the sun, ready to be carried away … to the watery depths of the lake where it would add to … siltation … Where I used to hunt in dense forest as a child, the open veld now lay forlorn, lifeless tree stumps jutting hopelessly from the soil like beckoning fingers imploring someone to cover the wounded earth. Kyle's catchment area was being threatened from all sides … on the portion of Morgenster farm given back to Chief Mugabe for village resettlement, the Bingura forest was fast disappearing, making way for row upon row of homesteads and cultivated fields. Some callous profiteers … stripped the steep Nyuni slopes of their protective mountain acacias to earn a quick buck from firewood, leaving the soil exposed to inevitable erosion and adding to the siltation of the lake. Among the upper reaches of the Popotekwe and Mutirikwi rivers … poorly controlled resettlement schemes led to river bank cultivation which, in times of flooding could only further compound the problems of Lake Kyle. (1998:15–16)

Daneel's sentiments were particularly provoked by 'the invasion of Mount Mugabe' (where Morgenster is located) by 'mindless', 'greedy' exploiters who 'desecrated the holy grove' by cutting firewood to sell. 'To make matters worse … squatters, ignoring threats of eviction, tore open the mountainside … cleared bush and started planting their maize

---

113 Matende 18/12/05.
114 'Police news' *Fort Victoria Advertiser*, 11/12/81.

and millet crops in places unsuitable for cultivation, triggering a process of erosion such as the mountain had never known' (1998:16). It is hard to ignore the resonances here with the technocratic, developmental, conservation imperatives long in play around Mutirikwi, that trace back through the NLHA and the traditionalism that followed it, to the centralisation of the reserves in the 1940s. There are also resounding echoes with white Rhodesian aesthetic sentiments about landscape, wilderness and watery shorelines, which Hughes suggests were deeply entangled with the need to establish a sense of white belonging (2010).

The real irony, however, is that many of the key players in his subsequent 'war of the trees', including VaZarira, Mudarikwa Murinye and Chief Mugabe, were amongst, closely aligned to or involved with the very 'squatters' to which Daneel was so opposed. Furthermore, one of the key war veterans in his AZTREC project was Cosmas Gonese (aka Weed Chakarakata), who had spent eight years in prison for his involvement in the events surrounding Sophia Muchini and the Victoria East farm attacks. Gonese and VaZarira both later split from Daneel's AZTREC to form a splinter group (Daneel 1998:118), and after they too parted company from each other, Gonese became involved in fast-track land reform and the national war veterans association.[115] However committed (or not) VaZarira, Gonese, Mudarikwa Murinye and many others were to his 'earthkeeping' project, with hindsight Daneel's movement appears like an effort to depoliticise land issues around Mutirikwi through the framework of 'indigenous conservation'. It seems unlikely it could have accommodated the political implications of the view (widely shared around Mutirikwi) that 'people who don't know the land can't look after it'. Given the long salience of Mutirikwi's affective, active and deeply contested landscapes of belonging, it is perhaps of little surprise that Daneel's enterprise faltered.

If Daneel's efforts were an unusual attempt to bring together so-called 'traditional' religion, chiefly authority, African Independent churches and *Chimurenga* legacies, into an energetic 'indigenous' conservation movement, then they also appear like a deliberate attempt to synthesise the many different, entangled registers of meaning and practice to do with land and water long salient around Mutirikwi. But how new and unique was this? Chiefs and mediums re-asserting territory and authority, people reclaiming ancestral graves and the landscapes of their childhoods, landless peasants 'squatting' on farms and state lands, or occupying resettlement schemes, have all long been situated within, engaged with, appealed to, contested or negotiated *across* different regimes of rule and registers of meaning co-existent in close proximity around Mutirikwi. Most of the different people I have discussed in this

---

[115] Gonese left Daneel's AZTREC amidst allegations of embezzlement. VaZarira joined his splinter AZTREC Trust because 'Gonese said "lets follow our real *chivanhu* [culture, tradition], because Professor Daneel's ZIRRCON included bishops, who did not respect us'. Later VaZarira left Gonese's group after her spirits Murinye and Zarira told her to, because Gonese had failed 'to find money to buy tobacco snuff or cloth ... Ambuya was used for nothing' (VaZarira 17/02/01).

book articulated their diverse positions and perspectives across broad repertoires of meaning and practice to do with land and water.

Perhaps the best example is Ambuya VaZarira. Her movements around Mutirikwi in the decades after independence, between Bannock-burn farm on Beza, Oatlands irrigation at Boroma, and finally, Mazare resettlement at Zvishumbe, connects with all the events I have de-scribed. As a senior Duma medium she has long had obligations to return to Zarira's *mapa* on Beza, as well as responsibilities towards the Murinye, Mugabe, Shumba and Chikwanda clans, and personal aspirations to the custodianship of Great Zimbabwe (Fontein 2006a). Although for some time involved in Daneel's AZTREC, in 2000 she attended a *bira* ceremony held by Samuel Haruzvivishe on Mzero farm, to 'sweep the *mapa*', mark-ing their second return to the *makuva* and *matongo* of their ancestors. In 2004, she led Mudarikwa's burial in Murinye's *mapa* on Boroma, and in 2005/06 she was drawn into the internal disputes that beset Chikwanda's chieftaincy, and their need to conduct a *bira* at Mafuse on Mkwari farm. She also lobbied politicians, officials and businessmen to support a high-profile visit to the Matopos to ask for rain. Furthermore, VaZarira's occupation of her Beza *mapa* on Bannockburn farm, where she lived for ten years with the permission of its white owner Mr Cov-entry, is a good example of how some claiming autochthonous links to landscape were able to negotiate access to land on white farms in the years after independence, even if that raised its own problems.[116] After her removal from Bannockburn in 1993 by its new owner, VaMakova, a prominent businessman and ZANU PF politician from Bikita, she lived at Oatlands below Boroma, before moving to her own plot on the Mazare resettlement where she now lives. Matende claims VaZarira was deeply involved in the establishment of Oatlands irrigation after the squatters had been removed. 'They worked very hard' Matende explained, 'espe-cially VaZarira, she went to the Matopos to ask for this land, and then to Joshua Nkomo, the vice president, and to the local government and the ministry of lands to ask for this place. It took them four or five years.'[117]

---

[116] VaZarira claimed that she was invited to live on Bannockburn because Mr Coventry was having trouble with *mhondoro* lions killing his cattle, the same lions that troubled war veterans on Beza in the 2000s, VaZarira 17/02/01, 16/08/01. Mr Coventry's wife, daughter of one of his farm workers, had a different account: 'In 1983 VaZarira asked to live on Bannockburn at the spot where the previous medium for her spirit Zarira is buried. Vernon Coventry said ok, and she was given a plot where she and her family could live. After a while there were too many people living with her and she had many cows (50 or 60). Problems started between her and Mr Coventry. Once Vazarira threatened him saying that she would send lions after him, and Vernon, said that was fine, he would shoot them. During the 1980s Vernon Coventry sold Bannockburn to Rex Chiwara. At first they seemed to get on better but later problems started between VaZarira and Chiwara too. Chiwara sold Bannockburn to Makova. Makova eventually evicted VaZarira. Makova was a political figure and once ZANU MP for Bikita', (Mai Coventry, Desmondale 01/11/05).
[117] Matende 18/12/05; VaZarira only lived at Boroma for two years, with her brother's son, until she was given plot 36 at Zvishumbe (Mazare) where she moved in 1996 (VaZarira 17/02/01).

VaZarira's movements and activities illustrate how some people were able to negotiate successfully across different regimes of rule and registers of meaning around Mutirikwi in the postcolonial period. But she is undoubtedly an exceptional person. In the 2000s her obligation to return to Beza, 'to clean the bones' of the first Zarira buried there, animated her relations with war veterans resettling farms north of the lake. During a *bira* at her home in June 2001 war veterans offered her a place 'where they say I should go to look after the *mapa*', insisting 'she nominate one person to go and stay there'. She replied angrily: 'And who does Beza belong to?' emphasising that it belonged to her ancestors, and only they can give out the land. Later she told me 'I am not interested in fast-track ... I want to go back there with *chivanhu*'.[118] Throughout 2005/06 her efforts to return to Zarira's *mapa* on Beza continued. But by December 2011 they had not yet born fruit. With her husband succumbing to blindness and herself noticeably older and frailer, it seemed increasingly unlikely.

PROMISES AND RETURNS IN THE 2000s

In the wake of war many anticipated futures that turned on promised returns around Mutirikwi were frustrated and disappointed. Some aspirations were realised, notably the return of Chikwanda's chieftaincy, and some of Nemanwa and Mugabe's lands on Mzero and Morgenster farms. Some, like VaZarira on Beza and Oatlands, and others on *minda mirefu* around Harawe and Boroma, successfully negotiated the reconfigured registers of meaning and regimes of rule in play in the 1980s and 1990s. But many could not. Many aspired returns were disappointed as 'squatters' and 'returnees' all around the lake were evicted and replaced with formal, technocratic resettlements. This chapter began with a discussion of Sophia Muchini and the Victoria East farm murders in the early 1980s, so it is fitting to return there in conclusion here.

One of the striking things about those events was the way that 'macro' concerns intertwined with the highly localised and specific. This is symptomatic of how the politics of land and water around Mutirikwi has always taken place, entangling the local and minute with larger-scale politics, interests and concerns. It reflects the way water flows, and how dams have effects at large and small distances, across geographical scales. Sophia Muchini made large statements about Great Zimbabwe's sacredness, the need to heal the country after war, and about the return of land appropriated by white Rhodesians. But she became minutely intertwined within local struggles between Nemanwa and Mugabe, and with NMMZ's efforts to re-establish itself at the ruins. She became involved with the opaque political machinations of leading ZANU PF figures like Herbert Ushewokunze, at a time when official policies of reconciliation, army integration, and rising concerns about 'banditry' and 'dissidents' were subject to deepening scrutiny. At the same time, local aspirations to return to the active ancestral landscapes of graves and

[118] Fieldnotes 29–30/06/01; VaZarira 18/08/01.

ruins, materialised a wave of squatting all around Mutirikwi, but particularly on its southern and eastern shores, where Charumbira, Nemanwa, Mugabe, Murinye and Chikwanda people attempted to reclaim lands lost 40 years before. Also part of the story of the killing of Chimuka Roux, and of other farm attacks during or after the war, are personal memories, grievances and injustices of Rhodesian rule, eviction and war.

When her homestead was raided, and later during her trial, Sophia Muchini declared that 'independence is a mockery' (Ranger 2010a:10). She accused '[Robert] Mugabe, [Simon] Muzenda and [Rex] Nhongo [i.e. Solomon Mujuru]', and the new government, of being 'enemies of the people', of 'having been bought by western money' and 'selling out' to the whites (Clark 1985:90). She warned there would be no peace until her concerns were resolved. In some respects she was right. Nearly all the issues animating her concerns, and the events in which she became entangled, re-emerged in the 2000s. Unresolved 'land thirst', and particularly the desire for the return of ancestral territories, so frustrated by the evictions of the 1980s, manifest new farm invasions and land occupations all around Mutirikwi. This immediately provoked complex boundary contests between rival chiefs and clans, and sometimes complicated succession disputes. Similarly, war veteran demands for the reburial of war dead from Mozambique and elsewhere, and for healing from the violence of war, were reanimated in new activities at Great Zimbabwe, Njelele and elsewhere (Fontein 2009b, 2010, 2014). Mediums and chiefs, even the spirits themselves, demanded ancestral graves and ruins, and the springs and rivers of *njuzu* be respected, as they became crucial to war veterans and new farmers resettling commercial farms north of the lake. Recurring droughts brought the ancestral legitimacy of the state into question again. Even Mkwari farm itself, where Chimuka and his wife were killed in 1981, and where Chikwanda's *mapa* Mafuse is located, became (like farms elsewhere) the centre of new struggles, as local political elite competed with each other and peasant 'invaders' to acquire A2 (medium-sized commercial) farms. Most of all, violence returned, as war veteran bases and militia camps brought fear and danger back to Mutirikwi's landscapes, especially in the 2008 elections (cf. Fontein 2010; Sachikonye 2011).

After Sophia Muchini's release, she returned to live in obscurity in a small homestead below Boroma, near Oatlands. Locals avoid her and most people consider her mad, or deeply troubled by *mashave* (alien or animal) spirits, despite evidence she had been immersed in their intense local disputes in the 1980s (Fontein 2006a:159–60). She is still sometimes seen walking in skins and bangles, along the road to Masvingo town. Yet the issues animating her activities in the early 1980s did not fade into notoriety as her reputation did. With the return to a more radical remaking of landscape and the state in the 2000s, long-delayed aspirations for return to ancestral graves, ruins and sacred places around Mutirikwi were materialised; even as the vagaries of social, economic and political life in that decade inevitably meant other aspirations tied to nationalism – for democracy, rights and development – did not fare so well. The 2000s promised the completion of a project of re-Africanising Mutirikwi's land-scapes. In the years after this research was done, and into a new decade, new discourses of 'indigenisation' began to focus not only on land and water around the lake, but also on its remaining infrastructure of game parks, hotels, sugar farms and even mines, around it and in the lowveld linked to it by water. Just as African pasts were never obliterated by the dam and its 'beautiful' recreational 'playground', nor by the industrial landscapes of the lowveld, these European pasts continue to co-exist with new and re-asserted orders, through the ghosts, ruins and graves of white occupation, and their rebounding traces of past imagined futures, meanings and rule still active and affective in Mutirikwi's emergent and troubled landscapes.

Given all the disappointed returns and frustrated futures around
Mutirikwi in the 1980s, it is hardly surprising that the land invasions
of 2000 began in Masvingo, soon after the constitutional referendum
of February that year (Sadomba 2011:170; Alexander 2006:186).[1] Commentators within and without Zimbabwe quickly identified this as a
critical moment, marking a rupture in Zimbabwe's postcolonial history.
While others argued the 'war veteran-led land revolution' had begun in
Svosve in 1998 (Sadomba 2011:119–49), the stories recounted in this
book suggest that much longer and more complex histories and historiographies are at play. The ongoing remaking of Mutirikwi's landscapes,
traced here, points to the active and affective co-existence of many
pasts and futures, and of past futures and future pasts, immanent and
emergent in the materialities of milieu. It suggests that rupture, change
and difference cannot be properly understood or even identified, except
relationally, in the context of the material, imaginative and discursive
endurances and continuities with which they are in tension, through
which they gain traction, make sense, and can be made sense of. This
offers a challenge not only to those who might identify the land occupations of 2000 as a decisive, and divisive, break in Zimbabwe's history, but
more broadly to the temporal (pre-colonial, colonial and postcolonial)
schemas through which Africanist scholars have conventionally ordered
African pasts and divided labour amongst themselves.

For many aspiring to return to the graves and ruins of forefathers and
past lives forged in the substance and form of Mutirikwi's landscapes,
the colonial period can appear as just a blip in longer continuities of
belonging that neither the grandiosity of the dam nor the white imagined futures it afforded (or that afforded it) could deny. But this blip did
not come to an end with independence in 1980, despite the euphoria
of that moment, and the aspirations of return that nationalism and
war had promised. The re-Africanisation of Mutirikwi's Europeanised
landscapes had to wait. If, for some, 2000 witnessed a rupture marking
the 'plunging', 'exhaustion' of developmental nationalism (Bond & Manyanya 2003; Campbell 2003), or a 'retreat from' or 'end of' modernity in

---

[1] In 2001 VaMhike, then chairman of Masvingo's war veterans association, told
me he had led the first occupations in Masvingo in 2000 (VaMhike 26/06/01).

favour of authoritarian nationalism (cf. Worby 2003), for many around Mutirikwi the rupture of 2000 marked a return to the aspirations of the 1970s and early 1980s, and to the delayed promises of independence. This was not land, ancestors and sovereignty at the cost of development, modernity and agricultural productivity, but new futures to be forged through material and imaginative engagements with multiple spatialities of meaning and rule. For many around the Mutirikwi, the fast-track-resettlement context of the early 2000s seemed to re-open access to state-making processes, revitalising the possibility of making the state work towards their interests, and the potentiality of both 'belonging to our roots' and being 'modern people'.[2]

There is no doubt that the genealogical geographies ascendant again after 2000 in the localised disputes of rival chiefs and clans around Mutirikwi, involve complex, highly politicised acts of historiography through which the presence of particular pasts, particular ruptures and particular endurances are given precedence over others. They are highly contested ways of ordering time and space, and movement through them. But this does not make them any less real, any less *substantial*. On the contrary, the very stuff-ness of these pasts – these genealogies turned into geography, of kinship and relatedness with the substance of soil – illuminates the affective, metonymic qualities of many different pasts (and futures) imbricated in the emergent politics of the present. These particular ways of doing history and politics point to the co-existence in close proximity of different temporalities, and of different regimes of meaning and rule to do with land and water aligned with them, anchored in, yet emergent and always becoming, through the political materialities of milieu. If temporal orderings come under question, so too are the techniques of difference and alterity involved in the politics of inclusion and exclusion revealed for what they are: processes of differentiation dependent on co-existent meanings, practices and shared material landscapes. The active proximity of different pasts and futures, and of different repertoires of meaning and regimes of rule, through the materialities of place and space do not eschew difference or change in favour of similarity or continuity so much as demand us to understand both at the same time.

In this book I have deliberately written the history of Mutirikwi backwards, starting 'now', going 'back', and then returning to the 'here and now', in order to defy normative linear temporalities and the determinist causalities they imply. This is neither a denial of human creativity in favour of an older kind of material determinism, nor a celebration of it in denial of the materialities that structure, enable and constrain human historicity. It is both and all these things. It is about History and historiography entangled and mutually dependent, and it is about the imbrication of matter and meaning, sovereignty and legitimacy in the politics of water, land and state-making. Through this lens, rain making and dam building, and everything these involve or invoke as different aspects of the ongoing remaking of Mutiriwki's landscapes,

[2] Manyanyi 05/06/06.

are not incommensurable regimes of meaning and rule, but rather decidedly commensurable in their shared historicity, political efficacies and ultimate indeterminacy. Just as the vagaries of weather really can determine the fortunes of those who claim to control it, so the excessivity of rain, run off and topography can defy the soil surveys, hydrological run-off and flow calculations, and cost-per-unit calculations of irrigation planners and dam builders. This was dramatically demonstrated again in early 2014, in neighbouring Chivi, when an unexpectedly heavy season of rainfall caused major flooding in the basin of the long-muted Tokwe Mukorsi dam, defying the rainfall and run-off estimations of hydrologists, and the 'phased process of relocation' planned according to it (Scoones 2014:1). The ongoing contestations that followed the emergency evacuation of thousands of people to make-shift holding camps, amid appalling conditions of dislocation and misery, reaffirm the consequentiality of milieu, 'of nonhuman entities and artefacts' (Moore 2005: 24) entangled with the politics of contested pasts and imagined futures, which has been a central recurring theme throughout this book. I will return to Tokwe Mukorsi below, but first some words on the ongoing remaking of Mutirikwi's landscapes in the late 2000s.

REMAKING MUTIRIKWI AFTER 2006

Not long after the referendum of February 2000, as commercial farms were invaded by war veterans and new farmers everywhere, Haruzvivishe, Mugabe, Murinye and Chikwanda people returned to re-occupy state lands all around the lake, including the recreational park at Mzero and the grazing areas of older resettlements around Boroma and Harawe. The *longue durée* of these thwarted aspirations in part explains the hope *with* optimism (cf. Deneen 1999) so palpable around Mutirikwi during 2005/06, once the rains finally came, making tangible and realisable, if only for a moment, a host of long-delayed imagined futures and promised returns that turned on land and water in diverse ways. But it did not last. In the following years, hunger and drought re-appeared, Zimbabwe's economy achieved new depths of despair and, in 2008, fear, danger and violence returned to Mutirikwi.

After 2005/06 I returned to Mutirikwi at three very different moments. My first return was in August 2008, during the exceptionally arduous post-election period of that year, when hyper-inflation was nearly at its worst, drought had returned, and ZANU PF's suspension of NGO activities exacerbated the hunger faced by brutalised rural folk. My second return was under very different circumstances, in November/December 2011, towards the end of the third year of Zimbabwe's Government of National Unity (GNU), when debates about yet another round of elections had already begun. The third was in December 2013, after the elections of that year had re-affirmed ZANU PF's dominance over Zimbabwe's political sphere. During those years, from 2006 up to and beyond the elections of 2013, Zimbabwe's political, social and economic situation shifted several times amid the 'severe ebbs and flows' of 'the battle for the state' that marked the GNU (Raftopoulos 2013:xi). I have argued throughout this book that the changes wrought by critical moments more often than not find traction only in the context of enduring continuities of meaning and practice, particularly as they relate to the active and affective political materialities of landscape. Here I will briefly reflect on some of those changes, and the continuities against which their significance can be judged, in the ongoing remaking of Mutirikwi's landscapes.

LANDSCAPES OF TERROR

2008 was a tumultuous year for people across Zimbabwe, and Masvingo was no different. With worsening inflation and a return to the recurrent droughts of the early 2000s, the optimism heralded by the rains of 2005/06 had disappeared. Exacerbated economic crisis, inflation topping an astonishing 350,000 per cent and worsening food shortages, meant confidence that ZANU PF could deliver its promises profoundly weakened, undermining support even in 'loyal' rural areas, and among new farmers and war veterans on resettled farms. Yet a new kind of optimism emerged, albeit briefly, prior to the combined parliamentary and presidential elections of March that year, as many around Mutirikwi turned to the MDC opposition parties;[3] particularly once unburdened of the charge that they would reverse land reform, an accusation often utilised with devastating effect by ZANU PF.[4] Some optimism also emerged from Simba Makoni's decision, at a late hour, to launch a new party of disillusioned ZANU PF stalwarts against President Mugabe; an unsuccessful project involving a number of senior, Masvingo-based war veterans and former army officers.[5] The MDC's unprecedented success in the March elections across rural Masvingo's ZANU PF strongholds (Mazarire 2013b: 83)[6] caught many off guard, especially Chief Charumbira and the veteran

---

[3] The MDC split into two factions in 2005. In Masvingo, MDC-T under Tsvangirai has had the greatest support.

[4] 'ZIMBABWE: Victory, "sweeter than a miracle!"', 03/04/08, *IRIN*, www.irinnews.org/report.aspx?ReportId=77600, accessed 05/10/14; 'Opposition thugs seek to reverse land reform', *Sunday Mail*, date uncertain. The MDC had been refuting this accusation since 2004, to little avail. 'We will not return farmers' land, says MDC', *Sunday Tribune*, 04/04/04.

[5] Such as Retired Major Kudzai Mbudzi, who became a leading official in Makoni's party in 2008, but later formed the shortlived Zimbabwe National Congress with Ibbo Mandaza, before rejoining ZANU PF in 2011; Daniel Shumba, a long-term ZANU PF member expelled after the infamous Tsholotsho events in 2004; and General Vitalis Zvinavashe, former commander of Zimbabwe's defence forces, who in April 2008 urged ZANU PF to concede defeat after the March elections; he died of liver cancer the following year.

[6] MDC's rural support in Masvingo had been growing for a while ('MDC membership soars in Masvingo' *zimbabwejournalists.com*, 27/08/07, accessed 05/10/14). Of Masvingo's 26 parliamentary seats, the MDC had previously held only one, in 2008 they won 13 seats (Mazarire 2013b:83).

Masvingo MP and historian, Stan Mudenge.[7] Both later worked hard to make up for it.[8]

But as ZANU PF demonstrated its 'ability to lose an election and stay in power' (Mazarire 2013b:88), its March 2008 election losses immediately heralded a return to violence and danger around Mutirikwi not witnessed since the war and the East Victoria killings of the early 1980s. New landscapes of terror emerged as militia bases were established, while intimidated rural people hastily draped their homes in ZANU PF paraphernalia to avoid militia attention, sometimes contributing to 'a broader complicity in the ... ruling party's violence' (Raftopoulos 2013:xix). The 2008 violence was unusual because the worst affected rural areas were in the Shona provinces ZANU PF long regarded as its own (cf. Sachikonye 2011). Masvingo province was terribly affected, with militia camps set up across its districts to beat, burn, and sometimes kill opposition supporters. I heard numerous accounts of the landscapes of terror established around Mutirikwi,[9] although it was widely agreed that Zaka, Gutu and Bikita districts were worse affected. In Nemanwa I heard the following account of what happened after the first round of elections that year.

> [T]hen the ZANU youth and war vets came. It was terrible. They would come to people's houses at night, and say everyone must go to the *sabhuku*'s house now. There was no way you could refuse. We all had to go. Then they said anyone who is MDC, come forward now. This also happened at the show ground, they told everyone from the MDC to step forward. Some people did that and got beaten, but many people just kept quiet. But it wasn't too bad. No one died here, not like in Zaka or Bikita. I was lucky, I didn't have any trouble. I just kept quiet, and then I put up those posters in the house there, like an insurance policy! Those youth set up their base near the GP, by that blue house. There was one war vet there, I know him, but I didn't know any of the youth because they would take them from somewhere else to set up those camps. That way it was

---

[7] Chief Charumbira was severely embarrassed by the results in his area, because 'as head of the council of chiefs, he had to explain to the president why in his area people voted for the MDC!' Fieldnotes 22–24/08/08).

[8] In April 2011 Mudenge 'promised his party leader ... to witch hunt people' who voted for the MDC (*Radiovop.com* 22/04/11, accessed 05/10/14), but died in October 2012 before he could fulfill his promise (*SWRadioAfrica* 05/10/12, accessed 05/10/14). Charumbira was deeply involved in efforts to re-establish ZANU PF control over rural Masvingo and repeatedly implicated in violence and electioneering. In February 2010, villagers from Charumbira's area were beaten for attending an MDC-T rally (*radiovop.com*, 07/02/10, accessed 05/10/14). In July 2010 houses belonging to four MDC supporters were burnt in Mushandike, allegedly on Charumbira's instructions (*Zimtelegraph*, 06/07/10). He also obstructed the constitutional outreach programme (*SWRadioAfrica*, 06/07/10, accessed 05/10/14), and 'ordered traditional leaders and ZANU leadership [in Masvingo] to buy votes from villagers using funds acquired from the indigenisation programme's community ownership scheme' (*radiovop.com*, 26/11/12, accessed 05/10/14), publically declaring that 'Traditional chiefs and ZANU PF are inseparable' (NewZimbabwe, 11/12/12). He held rallies for ZANU PF candidates in his area (*Daily News*, 04/06/13) and banned villagers from attending MDC rallies (*Daily News*, 19/07/13), and at same time 'castigated politicians for using food to buy votes' (*Newsday*, 20/07/13).

[9] Fieldnotes 22–24/08/08 and 28/11–22/12/11.

easier for them to do that violence. In their own areas they wouldn't be able to do that violence to people they know, *hasviiti!* [impossible]. But here was better, Zaka and Bikita is where houses were burnt and people were killed. You would find ZANU burning MDC houses, and then MDC youth would go and burn the houses of ZANU supporters. Maybe it was better here because of that police camp. Later some of those youth who were taking peoples' cattle, goats and chickens to eat at the bases were arrested by the police, once the elections were over.'[10]

Similar landscapes of terror were established on resettled farms north of Mutirikwi, as 'George' (pseudonym) explained in December 2011:

'George' tells me that during the 2008 elections, a base of ZANU PF youth was established right next to their home, at the borehole, just 50 yards away. 'They would collect young men, in their late teens and early twenties, and give them *mbanje* [cannabis] and *scud* [opaque beer] all day and then at the night, when they have got drunk, tell them to go and beat people, and even kill them ... Many people got killed. It was especially bad in Zaka, Gutu, and Bikita. I got into trouble with those people in that base there. I have a grown-up son who lives in Gweru. He came here to visit us. I did not know that he is an MDC person for this area. After my son went back to Gweru those ZANU guys came after me, and they wanted to beat me, saying your son is MDC and so on. But I said 'No, what my son does, I don't know anything about that. He is over 18, he is an adult. I have nothing to do with that'. They wanted to beat me but I was lucky because I was able to persuade them not to. They were beating people with long wooden poles. Just over there on what used to be Thomas's [pseudonym] farm, where he used to grow wheat, there was another base camp where people were killed. Here, this was a camp *yeddiscipline* [of discipline] only, over there, that was a camp *yekuuraya* [of killing]!'[11]

Although this violence was particularly concentrated in 2008's election period – between the March elections and the presidential run-off in June – and had eased by August that year, it would re-occur around Mutirikwi over the following five years, as 'selective violence', coercion and intimidation remained an important ZANU PF strategy (Raftopoulos 2013:xvii). This was especially the case after the war veteran leader Jabulani Sibanda arrived in Masvingo, and stayed 'to re-educate the ... rural electorate ZANU–PF-style on the consequences of voting for the opposition' (Mazarire 2013b:83).[12] Sibanda quickly became immersed

---

[10] Fieldnotes 22–24/08/08.

[11] Fieldnotes 28/11–22/12/11.

[12] 'Violence in Chiredzi and Zaka', *Zimbabwean*, 23/04/08; 'Three MDC members killed in Masvingo', *Zimbabwe Times*, 05/06/08; '7000 teachers flee from schools', *Zimbabwe Times*, 12/05/08; 'ZANU PF sets up torture bases', *radiovop.com*, 25/01/10, accessed 05/10/14; 'Zanu Pf youth militia forces villagers to join party', *radiovop.com*, 12/03/10, accessed 05/10/14; '10 arrested over political violence', *Daily News*, 05/05/10; 'Masvingo villagers get a hiding for attending MDC T Rally', *radiovop.com*, 07/02/01, accessed 05/10/14.; 'ZANU PF violence flares up in Masvingo', *Zimeye*, 16/12/09; 'Farmers tortured for not attending ZANU PF rally', *radiovop.com*, 07/11/10, accessed 05/10/14; 'Teachers beaten up because of elections', *Daily News*, 04/11/10; 'Four teachers severely beaten by ZANU PF youths in Masvingo', *swradioafrica.com*, 05/11/10, accessed 05/10/14; 'NGOs assisiting victims of violence', *Standard*, 30/10/10; 'Sibanda strikes fear among Zaka villagers', *Standard*, 17/10/10; 'Sibanda threatens to unleash terror', *Daily News*, 27/04/11; 'ZANU PF's controversial war vet in child soldier training', *radiovop.com*, 16/02/01, accessed 05/10/14; 'Villagers paying 2r a day for War

in Masvingo's long-running factionalism, challenging loyalties and rivalries between local war veterans, chiefs and ZANU PF groups.[13] War veterans and youth were not the only source of violence, coercion and intimidation in the years following 2008. In April 2010 ZINASU's (Zimbabwe National Student Union) treasurer was abducted by 'suspected state agents' in Masvingo town who 'dumped him at Lake Kyle and left him for dead'.[14] CIO agents and the army were also later implicated in a campaign of harassment against a lively local newspaper after it repeatedly reported on ZANU PF's festering internal struggles across the province.[15] In line with a broader militarisation of state institutions (cf. Alexander 2013), and ZANU PF's own deep-rooted links with the armed forces (cf. Mazarire 2013b), soldiers were repeatedly involved in harassing opposition supporters, and in mobilising or disciplining rural communities, especially leading up to the elections of 2013.[16] Violence, however, was not entirely one-sided, despite its obvious and heavy weighting. Sometimes opposition supporters retaliated by destroying

(contd)   "vet's" upkeep', *radiovop.com*, 11/05/11, accessed 05/10/14; 'Jabulani Sibanda takes his threats and intimidation to Masvingo', *MDC Information & Publicity*, 26/05/11; 'MDC tackles Jabulani Sibanda', *Daily News*, 12/07/11.

[13] 'War vet leader vows: 'I will not leave Masvingo', *radiovop.com*, 04/06/11, accessed 05/10/14; 'Sibanda targets chiefs in violent ZANU PF campaign', *Standard*, 05/06/11; 'Details of more ZANU PF infighting emerge', *swradioafrica.com*, 11/07/11, accessed 05/10/14; War Vets, ZANU PF clash over Sibanda expulsion', *radiovop.com*, 26/06/11, accessed 05/10/14; 'Jabulani SIbanda rips ZANU PF apart in Masvingo province', *swradioafrica.com*, 28/06/11, accessed 05/10/14; 'ZANU PF dismiss war veterans leader, Sibanda', *radiovop.com*, 20/06/11, accessed 05/10/14; 'War vets leader Sibanda taken to court', *Zimbabwe Metro*, 08/07/10.

[14] 'ZINASU treasurer dumped at Lake Kyle', *Nehandaradio*, 07/04/10, accessed 05/10/14.

[15] '"Raid" on Masvingo Mirror newspaper offices leaves staff uneasy', *swradio.com*, 20/06/11; 'Masvingo Mirror editor's defamation case thrown out', *radiovop.com*, 24/02/11; 'Soldier's 'ban' Masvingo weekly newspaper in Gutu', *swradio.com*, 18/01/11; 'Soldiers ban vendors from selling Mirror', *radiovop.com*, 16/01/11; 'Zim journo beaten up by ZANU PF thugs', *radiovop.com*, 06/12/10; 'CIO bars journalists from covering ZANU PF meeting', *SWradio.com*, 15/05/12; all accessed 05/10/14.

[16] 'Army summons chiefs', *Daily News*, 06/08/12; 'Army general abducts MDC-T official in Masvingo', *radiovop.com*, 11/01/11; 'Soldiers terrorise villagers for attending MDC rally', *Daily News*, 16/11/10; 'Police refuse to probe Army general', *Zimbabwean*, 14/01/11. Some violence was more to do with protests against poor pay and conditions ('Soldier run amok in Masvingo, beat up civilians', *radiovop.com*, 08/07/11, accessed 05/10/14), although they were also deployed to break or enforce strikes by teachers and other civil servants ('Soldiers chase teachers from schools', *radiovop.com*, 27/01/12, accessed 05/10/14). Also 'Mutasa admits soldiers' role in politics', *Standard*, 15/01/11; 'Demonstration by Zimbabwean soldiers for President Mugabe heightens concerns', *VOAnews.com*, 08/11/10, accessed 05/10/14; 'Army deployed to "assist" shambolic ZANU PF structures', *SWRadioAfrica*, 08/11/10, accessed 05/10/14; 'Police hunting down MDC-T Bikita executive', *radiovop.com*, 08/11/10, accessed 05/10/14; 'Soldiers declare Mugabe life president as panic sets in Masvingo', *radiovop.com*, 08/11/10, accessed 05/10/14; 'Soldiers threaten MDC legislator', *Daily News*, 13/10/10.

ZANU 'terror bases', as happened in Barahanga and Chikarudzo in March 2010, and other times two MDC factions were involved in their own internal squabbles.[17]

MOU, GPA AND GNU: ZANU PF REGROUPS

Reflecting how (as this book has discussed) power always involves the contested play of both sovereignty and legitimacy, ZANU PF's reliance on violence to avoid its 2008 election defeat also deeply undermined its political legitimacy. By August that year, under intense regional pressure from SADC, discussions between the MDC parties and ZANU PF were underway, with the Memorandum of Understanding (MOU) in July 2008, and the Global Political Agreement (GPA) in September.[18] With absurd levels of inflation, unremitting hunger, recurrent violence, and a cholera epidemic that killed far more people than election violence had (Mason 2009), a fraught Government of National Unity (GNU) was formed in February 2009. With the two MDC factions now partly represented in government, for some this led to another, hesitant moment of optimism, particularly after the moribund Zimbabwean dollar was abandoned, and inflation finally stabilised. Like the 'five men from Chief Murinye's area' who 'walked back' from Mozambique 'in anticipation of a bright future after … the formation of an all inclusive government',[19] some in Zimbabwe's expanding diaspora took the opportunity to return, although many did not, remaining distrustful of the new dispensation (cf. McGregor & Primorac 2010).[20]

With hindsight, this scepticism was justified. The GNU heralded nearly five years of intense political chicanery, during which ZANU PF restructured itself, and repeatedly obstructed MDC efforts to implement the GPA accords (Raftopoulos 2013). Besides continuing coercion, intimidation and sometimes violence across rural and urban areas, ZANU PF's strategy involved a deliberately obstructive kind of politics, the extension of informal patronage networks, and 'parallel government' (Kriger 2012:12), and the continued militarisation of state institutions. ZANU PF, however, also carefully nurtured its ideological agenda by refocusing

[17] 'MDC Supporters Demolish Zanu PF Torture Bases', *radiovop.com*, 26/03/10, accessed 05/10/14; '10 arrested over political violence', *Daily News*, 05/05/10; 'MDC-T activists in Court over violence', *Standard*, 26/03/11; 'Tsvangirai orders re-run of Masvingo Congress', *radiovop.com*, 07/04/11, accessed 05/10/14; 'Masvingo MDC factions make peace', *radiovop.com*, 17/04/11, accessed 05/10/14.
[18] 'ZIMBABWE: Memorandum of understanding signed by rivals' *IRIN*, 21/07/08.
[19] 'Five walk from Mozambique to celebrate Unity government', *radiovop.com*, 25/02/09, accessed 05/10/14.
[20] Despite Prime Minister Tsvangirai's call for diasporans to return ('Come home, Tsvangirai tells expats', *Independent* (UK), 20/06/09; 'Tsvangirai tells Britain's Zimbabwean exiles: It is time to come home', *Telegraph*, 20/06/09; 'UK Zimbabweans jeer Tsvangirai as he urges them to return home', *Independent* (UK), 21/06/09).

its rhetoric of patriotic history and the Third *Chimurenga*, accompanying land reform in the 2000s onto its 'policy of indigenisation' (Raftopoulos 2013:xv).

With recurrent waves of intimidation around Mutirikwi, 'villagers' sometimes responded by urging the MDC prime minister, Morgan Tsvangirai, 'to quit the GNU'. Other times ZANU PF officials were 'booed', and Masvingo's provincial governor Titus Maluleke was 'nearly assaulted' when he again banned NGO activities and suspended food distribution after poor harvests in 2012.[21] As ZANU PF busily regrouped across the province in anticipation of new elections, its shenanigans against its MDC 'partners' in the GNU continued.[22] It repeatedly obstructed the constitutional reform process (COPAC) and various other 'democratising provisions of the GPA' (Raftopoulos 2013:xvii), such as the Joint Monitoring and Implementation Committee (JOMIC), the Zimbabwe Human Rights Commission (ZHRC), and the oddly-named (and ineffectual) Organ of National Healing, Reconciliation and Integration (ONHRI).[23] ZANU PF also used forceful lobbying for the removal of sanctions to consolidate its former rural strongholds and re-establish its presence in urban areas.[24]

As ZANU PF redoubled its efforts to mobilise (and discipline) traditional leaders, Chief Charumbira restated his commitment to restoring chiefs' powers, arguing in July 2010 that 'Land belongs to the chiefs. That power ... was taken away from us in a criminal manner during the colonial era. Now that we have had land reform, we should have full power over the land'.[25] Apart from mobilising fiercely against MDC in his own area, he was also accused of destabilising the COPAC outreach program, 'allegedly moving around Masvingo province instructing participants how to

---

[21] 'Villagers urge Tsvangirai to quit GNU', *Zimbabwe Times*, 15/03/10; 'ZANU PF official booed by supporters', *Zimbabwe Times*, 24/02/10; 'Villagers tell governor off', *Zimbabwe Times*, 25/03/10; 'Masvingo residents give governor 96 hours ultimatum to reverse NGO ban', *radiovop.com*, 25/02/12; 'ZANU PF ban on NGOs in Zimbabwe self defeating', *nehandaradio.com*, 19/02/12, accessed 05/10/14; 'NGO ban sadistic, evil', *Daily News*, 10/03/12; 'MPs embarrass provincial governor', *Daily News*, 02/09/12.

[22] 'Chombo suspends Masvingo MDC councilor', *Daily News*, 07/11/12; 'MDC-T Youth march in Masvingo for activists release', *swradioafrica*, 20/01/12; also 'Chief involved in cheap politicking', 21/03/12, www.mdc.co.zw/index.php/news/42-rokstories/1437-chief-involved-in-cheap-politicking.html,   accessed 21/02/13.

[23] 'Zimbabwe Journos chased away from constitutional meeting', *radiovop.com*, 06/02/10; 'Public hearing on human rights bill abandoned in Masvingo', *swradio.com*, 21/07/11; 'Eight activists arrested as onslaught escalates in Masvingo', *radiovop.com*, 26/11/11; 'MDC MP drags ZANU PF chief to JOMIC', *radiovop.com*, 29/03/12.

[24] 'Tight security ahead of Mugabe rally, banks ordered to release funds', *radiovop.com*, 16/02/11; 'Zim Major General Rugeje disrupts university lessons', *radiovop.com*, 06/05/11; 'Masvingo villagers homeless after refusing to sign Mugabe's anti-sanctions petition', *radiovop.com*, 15/04/11; 'Villagers from anti-sanctions rally battling for life after lorry accident', *radiovop.com*, 21/03/11; all accessed 05/10/14.

[25] 'Jomic warns of land clashes in Matabeleland', *Newsday*, 07/07/10.

answer questions that promote ZANU PF views', despite being a 'senior COPAC delegate meant to be assisting the programme'.[26] He also promoted ZANU PF's indigenisation policies, demanding 'traditional leaders … sit on the boards of mining companies' in their areas 'to ensure local companies benefit from their resources'.[27] At ZANU PF's annual conference in December that year, he stated chiefs would 'continue supporting ZANU PF as it is the only party that brought back land', and 'pleaded with President Mugabe not to listen to critics of the indigenisation and empowerment programme'.[28] When the new (deeply compromised) draft constitution was eventually produced in 2013, Charumbira led a delegation of traditional leaders to complain to President Robert Mugabe about clause 15.3(2), which had allegedly been 'tampered' with in the 'chiefs' absence', and now stated: 'Traditional leaders shall have no authority, control or jurisdiction over land except communal land or over persons outside communal land unless the action arose within the area of the traditional leader's jurisdiction'.[29] They must have been confident that their concerns would be addressed, as they nevertheless 'expressed commitment to drum up for "yes" vote during the [constitutional] referendum'.[30] With all parties in the GNU canvassing for it, the new constitution passed a referendum largely unopposed in March 2013.

A NEW CHIEF MURINYE AND A NEW ACTING CHIEF MUGABE

This was the broader political context surrounding Matopos Murinye's failure in 2010 (before his own death the following year) to be permanently installed as Chief Murinye. The events of March 2010, when 'irate villagers' from Murinye destroyed 'ZANU PF terror bases' in Barahanga and Chikarudzo, hardly strengthened his position, particularly given his earlier suspension from ZANU PF for campaigning for independent candidates in the 2005 senate elections.[31] The subsequent struggles of his controversial successor, Ephias Munodawafa Murinye, with the area's new MDC MP, Jefferson Chitando (whose supporters were implicated in the Barahanga/Chikarudzo events) suggests there were political undercurrents to his appointment.[32] Nevertheless, the enduring resonances of

[26] 'Influential chief accused of destabilizing outreach program', *swradioafrica.com*, 06/07/10; 'Hidden story', *swradioafrica.com*, 07/07/10; both accessed 05/10/14.
[27] 'Chief demand board places in mines', *newzimbabwe.com*, 24/02/12; 'Local chiefs demand control of mines', *Harare 24news*, 25/02/12; 'Chief urges ZANU PF leaders to use indigenization policy to buy votes', *radiovop.com*, 26/11/12; all accessed 05/10/14.
[28] 'Chiefs to rally behind ZANU PF: Charumbira', *Bulawayo Chronicle*, 14/12/12.
[29] 'Copac draft riles chiefs', *Herald*, 04/02/13; 'Traditional leaders not happy with new constitution', *swradioafrica.com*, 04/02/13.
[30] 'President to meet chiefs', *Zimbabwe Mirror*, 17/02/13.
[31] 'MDC Supporters Demolish Zanu PF Torture Bases', *radiovop.com*, 26/03/10; 'Zanu PF night of long knives in Masvingo', *Newzimbabwe.com*, 04/07/06.
[32] 'Chief involved in cheap politicking', *MDC Information & Publicity*, 21/03/12; 'MDC MP drags Zanu (PF) Chief to Jomic', *The Zimbabwean*, 29/03/12; 'Masvingo

the tainted war legacies of Matopos's father, Mudarikwa Murinye, appear equally significant. The new chief, Ephias Murinye, himself told me Mudarikwa had been 'an uneducated chief', 'tricked by the whites' and 'used ... against the Murinye people', who 'came to see him as traitor'.[33]

This exemplifies the continuing salience of war legacies in Zimbabwe, and illustrates how the past continually intrudes upon the present, and change often only finds traction in the context of enduring continuities of meaning and practice. Ephias Murinye's subsequent controversies illustrate this further. He was immediately entangled in the ongoing the boundary dispute with Mugabe around Boroma, again manifest through contested genealogical geographies, disputed ward boundaries and the politics of food distribution.[34] Following the death of his father, the late chief, Matubede Mudavanhu was now acting Chief Mugabe. Ephias Murinye and Matubede Mugabe were involved in exactly the same struggles as their predecessors. Ephias's interferences in food-aid distribution around Boroma not only revisited older Murinye/Mugabe disputes, it also provoked the ire of villagers, much as Matopos Murinye's imposition of an agricultural ban in mourning for his father had done in 2005.[35] When Ephias interfered in food distribution, however, he was assaulted by hungry villagers and forced to seek refuge in the late Chief Mugabe's bedroom, where 'he even took off his *nyembe* [title/badge] and left it ... on the bed'.[36] Later Ephias was accused of 'arbitrarily ordering' villagers to 'pay a road levy',[37] and of 'selling' food aid and agricultural inputs for foreign currency, as both Matopos and Mudarikwa had been.[38] He also became 'sucked' into his own 'chieftaincy wrangle' when his brother tried to take legal action against his appointment.[39] And he quickly became mired in ZANU PF factionalism, becoming victim to ZANU PF youth violence himself after he was labelled a 'sellout' and an 'MDC chief', for allegedly advising people 'not to donate gifts for President Mugabe's birthday party'.[40]

(contd)   central MP arrested', *MDC Information & publicity*, 10/04/12; 'Chiefs part of ZANU PF's political arsenal', *Independent*, 05/01/12.

[33]   Chief Ephias Murinye, 19/12/11.

[34]   'Hungry Masvingo villagers assault their chief', *radiovop.com*, 12/12/10, accessed 05/10/14; 'Chief Murinye clashes with ZANU-PF DCC chair', *Daily News*, 30/11/11.

[35]   'Villagers protest against 6-week ban on field work', *Herald*, 18/07/05.

[36]   'Chief Murinye found in Mugabe's bedroom', *Masvingo Mirror*, 25/12/10; 'Hungry Masvingo villagers assault their chief', *radiovop.com*, 12/12/10, accessed 05/10/14; Also, Acting Chief Mugabe 16/12/11.

[37]   'Chief accused of abusing powers', *Herald*, 24/05/11.

[38]   'Chiefs suspended over inputs', *Zimbabwean*, 13/02/13; 'Masvingo school headmaster turned conman', *Harare tribune*, 09/04/09; 'Chief under probe for selling grain in forex', *fxupdates.com*, 14/11/08, accessed 01/07/09; 'Chiefs selling maize meal on black market', *radiovop.com*, 14/11/08, accessed 05/10/14; 'Cases of politicized food aid growing, says MDC', *Daily News*, 17/01/03.

[39]   'Chombo sucked in chieftainship wrangle', *Financial Gazette*, 21/10/11.

[40]   'Masvingo chief battling for life after assault by ZANU PF youths', *radiovop. com*, 22/02/11; also 'ZANU PF clash over mine and Mugabe Birthday bash', *radiovop.com*, 15/02/10; all accessed 05/10/14.

Despite assuring me in December 2011 that as 'an Adventist ... I do not deal with spirit mediums' he has also had to be responsive to the demands imposed by genealogical geographies and the immanence of the past as emergent through mediumship and the materialities of landscape.[41] In December 2011 Peter Manyuki told me Ephias had approached VaZarira for support several times 'in the early days, when they were still organising the *ushe* [chieftaincy], ... but was some time ago and ... he hasn't come back to visit Ambuya again'.[42] Like chiefs Chikwanda and Charumbira, Ephias was adamant that the authority of chiefs does not derive from mediums. 'I have not stopped her, VaZarira or anyone else, from continuing with their beliefs' he told me, 'but they must respect my belief. I was born a chief. I am not chief because of a spirit medium. I was born a chief, but my beliefs are my own, which I have chosen'.[43] It is quite possible he will be embroiled in the same kind of disputes Chief Chikwanda has had with VaZarira (if she still has the strength), even if, like Matopos and Mudarikwa before him, he too has his own disputes with Chikwanda and others to pursue.

Still, in securing his nascent chieftainship, Ephias too has engaged with the affective and active materialities of the past emergent in the form and substance of landscape. Like Matopos, he is planning to build a house below Boroma in order to cement Murinye claims to the area. Perhaps like Mudarikwa, he too will plan to be buried in Murinye's *mapa* on Boroma, as Matopos had desired but was, in the end, denied. It is likely he too will insist that taboos regarding the *mapa* be strictly respected, and could appeal across a variety of overlapping registers of meaning and regimes of rule to do so. This became apparent in late 2011 and early 2012, after Chinese contractors working on an Econet mast on the Boroma hillside, damaged very old graves amongst the rocks and caves of the area. This incited fierce contests across Boroma's various claimants. Museum authorities were alerted, and police intervened to protect the archaeology revealed by the contractor's bulldozers.[44] Incensed about the damage done, after 'they exposed my forefathers' remains', Ephias Murinye demanded Econet build him a 'fabulous homestead' in compensation. Acting Chief Mugabe accused Ephias of being 'greedy', arguing 'Boroma and Sviba are under my area and there is no way he can benefit from that Econet project'.[45] Chief Executive of the local council, Clemence Mwakarimba, who authorised the project, accused Murinye of 'extortion', and the DA warned 'these chiefs should not waste their time fighting to benefit from the Econet project because the area is under dispute'.[46] NMMZ later granted approval for the work to continue. But acting Chief Mugabe was equally angry about the 'scattered' human re-

41 Ephais Munodawafa Murinye 19/12/11.
42 Fieldnotes 13/12/11.
43 Ephais Munodawafa Murinye 19/12/11.
44 Tendai Musindo, then curator, NMMZ, 12/12/11; 'Econet forced to abandon project', *Masvingo Mirror*, 15/06/12.
45 'Econet forced to abandon project', *Masvingo Mirror*, 15/06/12.
46 Ibid.

mains and the destruction of 'relics from the shrine'.[47] In an unexpected and rare moment of unity, despite their continuing disputes, Mugabe and Murinye together summoned Econet to 'a traditional court' before neighbouring Chief Shumba (as a 'neutral arbiter'), to 'pay compensation to appease the Murinye and Mugabe ancestors whose remains were excavated when the booster was ... installed'.[48] When this failed, because Econet did not turn up,[49] Murinye and Mugabe went to the high court, claiming '2000 white cattle from Econet' in compensation.[50] Despite Mugabe's warning that such 'desecration of sacred shrines ... would result in plagues like diseases and famine', the case was thrown out of court with costs, after it was revealed Econet had 'signed a lease agreement for a 400 square-meter space with Masvingo Rural District Council', and both chiefs had been present when 'permission to build the base was given'.[51]

LAND GRABS, INDIGENISATION AND TOURIST REVIVAL AROUND MUTIRIKWI?

The graves exposed by Econet's activities at Boroma brought the presence of Mutirikwi's much older pasts back into the spotlight. While NMMZ focused on the archaeological remains,[52] both Murinye and Mugabe engaged with these material resonances through their own continuing contests over Boroma, with each other and the district council. The episode also illustrated how a new politics of 'indigenisation' had become intertwined with Mutirikwi's older materialities of belonging. As acting Chief Mugabe put it in December 2011:

> This issue of *miganhu* [boundaries] is a big problem, especially at Boroma. All the chiefs see this very fertile piece of land there and want it for themselves. At the moment there is all this talk of indigenisation, and in that strip of land there are all these hotels, from Ancient City [once George Sheppard's hotel] to Norma Jean's [MacDougall's last home Dunollie] and the [Kyle View] chalets. So this indigenisation law says that local people and their chiefs should get 10 per cent of those businesses. That is why there are all these problems there at Boroma. Murinye says it is his, we know it is ours; there is no way they could have crossed that Mutirikwi river. Even Charumbira is now saying all that land up to Boroma, and even Mutirikwi is his, from Mutirikwi to Mushandike, Charumbira claims is Charumbira land. So this issue of *miganhu* is coming together because of the indigenisation law that everyone is talking about.[53]

[47] 'Two Masvingo chiefs take Econet to court', *Nehanda radio.com*, 15/10/12, accessed 05/10/14; 'Chiefs demand 2000 white cattle from Econet', *Herald*, 08/11/12.

[48] Ibid.

[49] 'Econet scoffs at chiefs' demands', *Herald*, 06/12/12.

[50] 'Two Chiefs take Econet to court', *Nehanda Radio*, 15/10/12; 'Chiefs demand 2000 white cattle from Econet', *Herald*, 08/11/12.

[51] 'Masvingo Chiefs lose case against Econet', *Herald*, 10/12/12.

[52] Tendai Musindo, 12/12/11.

[53] Acting Chief Mugabe 16/12/11.

Through the new politics of indigenisation, Mutirikwi's contested genealogical geographies became entangled with the material legacies of the recreational landscapes white Victorians constructed in the 1960s and 1970s. Perhaps the antecedents to this re-configuration of Mutirikwi's different co-existent pasts was already apparent in Matopos Murinye's insistence in 2005/06 that the Ancient City hotel must allow his elders to appease ancestral graves at the site, to prevent trouble from ticks and George Sheppard's ghost. At any rate, it is striking that while in the 1980s appeals to the aesthetics of Mutirikwi's recreational landscapes had driven the evictions of squatters from its shores, by the early 2010s indigenisation appeared to merge appeals to autochthonous belonging with the material traces of what had once been 'Rhodesia's playground'.

Other aspects of Mutirikwi's multiple overlapping pasts too promised to reappear after 2008. Amid deep scepticism towards the GNU, some commentators suggested in late 2008 and early 2009 that the best alternative to political power-sharing was 'an internationally-sponsored, technocratically-based transitional authority' to re-establish basic public services, leading to new, supervised elections in due course.[54] Of course, technocratic planning and soil conservation had already re-appeared, as the *jambanja* of the land invasions transformed into fast-track land reform in the early 2000s. Contouring ridging, pegging and appeals to productive farming had become part of broader repertoires through which claims to entitlement were re-forged around Mutirikwi. In April 2012 the Natural Resources minister, Francis Nhema, again 'challenged traditional leaders to enact laws that protect the environment and promote the sustainable use of natural resources in their communities', echoing the technocratic roles with which chiefs had long been tasked.[55] The transitional authority some were advocating in 2008/09 envisaged a de-politicised, 'technical approach' spread across 'the entire governmental sphere', 'coordinated by a temporary administration' to stabilise state services and 'get food production going', before dealing with governance issues, constitutional reform, and new elections.[56] But it seems unlikely the technocratic and the political could be so easily isolated. There were moments during the GNU, when it appeared the influence of the MDC parties, might have allowed a more de-politicised, technocratic approach to land to appear. With 'thousands of families on the waiting list for formal resettlement' in Masvingo province, many of them 'irregularly resettled' on statelands, black-owned farms and national park land, there was some expectation in early 2009, amid reports of multiple farm ownership by ZANU PF elite, that a new MDC governor would immediately order a provincial land audit (cf. Scoones et al. 2010:30).[57] But no MDC governors

---

[54] Mary Ndlovu 'Zimbabwe on the edge of the precipice' *Pambazuka News* 17/12/08;'Interview: 'We would've set up compact, technocratic govt' Lance Guma speaks to Dr Simba Makoni' *Zimonline* 16/2/09, accessed 05/10/14.
[55] 'Enact laws to protect environment chiefs told' *Herald* 05/04/12.
[56] Mary Ndlovu *Pambazuka News* 17/12/08.
[57] 'Masvingo short of land for resettlement'. *Herald*, 14/08/07; 'Knives out as Mzembi accused of MDC links', *Zimbabwe Times*, 16/07/09.

were ever appointed and no new land audits commissioned, nor were the results of earlier, controversial, national land audits published.[58]

Yet in February 2012, the *Financial Gazette* reported that 'the days are now numbered for hordes of illegal land invaders after the inclusive government uncharacteristically directed police to bring to justice all those ... disrupting agricultural activities in Masvingo and other parts of the country'. A week before police had 'thumped a rag-tag group of war veterans led by self-styled commander of the land invasions, Francis Zimuto, alias Black Jesus' and now, 'after a lot of hesitation police had been given the green light to arrest all illegal land invaders ... to restore sanity in the farming sector'. Sopha Tsvakwi, permanent secretary in the ministry of lands and resettlement, announced that all new 'illegal land occupiers would be locked behind bars'.[59] Echoing these sentiments, Masvingo's MDC mayor, 'blamed the demise of the country's oldest town on the chaotic fast-track land reform which destroyed a once thriving cattle ranching industry that was the backbone of the city's economy'.[60] But these announcements were indeed 'uncharacteristic' of the GNU years, and the de-politicised, technocratic approach some sceptics advocated in late 2008 never materialised.

In many respects quite the opposite happened. The late 2000s witnessed a new wave of land occupations around Mutirikwi and the province (Scoones et al. 2010:35,199). These were often much less technocratic than fast-track had been, and more akin to elite land grabs than the promised returns to ancestral landscapes long animating localist politics around Mutirikwi. In 2008/09 anticipation that the 'inclusive government ... might end land-based patronage' provoked 'a range of speculative land claims by politically-connected elites' (Scoones et al. 2010:199). This new wave of land grabs meant many remaining white farmers, who had still held farms in 2005/06, were now removed. John Bolland lost his farm (Scoones et al. 2010:35) and the Mitchell's chicken farm, Barquest, was taken by the DA Felix Mazvizda.[61] Ronnie Sparrow was chased off his ranch neighbouring the Kyle game reserve by Alex Mudavanhu, a former ZANU PF provincial chairman, leaving its hungry lions to escape, 'sending shivers to the Chikwanda community' nearby.[62] While the Attorney-General Johannes Tomana took Malangani ranch, Chief Charumbira acquired Dyres ranch in Mwenezi, and Clemence Makwarimba took Brett Connar's Justice farm, 'as farm invasions continued in defiance of the GPA'.[63] With Masvingo's elites grabbing farms all around the province,

---

[58] 'Zimbabwe Minister sitting on explosive land audit report', *zimnetradio.com*, 20/07/09, accessed 05/10/14.

[59] 'Farm invaders face arrest', *Financial Gazette*, 24/02/12.

[60] 'Masvingo mayor blames land reform', *Independent*, 19/10/12.

[61] The invasion of Bolland's farm was discussed at a ZANU PF rally in Mazare, before the 2005 senate elections (Fieldnotes 05/11/05). 'ZANU PF's New farmer and the land question in Masvingo province', *Harare Tribune*, 24/03/09.

[62] 'Villagers live in fear of stray lions', *radiovop.com*, 26/08/09, accessed 05/10/14.

[63] 'Tomana takes over ranch in Masvingo', *Zimbabwe Times*, 27/06/09; 'Top ZANU PF official in land grab', *Daily News*, 14/10/10.

the new seizures 'provoked anger among war veterans in the province',[64] contributing to deepening factionalism (Scoones et al. 2010:35), as ZANU PF officials asserted '*jambanja* on *jambanja*' (Sadomba 2011:217) by evicting earlier occupiers. Former Governor Chiwewe's problems on Mkwari ranch and elsewhere deepened,[65] and Stan Mudenge became embroiled in similar disputes with war veterans and new farmers on Chikore farm.[66] These elite land grabs quickly became intertwined with the new politics of indigenisation and ZANU PF patronage (Raftopoulos 2013:xvii), particularly in Chiredzi, where elites' acquisitive focus shifted from sugar plantations to game ranches and lucrative hunting licenses.[67] The 'controversial indigenization minster', Saviour Kasukuwere, 'set his eyes on Masvingo province' and planned 'to acquire 51% shares in ... Bikita Minerals, sugar growing giant Tongaat Hulet, Renco mine and Malilangwe Trust',[68] further stirring the province's complex factionalism.[69]

There were critics of the indigenisation of lowveld game conservancies. While chiefs in Save complained 'the adopted program ... prioritised a few people ... at the expense of their communities', others worried about the threats posed to wildlife and particularly tourism.[70] Walter Mzembi,

---

[64] 'Tomana takes over ranch in Masvingo', *Zimbabwe Times*, 27/06/09
[65] 'Former Governor evicted from seized farm', *Zimbabwe Times*, 03/08/09; 'Court orders former governor to co-exist with Ganyani family', *Newsday*, 21/07/10; 'Police thump war veterans in Masvingo', *Radio VOP*, 13/02/12, accessed 05/10/14; 'Former Masvingo Governor booted out of farm', *Newsday*, 04/06/12; 'Minister, war vets' fight for farm', *Zimbabwean*, 23/01/13; 'Ex-governor Masvingo embroiled in land dispute', *newzimbabwe.com*, 05/02/12, accessed 05/10/14.
[66] '"War vets languish in prison" over land dispute', *radiovop.com*, 09/11/11, accessed 05/10/14; 'New twist to Mudenge-war vets land wrangle', *Daily News*, 03/05/10; 'Mudenge seeks to evict war vets from farm', *Zimbabwe Times*, 25/02/10; 'Mudenge elbowed out of farm', *radiovop.com*, 19/04/10, accessed 05/10/14.
[67] 'Chiefs grab sugar farms', *Zimbabwean*, 07/11/12; Top army officials and war vets jostle for farms'. *radiovop.com*, 05/06/09; 'Zimbabwe land reforms target wildlife reserves', *AFP*, 09/03/11; 'Wildife land reform enacted', *Zimbabwean*, 11/03/11; 'Mudenge fingered in conservancy destruction', *New Zimbabwe*, 04/04/12; 'CIO chief among ZANU PF officials linked to illegal hunting in Zim', *swradioafrica.com*, 17/10/12; 'Save invasions threaten US$30m safari business', *Standard*, 02/09/12; 'hunting licenses for Zim cronies', *www.iol.co.za*, 12/08/12, accessed 24/08/13.
[68] 'Indgenisation minister eyes take over of Masvingo firms', *swradioafrica.com*, 29/03/12; 'Minister loses patience with "defiant" Tongaat Hulett', *Mail & Guardian*, 20/04/13.
[69] 'ZANU PF officials fight over South African Sugar Milling Giant', *VOAzimbabwe.com*, 02/05/13; 'ZANU Big wigs in Masvingo face arrest – Kasukuwere', *radiovop.com*, 23/11/12; 'ZANU PF clash over Mine and Mugabe birthday bash', *radiovop.com*, 15/02/10; all accessed 05/10/14.
[70] 'Wildlife land reform policy will have huge impact on Tourism', *swradioafrica.com*, 09/03/11; 'ZANU ministers clash over Save', *Zimbabwean*, 17/10/12; 'Protect wildlife sanctuary', *Standard*, 28/08/12; 'Chiefs want conservancy seizure reversed', *newzimbabwe.com*, 03/09/12; 'ZANU PF factions take Save conservancy dispute to courts', *voazimbabwe.com*, 31/08/12; 'Conservancy slams 'criminal' handover of hunting permits to ZPF', *swradio.com*, 13/08/12; all accessed 05/10/14.

MP for Masvingo South, was a significant critic of the indigenisation of the lowveld's safari industry. Like (but often opposed to) Kasukuwere,[71] Mzembi rose quickly within ZANU PF's ranks during the GNU, much to chagrin of his factional opponents in Masvingo and elsewhere.[72] Considered a moderate, he urged 'Zimbabweans to grow beyond partisan politics and start tolerating divergent views' during the 2008 elections, adding that 'I have no problems working in an MDC government'.[73] Just a few months into the GNU, when reports suggested 'hordes of people [had] invaded land around the shores of Lake Mutirikwi', he announced government would 'remove all ... invaders' from 'the shores of lakes or reservoirs'.[74] Mzembi's critique of occupations around Mutirikwi focused on the threat posed to tourism, which he had been tasked to revive as the GNU's Tourism minister.[75] This mirrored criticisms of 'tourist site invasions' elsewhere, including the lowveld conservancies, and around Harare's Lake Chivero in 2011.[76] In July 2012 Mzembi warned parliament that 'without peace and stability we can kiss goodbye to any hopes ... of a tourism boom' or 'hosting ... the UNWTO [United Nations World Tourism Organisation] General Assembly in 2013'.[77] As he prepared for the 2013 UNWTO, he developed a vision of the whole of 'Zimbabwe as a tourism product' subject to 'admiration by other nations'.[78] This resonated with the role long played by aesthetics and recreational aspirations in the remaking of Mutirikwi's landscapes, and its legacies of eviction and return, but stood at odds with those agitating for indigenisation in the 2010s.[79] It also echoed NMMZ's concern that if people 'settled along the Mutirikwi dam' were not removed Great Zimbabwe would be 'de-listed' from the World Heritage List (Marongwe 2007:31).

Whether Mzembi is indeed a moderate reformer, as some suggested, remains to be seen. In 2010 he was deeply implicated in a scandal involving the disappearance of birthday gifts for President Mugabe, and

[71] 'Mzembi childish – Kasukuwere', *Newsday*, 22/04/14.

[72] 'Knives out as Mzembi accused of MDC links', *Zimbabwe Times*, 16/07/09; 'Chinotimba hits back at Mzembi', *radiovop.com*, 19/05/09; 'ZANU PF youths want Mujuru, Nkomo out', *radiovop.com*, 23/08/09, accessed 05/10/14; 'War veterans threaten recall of Mzembi', *Zimbabwe Times*, 31/12/09.

[73] 'Nguni, Mzembi and Kaukonde speak out against Mugabe', *Zimbabwean*, 05/06/08.

[74] 'Knives out as Mzembi accused of MDC links', *Zimbabwe Times*, 16/07/09.

[75] 'Save conservancy; Mzembi pleading for the masses', *Standard*, 09/09/12; 'Paida moyo', *Independent*, 06/07/12; Wildlife land reform policy will have huge impact on Tourism', *swradioafrica.com*, 09/03/11, accessed 05/10/14; 'ZANU ministers clash over Save', *Zimbabwean*, 17/10/12.

[76] 'ZANU PF criticizes tourist site invasion', *Mail & Guardian*, 28/01/11; 'Muckraker', *Independent*, 27/01/11.

[77] 'Paidamoyo Muzulu', *Independent*, 06/07/12.

[78] 'Zim A World Of Wonders', *Financial Gazette*, 28/09/12; 'Make Zimbabwe a tourist draw card', *Sunday Mail*, 24/04/11; 'Gvt moots new vic falls town', *Standard*, 14/05/13; 'UNWTO: Mzembi begs private sector aid', *Standard*, 08/07/13; 'Mzembi speaks on Masvingo airport', *Herald*, 24/07/13; 'Zim ready to host UNWTO', *Newsday*, 29/07/13.

[79] 'Paidamoyo Muzulu', *Independent*, 06/07/12.

in the harassment of local journalists that followed.[80] In February 2013, Mzembi became entangled in an attempt to take over RioZim's Renco mine in Masvingo South, after 'local villagers barricaded the main gate demanding an improvement in worker's conditions and community assistance'. Mzembi 'announced ... RioZim had not complied with indigenization obligations ... and hence they were taking over the mine'.[81] Whatever his reservations about 'indigenising' tourism, he was hardly opposed *in principle* to ZANU PF's indigenisation policies. Even when he urged the removal of 'hordes of people' re-occupying Mutiriwki's shores in 2009, he insisted 'we are not against the land issue but want to make sure ... we ... get as many tourists as possible'.[82] Similarly, when Mutirikwi's waters dropped to 'below 15 capacity' in October 2012, he blamed the sugar industries, declaring 'an ecological timebomb ... will explode anytime ... because ... water continues to be drawn unsustainably to irrigate sugarcane plantations in the lowveld'. 'I will push for ... an inter-ministerial committee to tackle the issue' he continued, 'because the drying up of the dam will ... impinge on tourism in a big way'. Furthermore, he insisted, there is 'need to apply an empowerment model on Lake Mutirikwi to benefit local communities'.[83] Mzembi therefore not only echoed the appeals to Mutirikwi's aesthetic, recreational landscapes that had driven the evictions of its returnees in the 1980s, but also invoked much older tensions over who should benefit from its waters, which had beset Victoria residents and lowveld irrigators since the 1940s, before the dam was even built.

AFTER JULY 2013

In the aftermath of the largely peaceful elections of July 2013, it became clear ZANU PF's efforts to regroup since 2008, by whatever means, had been astonishingly successful.[84] This time the opposition appeared

[80] 'Minister in trouble over missing Mugabe birthday gifts', *Zimbabwe Mail*, 12/04/10; Minister accused of stealing Mugabe's gifts', *Daily News*, 14/04/10; 'Police harass Masvingo journalist', *swradioafrica.com*, 10/05/10; 'Mzembi presses criminal defamation charges against journalists', *Standard*, 15/05/10; 'Case against Masvingo publisher and journalist thrown out', *radiovop.com*, 18/05/10; 'Court case against Masvngo journalist and editor thrown out', *swradio.com*, 19/05/10; 'ZUJ executive committee member accused of causing editor's arrest', *radiovop.com*, 15/05/10; 'Masvingo journalist on the run after threats', *radiovop.com*, 09/05/10; 'Police intimidate Masvingo journalist to reveal sources', *swradioafrica.com*, 11/05/10; all accessed 05/10/14.

[81] 'RioZim, Mzembi on collision course after ZANU PF takeover of Renco mine', *Zimbabwean*, 06/02/13. 'Mzembi vows to continue fight RioZim', *Newsday*, 13/03/13; 'High court orders Mzembi to leave gold mine', *newzimbabwe.com*, 11/02/13, accessed 05/10/14.

[82] 'Knives out as Mzembi accused of MDC links', *Zimbabwe Times*, 16/07/09.

[83] 'Lake Mutirikwi below 15% capacity', *Herald*, 11/10/12; 'Biggest inland dam in dire straits', *Southern Times*, 13/02/12.

[84] 'Western Backlash Rises Over Zimbabwe Vote', *radiovop.com*, 05/08/13; 'Scale of Zimbabwe vote theft surprised us all', Petina Gappah, *Gulfnews*, 05/08/13;

caught unawares. ZANU PF's political control over Masvingo was firmly re-established. It seemed likely indigenisation would be pursued, despite Zimbabwe's financial doldrums.[85] It remains unclear whether this will imbricate with, *or* deliver another challenge to, the long-promised returns to ancestral landscapes around Mutirikwi that fast-track reinvigorated in the 2000s. Many of Mutirikwi's returnees remain on state lands, without formal land offers or 99-year leases, and they could still be evicted. The Great Zimbabwe University has not yet been built.[86] The recreational potential of Mutirikwi's aesthetic landscapes still has traction, as do the technocratic imperatives of soil conservation and irrigation and, of course, the lowveld sugar industries. But Mutirikwi's older, ancestral landscapes of graves and ruins, caves and hills, rivers and *njuzu* remain active and affective. The material remains of all these pasts – all these different registers of meaning and regimes of rule – continue to have salience and efficacy in the ongoing remaking of Mutirikwi's landscapes.

In Harare ZANU PF's election success in 2013 spelled a new period of gloom and apprehension, with reports of panic buying as stock markets reacted strongly to rumours that the Zimbabwean dollar would be reintroduced.[87] This was followed by economic stagnation, deflation, and continuing unemployment, provoking a new exodus of Zimbabweans going abroad, as hope, optimism and opportunity withered again. It seemed unlikely 'Zim Asset',[88] ZANU PF's five year 'economic blueprint' for 'the turnaround and development of the economy', could achieve anything beyond revealing its own forlornness, as the ruling party's intense internal succession battles began to rage. Whether the same is true around Mutirikwi is less sure. A new period of hope *with* optimism may yet emerge, even if only briefly or only for some. This will likely depend less on government policies of indigenisation, tourism revival, or economic recovery *per se*, than on how they engage with the political materialities of its landscapes, with its multiple, co-existent, emergent

(contd) 'Why Robert Mugabe scored a landslide victory in Zimbabwean elections', Miles Tendi, *Guardian*, 05/08/13; 'Zimbabwe elections free, credible: AU', *Sapa-AFP*, 02/08/13; '"We did not say Zim elections were fair" – Zuma's Minister', *Zimbabwean*, 05/08/13; 'Mugabe elected SADC deputy chair', *Radio Dialogue*, 18/08/13; all accessed 05/10/14.

[85] 'Mugabe party vows to boost black ownership of Zimbabwe economy', *Reuters*, 06/08/13; 'Mugabe Plans to Transform Zimbabwe Through Wealth Transfer', *Businessweek*, 06/08/13; 'Robert Mugabe vows to continue Zimbabwe indigenisation', *BBC News*, 14/08/13; 'Indigenisation has to be flexible', *Independent*, 23/08/13.

[86] See www.gzu.ac.zw/index.php/about-the-university/location-of-gzu, accessed 25/08/13; 'Govt. stall church plans', *Daily News*, 13/03/12; 'Mugabe supporters grab university land', *universityworld news.com*, 16/01/11, accessed 05/10/14.

[87] 'Zimbabwe Stock Exchange Plunges 11% After Mugabe Victory', *Zimbabwean*, 05/08/13; 'Panic buying as Zanu (PF) wins', ,Zimbabwean 07/08/13; 'Zimbabwe faces tough future as economy falters after elections', *Standard Digital News – Kenya*, 12/08/13; 'Regional stability fears rise as Zimbabwean "exodus" reported', *SWRadioAfrica.com*, 17/08/13, accessed 05/10/14.

[88] 'Economic Blueprint unveiled', *Herald*, 17/10/13.

pasts and futures, and with the different repertoires of meaning and regimes of rule in active proximity around it. Perhaps not least of all, it will
depend upon the vagaries of water and rain.

This is what was demonstrated again in February 2014, with the
flooding at the Tokwe Mukorsi dam, which threatened a breach in the
unfinished dam wall, provoking fears of a major catastrophe. A national
disaster was declared and international relief mobilised. The planned
and 'orderly' phased relocation of people to Nuanetsi Ranch, was turned
by the 'massive scale of rainfall and rapid filling of the dam' into an
emergency (Scoones 2014:1), and 4,500 people were evacuated at short
notice, and placed in make-shift holding camps in the lowveld, under
deteriorating conditions and increasing political tensions. Echoing the
mis-estimations of engineers and hydrologists at Kyle in the 1950s and
1960s, engineers at Tokwe Mukorsi 'had discounted a once in 30 year
rain event', and projected 'the gradual filling of the dam' according to
'more common rainfall' patterns (Scoones 2014:1). The disaster therefore revealed again the excessiveness of rain, run-off and topography,
and the consequentiality of the milieu. But there are other parallels
too between Tokwe Mukorsi and the building of Kyle. Like Kyle, the
planning of the Tokwe Mukorsi too 'was always political, wrapped up
in national and local, lowveld wrangles' (Scoones 2014:1). Repeated
disruptions by disturbed *njuzu* too are said to have long marred this
effort in heroic engineering. Funding for the Tokwe Mukorsi has also
been a challenge, as was the case during the Federation when new forms
of contractor finance had to be developed to enable Kyle to go ahead.
When renewed funding was secured in recent years, it is Italian engineers who again led its construction, as at Kyle and Kariba. Like Kyle,
Tokwe Mukorsi was designed for lowveld sugar, not local communities,
although some of those displaced are supposed to become 'outgrowers
in new sugar plantations' (Scoones 2014:2). Questions remain, however,
about what benefits people around the dam in Chivi will receive from
the water flooding 'their ancestral lands, their homes, fields and graves'.
With a game park also being discussed for its immediate milieu, the parallels with the remaking of Mutirikwi's landscapes heralded by the Kyle
dam seem prodigious.

There is a difference though. In the years after Kyle was constructed,
and fifty-odd years on, those people actually displaced from Nyangani
and Chinango by the dam, and moved to new lands at Zano, often
seemed the least discontented of all those affected by the damming of
the Mutirikwi river. They do have recurring problems with hippos invading their fields from the protected waters of the lake, and with national
parks' paramilitary control over its milieu. And they still await long-
promised but never-delivered irrigation from the lake's waters. These
problems are serious and ongoing. But the people of Zano also remembered being relieved, even pleased, when they saw the fertile soils they
had moved to, and the ordered delineation of fields and homesteads prepared for them, and the compensation they received. Most were able to
reconcile the loss of their ancestral homes, graves and landscapes with

the opportunities their resettlement offered. Perhaps they bought-in to what the Europeanisation of Mutirikwi's landscapes and the building of the Kyle dam afforded. Tellingly, unlike many other groups and clans around Mutirikwi, they were not involved in the squatting of the 1980s, nor the opportunities of return that fast-track afforded in the 2000s.

This scenario seems highly unlikely to be repeated at Tokwe Mukorsi. After losing homes, belongings, cattle and crops, people evacuated from the floods endured months of deprivation, hunger, overcrowding and worsening health and sanitary conditions at the Chingwizi holding camp.[89] Tensions quickly rose, particularly when the government reneged on promises of compensation and four-hectare resettlement plots. Although conditions at the camp were deteriorating, people refused to move to the much smaller one-hectare plots the government pegged in Mwenezi without the compensation they had been promised. Ministers and officials visiting the camp were repeatedly heckled, booed and shouted down, there were riots, and police vehicles were burnt after Ignatius Chombo, Minister of Local Government, threaten to withdraw food aid if the people did not move to their allocated plots. In the cramped congestion of the camp, unrest and violence also arose between displaced villagers, as people who acquiesced to moving to the new smaller plots were accused of betrayal by others resisting the government's demands. With armed riot police deployed to the camp, it was revealed that funds gathered for compensation had been re-allocated to pay civil servants' wages. Later food storage facilities were moved from the holding camp to the new resettlement area, denying food to camp dwellers, and provoking further protests and hundreds of arrests. Many families chose to move back by themselves to the lands from which they had been evacuated.[90] There were also wider political reverberations as both President Mugabe and opposition MDC leader Morgan Tsvangirai, as well as ministers and local officials, were accused of ignoring the plight of the displaced at Chingwizi.[91] As access to the site was increasingly curtailed, rumours circulated that the flooding had been exaggerated in order to force the removal of people opposing phased relocation. These suggested that some people had been conveniently evacuated from the dam's proposed buffer zone and game park who had not been in danger from the rising floods, because they had been resisting formal resettle-

[89] 'Flood victims facing fresh hunger emeregncy', *SWRadioAfrica*, 19/03/14; 'Tokwe-Mukosi victims in food crisis', *Zimbabwe News Online*, 20/03/14; both accessed 05/10/14.

[90] 'Tokwe-Mukosi flood victims demand compensation', *SWRadio Africa*, 15/04/14; 'Angry Tokwe-Mukosi villagers riot', *NewZimbabwe*, 22/04/14; 'Flood disaster victims turn on each other at Chingwizi', *SWRadioAfrica*, 23/04/14; 'Ministers see hell', *Southern Eye*, 11/05/14; 'ZANU PF ministers booed out of Chingwizi camp', *SWRadio Africa*, 12/05/14; 'Tokwe-Mukosi flood victims being denied food aid', *SWRadio Africa*, 03/06/14; 'Minister flees angry villagers', *Newsday*, 16/07/14; 'Tokwe-Mukosi flood victims return to original homes', *Zimbabwe News Online*, 05/08/14.

[91] Although when Tsvangirai did try to visit, he was barred from entry; 'Tokwe-Mukosi flood victims demand compensation', *SWRadio Africa*, 15/04/14.

ment. Others worried they were being moved to provide cheap labour for a controversial ethanol project near the proposed resettlement site in Mwenezi.[92]

For now it seems unlikely people displaced by the Tokwe Mukorsi dam will be able to reconcile the loss of their ancestral homes, graves and landscapes with the opportunities resettlement offers in the way the people at Zano appear to have done. The vagaries of weather as well as the way resettlement was handled are partly responsible for that. 'Government never made any plan for the graves of our loved ones' one man explained. 'When I look at this lake, I think of my father, mother and grandparents', but 'I will never be able to see their graves again,' he said 'with tears rolling down his cheeks'.[93] Yet it is likely that, as around Mutirikwi, the graves, ruins and other material traces of past lives forged in the very substance of the soil – the co-existence of multiple pasts and futures immanent in the materialities of milieu – will continue to have salience and efficacy in unexpected ways for a long time to come.

This book has argued *against* simplistic linear temporalities that constitute History as a sequential series of ruptures leading from a determined past to the present and forward into the future. Dam building is both destructive and productive. It *is* a decisive and often divisive intervention into landscape, and sometimes, like rain making, a mighty demonstration of capacity and sovereignty. Yet while dams make History and shape historiography, they are also subject *to* these entangled, mutually dependent and open-ended processes. They are about contested legitimacies as much as performed sovereignties in an ongoing politics of inclusion and exclusion, belonging and state-making. Although dams harness water and remake landscapes, they are also made possible, constrained and confronted by the excessive materialities of land, water, climate and topography. The building of the Kyle dam was a decisive moment in the ongoing remaking of Mutirikwi's landscapes, but it did not obliterate the active and affective traces of earlier lives and regimes forged in the substance of milieu, nor could it wholly circumscribe the subsequent remakings these residues demand and make real. Similarly, the pasts and futures immanent through the dam's presence are not obliterated by recent, much delayed, efforts to reclaim and re-forge Mutirikwi anew. While the dam stands testament to a complexity of contested and incomplete past futures, it also makes possible, entangles with and, in part, structures current and future re-orderings of landscape and of the past. So it represents neither rupture nor continuity alone, but both at once. Likewise, when the Tokwe Mukosi dam finally takes its place alongside Kyle/Mutirikwi in a vast hydrological scheme devised and imagined many decades ago, it will be both a destructive and productive moment in the ongoing becoming of multiple, co-existent pasts and futures emergent through the political materialities of land and water.

---

[92] 'Did Tokwe-Mukosi Dam collapse? *Southern Eye*, 06/06/14; 'Tokwe-Mukosi man-made disaster cannot just be wished away', John Huruva, *Zimbabwe Situation*, 16/05/14; 'The struggle continues for Tokwe-Mukosi families', *Herald*, 06/05/14.
[93] 'The untold story of Tokwe-Mukosi', *Standard*, 24/03/14.

Bibliography

Abraham, D.P. (1966) 'The roles of Chaminuka and the Mhondoro cults in Shona political history' in Stokes, E.T. & Brown, R. (eds) *The Zambesian Past* (Manchester: Manchester University Press).

Adams, W. (1995) *Wasting the Rain: Rivers, People and Planning Africa* (London: University of Minnesota Press).

Agamben, G. tr. Heller-Roazen, D. (1998) [1995] *Homo Sacer: Sovereign Power and Bare Life* (Stanford CA: Stanford University Press).

—. tr. Attell, K. (2005) [2003] *State of Exception* (Chicago IL: Chicago University Press).

Akong'a, J. (1987) 'Rainmaking Rituals: A Comparative Study of Two Kenyan Societies' *African Study Monographs* (Kyoto) 8, 71–85.

Alexander, J. (1995) 'Things fall apart, the centre *can* hold; processes of post-war political change in Zimbabwe's rural areas' in Bhebe N. & Ranger T.O. (eds) *Society in Zimbabwe's Liberation War* (London: James Currey).

—. (2003) '"Squatters", veterans and the state in Zimbabwe' in Hammar et al. 2003, 83–118.

—. (2006) *The Unsettled Land: State-Making and the Politics of Land in Zimbabwe, 1893–2003* (London: James Currey).

—. (2013) 'Militarisation and State Institutions: "Professionals" and "Soldiers" Inside the Zimbabwe Prison Service' *Journal of Southern African Studies* 39, 4.

Alexander, J. & McGregor, J. (2000) 'Wildlife & Politics: CAMPFIRE in Zimbabwe' *Development & Change* 31, 605–27.

Appadurai A. (ed.) (1986) *The Social Life of Things: Commodities in Cultural Perspective* (Cambridge: Cambridge University Press).

—. (1988) 'Putting Hierarchy in its Place' *Cultural Anthropology* 3, 1, 36–49.

Aquina, M. (1965) 'The Tribes in Victoria reserve' *NADA* 9, 2.

Aschwanden, H. (1989) *Karanga Mythology* (Gweru: Mambo Press).

Barnard, A. (2006) 'Kalahari Revisionism' *Social Anthropology* 14, 1, 1–16.

Beinart, W. (2000) 'African History and Environmental History' *African Affairs*, 99, 395, 269–302.

Bender B. (1993) (ed.) *Landscapes, Politics and Perspectives* (Oxford: Berg).

—. (1998) *Stonehenge: Making Space* (Oxford: Berg).

—. (1999) 'Subverting the western gaze: Mapping alternative worlds' in Layton, R. Ucko, P. (eds) *The archaeology and Anthropology of Landscape* (London: Routledge).

—. (2001) 'Introduction' in Bender, B. & Winer, M. (2001) (eds.) *Contested Landscapes: Movement, Exile, Place* (Oxford: Berg).

Bender, M. (2008) 'For More and Better Water, Choose Pipes!' Building Water and the Nation on Kilimanjaro, 1961–1985' *Journal of Southern African Studies* 34, 4, 841–59.

Bent, J.T. (1893) *The Ruined Cities of Mashonaland* (London: Longman's Green).

Bernault, F. (2006) 'Body, Power and Sacrifice in Equatorial Africa' *Journal of African History*, 47, 2, 207–39.

—. (2010) 'Colonial Bones: The 2006 Burial of Savorgnan de Brazza in the Congo' *African Affairs* 109, 436, 367–90.

Berry, S. (2001) *Chiefs know their boundaries* (Oxford: James Currey).

Bertelsen, B.E. (2004) 'It will rain until we are in power: Floods, elections and memory in Mozambique' in Englund, H. & Nyamnjoh, F.B. (eds) *Rights and the Politics of Recognition in Africa* (London: Zed Books), 169–91.

Bond, P. & Manyanya, M. (2003) *Zimbabwe's Plunge: Exhausted Nationalism, Neoliberalism and the Search for Social Justice* (Harare: Weaver Press).

Bourdillon, M.F.C. (1987) *The Shona Peoples* (Gweru: Mambo Press).

Brandt, S. & Hassan, F. (eds) (2006) *Damming the Past: Cultural Heritage Management and Dams in Global Perspective* (Lanham MD: Lexington Books).

Bratton, M. (1978) *Beyond Community Development* (Gwelo: Mambo Press).

—. (1994) 'Land redistribution, 1980–1990' in Rukuni, M. & Eicher, C.K. (eds) *Zimbabwe's Agricultural Revolution* (Harare: University of Zimbabwe Publications).

Bratton, M. & Masunungure, E. (2006) 'Popular Reactions to State Repression: Operation Murambatsvina in Zimbabwe' *African Affairs* 106, 422, 21–45.

Brockington, D. (2002) *Fortress Conservation: The Preservation of the Mkomazi Game Reserve* (Oxford: James Currey).

Brown, B. (2001) 'Thing Theory' *Critical Enquiry* 28, 1, 1–22.

Burke, E.E. (1969) *The Journals of Carl Mauch 1869–1872* (Salisbury: National Archives of Rhodesia).

Buur, L. & Kyed, H.M. (2006) 'Contested sources of authority: re-claiming state sovereignty by formalizing traditional authority in Mozambique' *Development & Change* 37, 4, 847–869.

Campbell, H. (2003) *Reclaiming Zimbabwe: The Exhaustion of the Patriarchal Model of Liberation* (New York: Africa World Press).

Carrithers, M., Candea, M. Sykes, K., Holbraad, M. & Venkatesan, S. (2010) [2008] 'Ontology is just another word for culture' *Critique of Anthropology* 20, 2, 152–200.

Chambati, W. (2011) 'Restructuring of Agrarian labour relations after Fast Track Land Reform in Zimbabwe' *Journal of Peasant Studies,* 38, 5, 1047–68.

Chatterjee, P. (1993) *The Nation and its Fragments: Colonial and Postcolonial Histories* (Princeton NJ: Princeton University Press).

—. (1996) 'Whose imagined community?' in Balakrishnan, G. (ed.) *Mapping the Nation* (London: Verso).

Chaumba, J., Scoones, I. & Wolmer, W. (2003a) 'From *Jambanja* to Planning: The Reassertion of Technocracy in Land Reform in South-Eastern Zimbabwe?' *Journal of Modern African Studies* 41, 4, 533–54.

—. (2003b) 'New politics, new livelihoods: agrarian change in Zimbabwe' *Review of African Political Economy* 30, 98, 585–608.

Chung, F. (1995) 'Education and the War' in Bhebe, N. & Ranger, T.O. (eds) *Society in Zimbabwe's Liberation War* (London: James Currey).

—. (2006) *Re-living the Second Chimurenga: Memories From the Liberation Struggle in Zimbabwe* (Harare: Weaver Press).

Clark, H.A. (1985) *A Policeman's Narrative of Witchcraft and Murder in Zimbabwe* (Kent Town: Veritas).

Cleaver, F. (1995) 'Water as a Weapon: The History of Water Supply Development in Nkayi District, Zimbabwe' *Environment and History* 1, 3, 313–33.

Cliffe, L., Alexander, J. Cousins, B. and Gaidzanwa, R. (2011) 'An Overview of Fast Track Land Reform in Zimbabwe: Editorial Introduction' *Journal of Peasant Studies* 38, 5, 907–38.

Cohen, D.C. & Odhiambo, A.C. (1992) *Burying SM: The Politics of Knowledge and the Sociology of Power in Africa.* (London: James Currey).

Colson, E. (1971) *The Social Consequences of Resettlement: The Impact of the Kariba Resettlement upon the Gwembe Tonga* (Manchester University Press).

Cousins, B. (2006) 'Debating the Politics of Land Occupations' *Journal of Agrarian Change* 6, 4, 584–97.

—. (2009) 'A Reply to Mamdani on the Zimbabwean Land Question' in Jacobs, S. & Mundy, J. (2009) 'Reflections on Mahmood Mamdani's "Lessons of Zimbabwe"' *ACAS Bulletin 82*, http://concernedafricascholars.org/bulletin/issue82, accessed 27/05/13.

Cosgrove, D. & Daniels, S. (eds) (1988) *The Iconography of Landscape: Essays on the Symbolic Representation, Design and Use of Past Environments* (Cambridge: Cambridge University Press).

Daneel, M.L. (1995) (as Mafuranhunzvi Gumbo) *Guerrilla Snuff* (Harare: Baobab Books).

—. (1998) *African Earthkeepers* (Pretoria: Unisa Press).

Das, V. & Poole, D. (2004) *Anthropology in the Margins of the State* (Oxford: James Currey).

de Jong, F. & Rowlands, M. (eds) (2008) *Reclaiming Heritage: Alternative Imaginaries of Memory in West Africa* (Walnut Creek CA: Left Coast Press).

de Saussure, F. (lecturer), Bally, C. & Sechehaye, A. (eds), Harris, R. (tr.) (1983) *Course in General Linguistics* (La Salle IL: Open Court).

de Schlippe, P. (1956) *Shifting Cultivation in Africa* (London: Routledge).

Dean, M. (2001) '"Demonic societies": liberalism, biopolitics and sovereignty' in Hansen, T. & Stepputat, F. (eds) *States of the Imagination: Ethnographic Explorations of the Postcolonial State* (Durham: Duke University Press).

Dekker, M. & Kinsey, B. (2011) 'Contextualising Zimbabwe's Land Reform: Long-Term Observations from the First Generation' *Journal of Peasant Studies*, 38, 5, 995–1019.

Deleuze, G. & Guattari, F. ([1980] 1987) (trans. B.Massumi) *A Thousand Plateaus* (Minneapolis MN: University of Minnesota Press).

Delius, P. & Marks, S. (2012) 'Rethinking South Africa's Past: Essays on History and Archaeology' *Journal of Southern African Studies* 38, 2, 265–80.

Deneen, P.J. (1999) 'The Politics of Hope and Optimism: Rorty, Havel, and the Democratic Faith of John Dewey' *Social Research* 66, 2, 577–609.

Derman, B. & Ferguson, A. (2003) 'Value of Water: Political Ecology and Water reform in Southern Africa' *Human Organisation* 62, 3, 277–88.

Derman, B. & Hellum, A. (2007) 'Land, identity & violence in Zimbabwe' in Derman, B., Odgaard, R. & Sjaastad, E. (eds) *Conflicts over Land & Water in Africa* (Oxford: James Currey).

Derman, B. & Manzungu, E. (2012) 'Zimbabwe's water crises: the importance of environmental governance and a right to water' in Johnston, B. R. (ed.) *Water, Cultural Diversity and Global Environmental Change* (Dordrecht: Springer).

Derman, B. (2003) 'Cultures of Development and Indigenous Knowledge: The Erosion of Traditional Boundaries' *Africa Today* 50, 2, 67–85.

Derrida, J. (tr. Spivak, G.) (1974) *Of Grammatology* (Baltimore: Johns Hopkins University Press).

Dorman, S.R. (2003) 'NGOs and the Constitutional Debate in Zimbabwe: From Inclusion to Exclusion' *Journal of Southern African Studies* 29, 4, 845–63.

Domańska, E. (2006) 'The Return to Things' *Archaeologia Polona* 44, 171–85.

Drinkwater, M. (1989) 'Technical Development and Peasant Impoverishment' *Journal of Southern African Studies*, 15, 2, 287–305

—. (1991) *The State and Agrarian Change in Zimbabwe's Communal Areas* (London: Macmillan).

Duffy, L. (2005) 'Suffering, Shame, and Silence: The Stigma of HIV/AIDS' *Journal of the Association of Nurses in Aids Care*, 16, 1, 13–20.

Duffy, R. (2000) *Killing for Conservation: Wildlife Policy in Zimbabwe* (Oxford: James Currey).

—. (2008) 'Nature crime: in the shadow of conservation' Seminar paper, Centre of African Studies, University of Edinburgh, 29/10/08.

—. (2010) *Nature Crime: How We're Getting Conservation Wrong* (London: Yale University Press).

Duggan, W.R. (1980) 'The Native Land Husbandry Act of 1951 and the Rural African Middle Class of Southern Rhodesia' *African Affairs* 79, 315, 227–40.

Dzingirai, V. (2003) '"CAMPFIRE is not for Ndebele Migrants": The Impact of Excluding Outsiders from CAMPFIRE in the Zambezi Valley, Zimbabwe' *Journal of Southern African Studies* 29, 2, 445–59.

Eastwood, J.H.R. (1996) *After MacDougall* (Triangle: Triangle Ltd).

Edensor, T. (2005) *Industrial Ruins: Space, Aesthetics and Materiality* (London: Berg).

Engelke, M. (2007) *A Problem of Presence: Beyond Scripture in an African Church* (Berkeley: University of California Press).

Englebert, P. (2002) 'Patterns and Theories of traditional Resurgence in tropical Africa' *Mondes en Development* 30, 118–51.

Englund, H. & Nyamnjoh, F. (2004) *The Politics of Recognition* (London: Zed Books).

Evers, S. (2005) 'Trumping the ancestors: the challenges of implementing a land registration system in Madagascar in competing jurisdictions' in Evers, S., Spierenburg, M. & Wells, H. (eds) *Competing Jurisdictions: Settling Land Claims in Africa* (Leiden: Brill).

Fabian, J. (1983) *Time and the Other* (New York: Columbia University Press).

FAO & SAFR, (2000) 'Socio-economic Impact of Small holder Irrigation Development in Zimbabwe' (Harare: FAO).

Ferguson, A. & Derman, B. (1999) 'Water Rights vs Rights to Water: Reflections on Zimbabwe's Water Reforms From a Human Rights Perspective' Paper presented to American Anthropological Association, Chicago IL, available at http://pdf.usaid.gov/pdf_docs/PNACL428.pdf accessed 24/06/13.

Ferguson, J.G. (1999) *Expectations of Modernity: Myths and Meanings of Urban Life on the Zambian Copperbelt* (Berkeley: University of California Press).

—. (2002) 'Of Mimicry and Membership: Africans and the "New World Society"' *Cultural Anthropology* 17, 4, 551–69.

Filippucci, P., Harries, J., Fontein, J. & Krmpotich, K. (2012) 'Encountering the past: unearthing remnants of humans in archaeology and anthropology' in Shankland 2012.

Fisher, J.L. (2010) *Pioneers, Settlers, Aliens, Exiles: The Decolonisation of White Identity in Zimbabwe* (Canberra: Australian National University E Press).

Fontein, J. (2006a) *The Silence of Great Zimbabwe: Contested Landscapes and the Power of Heritage* (London: UCL Press).

—. (2006b) 'Languages of Land, Water and "Tradition" around Lake Mutirikwi in Southern Zimbabwe' *Journal of Modern African Studies*, 44, 2, 223–49.

—. (2006c) 'Shared Legacies of the War: Spirit Mediums and War Veterans in Southern Zimbabwe' *Journal of Religion in Africa* 36, 2, 167–99.

—. (2006d) 'Graves, Water and Chiefs: the articulation of memories and practises of landscape around Lake Mutirikwi' unpublished paper presented at History seminar, University of Zimbabwe, 02/06/06.

—. (2008) 'The Power of Water: Landscape, Water and the State in Southern and Eastern Africa: An Introduction' *Journal of Southern African Studies* 34, 4, 737–56.

—. (2009a) 'Anticipating the Tsunami: Rumours, Planning and the Arbitrary State in Zimbabwe' *Africa* 79, 3, 369–98.

—. (2009b) 'The Politics of the Dead: Living Heritage, Bones and Commemoration in Zimbabwe' *AsaOnline* 2 (available at www.theasa.org/publications/asaonline/articles/asaonline_0102.shtml, accessed 08/09/11).

—. (2009c) '"We Want to Belong to our Roots and we Want to be Modern People": New Farmers, Old Claims around Lake Mutirikwi, Southern Zimbabwe' *African Studies Quarterly* 10, 4, 1–35.

—. (2010) 'Between Tortured Bodies and Resurfacing Bones' *Journal of Material Culture* 15, 4, 423–48.

—. (2011) 'Graves, Ruins & Belonging: Towards an Anthropology of Proximity' *Journal of the Royal Anthropological Institute* 17, 4, 706–27.

—. (2012) 'Precarious Possession' unpublished paper presented at EASA conference, Paris.

—. (2014) 'Re-making the dead, uncertainty and the torque of human materials in northern Zimbabwe' in Stepputtat, F. (ed.) *Governing the Dead* (Manchester: Manchester University Press).

Fradenburg, L. O. (ed.) (1992) *Women and Sovereignty* (Edinburgh: Edinburgh University Press).

Fry, P. (1976) *Spirits of Protest* (Cambridge: Cambridge University Press).

Garbett, K. (1977) 'Disparate regional cults and a unitary field in Zimbabwe' in Werbner, R.P. (ed.) *Regional Cults* (London: Academic Press, 55–92).

—. (1992) 'From Conquerors to Autochthons: *Social Analysis* 31, 7, 12–43.

Gable, E. (2006) 'The Funeral and Modernity in Manjaco' *Cultural Anthropology* 21, 3, 385–415.

Garlake, P. (1973) *Great Zimbabwe* (London: Thames & Hudson).

—. (1983). 'Prehistory and ideology in Zimbabwe', in Peel, J.D.Y. & Ranger, T.O. (eds) *Past and Present in Zimbabwe* (Manchester: Manchester University Press).

Gathercole, P. & Lowenthal, D. (eds.) (1990) *The Politics of the Past* (London: Unwin Hyman).

Gelfand, M. (1959) *Shona Ritual: With Special Reference to the Chaminuka Cult* (Cape Town: Juta)

Gell, A. (1995) 'The Language of the Forest: Landscape and Phonological Iconism in Umeda' in Hirsch & O'Hanlon 1995.

—. (1998) *Art and Agency: An Anthropological Theory* (Oxford: Oxford University Press).

Geschiere P. (2005) 'Funerals and belonging' *African Studies* 48, 2, 45–64.

—. (2009) *The Perils of Belonging: Autochthony, Citizenship and Exclusion in Africa and Europe* (London: Chicago University Press).

Geschiere, P. & Nyamnjoh, F. (2000) 'Capitalism and Autochthony: The Seesaw of Mobility and Belonging' *Public Culture* 12, 2, 423–52.

Geschiere, P. & Jackson, S. (2006) 'Autochthony and the crisis of Citizenship: Democratization, Decentralization, and the Politics of Belonging' *African Studies Review* 49, 2, 1–7.

Gibb, A. & Partners (1948) 'Sabi-Lundi Development' (Salisbury, Government of Rhodesia).

Gibson, J.J. (1979) *The Ecological Approach to Visual Perception* (Boston: Houghton Mifflin).

Gluckman, M. (1958 [1940]) 'The bridge' in *Analysis of a Social Situation in Modern Zululand* (Manchester: Manchester University Press).

Gramsci, Antonio (1971) *Selections from the Prison Notebooks* (New York: International Publishers).

Gulbrandsen, Ø. (2012) *The State and the Social: State Formation in Botswana and its Precolonial and Colonial Genealogies* (Oxford: Berghahn Books).

Guyer, J.I, (1993) 'Wealth in People and Self-Realisation in Equatorial Africa' *Man* 28, 2, 242–65.

—. (1995) 'Wealth in People, Wealth in Things – Introduction' *Journal of African History* 36, 1, 83–90.

Hadzoi, L. (2003) 'Continuity and change in the powers of chiefs c. 1951–2000: case study of Gutu district', unpublished honours dissertation, University of Zimbabwe.

Hall, R.N. (1905) *Great Zimbabwe, Mashonaland, Rhodesia* (London: Methuen).

Hammar, A. (2003) 'The making and unma(s)king of local government' in Hammar et al. 2003.

Hammar, A. & Raftopoulos, B. (2003) 'Introduction' in Hammar et al. 2003

Hammar, A., Raftopoulos B. & Jensen, S. (eds) (2003) *Zimbabwe's Unfinished Business: Rethinking Land, State and Nation in the Context of Crisis.* (Harare: Weaver Press).

Hanlon, J., Manjengwa, J. & Smart, T. (2012) *Zimbabwe Takes Back its Land* (Sterling VA: Kumarian Press).

Hansen, T.B. & Stepputat, F. (eds) (2001) *States of the Imagination: Ethnographic Explorations of the Postcolonial State* (Durham: Duke University Press).

Harley, J.B. (1988) 'Maps, Knowledge and Power' in Cosgrove, D. & Daniels, S. (eds) *The Iconography of Landscape* (Cambridge: Cambridge University Press).

—. (1992a) 'Deconstructing the map' in Barnes, T.J. & Duncan, J.S. (eds) *Writing Worlds: Discourse, Text and Metaphor in the Representation of Landscape* (London: Routledge).

—. (1992b) 'Rereading the Maps of the Columbian encounter' *Annals of the Association of American Geographers* 82, 3, 522–42.

Harries, J. (2010) 'Of Bleeding Skulls and the Postcolonial Uncanny: Bones and the Presence of Nonosabasut and Demasduit" *Journal of Material Culture* 15, 4, 403–21.

Harries, J. & Fontein, J. (2010) 'The Matter of Bones' unpublished manuscript, University of Edinburgh.

Harrison S. (2004) 'Forgetful and memorious landscapes' *Social Anthropology* 12, 2, 135–51.

Hellum, A. & Derman, B. (2004) 'Re-negotiating water and land rights in

Zimbabwe: Some reflections on legal pluralism, identity and power', in Murison, J. Griffiths, A. & King, K. (eds), *Remaking Law in Africa: Transnationalism, Persons and Rights* (Edinburgh, Centre of Africa Studies, 2004) 233–60.

Henare A., Holbraad, M. & Wastell S. (2006) 'Introduction' in Henare A., Holbraad M. & Wastell S. (eds) *Thinking Through Things: Theorising Artefacts Ethnographically* (London: Routledge) 1–31.

Herzfeld, M. (1991) *A Place in History: Social and Monumental Time in a Cretan Town* (Princeton NJ: Princeton University Press).

Hirsch, E. (1995) 'Landscape: between place and space' in Hirsch & O'Hanlon 1995.

Hirsch E. & O'Hanlon, M. (1995) *The Anthropology of Landscape* (Oxford: Oxford University Press).

Hoag, H.J. (2005) 'The Damming of Africa' in Tempelhoff, J.W.N. (ed.), *African Water Histories: Transdisciplinary Discourses* (Vanderbijlpark: North West University).

Hobsbawm, E. & Ranger, T. (1983) *The Invention of Tradition* (Cambridge: Cambridge University Press).

Hodges, L.E. (1975) 'The Living Site of Adam Render' *Arnoldia* 7, 24, 1–9.

Hodges, M. (2008) 'Rethinking Time's Arrow: Bergson, Deleuze and the Anthropology of Time' *Anthropological Theory* 8, 4, 399–429.

Holbraad, M. (2006) 'The power of powder: multiplicity and motion in the divinatory cosmology of Cuban Ifa (or mana, again)' in Henare, A., Holbraad, M. & Wastell, S. (eds) *Thinking Through Things: Theorising Artefacts Ethnographically* (London: Routledge).

—. (2011) 'Can the thing speak?' OAC PRESS, Working Papers Series #7 (London: Open Anthropology Cooperative Press available at http://openanthcoop.net/press/http:/openanthcoop.net/press/wp-content/uploads/2011/01/Holbraad-Can-the-Thing-Speak2.pdf accessed 19/06/13).

Hoogeveen, J.G.M. & Kinsey, B.H. (2001) 'Land reform, Growth and Equity: Emerging evidence from Zimbabwe's Resettlement Programme – A sequel' *Journal of Southern African Studies* 27, 1, 127–36.

Huggan G (1991) 'Decolonising the map: post-colonialism, post-structuralism and the cartographic connection' in Adam, I. & Tiffin, H. (eds) *Past the Last Post: Theorizing Post-Colonialism and Post-Modernism* (London: Harvester Wheatsheaf).

Hughes, D. (2001) 'Water as a Boundary: National Parks, Rivers, and the Politics of Demarcation in Chimanimani, Zimbabwe' in Blatter, J. & Ingram, H.I. (eds) *Reflections on Water: New Approaches to Transboundary Conflicts and Cooperation* (London: The MIT Press).

—. (2006a) 'Whites & Water: How Euro-Africans made Nature at Kariba dam' *Journal of Southern African Studies,* 32, 4, 823–38.

—. (2006b) 'Hydrology of Hope: Farm Dams, Conservation, and Whiteness in Zimbabwe' *American Ethnologist,* 33, 2, 269–87.

—. (2006c) *From Enslavement to Environmentalism* (Seattle WA: University of Washington Press).

—. (2010) *Whiteness in Zimbabwe: Race, Landscape and the Problem of Belonging* (New York: Palgrave Macmillan).

Human Rights Watch (2003) 'Not Eligible: The Politicization of Food in Zimbabwe', 15, 17(A).

Humphrey, C. (1995) 'Chiefly and Shamanist Landscapes in Mongolia' Hirsch & O'Hanlon 1995.

Ingold, T. (1992) 'Culture and the perception of the environment' in Croll, E. & Parkin, D. (eds) *Bush Base, Forest Farm: Culture, Environment, and Development* (London: Routledge).

—. (1993) 'The Temporality of Landscape' *World Archaeology* 25, 2, 152–74.

—. (2000) *The Perception of the Environment* (London : Routledge).

—. (2005) 'Epilogue: Towards a Politics of Dwelling' *Conservation and Society* 3, 2, 501–8.

—. (2007) 'Materials against Materiality' *Archaeological Dialogues* 14, 1, 1–16.

—. (2011) *Being Alive: Essays on Movement, Knowledge and Description* (London: Routledge).

—. (2012a) 'Introduction' in Janowski, M. & Ingold, T. (eds) *Imagining Landscapes: Past, Present and Future* (Farnham: Ashgate).

—. (2012b) 'Dreaming of Dragons: on the imagination of real life', paper presented at Edinburgh University.

Isaacman, A.F & Isaacman, B.S. (2013) *Dams, Displacement, and the Delusion of Development: Cahora Bassa and Its Legacies in Mozambique* (Athens OH: University of Ohio Press).

Jacobs, S. & Mundy, J. (2009) 'Reflections on Mahmood Mamdani's "Lessons of Zimbabwe"' *ACAS Bulletin* 82 (http://concernedafricascholars.org/bulletin/issue82 accessed 27/05/13).

James, D. (2009) 'Burial sites, Informal Rights and Lost Kingdoms: Contesting Land Claims in Mpumalanga, South Africa' *Africa* 79, 2, 228–51.

James, W. (1972) 'The politics of rain control among the Uduk' in Cunnison, I. and James. W. (eds) *Essays in Sudan Ethnography: Presented to Sir Edward Evans-Pritchard* (London: Hurst).

Jedrej, M.C. (1992) 'Rain makers, women, and sovereignty in the Sahel and East Africa' in Fradenburg, L.O. (ed.) *Women and Sovereignty* (Edinburgh: Edinburgh University Press).

Jones, J.L. (2010) '"Nothing is Straight in Zimbabwe": The Rise of the Kukiya-kiya Economy 2000–2008' *Journal of Southern African Studies* 36, 2, 285–300.

Joy, C.L. (2012) *The Politics of Heritage Management in Mali* (Walnut Creek CA: Left Coast Press).

Kamete, A.Y. (2006) 'The Return of the Jettisoned: ZANU-PF's Crack at "Re-urbanising" in Harare' *Journal of Southern African Studies* 32, 2, 255–71.

Kaseke, E, (2006) 'The Revival of *Zunde raMambo* in Zimbabwe' *Vosesa Focus* 2, 1, (www.vosesa.org.za/focus/vol1_no4/index.html?article_3.html~content accessed 29/05/13).

Keane, W. (2003) 'Semiotics and the Social Analysis of Material Things' *Language and Communication* 23, 3–4, 409–25.

—. (2005) 'Signs are not the garb of meaning: on the social analysis of material things' in Miller, D. (ed.) *Materiality* (Durham, NC: Duke University Press).

Kinsey, B. H. (1999) 'Land reform, Growth and equity: Emerging evidence from Zimbabwe's Resettlement Programme' *Journal of Southern African Studies* 25, 2, 173–96.

Knight R. (1999) 'We are tired of promises, local politics and the fight for land in Zimbabwe' unpublished BA Development Studies dissertation, Brown University.

Kopytoff, I. (1986) 'The Cultural Biography of things: commoditization as process' in Appadurai A. (ed.) (1986) *The Social Life of Things: Commodities in Cultural Perspective* (Cambridge: Cambridge University press).

Kriger, N. (1992) *Zimbabwe's Guerrilla War: Peasant Voices* (Cambridge: Cambridge University Press).

—. (1995) 'The politics of creating national heroes' in Bhebe, N. & Ranger, T.O. (eds) *Soldiers in Zimbabwe's Liberation War* (London: James Currey).

—. (2003) *Guerrilla Veterans in Post-War Zimbabwe: Symbolic and Violent Politics, 1980–1987* (Cambridge: Cambridge University Press).

—. (2006) 'From Patriotic Memories to "Patriotic History" in Zimbabwe 1990–2005' *Third World Quarterly* 27, 6, 1151–69.

—. (2012) 'ZANU PF politics under Zimbabwe's "Power-Sharing' Government" *Journal of Contemporary African Studies* 30, 1, 11–26.

Krige, E.J. & Krige, J.D. (1943) *The Realm of a Rain-Queen* (Oxford: Oxford University Press).

Krmpotich, C., Fontein, J. & Harries, J. (2010) 'The substance of bones: the emotive materiality and affective presence of human remains' *Journal of Material Culture* 15, 4, 423–48.

Kuchler, S. (1993) 'Landscape as memory: The mapping process and its representation in a Melanesian society' in Bender, B. (ed.) *Landscape: Politics and Perspectives* (Oxford: Berg).

—. (1999) 'The place of memory' in Forty, A. & Kuchler, S. (eds) *The Art of Forgetting* (Oxford: Berg).

Kuklick, H. (1991) 'Contested monuments: the politics of archaeology in southern Africa' in Stocker, G. W. (ed.) *Colonial Situations: Essays on the Contextualization of Ethnographic Knowledge* (London: University of Wisconsin Press).

Kuper, A. (1982) 'Lineage Theory: A Critical Retrospect' *Annual Review of Anthropology* 11, 71–95.

—. (2003) 'The return of the native' *Current Anthropology* 44, 3, 389–402.

Lambek, M. (2002a) 'Nuriaty, the saint and the sultan: virtuous subject and subjective virtuoso of the postmodern colony' in Werbner, R. (ed.) *Postcolonial Subjectivities in Africa* (London: Zed Books).

—. (2002b) *The Weight of the Past: Living with History in Mahajanga, Madagascar* (New York: Palgrave Macmillan).

Lan, D. (1985) *Guns & Rain: Guerrillas & Spirit Mediums in Zimbabwe* (London: James Currey).

Landau, P. (2010) *Popular Politics in the History of South Africa 1400–1948* (Cambridge: Cambridge University Press).

Latham, J. (2002) 'A review of the water reform process in Zimbabwe: the case of the Manyame Catchment Council' in Manzungu, E. (ed.) *The Process and Dynamics of Catchment Management in Zimbabwe* (Harare: Save Africa Publications 21–43).

Latour, B. (1999) *Pandora's Hope: Essays on the Reality of Science Studies* (Cambridge: Harvard University press).

Layton, R. & Ucko, P. (eds.) (1999) *The Archaeology and Anthropology of Landscape: Heritage, Museums and Education* (London: Routledge).

Li, T.M. (2000) 'Articulating Indigenous Identity in Indonesia: Resource Politics and the Tribal Slot' *Comparative Studies in Society and History* 42, 1, 149–79.

Lonsdale, J. (1992) 'African pasts in Africa's Future', in Berman, B. & Lonsdale, J. *Unhappy Valley: Conflict in Kenya & Africa,* (London: James Currey) 203–23.

Low, D.A. & Lonsdale, J. (1976) 'Introduction: Towards the new order, 1945–1963' in Low, D.A. & Lonsdale J. (eds) *History of East Africa* (Oxford: Oxford University Press, 1976) 12–16.

Lowenthal, D. (1998) *The Heritage Crusade and the Spoils of History* (Cambridge: Cambridge University Press).

Mabedza, C.M. & Mawere, M. (2012) 'Dambo Cultivation in Zimbabwe' *Journal of Sustainable Development in Africa* 14, 5, 39–53.

Mafu, H. (1995) 'The 1991–92 Zimbabwean Drought and Some Religious Reactions' *Journal of Religion in Africa* 25, 3, 208–308.

Mamdani, M. (1996) *Citizen & Subject: Contemporary Africa & the Legacy of Late Colonialism* (London: James Currey).

—. (2008) 'Lessons of Zimbabwe' *London Review of Books* 30, 23, 17–21.

Manzungu, E. (2003) 'Global rhetoric and local realities: The case of Zimbabwe's water reform' in Chikowore, G., Manzungu, E., Mushayavanhu, D. and Shoko, D. (eds) *Managing Common Property in an Age of Globalisation: Zimbabwean Experience* (Harare: Weaver Press) 31–44.

—. (2004a) 'Environmental impacts of Fast-track land reform programme: a livelihoods perspective' in D. Harold-Barry (ed.) *Zimbabwe: The Past is the Future – Rethinking Land, State and Nation in the Context of Crisis* (Harare: Weaver Press).

—. (2004b) 'Water For All: Improving Water Resource Governance in Southern Africa' *Gatekeeper Series* 113.

Manzungu, E. & Kujinga, K. (2002) 'The Theory and Practice of Governance of Water Resources in Zimbabwe' *Zambezia* 29, 2, 191–212.

Mapira, J. (2011) 'Urban Governance and Mismanagement: An Environmental Crisis in Zimbabwe' *Journal of Sustainable Development in Africa* 13, 6, 258–267.

Marongwe N. (2003) 'Farm occupations and occupiers in the new politics of land' in Hammar et al. 2003, 179–182.

—. (2007) 'Redistributive land reform and poverty reduction in Zimbabwe' unpublished working paper for 'Livelihoods after land reform' project.

—. (2011) 'Who was Allocated Fast Track Land, and What did They do with it? Selection of A2 Farmers in Goromonzi District, Zimbabwe and its Impacts on Agricultural Production' *Journal of Peasant Studies* 38, 5, 1069–92.

Mason, P. (2009) 'Zimbabwe Experiences the Worst Epidemic of Cholera in Africa' *Journal of Infection in Developing Countries* available at http://jidc.org/index.php/journal/article/view/19755746 accessed: 21/05/13.

Masunga, B. Masocha, M. Kusangaya, S. (2004) 'Sustainability of Co-operative Fishing in Lake Mutirikwi' *Geographical Education Magazine* 27, 1–2, 60–69.

Matenga, E. (1998) *The Soapstone Birds of Zimbabwe* (Harare: African Publishing Group).

Matondi, P. (2012) *Zimbabwe's Fast Track Land Reform* (New York: Zed Books).

Mauss M. (tr. Cunnison, I.) (1954 [1923]) *The Gift: Forms and Functions of Exchange in Archaic Societies* (London: Cohen & West).

Mavedzenge, B.Z., Mahenehene, J., Murimbarimba, F., Scoones, I., & Wolmer, W. (2008), 'The dynamics of Real Markets: Cattle in Southern Zimbabwe following Land Reform' *Development And Change* 39, 4, 613–39.

Mawere, A. & Wilson, K. (1995) 'Socio-Religious Movements, the State and Community Change: Some Reflections on the Ambuya Juliana Cult of Southern Zimbabwe' *Journal of Religion in Africa* 25, 3, 252–87.

Maxwell, D. (1999) *Christians and Chiefs in Zimbabwe: A Social History of the Hwesa People 1870s–1990s* (Edinburgh: Edinburgh University Press).

Mazarire, G.C. (2003) 'Changing Landscape and Oral Memory in South-Central

Zimbabwe: Towards a Historical Geography of Chishanga c.1850–1990' *Journal of Southern African Studies* 29, 3, 701–15.

—.   (2008) 'The Chishanga Waters have their Owners': Water Politics and Development in Southern Zimbabwe' *Journal of Southern African Studies*, 34, 4, 757–84.

—.   (2010) 'A Social and Political History of Chishanga: South-Central Zimbabwe c. 1750–2000' unpublished DPhil thesis, University of Zimbabwe.

—.   (2013a) 'The *Gadzingo*: towards a Karanga expansion matrix in 18th and 19th century southern Zimbabwe' *Critical African Studies* 5.1, 4–16.

—.   (2013b) 'ZANU-PF and the Government of National Unity' in Raftopoulos 2013.

Mbembe, J.A. (2001) *On the Postcolony* (London: University of California Press).

—.   (2003) 'Necropolitics' *Public Culture* 15, 1, 11–40.

McCully, P. (1996) *Silenced Rivers: The Ecology and Politics of Large Dams* (London: Zed Books).

McGregor, J. (1995a) 'Introduction' *Environment and History*, 1, 3, 253–55.

—.   (1995b) 'Conservation, Control and Ecological Change: The politics and ecology of Colonial Conservation in Shurugwi, Zimbabwe' *Environment and History* 1, 3, 257–80.

—.   (2002) 'The Politics of Disruption: War Veterans and the Local State in Zimbabwe' *African Affairs* 101, 402, 9–37.

—.   (2005) 'The Social Life of Ruins: Sites of Memory and the Politics of a Zimbabwean Periphery' *Journal of Historical Geography* 31, 2, 316–37.

—.   (2008) 'Patrolling Kariba's Waters: State Authority, Fishing and the Border Economy' *Journal of Southern African Studies* 34, 4, 861–79.

—.   (2009) *Crossing the Zambezi: The Politics of Landscape on a Central African Frontier* (Oxford: James Currey).

—.   (2011) 'Rethinking the Boundaries of the Nation: Histories of Cross Border Mobility and Zimbabwe's New "Diaspora"' *Critical African Studies* 4, 6, 47–68.

McGregor, J. & Primorac, R. (eds) (2010) *Zimbabwe's New Diaspora: Displacement and the Cultural Politics of Survival* (Oxford: Berghahn).

McGregor, J. & Schumaker, L. (2006) 'Heritage in Southern Africa: Imagining and Marketing Public Culture and History' *Journal of Southern African Studies* 32, 4, 649–665.

McKittrick, M. (2008) 'Landscapes of Power: Ownership and Identity on the Middle Kavango River, Namibia' *Journal of Southern African Studies* 34, 4, 785–802.

McLaughlin, J. (1995). 'Avila Mission: a turning point in church relations with the state and the liberation forces' in Bhebe, N. & Ranger, T.O. (1995) *Society in Zimbabwe's Liberation War* (London: James Currey) 90–101.

Mercer, C. & Page, B. (2010) 'African Home Associations in Britain: Between Political Belonging and Moral Conviviality' *African Diaspora* 3, 1, 110–30.

Mercer, C. Page, B. & Evans, M. (2008) *Development and the African Diaspora* (London: Zed Books).

Meskill, L. (2012) *The Nature of Heritage: The New South Africa* (Chichester: Wiley-Blackwell).

Mhanda, W. (2011) *Dzino: Memories of a Freedom Fighter* (Harare: Weaver Press).

Miller D. (2005) 'Materiality: an introduction' in Miller D. (ed.) *Materiality* (London: Duke University Press) 1–50.

Mlambo, A.S. & Pangeti, E.S. (1996). *The Political Economy of the Sugar Industry in Zimbabwe, 1920–1990* (Harare: University of Zimbabwe Publications).

Moore D. (1998) 'Subaltern Struggles and the Politics of Place: Re-mapping Resistance in Zimbabwe's Eastern Highlands' *Cultural Anthropology* 13, 3, 344–81.

—. (2005) *Suffering for Territory: Race, Place and Power in Zimbabwe* (London: Duke University Press).

—. (2012) 'Progress, Power, and Violent Accumulation in Zimbabwe' *Journal of Contemporary African Studies* 30, 1, 1–9.

Morphy H. (1993) 'Colonialism, history and the construction of place: the politics of landscape in Northern Australia' in Bender, B. (ed.) *Landscape: Politics and Perspectives* (Oxford: Berg).

—. (1995) 'Landscape and the reproduction of the ancestral past' in Hirsch & O'Hanlon 1995.

Mosse, D. (2003) *The Rule of Water: Statecraft, Ecology and Collective Action in South India* (New Delhi: Oxford University Press).

—. (2008) 'Epilogue: The Cultural Politics of Water: A Comparative Perspective' *Journal of Southern African Studies* 34,4, Special Issue: Abstract 'The Power of Water: Landscape, Water and the State, *Southern and Eastern Africa*, 939–48.

Moyo S. (2001) 'The Land Occupation Movement and Democratisation in Zimbabwe: Contradictions of Neoliberalism' *Millennium – Journal of International Studies* 30, 2, 311–30.

—. (2011) 'Changing Agrarian Relations after Redistributive Land Reform in Zimbabwe' in *Journal of Peasant Studies* 38, 5, 939–66.

Moyo, S. & Yeros, P. (2005) 'Land occupations and land reform in Zimbabwe: Towards the national democratic revolution' in Moyo, S. & Yeros, P. (eds) *Reclaiming the Land: The Resurgence of Rural Movements in Africa, Asia and Latin America* (London: Zed Books).

Moyo, S., Chambati, W., Murisa, T., Siziba, D., Dangwa, C., Mujeyo, K. & Nyoni, N. (2009) *Fast Track Land Reform Baseline Survey in Zimbabwe: Trends and Tendencies, 2005/06* (Harare: African Institute for Agrarian Studies).

Mtetwa, R.M.G. (1976) 'The Political and Economic History of the Duma people of South-eastern Rhodesia, from early 18th century to 1945', unpublished PhD thesis, University of Rhodesia.

Mubvumba, S. (2005) 'The Dilemma of Governance: Government policy of traditional authority in resettlement areas 1980–2004 – the case of Guruve', unpublished BA dissertation, Department of History, University of Zimbabwe.

Mujere, J. (2010) 'Land, Graves and Belonging: land reform and the politics of belonging in newly resettled farms in Gutu, 2000–2009'. *Livelihoods after Land Reform in Zimbabwe* Working Paper 9 (South Africa: PLAAS).

—. (2011) 'Land, graves and belonging: land reform and the politics of belonging in newly resettled farms in Gutu, 2000–2009' *Journal of Peasant Studies* 38, 5, 1123–44.

—. (2012) 'Autochthons, Strangers, Modernising Educationists, and Progressive Farmers: Basotho struggles for belonging in Zimbabwe 1930s–2008' PhD thesis, University of Edinburgh.

—. (2013) 'Family Farms, Graves, and Belonging: Migrations and the Politics of Belonging among Basotho in Colonial Zimbabwe' *Conserveries mémorielles* 13.

Mukamuri, B. B. (1995) 'Local Environmental Conservation Strategies' *Environment and History* 1, 3, 297–311.

Murisa, T. (2011) 'Local farmer groups and collective action within fast track land reform in Zimbabwe' *Journal of Peasant Studies* 38:5, 1145–66.

Musemwa, M. (2006). 'Disciplining a "Dissident" City: Hydropolitics in the City of Bulawayo, Matabeleland, Zimbabwe, 1980–1994' *Journal of Southern African Studies*, 32, 2, 239–254.

—. (2008) 'The Politics of Water in Post-colonial Zimbabwe, 1980–2007' paper presented to African Studies Centre, Leiden, June).

Mutupo, P. (2011) 'Women's struggles to access and control land and livelihoods after fast track land reform in Mwenezi district, Zimbabwe' *Journal of Peasant Studies* 38, 5, 1021–46.

Muzondidya, J. (2007) '*Jambanja*: Ideological Ambiguities in the Politics of Land and Resource Ownership in Zimbabwe' *Journal of Southern African Studies* 33, 2, 325–41.

Navaro-Yashin, Y. (2002) *Faces of the State: Secularism and Public Life in Turkey* (Princeton University Press).

—. (2009) 'Affective Spaces, Melancholic Objects: Ruination and the Production of Anthropological Knowledge' *Journal of the Royal Anthropological Institute* 15, 1, 1–18.

—. (2012) *The Make-Believe Space: Affective Geography in a Postwar Polity* (Durham NC: Duke University Press).

Ncube, G.T. (2011) 'Crisis of Communal Leadership: Post-colonial Local Government Reform and Administrative Conflict with Traditional Authorities in the Communal Areas of Zimbabwe, 1980–2008' *African Journal of History and Culture* 3, 6, 89–95.

Ndoro, W. (2001) *Your monument, our shrine: The preservation of Great Zimbabwe, Studies in African Archaeology 19* (Uppsala: Department of Archaeology and Ancient History, Uppsala University).

Ngara, J. (1978) 'The Zimbabwe Revolution and the Internal Settlement' *Marxism Today*, November.

Nielsen, M. (2011) 'Futures Within: Reversible time and House-building in Maputo, Mozambique' *Anthropological Theory* 11, 4, 397–423.

Nkomo, J. (1984) *Nkomo: The Story of My Life* (London: Methuen).

Nugent P. (2008) 'Putting the History Back into Ethnicity' *Comparative Studies in Society and History* 50, 4, 920–48.

Nyathi, L. (2003) 'The Matopos Shrines: A Comparative Study of the Dula, Njelele and Zhame Shrines' unpublished History Honours Dissertation, University of Zimbabwe.

O'Gorman, E. (2011) *The Front Line Runs through Every Woman* (Woodbridge: James Currey).

Oomen, B.M. (2002) 'Chiefs! Law, power and Culture in Contemporary South Africa' PhD Dissertation, University of Leiden, Netherlands.

Packard, R. (1981) Chiefship and Cosmology: An Historical Study of Political Competition (Bloomington IN: Indiana University Press).

Palmer, R. (1977) *Land and Racial Domination in Southern Rhodesia* (London: Heinemann).

—. (1990) 'Land Reform In Zimbabwe, 1980–1990' *African Affairs* 89, 355, 163–81.

Peirce, C.S. (1955) *Philosophical Writings of Peirce* (New York: Dover).

Perman, T. (2011) 'Awakening Spirits: The Ontology of Spirit, Self, and Society in Ndau Spirit Possession Practices in Zimbabwe' *Journal of Religion in Africa*, 41, 1, 59–92.

Phimister, I. (1993) 'Rethinking the Reserves: Southern Rhodesia's Land Husbandry Act Reviewed' *Journal of Southern African Studies* 19, 2, 225–39.
—. (2012) 'Narratives of progress: Zimbabwean historiography and the end of history' *Journal of Contemporary African Studies,* 30, 1, 27–34.
Pikirayi, I. (2011) *Tradition, Archaeological Heritage Protection and Communities in the Limpopo province of South Africa* (Ethiopia: OSSREA).
Pilossof, R. (2012) *The Unbearable Whiteness of Being: Farmers' Voices from Zimbabwe* (Harare: Weaver Press).
—. (2013) 'Reinventing Significance: Reflections on Recent Whiteness Studies in Zimbabwe' unpublished manuscript, ECAS, Lisbon (June).
Pinney, C. (2005) 'Things happen: Or, from which moment does that object come?' in D. Miller, (ed.) *Materiality* (Durham, NC: Duke University Press) 256–72.
Potts, D. (2006) '"Restoring order"? Operation Murambatsvina and the urban crisis in Zimbabwe' *Journal of Southern African Studies* 32, 2, 272–91.
Posel, D. & Gupta, P. (2009) 'The life of the Corpse: Framing Reflections and Questions' *African Studies* 68, 3, 299–309
Povinelli, E.A. (2001) 'Radical worlds: The Anthropology of Incommensurability and Inconceivability' *Annual Review of Anthropology* 30, 319–34.
Primorac, R. (2005) 'History as Fiction: The "Third Chimurenga" and Zimbabwean Popular Novels' *BZS Newsletter* (May).
Pwiti, G. (1996) 'Let the Ancestors Rest in Peace? New Challenges for Cultural Heritage Management in Zimbabwe' *Conservation and Management of Archaeological Sites* 1, 3, 151–60.
Raftopoulos, B. (2003) 'The state in crisis: Authoritarian nationalism, selective citizenship and distortions of democracy in Zimbabwe' in Hammar et al. 2003.
—. (2007) 'Nation, Race and History in Zimbabwe' in Dorman, S., Hammett, D. & Nugent, P. (eds) *Making Nations, Creating Strangers: States and Citizenship in Africa* (Leiden: Brill) 181–194.
—. (ed.) (2013) *The Hard Road to Reform: The Politics of Zimbabwe's Global Political Agreement* (Harare: Weaver Press).
Raftopoulos, B. & Mlambo, A. (2009) 'Introduction: in Raftopoulos, B. and Mlambo, A. (eds.) *Becoming Zimbabwe: A History from the Pre-colonial Period to 2008* (Harare: Weaver Press).
Ranger, T.O. (1967) *Revolt in Southern Rhodesia, 1896–97* (London: Heinemann).
—. (1982a) 'Tradition and Travesty: Chiefs and the Administration in Makoni District, Zimbabwe, 1960–80', *Africa* 52, 3, 20–41.
—. (1982b) 'The Death of Chaminuka: Spirit Mediums, Nationalism and the Guerrilla War in Zimbabwe' *African Affairs* 81, 324, 349–69.
—. (1983) 'The Invention of Tradition in Colonial Africa' in Hobsbawm, E. & Ranger, T.O. (eds.) *The Invention of Tradition* (Cambridge: Cambridge University Press).
—. (1985) *Peasant Consciousness and Guerrilla War in Zimbabwe* (California: University of California Press).
—. (1999) *Voices from the Rocks: Nature, Culture & History in the Matopos Hills* (Oxford: James Currey).
—. (2003) 'Women and Environment in African Religion: The Case of Zimbabwe' in Beinart, W. & McGregor J. (eds), *Social History & African Environments* (Oxford: James Currey).
—. (2004) 'Historiography, Patriotic History and the History of the Nation: The Struggle over the Past in Zimbabwe' *Journal of Southern African Studies* 30, 2, 215–34.

—. (2007) 'City Versus State in Zimbabwe: Colonial Antecedents of the Current Crisis' *Journal of Eastern African Studies* 1, 2, 161–92.

—. (2010a) 'From Spirit to Body: Approaches to Violence and Memory in Zimbabwe' Lecture University of Illinois (14/10/10).

—. (2010b) 'Contested Heritage in Zimbabwe' Paper presented at conference 'Shaping the Heritage Landscape: Perspectives from East and Southern Africa', BIEA Nairobi (05/05/10).

—. (2010c) *Bulawayo Burning: The Social History of a Southern African City, 1893–1960* (Woodbridge: James Currey).

—. (2011a) 'Zimbabwean Diamonds' *Africa* 81, 4, 649–61.

—. (2011b) 'The Politics of Zimbabwean Christianity: Histories of interaction with a 'dignified' African spirituality' *BZS Zimbabwe Review* 11,1.

—. (2012) *Malindidzimu: A Guide to the People and Events Associated with the "View of the World", Matopos* (Bulawayo: Khami Press).

—. (2013a) *Writing Revolt: An Engagement with African Nationalism 1957–67* (Woodbridge: James Currey).

—. (2013b) 'Caves in Black and White: The Case of Zimbabwe', in Moyes, H. (ed.) *Sacred Darkness: A Global Perspective on the Ritual Use of Caves* (Boulder CO: University of Colorado Press).

Ranger, T.O. & Ncube, M. (1995) 'Religion in guerrilla war: the case of southern Matabeleland' in Bhebe, N. & Ranger, T.O. (eds) *Society in Zimbabwe's Liberation War* (London: James Currey).

Rennie, J.K. (1979) 'From Zimbabwe to a colonial chieftancy: four transformations of the Musikavanhu territorial cult in Rhodesia' in Schoffeleers, J.M. (ed.) *Guardians of the Land: Essays on Central African Territorial Cults* (Gweru: Mambo Press).

Reynolds, P. (1996) *Traditional healers and childhood in Zimbabwe* (Athens OH: Ohio University Press).

Richardson, C.J. (2007) 'How Much did Droughts Matter? Linking Rainfall and GDP Growth in Zimbabwe' *African Affairs* 106, 424, 463–78.

Rukuni, M. & Eicher ,C.K. (eds) (1994) *Zimbabwe's Agricultural Revolution* (Harare: University of Zimbabwe Publications).

Runia, E. (2006) 'Presence' *History and Theory* 45, 1, 1–29.

Rutherford, B. (2001) *Working on the Margins: Black Workers, White Farmers in Post Colonial Zimbabwe* (Harare: Weaver Press).

—. (2003) 'Belonging to the Farm(er): Farm workers, Farmers, and the shifting Politics of Citizenship' in Hammar et al. 2003.

—. (2008) 'Conditional Belonging: Farm Workers and the Cultural Politics of Recognition in Zimbabwe' *Development and Change* 39, 1, 73–99.

Sachikonye, L. (2011) *When a State Turns on its Citizens* (Harare: Weaver Press).

Sadomba W. Z. (2008) 'War Veterans in Zimbabwe's Land Occupations' PhD thesis Wageningen University.

—. (2011) *War Veterans in Zimbabwe's Revolution* (Woodbridge: James Currey).

Sadomba, W.Z. & Andrew, N. (2006) 'Challenging the Limits of the State's Market-based Land Resettlement Programme in Zimbabwe: Paper presented at Conference *Land, Poverty, Social Justice & Development* (ISS the Hague, Netherlands 9–14/01/06).

Sanders, T. (2008) *Beyond Bodies: Rainmaking and Sense Making in Tanzania* (Toronto : University of Toronto Press).

Saunders, C. (1977) *Murray MacDougall and the Story of Triangle* (Bulawayo: Triangle Limited).

—. (1989) (2nd edn) *Murray MacDougall and The Story of Triangle* (Bulawayo: Triangle Limited).

Sayce, K. (1978) *A Town called Victoria* (Salisbury: Books of Rhodesia).

Scarnecchia, T. (2008) *The Urban Roots of Democracy and Political Violence in Zimbabwe* (University of Rochester Press).

Schoffeleers, J.M. (ed.) (1979) *Guardians of the Land: Essays on Central African Territorial Cults* (Gweru: Mambo Press).

Schumaker, L. (2008) 'Slimes and Death-Dealing Dambos: Water, Industry and the Garden City on Zambia's Copperbelt' *Journal of Southern African Studies* 34, 4, 823–40.

Scoones, I. (1997) 'Landscapes, Fields and Soils: Understanding the History of Soil Fertility Management in Southern Zimbabwe' *Journal of Southern African Studies* 23, 4, 615–34.

—. (2008) 'A New Start for Zimbabwe?' 15/09/08 www.lalr.org.za accessed 29/05/13.

—. (2014) 'Dams, Flooding and Displacement: The Tokwe Mukorsi Dam' 17/03/14, http://zimbabweland.wordpress.com accessed 25/08/14.

Scoones, I. & Cousins, B. (1991) *Contested Terrains: The Struggle for Control over Dambo in Zimbabwe* (London: IIED Drylands Programme).

Scoones, I., Marongwe, N., Mavedzenge, B., Mahenehene, J., Murimbarimba, F. & Sukume C. (2010) *Zimbabwe's Land Reform: Myths and Realities* (Oxford: James Currey).

Scoones, I., Marongwe, N., Mavedzenge, B., Murimbarimba, F., Mahenehene, J., Sukume, C. (2011) 'Zimbabwe's land reform: challenging the myths' *Journal of Peasant Studies* 38, 5, 967–93.

Scott M. W. (2007) *The Severed Snake: Matrilineages, Making Place, and a Melanesian Christianity in Southeast Solomon Islands* (Michigan NC: Carolina Academy Press).

Seligman, C.G. & Seligman, B.Z. (1932) *Pagan Tribes of the Nilotic Sudan* (London: Routledge).

Shankland, D. (ed.) *Archaeology and Anthropology: Past, Present and Future* (ASA Monographs 48, London: Berg).

Shipton, P. (2009) *Mortgaging the Ancestors: Ideologies of Attachment in Africa* (London: Yale University Press).

Shoko, T. (2007) *Karanga Indigenous Religion in Zimbabwe: Health and Well-being* (Aldershot: Ashgate).

Shumba, E., Roberntz, P. & Kuona, M. (2011) *Assessment of Sugarcane Outgrower Schemes for Biofuel Production in Zambia and Zimbabwe* (Harare: WWF-World Wide Fund For Nature).

Shutt, A.K. (1997) 'Purchase Area Farmers and the Middle Class of Southern Rhodesia, c. 1931–1952' *International Journal of African Historical Studies* 30, 3, 555–81.

Sithole, B., Campbell, B., Doré, D. & Kozanayi, W. (2003) 'Narratives on Land: State–Peasant Relations over Fast Track Land Reform in Zimbabwe' *African Studies Quarterly* 7, 2–3, 81–95 (available at http://asq.africa.ufl.edu/sithole_fall03 accessed 02/02/15).

Sithole, M. (1979) (1st edn) *Zimbabwe: Struggles within the Struggle* (Harare: Rujeko Publishers).

Southall, A. (1953) *Alur Society: A Study in Processes and Types of Domination* (Cambridge: Heffer).

Spear, T. (2003) 'Neo-Traditionalism and the Limits of Invention in British Colonial Africa' *Journal of African History* 44, 1, 3–27.

Spierenburg, M.J. (2004) *Strangers, Spirits and Land Reforms: Conflicts about Land in Dande, Northern Zimbabwe* (Leiden: Brill).

—. (2011) 'The Politics of the Liminal and the Liminoid in Transfrontier Conservation in Southern Africa' *Anthropology Southern Africa* 34 (1–2), 82–89.

Stoler, A.L. (2008) 'Imperial Debris: Reflections on Ruins and Ruination' *Cultural Anthropology* 23, 2, 191–219.

Strang, V. (2004) *The Meaning of Water* (Oxford: Berg).

Tekere, E.Z. (2007) *A Lifetime of Struggle* (Harare: Sapes).

Thebe, V. (2012) '"New Realities" and Tenure Reforms: Land-use in Worker-Peasant Communities of South-western Zimbabwe (1940s–2006)' *Journal of Contemporary African Studies* 30, 1, 99–117.

Tilley, C. (2006) 'Introduction: Identity, Place, Landscape and Heritage' *Journal of Material Culture* 11, 1–2, 7–32.

Tischler, J. (2013) *Light and Power for a Multiracial Nation: The Kariba Dam Scheme in the Central African Federation* (New York: Palgrave Macmillan).

Tsikata, D. (2006) *Living in the Shadow of Large Dams: Long Term Responses of Downstream and Lakeside Communities of Ghana Volta River Project* (Leiden: Brill).

Tsing, A. (1994) 'From the Margins' *Cultural Anthropology* 9, 3, 279–97.

Turner, V. (1969) *The Ritual Process: Structure and Anti-structure* (Chicago IL: Aldine).

Ucko, P.J. (1994) 'Museums and sites: cultures of the past within education – Zimbabwe, some ten years on' in Stone, P.G. & Molyneaux, B.L. (eds) *The Presented Past: Heritage, Museums and Education* (London: Routledge).

UNAIDS/UNICEF/WHO (2004) 'Zimbabwe: Epidemiological Fact Sheets on HIV/AIDS and Sexually Transmitted Infections 2004 Update' Geneva available at http://data.unaids.org/publications/Fact-Sheets01/zimbabwe_en.pdf accessed 16/05/13.

Uusihakala, K. (2008) *Memory Meanders: Place, Home and Commemoration in an Ex-Rhodesian Diaspora Community* (Helsinki: University of Helsinki).

Vambe, M. (ed.) (2008) *The Hidden Dimensions of Operation Murambatsvina in Zimbabwe* (Harare: Weaver Press).

van der Merwe, W.J. (1953) 'The Day Star Arises in Mashonaland, Morgenster' Lovedale Press.

van Gennep, A. (1960 [1909]) *The Rites of Passage* (Chicago: University of Chicago Press).

Vijfhuizen, C. (1997) 'Rain-making, Political Conflicts and Gender Images: A Case from Mutema Chieftaincy in Zimbabwe' *Zambezia*, 24, 1, 31–49.

Viveiros de Castro, E. (1998) 'Cosmological Deixis and Amerindian Perspectivism' *Journal of the Royal Anthropological Institute* 4, 3, 469–88.

—. (2003) 'And' *Manchester papers in social anthropology* 7 (available at http://nansi.abaetenet.net/abaetextos/anthropology-and-science-e-viveiros-de-castro accessed 08/09/11.

von Schnitzler, A. (2008). 'Citizenship Prepaid: Water, Calculability, and Techno-Politics in South Africa' *Journal of Southern African Studies* 34, 4, 899–918.

Weinrich, A.K.H. (1971) *Chiefs and Councils in Rhodesia: Transition from Patriarchal to Bureaucratic Power* (London: Heinemann).

—. (1975) *African farmers in Rhodesia: Old and New Peasant Communities in Karangaland* (London: Oxford University Press).

Werbner, R.P. (1989) 'Regional cult of God above: achieving and defending the macrocosm' in Werbner, R.P. (ed.) *Ritual Passage, Sacred Journey: The*

Process and Organization of Religious Movement (Washington DC: Smithsonian).

—. (1991) *Tears of the Dead: The Social Biography of an African Family.* (Edinburgh: Edinburgh University Press).

—. (1995) 'In memory: a heritage of war in south-western Zimbabwe' in Bhebe, N. & Ranger, T.O. (eds) *Society in Zimbabwe's Liberation War'* (Oxford: James Currey) 192–205.

—. (1998) 'Smoke from the barrel of a gun: postwars of the dead, memory and reinscription in Zimbabwe' in Werbner, R.P. (ed.) *Memory and the Postcolony: African Anthropology and the Critique of Power* (London: Zed Books).

—. (1999) 'The reach of the postcolonial state: development, empowerment/ disempowerment and technocracy' in Cheater, A. (ed.) *The Anthropology of Power: Empowerment and Disempowerment in Changing Structures* (London: Routledge).

—. (2008) 'Ask Max' *The Social Ant* 1, 3, 2–3.

Williams, R. (1977) *Marxism and Literature* (Oxford: Oxford University Press).

Wilson, K.B. (1995) '"Water used to be Scattered in the Landscape" Local Understandings of Soil Erosion and Land Use Planning in Southern Zimbabwe' Special Issue on Zimbabwe, *Environment and History* 1, 3, 281–96.

Wittfogel, K.A. (1957) *Oriental Despotism: A Comparative Study of Total Power* (Yale University Press).

Wolmer, W. (2003) 'Transboundary Conservation: The Politics of Ecological Integrity in the Great Limpopo Transfrontier Park' *Journal of Southern African Studies* 29, 1, 261–78.

—. (2007) *From Wilderness Vision to Farm Invasions: Conservation & Development in Zimbabwe's South-east Lowveld* (Oxford: James Currey).

Worby, E. (1994) 'Maps, Names and Ethnic Games: The Epistemology and Iconography of Colonial Power in Northwestern Zimbabwe' *Journal of Southern African Studies* 20, 3, 371–93.

—. (1998) 'Tyranny, Parody, and Ethnic Polarity: Ritual Engagements with the State in Northwestern Zimbabwe' *Journal of Southern African Studies* 24, 3, 561–78.

—. (2003) 'The end of modernity in Zimbabwe? Passages from development to sovereignty' in Hammar et al. 2003.

Zamchiya, P. (2011) 'A Synopsis of Land and Agrarian Change in Chipinge District, Zimbabwe' *Journal of Peasant Studies* 38, 5, 1093–1122.

EASTERN AFRICAN STUDIES

These titles published in the United States and Canada by Ohio University Press